Fight the Power:

A Memoir of the Sixties

Eric Leif Davin

DavinBooks

Pittsburgh, Pennsylvania

Also by Eric Leif Davin

Sweet Sorrows & Violent Delights:
Fantasy & Science Fiction
(Lulu.com, 2009)

Walk Like A Man:
A Memoir of Machismo
(Lulu.com, 2008)

American Labor History Made Easy!
(Lulu.com, 2008)

Partners in Wonder:
Women and the Birth of Science Fiction, 1926-1965
(Lexington Books, 2006)

Pioneers of Wonder:
Conversations With the Founders of Science Fiction
(Prometheus Books, 1999)

Created Equal:
Democracy Comes to the Industrial Heartland,
1914-1948
(Forthcoming from Lexington Books)

DavinBooks
Box 90087
Pittsburgh, PA 15224

Copyright 2008
All Rights Reserved

ISBN 978-0-578-01394-7

Front Cover: Peace sign in the sky over Boston, October 15, 1969. Photo by Eric Leif Davin.
Back Cover: Eric and Annie, Phoenix, Christmas Eve, 1968.

Thanks to Laura Campbell for editorial suggestions.

Power Never Sleeps

Bodies writhe on the bed,
    Locked in hand-to-hand combat,
        Wrestling on a battlefield
            Where Power fucks,
                But Power never sleeps.

Power prowls
    In the trenches of the family.
    Power howls
        In the trenches of the schools.
        Power lurks
            In the trenches of the church.
            Power shills
                In the trenches of the corporation.
                And Power kills
                      In the trenches of the city.
                        But Power never sleeps.

Power destroys the village
        To save the village.
    Power enshrines privilege
        In the name of freedom.
    Power says it's for the best,
        But it's for the worst.
    Power seeps
            Into our heads,
And Power creeps into our beds...

                But Power never sleeps.

* CONTENTS *

Introduction
Raised in Anger

Part One

That Old Time Religion

Come Unto Jesus	15
For Thou Art With Me	22
Alone Against God	27

Part Two

Better Dead Than Red

Soldier Boy	49
The Dragon Lady	52
A Rendezvous With Death	57
A Choice, Not an Echo	62
Gulf of Tonkin Incident	69

Part Three

You Don't Know Jack

Hope in a Hopeless Land	75
Mountain Meadows	80
Like a Brother	87
Thus I Refute Jehovah	93
The Abolition of Toleration	98
Apostasy	103

Part Four

The Doors of Perception

Light My Fire	111
One Fine Day	116
Strangers in the Night	118
A Fine and Private Place	122
The Great Fear	127
The Superstitions	130
Damsel in Distress	134
Mojo Man	138
Vision Quest	147

Final Exam 152
Rite of Passage 155

Part Five

Decline and Fall

Against the Wind 161
The Happening 167
Paranoia Strikes Deep 171
Here Comes the Night 175
Paint it Black 178
The Sharpest Thorn 180

Part Six

Resurrection

The Lower Depths 185
Sandbox Politics 190
The Call to Resist 199
Dark Lady 203
Thou Art the Man 208
A Rose From the Ashes 213
Blood Nativity 216
Freedom Road 220
Chattanooga Stonewall 225
Sarasota Summer 228
Misbegotten 231
Blood Money 237

Part Seven

Smoke From a Distant Fire

Ho Chi Minh at Versailles 241
From Protest to Resistance 244
The Acid Vat 249
Famous for Fifteen Minutes 251
The Most Dangerous Man in Phoenix 255
Signs and Portents 259
Arrogant Ignorance 265
The Tet Offensive 270
Disappearances 284
Ancient Fire 287
Petroglyphs of Wupatki 290
Passing as a Pig 294
The War at Home 300

Finger on the Trigger	303
Fender Benders	306
Across the Mojave	308

Part Eight

Children of the Revolution

The Grovel-In	313
Carlo the Magnificent	317
Civics Lesson	322
Hearts and Minds	325
Peace on Earth	328
Endless War	332
The Long March	339
The Autocrat of the Dinner Table	345
Honor	351
Give Peace a Chance	357
Fork in the Road	365
Love in the Ruins	369
Ravaged Beauty	372
Cast Your Fate to the Wind	373

Part Nine

Babylon Burning

A Cowboy in Cambridge	379
A Walk on the Moon	385
The Cost of Freedom	394
The Partisan	406
To Liberate the Oppressed	417
Ways of the Weak	421
Duty	433
Farewell to the Sixties	440

Introduction

Raised in Anger

From my earliest memory I was beaten. I don't remember any of the sins for which Elmer, my giant construction worker step-father, beat me. But I remember his beatings. His leather belt slithered out of the loops at his waist like a snake. I twisted this way and that, crying, as its sharp sting bit into me on my arms, my back, my legs, but there was no escape.

Once, when I was eight, his doubled-up belt broke in two as he was whipping me in my bedroom. He towered over me, surprised and puzzled by the broken leather strap in his hand as I cowered at his feet, hoping the broken belt meant my beating had ceased. And then he slugged me so hard I was thrown across the king-sized bed to slap up against the wall on the other side and crumple to the floor.

My mother also believed good parenting meant lots of beatings. Like Elmer, she had been raised on the principle: "Spare the rod, spoil the boy." Therefore, the rod would not be spared.

However, it didn't need to be a rod. Anything would do. She became enraged easily and often and grabbed whatever was at hand to carry out her beatings. Once, in a fit of rage at my younger brother Denny, she picked up the telephone from its little table beside the living room sofa and beat him with it, pounding it into his head and body over and over.

If Mom felt I was in need of memorable instruction, she used a good switch stripped from a tree in the yard. To insure that I would visualize exactly the terror in store for me, part of my punishment was for me to prepare the switch she would use on me. I was sent to get the kind she preferred -- thin and perhaps two feet long. I stripped off the leaves and tiny twigs, as I'd been taught to do, until it was straight. I swished it through the air to make sure it was supple enough for the purpose. Then I brought it to her. She carefully examined it to make sure I'd properly prepared the instrument of my punishment. She swished it through the air to make sure it had a snap to it. Then she gripped my thin upper arm with one hand to hold me still and laid into me with the switch in the other. I screamed and twisted trying to escape the stinging switch, but I couldn't get away from her grip or from the switch raising red welts on my bare legs.

"Please, please, I won't do it again! I won't do it again!" I cried, though I can't remember what I'd done.

"I know you won't," Mom said through gritted teeth, her arm working like a metronome, "I *know* you won't when I get through with you!" I screamed and danced as the blood ran down my legs and Mom whipped me until her arm was too tired to whip any more.

But my parents were merely passing on a long regional tradition. We lived in Phoenix, Arizona, but both came from the South, a violent and savage land. Elmer was a Missouri farm boy from Jackson County, the same part of Missouri that was ravaged by rebels Frank and Jesse James when they rode with William Quantrill's Confederate Raiders during the Civil War. Missouri was a slave state and tried hard at the beginning of the Civil War to secede from the United States and join the Confederacy. Only military force kept it in the Union. But military force wasn't enough to suppress Confederate sentiment, and for the entire war's duration the state was torn by murderous guerrilla fighting.

Mom was also from a slave state, Tennessee. But Tennessee was successful in leaving the United States and joining the Confederacy. And parents there, as in Missouri, believed in beating their children. The violence needed to maintain a slave society seemed to have seeped into all cultural relations. Mom recalled that her Cousin Louise, Grandfather Frank's sister Mary's daughter, was often brutally whipped by her father. "Cousin Louise's father lashed her with his belt like he was whipping a slave," Mom said. "He gave her what we called a 'real Southern beating.'"

So, the regional tradition of "real Southern beatings" was also a family tradition. In Mom's family, parents had beaten children as far back as memory went. Her father, my Grandfather Frank, whipped Mom with his leather razor strap when she was as young as four. And Grandfather Frank had been beaten by *his* father. It took extraordinary circumstances for a child to escape a beating from Grandfather Frank's father. One time when Grandfather Frank managed to do so was just before America entered World War I in 1917.

Grandfather Frank and his brother Charlie, both teenagers, were cutting timber out in the north Georgia backwoods where they lived. They'd chopped down a tree and shorn it of limbs. Then Charlie began "walking" the log down the mountain side for Frank to catch and load onto their mule-drawn wagon. Charlie lost control of the log. It hit Frank's leg and broke it.

Charlie got Frank home in their wagon and put him to bed. But, when their father came home he noticed that Frank hadn't done his farm chores. So, he went into the house, found Frank in bed, and told him to get up and get his work done. Frank said, "Pa, I can't."

"Well," Mom recalled, "you didn't say no to my grandfather. He got his strap and was going to give Daddy a licking he wouldn't forget. Daddy said, 'Please, Pa, don't whip me. I'm sure my leg is broken.'"

Which it *was,* so Grandfather Frank escaped a whipping that one day.

But, Grandfather Frank regularly whipped his own children, including my mother.

As did my mother's mother. As with Mom, her own mother favored switches. Once, when Mom had been the cause of a pot of beans burning, her mother whipped her especially long and hard. "She cut a switch and switched my arms, legs, back, face -- wherever she could hit me," Mom recalled. "She was like a mad person. I had blood oozing out of welts all over my body." Just as I have never forgotten Mom's similar mad whippings of me, so Mom never forgot this whipping by her own mother and remembered it with bitterness as she looked down into her mother's open coffin after her death in 1939.

Mom also remembered a day in the early 1930s when she was only six or seven. A bill collector knocked on the door while her mother was ironing. Her mother hid and told Mom to tell the bill collector no one was home.

Mom answered the door and said to the bill collector, "My mother told me to tell you that she isn't home."

When the bill collector left, her mother gave Mom what she remembered as one of the worst "no holds barred" beatings of her life. Mom was covered in bruises, even on her face. Afterward, she just lay in bed, moaning in pain, thinking that it would be better to die than feel the hurt she was feeling.

And then Mom did it to me. By the 1950s, it was Mom who hid behind the door when the bill collector came knocking. She told me to answer the door and tell him she wasn't home. Without knowing that I was playing her own childhood role and repeating her own childish words, I told the bill collector that, "My Mother told me to tell you she isn't home."

After the bill collector left, Mom beat me viciously, exactly as her own mother had beaten her a quarter century before. The tradition went on and on, down the generations. Parents beat children who became parents who beat children who became parents who beat children.

But the beating from my mother I remember most clearly was the last one, the time the beatings finally stopped. By then I was no longer a little boy to whom she could take a switch stripped from a tree in the yard. By then I was a teenager, bigger and stronger than her.

Habits of submission die hard and, after years of being beaten, I was used to it and accepted it. Mom was screaming insanely and, as usual, grabbed the first thing which came to hand. We were in the kitchen and what came easily to hand was her broom. She held it by the long handle and beat me about the head, shoulders, and upraised arms, screeching her rage all the while. She was as consumed with anger, perhaps, as her own mother had been when she beat Mom back in the Thirties.

Then I decided I'd had enough; that I wasn't going to let her beat me any more. I grabbed the broom in mid-swing, twisting it out of her hands. What happened next was surprising, stunning. Instantly Mom cowered against the wall, hands raised protectively over her head, face white with fear, still screaming, but now with terror: "You'd better not hit me!" she screeched, "You'd better not hit me!"

The idea that I might hit *her* with the broom shocked me. I wasn't going to hit her. I wasn't holding the broom in a threatening manner. I'd not taken a step toward her. I'd not even made any threatening noises. All I'd done was take the broom away from her so she couldn't beat me with it any longer. And now she was creeping fearfully away from me along the wall, half begging, half threatening that I'd better not hit her with the broom I held in my hands.

"I'm not going to hit you. I just don't want *you* hitting *me* any more. I've had enough and it's going to stop. You will never hit me again."

I threw down the broom and walked out of the kitchen.

What stays with me from this last beating is the huge mental gulf between us. I could not conceive of hitting my mother. My mother, however, could not conceive of me *not* hitting her, once I had the chance. In the midst of beating me, she couldn't imagine that I simply wanted to stop the beating. Once the broom was in my hands, all she could imagine was my doing unto her as she had been doing unto me.

So few of us, it seems, can imagine anything else. The oppressor finds it inconceivable that the oppressed just wants to end the oppression. The oppressed may be moved by a dream of freedom or of equality -- but the oppressor is so accustomed to oppressing that he (or she) can imagine no other way of relating: Dominance or submission. Us or them. Beat or be beaten.

In 1966, when I was a student at Phoenix Community College, Richard Goldberg, my favorite history teacher, invited Alexander Kerensky to speak. Kerensky had led the liberal democratic Provisional Government after the overthrow of the Russian Czar in 1917. After Kerensky's speech, some of Mr. Goldberg's students were invited to have dinner with him and the white-haired Kerensky. I was one of them.

Over dinner with Kerensky we discussed the Russian Revolution and how Kerensky had allowed Vladimir Lenin and his Bolshevik comrades to agitate unmolested against the Provisional Government. In July, 1917, Lenin even orchestrated an attempted coup against Kerensky. When the coup was suppressed, Lenin told fellow Bolshevik Leon Trotsky, "Now they will shoot us all, it is the right moment for them." After all, it's what the Czar had done to failed revolutionaries. It's what Lenin would have done to Kerensky, if the tables had been turned. It's what Lenin *did* do to his opponents, once he came to power.

No doubt to Lenin's puzzlement, Kerensky didn't shoot him and Trotsky and their Bolshevik comrades. Unlike the Bolsheviks, Kerensky was a democrat who didn't believe in murdering his political opponents. Luckily for him, Kerensky escaped into exile before Lenin could shoot him after Lenin came to power.

At the time of our dinner, I, like Lenin, also found it difficult to understand Kerensky's democratic point of view. By then I'd had enough "real Southern beatings" to know what you should do once you had the whiphand.

I remember a documentary of a Ku Klux Klan rally in Mississippi sometime in the Sixties. The speaker, whipping up racist fury among his listeners, told them, "The nigger doesn't want something *like* what you've got! He wants *what* you've got!" His fellow Klansmen bellowed their agreement. They were so habituated to demeaning others on the basis of race they they could imagine no other way of relating. The only difference possible was in who was on top. Martin Luther King's "Dream" was, to them, a subterfuge, lying rhetoric concealing the lust for revenge they were sure every black man harbored. Don't give up your guns, brothers!

When I read stories or look at cartoons from the Victorian Age, I marvel at male images of the Woman Suffrage Movement. Women wanted the vote, they wanted political equality. To many nineteenth century men, that, too, seemed to be lying rhetoric concealing a lust for power and revenge. They were so accustomed to the norm of male dominance and female subordination that they could not conceive of gender equality. All they could imagine was a role reversal.

And so the tabloids painted fantastical pictures of men in muttonchops and aprons washing dishes, minding the baby, and being bossed by swaggering women who rushed off in their bloomers to fight wars between all-female armies. The suffragists were portrayed as what an earlier church leader called, "A monstrous regiment of women!"

No doubt there was an element of rhetoric to such images and language. But we are lost in that same conceptual gulf which separated my mother and me if we cannot accept those fears as sincere. If the rhetoric was a powerful mobilizer of reaction -- it was only because it spoke to genuine fears; it reflected a genuine world view.

Racist Klansmen may have sincerely believed the black man was genetically inferior; Victorian males may have honestly believed women were divinely or biologically ordained for a subordinate position. But those men also knew that they were on top. They knew the others were on the bottom. And while the oppressed may dream of freedom or equality, too often the oppressor -- of all races, sexes, classes, and ages -- can only conceive of a reversal of the status quo and they fear the revenge of the oppressed.

Which, of course, has happened. Yet, contrary to the fears of the oppressor, not always. Decades of Franco fascism in Spain was replaced by a long-repressed socialism which proved to be benign. The collapse of Communism in Eastern Europe did not result in mass roundups and firing squads in Poland, the Czech Republic, or eastern Germany. The rise of Nelson Mandela to the presidency of South Africa did not bring about the predicted massacre of whites.

Nor, for that matter, did woman suffrage result in the social or economic subordination of men. Nor did the legal and political equality of blacks made possible by the Civil Rights Movement result in the dispossession and enslavement of the white race -- Aryan Nation demagogues to the contrary.

There are many very real material obstacles to equality. The power -- military, political, financial, institutional -- is in the hands of the oppressors.

But there is also a psychological obstacle in the minds of the oppressors, a belief which makes them fight all the more fiercely to hold on to their power. Their world of oppression, handed down through generations, shackles their imaginations. In a world of hierarchy, they cannot imagine its end. It is either dominance or submission; us or them; beat or be beaten. They cannot conceive that the oppressed may just want to -- finally -- stop the beating.

They cannot conceive that the oppressed may just throw down the broom and walk away.

Part One
That Old Time Religion

Come Unto Jesus

"It's so easy to step forward," the preacher said. "Step forward and accept the love of Jesus. Gently, tenderly, Jesus is calling, calling, 'O, Sinner, come home.'"

It was Sunday, the last day of Summer Bible Camp. All around me bodies were swaying, people were crying, the choir was singing behind the preacher, and young sinners were stepping forward to escape eternal damnation by accepting Jesus as their personal Savior. It'd been like this every day for a week.

And for a week I'd held out.

But today was my last chance to be saved from eternal hellfire. Tomorrow we would all go home. So today was my last chance to accept the love of Jesus, Who loved me deeply, tenderly, and Who only wanted to save my eternal soul.

And all I had to do was return His boundless love, love Him as He loved me.

And now, everyone else had stepped forward. I, alone, had not stepped forward. The camp counselors stood around me, gently touching me on the arms, the shoulders, gently urging me to step forward and be saved from eternal torment. I was the lone lost sheep left to be saved.

"It's so easy to step forward unto Jesus and everlasting life," the preacher repeated.

So easy to step forward.

****

In the summer of 1960, my younger brother Rick and I went to summer camp. We were alone among the seven brothers who ever did so. It was because Rick and I were good Christians. I was 13 that summer and had just graduated from Orangedale Elementary School in Phoenix, Arizona. In the fall I would enter North Phoenix High School. There was just enough time that summer for my soul to be saved.

We were Southern Baptists. Always had been. At least Mom and her seven sons were. I never knew Elmer, my step-father, to attend church. He went to his tavern on Sundays. However, like everyone else, he paid lip service to Jesus.

Mom had been raised in Chattanooga, Tennessee as a Southern Baptist. I was five when she moved to Phoenix, taking me and my brother Bruce with her. As it turned out, a lot of Southerners moved to Phoenix. Arizona had always been sympathetic to the South. Arizona was formed from territory stolen from Mexico during the Mexican War of the 1840s. That war had been fomented by Southern slavelords who wanted more land to expand their Slave Empire all the way to the Pacific. And, indeed, before the Civil War, New Mexico Territory, of which Arizona was then a part, voted come in as a slave state when it entered the Union.

Then the Civil War erupted. In the summer of 1861 a Confederate army from El Paso commanded by General Henry Hopkins Sibley invaded New Mexico, moving up the Rio Grande to Albuquerque and Santa Fe, both of which it captured. The rebels wanted to seize the rich silver-mining districts of Colorado Territory next. However, "Sibley's Brigade" was turned back at Glorietta Pass east of Santa Fe by Union volunteers coming down from Colorado.

At the same time as the New Mexican invasion, a Confederate column detached from Sibley's "Army of New Mexico" entered southern Arizona and occupied Tucson. A hotbed of pro-secession sentiment, Tucson welcomed the Confederates as liberators. Indeed, in August, 1861, even before Confederates forces entered the territory, Tucson had passed an ordinance of secession, officially leaving the United States of America and joining the Confederacy. That same month, Sibley's Confederate forces in southern New Mexico formally proclaimed the formation of Confederate "Arizona." This was the first time that the term "Arizona" was used to designate the region. Confederate "Arizona" would be all territory south of the 34th Parallel, which meant modern-day Phoenix and everything south of it, with Tucson as the temporary rebel capital.

In March of 1862, Confederate forces moved north from Tucson and occupied the Pima Indian villages on the Gila River. Next they moved west, down the Gila River toward Ft. Yuma, on the Colorado River.

However, a force of California Volunteers stopped the rebels on March 29 in a skirmish at Stanwix Station, about half-way between Phoenix and Yuma. This clash in Arizona's western desert was the western-most land battle of the Civil War. There was a subsequent skirmish on April 15 at Pichacho Peak, about half-way between Phoenix and Tucson. After the fight at Pichacho Peak, Confederate forces pulled back to New Mexico and, later, to Texas. On May 20, 1862, the California Volunteers occupied Tucson -- and the good people of Tucson prudently decided to remain in the United States, after all.

I've always been in love with history, so I've been to all three of these battlefields, Glorietta Pass in New Mexico, and Stanwix Station and Pichacho Peak in Arizona. You have to know what you're looking for, as nothing except historical markers designate them. For Stanwix Station, there isn't even a historical marker.

The desert between Phoenix and Yuma is flat and boring, boring, boring. Go due west out of Phoenix toward Buckeye. Turn south on Route 85 to Gila Bend. Get on Interstate 8, which is a straight run into Yuma and, eventually, San Diego. West of Gila Bend is a teeny village called Sentinel. Stop at the first rest stop after Sentinel. Look all around you at the flat and boring desert. If you have a map, your map may identify the surrounding wasteland as Stanwix Flats. In the old days, there was a stagecoach watering station there. That reststop is as close as you'll get to Stanwix Station, site of the westernmost battle of the Civil War. As I said, you have to know what you're looking for.

The desert between Phoenix and Tucson on Interstate 10 isn't *quite* as boring. Perhaps the most interesting part of it is Pichacho Peak, which is now a state park. Stop and look around. It has RV camping and nice desert flora. And there's a gift shop. Buy some petrified wood, saguaro honey, and a couple of rattlesnake rattles.

Glorietta Pass, billed as the "Gettysburg of the West," is east of Sante Fe off of Interstate 25. Even the locals have trouble finding it. Right now there are just some dilapidated old ranch buildings dating from the time of the battle. The site is U. S. Park Service land and is administered by the nearby Pecos National Historical Park.

Pecos is a prehistoric pueblo Indian ruin and, in some ways, the birthplace of Southwestern archeology. The entire chronology of prehistoric Southwestern pottery styles was worked out by archaeologists digging in Pecos pueblo's trash. For centuries the pueblo dominated the main pass between the Rio Grande Valley and the Great Plains. This was why the Spanish Conquistadores made a point of capturing it. Later, after the Great Pueblo Revolt of 1680, the Indians abandoned it, fearing Spanish retaliation. The ruin itself is fun to walk around and has an underground kiva, the equivalent of an Indian church, into which you can climb. The Visitor Center also has an excellent little theater which shows a film on the history of the Pecos Pueblo Indians. And the museum not only has a fine exhibition on the Pueblo Indians, but murals telling the entire story of the Battle of Glorietta Pass, the high tide of the Confederacy in New Mexico.

After the end of the Civil War, a lot of defeated Confederates migrated west. Jesse James, who, along with his brother Frank, rode with Quantrill's Confederate Raiders during the war, stayed around Missouri. But "Doc" Holliday, a Southerner who fought with Wyatt Earp at the OK Corral in Tombstone, Arizona, did not. And the first "adult" Western novel ever written is entitled *The Virginian*. This migration of Southerners continued unabated for 100 years. Mrs. Hearle, the old pioneer who once owned all the land around our white stucco house on 52nd Street in Phoenix, had come out from Virginia in a covered wagon in the 1890s. Another nearby family came from Georgia, which was where Mom's family had originally come from. On Mom's side of the family, I come from a long line of Georgia rednecks going back to the Confederacy and beyond. So, there were Southerners all around us.

Because of this, Mom had no problem finding nearby churches which preached the same brand of hellfire Southern Baptism in which she had been raised. And so, although raised in Arizona, we kids also were raised as Southern Baptists.

Mom was firm in her faith, and so did not need to attend church every Sunday. Besides, there were young children and infants she had to take care of at home. Elmer rose early and disappeared on the weekends, so he was not available for babysitting. Indeed, the children were never alone with Elmer. Looking after children was not something a real man did. Not when there were eager women waiting for him in the tavern.

And there was no money to hire a babysitter.

But it was important to Mom that her sons be raised properly in the church.

And so, those of us who were old enough to walk to church on our own -- me, Rick, and Bruce -- always had to go, while Mom stayed home with the younger ones.

It was a long walk in the blazing Arizona sun to Sherwood Heights Baptist Church, the closest Baptist church. And it was just as long walking back. We always wore suits, with jackets and ties. And, of course, we had to arrive back home dressed just as neatly as when we left. That meant no playing along the way, going or coming. The walk to and from church each Sunday was just as much torture as church itself.

Sherwood Heights Baptist Church was close to 56th Street and Thomas. The city of Scottsdale began just on the other side of 56th Street. Then, as now, Scottsdale was an upscale suburb of Phoenix. A better class of people lived there than in the eastern neighborhoods of Phoenix where I lived. And the entire area of Scottsdale beyond 56th Street and bounded by Thomas to the north and Oak Street to the south, where the Papago Military Reservation began, was given over to a huge middle class housing tract known as Sherwood Heights Estates. Some of the kids in my class at Orangedale, such as our eighth grade class valedictorian Tom Jacobsen, who later went to Berkeley, lived there.

But there was no Sherwood Forest anywhere near Sherwood Heights Estates. There was no forest of any kind. The entire subdivision had been plopped down in a desert expanse and given an idyllic name by the developer. And since our Baptist church was near 56th Street and Sherwood Heights Estates, the same public relations pressure was behind our church being named Sherwood Heights Baptist Church.

Once we arrived after our long walk in the sun, we attended Sunday School. We studied the Bible, we learned our Christian lessons. And then we went to regular church services with the adults. We listened to the preacher's sermon, we bowed our heads in prayer, we stood and sang the hymns. And then we walked home.

And we did this without fail, Sunday after Sunday after Sunday, three grade school boys arriving on their own, alone, thirsty from their long walk in the sun and thirsty for the Word of the Lord. Obviously, we were good Christian lads, worthy of support.

So, that summer of 1960 the congregation passed the hat and raised enough money to send the two oldest of us, me and Rick, to a Baptist summer camp up in the Prescott mountains named Prescott Pines. This camp was supported by Baptist congregations throughout Arizona and, while there would be lots of children from all over the state, few would be from any one congregation. Rick and I were the only ones from Sherwood Heights Baptist Church.

Prescott Pines was in operation all summer long, but it was organized by age groups. Each age group attended for one week over the course of the summer. Rick was younger than me and his 11-year-old age group went before mine. It was good that we went separately, as I had my morning paper route and it meant Rick would be able to take over my route when he returned and it was my turn to go.

Rick came back from Prescott Pines with exciting tales. There was more food than you could imagine! There were late night pillow fights fought by entire armies of kids! You could get lost in the woods!

I was eager for my turn.

And so it came to pass.

And Rick was right about everything he said. He just didn't tell everything.

Going to this Baptist summer camp was the first time I'd been out of the Sonora Desert in which Phoenix is located. Going north from Phoenix, the entire ecology changes once you climb the Mogollon Rim escarpment to higher elevations. First, you enter range land. Soon after, you enter pine tree country. If you keep going north, you'll come to Flagstaff, at 7,000 feet one of the highest cities in America. It is surrounded by the San Francisco Mountains, the highest in the state, and its mountain locale makes it one of the coolest spots in Arizona.

But, if you veer to the west after reaching the top of the Mogollon Rim, you'll come to Prescott. At that time Prescott was a small and attractive town nestled among mountains covered to the horizon with pine trees. Until 1889, when Phoenix replaced it, Prescott had been the Territorial capital of Arizona. Arizona's Senator Barry Goldwater came from a mercantile family which owned the prestigious Goldwater stores and the very first Goldwater store had been in Prescott. And it was here that the Arizona Baptists had their children's camp.

The camp consisted of scattered log buildings in a dense pine forest. There was a dining hall, a one-room store filled with Jesus artifacts, and open-air meeting areas with benches made of logs sawn in half and supplied with wooden pegs for legs. The dorms dotted the forest, with the boys' dorms in one place, the girls' in another.

And everywhere there were alien pine trees. When I looked up, there was a canopy of pine branches blocking out the sky. I walked on a springy bed of pine needles. The air was saturated with the scent of pine resin. I put my nose to a tree trunk and inhaled deeply, filling my nostrils with the smell of it. Pine cones littered the ground. I picked up a pine cone and marveled at its sharp points pricking my fingers. I put it in my pocket as a souvenir of this strange land.

And, just as Rick had told me, there was a gigantic pillow war. The boys in my dorm battled the boys in the adjoining dorm one night after the counsellors left us. There must've been 40 boys whacking each other with pillows in the hallway which divided the two dorms. Because the battle line between the two small armies was clotted with combatants, not everyone could fight at once. So, some of us from our side snuck around to the rear of the other, climbed in the window of their bathroom, and then charged out of their bathroom into their rear. We had them on two fronts and pummelled them without mercy. When camp counselors finally responded to the noise and stopped the battle, both dorms were ankle deep in pillow feathers. It was the best pillow fight I've ever been in.

The counselors woke us at dawn every morning. I didn't mind. I had to get up *before* dawn in Phoenix to deliver my newspapers. We showered and dressed and trooped down to the dining hall, which was filled with hundreds of kids already eating breakfast.

Food was scarce in our house. My brothers and I were always hungry. Often there would be nothing to eat but a loaf of brown bread. I'd grab a couple of slices and eat them on the way to school. Sometimes we had a jar of French's yellow mustard. When that happened, my brothers and I took two slices of bread and slathered them thick with mustard, then slapped them together into a mustard sandwich.

Once, when I was visiting a friend, I found an ornamental glass bowl of candy on the dining room table. Over the course of my visit I made frequent trips past the bowl, grabbing a handful of candy each time. It was almost empty by the time my friend noticed it. He yelled at me that he was going to get in trouble because you weren't supposed to *eat* the candy! It was just for looks! That was hard for me to understand.

But at the camp there was more food than I'd ever seen in my life! And it was there to be eaten! There was scrambled eggs, sausage, ham, bacon, toast and jelly, waffles, pancakes, pitchers of maple syrup, pitchers of orange juice, pitchers of milk -- and we could eat all we wanted! I scarfed down the food as fast as I could so I had enough time to go back for seconds and then thirds. When breakfast was finally over, I stuffed my pockets with biscuits which I later hid under my pillow back in the dorm.

All of this was as Rick had related.

But Rick didn't tell me about the price we had to pay for the food and the pine trees and the pillow fights. We had to attend Sunday School every single day of the week! After breakfast we were herded off to open-air religion classes. There were Bible lessons, parables, sermons, songs. And, at the early afternoon end of each session came salvation time. A revival atmosphere broke out. People were singing gospel music and shouting hosannas, the preachers and counselors were urging us to come forward, come on down front, kneel and accept Jesus as our personal Savior as the preacher laid on the hands and the assembly prayed over us.

And, every day, kids went down front to kneel and accept Jesus into their hearts. We were all expected to do so. With all the singing and shouting and praying and exhorting, it was hard not to step forward like everybody else to be saved.

But I resisted. I didn't believe any of this superstition. I only made that long hot trek to Sherwood Heights Baptist Church every Sunday because I was forced to. I knew there was no divine Christ, there was no God, there was no Satan, there were no angels, there were no devils, there was no afterlife, there was no heaven, and there was no hell. It was all just the bullshit Oogie-Boogie stupid-stition of ignorant savages. I hated it all and I hated having to pretend that I believed any of the lies that everyone else took as "gospel Truth." I hated everything about Christianity, which I viewed as the greatest evil ever to plague humanity, and I hated everything about the church, which preached the Christian gospel of lies. I hated being forced to go through all the motions of belief. I hated having to kneel in church when the congregation prayed. I hated having to stand with them when they stood to sing.

But I no more prayed their prayers or sang their hymns when I kneeled and stood than I recited the Pledge of Allegiance when I had to stand with my class every day and salute the American flag. I made up prayers and lyrics and pledges to blaspheme everything I was supposed to be pledging myself to. But, I kept these blasphemies to myself and blended into the herd for the sake of survival. And then I hated the church for forcing me to be a hypocrite.

But going down front to accept Jesus as my personal Savior was stepping out of the herd. I could hide in the herd and pretend to be one of them. But I couldn't hide if I was standing in front of the herd. If I was kneeling in front of them to accept Jesus as my personal Savior, it was a personal statement of belief made while everybody watched.

And it would be a public act of hypocrisy. I hated the anonymous hypocrisy the church forced upon me as a continual part of life. However, at least I could be a private heretic and mouth blasphemies when I was supposed to be praying or singing. But, to say I believed in Christ when I did not, before the entire congregation, would make me just as hypocritical as all of them.

And I despised them all for being hypocrites. I knew of no hypocritical atheists. All the hypocrites I knew were good God-fearing Christians. They all said one thing publicly, and then did the opposite in their private lives. I'd never met a single Christian with any morals or ethics. Every Christian I knew was a lying, immoral, unethical, hate-filled savage. Their lies and their hypocrisy and their cruelties and their hatreds and their ignorant superstitions disgusted me. No truly moral or intelligent person, I felt, could ever be a Christian.

And so, because I believed in morality and honesty and intelligence, I refused to be a Christian and accept Jesus as my Savior. I'd lose my self-respect to publicly do so. It would be a betrayal of everything I believed in. It wouldn't be right. It would be like swearing allegiance to Adolf Hitler.

So I refused to go forward and be saved. Jesus may have loved me, but I did not love Him. Rather than pretend I did, I'd rather burn in their imaginary eternal hellfire.

But it became harder and harder to resist. The pressure to step forward was unremitting. And every day, more and more kids stepped forward. Every day there were fewer and fewer who had not stepped forward.

Until, finally, there was only me. In late night prayer sessions the counselors prayed with me and over me, that I might be saved from eternal damnation. Attention was lavished upon me in the daily Sunday School. When the preacher pleaded with sinners to come forward, he directed his pleas straight at me.

And today, Sunday, the Lord's Day, was the last day at camp, the last day in which my eternal soul could be saved from eternal torment. It was my last chance for eternal salvation. Jesus was calling me, O, Sinner, come home! All eyes were on me. The choir was singing just for me. The preacher was preaching just for me. The counselors who had prayed so fervently for me, night after night, were standing beside me, hoping and praying I would be saved from the dark Satanic Pit. All of them wanted me to be saved for eternal Life.

But, it wasn't up to any of them. It was all up to me. Only I could made the decision to accept the love that Jesus carried in his bosom for me. Only I could save myself. Only I could step forward.

I was trembling and shaking and tears were running down my cheeks. The counselors around me patted me and hugged me in sympathy. They knew the torture I was going through as Satan tried to hold me back from taking the loving hand of Jesus. Satan wanted to claim me as one of his own. But the counselors wanted me to know that they were with me in my struggle with the Evil One. All of them loved me and wanted me to accept their love. They knew it was hard, for have not we all sinned and fallen short of the Glory of the Lord? We are all fallen sinners, but we all can be saved from eternal hellfire if we but reach out and accept the love that Jesus has for us.

All eyes were on me. The choir was singing just for me. The preacher was preaching just for me. The counselors were waiting just for me. The boys in my dorm, who had already gone forward, kneeled, and accepted the eternal love of Jesus, were looking only at me. They all urged me forward. All were waiting for me to step forward and accept the love of Jesus. All were waiting for me to step forward and be saved. All were waiting. Why was I not stepping forward? Why was I resisting?

    It was so easy to step forward.
    Jesus was waiting.
    It was so easy to step forward and accept his love.
    Why was I waiting?
    It was so easy to step forward and be saved from eternal punishment.
    I stepped forward, kneeled like one who believed, and accepted Jesus as my Savior.

For Thou Art With Me

By the summer of 1962, Mom was beginning to have problems with the Sherwood Heights Baptist Church. She said the Sherwood Heights Baptists believed in things that weren't in the Bible, which, as the Word of God, was the final authority on all things religious. For example, the Sherwood Heights Baptists did not believe in going to the movies on Sunday, the Lord's Day. But that wasn't in the Bible, Mom said.

And so Mom bought a book which explained the teachings of all the Christian denominations and began studying it. She became particularly interested in the Seventh-Day Adventists. This was because Dr. Rosenquist, who delivered all four of my younger brothers, was a Seventh-Day Adventist. Mom had begun going to see him when she was pregnant with Mike, who was born in 1955. She had done so because, as with Jews, for Seventh-Day Adventists the Lord's Day, the Sabbath, is Saturday. That meant Dr. Rosenquist's Scottsdale clinic was open on Sundays. And Sunday was the one day of the week Mom was able to persuade Elmer to delay going to his current favorite tavern long enough to take her to Dr. Rosenquist's for checkups.

So Mom contacted the Seventh-Day Adventists and two of their missionaries began coming to the house to discuss their beliefs. One of their beliefs was complete abstinence from alcohol and tobacco. Not only were alcohol and tobacco moral evils, but they were unhealthy. Long before the Surgeon General announced that there was a link between cigarettes and lung cancer, the Seventh-Day Adventists (like the similarly abstemious Mormons) were already preaching this. One night, to illustrate the consequences of cigarette smoking, the Adventist missionaries brought a film projector and a color 8-mm film depicting an operation for lung cancer. They set up the projector and a portable screen in our living room and began showing the film.

I began to feel queasy as the lung cancer patient in the film was prepped for surgery. We were right there, in the operating room, looking over the doctors' shoulders, as they cut through the guy's skin and sternum with a buzz saw. Blood began to flow. In full color. Then they applied a huge vice and actually pried apart the guy's rib cage. Inside was the guy's beating heart and, on both sides, his cancerous lungs. They were slimy, bloody, veined, and glistening. The narrator directed our attention to the cancerous mass growing on the lungs like a putrid cauliflower.

I felt the blood drain from my brain. "I'm going to faint," I managed to whisper. And then darkness closed over me and I toppled face-first out of my chair toward the floor.

One of the missionaries caught me before I hit the floor. He carried me into my parents' bedroom and laid me on their bed. Mom came with a cold washcloth and placed it on my forehead. Then they closed the door and left me to lie alone in the darkened room. After the blood returned to my brain, I continued to lie on the bed, not moving, as the bloody images of the cancerous lungs replayed themselves in my mind. If a picture is worth a thousand words, perhaps a moving picture is worth a million. I'd never felt any desire to smoke, as there were no cigarettes in our house. Mom did not smoke nor, except for a rare cigar, did Elmer. But that film confirmed my revulsion for the practice. In this case, the missionary work was successful. I never became a smoker. But neither did we become Seventh-Day Adventists.

Even so, Mom continued to read her book and continued to search for a Christian church she could believe in more fully. And, as she became less adament about church attendance, I and my next-older brothers, Rick and Bruce, began going less and less often to Sherwood Heights Baptist Church.

Then, in the spring of 1963, Mom contracted cervical cancer. In May of that year she went in for surgery to remove the cancer and, simultaneously, have a hysterectomy. Dr. Rosenquist had discovered that fibroid tumors also filled both her fallopian tubes and he recommended a hysterectomy. Elmer refused to permit it. "Then she'd no longer be a 'she,'" he said. "She'd be an 'it.'"

Dr. Rosenquist consulted with his colleagues. They all agreed on the hysterectomy. Dr. Rosenquist called in Elmer for a talk and told him that Mom was going to have the hysterectomy, whether he agreed or not. Reluctantly, Elmer agreed. "But, you're depriving me of a wife," he told Dr. Rosenquist.

The surgery was scheduled at Tempe Clinic where my youngest brothers Pat and Bradley had been born. Elmer drove Mom to the clinic and signed the papers and started to leave. The nurse asked him where he was going. He said he had to get to work. She told him Mom was having major surgery and he needed to be there for her. He refused. He said he didn't approve of the surgery and he didn't give a damn whether she lived or died. Then he left.

As Mom was lying on a gurney in a hospital hallway, awaiting prep for her surgery, a woman visiting a family member noticed her. "Are you here alone?" she asked Mom.

"Yes, I am. I'm here for cancer surgery."

"You shouldn't have to face that alone." The woman took Mom's hand and held it between both of hers. "I'll stay here with you until you go into surgery," she said. "And I'll be here waiting for you when you come out."

As the woman held Mom's hand, Mom began to cry. "There, there," the woman said. "You're in God's hands, now. Let us pray together."

And so, as the woman stood beside Mom's gurney, the two women held each other's hands, closed their eyes, and the woman led Mom in reciting Psalm 23. They prayed together for the Lord to have mercy on Mom in her time of need and to bring her safely through the Valley of the Shadow of Death. "And I shall fear no evil," the woman prayed with Mom, "for Thou art with me. Thy rod and thy staff comfort me."

And God was with Mom and He did have mercy and He did bring her safely through the Valley of the Shadow of Death.

Following her surgery, Mom was put in the Intensive Care Unit (ICU). And, as she had promised, the woman was there in the ICU, waiting for Mom, when Mom regained consciousness after surgery. And the woman was there with Mom for every one of the days Mom spent recuperating in the ICU. And, after 18 days in the ICU, she came home. She'd lost a lot of weight. She was pale and weak. She was tired all the time. But she got up before dawn every morning and fixed Elmer breakfast and prepared his lunch box for him. It was what he expected her to do. It was what she felt obligated to do. It was her wifely duty, despite hysterectomy and cancer surgery.

The woman from the hospital came to visit Mom at home. They prayed together for Mom's quick and full recovery every time the woman came. And she talked to Mom about her God. It seems this good Christian woman was a member of the Church of Jesus Christ of Latter-Day Saints, a Mormon. She told Mom about the beliefs of the Mormons. Mom was not completely unfamiliar with the Mormons. Her boss at Bausch & Lomb, Rudy Mortenson, was a bishop in the Mormon church. Nilas Johnson, Mom's best friend, was also a Mormon. All of them, like the woman who walked with Mom through the Valley of the Shadow of Death, were good Christians. Indeed, they were the best Christians Mom had ever known.

And so Mom told the Mormon woman that she'd like to learn more about the Mormon faith. After that, two Mormon "Elders," missionaries still in their teens, began coming by the house. The first thing they told Mom was that the body is the temple of God, and it should not be polluted. Therefore, Mormons did not use alcohol, tobacco, or caffeine. The first two were fine with Mom, as she didn't smoke or drink, anyway. But, she loved her morning coffee. The teenage Elders assured her that a caffeine-free drink called "Postum" tasted much the same. But, we also had to give up tea and most soft drinks -- except Dr. Pepper -- because they contained caffeine. Mom decided she could live with that. What we kids thought about it was irrelevant.

Then Mom asked about the multiple wives she'd heard Mormon men were allowed to have, as many as they wanted. The teenage Elders assured Mom this was no longer the case. The president of the Mormon church is a living prophet. Thus, like the Pope, he is in direct communication with God. And, from time to time, God speaks to him through revelations, as God also does to the Pope. And in 1890 the prophet at that time received a revelation from God in which God said that Mormons should stop practicing plural marriage. So, Mormons stopped practicing plural marriage -- except for a handful of renegades on the Arizona-Utah border and others who left for Mexico, who never accepted the revelation as legitimate.

That satisfied Mom. However, there was more to it than that. The rest of God-fearing Christian America never did like Mormon polygamy. That's one of the reasons a mob of God-fearing Christians murdered the Mormon founding Prophet Joseph Smith and his brother Hiram and drove the remaining Mormons out of the East. They also didn't like that the territory of Utah, where the Mormons then settled, gave women the vote in territorial elections in 1870. Only Wyoming was earlier, in 1869. The reason Utah did this was because then each Mormon husband's vote was multiplied many-fold as his obedient wives voted the way he told them to vote. So, there was no way that Utah was ever going to become a state as long as the Mormons continued to practice polygamy.

But, the good Mormon men liked having all their wives, and they were in no hurry to become a state, anyway. Then, in 1887, the U. S. Congress had passed the Edmunds-Tucker Act, which mandated the federal seizure of all assets of the Mormon church, except chapels and cemeteries, because Mormons continued to practice polygamy. This law also penalized all Mormon males with multiple wives with five years in prison for each day they remained married to a multiple wife.

Being good Christians, the Mormons continued to obey the commands of the Lord and defied the federal government. They remained with their wives. Finally, however, after three years, the then-current Mormon prophet-president had a revelation from God. And God said they should cease practicing polygamy. This would make it possible for them to avoid prison, get their property back, and also become a state within the United States. So that is why, in 1890, the Mormons became monogamous. And, as a reward, besides avoiding prison and getting the church property back, in 1896 Utah Territory was allowed to become a state. God is good. God is just. He always knows what is best.

Next Mom asked about Mormon attitudes toward blacks. According to Mormon theology, the teenage missionaries told Mom, we all lived prior lives before being reincarnated on this Earth. However, some people did not live goodly lives in that prior existence. Thus, when they came into this world, they were marked with black skins to denote their sinful former lives.

But, being good Christians, the Mormons did not hold their former sinfulness against blacks. Blacks were welcome to join the church. But, because of their sinful former lives, and upon God's command, black males could never become members of the priesthood, for which all white boys were eligible when they reached the age of twelve. Thus, blacks remained second-class citizens within the church. (However, in 1978, long after the Mormon missionaries explained black inferiority to us, God spoke to the then Mormon prophet-president about this, and blacks, despite their sinful previous lives, were thereafter allowed to join the priesthood and become Mormon missionaries. Besides being good and just, God is also forgiving. And He also seems to change his mind a lot.)

The teenage Elders then went on to say that, just as we lived prior lives before coming to this world, so we will live again after we leave this world. Only, instead of becoming angels in God's Heaven, we will become gods ourselves. God, Himself, was once a mere mortal like you and me, they said. Then he died and became the God of our world. But, there are infinite worlds. And, if we live saintly lives, after we die we, too, will eventually become the God of one of these infinite worlds. We will have the power of life and death over the people of our world, to whom we will dispense justice and mercy and forgiveness. That will be our eternal reward.

The teenage Elders also discussed the *Book of Mormon*, their supplement to the Bible. Christians have a supplement to the Jewish Bible, which they call the "New Testament." In Christian theology, it is just as much the Word of God as anything in the Jewish "Old Testament," as Christians term it. Mormons, being Christians, of course accept the New Testament. But, just as God had earlier added a "New Testament" to his "Old Testament," the Mormons believe that God had later added an even "Newer Testament" to the two older Testaments. And this "Newer Testament" was the *Book of Mormon*, whence the Mormons get their nickname.

The *Book of Mormon* is a history of the Ten Lost Tribes of Israel in the New World. In 722 B.C. the Assyrian king Sargon II destroyed Samara, the capital of Israel, and obliterated the entire kingdom of Israel. While a separate Jewish kingdom centered on Jerusalem, called Judea, continued to exist, Israel's King Hosea and tens of thousands of his subjects, comprising ten of the original twelve tribes of Israel, were shipped off into enslavement east of the Tigris and Euphrates Rivers, where they disappeared into legend as the Ten Lost Tribes of Israel.

The Mormons, however, know what happened to them. It seems the Lost Tribes wandered across Asia to Alaska and down the Western Hemisphere to populate North and South America. They reached a high level of civilization, of which Mayan temples and Anasazi ruins and Ohio Valley burial mounds are mute testimony. Jesus visited these Jewish descendants to preach Christian salvation during the three days he was in the tomb after his crucifixion. After that, there was a great war which engulfed the entire Western Hemisphere, and most of these Lost Israelites killed each other. Only the so-called American Indians survived, as a debased and pitiful remnant of these once mighty people.

This seems like a bizarre belief today, but when Joseph Smith founded the Mormons in the early nineteenth century, this idea was widespread. In the 1965 Jane Fonda-Lee Marvin Western, *Cat Ballou,* Fonda's father is always spouting pidgin Hebrew at their Indian hired hand because an itinerant lecturer at a local Chautauqua had explained how the Indians were descended from the Lost Tribes of Israel -- so the Indian hired hand should've been able to understand Hebrew. If you didn't know this was a common belief of the time, you'd think it was just an eccentricity of the screenwriters. What Smith did was pick it up and build an entire theology around it.

And, it is because the Indians are the remnants of the Lost Tribes that the Mormons have a special responsibility to convert them to the true Word of God. Therefore, Mormons obsessively proselytize on Indian reservations and eagerly adopt Indian children into their own homes to raise as proper Mormons.

The Mormons know all of this history because an Indian historian named Mormon incised it all on plates of gold around 400 A.D. in a now-lost Native American written language.

(It must have been difficult to make revisions and corrections on those golden plates, I thought.) Then Mormon buried the golden plates in upstate New York.

Beginning in the 1820s, however, God began sending sacred dreams and heavenly manifestations to Joe Smith, who just happened to live in upstate New York. Then, in 1827, God sent a vision to Smith showing him where Mormon's golden plates were buried. After Smith dug up the golden plates, the Angel Moroni helped Smith translate the lost Indian written language into English. Smith published the resulting 600-page *Book of Mormon* in 1830 and founded the church based upon the book that same year. He became the first prophet of the new church and, based upon God's continuing revelations to him, began to take many wives, as God ordered, as did his eager male followers.

Mom asked where the original golden plates upon which the *Book of Mormon* was written were kept. The teenage Elders explained that, unfortunately, after Smith had translated the unknown Indian language into English, the Angel Moroni took the Indian historian's golden plates up into heaven. However, men that Smith had recruited into the church swore they saw the golden plates before Moroni claimed them for God.

I guess this all made sense to Mom, because in October, 1963, she converted and was baptized into the Church of Jesus Christ of Latter-Day Saints. And since Mom considered all of her children mere extensions of herself, we, too, were forced to become Mormons. We had no say in the matter. It was something like the 1648 Peace of Westphalia I'd read about, which ended another stupid religious war between Catholic Christians and Protestant Christians. Westphalia established that each German princeling could determine the creed of his subjects. Mom was our princeling, so we had to go along with whatever religion she chose. In due time, we were baptized into the Mormon church. Only my youngest brother, Bradley, who was just three, escaped baptism, as he was considered too young to make a mature decision on the matter. Instead, a blessing ceremony was performed over him.

And so we began attending the local Mormon church every Sunday. Once more we began the long treks to church in the hot Arizona sun. This time, however, Mom went with us, as now the youngest brothers were also old enough to go to church.

It didn't make any difference to me. I remained just as much a secret heretic after becoming a Mormon -- someone they called a "Jack" Mormon -- as I'd been while a Baptist. As far as I was concerned, one Christian sect was just as crazy as another so, like an obedient subject, I accepted Mom's Westphalian mandate.

Elmer, of course, already belonged to the Church of the Sunday Tavern, and so did not become a Mormon. There was no way on God's green Earth that he was going to give up his tavern life. Nor was he giving up the Copenhagen-brand chewing tobacco to which he was addicted and which ate away his gums. Besides, the Mormon church required tithing. All members had to turn over 10% of their income to the church. Elmer wouldn't spend 10% of his income on his own family, he'd be damned if he'd give 10% of his income to a church.

But, it hardly mattered that Elmer didn't become a Mormon. He and the family lived separate lives, anyway. He merely used the house as a mail-drop and a place to store his clothes.

Alone Against God

The Wandering Jew

Citizen of two worlds.
        Or four. Or more.
Lost in the ozone,
        Flying beneath the radar.
Neither this nor that,
        Yin nor Yang,
                All one thing nor another,
In the world,
        But not of the world.
I am the intimate stranger
        in a strange land.
        I know the rules
             Which do not bind me.
        I know the names
             Which do not name me.
        I know the customs and rituals
             Of friends and lovers,
                  Neighbors and comrades,
                        Sisters and brothers,
                            Of families
                Which do not call me home.
I am the visitor to the lodge,
        The tourist out of season,
            The reporter on assignment.
I walk among the savages,
        The familiar anthropologist,
            Received and accepted.
Hunter in the hunt,
        Chanter in the dark,
            Dancer in the firelight,
                A man of the tribe, gone native,
But for my skin beneath the lurid facepaint.
        I am the White African,
             The Indian Cowboy,
                The Female Man.
I am the Jewish Goy
        Who celebrates both Christmas and Chanukkah,
            The Winter Solstice,
                And the Miracle of the Lights.
I am the Wandering Jew

> Wondering,
>   As I wander,
>   If the Messiah will ever come.
> Bless me, Father, for I have sinned.
>   Hail, Mary, full of Grace,
>   Blessed art Thou,
>   And the fruit of thy womb, Jesus,
>   Blessed Jesus, walk with me,
>   Next year in Jerusalem.

****

Call me "Israel" -- "One Who Wrestles With God." That is the name that Jacob took after his long night of wrestling with the angel of the Lord. It may as well have been mine.

My mother once told me, after I'd grown up, that although she tried very hard to do so, she'd found it difficult to ever love me. She wanted a child who was pliable and obedient. From the cradle I was stubborn and disobedient. But perhaps the biggest reason she found me unlovable was that I rejected what she loved the most. Most of all she loved God. But I did not love God. I only pretended that I did. Besides being one who wrestled with God, I guess that also made me a *converso*.

In 1492 Columbus sailed the ocean blue. And Spain expelled the Jew. And those Jews who did not leave were forced to convert to Christianity. But many, it was thought, remained secret Jews, converts -- *conversos* -- in name only. They still practiced Judaism at home, in their private lives. And to search out and destroy such secret unbelievers, King Ferdinand established the Spanish Inquisition.

I, too, hid from the Inquisition, a *converso* in name only. But I did not have a secret faith to fall back upon. I was steeped in Southern Protestantism, raised as a Southern Baptist transplanted to Arizona, where we'd become Mormons. But, I was always a *converso* Baptist and a *converso* Mormon because, from my earliest memory, I never believed any of it. So, I was an unbeliever in the truest sense. I had never been a True Believer in any religion.

Indeed, I was not only an atheist, I was an anti-theist. I saw religion -- *all* religion -- as the oldest and greatest tyranny. It not only tyrannized over us now, in *this* life, but claimed to have the power to tyrannize over us in the *next* life, as well -- for all eternity! It was thus a tyranny worse than Hitler's. Hitler just aimed for a Thousand-Year Reich. But God -- under whatever name you called Him -- claimed to be an Omnipotent Fuehrer who ruled over an Eternal Reich. What could be more hateful?

If I'd been raised in some Muslim land, I'd have been just as hostile to Islam. Indeed, the very word "Islam" is Arabic for "submission." I refused to submit to any spiritual tyrant. Perhaps, for this reason, I'd have been stoned to death in days of old by the Muslim faithful, as those who disobey are still stoned today, in some places, by those who revere Allah, for Islam is as hateful and intolerant of disbelief as is Christianity. In the Koran, Sura 8:12, the Prophet Mohammed himself, speaking for Allah, the Beneficent, the Merciful, says , "I will cast terror into the hearts of those who disbelieve. Therefore, strike off their heads and strike off every fingertip of them." Allah, then, the Great Terrorist God, is just as abhorrent as the Judeo-Christian God. But, of course, they are both supposedly one and the same, so this makes sense.

There seemed to me to be two perfectly logical and non-spiritual reasons for why religion is a universal human phenomenon. The first of these is that humans seem to have an innate cognitive need to seek order in even the most chaotic phenomena. We find it hard to remember or make sense of random bits of information. So, we try to *make* sense out of it. This is why we see patterns in clouds and shapes in ink blots.

And this is why mnemonics work. They meet our cognitive need for order. Mnemonics are memory devices which impose an easily remembered pattern on otherwise chaotic and hard to remember data. For example, you might find it hard to quickly rattle off all the names of the Great Lakes, because such a list is completely random. You might have to think about it, you might try to picture a map of the lakes in your mind, then you might stumble through their names and wonder if you got them all.

But, suppose I told you it would be possible to quickly and easily remember them forever if you simply remember the acronym HOMES. Each letter stands for one of the lakes: Huron, Ontario, Michigan, Erie, and Superior. Suddenly the random information is orderly and has a pattern. And, because of that, you can quickly and easily make sense of and recall the information. However, like cloud patterns and shapes in ink blots, mnemonic devices like this have no inherent meaning. They are just artificial patterns we *impose* on chaos in order to make sense of it.

Likewise, primitive humans looked around themselves and saw mystery and chaos everywhere. So, for their own psychological health, they began to concoct explanations for these mysteries. They began to attribute agency and meaning where no agent or meaning existed. Someone, or some *thing,* had to have made things happen: The rain to fall, the crops to fail, babies to be born, and the children to die. There had to be a *reason* for these things.

And so primitive humans invented ghosts and demons and monsters under the bed, gods, goddesses, Jehovah and Allah. And it was these ghosts and demons and monsters under the bed who did whatever it was the early humans were trying to explain -- for reasons of their own, "for the Lord works in mysterious ways." But, at least the primitives knew who was *doing* it. And so, every religion in every culture, no matter how primitive, seems to believe in invisible beings -- ancestors, spirits, ghosts or gods -- who intentionally *do* things to us, or for us, or around us.

Of course, this human cognitive need to make sense out of chaos also, eventually, gave rise to naturalism, which argues that there is but one world, the natural world. The philosophy of naturalism arose in the sixth century B.C. among the pre-Socratic Milesian philosophers, including Thales, Anaximander, and Anaximenes. They rejected Greek myths as explanations for the world and argued that nature was a self-contained system that operated according to laws which could be understood by human reason. Thus, it was not necessary to postulate the existence of something outside the natural world -- something supernatural -- to understand how nature worked. Understanding could be found within the natural world itself. From this, it follows that the supernatural does not exist: There are no gods or God, no immortal souls, no afterlife, no heaven, no hell, no ghosts, witches, and demons. Imagine!

This worldview is the beginning of history. The word "history" in its root sense means "inquiry." Thus, the historical worldview rejects myth. Herodotus is often called "the Father of History," but, in fact, there is much which is entirely mythological in his work. Instead, history really begins with the later Thucydides and his account of the Peloponnesian War. It was Thucydides who, for the first time, endeavored to inquire about and to record a series of verifiable and dated events which fit together in a cause and effect story.

This worldview, therefore, resulted in the first discernable "atheist" (literally, "not theist") beliefs. And, with the questions of the Greek philosopher Epicurus (341-271 B.C.), we also have the first explicit doubts about the existence of God or gods in general. It was Epicurus who first asked the basic questions concerning theism which have never yet, almost 2,500 years later, been satisfactorily answered:

"Is God willing to prevent evil," he asked, "but not able?

"Then he is not omnipotent.

"Is He able, but not willing?

"Then He is malevolent.

"Is God both able and willing?

"Then where does evil come from?

"Is He neither able nor willing?

"Then why call Him God?"

It is also with the the naturalistic worldview of the ancient Greeks that we find the origins of science. Science, like history, is based on rationality, which is an outgrowth of the naturalistic worldview. Rationality presents explanations based on reason, evidence, and arguments open to examination and evaluation, acceptance or rejection, on the basis of facts and principles available to all. Thus, science seemed to give me better explanations for the mysteries of life than religion. This was because, unlike religion, the scientific method of research and verification allows us to *test* our patterns and explanations and refine them or discard them if they prove unable to explain the data. This is the very basis of the naturalistic-based rational worldview.

Religion, on the other hand, can never be tested and can never be substantiated or repudiated by experiment. That meant, for me, that it was useless as an explanatory tool. Religion is, in essence, irrational. We pride ourselves on calling our species *homo sapiens* -- thinking hominids -- and claim our ability to think rationally distinguishes us from all other animals. But few of us are entirely rational. Instead, our lives are in the grip of emotions and feelings, which shape our thoughts. And thoughts based on emotions and feelings are mostly immune to rational argument.

So, I realized rational arguments against religion would never convince anyone around me. But, I couldn't stop myself from coming up with rational objections to what I was taught. In fact, I could do no else, because I believed in rationality as the basis of all thought.

The second reason religion came into existence, it seemed to me, and continues its existence, is also emotional and psychological. Perhaps it evolved as a survival mechanism, but, for whatever reason, every single one of us believes, deep down, that it's all about *me*. We all feel that we are the Center of the Universe and, when we move, the universe moves with us. Whereas, everyone else out there is actually just a bit player in the drama of our own lives.

And, since it's all about *us,* what sense would there be in the Center of the Universe ceasing to exist? The universe itself would then crease to exist. Therefore, some essential part of us, the soul, let's say, doesn't die and will live on for eternity in an afterlife following this life. How could it be otherwise, if we are the Be-All and End-All of Creation? And religion explains the nature of this continuing eternal life of the Center of the Universe.

But, at the very same time, we are tortured with doubt about this belief. What if we *aren't* the Center of the Universe? Thus, we entertain two contradictory tenets -- it's all about *us,* but maybe it *isn't* -- and so we suffer the psychic anxiety of what psychologists term "cognitive dissonance," believing two contradictory things simultaneously. "Anyone can become a millionaire -- but the game is rigged and it's all in who you know."

And, it is because we want to dissolve this dissonance and reconcile our contradictory beliefs that we whore after celebrities, the rich and the famous, and worship the Golden Calf of fame. This is because it seems that the celebrity has what we want, what we believe we rightly should have, the celebrity is the acknowledged Center of the Universe. But, if we can perhaps get close to the celebrity, get his autograph or get our picture taken with her, or if we can be like him or wear the same clothes she does, then we can move closer to the Center of the Universe, where we believe we rightly belong. Perhaps some of the fairy dust will even rub off on us.

This worship of the Golden Calf of fame and celebrity in an attempt to get closer to the Center of the Universe is thus the final basis of religion. The pagan gods were the first big celebrities of primitive humans. Then, with the emergence of monotheism, God became the Ultimate Celebrity; and, if you could get closer to God, you'd get closer to the Center of the Universe, the Alpha and the Omega, the Beginning and the End of Everything. You'd get closer to where you really, deep down, always believed you should be.

In any case, these are the conclusions I came to as I thought about religion as a kid. And all of these conclusions led me to doubt religion as being anything other than a manifestation of our psychological needs and fears. And I thought my doubt was a good thing, because I also felt that all freedom of thought begins with doubt.

But, I had to keep such thoughts and doubts to myself. It was dangerous to doubt, it was dangerous to question. Everyone around me, my family and all my friends and everyone in the neighborhood and at school -- *everyone* -- was a True Believer. They were all faithful, while I was *reasonable,* although my mother always felt I was unreasonable. I was thus a lonely foot soldier in the eternal war between faith and reason, two incompatible ways of understanding human existence. This made me feel, like Moses after he fled the wrath of Pharaoh and lived among the foreign Midianites, that "I was a stranger in a strange land" (Exodus 2:22).

However, even though I was a lone partisan lost behind enemy lines, my morale was high. I felt I was on the winning side.

Perhaps my reading, which I remember always doing, led me into the ways of unbelief. Early on I became an avid science fact and science fiction reader. It would be incorrect to say that reading science fact and fiction undermined my religious faith, as I never had any faith to undermine. But it did *confirm* my unbelief. The science presented more compelling explanations for the mysteries of the cosmos, while the fiction sometimes presented stories which directly questioned religious belief. One such subversive story I remember with vividness was Arthur C. Clarke's Hugo-winning 1955 short story, "The Star."

In this classic story, which I must have read in a reprint anthology or a collection of Clarke's short fiction, a human exploration party lands on a dead planet circling the remnants of a star which went nova eons before. The party discovers that the planet-wide civilization which flourished before that stellar explosion created beautiful works of art, built magnificent cities, and left all indications of having been a wise and noble people. And then their star exploded and destroyed them and all they had accomplished.

Then further calculations of when the nova occurred and how it would have been seen from Earth revealed that this exploding star had to have been the Star of Bethlehem, suddenly appearing in the night sky over ancient Israel. Of course, a Christian sees the appearance of the Star of Bethlehem as a purposeful act of God. Which had to mean, then, that God purposely wiped out this wonderful civilization simply to give a sign to the Three Wise Men and lead them to the Christ child. The story is told from the viewpoint of a believing Christian, who wrestles with why God would have genocidally destroyed billions of such wise and wonderful people for such a trivial purpose. Since I was not a believing Christian, I read it simply as confirmation of God's capricious and murderous nature.

Being a reader of science fiction became yet one more way in which I was socially isolated, because everyone I knew laughed at it. "How can you *believe* in that crap?" people asked. "UFOs and aliens and outer space monsters?"

I answered that I *didn't* believe in "that crap." It is called science fiction, I said, because it is *fiction*. It seemed that most everyone who objected to my reading material didn't actually read *anything* themselves. As a consequence of being non-readers, they assumed that one had to believe in the *literal truth* of fiction in order to enjoy it. They didn't understand that fiction was an acknowledged lie -- *which told the truth.*

I enjoyed reading about time travel to the distant past and alternative history in parallel worlds and faster-than-light space flight, but I knew they were scientific impossibilities. They were fictions, and I did not confuse fiction with fact. And I did not feel that one had to believe in the *literal truth* of a short story or a novel in order to enjoy it and learn from its *metaphorical truth.* So I saw science fiction as metaphorical, as a way of talking about things you cared about. Or as a literature read simply for enjoyment. But not as something you had to literally *believe* was *real* in order to enjoy it or to use metaphorically.

Instead, when it came to *belief,* what I believed in was science fact. Late at night in my bedroom in our white stucco house on 52nd Street in Phoenix, with my family asleep around me, I read with a flashlight under the covers when I should have been asleep myself. I read H. G. Wells writing about history and science, and I read H. G. Wells when he wrote science fiction. I became, like H. G. Wells, a convert to the Enlightenment and the Scientific Revolution. I believed in *data,* data which one could observe, analyze, test, and repeat. I believed, in other words, in the scientific method. This intellectual discipline, I believed, was the only way we have of discovering new information. And new information, I believed, was the driving force of human progress, so I was always hungry for new information.

Religion seemed to be the complete opposite of what I'd come to believe. It stood in the way of human progress. It was merely another form of superstition -- and I disdained all things supernatural. I did not believe in God or Satan. I did not believe in ghosts and prophecy and gods and demons. I did not believe in heaven, hell, souls, or spiritual immortality. They were simply manifestations of irrational superstition.

And, yes, my mother was deeply superstitious. She once told me about spending time at her Aunt Flossie's Tennessee farm one summer in the early 1930s when she was eight or nine. "One of their little chicks died," she said, "so we kids made a casket for it out of a shoe box. We dug a grave out near the swing and had a funeral for it. We even planted a baby cedar tree at the head of the grave.

"That night at the supper table we told what we'd done. Aunt Flossie said, 'Oh, Child, you ought not to have done that. When the tree grows as tall as you girls, you will all die.' Well, that night when we got up to use the slop jar, the chamber pot, we sneaked out and pulled up the durn tree."

In 1939, when my mother was 14, her own mother died. Mom idly began counting the number of cars in the funeral procession. By the time she got up to 35 cars Aunt Flossie said, "Oh, Tootsie," as Mom was called by her family, "don't count the cars. If you do, you will die at the age that the cars total." So, her entire 35th year, which was in 1960, Mom lived in fear and trembling, as she was sure she would die before the year was over.

Aunt Flossie also told Mom she would die if she looked at a full Moon. It seems Aunt Flossie was obsessed with death and dying -- as my mother also became. Almost anything could cause an early death. No doubt Aunt Flossie would have been particularly perturbed by me looking at the full Moon with binoculars, as I often did on clear Arizona nights. Surely, I was courting certain death.

To me, there seemed to be little difference between Mom's superstitions and her religious beliefs. And her religious faith colored every aspect of her life, no matter how mundane. For example, my fondest childhood memories are of lying under the covers in bed and listening to Mom rocking in the living room late at night and singing the good ol' Gospel songs, the only songs she ever sang, as she tried to lull my younger brothers to sleep in her arms.

And perhaps I, too, was eventually lulled into sleep and dreams of an Old Rugged Cross, on a hill far away, the symbol of suffering and shame, or the Rock of Ages, cleft for me, or of climbing Jacob's Ladder, every rung going higher, higher.

I still know and love these songs. I suppose one could call me a hymn-loving heathen. But I resisted singing them in church, even though I was always told I had a good singing voice. I felt that if I sang the songs long enough, I might eventually begin to believe them. Even so, standing in Sherwood Heights Baptist Church, surrounded by all the True Believers, a stranger among strangers, I was expected to sing, as if this *converso* was one of them.

So I sang those good ol' Gospel songs. But I sang in a low, almost inaudible voice, a voice even I could hardly hear. And I ad libbed sacrilegious verses as we went along, so that every time I was compelled to stand and sing, I reaffirmed my blasphemy. "Let us praise God all sheep here below, let us all refuse to know, all the hatred that He shows, all the lies that He tells, all the babies that He burns in Hell. A-men."

I had to keep my unbelief secret in Sunday School and at Vacation Bible School, which I attended during the summer. The congregation gave me a cheap Bible inscribed from "Sherwood Heights Baptist Sunday School." I still have this Bible. It was new when I received it, but now it is much worn, with the rigid covers separated from the binding, as I read this Bible in its entirety many times, both Old and New Testaments, and annotated it thoroughly.

This was perhaps more than the True Believers ever did, even though they accepted as an article of faith that it was the literal Word of God. One would think True Believers would want to know, intimately, what God said for their eternal benefit. But, they didn't *have* to know what was in the Bible. They simply believed whatever they were told was in it. It seemed they knew very little, but they believed very much.

But I questioned. So, in order to know the enemy, I had to know the Bible.

For this reason, I was always a good Bible student; I was the best. I won Sunday School awards for being the first to memorize the correct sequence of all the books of the Bible (best sequence: "Joshua, Judges, Ruth" -- yeah, Joshua *would* be judgmental, especially of a woman, I thought); for discovering the shortest sentence in the Bible ("Jesus wept," John 11:35); for knowing that Sarah, Father Abraham's wife, is the only woman in the Bible whose age at death is given: 127 years.

And then I asked questions, assuring my teachers I was sincere.

"If Moses wrote the Pentateuch, the first five books of the Bible, why does it end by saying that no one knows to this day where Moses was buried?

"It says in Genesis 1:16 that God didn't make the Sun and the Moon until the fourth day. In that case, how long were those days before there was a Sun to measure day and night?

"And if Cain and Abel were Adam and Eve's only children at the time Cain was exiled, why does it say in Genesis 4:17 that Cain found a wife in the Land of Nod? Where did these Nod people come from?

"And why are there two different Creation stories in Genesis? In Genesis, Chapter One, God creates plants before Adam and Eve. In Chapter Two, He creates them after Adam and Eve. In Chapter One, God creates animals before Adam and Eve. In Chapter Two, He creates animals after Adam and Eve. In Chapter One, God creates Adam and Eve at the same time. In Chapter Two, He creates Eve later, pulling her from Adam's rib cage. Which is the truth? Did God get confused and forget what he did when?

"And if God stopped the Sun from going down so Joshua could have more time to slay his enemies, that means God stopped the Earth from spinning. But forward momentum would have kept the Earth's surface moving forward, just like our bodies keep moving toward the dashboard if the driver of our car slams on the brakes. The entire surface of the Earth would have kept moving toward the dashboard. Wouldn't there have been unimaginable global destruction everywhere if the Earth just suddenly stopped spinning and the surface kept spinning? And wouldn't we have evidence of that massive destruction in the geological or historical record? But the Bible doesn't say 'And there were great earthquakes in the land'."

"It was a miracle," my Sunday School teacher told me. She was an older lady who looked to my young eyes like she'd been teaching Sunday School since the time of Moses. "A miracle is something which defies physical laws. God is not bound by the laws of physics, because He created those laws. He is above the laws. Therefore, He can do anything, even if it seems impossible. With God, all things are possible."

"But if God can do anything, why does it say in Titus 1:2 that God 'cannot lie'? If God can't lie, then God is not all-powerful. And if God is not omnipotent, is he really God? And doesn't that seem like a lesser standard of morality than we live by?"

"What do you mean?"

"Well, God *cannot* lie. I *can* lie, but I *choose* not to. Doesn't the fact that God has no choice in the matter, but I do, and I *choose* to do the right thing -- doesn't that imply a higher standard of morality on my part?"

"Are you putting yourself above God?"

"No, ma'am. I'm just trying to do as the Apostle Paul instructed us to do in First Thessalonians, 5:21, 'Prove all things; hold fast that which is good.'"

"You can hold fast the revealed Truth of the entire Word of God."

"But, what is the truth in Titus 1:12? The Apostle Paul says there that, when he visited Crete, a Cretian prophet told him that 'The Cretians are always liars.'"

"If the Apostle Paul says that is true, then it was true."

"But the person who said that was a Cretian. And if what he said was true, that meant he had to be telling a lie. But, if he was telling a lie, then what he said about Cretians *always* lying wasn't true. Because he was a Cretian who was, at that point, telling the truth about Cretians. But if he was telling the truth, that Cretians always lied, then he wasn't telling the truth, he was lying. Because he was a Cretian. And so he had to be lying. And so what he said was true. So, what is the truth in this passage? I just want to know."

"I don't follow you in all of that."

"Well, then, here's a question you may be able to answer. What about Eve? If Eve was created from Adam's rib, as Genesis Version Number Two said, did she have a belly button? Since she was never in a womb, she would not have needed an umbilical cord, and so would not have needed a belly button. And if God created Adam from a handful of dust, Adam was never in a womb, either. So, did Adam have a belly button? And if Adam was created in God's image, and Adam *did* have a belly button, does that mean God has a belly button? And if God has a belly button, does that mean he had an umbilical cord in His mother's womb? And, if He did, who was God's mother?"

"Eric, God did not have a mother. God just *is* and always has been. Does not the Apostle Paul say in Hebrews 11:1 that 'faith is the substance of things hoped for, the evidence of things not seen?' We have to accept some things on faith, even if we can't understand or prove them."

"But that contradicts what the Apostle Paul said in First Thessalonians, 5:21, 'Prove all things.' Which saying by Paul am I supposed to believe?"

"You're supposed to believe that faith is the evidence of things not seen, and by faith we prove all things. So, have faith and just *believe* in the Lord."

"If I believe in the Lord, will He believe in me?"

"Eric, you're being blasphemous and you're disrupting the class. You should just love and fear God more and accept things on faith."

"But if God is infinitely good, why should I fear Him?"

"Eric, that's enough. Stop disturbing the class with these nonsense questions."

For my part, I didn't believe that faith was capable of proving anything at all. In fact, faith *avoids* proof, faith is certain in the complete *absence* of proof. It just accepts, without question. It is the direct opposite of science, which *does* prove things on the basis of evidence, and yet remains uncertain of final truth, remains open to the possibility of being proved wrong. But faith is never open to the possibility of being wrong. Faith does not accept the validity of evidence. Thus, it was just double-talking gibberish for the Apostle Paul to speak of faith as some kind of evidence, seen or not.

But, I didn't express such inner doubts. Such rational objections would have fallen on deaf ears. Instead, I turned to the Bible.

"But, why should I believe you when you tell me all this?," I said. "Doesn't God tell us that we shouldn't listen to any woman teacher? And shouldn't *you* be listening to *me,* instead?"

"Where did you get *that?*"

"From the Word of God. Timothy 2:11-14 says, in part, 'A woman should learn in quietness and full submission. I do not permit a woman to teach or to have authority over a man; she must be silent.' And 1 Corinthians 14:34-35 says that is is 'disgraceful' for a woman to speak in church. Besides, teaching is a form of work, and Exodus 35:2 says all who work on the Sabbath should be put to death. Don't you believe in the Word of God?"

"Eric, let's just get on with our Bible lesson for today."

And so I persisted in disturbing the Sunday School peace, week after week. Over time, it became harder and harder to pretend I was a True Believer. I'm sure that, after awhile, my persistent questions in Sunday School made it clear that I wasn't sincerely seeking God.

Mom, at least, eventually discovered the truth.

In December, 1964, once, and only once, after we'd lived in Phoenix a dozen years, we visited Mom's family back in Chattanooga, Tennessee, for Christmas. By then I was asking questions of faith even more adamantly. But in Chattanooga I fell in love with the most beautiful Bible I'd ever seen. It belonged to Mom's brother, Uncle Harold. It had gilt edges, was bound in soft white leather, had a deep blue ribbon as a book mark, and was so small it fit in my palm. It felt wonderful just lying there in my hand. The type was tiny, but it could still be read. I could easily slip it into the rear pocket of my jeans. When I saw Uncle Harold's Bible, I *really* wanted a Bible just like his.

So, when Uncle Harold asked what he could get me for Christmas, I said, "I love your little Bible, Uncle Harold. Please give me a Bible just like it so I can always carry it with me. It's the only thing I want."

"Don't give him a Bible!" Mom ordered. "He'd only use it to argue *against* the Bible."

I felt like Mom had stabbed me in the heart. She was absolutely right. I *did* want the small Bible so that I'd be able to whip it out and cite chapter and verse in my ceaseless confrontations with the True Believers.

But I also wanted the Bible because it was so beautiful and I loved the look and feel of it. And I also wanted the Bible because it would have been just like the one Uncle Harold, whom I admired, owned and loved.

Mom's command to Uncle Harold hurt so much I couldn't even justify or defend my request. I just stood in stunned silence. And Uncle Harold did not give me a Bible like his for Christmas.

And I felt more alone than ever.

But I did not stop "arguing against the Bible."

What bothered me even more than all the logical contradictions and silly absurdities of the Bible were the stories of God's sadism and cruelty. It seemed to me that the existence of evil -- and of evil atrocities like the Holocaust -- was either the ultimate refutation or ultimate condemnation of God. Agreeing with Epicurus, I felt there were only two possibilities: The first was that God was benevolent, but was powerless to abolish evil. In which case He was not the omnipotent Ruler of the Universe, and therefore He was not God.

The second possibility was that God *was* the omnipotent Ruler of the Universe, but He did not wish to abolish evil. And if God had the power to do so, but did not wish to abolish evil, that was the most evil act conceivable. In which case, He, Himself, was Evil Incarnate, a sadistic demon who ruled the universe and delighted in watching the sufferings of His creations. People in my church were always preaching that God was a kind and benevolent Father. But most of what God did in the Bible contradicted what I was told about Him. Most of what God did in the Bible confirmed the hypothesis that God was a malevolent all-powerful Demon who delighted in torturing us.

For example, why should an omnipotent Being feel the constant need for revenge against his puny creations? How could they possible harm him? And yet the Bible is rife with instances of God saying things like, "And I will execute great vengeance upon them with furious rebukes; and they shall know that I am the Lord, when I shall lay my vengeance upon them (Ezekiel 25:17)." It's like, "Whoa, you don't know who you messed with and you're gonna be sorry you hurt me after I get through with you!" This doesn't sound like a compassionate all-powerful Father. It sounds like a petulant little boy.

And what about Moses and Pharaoh? God told Moses to go to the Pharaoh and tell him to let the Jews go free out of the land of Egypt -- or else!

But God is all-knowing, and He already knew how Pharaoh would react. He knew Pharaoh would immediately allow all the Children of Israel to leave. So He also told Moses, in Exodus 4:21 and again in Exodus 7:3, that, "I will harden his heart, that he shall not let the people go" and "I will harden Pharaoh's heart..."

And God did just as He said He would do. To impress Pharaoh with God's power, Moses threw down his staff before Pharaoh and it became a snake. But (Exodus 7:13, 22), God "hardened Pharaoh's heart, that he harkened not unto" Moses and his brother, Aaron.

So God unleashed his first plague upon Egypt, the plague of frogs. And Pharaoh immediately cried "Uncle!" "Then Pharaoh called for Moses and Aaron," we are told in Exodus 8:8, "and said, Entreat the Lord, that he may take away the frogs from me, and from my people; and I will let the people go, that they may do sacrifice unto the Lord."

But God hardened Pharaoh's heart again, so that he changed his mind. And so it went, plague after plague. After each plague Pharaoh said "Go! Leave! Get outta here!"

But then God always intervened to harden Pharaoh's heart (Exodus 9:12, etc., etc.) so that he changed his mind.

Finally, God, the All-Powerful Puppet Master, escalated His sadistic torture to the killing of all the Egyptian first-born. And we have the confession of the Supreme Sadist of His authorship of all these pointless tortures and murders right there in the Word of God!

So, why do we blame Pharaoh for not letting the Jews go? He had no say in it at all. It was all God's doing. God deliberately intervened to harden Pharaoh's heart and reverse his decisions, just so He could continue inflicting sadistic plagues on the Egyptians.

Then, once Moses and Aaron led the Hebrews out of Egypt, God didn't let either of his faithful servants enter the Promised Land. This was punishment for some petty infraction of His rules. It seems God had determined that Aaron, now an old man, was not sufficiently deferential to His Divine Nibs. So God ordered Moses to strip his brother Aaron naked and leave the old man on a mountain top to die of exposure. By tradition, the mountain upon which Aaron was left shivering to die for his disrespect toward our All-Powerful and All-Loving God is called Jebel Haroun ("Mt. Aaron," in Arabic), and can be visited in southern Jordan. It is about a two-hour donkey ride south of the popular tourist destination of Petra.

Later, Moses had to peer longingly at the Promised Land from a mountain top as the Children of Israel proceeded on without him, having left him behind to also die alone. It is because of this abandonment, I guessed, that the last book of the Pentateuch tells us no one knows where Moses is buried. Perhaps, because he was left alone, he wasn't even buried. Perhaps vultures picked his bones clean.

Moses and Aaron were not the only ones our petty and petulant God refused to let enter the Promised Land. God did not allow a single one of those who risked the Exodus out of Egypt, believing in and searching for the Promised Land, actually to enter into the Promised Land. It seems God had lied to them when He "promised" them they'd reach the Promised Land. They never saw it because God judged every last one of them as slackers who worshipped the Golden Calf or displeased the admittedly jealous Lord God with other offenses. That's *why* God left them to wander in the wilderness for forty years. Time was needed for them to die off.

It's not all that far from Egypt to Israel, even on foot. Joseph, Mary, and the baby Jesus fled to Egypt on foot and on donkey when King Herod was killing all the babies. But God turned a few days' journey into a forty-year-trek so all the Exodus Jews would die off. God lured them out of bondage in Egypt with the promise of a land flowing with milk and honey. What He gave them instead was death in the desert.

When the wandering Jews finally reached the border of the Promised Land, God commanded then-leader Joshua to mass circumcise all Jewish males -- circumcision being a sign of the "covenant" between God and the Jews -- because not a single circumcised Exodus Jewish male remained alive. They were all dead in the wilderness, from Moses and Aaron on down. So much for God's forgiveness, supposedly one of His great traits. I'm not making any of this up. It's all there in Joshua 5:2-9. The Bible is full of these lessons in why you should *not* believe in or follow leaders, especially Divine Leaders. They usually repay your loyalty with betrayal.

Once in the Promised Land, God ordered the Jews to exterminate "utterly" the people they found there, man, woman, and child. On God's orders, the Jews killed King Sihon and his people, the Amorites: "And we took all his cities at that time, and utterly destroyed the men, and the women, and the little ones, of every city, we left none to remain" (Deuteronomy 2:34). We're talking genocide here!

When King Og of Bashan stood in the path of progress, "...they smote him, and his sons, and all his people, until there was none left him alive; and they possessed his land" (Numbers 21:35). "And we utterly destroyed them...utterly destroying the men, women, and children, of every city" (Deuteronomy 3:6). The entrance of the Jews into the Promised Land was a bloody and violent "ethnic cleansing" of the land.

The Midianites fared a little better. Perhaps this was because the Midianites had sheltered Moses when he first fled the Pharaoh's wrath. Remember Exodus, Chapter Two? Midia was where Moses was a "stranger in a strange land." But, he didn't remain a stranger for too long; he married Zipporah, a Midianite woman. Maybe this was why, later on, God let the Midianite women live. They were good for procreation.

On the other hand, following God's orders to the letter, the Jews murdered all the Midianite males, man, boy, and infant. I guessed this was so there would be no competition for the Midianite women. So, after slaughtering all the in-laws of Moses, the Jews enslaved the Midianite women and girls and looted the Midianite cattle, sheep, and goods (Numbers 31:7-9).

Sometimes God ordered that even the herds of cattle and flocks of sheep be slaughtered, along with their masters, and this was why God had a falling out with King Saul. After he carried out God's orders to exterminate the Amalekites, Saul distributed their herds and flocks among the Israelites, instead of butchering them, as God had ordered.

Whereupon omniscient God, who should have known beforehand that Saul would defy His orders, whined to the prophet Samuel, "I repenteth me that I have set up Saul to be king: for he is turned back from following me, and hath not performed my commandments" (I Samuel 15:11). God rejected Saul and enthroned David, whom He could rely on to kill as directed.

So it went, tribe after tribe, nation after nation, falling under the sword of the Israelites. Men were slaughtered, babies were butchered, women were raped and enslaved on God's orders. God was as pitiless as pestilence, ferocious as famine. The confessions of the bloody-handed mass murderers, God's willing executioners, are all there in the Pentateuch and the subsequent books. In fact, I went through the Bible page-by-page and counted up all the people God murdered or ordered to be murdered -- excluding the famines and plagues God sent down on a regular basis, and the eradication of Sodom and Gomorrah for their lascivious lifestyle, and Noah's Flood (by which God genocidally murdered everyone on Earth except for a blessed eight in Noah's Ark) -- and realized that God's slaughter record quickly reached or exceeded Holocaust proportions. I concluded that He's the greatest mass murderer in history. It's a wonder the human species survived God's mass extinctions.

Satan, on the other hand, is responsible for only ten deaths. He kills Job's three daughters and seven sons -- with God's permission. We are supposed to hate Satan and love God, but who is the greater monster? Who is more evil? It was clear to me that the only reason such a compulsively homicidal psychopath had been able to get away with mass murder is because winners write the history books. In doing so, they get to make themselves the heroes of their own stories, while demonizing their opponents. After all, isn't the Bible called the "Word of God"? We only hear His side of the story. Where is Satan's Bible?

In church we were supposed to sing hosannas praising God's genocide because the victims had it coming. They were wicked and committed sins of various natures. Isn't it strange, I thought, that in our modern age of secular humanism, most of us have come to see the death penalty for criminals as immoral on principle? But in past times, such as the medieval "age of faith," when all men believed in God and the Church ruled, devout Christians considered it their moral right to torture sinners and criminals, to sentence them to barbaric deaths and burn them alive. Godly people of that era called such human bonfires *autos de fe,* "acts of faith." No wonder it was known as the "Dark Ages," I thought.

Are we really supposed to think that the babies and young children of Sodom and Gomorrah were wicked and sinful and they deserved to be incinerated with hellfire from heaven? Can all the babies and children of the world have been wicked and sinful enough in God's eyes to deserve to be killed in their millions by Noah's Flood? Or maybe we are not supposed to think about the victims of God's murders at all?

God justifies the ethnic cleansing of the Promised Land of its former inhabitants because they -- and their babies and children -- didn't worship the self-confessed jealous and sadistic God of the Jews. But whose fault was that? Didn't God Himself choose not to reveal Himself to the heathen who previously owned the Promised Land? Therefore, didn't God Himself create the excuse for the genocidal slaughter the Jews committed in order to empty the Promised Land of its prior tenants?

I asked myself, "What about all the other myriad peoples of the Earth who knew not the Lord?" Christian theology allows no salvation but through Christ. "Whosoever believeth in him," says John 3:16, "should not perish, but have everlasting life." Think of the Indians of the Americas, the natives of Africa, the Polynesians, the Australian Aborigines, the millions of Asians who lived before the time of Christ or who never had a chance to get to know Christ. Think of the millions of Muslims, Hindus, Buddhists, Taoists, Confucianists, Shintoists, animists, atheists and agnostics, not to mention Jews, who live moral and honest lives, and yet deny the divinity of Christ.

The Bible promises me that God will burn all these moral, honest, hard-working people in everlasting hellfire. God does not cherish those who live moral, honest, generous, and merciful lives. God cherishes only those who believe in Him. In you fail Him in this "act of faith," God will punish you with eternal pain, even though all of mankind calls you a saint. If you profess a faith in this murderous God, you will live in eternal bliss, even though your crimes be as black as the pit of hell. Hitler only burned six million Jews. God will burn six billion or more people who, throughout the world and throughout time, did not know or accept Him or His only begotten Son. Indeed, "beneficent" God must really hate us, because He will condemn the vast majority of humanity, regardless of their virtues, to eternal torment and damnation.

To be constantly abused and tormented thus by a heavenly Father -- while being assured incessantly that the abuser and torturer truly loves us -- is a prescription for deranging perceptions of reality and instills insanity in the victims. It seemed far better for our mental health to know straight out that we are in the hands of a malevolent demon.

The Jews, God's Chosen People, were, in this respect, indeed the Children of God. They hardly needed God's commands to murder and pillage. They were quite willing to do it on their own. The story of Dinah and Shechem, told in Genesis, Chapter 34, is a good example. Shechem, the son of a local chief named Hamor, either raped or made love to Dinah, daughter of Jacob, with the result that Jacob and his sons were in an uproar over Dinah's "defilement." (The King James Version of the Bible is unclear on whether this was rape or consensual sex. It simply says Shechem "lay with her, and defiled her." It's possible Jacob and his people considered even consensual sex with someone outside the tribe a "defilement.")

When Hamor and Shechem visited Jacob to smooth things out, Hamor told Jacob that Shechem, his son, loved Dinah, who was still back in their town, and wanted to marry her. If Jacob agreed to let them marry, Hamor and Shechem would pay any bride price Jacob asked and also share their land with Jacob and his people.

It seems to have sounded like a good deal to Jacob and his sons, Levi and Simeon; they agreed to this proposal...on one condition: Shechem and all the other men in Hamor's town would have to be circumcised first. Shechem must have really loved Dinah, because he and Hamor agreed to Jacob's conditions. (I guessed all the men of the town had to go along with whatever their chief, Hamor, said.)

Following the mass penile cutting of Shechem and all of his tribesmen, "when they were in pain" and incapacitated, Jacob's sons entered the town and murdered every last man. Then

Levi and Simeon plundered the town, stole all the livestock, and seized all the women and children as slaves. Then they took Dinah back home to Papa Jacob.

Isn't this a story about how Jacob and his sons, the collective fathers of the Chosen People, lied, encouraged strangers to convert to Judaism only to make it easier to murder them all (including the innocent men who had nothing to do with Dinah), pillaged the property of well-meaning unfortunates, and enslaved the women and children who survived? And these are the Children of God? The only honorable and admirable people in the story are Hamor and Shechem, the murdered pagans I was supposed to abhor.

God is, of course, silent on these atrocities committed by his Chosen Ones. God seems to speak up only to encourage more blood and gore. For instance, there's God's raging homophobia. Gays seem to have been some of God's creations he wasn't pleased with. So, very clear laws were handed down about how to deal with such "abominations," as Leviticus 18:22 terms a man lying "with mankind, as with womankind." And, of course, the penalty for such an abomination is death. In Leviticus 20:13 we are told, "If a man also lie with mankind, as he lieth with a woman, both of them have committed an abomination: they shall surely be put to death."

What the early Jews reviled, those later Jews-turned-Christians also reviled. In Romans 1:27 the Apostle Paul rails against "men, leaving the natural use of the woman, [and who] burned in their lust one toward another; men with men working that which is unseemly..." Lesbians are just as bad. In Romans 1:26 Paul attacks the "vile affections" of women for each other, "which is against nature."

Those who "defile themselves with mankind," as Paul again describes gays in 1 Timothy 1:10, shall not go to Heaven. The "effeminate, nor abusers of themselves with mankind shall not inherit the kingdom of God," he again says in 1 Corinthians 6:9. I wondered, why would they want to? Why would they want to sit on the right hand of a God who hated them?

And then there was God's S&M relationship with Job, one which seemed particularly protracted and perverse to me. What was God's purpose in inflicting all those woes and the murders of Job's children on His good and faithful servant? Was it simply to see how far He could push Job before Job broke? Was it to win a bet with the Devil about how long masochistic Job would continue worshipping the sadistic source of all his misery? In any case, God, the Omnipotent Sadist, intensified His tortures little by little.

But, it gets worse.

God is all-knowing. He *knew* ahead of time that Job wouldn't break. Therefore, all God's infliction of torment was completely pointless as far as discovering how Job would react.

Knowing the outcome, God went ahead and tortured Job anyway. It was clear to me that only an evil sadist would treat his faithful friend as God treated Job.

I read all the ways God tortured Father Abraham who, like Moses, Aaron, and Job, was also His faithful servant. Father Abraham was so faithful he is considered the First Jew, the one with whom God made the initial Covenant and took Abraham's descendants as His "Chosen People." In his celebrated work *Fear and Trembling,* which I read many years later, the Danish philosopher Soren Kirkegaard uses the story of Abraham's willingness to slaughter his son Isaac on God's command as a wonderful example for us all. It illustrates, Kirkegaard says, how we, like Abraham, must abandon reason and our own moral judgment and take a "leap of faith" in order to serve God. Even as a young adult this seemed to me like a strange argument for a philosopher to make.

The story of Abraham and Isaac seemed to me to also portray God as an evil and insecure sadist. Perhaps, I thought, it's *because* God *is* so insecure that He tests the loyalty of his subjects and punishes them if they waver. Throughout the Old Testament, God constantly punishes His

Chosen People for one trivial reason after another, or for no reason, as in Job's case and Abraham's, for the purely sadistic pleasure it gives Him. I thought it no wonder later when I heard long suffering Tevye, in *Fiddler On the Roof,* ask God, "Couldn't you choose someone else, just once?"

I concluded on the basis of His word, as set forth in the Bible, that God is more sadistic than any mortal could possibly be because God is omniscient. Therefore, as with Job, God *already knew* that Abraham would pass His loyalty test. Abraham's obedience was therefore never in question. It was all a charade. I asked myself, what kind of divine being would allow Abraham and Isaac to climb that mountain, collecting firewood all along the way with which to incinerate Isaac, with Abraham grieving all the way with the knowledge that he will soon murder the beloved and obedient boy by his side? What kind of moral monster would allow this emotional suffering of a faithful servant, when the omniscient Divine One already knew that Abraham would pass His test? These tortures, which God inflicted on Job and Abraham, are simply the perverse and pathological actions of a sick sadist who pulls the wings off flies for the sense of power and pleasure it gives Him.

And what about Abraham? We commonly label parents who set out to murder their own children because "God told me to" as insane; we don't hold them up as moral exemplars to be emulated. Today a claim of this sort, anywhere in the land, results in a court order for a long stay in a mental hospital for the murderous parents.

I saw Abraham, whom Kirkegaard holds up as a model for us all, as a morally misguided executioner who provides an example only of something we should all reject. Abraham abandons his own reason and moral reservations and instead trusts blindly in the benevolence and wisdom of his Fuehrer. Abraham is the kind of True Believer dictators, from Hitler to Comrade Stalin to Chairman Mao, love. Dictators all want "Good Germans," who sacrifice their own reason and moral judgment to do as they are told. They want faithful servants ready raise the sword, pull the trigger, and murder their own children if ordered to do so. To my young eyes, the First Jew looked like a Good German who tells us he was "just following orders" as he committed a barbaric act. The only reason Father Abraham doesn't murder Isaac, his own beloved son, is because God gives him a countermanding order.

Woody Allen jokes about the true nature of God in his short story, "The Scrolls." In it, Allen retells the story of Abraham and Isaac. Faced with the choice of murdering his son or disobeying God's orders, Abraham thinks the choice is obvious. "To question the Lord's words is one of the worst things a person can do," he says, as he prepares to murder his son.

God is outraged that Abraham takes the command to sacrifice Isaac seriously. "I was just joking," He says. Does Abraham have no moral conscience at all?

In his defense, Abraham says that at least his willingness to follow orders and murder his own son shows that he loves God more than his own son. God scoffs at Abraham's defense. All it really proves, says God, is "that some men will follow any order no matter how asinine as long as it comes from a resonant, well-modulated voice."

I say Kirkegaard was wrong to admire Father Abraham for his murderous blind obedience. Rather, Father Abraham's readiness to murder on command should be deplored as morally reprehensible by anyone with any ethical awareness. Such obedience must be held up as an example of what *not* to do. We must defy any sadistic dictator who orders us to murder our own children and cook their flesh, even if so commanded by a resonant, well-modulated voice.

I see the sacrifice of Isaac, which God demands of Father Abraham, as a preview of God's murder of His own only begotten Son, Jesus. (BTW, if God is omnipotent, why couldn't he simply beget another Son?) This Ultimate Sacrifice is the epitome of both irrationality and of cruelty. I was told it was needed to redeem humans from their Original Sin, which began with Adam and Eve, as Paul claims in Romans, 5-7. Somehow, humans couldn't "get right" with God until Jesus took on all of humanity's sins and allowed His Father to torture and murder Him, thus exhausting God's venom and hatred of humanity (Romans, 8:3; Corinthians 5:21).

I have never been keen on blaming children for the sins of their parents. But let us suppose this bloody sacrifice could serve some redemptive purpose. Why blame Judas for betraying Jesus, then? After all, he simply did what Jesus and God wanted and needed him to do. The recently published -- and certifiably authentic -- Gospel of Judas argues exactly this position and says that Judas was the most faithful Apostle, the one Jesus trusted the most to carry out the necessary "betrayal."

By extension, I wonder why Christians blame the Jews for, supposedly, demanding the release of Barabbas instead of Jesus? (The account in John 18 specifically refers to "the Jews" making this demand, as if Barabbas and Jesus, Himself, weren't Jews.) Asking the Romans to release Barabbas and kill Jesus was what Jesus and God wanted and needed the Jews to do. For that matter, why blame the Romans for torturing and killing Jesus? Wasn't Roman complicity in crucifying Jesus needed to win redemption for Mankind? Blaming any of them is illogical. All were acting as required for the Divine Plan to manifest itself fully. It seemed to me that True Believers should applaud these Christ killers.

The One whom Christians might justly blame for the crucifixion of Christ is Christ Himself, who wanted it, sought it, needed it. Or, they might blame God, His Father, for concocting such a bloody, barbaric, sadistic and psycho way of delivering us from our Original Sin. I asked myself, was this bloodfest the best God could think up? Why couldn't He just say, "OK, guys, I forgive you for what your parents did long before you were born. Forget about it. Let's be friends from now on." Was such magnanimity impossible for God?

Finally, if Jesus died for our sins, I wondered why we still face going to Hell if we sin? What was his Atonement all about if not to save us from the eternal flames of hell? If we *still* have to pay for our sins, His Ultimate Sacrifice seemed completely irrelevant and illogical to me. And if the Ultimate Sacrifice was completely irrelevant to our ultimate eternal destinies -- then God's orchestration of this bloody murder seemed even more gratuitously sadistic and cruel.

The God of the Bible I read was no just, loving, and benevolent God. Rather, God's universe was ruled by an omnipotent sadistic Demon. Some of the beliefs of the ancient Christian Gnostic sects -- later deemed heretical by the official Church -- that the Supreme Creator of the Universe is actually an Evil Divinity and that our life here on Earth is a sentence in Hell seemed perfectly reasonable to me. Only an essentially evil force, they reasoned, only divine depravity, could effect such a cataclysm of human suffering. I still maintain, as I did at ages 12 and 13, that either God is not God, because He can't stop evil and so is therefore not omnipotent, or these "heretical" Gnostics were right and God is a Demon.

OK, I wasn't a biblical scholar. I had no idea how many angels could dance on the head of a pin. I was just a kid trying to make sense of everything I was being taught. And all of it just seemed so wrong to me. How could any person with any shred of ethical sensibility worship such a malignant and malicious God? This God was an insane sick-o, a pathological genocidal killer. He was worse than Gary Gilmore. He was worse than Dr. Josef Mengele, who tortured and murdered Jewish children at Auschwitz. He was worse than Idi Amin. He was worse than Saddam Hussein. He was worse than Hitler, Stalin, and Mao combined, all of whom God, I was taught, had created in His image.

To me, mindless faith seemed to rob True Believers of ethical awareness because, knowing all that we knew about God, from the Bible, the sacred and truthful Word of God itself, we were commanded to love and worship Him. As a result of such compulsory love and mandated worship, the Inquisition was founded, the witches burned, the heretics annihilated, the Crusades launched, the Jews exterminated, and Catholic Christian slaughtered Protestant Christian in horrific wars of religion.

Genesis 18:25 asks the relevant question, "Shall not the Judge of the all the earth do right?" Common sense and simple morality would say, yes, He should. So if God wanted *me* to love and worship him, He would have to confess His myriad sins and ask for my forgiveness.

But I was alone in waiting for God to confess His sins. Everyone I knew was a True Believer in the Psycho God; they saw no need for God, the Ultimate Serial Killer, to confess and beg forgiveness.

The only allies I found were among people long dead. Somehow I discovered Mark Twain's *Letters From the Earth* and *The Mysterious Stranger* and *The War Prayer.* You won't find the sentimental nostalgia of *Tom Sawyer* in these writings. You'll find the caustic heresy of a pen warmed up in Hell. In his 1890 essay, "Bible Teaching and Religious Practice," Twain comments on the "infallibility" of the Word of God by observing that, "During many ages there were witches. The Bible said so. The Bible commanded that they should not be allowed to live. ['Thou shalt not suffer a witch to live." Exodus 22:18.] Therefore the Church, after doing its duty in but a lazy and indolent way for eight hundred years, gathered up its halters, thumbscrews, and firebrands and set about its holy work in earnest. She worked hard at it night and day during nine centuries and imprisoned, tortured, hanged, and burned whole hordes and armies of witches, and washed the Christian world clean with their foul blood.

"Then it was discovered that there was no such thing as witches, and never had been. One does not know whether to laugh or to cry."

In *The War Prayer,* Twain brings a messenger from God to visit a congregation praying for victory in war. The messenger makes clear to the congregation exactly what they have prayed for. God, says the messenger, hears both the spoken and unspoken parts of that prayer and had commanded him to put into words their unspoken desires:

"O Lord, our Father, our young patriots, idols of our hearts, go forth to battle -- be Thou near them! We them -- in spirit -- we also go forth from the sweet peace of our beloved firesides to smite the foe. O Lord, our God, help us to tear their soldiers to bloody shreds with our shells; help us to cover their smiling fields with the pale forms of their patriot dead; help us to drown the thunder of the guns with the shrieks of their wounded, writhing in pain; help us to lay waste their humble homes with a hurricane of fire; help us to wring the hearts of their unoffending widows with unavailing grief; help us to turn them out roofless with their little children to wander unfriended the wastes of their desolated land in rags and hunger and thirst, sport of the sun-flames of summer and the icy winds of winter, broken in spirit, worn with travail, imploring Thee for the refuge of the grave and denied it -- for our sakes who adore Thee, Lord, blast their hopes, blight their lives, protract their bitter pilgrimage, make heavy their steps, water their way with their tears, stain the white snow with the blood of their wounded feet! We ask it, in the spirit of love, of Him Who is the Source of Love, and Who is the ever-faithful refuge and friend of all that are sore beset and seek His aid with humble and contrite hearts. Amen."

The messenger departs. "It was believed afterwards," Twain concludes, "that the man was a lunatic, because there was no sense in what he said."

Twain says that he was urged not to publish *The War Prayer*, written in 1904-05, because it was too heretical. Twain finally conceded because, he said, "I have told the whole truth in that, and only dead men can tell the truth in this world. It can be published after I am dead." And so it was done. Twain died in 1910 and the essay finally appeared in Twain's 1923 collection, *Europe and Elsewhere.*

I also discovered a collection of speeches by Twain's contemporary, Robert G. Ingersoll, which I marked up heavily. Ingersoll was a noted Gilded Age politician who earned the title of "The Great Agnostic." He traveled extensively on the lecture circuit railing against the inanities and contradictions of Judaism, Christianity, and the Bible. "There is no way to ever know or prove that there is or is not a God." He said. "It's just a matter of personal opinion." Because no one could know or prove there is or is not a God, he was honest enough to say he was agnostic on the question. His argument made sense to me. And, to my knowledge, no agnostic has ever burned a pagan, heretic, or unbeliever at the stake.

To Ingersoll, the fundamental beliefs of Christianity were as crazy as they were to me. "The notion that faith in Christ is to be rewarded by an eternity of bliss," he said, "while a dependence upon reason, observation, and experience merits everlasting pain, is too absurd for refutation." And yet, such belief was, after all, *not* too absurd for refutation, because Christians clung to it yet a hundred years after Ingersoll died.

Ingersoll paid for his dependence upon reason. Once, a reporter visited him in his home and commented on his extensive and eclectic library. The reporter asked Ingersoll how much his library cost him. Ingersoll glanced over his rows upon rows of books and said, "These books cost me the governorship of Illinois, and maybe the presidency of the United States, as well."

Ingersoll championed Thomas Paine, as did Mark Twain, who wrote that, "It took a brave man before the Civil War to confess he had read *The Age of Reason."* So I searched for and found Thomas Paine's *Age of Reason*, written in 1793 and 1794 just before and during the ten months Paine was imprisoned in an eight-by-ten French prison cell awaiting possible execution by the revolutionary government.

Thomas Paine is today remembered mostly, and justly, for *Common Sense,* his defense of American independence from Great Britain. He is revered as a fierce champion of liberty, in some ways even more devout in his devotion to that ideal that others of our Founders. Benjamin Franklin is reputed to have once said to Paine, "Where liberty is, there is my country." Paine replied, "Where liberty is not, there is mine."

However, for me, Paine's most revolutionary work is *The Age of Reason.* His unjustly neglected work is a detailed and critical dissection of the Bible. Paine summarized my own feeling about religion: "All national institutions of churches," he said, "whether Jewish, Christian, or Turkish, appear to me no other than human inventions, set up to terrify and enslave mankind, and monopolize power and profit....I do not believe in the creed professed by the Jewish Church, by the Roman Church, by the Greek Church, by the Turkish Church, by the Protestant Church, nor by any church that I know of. My own mind is my own church."

Like Ingersoll, I embraced Thomas Paine as an ally on the side of Reason in my long and lonely war against Christian Unreason. While Thomas Paine was not a Christian, he seemed a far more moral man than any Christian I'd ever met. "To do good is my religion," he said, "I believe in the equality of man; and I believe that religious duties consist in doing justice, loving mercy, and endeavoring to make our fellow creatures happy." Paine's ideals seemed to me to be the only values worth espousing.

I cut a frontispiece portrait of Thomas Paine out of one of his books, framed it, and put it on an altar to intellectual freedom in my room. And in the front of the Bible the Sherwood Heights Baptist Sunday School had given me I wrote my secret *converso* name: "Thomas Belial Dagon." "Thomas" after the intellectual liberator Thomas Paine. "Belial," after a biblical demon. And "Dagon," after a rival god to God in Canaan Land.

Chosen People for one trivial reason after another, or for no reason, as in Job's case and Abraham's, for the purely sadistic pleasure it gives Him. I thought it no wonder later when I heard long suffering Tevye, in *Fiddler On the Roof,* ask God, "Couldn't you choose someone else, just once?"

I concluded on the basis of His word, as set forth in the Bible, that God is more sadistic than any mortal could possibly be because God is omniscient. Therefore, as with Job, God *already knew* that Abraham would pass His loyalty test. Abraham's obedience was therefore never in question. It was all a charade. I asked myself, what kind of divine being would allow Abraham and Isaac to climb that mountain, collecting firewood all along the way with which to incinerate Isaac, with Abraham grieving all the way with the knowledge that he will soon murder the beloved and obedient boy by his side? What kind of moral monster would allow this emotional suffering of a faithful servant, when the omniscient Divine One already knew that Abraham would pass His test? These tortures, which God inflicted on Job and Abraham, are simply the perverse and pathological actions of a sick sadist who pulls the wings off flies for the sense of power and pleasure it gives Him.

And what about Abraham? We commonly label parents who set out to murder their own children because "God told me to" as insane; we don't hold them up as moral exemplars to be emulated. Today a claim of this sort, anywhere in the land, results in a court order for a long stay in a mental hospital for the murderous parents.

I saw Abraham, whom Kirkegaard holds up as a model for us all, as a morally misguided executioner who provides an example only of something we should all reject. Abraham abandons his own reason and moral reservations and instead trusts blindly in the benevolence and wisdom of his Fuehrer. Abraham is the kind of True Believer dictators, from Hitler to Comrade Stalin to Chairman Mao, love. Dictators all want "Good Germans," who sacrifice their own reason and moral judgment to do as they are told. They want faithful servants ready raise the sword, pull the trigger, and murder their own children if ordered to do so. To my young eyes, the First Jew looked like a Good German who tells us he was "just following orders" as he committed a barbaric act. The only reason Father Abraham doesn't murder Isaac, his own beloved son, is because God gives him a countermanding order.

Woody Allen jokes about the true nature of God in his short story, "The Scrolls." In it, Allen retells the story of Abraham and Isaac. Faced with the choice of murdering his son or disobeying God's orders, Abraham thinks the choice is obvious. "To question the Lord's words is one of the worst things a person can do," he says, as he prepares to murder his son.

God is outraged that Abraham takes the command to sacrifice Isaac seriously. "I was just joking," He says. Does Abraham have no moral conscience at all?

In his defense, Abraham says that at least his willingness to follow orders and murder his own son shows that he loves God more than his own son. God scoffs at Abraham's defense. All it really proves, says God, is "that some men will follow any order no matter how asinine as long as it comes from a resonant, well-modulated voice."

I say Kirkegaard was wrong to admire Father Abraham for his murderous blind obedience. Rather, Father Abraham's readiness to murder on command should be deplored as morally reprehensible by anyone with any ethical awareness. Such obedience must be held up as an example of what *not* to do. We must defy any sadistic dictator who orders us to murder our own children and cook their flesh, even if so commanded by a resonant, well-modulated voice.

I see the sacrifice of Isaac, which God demands of Father Abraham, as a preview of God's murder of His own only begotten Son, Jesus. (BTW, if God is omnipotent, why couldn't he simply beget another Son?) This Ultimate Sacrifice is the epitome of both irrationality and of cruelty. I was told it was needed to redeem humans from their Original Sin, which began with Adam and Eve, as Paul claims in Romans, 5-7. Somehow, humans couldn't "get right" with God until Jesus took on all of humanity's sins and allowed His Father to torture and murder Him, thus exhausting God's venom and hatred of humanity (Romans, 8:3; Corinthians 5:21).

I have never been keen on blaming children for the sins of their parents. But let us suppose this bloody sacrifice could serve some redemptive purpose. Why blame Judas for betraying Jesus, then? After all, he simply did what Jesus and God wanted and needed him to do. The recently published -- and certifiably authentic -- Gospel of Judas argues exactly this position and says that Judas was the most faithful Apostle, the one Jesus trusted the most to carry out the necessary "betrayal."

By extension, I wonder why Christians blame the Jews for, supposedly, demanding the release of Barabbas instead of Jesus? (The account in John 18 specifically refers to "the Jews" making this demand, as if Barabbas and Jesus, Himself, weren't Jews.) Asking the Romans to release Barabbas and kill Jesus was what Jesus and God wanted and needed the Jews to do. For that matter, why blame the Romans for torturing and killing Jesus? Wasn't Roman complicity in crucifying Jesus needed to win redemption for Mankind? Blaming any of them is illogical. All were acting as required for the Divine Plan to manifest itself fully. It seemed to me that True Believers should applaud these Christ killers.

The One whom Christians might justly blame for the crucifixion of Christ is Christ Himself, who wanted it, sought it, needed it. Or, they might blame God, His Father, for concocting such a bloody, barbaric, sadistic and psycho way of delivering us from our Original Sin. I asked myself, was this bloodfest the best God could think up? Why couldn't He just say, "OK, guys, I forgive you for what your parents did long before you were born. Forget about it. Let's be friends from now on." Was such magnanimity impossible for God?

Finally, if Jesus died for our sins, I wondered why we still face going to Hell if we sin? What was his Atonement all about if not to save us from the eternal flames of hell? If we *still* have to pay for our sins, His Ultimate Sacrifice seemed completely irrelevant and illogical to me. And if the Ultimate Sacrifice was completely irrelevant to our ultimate eternal destinies -- then God's orchestration of this bloody murder seemed even more gratuitously sadistic and cruel.

The God of the Bible I read was no just, loving, and benevolent God. Rather, God's universe was ruled by an omnipotent sadistic Demon. Some of the beliefs of the ancient Christian Gnostic sects -- later deemed heretical by the official Church -- that the Supreme Creator of the Universe is actually an Evil Divinity and that our life here on Earth is a sentence in Hell seemed perfectly reasonable to me. Only an essentially evil force, they reasoned, only divine depravity, could effect such a cataclysm of human suffering. I still maintain, as I did at ages 12 and 13, that either God is not God, because He can't stop evil and so is therefore not omnipotent, or these "heretical" Gnostics were right and God is a Demon.

OK, I wasn't a biblical scholar. I had no idea how many angels could dance on the head of a pin. I was just a kid trying to make sense of everything I was being taught. And all of it just seemed so wrong to me. How could any person with any shred of ethical sensibility worship such a malignant and malicious God? This God was an insane sick-o, a pathological genocidal killer. He was worse than Gary Gilmore. He was worse than Dr. Josef Mengele, who tortured and murdered Jewish children at Auschwitz. He was worse than Idi Amin. He was worse than Saddam Hussein. He was worse than Hitler, Stalin, and Mao combined, all of whom God, I was taught, had created in His image.

To me, mindless faith seemed to rob True Believers of ethical awareness because, knowing all that we knew about God, from the Bible, the sacred and truthful Word of God itself, we were commanded to love and worship Him. As a result of such compulsory love and mandated worship, the Inquisition was founded, the witches burned, the heretics annihilated, the Crusades launched, the Jews exterminated, and Catholic Christian slaughtered Protestant Christian in horrific wars of religion.

Genesis 18:25 asks the relevant question, "Shall not the Judge of the all the earth do right?" Common sense and simple morality would say, yes, He should. So if God wanted *me* to love and worship him, He would have to confess His myriad sins and ask for my forgiveness.

But I was alone in waiting for God to confess His sins. Everyone I knew was a True Believer in the Psycho God; they saw no need for God, the Ultimate Serial Killer, to confess and beg forgiveness.

The only allies I found were among people long dead. Somehow I discovered Mark Twain's *Letters From the Earth* and *The Mysterious Stranger* and *The War Prayer.* You won't find the sentimental nostalgia of *Tom Sawyer* in these writings. You'll find the caustic heresy of a pen warmed up in Hell. In his 1890 essay, "Bible Teaching and Religious Practice," Twain comments on the "infallibility" of the Word of God by observing that, "During many ages there were witches. The Bible said so. The Bible commanded that they should not be allowed to live. ['Thou shalt not suffer a witch to live." Exodus 22:18.] Therefore the Church, after doing its duty in but a lazy and indolent way for eight hundred years, gathered up its halters, thumbscrews, and firebrands and set about its holy work in earnest. She worked hard at it night and day during nine centuries and imprisoned, tortured, hanged, and burned whole hordes and armies of witches, and washed the Christian world clean with their foul blood.

"Then it was discovered that there was no such thing as witches, and never had been. One does not know whether to laugh or to cry."

In *The War Prayer,* Twain brings a messenger from God to visit a congregation praying for victory in war. The messenger makes clear to the congregation exactly what they have prayed for. God, says the messenger, hears both the spoken and unspoken parts of that prayer and had commanded him to put into words their unspoken desires:

"O Lord, our Father, our young patriots, idols of our hearts, go forth to battle -- be Thou near them! We them -- in spirit -- we also go forth from the sweet peace of our beloved firesides to smite the foe. O Lord, our God, help us to tear their soldiers to bloody shreds with our shells; help us to cover their smiling fields with the pale forms of their patriot dead; help us to drown the thunder of the guns with the shrieks of their wounded, writhing in pain; help us to lay waste their humble homes with a hurricane of fire; help us to wring the hearts of their unoffending widows with unavailing grief; help us to turn them out roofless with their little children to wander unfriended the wastes of their desolated land in rags and hunger and thirst, sport of the sun-flames of summer and the icy winds of winter, broken in spirit, worn with travail, imploring Thee for the refuge of the grave and denied it -- for our sakes who adore Thee, Lord, blast their hopes, blight their lives, protract their bitter pilgrimage, make heavy their steps, water their way with their tears, stain the white snow with the blood of their wounded feet! We ask it, in the spirit of love, of Him Who is the Source of Love, and Who is the ever-faithful refuge and friend of all that are sore beset and seek His aid with humble and contrite hearts. Amen."

The messenger departs. "It was believed afterwards," Twain concludes, "that the man was a lunatic, because there was no sense in what he said."

Twain says that he was urged not to publish *The War Prayer*, written in 1904-05, because it was too heretical. Twain finally conceded because, he said, "I have told the whole truth in that, and only dead men can tell the truth in this world. It can be published after I am dead." And so it was done. Twain died in 1910 and the essay finally appeared in Twain's 1923 collection, *Europe and Elsewhere.*

I also discovered a collection of speeches by Twain's contemporary, Robert G. Ingersoll, which I marked up heavily. Ingersoll was a noted Gilded Age politician who earned the title of "The Great Agnostic." He traveled extensively on the lecture circuit railing against the inanities and contradictions of Judaism, Christianity, and the Bible. "There is no way to ever know or prove that there is or is not a God." He said. "It's just a matter of personal opinion." Because no one could know or prove there is or is not a God, he was honest enough to say he was agnostic on the question. His argument made sense to me. And, to my knowledge, no agnostic has ever burned a pagan, heretic, or unbeliever at the stake.

To Ingersoll, the fundamental beliefs of Christianity were as crazy as they were to me. "The notion that faith in Christ is to be rewarded by an eternity of bliss," he said, "while a dependence upon reason, observation, and experience merits everlasting pain, is too absurd for refutation." And yet, such belief was, after all, *not* too absurd for refutation, because Christians clung to it yet a hundred years after Ingersoll died.

Ingersoll paid for his dependence upon reason. Once, a reporter visited him in his home and commented on his extensive and eclectic library. The reporter asked Ingersoll how much his library cost him. Ingersoll glanced over his rows upon rows of books and said, "These books cost me the governorship of Illinois, and maybe the presidency of the United States, as well."

Ingersoll championed Thomas Paine, as did Mark Twain, who wrote that, "It took a brave man before the Civil War to confess he had read *The Age of Reason."* So I searched for and found Thomas Paine's *Age of Reason*, written in 1793 and 1794 just before and during the ten months Paine was imprisoned in an eight-by-ten French prison cell awaiting possible execution by the revolutionary government.

Thomas Paine is today remembered mostly, and justly, for *Common Sense,* his defense of American independence from Great Britain. He is revered as a fierce champion of liberty, in some ways even more devout in his devotion to that ideal that others of our Founders. Benjamin Franklin is reputed to have once said to Paine, "Where liberty is, there is my country." Paine replied, "Where liberty is not, there is mine."

However, for me, Paine's most revolutionary work is *The Age of Reason.* His unjustly neglected work is a detailed and critical dissection of the Bible. Paine summarized my own feeling about religion: "All national institutions of churches," he said, "whether Jewish, Christian, or Turkish, appear to me no other than human inventions, set up to terrify and enslave mankind, and monopolize power and profit....I do not believe in the creed professed by the Jewish Church, by the Roman Church, by the Greek Church, by the Turkish Church, by the Protestant Church, nor by any church that I know of. My own mind is my own church."

Like Ingersoll, I embraced Thomas Paine as an ally on the side of Reason in my long and lonely war against Christian Unreason. While Thomas Paine was not a Christian, he seemed a far more moral man than any Christian I'd ever met. "To do good is my religion," he said, "I believe in the equality of man; and I believe that religious duties consist in doing justice, loving mercy, and endeavoring to make our fellow creatures happy." Paine's ideals seemed to me to be the only values worth espousing.

I cut a frontispiece portrait of Thomas Paine out of one of his books, framed it, and put it on an altar to intellectual freedom in my room. And in the front of the Bible the Sherwood Heights Baptist Sunday School had given me I wrote my secret *converso* name: "Thomas Belial Dagon." "Thomas" after the intellectual liberator Thomas Paine. "Belial," after a biblical demon. And "Dagon," after a rival god to God in Canaan Land.

If my heroes and allies were not long since dead, they were far away. Indeed, they were across the ocean in England. I found Bertrand Russell's 1927 book, *Why I Am Not A Christian* and it gave me hope. Russell was a pacifist and had been a conscientious objector during World War I. "Many people," he observed of that war, "would rather die than think; in fact, they do." Of Christianity he wrote, "The Christian god may exist, so may the gods of Olympus, or of ancient Egypt, or of Babylon. But no one of these hypotheses is more probable than any other.... What is wanted is not the will to believe, but the will to find out, which is the exact opposite."

So I also cut out a color frontispiece portrait of Bertrand Russell I found in a book, mounted it, and placed it at my Freedom Altar beside the portrait of Thomas Paine.

By 1965, I was fighting the climactic battle of this long personal war of reason against faith and needed to know that Bertrand had never wavered. On November 22, 1965, I wrote to him at an address I found in the public library. "I'm alone out here in Godly Arizona. I've got to know. Are you steadfast? In 1927 you wrote that you were not a Christian. Are you still not a Christian?"

He quickly replied. In a letter on Bertrand Russell Peace Foundation stationery dated December 7, 1965, he wrote, "People will tell you that my views on religion are no longer those expressed in 'Why I Am Not a Christian.' This is totally untrue. My views on religion have not changed since 1890."

I was not alone.

Part Two
Better Dead Than Red

Soldier Boy

When I was eight or nine and we lived on 52nd Street in Phoenix, a young couple lived nearby. They were perhaps in their mid-twenties and he "rough housed" with me whenever he visited. It was great fun and I didn't know any other adult male willing to play around like that. He was also a member of the Army National Guard, a "Weekend Warrior," as he called it.

During one visit, as he sat in our living room easy chair watching TV, I snuck up on him with my toy rifle equipped with a detachable floppy rubber bayonet. He didn't hear me as I stood silently by the doorway into the living room. When I was sure he was completely at ease and distracted by the TV, I yelled "Charge!" and burst into the living room. I ran straight at him with my rifle thrust forward ready to stab him with my rubber bayonet.

I'd obviously caught him by surprise. He was shocked into immobility and just sat there, staring at me as I ran toward him. But as I reached him, almost stabbing him with my rubber bayonet, in a flurry of hands and feet he wrenched away my rifle and swept my feet out from under me, so that I was suddenly flat on my back in front of his chair. He held my rifle in his hands, pointing the rubber bayonet down at my throat. And he still just sat in the easy chair, not having moved except for his hands, which had taken my rifle, and his feet, which had tripped me.

"Wow!," I said, vastly impressed. "How did you *do* that?"

And he showed me the ballet his hands and feet went through to wrest my rifle away from me, knock me on my butt, and point my own bayonet at my throat.

"Where did you learn this?"

"In the Army. Hand-to-hand combat. And I still practice at Guard encampments. It's very useful for when kids charge you with their rubber bayonets."

I decided then that I wanted to learn to fight the U. S. Army way.

So, when I entered North High in the fall of 1960, I immediately signed up for the Reserve Officer Training Corps, ROTC Among other things, this meant that I learned how to handle the M-1 Garand, the real-life prototype of my toy rifle.

The M-1 Garand is the rifle that won World War II, at least to hear American vets tell it. Almost every American soldier in Europe and the Pacific carried the M-1, which, at 11-pounds, was heavy enough to deliver a killing hit even at 1,000 yards, the length of ten football fields.

The M-1 was originally designed to accept a top-loading, eight-round, self-ejecting ammunition clip. This clip was pushed into the top of the receiver with the thumb of the right hand, after having slammed back the bolt until it caught in an open position. Inserting the clip depressed the follower, which released the retracted bolt. Under hundreds of pounds of pressure, the sprung bolt then slammed the receiver shut. If you weren't fast, or if your thumb was not positioned correctly, the bolt also smashed your thumb. In some cases, the bolt could even break your thumb.

Like everyone, I was most in danger of smashing my thumb as we stood in formation for rifle inspection. On command, with our rifles held diagonally across our chests, we slammed our bolts back with the heel of our left hands so that they caught in the open position. Then our commanding officer -- an actual member of the United States Army -- walked slowly down the line, looking into the empty receiver of each cadet's rifle as we stared straight ahead.

When he finished, the command was given to release the bolt. This was done by holding the diagonal rifle with the left hand about midway on the stock. Then, with the edge of your right hand against the retracted bolt, you reached into the open receiver with your right thumb and depressed the follower at the bottom of the chamber. This immediately released the bolt, which slammed shut. If your right hand wasn't quick in getting out of the receiver, you got a smashed thumb. My thumb was smashed enough times that I learned to be fast.

At age 13, when I began ROTC, I was still small and the M-1 rifle seemed huge. And, at 11-pounds, it seemed tremendously heavy. When holding it in the present arms position in front of my chest for what felt like an eternity, the rifle just grew heavier and heavier. But, by the end of that year I could slap it into the various positions on command just as well as any other recruit.

I was also familiar enough with it that I was able to completely disassemble and reassemble the M-1 blindfolded. That sounds impressive, I suppose, but not to anyone who has ever handled a rifle. It's just routine. Every ROTC recruit was expected to be able to perform this task as a matter of course. And, as it turned out, the M-1 wasn't all that complicated. It soon became easy for me to quickly disassemble and reassemble the rifle by touch alone. Perhaps every task seems easy if you know it well enough to do it blindfolded.

But, I was never enamored of weapons and I didn't join ROTC in order to become an expert in an old World War II rifle which the U. S. military had, in fact, stopped making in 1956. I joined ROTC because I wanted to learn hand-to-hand combat the way the Army taught it. I felt like I was fighting a personal war every day of my life, and knowing how to fight hand-to-hand would be far more useful to me than any gun could ever be.

And so I studied the official U. S. Army combat manuals we were given and I practiced lethal blows and I listened and watched closely when our commanding officer showed us what to do. If two men are coming at you, don't just stand there and wait for them! Run toward one at an angle, so you're running away from the other one while drawing your target toward you. Take out the one you run toward, then turn on the remaining one.

Don't slug someone on the chin with your fist, like they do in all the Westerns. You might break the bones in your hand. Come up from below and smash the chin upward with the heel of your hand.

Better than the chin, smash the nose. If you smash the nose with a swift upward thrust of the heel of your hand, you can possibly ram bone splinters from the fucker's broken nose up into his brain, killing the fucker.

Or jab the eyes, blinding the fucker.

Aim for anything soft and fragile.

Kick the knee at a side angle, breaking it and crippling the fucker. That'll take him down.

Or kick the fucker in the balls, fast and hard. That'll also take him down. Then kick him in the face when he's down.

Or, if you flipped the fucker to the ground, while still holding his arm at the wrist, break the fucker's arm by stomping the outside of the elbow while simultaneously pulling his arm toward you by his wrist in the opposite direction in which the arm bends. You'll snap the fucker's arm like a dry twig.

Or, while still holding his arm, with him on the ground, kick him hard in the armpit with the toe of your shoe. Do it two or three times, fast and hard. That's possibly fatal.

This was not gentlemanly fisticuffs. This was not Marquis of Queensbury boxing. This was kill-or-be-killed fighting. It was fighting to maim and seriously injure. And that's what I wanted. I wanted to be able to smash noses, gouge eyes, kick balls, and break bones. I wanted to be able to take a bayonet out of an attacker's hands, knock him on his ass, and put the bayonet to the fucker's throat without breaking a sweat.

And so I practiced and practiced and practiced so that the moves, the blows, the kicks would become second-nature to me. I didn't want to have to think about them. I wanted them to be habit. I wanted to be an instinctual fighter, because no one has time to think in a fight.

The German philosopher Frederich Nietzsche wrote that what does not destroy you makes you stronger.

Being beaten at home and at school did not destroy me.

It made me a soldier.

The Dragon Lady

"Do you resent the American press referring to you as 'The Dragon Lady'?" I asked Madame Ngo Dihn Nhu, the nominal First Lady of the Republic of Vietnam. Madame Nhu was the sister-in-law of President Ngo Dihn Diem, the South Vietnamese military dictator. Diem's brother, Ngo Dihn Nhu, head of Diem's secret police, was his right-hand man. As Diem was unmarried, his brother's beautiful and elegant wife, Madame Nhu, came to perform the role of First Lady. As such, she was touring the United States on a goodwill mission to bolster support for her family's rule. On Friday, October 25, 1963, her tour brought her to the Westward Ho, Phoenix's premiere hotel.

At the beginning of *Psycho,* his 1960 movie, Alfred Hitchcock glides across downtown Phoenix in a breathtakingly long pan to zoom in through an upstairs window of the Westward Ho, where the camera finds Janet Leigh making love. But this was 1963 and I was downstairs in the Turquoise Room in a crowd of 700 Republicans who had bought $2 tickets to hear Madame Nhu plead her family's case, and I doubted Janet Leigh was upstairs making love.

Madame Nhu's family needed all the American goodwill it could get in late October, '63. It had gained a reputation for corruption and brutality, especially since protesting Buddhist monks had begun burning themselves to death in Saigon. Diem's government was already fighting a Communist insurgency in the countryside. The insurgents, called "Vietcong" by the press, seemed to be gaining ground, despite the presence of 16,000 Green Berets President Kennedy had sent to train and advise Diem's army.

In response to Vietcong advances, and perhaps following the advice of Green Beret counter-insurgency specialists, Diem had launched a "strategic hamlet" program to isolate the rural peasants from the Vietcong guerrillas. In his "Little Red Book" of quotations, Chinese Communist leader Mao Tse-tung had said the guerrilla moved among the people "like a fish swam through water." Diem's strategic hamlet project was designed to dry up the pond, empty it of water, and thus expose the guerrilla-fish. Entire villages were uprooted, their inhabitants forcibly relocated into barbed-wire encampments. But Diem's program had only increased support for the Vietcong among the villagers.

Then the Buddhist monks began immolating themselves. President Diem, Madame Nhu, and their entire family, were French-educated Catholics. But Vietnam was predominantly Buddhist, and the Buddhists charged Diem's government with religious persecution. Starting in May of 1963, Buddhist monks had begun demonstrating against Diem's government. Sometimes, to demonstrate the sincerity of their protests, they poured gasoline over themselves and lit a match as they meditated in the lotus position. The monks went up in flames, calmly meditating, until the charred ash of their corpses toppled over. Recorded by American TV crews, these self-cremations horrified viewers all over the world and were a public relations disaster for the Diem government.

That's when the American news media began referring to Madame Nhu as the "Dragon Lady," in a reference to the exotic villainess in the old "Terry and the Pirates" comic strip. "Terry" was a 1930s adventurer in the Orient who flew freight -- and anything else -- in his ramshackle airplane in and out of Asian and South Pacific locales just one step ahead of the authorities. Or one step ahead of the numerous bad guys he encountered as a routine part of his sometimes shady business. The Dragon Lady -- beautiful, alluring, dangerous -- was one of those dubious characters he encountered.

Madame Nhu seemed to be just as beautiful and alluring. With her clinging dresses, Ray-Ban shades, and teased coiffure, she looked like a member of the Ronettes. But, she was also as dangerous and as brutal as the Dragon Lady. As the Diem regime became more repressive, the American media found the label an apt title for Madame Nhu.

On August 25, 1963, Diem retaliated against the growing Buddhist protest movement by launching raids on Buddhist temples throughout South Vietnam, arresting Buddhist monks *en masse*. Anti-government demonstrations merely escalated. President Kennedy decided that Diem had become a liability. Kennedy felt Diem's increasingly unpopular government could not withstand the strengthening Communist insurgency, as well as the opposition of non-Communist elements of the population. But, South Vietnam was not a democracy. It was a military dictatorship. There were no free elections in South Vietnam. If there had been, Communist leader Ho Chi Minh would probably have won. The only possible indigenous pro-Western force which could replace Diem was his own military.

For this reason, and on Kennedy's orders, in late August Henry Cabot Lodge, Jr., America's ambassador to South Vietnam, publicly announced that the United States would welcome any military coup against the Diem government which "had a good chance of succeeding." It was the green light for a military coup.

In an effort to forestall that coup, the Dragon Lady appeared in the Turquoise Room of the Westward Ho on October 25, encouraging Americans to support her family back in Saigon.

It was a Friday night and I'd hitchhiked into downtown Phoenix. I'd caught a ride with an Arizona State University student driving home after his classes. That day he had attended, as a heckler, a John Birch Society rally at ASU. That rabidly conservative political group supported the Diem government. The student who gave me a ride, however, did not. When he discovered where I was headed, he gave me many reasons why the Diem "regime," as he called it, should be replaced. I didn't know enough to argue with him, but I wasn't persuaded either. I was politically conservative and anti-Communist; it seemed to me we had to stick with Diem against the Commies.

I got to the Westward Ho early. There were ten well-dressed, well-groomed students from the ASU Young Democrats picketing outside the Westward Ho. Five were co-eds, five were boys. Two of the boys were black, although in those days they were still called "Negroes." "No Nhus is good news," read one of their signs. "Is this 'Burn-a-Buddhist' Month?" asked another.

Inside the lobby was already full of Republicans awaiting Madame Nhu. A chanteuse was singing in the Copper Room just off the lobby. One bejeweled and befurred matron encountered another near me. "My dear!" she exclaimed. "What are *you* doing here?"

"I came with my husband to see Madame Boo, or whatever her name is. He said she's followed everywhere by a band of Communist assassins just waiting to get her. So, she may be dead soon and we may not get to see her alive again."

Just before 8 o'clock we were ushered up to the second floor Turquoise Room to meet "Madame Boo." Preceded by busy newspaper and TV cameramen, she finally appeared to thunderous applause and glided down the central aisle. On this occasion Madame Nhu didn't look like a member of the Ronettes. Draped in a white silk ao-dai, Vietnam's traditional ankle-length dress, she was as graceful as a geisha. Peeking from beneath her hem were matching white high heels. Even with the heels, at 5'2" she was still petite, . She smiled and waved to the crowd as she moved slowly toward the platform.

Behind her came Dihn Le Thuy, her demure 17-year-old daughter, dressed in a Western-style white blouse and white skirt. Behind Le Thuy came a young man who was, I learned later, the Vietnamese Observer to the United Nations. The Soviet Union, as a permanent member of the powerful Security Council, had vetoed South Vietnam's admission to the United Nations. So, instead of an ambassador, South Vietnam had only an "Observer" at that body. The three moved slowly down the aisle to the stage and took their seats. It was an impressive entrance.

An official from the local Republican Party organization took the microphone to explain that Madame Nhu had come to Phoenix simply to present "the truth" about events in Vietnam.

The Republicans thundered their approval. They were all for "the truth."

The Republican politico was followed by a representative of *The Arizona Republic,* the newspaper I'd delivered every dark morning for three years. The newsman said his newspaper, which co-sponsored the event, was also interested in "the truth." "Here in Arizona," he said, "newspapers are truly independent. You will not find managed news in Arizona."

The Republicans thundered their approval. They knew the newsman was referring to the Kennedy Administration's reputed masterful management and manipulation of the news media.

The "impartial" newsman then introduced the Dragon Lady, and I took out my notebook. In halting yet precise English, Madame Nhu justified her family's government, which she linked with the country of Vietnam itself. She thanked the American people for the warm welcome she had received on her American tour, which was more, she said angrily, than she had received from the American government. The Kennedy Administration, she said, had refused to extend an official welcome her on her tour of the United States.

Madame Nhu then went on to defend her brother-in-law against the charges lodged against him by the "managed news" of America. Roman Catholics like her and her family did not control South Vietnam, she said. The strategic hamlets, of which there were now 45, were working. Furthermore, "we are conquering" the Vietcong guerrillas. "Don't be misled by one or two headlines about lost battles in *The Washington Post* . There are bound to be lost battles in every war. But the side that wins the most battles will win the war. Free Vietnam will win if we are not betrayed by our friends and allies. I come to America bringing good tidings. I come to America to tell the truth. We are winning and the end of this war is so near."

The Republicans thundered their approval. They, too, wanted the war in Vietnam to be won that year, or next year, 1964, at the very latest.

"The Communists created the so-called 'Buddhist crisis,'" she continued. "They incited fanatics to commit suicide for a religion that has never been threatened. Even so, we are crushing the subversive warfare which now threatens your own country, as well.

"But now that victory is so near in our common struggle, we are being stabbed in the back by the American government itself. On August 25, the Voice of America radio in Vietnam issued a direct invitation to the Vietnamese armed forces to overthrown the Vietnamese government. Imagine your own reaction if the Vietnamese government issued an invitation to the American armed forces to overthrow President Kennedy. Would the American people permit such a thing? It seems in the world today, only those who favor Communism are safe. Those who bravely stand against Communism are assaulted from both sides."

The Republicans thundered their approval. They knew that all anti-Communist, patriotic Americans were a persecuted minority, "assaulted on all sides."

"I come to speak the truth," the Dragon Lady continued. "I come to ask your support. Our cause is just. We are fighting for our independence. Help us."

The Republicans thundered their approval.

And then she took questions. A forest of hands went up, mine among them.

"Do you speak as a leader for the majority of Vietnamese?" someone asked.

"I feel I have the right to speak for more than half the population," she answered. "After all, in Vietnam women vote, and women are more than half the population. And I am the unchallenged leader of Vietnamese women."

The Republicans laughed. They were pleased that Dragon Lady had a sense of humor.

"If you were an American citizen, who would you vote for in next year's presidential election, Rockefeller, Goldwater, or Kennedy?"

"We do not want anyone to interfere in the internal affairs of our nation. Therefore, I do not think I should interfere in the internal affairs of *your* country."

The Republicans thundered their approval.

"How do you weed out the subversive Buddhist monks?"

Madame Nhu had trouble understanding the phrase, "weed out." After *The Arizona Republic* newsman explained it to her, she said, "Buddhism in our country is not like Buddhism in other countries. Buddhists are supposed to be pacifists, but when we raided the pagodas in August we found machine guns, mortar shells, and even plastic bombs under the statues of Buddha himself. So, these Buddhist monks are not true Buddhists. We know the difference."

"Why didn't you meet with Ambassador Lodge in Saigon before you left?"

"In my country, as in yours, a woman does not go to see a man."

The Republicans laughed.

"What do you think about the managed news in America?"

"I want to know how they do it."

The Republicans laughed, the newsman at her side joining in.

And then she pointed to me. "Do you resent the American press referring to you as 'The Dragon Lady'?" I asked Madame Nhu.

She turned to *The Arizona Republic* newsman next to her for clarification of my question. It was clear she knew little of American popular culture, had never read "Terry and the Pirates," and had no idea who the Dragon Lady was. Even so, she answered my question as best she could.

"I did not know that Americans called me the 'Dragon Lady'," she said. "But the title is complimentary, because it is a wonderful animal. In Asia, the dragon is lucky symbol. So, it is good to be called the 'Dragon Lady.' Besides, my name isn't really 'Nhu.' That is my husband's name, and it really doesn't fit me. 'Nhu' means 'sweet' -- and I am not sweet. I am a dragon."

She may not have known who the Dragon Lady was, but at that moment Madame Nhu sounded exactly like her. The Republican crowd roared in appreciation.

The journalist from *The Arizona Republic* then interrupted to say that Madame Nhu and her daughter had to catch a plane to Los Angeles. The Dragon Lady stepped down from the stage to a standing ovation from the assembled Republicans.

She left the way she had entered, down the center aisle. As she moved slowly up the aisle, to continued applause, she paused briefly here and there to shake hands and say a few words with members of the audience.

As she came closer, I held out my hand. She took it between both of hers and cradled it. Her hands were soft and warm. "You are the boy who said I was the Dragon Lady."

"Yes, I am."

"Thank you," she said with a smile. "I am proud to be your Dragon Lady." She squeezed my hand and then released it, moving on. As she left, my skin tingled where her red nails scraped along my wrist.

A week later, on November 1, 1963, the Dragon Lady was in Beverly Hills when her brother-in-law was overthrown in Saigon by a military coup supported by the Kennedy Administration. Soldiers invaded the presidential palace and seized Ngo Dihn Diem, as well as the Dragon Lady's husband, Ngo Dihn Nhu. They were dragged outside and shot. Their bloody bodies were tossed into the back of a car and driven away from the palace. A new military strongman, more acceptable to President Kennedy, was installed.

The Vietnamese call the war which followed this coup the "American War," as America became mired deeper and deeper in Vietnam. This war, the longest war America has ever fought, lasted until 1975, killing over 58,000 Americans and more than three million Vietnamese.

I didn't realize at the time that this emerging "American War" would also become *my* war.

A Rendezvous With Death

November 22, 1963: For many of us, it was the beginning of "The Sixties," that turbulent era of assassinations and attempted assassinations, of protest and repression. I'd been suspended from North Phoenix High for inciting a riot in the cafeteria, so I was home alone, sleeping. Bill, the self-employed carpet cleaner from two houses down, barged into my bedroom to jerk me awake. "Kennedy's been shot!"

I turned on the radio. It was filled with breathless newscasters giving scrambled accounts of the murder of President John F. Kennedy, shot down in the hot Texas sunlight of Dallas. As Bill listened with me, he began elaborating on the fiendish tortures he felt should be inflicted on the bastard Commie who pulled the trigger. He was sure it was a Commie. I had no reason to doubt him. We were fighting a long Cold War against them. Who else could it be?

In later years I became a journalist and in 1983, as the 20th anniversary of Kennedy's assassination approached that November, I and a colleague, Anita Alverio, became interested in asking the people we interviewed about that day: Where they were, what they were doing, how it affected them. Without exception, they all knew exactly where they were when they heard the news from Dallas. This is what they told us:

In Chicago it was raining hard on November 22, 1963, and comedian and black activist Dick Gregory had cancelled his 9 a.m. flight into Pittsburgh, where he had a gig. A "psychic" comedy writer on his staff predicted that morning that the President would be shot. To kid his friend, Gregory pretended to cancel his scheduled talk that night at the University of Pittsburgh, meanwhile booking himself onto an afternoon flight. In the cab riding home, Gregory heard on the radio that the President had, indeed, been shot.

In Saigon, it was not yet dawn. Author David Halberstam, on assignment for *The New York Times,* was shaken awake by his photographer friend Horst Faas. Faas told him he wouldn't go out on helicopter patrol to shoot pictures that day, as he usually did. "Why not?" Halberstam asked.

"They shot Kennedy," Faas replied.

New York folk singer David Bromberg heard the news as someone rushed into his history class at Columbia University shouting that the President had been shot. He thought it was a prank.

Many others, like Bromberg, also thought it was some sort of gruesome hoax, in very bad taste. Canadian rock singer Rick Danko, of The Band, was, like me, also asleep, although in a Toronto hotel room and a few hours further into the day. A week before, fellow Band member Levon Helm had awakened Danko screaming hysterically, "The Russians just nuked New York City!" Danko was determined to not be fooled again when Helm woke him with the news that Kennedy was dead. He just rolled over and told Levon Helm to go to hell.

But even those with no reason to suspect a joke found the story unbelievable. Canadian novelist Margaret Atwood, then a secretary in a market research company, was at her typewriter in the company office. She had discovered that she could do her job in the morning and pretend to do it in the afternoon while actually working on her first novel.

Atwood put down her cup of coffee and stared in disbelief at the news on the TV. When it appeared to actually be true, she thought to herself, "Yes, that's the kind of thing Americans do from time to time. They killed Lincoln, didn't they, and they shot a couple of other presidents, right?"

But to most of us, those other assassinations were ancient history, having little to do with the present, little to do with the America we knew. Marion Damick, of the Pittsburgh office of the American Civil Liberties Union, felt just the opposite of Atwood. "Foreign countries do that," she thought, "but it isn't something that happens in the United States. We're more rational and civilized."

But, we weren't more rational and civilized. Suddenly, exceptional America was like all other countries. And, perhaps for that reason, citizens of other countries seemed to feel a rare kinship with America, similar to what happened, briefly, after 9-11. Folk singer Pete Seeger was in Japan on a world tour. Seeger and Kennedy had been in the same class at Harvard, although their paths had seldom crossed, and, later, Seeger disagreed with Kennedy on most matters. Yet in Japan, India, and Africa, on his tour, strangers saw Seeger merely as an American and stopped him on the streets to silently press their hands into his in sympathy. In Nigeria, a man stopped Seeger's wife in the market place and said over and over the only word he knew in English: "Kennedy... Kennedy."

Author Michael Harrington and his wife were flying from Warsaw to Milan, Italy, that day. President Kennedy had read Harrington's book, *The Other America,* sometime in February or March and, moved by it, had started in motion what would later become President Johnson's War on Poverty. But, Harrington didn't know that at the time. He'd been in Europe since January and was out of touch with what was happening in America. After unpacking in their hotel room, the Harringtons went downstairs to the dining room. The waiter quietly approached their table and said to them, "They have just killed Kennedy."

Wanting to find out more, Harrington and his wife hurried to the Milan office of the Associated Press. As with the Seegers, strangers by the score stopped them on the streets of Milan to express their sorrow. At the Associated Press office everyone was Italian, but they cleared a desk for the Harringtons and brought the news to them first as it came off the wire. The next day, Harrington remembered, led first by the Communist Party, all the myriad political parties of Milan displayed gigantic posters on their headquarters expressing their grief.

Some few Americans welcomed the news from Dallas. Ron Weisen, last president of the Homestead, Pennsylvania, Local 1397 of the United Steel Workers of America, was drinking with some buddies at the Circle Bar in Pittsburgh's Market Square when the news came on the TV that Kennedy had been shot. A woman stood up and said, "I hope he dies." Weisen was shocked.

For musician Charlie King, a young Boston Irish-Catholic Republican whose parents had voted for Nixon, the major feeling was dismay that Johnson would be taking Kennedy's place. He and his family felt Johnson was even more liberal than Kennedy, and that spelled disaster.

For others, the news was merely curious. In Milan, Michael Harrington finally found some other Americans in his hotel bar. He thought he would feel some camaraderie with them, but they were Texans, having a very dispassionate discussion of the probable rifle sight used to kill Kennedy. He and his wife quickly left.

For some, there was fear. Writer and Left political activist Sidney Lens arrived at Amherst College in western Massachusetts to discover that his scheduled speech had been cancelled because of the assassination. He called his wife to tell her he would be catching a plane home early and discovered a hornet's nest back home. Lens was one of the founders of the "Fair Play for Cuba Committee." Although Lens had never heard of him, Lee Harvey Oswald, the accused assassin, was said by the news media to be a member of that organization. Mrs. Lens was besieged with calls from *Time, Life, The New York Times,* and the radio and TV networks, all wanting to know if Lens knew Oswald and what Oswald's relationship to the Committee might be.

At the airport, Lens sat next to a couple of truck drivers and eavesdropped on their conversation. Their foul mood frightened him. Like my neighbor Bill, they were describing the most grotesque tortures imaginable to be performed on Oswald and all associated with him. "I just wondered whether Lyndon Johnson would order a wave of arrests of suspects that night. If so, perhaps I should stay away from home for a few days to see what happens..."

But, for the most part, there was an intense desire to get home, to cluster, to huddle, to draw together as if for protection. "It was so strange to be in a foreign city," recalled Harrington. "We wanted so much to be with Americans. All the Americans in Europe were phoning each other that night."

In America itself, husbands and wives called each other at home or at work. Strangers spoke with strangers. One such stranger approached science fiction writer Isaac Asimov in New York's Metropolitan Museum of Art as he was studying a model of the Parthenon for a book he was writing. The stranger told Asimov the news and Asimov immediately went home.

Radical film maker Emile de Antonio was recuperating from a knee operation in the elegant New York City estate of a friend, a mansion equipped with a French maid, a cook, and elevators between floors. He answered the phone. He recognized the fey voice. It was his friend, pop artist Andy Warhol. "Oh, Dee," Warhol said, drawing out the "eeee." "You'll just never guess what happened."

Expecting celebrity trivia, de Antonio said, "Tell me, Andy, what just happened?"

"The president's just been shot."

"C'mon, Andy, cut the bullshit."

"Oh, Dee, you'd better turn on the TV."

He discovered Warhol wasn't bullshitting.

In New Jersey, Alberta Arthurs, of the Rockefeller Foundation in New York, was very much a "new parent" with a son the same age as "John-John," the president's son. A neighbor ran over with the news. "Then she and I and our little children huddled in front of the television set and just watched and watched and watched with a kind of horrible fascination. People began to cluster almost self-consciously, it hit so hard."

Perhaps one reason Kennedy's assassination hit so hard was because it was the first national tragedy the nation shared as it was actually happening. The bombing of Pearl Harbor was reported after the fact. The death of President Franklin D. Roosevelt was announced after it happened. But President Kennedy's death was experienced, minute by painful minute, by the entire nation as it watched the television coverage. Harry Grant, a Pittsburgh architect, recalled, "We kept getting reports that he wasn't dead....then he was....then he wasn't....then he was again. It was a continuing thing. The next day I stayed home and watched television. I saw Jack Ruby kill Oswald as it actually happened."

Historian Albert McLean, of Pittsburgh's Point Park University, also watched the murder of Oswald. He was both shocked and fascinated. "I'd never seen anyone killed before and I shared this experience with millions and millions of other Americans who, because of television, were also with me right there, on the scene. We were conscious of participating in history at the very instant it was being made."

But also, for many Americans, it hit hard because there was a personal identification with Kennedy. "We were coming out of the Eisenhower years," remembered Marilyn Levin, former director of the Pittsburgh Film Makers. "They were so boring. Suddenly, everything just seemed to sparkle with the Kennedys, like we were in Wonderland. Kennedy, with his call for self-sacrifice for a greater good, made us care about the country for the first time."

Kennedy was indeed everything Eisenhower was not: Young, rich, handsome, sophisticated. Especially for so many of the young, it was hard not to be attracted by the Camalot glamour of Kennedy and his beautiful wife, Jacqueline. "The first time I ever admitted I wore a size 10 shoe," journalist Charlene Hunter-Gault told Anita, "was when I found out Jackie also wore size 10."

Charlene Hunter-Gault is also black and, as a veteran of the Civil Rights struggle in the South, saw real possibilities for racial justice in the Kennedy White House. "The Kennedys weren't as strong on Civil Rights as they could have been, but they made you feel there was potential for all of us. I mean, 'Ask not what your country can do for you, ask what you can do for your country.' We really believed that. John Kennedy was part of my dreams of what a better America could be at that point."

When she heard the news from Dallas, Hunter-Gault was nursing her seven-day-old baby girl. "I was crushed. I went totally to pieces. My mother had to take my child away from me as I broke down and wept."

Linnie Stovall was a young and pregnant Army wife on a military base in Hawaii. She heard the news as she ironed. "It was very personal," she recalled. "Like a personal threat. It was like the death of a king. You thought of the president as invulnerable, almost above human concerns. But, if he could be shot, surrounded by all that security, then anyone could be shot. I could be shot."

"I felt out of control of my life," remembered Mary Alice Gorman, owner of the Mystery Lover's Bookshop in Oakmont, Pennsylvania. "Somehow, that moment marked me and my peers. We realized that daddy was gone, that nothing could be counted on forever, that even the president, the most powerful man on earth, wasn't in total control."

Michael Harrington, who died of cancer in 1989, agreed. "I think everyone is frightened of accidents, of cancer, of the precariousness of life," he told me. "And to have a handsome and charismatic young man at the height of his powers, and with a seemingly endless vista of accomplishments opening up, suddenly cut off by an assassin's bullet, spraying his young wife with his own blood.... I think everybody, at that point, felt their own mortality....

"Kennedy was the Chosen One, the Prince, the leader. I think here we're getting at a stratum of our consciousness which goes back to the notion of the Mysterious, the Sacred and the Holy. Perhaps more than most leaders, Kennedy symbolized vitality and life....and on that day he became a symbol of death -- our death."

Indeed, as if there were some mystic union between leader and led, between the president and the nation, life ceased with Kennedy's death. Work stopped, shops closed, students were sent home. Historian Philip Foner was researching a book in the Newspaper Division of Washington, D.C.'s Library of Congress. Like everyone else, Foner gathered up his papers and went home.

Randy Harris was eight at the time and lived in Homestead, Pennsylvania. A day or two after the assassination, his parents took him to a movie in nearby McKeesport, just to escape the omnipresent funeral coverage on TV. The theater was closed.

Alberta Arthurs and her husband took their son into New York City for lunch. "Manhattan was dead," she recalled. "Nobody was there. It was absolutely deserted. There was silence everywhere."

Stu Cohen was living in a dorm at the University of Pittsburgh. "It was right before the Thanksgiving weekend," he remembered. "Pitt had a football game that weekend, but it was cancelled. Students walked around in a daze wondering how they would get home. There was a lot of concern about transportation: Would the trains still run? Would the planes still fly?"

So universal was the expectation that the nation's life, like the President's, would cease, that Isaac Asimov was surprised to learn that his scheduled speech before a Mensa group that night was still on. "I was not in the mood to talk, but I told them I would show up, just on the off chance that someone would be there. But, I really didn't think anyone would come. Well, they filled the darn hall. What I hadn't realized was that people wanted to escape the brutal reality of the news. And, once I began speaking, I, too, forgot.

"But, I felt I had embarrassed myself by going on as if nothing had happened. For ten years thereafter I observed my own version of the memory of that day. I refused to give any talk anywhere on November 22. Every year, someone would ask me to talk on November 22. Always, I refused."

"It haunts me still," Gail Pressberg, director of Middle East Programs for the American Friends Service Committee, said. "For my generation, it was the crack in the world, when things started coming apart. The world would never be the same again."

"It's strange," Pete Seeger told me. "My uncle, Alan Seeger, was killed in the First World War. He wrote a poem shortly before he was shot, which Kennedy admired tremendously." Without prompting, Seeger began reciting from memory the poem Kennedy admired so much: "I have a rendezvous with Death," he began, "At some disputed barricade...."

And then he stopped, unable to go on.

I later found a 1918 edition of Alan Seeger's complete poetry, published shortly after his death. It contained the poem that Pete Seeger had memorized. And I, too, memorized the poem President Kennedy had so admired....

>"I have a rendezvous with Death
>At midnight in some flaming town,
>On some scarred slope of battered hill,
>And I to my pledged word am true,
>I shall not fail that rendezvous."

A Choice, Not an Echo

The modern American political universe began to take shape in the 1964 presidential election which shortly followed Kennedy's assassination. That election revealed that the power center of American politics was beginning to shift south and west, although Kevin Phillips had not yet coined the term "Sun Belt" and had not yet discerned "The Emerging Republican Majority" based on that Sun Belt. But that year, for the first time, the candidates of the two major parties, Democrat Lyndon Johnson of Texas and Republican Barry Goldwater of Arizona, both came from the Southwest. And the Deep South, the heretofore Democratic states of Louisiana, Mississippi, Alabama, Georgia, and South Carolina, all voted Republican that year, beginning the transformation of that region into the Solid Republican South it is today.

With the Goldwater candidacy, we began to see an ideological polarization of the two parties which has persisted and intensified until today. The Democratic Party has become more liberal, especially with the defection of the South, and the Republican Party has become more conservative, with the marginalization and eventual elimination of liberal Northeastern Republicans, represented by politicians like New York Governor Nelson Rockefeller and Pennsylvania Governor William Scranton. Goldwater offered a clear conservative choice for voters, instead of the liberal echo of the Democrats these Northeastern Republicans were portrayed as offering. True, Johnson eventually won the election with the biggest landslide since FDR beat Alf Landon in 1936, and it seemed this "Choice" had completely destroyed the Republican Party. It was in the 1964 election that Ronald Reagan, campaigning for Goldwater, emerged as the future leader and shaper of the Republican Party. The party rebuilt itself from the ground up on Goldwater's clearly-presented conservative principles, leading to the eventual Reagan Revolution and the triumph of the Bushes.

Arizona had been politically conservative long before 1964. Indeed, Arizona is the most Republican state in America. In the 14 presidential elections in the half century between 1952 and 2004, Arizona went Democratic only once. No other state can match that record. Growing up, everyone I knew who expressed any political opinion was a conservative.

And so was I.

It was naturally assumed that everyone else also thought like us. Except, of course, those damn Eastern elitist Democrats and their Northeastern liberal Republican "echoes," who ran everything.

Ours was primarily a "small government" conservatism. I'd never read, nor did I know anyone who'd read, John Locke's 1690 *Second Treatise of Civil Government*. That being the case, I didn't know that he'd written, "The natural liberty of man is to be free from any superior power on earth," and that men are "by nature all free, equal, and independent." But we all knew that the Declaration of Independence began by saying, "We hold these truths to be self-evident, that all men are created equal." We took that as meaning not dependent upon the will of any other man. To us, that was a self-evident truth. It was the heart and soul of our conservatism.

Perhaps it was John L. O'Sullivan, who coined the term "Manifest Destiny," who also first said, "That government is best which governs least." He said something much like this, anyway, in the debut 1837 issue of his *United States Magazine and Democratic Review*. But, with Henry David Thoreau in his 1849 essay on "Civil Disobedience," I'd have taken it further and said, "That government is best which governs not at all."

Because we believed this was the ideal upon which America was founded, we loved America. Because we believed that Communism was all about totalitarian dictatorship, we hated the Russians and, of course, "Red China." Patriotic anti-Communism was the extent of our international political sophistication. I'd guess that most people I grew up around knew as much about international politics as my brother Rick. One day he told me he'd seen some Russian diplomats on TV and he was surprised that they looked just like us.

"What'd you expect them to look like?"

He shrugged. "I thought they'd be red. Isn't that why we call them 'Reds'?"

"Well, what color do you think the Red Chinese are?"

He frowned. "I dunno. I never thought about it before."

And that was typical. The people I grew up with just didn't think too deeply about such things, even at a primitive level. Deep thoughts just never came to them.

Today, to speak of political conservatism is to speak of God and "family values." It may be difficult, therefore, to believe that one could be a political conservative without also being religious. But David Hume was a conservative atheist. George Santayana was a conservative atheist. And I was a conservative atheist. At 13, I'd been bullied into accepting Jesus as my personal Savior by Southern Baptists transplanted to Prescott, Arizona, but they'd not won my heart and my mind. I remained a conservative atheist who disdained as benighted all the religious and social mores I was supposed to revere. So, to believe that a political conservative has to be religious is to mistakenly believe that conservatism is, or was, a monolithic ideology.

It is also to overlook the power of regionalism in American history and politics. There are two very different political variants of conservatism in America. These are social conservatism and minimal government conservatism. The latter could also be called individualistic or laissez faire or perhaps libertarian conservatism. In the late Fifties and early Sixties, these conservative variants were allied in a civil war within the Republican Party against what conservatives of both stripes called "the Eastern Establishment."

The Eastern Establishment was located in that corridor which ran from Boston down through New York and Philadelphia to Washington, D.C. This Eastern Establishment had controlled the Republican Party national machinery since at least 1940. That year it had pushed through the presidential nomination of Wendell Wilkie. It had nominated New York attorney Thomas Dewey in 1944 and 1948, and it had backed Eisenhower against Ohio Senator Robert Taft in 1952. In addition, it controlled the most important Republican governorships, such as that of New York, governed by Nelson Rockefeller, and Pennsylvania, governed by William Scranton. Indeed, both Rockefeller and Scranton were frontrunners for the party's nomination in 1964.

The conservatives who opposed the Eastern Establishment were and are closely associated with two regions which both have reason to resent the long political and economic dominance of the Northeastern region. Social conservatism is closely associated with the South, while minimal government conservatism is closely associated with the West. It is the alliance of these two regional conservatisms which has brought the Republican Party to power for most of the years since 1968. More specifically, it is the alliance of these two regional conservatisms which has made possible the political dominance of America by the South. When I was a kid, there was a well-known saying, "Save your Confederate money, boys. The South will rise again!" Indeed, it has. So dominant is the South that, in the 40 years between 1968 and 2008, the only two Democrats elected president were Southern governors, Jimmy Carter and Bill Clinton.

Primarily, however, the South has come to dominate America over the last 40 years by capturing the Republican Party and then using that party as its vehicle to power. Today, the leadership of the Republican Party at all levels is almost completely Southern. And, partly because of this, the Republican Party has come to espouse the social conservatism of the South.

Although born in the South and raised in the religion of Southern social conservatives, I was not a social conservative. I was a bone-deep Southwestern libertarian conservative. I was deeply suspicious of the state, I hated all coercive authority, and I elevated individual liberty above all other values. There were powerful elements within the Republican Party which also reflected these viewpoints. Business, of course, a major Republican constituency, always wanted the state to leave it alone, and so espoused a laissez faire philosophy. But good ol' American individualism also found its champions within the Republican Party.

No doubt I absorbed the ideal of American individualism through the very air I breathed, but most of the reading I was doing at that time also reinforced these values. I read historical fact and fiction, but mostly I read science fiction. And the science fiction of the Fifties was filled with paranoid stories about future dystopias, political dictatorships, and mind-controlled conformist hells opposed by a small handful of heroic individualists.

Perhaps the story which exemplifies this conformist hell motif most in current memory is Jack Finney's classic, *The Invasion of the Body Snatchers*. Published as a Dell paperback in 1955, Hollywood quickly purchased it for a 1956 film, directed by Don Siegel and starring Kevin McCarthy and Dana Wynter. In it, an alien life-form slowly turns the population of an entire California town into literally brain-dead conformists. Finally, only a single heroic individual is left to warn society of its impending doom. *Body Snatchers* stands as the most evocative vision of Fifties science fiction's paranoia about conformity.

Even more powerful, for me, was George Orwell's *1984* with its depiction of a totalitarian society ruled by the omnipresent Big Brother. Because I became acquainted with Orwell as a science fiction writer, I also read his small classic, *Animal Farm*, which intensified my distrust and suspicion of all totalitarian ideologies that subordinated the individual, even in the name of the common good. Because I realized Orwell's novel was a parable about the Soviet Union, it simply heightened my great distrust of Communism.

It wasn't just my reading and American individualism that encouraged my anti-government ethos. My orientation was also bolstered by the politics of my region. The American West has always chafed under Eastern domination. In the 1890s, the Great Plains was the heartland of populism. Long before I was a kid in Arizona, that Western populism had been reoriented away from attacking Eastern economic institutions and into suspicion of and opposition to the federal government. It was the federal government, back East in Washington, D.C., which we in the West now saw as the great enemy of Western freedom.

True, the rise of the Southwestern region of the Sun Belt would not have been possible without massive federal investment. It was federal tax dollars which built the Boulder Dam, the Hoover Dam, and the Glen Canyon Dam. It was federal tax dollars that Arizona Senators Carl Hayden and Barry Goldwater channelled by the billions into the Central Arizona Project, which brought water to Phoenix and Tucson and made possible the spectacular growth of those cities.

But we conveniently overlooked such federal largesse. What we saw were the restrictions and regulations and barriers. The federal government is the biggest landowner in the West. For example, the feds own 57% of Utah and 87% of Washington County, in southwestern Utah around St. George, one of the five fastest-growing counties in America. The federal government also owns 37% of Colorado, 42% of New Mexico, 42% of Wyoming, 45% of California, 48% of Arizona, 50% of Idaho, 53% of Oregon, 85% of Nevada, and 90% of Alaska. The federal government also controls a huge percentage of Western natural resources needed for economic growth. We deeply resented this dominance.

And our political leaders expressed that resentment, decade after decade. That is why President George W. Bush's 2006 budget mandated that the U. S. Forest Service sell 300,000 acres of government land in the West to private interests, while also requiring the Bureau of Land Management to raise $350 million from auctioning off public land in Western states. Meanwhile, the Congressional delegations from Western states were pushing for even greater sell-offs of public land.

Once you realize these things, it should not surprise you that America's most successful conservative leaders since World War II -- Barry Goldwater, George Wallace, Richard Nixon, Ronald Reagan, and the two Bushes -- have come from these two regions, the South and the West. Furthermore, Goldwater, Nixon, and Reagan all came from Arizona or California.

Barry Goldwater was my political hero all through high school, from 1960-64. However, objectively, I should not have been a Goldwater supporter. I was a working class kid from an impoverished home with a construction carpenter step-father who belonged to a union. Meanwhile, over his entire political career Barry Goldwater fought a war against people like me. The Goldwater family always opposed unionization of their fancy department stores. In the 1940s, Barry himself campaigned for legislation outlawing closed (union) shops in Arizona. After he was elected to the U. S. Senate in 1952 he built a reputation on the anti-labor views he advocated in that chamber. Politically, Goldwater was actually my enemy.

But neither I nor anyone I knew had any "class consciousness." Despite being the stepson of a unionized construction worker, there was nothing in the time or place I was raised which made me aware that I belonged to a "working class" which, politically, had very different material interests from "capitalist" merchants like the wealthy Goldwater family. So, I knew absolutely *nothing* about Barry's anti-working class views and actions.

Likewise, I knew nothing about Barry's attitudes toward the Civil Rights Movement. I lived in an all-white world. All of East Phoenix, where I lived, was white. The only time I saw blacks or Mexicans was when I ventured into downtown Phoenix. Every elementary school I attended in Phoenix was all-white. North High was all-white. Thus, during its entire existence, I hardly knew there was a Civil Rights Movement. In any case, it was all happening far away, in the South, and had nothing to do with my life in Arizona.

As what was to become the Civil Rights Act of 1964 worked its way through Congress in 1963, I knew nothing about it, or that Barry opposed it. And, when it finally came up for a vote, I did not know that he voted against it.

But white Southerners knew. That's why Goldwater eventually swept the Deep South states I mentioned previously in the 1964 election. These states had been Democratic since the end of the Civil War a hundred years before. But in Mississippi that year, the Republican Goldwater won an overwhelming 87% of the vote. President Johnson confessed privately that, in signing the 1964 Civil Rights Act into law, he had lost the South for the Democratic Party for a generation. In reality, it would be for longer than that. That year, 1964, was the beginning of the transformation of the South into the Republican fortress it remains to this day.

For example, South Carolina, Alabama, and Mississippi went Republican in all seven presidential elections from 1980 to 2004. Louisiana and Georgia went Republican in five of those seven elections. The leadership of the Congressional Republican Party is entirely Southern, from House Speaker Newt Gingrich, of Georgia, who engineered the 1994 Republican takeover of the House of Representatives, to Senator Bill Frist, of Tennessee, the Senate Majority Leader until the Democratic takeover of the Senate in 2006.

Instead of these racial issues, the issues which dominated political discussions in Arizona were international Communism and Big Government control of our lives. And, despite his vote against the Civil Rights Act, Barry was not a social conservative. He voted against the 1964 Civil Rights Act, he said, because it gave too much power over the states to the federal government. Further, he declared that "I'm frankly sick and tired of the political preachers across this country telling me as a citizen that if I want to be a moral person, I must believe in A, B, C, and D."

Rather than being a social conservative, Barry was a libertarian anti-Communist. This, for me, trumped everything else. Barry had gained a reputation in the Senate as a rabid McCarthyite. We knew, therefore, where he stood on Communism. And we also knew where he stood when it came to Big Brother. We knew these things not only because of what he did in the Senate, but because we'd read his book.

When I read Barry's 1960 political treatise, *The Conscience of a Conservative,* I approved of what I found in it. He advocated escalating the on-going fight against Communism in Vietnam by bombing Communist North Vietnam. He advocated withdrawing from the United Nations because it imposed a world government, with all its rules and restrictions, on America. And he advocated a minimum government conservatism which meshed with my own.

These views must have meshed with those of many others, also, as the book sold extremely well for a political tract. Its success was the main reason Goldwater became a national spokesman for the conservative movement. Only much later did I discover that Barry himself never wrote it; it was ghostwritten by a fellow traveler named Brent Bozell.

But, at the time, we all thought Barry wrote it and it made Barry our boy, so I supported him. This was the one area in which Mom and I agreed. Of course, she was a good ol' Southern social conservative and I was a sunny Southwestern libertarian conservative, but Barry was our mutual leader. Barry, we thought, had *principles.*

I never liked that other Western conservative, the Californian Richard Nixon. He never seemed to have any principles at all. Even though he carried Arizona in 1960, I felt nothing for him when he lost that year's presidential election to Kennedy. Then he ran for Governor of California in 1962 and also lost. That seemed to finish him. He gave a press conference and said he was retiring from politics. "Now the media won't have Nixon to kick around anymore," he sniffled. What a pathetic whiner. It was good that he was gone. He was the only other conservative politician who might have challenged our boy Barry, the only *real* man in politics.

But Barry was a reluctant presidential contender in 1964. After all, he had a safe senatorial seat up for re-election that year. Why should he risk it in a long-shot race for the White House against an incumbent? Therefore, our champion had to be persuaded to run. He had to be drafted by "the Movement."

The Movement was a swirling current of conservative dissent which manifested itself in diverse ways. New conservative organizations, such as the Minutemen and the John Birch Society, appeared on the scene. They called for the impeachment of liberal Supreme Court Chief Justice Earl Warren, minimal government, the abolition of all foreign aid, withdrawal from the United Nations, and militant anti-Communism.

Within the Republican Party, the Movement was centered around the national Young Republican organization, which was almost a party within the party. While the National Committee of the party was controlled by the Eastern Establishment, young conservatives controlled the Young Republicans. And these young conservatives planned to use the Young Republicans eventually to seize the Republican Party in the name of Sun Belt conservatism.

To do that, they needed a leader. Barry Goldwater was the obvious choice. Almost from the end of the Republican convention in 1960 the Young Republicans had begun organizing to draft Barry as their reluctant champion. They carefully put down roots across the country. They founded new chapters. They began to grow in size.

On the Fourth of July, 1963, over 7,000 representatives of the National Draft Goldwater Committee rallied in the Washington, D.C. National Guard Armory and called for Barry to come forward and accept their leadership. Barry, however, was not there. He had not yet decided to be their leader. But, he could not ignore them. A well-established movement with active chapters in 32 states was clamoring for him to become its leader. In some states, the draft Goldwater movement had already captured the Republican Party apparatus. In South Carolina, for example, the State Republican Committee announced that the Republican Party in South Carolina was now the official Draft Goldwater Committee for the state. *Time, Life, Newsweek* all featured Barry on their covers because of the "Draft Barry" movement.

By the late summer of 1963, Barry was leading the polls as the frontrunner for the Republican nomination. And it finally seemed that Barry was moving toward accepting the call to carry the banner of conservatism against John F. Kennedy in the 1964 election.

Then came Dallas. Vice President Lyndon Johnson became the new president and the new Democratic opponent in the 1964 election. Barry had second thoughts. But not for long. The Movement which had drafted him as its leader was composed of True Believers and it was beyond Barry's control. It was a juggernaut already in motion and it could not be stopped.

So, on January 3, 1964, Barry called a press conference on the balcony of his desert hilltop home in the wealthy Phoenix suburb of Paradise Valley. He announced to the news media that he was formally a candidate for the Republican presidential nomination. And the Movement shifted into overdrive to win that nomination for him against the Eastern Establishment's candidates, New York Governor Nelson Rockefeller and Pennsylvania Governor William Scranton.

Barry would go on to win control of the Republican Party and the subsequent presidential nomination in two ways: First, there was that early announcement of his candidacy, long before Rockefeller and Scranton joined the fray. This developed early momentum for him.

Second, the Movement simply out-organized the Eastern Establishment in the primaries and state nominating conventions. True Believers are always more fanatical about organizing than wishy-washy moderates. Thus, the latter were already defeated by the time of the national nominating convention in San Francisco that summer, a convention which chose Barry on only one ballot. It was the beginning of the end for the moderate Republicans who had controlled the party's nomination process since 1940. They just did not yet realize that they were dinosaurs headed for extinction.

As part of that ultimately successful primary campaign, the local organization in Phoenix developed a permanent presence by early 1964. It began recruiting high school kids into a new group called "Youth for Goldwater." Three of my classmates from Orangedale Elementary School who'd gone on to North High with me joined, including Tom Jacobsen, our eighth grade valedictorian. Then Tom asked me to also join. I was glad to do so. Anything for Barry. I even suggested a slogan for Barry: "AuH2O in MCMLXIV" -- the chemical notations for gold and water and the Roman numerals for 1964. The campaign didn't adopt it. No doubt it was too obscure. Instead, it chose, "A Choice, Not an Echo."

It was because we belonged to "Youth for Goldwater" that the four of us ended up in February, 1964 carrying banners for Barry at the Phoenix Municipal Stadium next to Papago Park just across the road from the Phoenix Zoo. It was the first Phoenix rally for Barry's presidential campaign after his announcement and we were there to support him by creating a spectacle. There must've been a thousand of us "Youths" on the field, all wearing identical white cowboy hats with huge "Barry in '64" buttons on the front and each one of us carrying a banner flapping in the breeze. The entire field was an ocean of Barry banners.

And there must've been tens of thousands cheering in the stands, cheering and stomping. There were some warm-up speakers, but the crowd kept up a clapping beat which drowned them out: "Bar-ry, Bar-ry, Bar-ry!"

The speakers soon disappeared and Barry Goldwater, "the next President of the United States," was driven onto the field in a limousine convertible, waving to the crowd like a Roman emperor celebrating a triumph as his chariot rolled slowly through the ocean of banners. The roar from the stands assaulted us and we joined in, cheering as loudly as we could as we bounced our banners up and down.

The limousine stopped at homeplate, where a platform had been erected for Barry. He ascended the platform and waved to the crowd and the TV cameras, his back to us. It must've been a wonderful sight for those in the stands and those watching the rally on TV to see us "Youths" standing in our white cowboy hats and with a thousand banners behind Barry as he began his campaign speech. The crowd in the stands went crazy over him.

I don't remember what Barry said that night. Perhaps it was then that he first declared that he offered America a "choice, not an echo." Perhaps the speech was written by his usual speech writer, Karl Hess. It was Hess who wrote the most famous line attributed to Barry, which Barry voiced in his Republican presidential nomination acceptance speech in 1964 at San Francisco's Cow Palace Auditorium. Replying to the Democrats, who labelled Barry as too ideologically "extremist" for the presidency, Barry thundered back, "Extremism in the defense of liberty is no vice, and moderation in the pursuit of justice is no virtue." The convention went wild over Barry's words. Or, rather, Karl Hess' words.

And, true to *his* minimal government principles, Karl Hess later became a left-wing anarchist who dropped out of the capitalist system to live in a Washington, D.C. hippie commune. There he lived off the grid by bartering his labor instead of using money. I could understand that. It is but a few steps from libertarianism to anarchism.

But, though I don't remember what Barry said, I do remember the excitement and the adrenalin that pumped through me. It was my first political rally and it was exhilarating to be present at the beginning of a great crusade to save America. That night, on the edge of the Papago desert in Phoenix, I felt that I was witnessing the birth of a powerful new political force. I was sure that America's future belonged to this new conservative movement which, in a small but proud way, I was helping to launch.

Gulf of Tonkin Incident

The Commies attacked me with all the fury of those who hated America. "Kill the bastard!" the old farts screamed. "Shut the fuck up! Get down from there!"

They were shaking their wrinkled fists and shambling toward me as I stood defiantly at the podium. Some were already climbing the stairs of the speaker's platform to pull me down. From the back I saw Jerry shoving them this way and that as he fought his way toward the front to help me escape the Commie mob. I didn't know if he'd make it in time. The United States Navy was fighting the Commies in the South China Sea and Jerry and I were fighting them on this California beach. But it was the same battle.

Jerry's uncle had warned us not to get mixed up with these Commies. "Don't go down there," he said. "You don't know what you're messing with. They're all members of the Communist Party. You'll only get into trouble if you fall in with Commies."

So, of course, we had to go see the Commies.

It was August 8, 1964. I was 17 and I'd recently graduated from North Phoenix High School. Except for one week at the Baptist summer camp in Prescott, after I graduated from grade school, and an attempted runaway during high school, which ended up in the Prescott jail, I hadn't been out of Phoenix since I was five, when Mom, me, and my brother Bruce arrived from Chattanooga, Tennessee. Phoenix was a stifling prison, and I wanted out.

Jerry suggested we visit Los Angeles, where he had an uncle who lived near the beach. Jerry Campbell was my best friend. He was an unemployed grade school drop-out who lived in an abandoned chicken coop near me on my street and who survived by stealing. He said his L.A. uncle would let us crash in his home for a time, so I readily agreed. I had no job and nothing better to do. Besides, I'd never seen the ocean.

When I told Mom I'd like to spend some time in L.A., just to get out of Phoenix for a while and see the ocean, she didn't object. In fact, she said she'd pack a suitcase for me.

She pulled a suitcase out of the closet and tossed it on the big bed she shared with my young brothers Pat and Brad and asked me what I wanted to take. "Whatever you think I'd need," I said.

She began loading in underwear, socks, and shirts, which she slowly folded. She kept packing in clothes until the suitcase began to bulge. As she did this, silent tears were trickling down her cheeks. I was surprised. And then I realized that she saw my L.A. visit entirely differently than I did. Like me, she had no idea what I might do after high school. College had never been mentioned as a possibility. It was beyond our mutual conceptions. No one we knew went to college. So, for her, she was engaged in a major life transition ritual. Her oldest child was now 17 and had graduated from high school. It was clear that he was now leaving home and leaving her forever, to begin his life as an adult. "Mom," I said, "that's enough clothes. I'll only be gone for a week or two."

"You never can tell."

Hard to argue with that.

Jerry's uncle didn't know we were coming, but he took us in readily enough. At least he didn't have a chicken coop. Instead, he had a living room floor. We threw blankets on his floor and crashed there. The mighty Pacific was only a ten-minute walk from his front door, so we visited the beach on a daily basis. The pounding and noise of the surf mesmerized me. Coming from the desert, I couldn't swim, but I waded along the beach and out into the surf as much as I dared. And both of us spent a lot of time just sitting on the sand and ogling the tall and tanned California girls striding along the beach in their bikinis.

And then, on August 2 and August 4, the North Vietnamese Commies launched what we were told were unprovoked attacks against two American destroyers on routine patrol off the coast of North Vietnam in the international waters of the Gulf of Tonkin. President Johnson was especially incensed about the August 4th attack, which suggested that the first attack had not been an accident. The North Vietnamese Commies were deliberately targeting American warships.

Based on that second attack, Johnson went before Congress and asked for authorization to respond appropriately. It was another Pearl Harbor, where Asians had once more launched a surprise attack on American ships. On August 7, Congress almost unanimously passed a "Resolution" authorizing Johnson to take "all necessary steps" to respond this unacceptable Communist aggression in Vietnam.

In the meantime, the old Commie farts down on the beach had been raising hell about this Gulf of Tonkin incident for the last couple of days. They had a ramada -- an open-sided shelter -- with a concrete speaker's platform, a podium, microphone, and speakers. Jerry's uncle said they were always ranting and raving about something down there. It was their Hyde Park soap box. Any day you went down you could hear Social Security Commies screaming like it was still the 1930s. We were sure they'd be waving their canes and having heart attacks over the Gulf of Tonkin Resolution, so Jerry and I had to go down to see the circus.

The beach ramada was jammed with more than the usual number of radical old fogies. Even before we got there we could hear some geezer yelling hysterically into the microphone, cheered on by his fellow pensioners. The agitated crowd was spilling out of the ramada. They were all yelling and screaming. Some were pounding the sand with their canes and walkers. They were really worked up over the Resolution. Since they probably all had high blood pressure, I marveled that some hadn't already keeled over from strokes.

Jerry and I pushed our way into the crowd. Bodies parted to make way for the two kids who'd come to hear what their seniors had to say.

The hysterical geezer at the microphone was working himself up into a spittle-flying froth about the so-called "lies" of the Johnson Administration. "Those weren't 'innocent' warships," he yelled. "They were on a spy mission. The North Vietnamese were simply defending their territorial waters. It's all a God-damned lie so this fascist capitalist Administration can take us into another colonial imperialist war against the Vietnamese people!"

The geezer worked himself up into such a rage that the veins were pulsing along his neck and on his bald pate. I expected him to topple over from a stroke any second. He went on and on as his comrades cheered, clapped, and urged him on to ever greater attacks on the government. It seemed America just couldn't do anything right. Our ships had been attacked, but we were the bad guy. Anything the president said was a lie.

And the more the hysterical geezer spewed his spittle, the madder I got. America had been attacked out of the blue, just like at Pearl Harbor, and all these God-damned Commie traitors could do was run down America and side with the enemy.

The frothing geezer finally ran out of steam and surrendered the mike to another comrade, who was acting as a moderator. "Who's next?" the moderator asked. There was a forest of waving, liver-spotted hands as the comrades all yelled to be next.

I raised my hand, too. "I'd like to speak!" I yelled. "Let me speak!"

The old comrades around me took up my cause. "Let him speak!" they yelled. "Let the boy speak! He has to fight the capitalist wars! Let the one who has to fight speak! Let youth speak!"

Heads turned, hands came down, and the moderator beckoned me forward. "Come on up, son. Let's hear what you have to say. You're the one who'll have to fight in this capitalist war."

You're damn right, I said to myself. I'm the one who'll fight, not you old farts. I was still 17 and too young for the draft, but I knew that, when called, I would serve willingly, wherever my country needed me. I was a patriot, unlike these Commie traitors.

The old Commies cleared a path for me as I made my way forward. Wizened hands reached out to clap me on the back. "Go to it, son! Give the bosses hell!"

The moderator stepped back and I stood alone at the microphone before the crowd of old Commies. They fell silent and looked eagerly toward me to hear what "youth" had to say about the Gulf of Tonkin Incident. I gripped the gooseneck mike in my fist and said, "The President of the United States of America would not lie to the American people!"

Mouths fell open in shock.

"America has been attacked!"

People began to grumble.

"It's time for all those who love America to come to her defense!"

Voices began to rise.

"Only a God-damned traitor would side with the Communist enemy in Vietnam!"

The mob began to howl. "Get that God-damned bastard down from there!" one yelled. "Get away from that mike, you sonuvabitch!" screamed another. The Commies began surging forward, and that's when Jerry began pushing his way through the angry mob toward me.

A couple of old Commies climbed onto the platform and grabbed me, pulling me away from the mike. I shoved through them and jumped down into the mob of gesticulating geezers. I began shoving this way and that, plowing a path through them.

Then Jerry reached me. He turned around and we began fighting our way together out of the crowded ramada. Blows were landing on my head and shoulders as the angry Commies hit us with their feeble fists and whacked us with their canes. We hunched up our shoulders, bowed our heads, and plowed on, pushing our way through the crowd.

Then we broke free and ran for the boardwalk. Some of the Commies hobbled after us, screaming and waving their canes. We easily outran them. When we reached the boardwalk, I turned and faced the pursuing Commies, most of whom had given up the chase as hopeless. "The President of the United States does not lie to the American people!" I yelled at the Commies.

"What the fuck do you know?" one yelled back. "Do you know who the Rosenbergs were, you stupid shit?" He gave me the finger.

"Commie traitors just like you!" I shot back, and gave him the finger in return. I had no idea who the Rosenbergs were, but I guessed I was probably right.

The old Commies began drifting back to the ramada. I could hear the moderator already inviting another comrade to the mike to denounce the coming imperialist war in Vietnam.

Jerry grinned at me. "You sure riled 'em up. I thought they were gonna start dropping like flies from heart attacks."

"Too bad they didn't. Fewer Commie traitors to worry about."

Part Three
You Don't Know Jack

Hope in a Hopeless Land

Like I told Mom when Jerry and I went to L.A., it was just to see the ocean. We saw the ocean. And also found the Commies. After returning, I prowled the neighborhood with Jerry at night and then slept till noon. I didn't have a job, so there wasn't much else to do. Perhaps if Elmer, my construction worker step-father, had given a shit, he could've gotten me a construction job, doing *something,* at Arizona Sand & Rock, where he worked. But, he didn't give a shit.

After waking I walked to the nearby Orangedale Elementary School and lifted weights until I was exhausted. They had a summer program to keep kids off the streets, and a weight room was one of the lures. Then I walked to the branch library at Thomas Mall, where I read until it closed. Then I hooked up with Jerry and we searched for trouble. At last, reluctantly, late at night, I returned home. There I crashed in my lower bunk, with Brother Rick on top, and slept till noon. I was marking time until something happened.

Finally, early in the morning of September 21, 1964, something happened.

A stranger was standing over me, shaking me. "Eric, wake up. Get up and get dressed. You're going to college."

It was gawd-awful early in the morning. Bleary-eyed, I looked up. It was Terry Lee, Bishop Lee's oldest son, just returned from his two-year mission for the Mormon church. Every Mormon boy -- and now, sometimes, every girl also -- is expected to go on a two-year self-financed tour of duty as a missionary when he turns 18. This is why you see these clean-cut kids in white shirts and ties knocking on doors all over America. And now, one of the returned Mormon missionaries, the Bishop's son, was standing over my bed, telling me to get up and get dressed, as I was going to college. I guessed he was still feeling like a missionary. "Whaddya mean, 'going to college'? I never applied to college."

"Well, you're going, anyway. Today is registration at Phoenix College for the Fall term. I'm taking you down to register you. So let's go, c'mon, get up and get dressed."

So I got up and got dressed.

Today, there are two-year junior colleges all over the Phoenix metropolitan area. But in 1964, Phoenix College was about it. It was the first and biggest of the local community colleges. Founded in 1920, it is in fact one of the oldest community colleges in the nation. It looked a lot like North High, from which I'd just graduated, and there was a reason for it. The current campus occupies a 30-acre tract facing Thomas Road, with Encanto Park on the other side. The buildings which occupied this campus in the 1960s were, like North High, completed in 1939 as a WPA work project. And anyone who was a high school graduate could enroll. I was a high school graduate. I was eligible.

Mormons believe in education. Interestingly, although they have a high rate of college graduates, the church seems to have successfully inoculated them against the liberalization of thought and attitude which usually comes with a college education. Perhaps this is because so many of them go after technical degrees. That was certainly the case with Terry Lee. He planned to be a dentist, and that's exactly what he became.

Besides believing in education, the Mormons believe in taking care of their own. Although the bishopric is, like all church positions, completely voluntary and unpaid, Bishop Lee was an energetic shepherd who expended a lot of time and energy looking after his flock. When he discovered that Mom and the rest of us walked the long distance to church each Sunday, he intervened. He personally co-signed a car loan so that Mom could buy a car. Then he made sure she got her driver's license. Then Mom began proudly driving the family to church on Sunday.

Then she began driving other places, as well. Elmer, my step-father, didn't like it, and there were some knock-down, drag-out battles. But Mom kept her car, and it was the beginning of her liberation from the prison of the home. Elmer cursed the Mormon church and swore Mom would live to regret owning a car.

And, when Bishop Lee learned that I'd graduated from high school, was unemployed, and was just hanging out and getting into trouble at night, he intervened once more. Still 17, I was too young to go on a mission, so instead, Bishop Lee sent his son to pull me out of bed and drag me to school. Being a dutiful returned-missionary son, Terry Lee obeyed.

And, having nothing else to do, I also obeyed. I'd never heard of Phoenix College. Even if I had, I'd not've thought of applying. Going to college was beyond my comprehension. I didn't know people who went to college. Certainly no one in my family. So college was never mentioned at home as a possibility. I assumed that college was too expensive for people like me. I'd never heard of scholarships, or government-backed student loans, which were only just coming into existence. All I knew was that I was a poor boy with no money, Mom had no money, and Elmer wasn't about to cough up a single penny for my education. He never had during high school, and there was no reason to believe he'd suddenly become a philanthropist just because I wanted to go to college.

I mentioned this to Terry Lee as he drove us to Phoenix College. "Not to worry," he said. "Tuition at Phoenix College is only $27 per semester. You can come up with $27, can't you?"

I was stunned that it was so cheap. I had no idea. "Yeah, I can come up with $27."

At that time, Phoenix College was about as large as North High. The campus was also, like North High, on Thomas Road, although further on down, on the other side of Central Ave. Even the WPA buildings looked like those at North High. It seemed the only real difference was that the students were a bit older and they could smoke. It was a high school with ashtrays. It felt familiar as soon as Terry Lee drove up.

Terry walked me through registration, then disappeared to register himself. In those pre-computer days, registration meant approaching various tables, where the actual teachers of each course sat waiting to register students into their upcoming classes, and signing up for a course. I say "teachers" because virtually none of them had a Ph.D. All you needed to teach in a junior college was a Master's, or the equivalent of graduate study, perhaps a few courses beyond the Bachelor's. So, most of these people were hardly "professors."

I liked this registration procedure, as you could check out the teachers and decide whether you might like them. The flip side was that they could also check you out and had the authority to arbitrarily bar you from their class, if they so desired. I was scruffy-looking that day. I'd decided to grow a beard and was about 10-days into it. The tonsorial changes of the Sixties had not yet swept across Phoenix in 1964, and beards were almost universally derided. Perhaps it was an echo of Phoenix's conservative Fifties antipathy to the Beatniks. In any case, the teacher for one course I wanted to take refused to register me because of my beard. "You can take my course when you shave it off," he said.

"Then I guess I'll never take *your* course." I stifled my urge to add, "asshole."

Seething, I walked over to the English Department tables. All of the teachers behind the English tables were women. "Can you believe I'm not allowed to register for a course because I have a beard!? I thought Phoenix College was supposed to be something more than a high school."

One of the teachers with long dangly earrings slapped a registration form down in front of me. It was for Introduction to American Literature. "Then you can sign up for *my* course. You're *just* the kind of student I want!"

I smiled at her. She smiled back. She was thin, blonde, looked to be in her fifties, and her huge dice cube earrings bobbled beneath her ear lobes every time she moved. I liked what I saw.

"What's your name?"

"I'm Dr. Mary Maher, the only Ph.D. in the English Department. I want students like you and I'm sure we'll get along fine."

"I'm sure we will," I replied, and signed up for her course. And we did get along fine. It was Mary Maher who gave me poetry books from her personal library. It was Mary Maher who took me to my first high-class restaurant where she bought me my first lobster and showed me how to crack open the claws for the meat inside. And it was Mary Maher who brought the poet Donald Hall to Phoenix College for a reading and then took him and her favorite student out to a fancy dinner on the English Department's tab.

Donald Hall, a co-founder of *The Paris Review,* went on to become America's poet laureate. At that time he was just a New England poet who, I thought, was not all that impressive. I wasn't impressed with his poems and I wasn't impressed his typical arty-farty zombie monotone "poetical" reading of them. Poetry began as a spoken art form, so why is it that so few poets know anything at all about the public reading of poetry? If you ever attend a poetry reading, listen as the poet begins to read. Just as adults speak to babies in an artificial "baby voice," so poets speak to their audiences in an artificial "poetry voice." His or her voice automatically rises in pitch and takes on an affected zombie monotone totally different from that poet's normal voice. There is no inflection, there is no emotion, there is no music in the voice. It is completely without nuance, completely boring, and completely soporific. It's hard to stay awake while listening to poets who affect this "poetic style." When poets begin their monotone drone, run for the exits!

Lest you think I'm a complete Philistine, let me acknowledge that there are exceptions. I know because I've heard them, and because I've heard them, I know the aural power of great delivery. Allen Ginsberg, towards the end, recited his poetry in a sing-song style which he accompanied with a small accordion-like harmonium. His poetry was meant to be delivered in a trance-like incantatory style. It was interesting and it worked.

But the first time I was truly moved and excited by a poetry reading was when I heard Anne Sexton, backed by a three-piece jazz combo, read her poems. It was a revelation. Her words moaned and groaned and you heard the music in and under her words. And Marge Piercy knows how to do it, as does Erica Jong. I've attended packed readings by both of them, and they can move you even without the jazz combo backup. Why is it that so many of the best poetry performers are women?

But even the lesser women poets fall into the zombie monotone "poetic style," which grates on the ear as a mockery of authentic oral communication. You can't hear their meaning for their zombie act. Is it any wonder that most people don't give a damn about poetry? Most poetry has become impossibly esoteric and opaque on the page, and then the poets themselves turn people off with their artificial hoity-toity zombie monotone public readings. Poetry originated as a spoken art form for the common people, and if poets don't know how to read their poems aloud in public so that common people can "hear" them, how can they really be called poets? They're just the living dead who retain the ability to speak.

Most academic poetry and academic poets are therefore a lost cause. They write in their little magazines only for each other and are paid only with a couple of free copies of the journal which contains their scribbles. They have refined themselves almost out of existence. So, I say let the academic poets masturbate alone in their ivory towers. The real hope for poetry rests with performance artists and slam poets like Todd Alcott, Bob Holman, Taylor Mali, and Sherman Alexi, who is one fucking funny guy. They are among the few who know how to speak so that ordinary people can "hear" them.

End of working class rant.

So, when Mary asked the portly Donald Hall, at dinner, to explain the use of metaphor in his poetry, I wasn't much interested in his reply. He may as well have just etherized me on the table. It was just bullshit academic jargon as far as I was concerned. If he couldn't explain his "poetical truth" so that an ordinary mortal like me could understand it, then there was no "truth" in it. The truth is always simple, and easily understood. If not, then it isn't the truth. "The art of art is simplicity," the poet Walt Whitman said.

Instead of his jargon, what stays with me is Donald Hall's fierce concentration on his food. He shoveled it in non-stop, fast and furious. Even his exegesis of his use of metaphor was thrown out between huge mouthfuls of food as he gulped down his dinner as if it might be his last. Years later, in a *Paris Review* interview, Donald Hall recounted a memorable lunch with Brooklyn poet Marianne Moore. "On a tray she placed three tiny paper cups and a plate," he recalled. "One of the cups contained about two teaspoons of V-8 juice. Another had about eight raisins in it, and the other had five and a half Spanish peanuts. On the plate was a mound of Fritos....What else did she serve? Half a cupcake for dessert, maybe? She prepared a magnificent small cafeteria for birds."

Given Donald Hall's huge hunger for Mary Maher's dinner, that lunch with Marianne Moore must have been sheer hell. Perhaps that's why he remembered it so vividly. From his humongous appetite, I surmised that poets were poorly paid in America.

But English teachers who love poetry are paid a little bit better. And sometimes they even have a student write a poem singing their praises, as I did for Mary Maher:

****

Mary Maher Should Be Mayor

Mary Maher should be mayor
    Of a village, burg, or town
        And in a passing day or
            Two she'd bring it much renown.
She is the land's most widely read,
    Books fill her car and house.
        Books are piled up on her bed
            There's no room for a mouse!
She knows most any poet,
    Olde English or brand new,
        And wouldn't you just know it?
            She knows Will Shakespeare too!
She felt the fleece that Jason sought,
    Labored long with Hercules,
        She knows the place where Beowulf fought,
            And all the plays of Sophocles.
She toured the dark Inferno

>   With Dante as a guide,
>   She read with Victor Hugo,
>   Told Tartuffe that he lied.
>   She told a whopping tale or two
>   With Chaucer by her side,
>   And she knows much more than I do,
>   Like why Niobe cried.
>   Tom Paine, Mark Twain, and Citizen Kane,
>   Then there's Edgar Allan Poe.
>   She calls Miss Austen simply, "Jane."
>   Is there any one she doesn't know?
>   She's taught them all in classes
>   All across the land,
>   Brought wisdom to the masses,
>   Now she deserves a hand!

****

Mary cried when I gave her the poem. She loved poetry so much -- but in her entire life, no one had ever written a poem for her. Nor would anyone ever again.

So, it turned out that Phoenix College was my on-ramp to higher education and poets like Donald Hall. And to teachers and friends like Mary Maher and Richard Goldberg, the first history teacher I ever had who actually *cared* about history. It was Richard Goldberg, for example, who brought Russian revolutionary Alexander Kerensky to speak at Phoenix College and who invited me, also his favorite student, to have dinner with the two of them.

It was all a complete accident. I had no plans to go to college, ever. It wasn't in the game plan. It happened only because I was a Mormon.

Mountain Meadows

"There are none virtuous but the powerless. And even they are criminal in their dreams."

-- Michael Bakunin

****

I was a Jack Mormon -- an unbeliever -- from the beginning but, so long as I kept my unbelief to myself, I had friends and I had a community to which I belonged. Sometimes I wished I could have believed. It's lonely being a doubter, especially a secret doubter. But I never desired friendship and community enough to stop thinking.

Even when I began studying to become a Mormon missionary, I continued to doubt.

Every college campus in the West, including both four- and two-year colleges, has a nearby off-campus meeting place for that school's Mormon students. These are called "Institutes of Religion." The Latter-Day Saint (LDS) Institute of Religion at Arizona State, in Tempe, was huge, as big as a church. The Phoenix College Institute of Religion, on the other hand, was small. In fact, it was merely a cinderblock house in a subdivision just across a street from the campus.

The living room of this house was used as a classroom, with folding chairs and an accordion divider to close it off during classes. The two bedrooms were furnished with desks, filing cabinets, and phones and were used as offices for the administrators. The kitchen remained a kitchen and the rear "family room" became the social center for the Mormon students who dropped by. This room had a soft drink machine which dispensed only Dr. Pepper, juices, and other non-caffeinated drinks, caffeine being as forbidden to Mormons as alcohol and tobacco. In the rear of the house was an enclosed backyard with several Ping-pong tables on a concrete patio for socializing. The Institute was like a Mormon club house or a sorority-fraternity house, where one could have fun with co-religionists, a welcome haven from the anonymity of the larger campus.

I spent a lot of time at the Institute, pretending to be a Mormon. I had no other friends at the school, I knew no one else. But, it was difficult being a *converso*. Once, in the heat of discussion, I said "damn." There was an awkward silence. I knew instantly that my mask had slipped. Good Mormon boys and girls don't use profanity. It was if I were a Jew in a Nazi officers' club, passing as Aryan, and had suddenly said, "Oy vey!" But, I only slipped that once, and it was because I was emotional. I was otherwise exceedingly circumspect. I had long practice in concealing my apostate nature.

But, the Institutes of Religion are used for more than just student socializing. They are also centers of "extra-curricular" instruction for Mormon college students. All Mormon students are encouraged to enroll in courses at the Institute, in addition to their "regular" courses at the adjacent college.

I signed up for the only two courses which remotely interested me. The first of these was "Missionary Training." I was still 17, so I was, for the time being, exempt from too much pressure to go on my two-year mission. When asked my plans, I explained that I'd go when I graduated from Phoenix College, at age 19. In the meantime, I would train for my mission.

Of course, I had no intention of ever going on a mission for the Mormon church, but I'd cross that bridge when I came to it. In the meantime, I thought it was a good idea to know the enemy I secretly opposed as intimately as possible. So, a spy in the enemy camp, I wanted to know what missionaries were expected to do.

Truth to tell, I remember very little about the techniques taught in this class, although the returned missionaries who taught the course said I'd make a good missionary. What I remember most is the effective social and mind control the church exercised over its teenage missionaries.

These missionaries, all paying their expenses out of their own pockets, could be sent anywhere in America or, indeed, the world. As a result of proselytizing, there are a lot of Mormons, for instance, in Great Britain.

Once out in the field, they were isolated from their families of origin as much as possible. They could write and receive as many letters as they wished, but phone calls were very few and very far between and, of course, there were no visits home, nor visits by parents to their children in the field. It was a two-year imposed separation from family even more complete than the military, where you at least have furloughs.

The adopted family for the missionary became the new Mormon community in which he found himself. Even more, his adoptive family was the fellow missionary with whom he was paired. Mormon missionaries are never alone. As with the original Twelve Apostles, they always travel in twos. Furthermore, these two live together, eat together, work together, pray and play together. They are joined at the hip. This is not only for mutual support, it is also so that they can keep watch on each other. Each is the other's keeper, making sure that there is no mutual slacking off of missionary zeal and work.

A missionary is assigned a certain region, such as Northern California, Western Pennsylvania, or the Phoenix metro area. Every six months, however, he is reassigned to a different part of that region, so that he doesn't become too familiar with the turf he was originally assigned -- and therefore slack-off. Further, every three months the missionary is assigned a new partner, to whom he will also become joined at the hip. This is to guard against the original pair becoming too familiar with and trusting of each other, and therefore negligent in their vigilance of each other. When given a new partner, the missionary maintains the zeal expected of him around this stranger, at least until he can begin to feel out his partner. But, by then, of course, he is reassigned to a new partner and the dance of acquaintanceship begins all over. The church knows what it is doing.

In 1964 in the densely populated East, missionaries got around by public transit. In the sprawling West, where public transit was a joke, missionaries drove Nash Ramblers owned by the church. There were two reasons for this. First, the Nash Rambler was a small car which economized on gas. Second, it was manufactured by the American Motors Corporation (AMC), of which Mormon George Romney was president and chairman from 1954-1962. Romney had made sure the Mormon church got a good deal when it purchased and re-purchased its fleet of Nash Ramblers. Romney was no longer head of AMC by 1964 -- he was the Republican governor of Michigan from 1963-1969 -- but the church was still getting a good deal from the car company he'd headed. His son, Mitt Romney, later became the Republican governor of Massachusetts and, like his father in 1968, Mitt was a candidate for the 2008 Republican presidential nomination.

As the Mormon missionaries drove their Nash Ramblers, the two missionaries were expected to put their travel time to good use. Not a minute was to be wasted. The one in the passenger seat wasn't just daydreaming, staring out the window, or engaging in idle chatter with his partner. He was memorizing pertinent passages from the Bible and the Book of Mormon. There was always a lot to memorize. The passenger quizzed his partner, the driver, on those same passages. Every single waking moment had to be devoted to the church and becoming a better missionary.

It was an intensive two-year immersion in church teachings, the function of which was to turn the teenage missionaries into fully committed Mormons as much as it was to win new converts. It is said of the Marines that, "Once a Marine, always a Marine." The same can be said of the missionary experience. "Once a missionary, always a missionary," and the missionaries returned from their missions filled with proselytizing zeal. After taking this course in Missionary Training, I was more certain than ever that I'd never go on a mission for the church.

The other course I took at the Institute of Religion was "History of the Church." Taking their cue from the early Christian martyrs, my teachers presented the history of the church as the story of the righteous persecuted. It's an emotionally compelling narrative. And there is a large element of truth to it.

Of all the Protestant sects founded in America in the nineteenth century -- the Seventh-Day Adventists, the Christian Scientists, the Jehovah's Witnesses -- Mormonism was perhaps the most successful. It was also the most persecuted. Violent neighbors drove the Mormons out of upstate New York, where the sect was founded, out of Indiana, out of Missouri, and out of Illinois.

The 1830s, for example, witnessed a decade of conflict between Mormons and Missouri settlers which came to be known as the "Mormon Wars." Mormons had moved to Missouri because the Prophet Joe Smith believed the Garden of Eden was in Missouri. Instead of Eden, the Mormons found war. This low-level guerrilla war culminated on October 27, 1838, when Missouri Governor Lilburn Boggs issued an executive order, which Mormons now call the "Extermination Order," running Mormons out of his state. In his order to the commander of the state militia, Governor Boggs said that Mormons were "in the attitude of an open and armed defiance of the laws and having made war on the people of this state...their outrages are beyond all description." Therefore, Mormons "must be exterminated or driven from the state."

And so they were. Several thousand members of the Missouri Militia were called up and hundreds of Mormon men, women, and children are thought to have been massacred. At least 12,000 Mormons were driven out of Missouri by fire and gun to the safety of the Mormon city of Nauvoo, Illinois, just on the other side of the Mississippi River.

But, Nauvoo was only a temporary refuge. Mormons were as unwelcome in Illinois as they'd been in Missouri. In 1844 Joseph Smith and his brother Hiram were seized and imprisoned -- only to be dragged from their jail cells by a crazed anti-Mormon mob and lynched. This was why Mormon remnants regrouped under the leadership of Smith successor Brigham Young and trekked westward to Utah's Great Salt Lake, where there was no one around to bother them. Only there, in the desert wilderness, did they find peace.

So, there is truth to the official narrative of the righteous persecuted for their faith, which links the Mormons with the very first Christians.

However, the Mormons did and do have strange theological ideas which set them apart from other Christians, including the belief that all Mormons will become omnipotent gods in the afterlife, as long as they lead righteous lives in this life. Indeed, God himself -- yes, *our* God -- is a flesh and blood man living on a particular planet out in the cosmos who led a virtuous life and therefore became God of Earth. Furthermore, the martyred Joe Smith will sit at the right hand of Jesus on Judgment Day and help determine whether each and every one of us will go to heaven or hell.

But all of the above mentioned new nineteenth century sects had their own particular strange beliefs. And none of them were persecuted as fiercely as the Mormons, none of their founders were murdered by lynch mobs. Why did the Mormons, alone, arouse such hostility?

The Mormons say it was because the godly are always persecuted by the ungodly. However, it was actually no doubt because of the Mormon practice of polygamy. Joe Smith was an energetic and charismatic young man. He had solidly established the Mormon church before the age of 25. Evidently, he was also a lusty young man. He claimed, as did all of his successors as heads of the church, that he was in continuous contact with God. Further, he claimed that in one of His revelations, God told him to impregnate as many women as he could in order to establish "a Righteous race...upon the Earth."

Therefore, much to the distress of his first wife, Emma, Joe Smith married 30 women and righteously impregnated 20 of them. These simultaneous wives in turn did their righteous duty and gave the Mormon Prophet 57 children.

His male followers devoutly emulated their Prophet and also sired many children on multiple wives. Brigham Young, for example, had 27 wives. Another leading Mormon, Heber Kimball, had 43 wives. They took these wives because they had been ordered to do so by God, Himself. Joe Smith told them so.

And this was the main reason their neighbors drove them out of settlement after settlement, from New York to Indiana to Missouri to Illinois. Mormon polygamy offended mainstream religious beliefs. As one Illinois Congressman said at the time, Mormon polygamy was "a crime against Christianity." The early Mormons weren't persecuted because they were so righteous. They were persecuted because, in the eyes of other Christians, they were so immoral.

At the same time that I was studying the official history of the church at the Phoenix College Institute of Religion and absorbing the persecution narrative, I was also studying the "hidden" history of the church and discovering the real reasons for that persecution. Much of what I learned came from my secret reading of Fawn Brodie's well-known 1945 biography of Smith, *No Man Knows My History,* the title taken from one of Smith's statements. I'd checked it out of the Phoenix College library, where any Mormon student could have also found it. It is indeed, however, an unknown history of the Mormon Prophet, at least to Mormons, as I never knew of any Mormon student who read it.

Fawn Brodie was born into a prominent Mormon family. Indeed, her uncle became the Mormon prophet-president in 1950. As such, he was successor to Joseph Smith and was on speaking terms with God. Fawn Brodie could therefore be trusted with access to various church documents never before seen by biographers and historians.

However, her resulting biography portrayed Smith and his supernatural claims in a overtly skeptical light. Unlike the laudatory presentations of the church, which revered the Prophet and his hundreds of revelations from God, Brodie discounted his revelations and portrayed Smith as all-too-human. Reading her biography, one can only view the Prophet either as someone who was very seriously mentally deranged, or as an amazingly charismatic charlatan. I thought the interpretation of the Mormon Prophet as a charismatic charlatan more convincing.

Of course, the Mormon church was appalled by the biography and regretted granting Fawn Brodie access to its archives. The church therefore excommunicated her in 1946, despite her family's influence within the church, and commissioned a rebuttal pamphlet entitled, *No, Ma'am, That's Not History.* I read it, also, and concluded that, yes, Brodie's biography really *was* history. Her portrait was factually convincing, the rebuttal merely spluttering.

Then I read on and learned about the Mountain Meadows Massacre which, of course, my Mormon teachers of church history never mentioned. The Mountain Meadows Massacre vindicated Lord Acton's famous warning about power. "Power tends to corrupt," he said, "and absolute power tends to corrupt absolutely." The Mormons may have been a persecuted and powerless minority in the East, but out West, in Utah, they were the power -- and it seems they used that power to avenge their treatment back East.

The Mountain Meadows Massacre was one of the most brutal and notorious mass murders of the nineteenth century. In 2007 Jon Voigt starred in *September Morning,* a feature film on the massacre, which is now available on DVD. The killings were the culmination of several days of events, ending on September 11, 1857. During those days leading up to the infamous slaughter on 9-11, 1857, Mormons in southern Utah attacked a wagon train of Arkansas settlers traveling from the hated Missouri to California. After a series of skirmishes, the pioneers agreed to surrender to their Mormon attackers. After they did so, in a period of 30-minutes the Mormons exterminated the entire wagon train. In a frenzy of bloodshed, the Mormons shot, stabbed, and beat to death with rocks the 137 men, women, and children of the wagon train. Then they stripped the corpses of their clothes and possessions, which they sold at auction to other local Mormons. They finally tossed the naked bodies into two large piles for the bugs and the birds to feast on.

The Mormons spared only 17 children under the age of ten. The Mormon murderers felt that children of such young age would not be able to remember the murder of their parents. As Argentine military killers did with the children of the dissidents they murdered during Argentina's "Dirty War" of the 1970s, the Mormon killers farmed these children out to families of the killers. In the case of the Argentine killers, the children were raised to be good, God-fearing supporters of the military junta which had killed their parents. In the case of the Mormon murderers, the children were to be raised as good, God-fearing Mormons.

At first, the Mormons blamed the blood orgy on local Paiute Indians. This stance changed when it became clear that local Mormons were deeply involved. The official church position even today disputes historical claims that church president and Utah territorial governor Brigham Young ordered the massacre in an effort to keep non-Mormons out of Utah.

What we do know for certain is that the wagon train experienced a number of attacks over those days -- either by Paiutes, a mixture of Paiutes and Mormons, or by Mormons dressed as Paiutes. After several days, the party attacking the wagon train displayed a truce flag, carried by local Mormon leader John D. Lee -- a distant relative of my own Bishop Lee. He told the settlers that the Mormons had "controlled" the Paiutes, who were supposedly attacking them, and that if the pioneers surrendered their weapons, and came out with the Mormons, they would be safe.

So the pioneers surrendered their weapons to the Mormons and marched out in single file, with a Mormon walking by each man, supposedly for safety. After they had emerged from the circle of wagons, each Mormon turned to the pioneer walking beside him and killed him, either by shooting him, stabbing him, or beating him in the head with a rock. John D. Lee then personally supervised the murder of all the sick and wounded pioneers, who were riding in a separate wagon. Only the 17 youngest children were spared, to be carried off and given to Mormon families.

These facts are not in dispute. Other issues remain murky. For instance, did John D. Lee and the local Mormons act on their own? Or were they following church orders from on high?

The year 1857 was a tense one for the Mormons. That spring U.S. President James Buchanan had deposed Brigham Young as Utah's territorial governor and replaced him with a non-Mormon. Young ignored the president's orders and continued as territorial governor. Buchanan declared the Mormons in rebellion against the United States and dispatched U.S. Army troops, busy fighting Indians on the Great Plains, to enforce his orders in Utah.

However, Buchanan's troops had not arrived when the Mountain Meadows Massacre began, so Young still held his position and powers at that time. Indeed, he declared martial law throughout the territory and on September 15, four days after the massacre, issued an order banning all U.S. troops from entering Utah. It's clear that the Mormons were suspicious of and hostile toward any non-Mormons entering their territory even before the unfortunate wagon train crossed into Utah.

Because Brigham Young refused to relinquish his position as territorial governor and had forbidden federal troops from entering Utah, there were no non-Mormons in a position of authority in the territory at the time of the massacre, or immediately after, who might have conducted an independent investigation of the events.

When the U.S. Army finally reached Mountain Meadows, the soldiers erected a monument to the massacred pioneers. The monument placed the blame for the massacre squarely on the Mormons. On it were also the words, "Vengeance is mine, saith the Lord, and I will repay."

Four years later, in 1861, with the United States distracted by the Civil War in the East, Brigham Young visited the massacre site and ordered the Army monument to the pioneers demolished. "No," he said, looking on the monument's rubble, "vengeance is mine, and I have had a little of it."

Only 20 years after the massacre, in 1877, was one man finally prosecuted for the murders. That man was John D. Lee, the high-ranking lieutenant of Brigham Young's who confessed to leading the local Mormons in the attack on the wagon train. Prior to the massacre, Lee had been adopted by Brigham Young as a "spiritual son," and Lee described himself as "clay in the hands of the potter" when it came to obeying the orders of his church leaders. He was used to following such orders and, in his written confession, stated that he had received just such written orders to carry out the massacre from church elders. He did not, however, name his "spiritual father," Brigham Young, as the ultimate source of these orders.

As was the means of capital punishment in Utah, then and later, John D. Lee was executed by a firing squad. Up until the moment the bullets hit him, Lee insisted that he was a loyal Mormon and was being sacrificed, he said, "for the sins of others." Whatever the truth of the matter, it remains the darkest stain on Mormon history.

I discovered the story of the Mountain Meadows Massacre on my own. My Mormon teachers at the Institute of Religion did not even give me the official version of this story. As far as my course in church history was concerned, it never happened. Instead, Mormons were presented as always being the godly "saints," persecuted for their faith. With or without church orders, Mormons had never harmed any others. Just as Japanese history books teach a victim version of World War II, in which children are taught about the horrors of Hiroshima and the fire bombing of Tokyo, but never about the Japanese Army's enslavement of thousands of Korean, Chinese, and Filipino women for use as sex slaves, or about the Rape of Nanking and the attack on Pearl Harbor, which led to Hiroshima, so Mormons are never taught about their own atrocities. They were always the victims of the gentiles, as they call non-Mormons, never the victimizers.

This conscious act of omission deliberately distorted the history of the church. What I was taught was therefore a lie. Brigham Young may or may not have ordered his loyal lieutenant and spiritual son, John D. Lee, to massacre the pioneers at Mountain Meadows in 1857. But, by pretending it never happened, my Mormon teachers of church history certainly lied about it a hundred years later.

Power tends to corrupt, said Lord Acton.

He was right.

Like a Brother

If Gerald Noble had been an actor in a Western, he'd have worn a white hat. In fact, the first time I saw him I thought he looked exactly like Hank Worden, the great old character actor who appeared as John Wayne's buddy in 14 Westerns, including *True Grit* and *The Alamo.* In Wayne's 1956 classic, *The Searchers,* Worden portrayed Wayne's pard "Mose Harper." Mose was always there for the Duke, in a quiet, unassuming way.

Gerald Noble was almost the exact opposite of Jerry Campbell, my pard with whom I'd fought the California Commies just a couple of months earlier. Just returned from his two year mission for the Mormon church, Gerald was still fired up with faith and zeal. He was a member of my local congregation, which meant he lived not too far from me, just on the other side of the big Crosscut Canal in one of the myriad cinderblock subdivisions which sprinkle Phoenix.

Like me, Gerald was also a freshman at Phoenix College and frequented the off-campus LDS Institute of Religion. Perhaps I met him there, but more likely I met him at church. For some reason, maybe because we were both lonely and shared Phoenix College and church membership, we became friends. Indeed, we began spending so much time together we may as well have been two missionaries together on a mission.

Gerald was not academically gifted, but he worked with missionary fervor at being a good student. School was his new mission. Perhaps sheer determination and missionary discipline brought him good grades, but he sometimes had problems thinking logically. For example, Gerald was more religiously than mathematically adept. The Mormon church expects all members to sign over 10% of their gross income to the church, a religious tax called "tithing." So, when Gerald got his student loan for the year, he immediately signed over 10% of it to the church as his dutiful tithe on income.

I pointed out to him, however, that his loan wasn't actually "income." It wasn't *his* money. It was the *bank's* money, simply lent to him, and he'd have to pay 100% of it back, plus interest, out of future income. And, on that future loan-repayment income, he'd naturally pay his 10% tithe to the church. Which meant that he'd actually end up paying 20% of this particular income unit to the church, double what the church asked of him.

Gerald couldn't follow the math and was, instead, offended. He believed I was discouraging him from paying his rightful 10% tithe to the church. He all but said, "Get thee behind me, Satan!" and I realized I was skating on thin ice, exhibiting a possibly disloyal attitude toward the church, so I dropped it.

Gerald, and his younger brother, Gary, who also attended Phoenix College, had the worst cases of acne I've ever seen on anyone. Pustules covered their faces, necks, chests and backs. Gerald was always popping them, to drain the pus and then medicate them, but nothing seemed to diminish their number. There were always new ones, which routinely popped on their own under the pressure of the built-up pus. When they did so, they stained Gerald's underclothes with oozing pus and blood.

Gerald's underclothes were a sort of cut-off cotton Long Johns called "temple garments," worn in both winter and summer. These garments are like magic underwear. Mormons believe they protect the wearer from knives, fire, and a host of other lethal dangers. They also must be worn when visiting the local Mormon temple.

Each region of Mormon settlement has an enormous and ornate temple to serve the numerous churches in its vicinity. The Mormon temple for the Phoenix metro region was and is located in the suburb of Mesa, a town originally settled by Mormon pioneers. Weddings and baptisms take place in the temple, including baptisms for the dead.

Common to all Christian denominations is the belief that, if you don't accept Jesus as your personal savior, you'll go to Hell and burn forever in the unquenchable fire, where the worm dieth not. There is no way to heaven, Jesus said, but through him. Which means all those currently in the world who have not accepted Jesus will burn in eternal hellfire once they die. It also means all those in the past who never had a chance to hear the teachings of Jesus and accept him will also burn in eternal hellfire, through no fault of their own. This includes all members of your family, down through the long past.

Of course, each Christian sect believes that it, and it alone, has sole possession of the truth. Which means all the other Christians who don't accept that sect's party line are wrong and doomed to eternal hellfire, along with all those Jews, Hindus, Sikhs, Jains, Buddhists, and Muslims who aren't even Christians at all. This is not to mention the Chaldeans and Zoroastrians and all the Roman legionaries who worshiped Mithra. Let's not even get into the Viking gods and all the others. Just too many of them.

Since we're talking about Mormon beliefs here, not only will all these people who belong to other faiths burn in eternal hellfire, but all the members of your family tree who never had a chance to accept Mormonism, meaning anyone who lived before Joe Smith invented it in 1830, will also burn in eternal hellfire.

Since it is estimated that about 100 billion humans have lived and died since the beginning of the human race, and most of them never heard of Jesus, much less Joe Smith, we're talking about many billions of people writhing in eternal hellfire, while a minuscule fraction will flap their wings happily forever among the heavenly host as they wing their ways to becoming gods of their own little worlds. I always thought this belief was an "unchristian" doctrine of callous cruelty, but there you have it. That's just the way it is. If you're Christian, you must accept as right and just the eternal agony of these innocent billions, most of whom will be eternally tortured for the sin of being born too soon.

This monstrous doctrine of demonic cruelty, which festers at the heart of Christianity, should torment the consciences of all good Christians, but they seem to be able to accept it with amazing unconcern and equanimity. It is a singular lack of empathy for other human beings. Christians just turn off their minds when it comes to thinking through the theology they espouse and never ponder the full implications of their beliefs.

But the Mormons have a way of dealing with this doctrine of cruelty which makes them a little less monstrous than all the other Christian sects. All Mormons in good standing can go to a temple and undergo a surrogate baptism for their ancestors, as far back as they care to trace their genealogy. You can baptize all of your current relatives into the Mormon faith, even though they don't want you to do so. And you can retrospectively baptize all of your family tree into the Mormon faith, back to Adam and Eve if you wish, thus saving them from eternal hellfire.

This substitute baptism isn't just limited to your ancestors. You can baptize any dead person you want into the Mormon faith, including celebrities, heroes, villains, and complete strangers. The Mormon church compiles an International Genealogical Index of people waiting to be surrogately baptized. King Herod, Genghis Khan, Al Capone, Adolf Hitler, Joseph Stalin, Mao Zedong, and even Mickey Mouse have all been listed on the Index awaiting their turn to become posthumous Mormons. You could, if you wished, baptize dead Popes into the Mormon church, beginning with St. Peter. Perhaps someone already has, for all I know.

And, when you undergo this proxy baptism for your ancestors, Catholic saints, or mass murdering deceased dictators, you wear the cut-off Long John temple garments that Gerald wore.

But, you have to be among the elect, the purest of the pure, to even step inside a temple. Since I was never among the purest of the pure, I've never been inside a Mormon temple. Nor have I ever worn temple garments, which always looked exceedingly uncomfortable to me, especially for the long hot Arizona summers.

And the idea of them stained with Gerald's pus and blood made them seem even more unattractive. Good Mormon missionary boy that he was, Gerald had a large supply of temple garments, changed them daily, and was always cleaning them. He did the best he could with the poor card genetics handed him.

But, these poor genetics which affected his looks did not stop Gerald from becoming a college actor. I've never known another Mormon actor, as most were interested in more technical careers. Indeed, Gerald himself eventually became an automobile air conditioner repairman and then an auto mechanic. But, in college, he stretched himself. He was never a stage star, he looked too much like the star's sidekick for that, but he was a serviceable character actor. At Phoenix College I watched him perform as the poor snook in the two-man one-act Edward Albee play, "Zoo Story." He was also a Doughboy who was slaughtered while advancing into the machine guns of No Man's Land in the play, "Oh, What a Beautiful War!"

Nor did Gerald's looks stop him from dating, despite certain effeminate mannerisms. Mom was certain that Gerald was, as she said, "queer." He just didn't act masculine enough, in her eyes, to be a real man. So he had to be a homo, and she was dubious of my hanging around with him.

I assured Mom that Gerald was not queer. Perhaps because of his missionary confidence, Gerald always had plenty of dates with good Mormon girls. As they *were* good Mormon girls, nothing ever went beyond kissing. Gerald once told me how he dealt with the passions worked up in the heat of the night by heavy petting in the two front seats of his tiny VW Beetle. As he and his date reached a level of arousal where it was clear something a lot beyond kissing was going to happen -- who knows, perhaps he'd touch her breast next, or perhaps even reach between her legs? -- he excused himself. He told her he was going to walk around until he calmed down, and he advised the girl to just sit there, with the window down, and cool off.

Then Gerald walked somewhere behind his Beetle, unzipped his pants, unbuttoned his temple garments, and his hard prick popped out like a party favor. He jacked off until he came, usually pretty quickly. Then he cleaned himself off with his hanky, which he tossed into the bushes, and zipped up. He walked back to his car, where his good Mormon girl was waiting for him. And all was well, passions had cooled, temptations had passed. Both had successfully preserved their purity for their future spouses. Gerald eventually married a good Mormon girl from Brigham Young University and they had five children together, a goodly number for good Mormon parents trying to enlarge the numbers of the righteous race.

Having a car, even a small one like Gerald's Beetle, helped in getting dates. I, of course, did not have a car, so I depended on Gerald when we went to dances together. This was the spring tide of the British Invasion, 1964-65. The Beatles and the Stones and the Dave Clark Five were revolutionizing the sound of rock and roll. Mormon kids were not immune to the pop charts and wanted to rock out as much as any other kids.

Their parents and the church wanted them to do it demurely and safely, so the church sponsored Saturday night dances at various local Mormon churches. Mormons may be "fundamentalist" in many ways, but at least they have nothing against dancing, as shown by Mormon singer Marie Osmond performing on the TV hit *Dancing With the Stars* in 2007. Terry Lee, Bishop Lee's son, was a great ballroom dancer and everyone stood back to watch him and his steady girlfriend strut their stuff on the dance room floor.

These church-sponsored dances were always jammed, because they were the only dances parents approved and Mormon kids could attend. There was always a live band covering the latest Brit hits, but there were also adult chaperons and everyone could be sure that nothing happened except dancing. At least at the dances. What happened in VW Beetles afterward was beyond their control.

After one of these Saturday night dances, Gerald and I were too awake and restless to go home. We wanted to do something. If I'd been hanging with Jerry Campbell, the something would have been illegal. But, I was with Gerald Noble, a good Mormon boy. Whatever we did could be wild and wacky, but it had to be legal.

Somehow we concocted a plan to drive up to the Grand Canyon, which neither of us had ever seen. It was perhaps a four hour drive up, four hours back. It was winter, so the rim of the Canyon would be blanketed in snow. We'd pack snow on the hood of the Beetle, which covered the trunk. As the engine was in the rear, there would still be some snow on it when we drove straight to church in the morning. As Gerald parked prominently in the church's parking lot, just as all the parishioners were arriving, people would marvel at the snow. It didn't snow in Phoenix, even in the winter. How could there be snow on Gerald's car? And then we'd tell them we drove up to the Canyon and back last night, just for the heck of it. Not as exciting as stealing the flag from the local Playboy Club, which I did with Jerry Campbell when I was in high school, but it had the virtue of being legal.

So, Gerald and I roared off into the night, heading north out of Phoenix. We climbed the Mogollon Rim and passed through Cordes Junction a lot faster than I had on my bicycle when I'd ran away from home to Prescott about two-and-a-half years earlier. We stopped in Flagstaff in the early morning and filled up on gas. Then we headed north out of Flagstaff on the lonely pine forest road to the Canyon. Today, because of Republican cutbacks in funding, you have to pay to get into the Canyon, just like you have to pay to enter every other National Park. But, in those days, the people's parks were free to the people.

We drove to a parking lot on the North Rim and got out to peer at the vast chasm. It was a moonlit night, and the Canyon was splashed with the ghostly light of the full moon. You can't really see much viewing the Canyon by moonlight. The far vistas are lost in the darkness. Even so, we'd not seen the Canyon before, and what we saw was impressive. There wasn't a soul around and the only sound was the wind and an occasional hoot owl.

Then we set to work packing the hood and top of the Beetle with snow. As expected, the entire Rim was deep in the stuff. We'd just driven up from a Saturday night dance in the desert, so we weren't clothed for the snow, nor did we have gloves. Our hands quickly turned numb from the ice and snow, but our enthusiasm for the joke kept us piling it on the hood and packing it down to minimize the evaporation. Because the engine was in back, there'd be no engine heat seeping up through the hood to melt the snow. The only problem was the curvature to the car as a whole. The VW Beetle had an almost semi-circle shape to its hood and top, sloping down to the rear engine, all of which made it a bit top-heavy and unstable.

Then we headed back to Phoenix. We had just enough time to make it to church services. We again passed through Flagstaff, down through the range land around Cordes Junction, and down the Mogollon Rim to the Sonora Desert below.

By then Gerald had been driving a long time. In addition, he'd jerked around on the dance floor and flirted extensively at that night's dance which, in turn, had come at the end of a long day. I, too, was tired. Only adrenalin had kept us going. Now that was wearing off and Gerald felt he was too tired to drive any more. He decided to hand it off to me. I had a license, but I wasn't confident of my driving skills. "Gerald, I've never driven a VW before."

"There's nothing to it. And there are no other cars on the highway. All you have to do is aim it straight ahead and keep the car on the road."

So, we switched places and Gerald monitored me as we drove through the night. And he was right. It was easy and uneventful. Eventually, he dozed off and I was driving alone on a lonely highway. We were still some distance out in the desert, but approaching the outskirts of Phoenix nonetheless.

The eastern sky to our left began to lighten as I drove ever south toward Phoenix. Then the sun began peeking up over the horizon. The bright desert sunlight lit up the interior of the Beetle and aroused Gerald. Blearily, he opened his eyes and looked around. He suddenly pointed to an exit I was fast approaching and said, "That's our exit! Take it!"

It seemed we were still too far from the city to get off the highway, but I swerved to the right to take the exit.

Then Gerald said, "No, it's not our exit! Don't take it!"

I was almost off the highway and onto the exit, so I swerved back to the left to get back on the highway before it was too late. I was going too fast and I turned too abruptly. Forward momentum toppled the Beetle and suddenly we were spinning, spinning, over and over down the highway and then off the highway and down an embankment. It all happened so incredibly fast. There was nothing we could do but wait until the twirling chaos ended. The Beetle banged and spun and bounced down the embankment, while we swirled inside, held in place by our seat belts.

Suddenly, the whirligig smashed to a stop. The Beetle was lying somewhat on its right side at the bottom of the embankment. The passenger door was broken open. I was hanging at a slant, tied to my seat by my seat belt. I unbuckled my belt and gravity pulled me out of the smashed Beetle, over Gerald, to the ground where the broken door stopped my slide --

And then the world faded away into blackness.

I don't know how long I was unconscious. Slowly I awoke. And I was aware that I *was* waking up. And I remembered the spinning wreck of the Beetle. And vast relief flooded over me like blessing water. "Thank God," I muttered. "It was just a dream. It was just a dream."

And then I awoke fully to find myself on the cold ground. The smashed wreckage of the Beetle was beside me. And Gerald was dangling, unconscious, half out of the Beetle, still held to his seat by his seat belt. He was obviously hurt, but I didn't know how badly.

And then despair swept over me, replacing my relief. It wasn't a dream after all! It'd really happened! "Oh, God, no! Oh, God, no!"

I looked at Gerald. He was snoring as he dangled. It seemed odd, but at least he was breathing, he was alive. I later learned that it's not uncommon for those knocked unconscious to snore. The right side of his face was covered with blood and I knew I was responsible for hurting him. I was responsible for totalling his car. I was responsible for everything.

I looked up to the top of the embankment down which we'd rolled. There were people up there. "We need help! Please help us!"

"We don't dare!" one of them yelled back. "But there's an ambulance on the way!"

Then I passed out again.

When I next awoke, I was in a hospital bed. Mom was there. Elmer was not. I learned that I hadn't been hurt that much. I had a cut on my left forearm and I had pneumonia from lying unconscious for too long on the cold ground in the dawn chill. But the seat belt had saved me from further harm.

Gerald wasn't as lucky. Because the car had toppled and rolled to the right, his face had smashed into the passenger window and perhaps something else. His right cheek bone had been shattered and he had a concussion. Otherwise, he was OK. His seat belt had also saved him from something worse.

Gerald was in the same hospital with me, just down the hall. I insisted on seeing him. Mom said it was too soon, I was too weak to walk, there might be undiscovered trauma which exertion would worsen. "Then get me a wheelchair," I said.

Mom helped me into a wheelchair and then rolled me down the hall to Gerald's room. Gerald was awake as I rolled in. The entire right side of his face looked bruised and pulverized. He moved his head a fraction, glancing over at me. He said nothing. I was overcome with tremendous guilt. I wished it had been me, instead of Gerald, whose face had been smashed.

I rolled up to his bedside. I clasped his right hand in mine and cupped it. "Gerald, I am so terribly sorry. I wish it was me in your place."

Gerald squeezed my hand weakly. "It's OK," he whispered. "It's OK."

And then the tears I'd been fighting to hold back flooded down my cheeks. I bowed my head and cried. At that moment I felt closer to Gerald than I'd ever felt before. I loved him like a brother. For a long time I sat there in my wheelchair next to Gerald's bed, holding Gerald's hand as he held mine.

Thus I Refute Jehovah

"Dan the Man," as he called himself, was the opposite mirror image of Gerald Noble. He seemed to have everything going for him. He was blond, over six feet tall and, because he was a body builder, looked like a muscular Glen Campbell. And instead of a VW Beetle, Dan drove a behemoth Olds 88.

But, whereas Gerald had a wide circle of friends and acquaintances because he was imbedded in the Mormon community, Dan had no friends. Also, whereas Gerald had a missionary's self-confidence, Dan was wracked by insecurity and self-doubt. Perhaps that's why he called himself "Dan the Man." He was compensating. Maybe that's why he also became a weight lifter. That was certainly why I lifted weights. And Dan's self-doubt was almost certainly the reason he had no friends.

I met Dan in one of my public speaking classes. He was a good speaker, perhaps another effort to overcome his lack of self-confidence. But, there were a lot of good speakers in that class, so that didn't particularly attract my attention. One day, though, he was hanging around after class was dismissed. I bought a Babe Ruth from one of the snack food dispensers which dotted the Phoenix College campus. I tore the wrapper and began munching on the Babe Ruth.

"Give me a bite of your Babe Ruth, asshole," Dan demanded. Dan, as I soon learned, had the foulest mouth I've ever heard on *anyone*. Every sentence was liberally sprinkled with profanity.

"You go to hell," I said. I spoke differently when I wasn't around Mormons.

"I can't do that, asshole. I don't believe in hell."

"Well, neither do I, shithead."

Then we both laughed. And so I discovered that Dan was a militant atheist, the first avowed atheist I ever met. Finding him was like finding another countryman in a land of strangers. It was the beginning of a beautiful friendship, and when I wasn't hanging with Gerald, I was hanging with Dan.

Talk about being schizoid! I was two different people with each of them. I felt like a "real" person when I hung with Dan and a *converso* when I hung with Gerald. It was like moving between alien worlds. As I grew more confident about the collegiate world at Phoenix College, I think I'd have quickly left the church but for Gerald. Only his friendship kept me a Mormon.

I think, for the most part, men don't have friends. They have buddies. Buddies are for joking around with and doing things with. So, men have work buddies, drinking buddies, hunting buddies, sports buddies. But, they don't have many friends, people they are intimate with. This is because intimacy isn't a male thing. Especially intimacy between men. Intimacy between men is always suspected of being covertly homosexual. Guys aren't *really* supposed to like each other a lot unless they're fucking each other.

That may have been one of the reasons Mom thought Gerald was "queer." I spent way too much time with him. At least at that time, paranoid parents were the first to raise the queer flag if their sons had close male friends. It was a fear which haunted parental minds. Is my son queer? No doubt plenty of sons got the message, even if only subliminally, and this contributed to a certain distance they maintained with their male friends.

As I began spending a lot of time with Dan, questions of sexual orientation arose in his parents' minds. One night, he told me, they straight out asked him if he was having a queer relationship with me. He was shocked. How could his parents think that of him? How could they know so little about him?

Dan was shocked because he was obsessed with girls. So was I. Hey, we were both male teenagers. But Dan had a lot more success than me, despite his self-doubt. He didn't have friends -- but he had *girlfriends*. It seems his physical attributes -- being a blond and handsome body builder -- overcame his uncertainties. All he had to do was tentatively ask a girl out and she was soon wrapping herself around him in his Olds 88. And, unlike Gerald, who had to take a jack-off break to cool off, Dan the Man always consummated.

But, not until he'd asked the girl to marry him. Dan was a serial fiance. Every girl he asked out he also asked to marry him. If she declined, which few did (which always amazed me), he stopped dating them. If they accepted, he immediately bought them an engagement ring, which they proudly showed to all their girlfriends.

Then they fucked.

The engagement lasted a couple of weeks, a month, maybe two months, three months. Then Dan broke it off and he was once again looking for a fiancee to fuck. This must've been an emotionally wrenching experience for both parties, but Dan seemed to weather each break-up well enough. I told him that casual dating surely had to be less stressful than such serial engagements.

That didn't stop him from asking the next girl he really wanted to fuck to marry him. I don't know what religion his parents were, but they evidently instilled a strong strain of sexual morality into him which Dan wasn't able to shake free of, despite his aggressive atheism.

In addition to the emotional cost of being a serial fiance, it was also materially expensive. This was because Dan always let his ex-fiancees keep their engagement rings. I told him this was exceedingly profligate. The least he could do was ask the girl to return the ring. Then he could present it to the next girl he wanted to fuck. He could get down on bended knee, open the ringbox which he could always carry in his pocket along with rubbers for such horny emergencies, hold out the ring to the girl and say, "Madam, will you do me the honor of becoming my wife and allow me to fuck you until we marry?"

But, he never did. Perhaps he felt guilty for dumping his fiancees and let them keep the rings as consolation prizes. In any case, he always bought a new diamond engagement ring for the next fiancee. Eventually, there were a lot of girls at Phoenix College who had received what Marilyn Monroe called "a girl's best friend."

Dan spent freely in other ways. For instance, he bought a gym membership which allowed him to bring in guests for workouts three times a week. I became his regular guest and we worked out together at his gym Monday, Wednesday, and Friday afternoons.

As we encouraged each other to life heavier and heavier weights, we quizzed each other on theological arguments, honing our rhetorical skills like two missionaries on a mission, although our mission was to sow doubt and unbelief. We'd take turns, as if we were debaters, arguing for and against God. For example, while he was pumping out barbell curls, I might present the argument from First Cause, the Cosmological Argument, which goes like this: Complex things don't just happen, someone had to make them, someone "caused" them to come into existence. Which meant there had to be a God to make the universe, the most complex thing of all. God, then, is the First Cause of everything.

I'm still getting this today from black ladies in my neighborhood when they ring my doorbell for the Jehovah's Witnesses, although they probably don't call it by anything as fancy as the "Cosmological Argument." I tell them they're casting their pearls before a swine, because I don't believe in God.

They'll look startled for an instant, then point to a car out on the street. "See that car?" they'll say. "It's too complex to have just happened. Someone had to make it. The same with the even more complex universe. Just as that car didn't just happen, the universe didn't just happen. Someone had to make it, and that someone is God."

To which I reply the same way Dan replied, pumping out his barbell reps, when I gave him the Cosmological Argument.

"OK, let's accept that. Complex things don't just happen. Someone has to make them. And anything that could make the universe has to be even *more* complex than the universe. So, according to your logic, someone had to make God. So, I ask *you,* who made God?"

At that point, the logic of the black ladies always runs into a stonewall. "Oh, no!" they say, shocked at my blasphemy. "No one made God! The Lord Jehovah has *always* been here."

Then, as Dan said to me, but omitting his profanity, I reply, "It makes just as much sense to think the universe has always been here as to believe God has always been here."

And the Jehovah's Witness ladies can see they'll get nowhere with me, so they tell me to have a good day, turn, and leave. I wish them success converting someone else as they walk down my steps.

Then, back in the gym, as I did *my* barbell curls, Dan would present another argument, say, Pascal's Wager. Blaise Pascal was a French philosopher who died in a Catholic convent in 1662 at the age of 39. He felt it was impossible to prove the existence of God. Nonetheless, he argued that one *ought* to believe in God's existence, simply as a matter of probability. He felt that belief in God amounted to a wager. And the wager goes like this:

If God *does* exist and the Holy Scripture is true, then belief in him will give you infinite happiness in the afterlife. If, on the other hand, God *doesn't* exist, but you believe that he does, all you lose is the time you spent in church and the very finite pleasures of smoking and drinking and whoring. Even if you think the possibility of God's existence is near zero, Pascal said you should still believe. This is because, mathematically speaking, any finite percentage of infinity is still infinity, so you have infinite bliss to win for mere finite sacrifice. Betting on God's existence is thus the rational thing to do if there is anything more than an absolute zero chance of it being true, which, of course, just *might* be the case. It'd be foolish not to bet on God.

"That's good," I said to Dan, as I pumped out my reps with the barbell, "It sounds very rational. But for Pascal's Wager to work, you have to beg the question and grant much of what he wants to prove: That, if God exists, He is infinite, omniscient, omnipotent, and the Bible is His absolute Word. But, what if God exists, but doesn't really give a damn about human behavior and belief? So, if He doesn't care what we think, then we *won't* burn in eternal hellfire for not believing in Him. Or, what if God exists, but isn't an infinite and omnipotent being? In that case, He wouldn't be able to torture us for eternity for not believing in Him.

"But," I said, pumping out my last rep, "there are even more serious refutations. Pascal was a Catholic and assumed that the Christian God was the only alternative. He assumed there was only one God, the Christian God.

"But, there have been and are many possible God candidates. What if Allah is the real God, and demands adherence to the Koran for salvation? What if the Hindu gods -- Lord Krishna, Lord Shiva, and the elephant-headed Lord Ganesha -- are the real gods? What if Mithra is the real God? What if Osiris and Horus and all the ancient Egyptian gods are the real gods? What if Baal and Dagon, the gods of the Philistines, are actually the real Gods of the Universe? And the list goes on. According to Pascal's Wager, we shouldn't take a chance. We should believe in all of them and follow their precepts if there is slightest non-zero chance that one of them might be the real God.

"But, they're all also mutually exclusive. They can't *all* be right. Only *one* can be God. And they'll all damn you to infinite hell for believing in anyone but them. 'Thou shalt have no other god before me,' said God. Remember?

"So, the best and ultimate refutation of Pascal's Wager is that it is impossible to implement. We'd have to believe in an almost infinite number of God candidates to abide by it, and doing so would damn us to hell because they all claim absolute devotion from their believers. It's a Catch-22 situation and so, logically, can't be implemented. Not very good thinking for a famous French philosopher."

"OK, smart-ass," Dan said, as he took the barbell again for his reps. "Then you give me a good fucking argument for God's existence."

"The classic Ontological Argument, created in the Middle Ages and still going strong. God is, by definition, perfect. And it is more perfect to exist than to not exist. Therefore, logically, God must exist."

"Bullshit! I can imagine a perfect *Playboy* Playmate named Blowjob Betty, with all the attributes of idealized female perfection, who, if she is going to be perfect, also loves to blow me. The Ontological Argument would then say that, if she is perfect, then she *has* to also exist, as existence is part of perfection. But, just because I can *imagine* such a perfect woman doesn't mean that she actually *does* exist. Likewise with God. Just because we can *imagine* such a perfect being doesn't mean it actually *exists.* There's no logical correlation between 'perfection' and existence at all. It's just empty rhetoric."

And so it went, back and forth, back and forth, as we pumped iron and refuted God.

Afterward, Dan bought me a thick juicy steak. We had to eat right, he said. Steak for the protein, salads for the greens. If we were at his house, he'd fix us scrambled egg sandwiches on toasted whole wheat. For snacks, he'd pop unbuttered popcorn. "Eat, you fucker," he told me, "ya gotta keep up your strength."

All of this cost money, so Dan was always hatching money-making schemes. And, as I had little money of my own, I was always his partner in these ventures. After classes, we'd hop into his Olds 88 and drive to one of the endless new cinderblock subdivisions sprouting around Phoenix. They all had tiny address numbers on their doors or the walls next to the doors. But, those were hard to see at night.

"What if you had an emergency one night and had to call the cops, the fire department, or paramedics?" Dan asked the homeowner who came to answer the doorbell. "Minutes, *seconds*, could mean the difference between life and death. They need to be able to find your house quickly in the dark."

"So," the dubious homeowner replied, "what do you suggest?"

"This," I said, holding up a set of numerical stencils. "We'll stencil your address out there on the cement berm of your property with permanent water-proof black paint."

"The cops can really see these babies at night," Dan added. "Only four dollars."

Sometimes we made a sale, often times we didn't. It was all a question of numbers. Ring enough doorbells and you could accurately figure the odds of making whatever target amount of money you set for yourself.

And, when we got tired of tramping from one house to another in the blazing Arizona sun painting stencils on people's curbs, Dan the Man came up with another money-making idea. He had an endless supply of them.

And so it went. If I wasn't at the Mormon Institute of Religion with Gerald, or with him at a Mormon dance, I was with Dan, pumping iron and refuting God.

And, because I felt I had so much in common with him, because I felt so at ease around him, I came to feel as close to Dan as I did to Gerald.

But, it was something we didn't talk about. Because intimacy isn't a male thing. Especially intimacy between men. As I said, it's always suspect. Because guys aren't supposed to *really* like each other a lot unless they're fucking each other. And already his paranoid parents thought he was queer, just as Mom thought Gerald was queer.

So, how *does* a straight guy let another straight guy know he really appreciates him?

First, don't say it in private, especially don't say it in a men's room. Say it in public, where there are witnesses, so everyone knows you're not trying to hide anything unmanly. The best place to say it is at an already emotionally charged event, such as a wedding or a funeral. Then, as the women are weeping all around you, it's OK to momentarily loose control and choke up.

Second, keep it brief. Say, "I really love ya, guy," as you struggle to control your emotions. It's OK to punch him gently on the upper arm as you say this. And that's it. Nothing else. Then forget about it.

Because intimacy isn't a male thing.

Especially between men.

The Abolition of Toleration

Ronald Reagan strode onto the national political scene one month after I enrolled at Phoenix College. At the time, the Goldwater presidential campaign was faltering. The Draft Goldwater Movement steamrollered opposition within the Republican Party in order to gain Goldwater's nomination that summer, but even a blind man could see that Barry was headed for disaster in the November election. Nor did his cash-strapped campaign have enough money to begin countering the anticipated debacle with a series of TV ads. Reagan did what he could to change all that.

No need to go into a long bio on Ronald Reagan. We all know who he was. At the time, however, he was mostly known, if anyone knew him at all, as a fading B movie star. He'd been president of the Screen Actors Guild and still had two years on his contract as the host of a TV Western anthology show. Who knew what he'd do after that? His career was pretty much over.

So Reagan reinvented himself. He became a capitalist apologist for General Electric, a full-time PR flack to both the world at large and G.E.'s own employees. He travelled from plant to plant praising American capitalism and attacking Godless communism in what came to be known as "The Speech." Honing and polishing and delivering "The Speech" over and over, it became second nature to him. And it also became his ticket to political power.

From the beginning of his Hollywood career Reagan had been interested in politics. That's what had led him to run for president of the Guild. But his ambitions were much higher than that. Indeed, they were national in scope. Reagan had been, he liked to remind everyone, a life-long registered Democrat. No more. By 1964, he'd become a zealot for Goldwater and conservative Republicanism. He perceived in the faltering of the Goldwater campaign an opportunity to promote himself. He'd be Shane, single-handedly facing down the bad guys and saving the good guys, before donning his white hat and riding out of town alone. Out of his own pocket Reagan purchased prime time on the TV networks for a major speech on the choice facing America in the upcoming election. That choice was starkly contrasted in "The Speech," which he delivered on Tuesday, October 27, exactly one week before the 1964 election.

With Gerald at his house I watched Reagan deliver "The Speech." Like all Mormons, Gerald was politically conservative. At least I had that in common with him. Reagan stunned and impressed us. As it turned out, he stunned and impressed people all across the nation. It was a powerful performance. We were used to boring speeches by boring politicians. But Reagan was a professional actor, not yet a professional politician. So, he acted. And we were enthralled.

"The Speech" was long, but the theme was clear. The upcoming election, Reagan said, offered America a clear and simple choice. That choice was between individual freedom and "the ant heap of totalitarianism" represented by Johnson and the Democrats. Given that choice, which would *you* choose? For me, as a libertarian conservative, it was a no-brainer. Less than three months earlier, on August 8, I'd battled California Commies over essentially the same choice. I chose Reagan and individual freedom over the ant heap collectivism of Democratic totalitarianism.

Unfortunately, I was too young to vote. I was still 17 and the voting age had not yet been lowered from age 21. Nor did I have any money to contribute to Goldwater, as Reagan requested at the end of his speech. However, plenty of other conservatives did. Over a million dollars quickly poured in to the Goldwater war chest, a huge amount at the time.

As for Reagan, it was the performance of his life. Never again would he be so eloquent and charismatic, not even when he was running for president himself. The performance made him a conservative hero overnight, just as he hoped it would, and it catapulted him into the front ranks of conservative champions.

A week later Goldwater went down in flames. He would lick his wounds and, two years later, regain his seat as U.S. Senator from Arizona, but he would never again be a contender for national office. His day was done.

For Reagan, on the other hand, it was "morning in America." Two years later, in 1966, he ran for governor of California on a campaign of cleaning up the mess at Berkeley. The university and the city, he claimed, had surrendered to student radicals. He intended to set things right. That was exactly what a majority of Californians wanted to hear. He swept into office and sent the National Guard onto the Berkeley campus to restore order.

Then he used the California governor's mansion as a springboard to the White House. A decade later, in 1976, Reagan challenged sitting Republican president Gerald Ford for the party's nomination. He failed to topple Ford, but he did win the party's nomination four years after that, in 1980. Then, just 16 years after he burst upon the political scene as a champion for Goldwater, Reagan flushed Democrat Jimmy Carter out of the White House and launched a long-delayed counter-revolution against the New Deal that came to be called the "Reagan Revolution." Just a dozen-and-a-half years after Goldwater had gone down in a staggering defeat, Ronald Reagan was elected President of the United States on a platform which was basically the same as Goldwater's. In a sense, Goldwater finally won in 1980...and the conservative revolution he campaigned for was underway.

I suppose I did my part as a foot soldier in the Movement. I had no money, I had no influence beyond a small circle of acquaintances. But, as Republican Teddy Roosevelt once said, you "do what you can, with what you have, where you are." You blossom where you're planted. I did what I could to blossom by taking public speaking classes at Phoenix College.

The routine was the same as it had been when I'd studied speaking at North High; students delivered impromptu and expository speeches in class. I joined the school's debate team and was chosen to compete in inter-collegiate speech tournaments which took me out of the prison that was my life in Phoenix frequently. Selected debaters travelled to tournaments all over the Southwest, to Utah, New Mexico, Colorado, Texas. The first time I ever flew was when our debate squad boarded a small niche airline for a short hop to Colorado.

My first year debaters argued capital punishment. My teammate in these debates was Gerald. His two years as a Mormon missionary gave him good stage presence. He was calm, organized, articulate. But presentation is only part of the game. You have to have something to *present*. So Gerald and I spent endless hours in the library compiling data on capital punishment: The logic of it, the illogic of it; its effectiveness as a deterrent, its ineffectiveness as a deterrent. Each bit of information, each argument, was entered on a 3" x 5" file card, which we then placed in long metal portable file boxes. We had one box for arguments in favor of capital punishment, another box for arguments against capital punishment.

Then, after endless hours of digging up this information, we spent another eternity pawing over and over these cards, memorizing the material on them, so that, in the heat of debate, we could instantly go to the exact card holding the exact information we needed to rebut the argument just presented by the other side. It sounds like a very male activity, and most debaters *were* mostly male, but there were also female debaters who held their own. In those days, however, male teams debated male teams and female teams debated females. Collegiate debating was strictly segregated along gender lines.

Debate tournaments also featured orations on topics of the speaker's choosing. Prepared speeches depended more on delivery and persuasiveness, rather than alacrity in factual rebuttal of a rival. And I excelled in oration and won first place in oratory at the College of Eastern Utah Regional Speech Tournament in the spring of 1966.

I delivered one of two speeches I had written for these tournaments. In retrospect, the topics may seem contradictory, but I saw no incompatibility at the time. The first speech was entitled "Pax Americana." The world has always been a dark and dangerous place, I said. But, at certain times, one power has held such hegemonic sway over the world that it has been able to enforce peace and harmony, to the greater benefit of all. This was the case at the height of the Roman Empire, when Rome was able to enforce a "Pax Romana," a "Roman Peace," upon the lands surrounding the Mediterranean Sea. Protected by the umbrella of Roman might, trade flourished, people prospered, culture entered a Golden Age, and populations increased.

A lesser version of the "Pax Romana" existed during the nineteenth century, when the British navy ruled the seas and the sun never set on the British Empire. Yes, there were brushfire wars on the fringes of the Known World. But there were no major conflicts, at least in Europe, for a hundred years between the defeat of Napoleon at Waterloo in 1815 and the outbreak of World War I in 1914. This British hegemony over much of the Known World, and the peace it enforced, is sometimes termed the "Pax Britannica," the "British Peace."

In my first speech, I called for a similar harmony, only with America as the enforcer of peace. Being a patriotic American, I had no trust in the United Nations as a body capable of securing world peace. Only America, the sole superpower of the non-Communist world, had the power to enforce global peace, for the benefit and prosperity of all. Only America, I argued, had the benign desire for the betterment of all the world's peoples. America was a "city on a hill" where the good guys held sway, and, luckily, these good guys also happened to be the most powerful guys around. America could be trusted to use this power wisely and justly to do what the United Nations could not, establish world peace through a "Pax Americana," an "American Peace."

I don't remember if I even knew the concept of "imperialism" at the time, but that was what I was advocating: American imperialism. However, I was not arguing for any selfish aggrandizement of American power or wealth. I was arguing, although I didn't use his words, for the acceptance of what Rudyard Kipling, in his famous Victorian Era poem, had called "The White Man's Burden." That burden, Kipling said, was the burden of parenthood. The Western societies were the most advanced on earth. The Western societies, therefore, had an obligation to bring civilization and democracy to the other peoples of the earth. Kipling sincerely believed in the burden of Western parenthood. So did I.

In retrospect, it's clear I was still not fully aware of Lord Acton's warning: "Power tends to corrupt." And absolute power, absolutely. The belief in American exceptionalism has a long tradition and I was part of that tradition. I thought America could be trusted to use its power for the benefit of all. Most Americans still think that today.

But, it wasn't my "Pax Americana" oration which won first place in the tournaments. It was my other speech, "The Abolition of Toleration." I'd say I was a "compassionate conservative," if the phrase wasn't such a cruel joke today. In "Abolition" I decried what I saw as a rising trend of intolerance in the middle of the Sixties. True, the Civil Rights Act of 1964 and the Voting Rights Act of 1965, then wending its way through Congress toward Lyndon Johnson's pen, successfully capped the Civil Rights Movement. But they did not bring an end to strife and conflict. Instead, it seemed that hatreds lingered, that passions were becoming more inflamed every moment, that backlash against racial justice laws and movements was intensifying.

Habituated as I was to thinking in biblical terms, even as I rejected the Bible, I wrote a presentation around one of the few admirable actions of Jesus that I could find in the Gospels.

The Jesus of the various Gospels comes across as one contradictory guy. He is sometimes merciful and magnanimous. Unless you cross him, unless you doubt his teachings. Then he has it in for you. Like all prophets, Jesus is completely intolerant of anyone who doubts Him. The Mormon Prophet Joe Smith raged against any who challenged his authority, and so does Jesus. In the Gospels, Jesus condemns anyone who doubts his mission to everlasting torment in Hell.

I felt anyone who believed in Hell was ethically deficient and emotionally stunted, exhibiting a complete lack of mercy and empathy. How could anyone be truly humane who also believed in eternal punishment without the hope of redemption? Even our own flawed penal system believes in rehabilitation and redemption.

Not so Jesus, at least for doubters. He expresses only vindictive fury against any who question him. "Ye serpents, ye generation of vipers," he rages, "how can ye escape the damnation of hell?" For those who challenge his message, there will be no forgiveness: "Whosoever speaketh against the Holy Ghost," Jesus declares in Matthew 12:32, "it shall not be forgiven him neither in this world nor in the world to come."

And at the time of His Second Coming, he says, he will divide the sheep (the good) from the goats (the bad) and he will say to the goats, "Depart from me, ye cursed, into everlasting fire." To make that very, very clear, he repeats himself, "And these shall go away into everlasting fire."

Further, Jesus declares that, "If thy hand offend thee, cut it off; it is better for thee to enter into life maimed, than having two hands to go into hell, into the fire that never shall be quenched; where the worm dieth not and the fire is not quenched." There's a lot of this everlasting unquenchable hellfire, over and over, in the teachings of Jesus.

And also a lot of wailing and gnashing of teeth. "The Son of Man shall send forth His angels," Jesus says in Matthew 13:41-42, "and they shall gather out of His kingdom all things that offend, and them which do iniquity, and shall cast them into a furnace of fire; there shall be wailing and gnashing of teeth." Jesus seems to get a lot of pleasure out of imagining this wailing and gnashing of teeth that all those who doubt him are going to be doing. The wicked shall be cast into "a furnace of fire," he says again in Matthew 13:50, where "there shall be wailing and gnashing of teeth." He really gets worked up over this. This hardly seemed to me the attitude of a loving and caring father, the image of Jesus so often presented to us.

This doctrine of cruelty seemed to me a manifestation of insecurity on Jesus' part or on the part of the writers of the Gospels. If Jesus really was "God," then he knew everything and therefore knew that he was absolutely right in his teachings. He should have had supreme self-confidence in himself and his teachings. And if you are absolutely secure in your knowledge, it seems to me you accept doubt and dissent with calmness and equanimity. They can't possibly shake your certainty.

Compare Jesus' reactions, when faced with doubters, to those Socrates displayed when faced with those who questioned his teachings. Socrates accepted dissent and doubt with the benign calmness one expects in one sure of himself. But Jesus raged with unceasing fury against any who questioned his words. Raging fury against doubters seems indicative of one who isn't certain of his beliefs and his authority, rather than of one who is completely convinced of his teachings and authority. Basic psychology, then, when applied to Jesus, seems to encourage the very doubt Jesus fulminates against.

But, if you don't challenge his authority, Jesus can be quite tolerant. And those are the passages I chose to focus on, the teachings I tried to emphasize. It was the best I could do to use Christianity against Christian intolerance. Specifically, since capital punishment was the debate topic for that year, in my oration I chose the only passage in the Bible in which Jesus expresses an opinion on capital punishment. It is the story of the woman taken in adultery in John 8:1-11:

"Jesus went unto the Mount of Olives. And early in the morning He came again into the temple, and all the people came unto Him...And the scribes and Pharisees brought unto Him a woman taken in adultery; and when they had set her in the midst, they say unto Him, 'Master, this woman was taken in adultery, in the very act. Now Moses in the law commanded us, that such should be stoned: but what sayest thou?'

"So when they continued asking Him, He lifted up Himself and said unto them, 'He that is without sin among you, let him first cast a stone at her.'

"And they which heard it, being convicted by their own conscience, went out one by one...even unto the last: and Jesus was left alone, and the woman standing in the midst.

"When Jesus had lifted up himself, and saw none but the woman, He said unto her, 'Woman, where are those thine accusers? Hath no man condemned thee?"

"She said, 'No man, Lord.'

"And Jesus said unto her, 'Neither do I condemn thee: go, and sin no more.'"

This is the most humane passage in the entire blood-soaked Bible. It is the most "Christian" passage in the entire "unchristian" New Testament. And it is this compassionate passage around which I wrote my second oration, "The Abolition of Toleration," which won me first place at oratory tournament after oratory tournament.

Do what you can. With what you have. Where you are.

Apostasy

The Hill

There is a dark and lonely hill.
And we live in sorrow
    Beneath that dark
        And lonely hill.
            Because we live in time.
And where there is time,
    There is loss.
And where there is loss,
    There is sorrow.
And so we live in sorrow,
    Beneath that dark
        And lonely hill.
And, in time,
    All must climb
        That dark
            And lonely hill.
Rich man, poor man,
    Beggar man, thief.
The Prince and the Pauper,
    The Commander-in-Chief.
The tramp and the lady,
    Madonna and Child.
The good, the bad,
    The meek and the mild,
In time,
    All must climb
        That dark
            And lonely hill.

****

In the spring of 1965, near the end of my first year at Phoenix College, I was walking from one class to another across campus. A Mormon acquaintance from the Institute of Religion whom I only knew by sight approached me. "Hi, Jack," he said as he passed.

I turned toward him. "Excuse me?" He stopped and turned back to me. "My name isn't Jack, it's Eric."

"I know."

"OK, well, see you then." I turned to go.

"Yeah, see ya, Jack," he said, and continued on his way.

And then I got it. A "Jack Mormon" is what Mormons call an apostate, someone who has defected, someone who has renounced and abandoned his faith altogether. "Jack," for short. From now on, as far as the Mormons were concerned, my name was "Jack."

I knew it would come to this eventually. I couldn't continue living as a *converso*, a pretend Mormon, pretending to have a faith I could never embrace. The only reason it hadn't come sooner was because of my friendship with Gerald. What brought it to a head was "the talk," the long-dreaded talk about when I would go on my mission. I'd been 18 for a few months and I was finishing a full academic year at Phoenix College. As far as the church was concerned, it was time to take an academic sabbatical and go preach the faith.

I'd mentioned the imminent mission obligation to Dan. "Just tell 'em to fuck themselves in the ass," he said. "Tell 'em you don't believe in their bullshit Christ and you don't believe in their fake bullshit prophet, Joe Smith."

"Aw, Dan, it isn't as easy as that. My mother is Mormon, my brothers are Mormon, and I still have to live with them no matter what. I dance with Mormon girls. I have a Mormon social circle on campus at the Institute of Religion. And the only other real friend I have besides you is a returned Mormon missionary. I'd be isolating myself from all of them."

"You're already isolated from them because you don't believe in anything *they* believe in. You're only *pretending* to be one of them. You're living a lie and it'll just get harder to leave the longer you live it. Stop lying, you fucking hypocritical asshole."

His words stung. Because it was the truth. I was living a lie and I was a hypocrite. I had to break with the church.

But I procrastinated. I agonized over how to make the break. I wondered if I could still be friends with Gerald if I told him I was only a pretend Mormon. I decided I probably could not. He was too devout. It'd be the end of our friendship. And so I agonized some more. What was the right thing to do? It wasn't clear to me. Doing the right thing seldom is.

True Believers object that, without the Bible or the Church or God's will, all we have is "relativistic morality," that anything goes. That's a load of crap. You don't have to believe in God to know that robbing a bank is wrong and, atheist or True Believer, you'll go to jail if you do it. That's because we have laws, passed by legislatures and enforced by the police and the courts. And we've had laws ever since the Babylonian king Hammurabi handed down his famous Code, the first written laws, almost four thousand years ago. But Hammurabi never heard of Jesus or Jehovah. He just knew he wanted an orderly society over which to rule. And don't tell me no one knew it was wrong to kill before Moses came down from the mountain top with his Ten Commandments telling us "Thou Shalt Not Kill."

Regardless of the existence of human-made laws, True Believers can't escape from the reality that ethical decisions, finally, still come down to individual choice. Just because Abraham set out to obey God's order to murder Isaac, his son, did not absolve Abraham from the responsibility of making a moral choice. If a mother murders her children today because, she says, "God told me to do it," her lawyers will claim insanity -- the judge and jury will probably agree. How did Abraham decide he wasn't going insane?

Abraham also had to decide whether the voice ordering him to kill his son was actually the voice of God -- or was the voice commanding him to perform such a demonic deed actually that of Satan? Joan of Arc followed her voices into battle in the belief that she was following God's commands. But, at her trial, her inquisitors asked her how she *knew* her voices came from God, and not from Satan. She'd never considered that possibility previously and, for a while, she wavered before deciding they were indeed from God. She had to consider the possibility that they were satanic and, in the dark night of her soul, she made a decision.

But there is no record of Abraham undergoing a dark night of *his* soul as he considered the possibility that the voice which commanded him to murder his son came from Satan. How did he decide he was listening to God, and not Satan? How did he make that moral choice?

The moral choices for a devout believer like Abraham don't end there. If he decided that he wasn't going insane, that he was really listening to the voice of God, he had to decide whether God was serious or whether, as in the Woody Allen story, God was just joking.

If he finally concluded that he wasn't insane, that the resonant, well-modulated voice was actually God's, and that God was serious, Abraham then had to choose whether or not to obey that resonant, well-modulated voice. Isaac was completely innocent of all wrong-doing, as innocent as a new-born lamb, which is why God said he had to be murdered as a sacrifice. Abraham had to decide if murdering his innocent son was right or wrong. To say you are obeying God's will does not absolve you from the moral responsibility of choice.

If you are convinced that God has ordered you to slowly, slowly, lower a person you know to be completely innocent of all wrong-doing -- say, a new-born infant -- into a vat of sulfuric acid which burns away the body of that infant inch by inch until the infant dies a horrible, screaming, flailing death -- would it be OK, simply because God ordered you to do so? Would you believe that you were absolved of the responsibility for torturing and murdering that infant, just because you were following orders? Would you believe you had no moral decision to make at all concerning the infant's horrible death? That you were obviously doing the right thing because you were killing on God's orders?

Just deciding to "follow the will of God" doesn't relieve you from the responsibility to decide whether your actions are right or wrong. The 9-11 suicide hijackers were True Believers who flew their commandeered planes into the World Trade Center and the Pentagon chanting the name of God, absolutely convinced that they were following God's orders. Millions of their co-religionists believed they were right. We, and millions like us, believe they were wrong. Which of these many millions were actually right?

So, it doesn't matter whether you are a True Believer or not, things are not handed to you on a silver platter. You are not absolved from moral responsibility. It's still up to you, finally, to decide what is right and what is wrong. If the right decision was obvious, then we'd never be in doubt or disagreement. If it was easy, then ethical philosophers from Aristotle to Kant to the Utilitarians wouldn't have continued thinking and writing about the basis of morality for thousands of years. Someone would have hit on the obviously "right" formula millennia ago.

So, whether you are a True Believer or not, it still comes down to individual choice. You have to choose, even if your choice is to just follow the orders of God.

So, how do you choose? Because it is an individual decision, we all have to climb that dark and lonely hill by ourselves. No one else can climb it for us.

This is how I came to climb it:

Empathy, I decided, is the beginning of all morality. There must be a concern for the welfare of others. Self-interest cannot be completely sovereign, because "doing the right thing" always entails the possibility of acting against one's own self-interest. We recognize that those who are completely indifferent to the welfare of others are mentally ill psychopaths. But, we all exist somewhere along that emotional and psychological continuum, from the complete altruism of St. Francis of Assisi to the complete psychopathology of Adolf Hitler. And the ideal is to push as much toward the altruistic end of that spectrum as we possibly can.

There is nothing particularly earth-shattering about this insight. It is what some, beginning with the Chinese philosopher Confucius thousands of years ago, have called "The Golden Rule." "Do not do to others what you would not want done to yourself." You realize that some things are good or bad for us. Empathy, a feeling for the welfare of others, makes us realize that these same things must also be good or bad for others. So, we don't do those bad things. Instead, we do the good things. All human cultures have a version of this Golden Rule, and studies have even discovered a version of such empathetic feelings among chimpanzees and other lower primates, suggesting it may even have a genetic basis. Perhaps, in order to live and prosper in social groups, we must have some such rule encoded in our DNA. There is no place for a rogue elephant in a social group.

A rule like this is what Immanuel Kant termed a "categorical imperative." An imperative is any kind of command or principle. A categorical imperative is a principle of universal applicability, not specific to any one person or situation, interest or desire. It applies to everyone and everything. So, we strive to be consistent in our application of this universal imperative, regardless of the circumstances. In other words, we try not to be hypocrites, who say one thing, but do another. And so being a hypocrite seemed to me, as it does to many others, to be categorically wrong.

But, as usual, such things are easier said than done. If it was easy to live by the Golden Rule, there would be no such thing as hypocrites. If it was easy to know how best to insure the welfare of others, as well as ourselves, there would be no moral quandaries. If it was easy, we would all agree on what needs to be done -- and we would do it.

But, it is in the nature of things that it is never easy to do the right thing, at any level.

For example, one wants to know the truth. Since it is good for ourselves to know the truth, it follows that it is also good for others to know the truth. Telling the truth, then, is a categorical imperative and the Golden Rule requires us to tell others the truth.

But it's never as simple as that. What if the truth harms us? Do we tell it anyway? What if the truth harms the person we tell it to? Empathy mandates that we should be concerned about the welfare of others. Do we tell the whole truth, and nothing but the truth, and harm that person, just because it *is* a categorical imperative? Or do we decide to protect someone from a truth which, we believe, would harm them? In this case, our empathetic concern for the welfare of others is in conflict with the imperative to tell the truth. Which is more ethical? Or, do we tell a partial truth? If so, how do we parse the truth, how do we decide how much to tell?

These are hard choices. The solution is seldom obvious and seldom easy.

Which is why I delayed in telling Gerald the truth about my religious beliefs. I was sure the truth would destroy our friendship. Which was more important in this situation, the truth or our friendship? I didn't know.

When the church asked Gerald to talk with me about my upcoming mission, I could delay action no longer. Gerald was a member of my local congregation, a returned missionary, "an elder" who knew the ropes, a close friend, so the congregation thought they were doing me a favor by asking Gerald to talk with me about my mission. Instead, they just made it that much harder for me.

Gerald asked me to meet with him about my mission after Sunday service. During the service I was oblivious to anything anyone said, thinking about the upcoming meeting with Gerald. I wanted to avoid the entire matter.

Gerald greeted me with a huge smile when I opened the door to the meeting room. "Hello there, elder," he said, shaking my hand firmly like a good missionary. "I've been making plans for you." Gerald was being a bit premature in calling me "elder." Female Mormon missionaries are called "sisters," but male Mormon missionaries are not called "brothers." Even if they're the same age or younger than their "sisters," they are called "elders." The missionary who had converted Mom and the rest of us to Mormonism was "Elder Schroeder," an 18-year-old kid. I was not yet a Mormon elder. Nor would I ever be.

I sat down across from Gerald. He had a lot of handwritten notes in front of him, evidently of things he wanted to say to me about his own experiences as a missionary. He was beaming at the prospect of prepping his best friend for the mission field. His smiling face was slightly irregular. He had a left cheek bone, but no right cheek bone. His acne scarred right cheek was flat. It wasn't particularly noticeable. Any stranger who met him might miss it altogether. But Gerald was highly conscious of it. He hadn't said anything to me about it, but he was always examining himself in the mirror, comparing the two sides of his face.

And I was highly aware of it, because I was responsible for it. I was the one who drove us both off the highway in his VW Beetle. Every time I looked at him I felt guilty as hell about the accident. I felt I owed him something. Perhaps I owed him a mission.

"Have you thought of where you might like to go?" Gerald asked.

There was no way to avoid it. I decided to just blurt it out. Those who bite the bullet need not eat the gun. "Gerald, I'm not going."

Gerald stopped shuffling his notes and looked at me. "Is it finances?" Every missionary is expected to pay his or her own expenses for the two year mission.

"No, it's not finances. I'm not going because I don't believe in the mission."

"I don't understand."

"What I mean is, I don't believe in the church."

There was shock and confusion on Gerald's irregular face. I felt like I was confessing a mortal sin to my best friend, but I had to push on.

"Gerald, I've always had my doubts. I just don't believe. And it would be hypocritical of me to go on a mission and preach something I don't believe in. I just can't do it."

"Have you given this a lot of thought?"

"More than you can imagine."

"What can I say to change your mind?"

"Nothing. I know I'm disappointing you, but I've made up my mind. I'm not going."

"Why don't we pray about it together? Ask the Lord for guidance?"

"Prayer won't help, and neither will the Lord. I don't need any guidance, because I've already made my decision. I can't go on pretending to believe when I really don't. I'm leaving the church. This is the last time I'll step inside this building."

Gerald sat in silence. I could see that he was searching for something to say.

I broke the silence. "Gerald, please believe me that it really hurts me to say what I've just said. I didn't want to say it, but I had to. I just can't go on living a lie."

"Then you're doing the right thing."

"I know."

But the "right thing" felt like I was betraying my brother.

Part Four
The Doors of Perception

Light My Fire

In March, 1965, during my second semester at Phoenix College, President Lyndon Johnson began sending U.S. ground troops to Vietnam. He felt the Gulf of Tonkin Resolution gave him the authority to do so.

The Constitution gives Congress the sole power to take America into a war. The Founders felt that war was such serious business that, since this is a democracy, only the body which most closely represents the people should make such a serious decision.

But the last time Congress declared war on anyone was following the Japanese attack on Pearl Harbor. The next day, December 8, 1941, Congress decided that America was at war with the Empire of Japan.

The Korean War wasn't officially a war. It was a "police action," so President Harry Truman felt he didn't need a Congressional war declaration.

The Vietnam War was...what? The longest war America has ever fought. The fourth most costly war in terms of American casualties, after the Civil War and the two World Wars. And the only war that, so far, America has lost. At least Korea was a stalemate.

Despite the fact that the war escalated steadily in the mid-1960s so that, by 1968, Johnson had well over half-a-million -- 543,000 -- troops fighting in that tiny far away country -- Vietnam, like Korea, was never officially a war. Constitutionally, America has not fought a war since World War II. Korea, Vietnam, Grenada, the Persian Gulf, Afghanistan, Iraq -- despite what they may have been in reality, as far as the Constitution is concerned, they were never wars.

Instead of declaring war, Congress has simply handed the imperial president a blank check to do whatever he sees fit. That's what the Gulf of Tonkin Resolution of August, 1964 had been. "Do whatever you think needs doing, Lyndon," Congress said.

What Lyndon thought needed doing was the biggest war since World War II. October-November, 1965, the fall semester of my second year at Phoenix College, brought the first major battle of this "American" phase of a long colonial war which had been going on in Vietnam since the end of World War II. From October 19 to November 26 the U.S. First Cavalry Division fought Communist guerrillas in the Ia Drang Valley. At the height of the fighting, in mid-November, more than 240 American soldiers were killed, and only American air power saved the First Cavalry Division from complete annihilation.

In response, General William Westmoreland, the top American commander in Vietnam, complained to Washington that the 185,000 soldiers he had on hand weren't enough to win the war. He needed more. So on November 30, Defense Secretary Robert McNamara recommended that Johnson send more, lots more -- 400,000 soldiers more -- by the end of the coming year, 1966. He felt that would be enough to win the war. Johnson agreed to send those troops. However, this meant that draft quotas had to also be stepped up, big time.

Johnson also agreed to step up the war in other ways. On December 20th, 1965, he gave field commanders permission to pursue guerrillas into neighboring Cambodia and to order air strikes and artillery barrages into Cambodia. American forces had already been strafing and bombing the Ho Chi Minh Trail in Laos since May. By Christmas of '65, America was flying 1,500 bombing sorties a week over North and South Vietnam. Eventually, America would drop more bombs on Vietnam and fire more artillery shells on Vietnam than it dropped and fired on all fronts during all of World War II. In this sense, Vietnam was bigger than World War II.

The bombing and shelling never had much effect. On Christmas Eve of '65, the Defense Intelligence Agency reported that the 1,500 sorties per week had been unsuccessful in crippling the North Vietnamese economy or stopping North Vietnam from moving supplies south on foot. For the entire duration of his presidency, Johnson's response to these failures was to ratchet the war up yet another notch. Someone, I don't know who, once defined insanity as, "doing the same thing, over and over, hoping for a different result." If so, then Johnson and the American military command were insane throughout the Sixties. It's what Graham Nash, of Crosby, Stills, and Nash, would come to call "military madness."

As Johnson steadily escalated the war, opposition to it at home, including scattered incidents of draft card burning, also escalated from 1965-67. Since Democratic and Republican representatives in Congress were both gung-ho for the war, Congress decided to put a stop to draft card burning. On August 31, 1965, just as I returned from a summer job in the Arizona canteloupe fields for my second year at Phoenix College, Congress made it a crime to burn draft cards. In October, David J. Miller, age 22, became the first person arrested and convicted under the new law. He was sentenced to three years in prison, followed by two years of probation.

Like most Americans in late 1965, I really didn't know what the war in Vietnam was all about. The widespread college campus teach-ins to educate students about the origins and nature of the war were yet to come. So I continued to see it in simple black-and-white terms. We were fighting for freedom against world Communism. I was a conservative American patriot, so I, of course, supported the war.

But, being a working class kid, even though I wasn't consciously aware of being "working class," there was a part of me which felt that a real man doesn't take shit from *anyone.* Not even from the United States government. And, if you refuse to take shit from the United States government, that means you're an anarchist. Perhaps I was a conservative anarchist. Another word for conservative anarchism is "libertarian." Working class conservative libertarian may more precisely describe my outlook. I didn't know these words, "anarchist" and "libertarian," at the time.

But, I *did* know the words of the Founders, men like Thomas Paine and Benjamin Franklin. It was Franklin who said, "Those who desire to give up freedom in order to gain security will not have, nor do they deserve, either." And it seemed to me that laws being passed by Congress -- such as the one making it a crime to burn draft cards, making it a crime not to have your card on your body at all times -- were curtailing American freedom. And any American patriot would fight for American freedom against whoever threatened it. Which meant that I was more angered by the new draft card law than I was by what was going on in Vietnam, of which, in any case, I was mostly ignorant.

I was 18 that fall. As soon as I'd turned 18 I'd registered for the draft. At that time, anyone enrolled in a college program leading to a degree -- including a community college student -- was automatically given a student draft deferment. It didn't matter if you were on the verge of flunking out, you got the deferment. It would not be until March of the next year, 1966, that scholastic performance became a basis for awarding a student deferment. So, I was automatically given the student deferment when I registered.

I was lucky to have been a Mormon. If Bishop Lee's son hadn't dragged me out of bed on September 20th of 1964, I wouldn't have gone to college. Then, when I registered for the draft, I'd have been classified I-A, prime beef, the first to be drafted, like so many other working class kids like me who weren't in college. Because I was unemployed and aimlessly drifting after high school, I'd probably have gone when called up after Westmoreland asked for 400,000 troops by the end of 1966.

But now I had a student deferment, and I knew that the only thing that kept me from being Grade A prime beef for the war machine was the fact that I was paying $27 per semester to go to Phoenix College. So, just as Phoenix College had kept me from going off at age 18 to be a Mormon missionary -- for which I'd have obtained a two-year ministerial deferment from the draft, to be followed, no doubt, by a student deferment -- so Phoenix College was also keeping me from going off to Vietnam. It was worth the $27.

I experienced some "cognitive dissonance" nevertheless -- two more words I didn't know at the time -- in my situation as a working class college student. Having always read, I was feeling more at home at Phoenix College than I had in the anti-intellectual atmosphere of North High. But, being working class, there was always a part of me that felt I didn't belong at Phoenix College, or any other college. That I *really* belonged out there in the working class, doing some kind of "real" work that Elmer, my carpenter-construction worker step-father, would respect. Had Terry Lee not pulled me out of bed and driven me down to Phoenix College the previous year, I'd have tried to become an operator of heavy construction equipment. Before I was drafted. And then, maybe, I might have operated that kind of equipment in the Army.

But, now there I was, at Phoenix College, protected from the draft by my student status.

Even so, none of these circumstances made me like the new draft card law any better. Nothing could have quelled my resentment at the new curtailment of individual liberty aimed specifically at young men my age.

In the fall I returned to the college debate squad and, once more, travelled to other schools in other states for debates and speeches. We spent as much time on the road as any of the school athletes. A big difference, however, is that we were co-ed. True, we had gender-segregated debate teams, tournament matches, and motel rooms. Nevertheless, the camaraderie of the road gave us a chance to know members of the opposite sex a bit more intimately than what would otherwise have been the case.

There was a cute girl debater I liked named Josephine. Everyone called her "Josie." Her family consisted of her and her mother. If I ever knew what happened to her father, I've forgotten. In many ways she was entirely conventional: Typical early Sixties over-done make-up, with too much face powder; the hard hair of a beehive hair-do which felt to me like barbed wire from all the spray needed to keep it piled up on top of her head. She looked like a member of the Shirelles. I didn't like that.

But she was sweet and she was intelligent, else she would not have been on the debate squad. That, I did like. So I devoted a fair amount of time, both on trips and on campus, to bedding her. I eventually succeeded, and she turned out to be not as conventional as I'd first thought. For instance, despite her long resistance, she wasn't a virgin.

And, once in bed, she was fun and relaxed and eager. We made love in her bedroom on hot Arizona afternoons while her mother was at work. I pushed the envelope, always trying new things, and Josie always welcomed them with enthusiasm. Afterward, we'd lay panting in each other's arms, listening to the world go on about its business outside her window. "If your mother comes home early," I said after one afternoon delight, "I'm fucked."

"No, *I'm* fucked," she giggled, "and *you're* the fucker!"

I began tickling her, and then things got out of hand....

But, while I liked her and enjoyed being with her and I was avid to make love to her in her bedroom as those fall days declined toward winter, I wasn't in love with Josie. I sometimes felt guilty about that. She was my first college girlfriend, my first extended sexual relationship, and, because of that, I felt I *should* have been in love with her. But you can't force yourself to love. The feeling either comes on its own, or it doesn't. In the meantime, we enjoyed each other's company, both in and out of bed.

One evening on the road our debate squad stopped at a diner for supper. We were either on our way to or coming home from a tournament. It was late, winter was coming on, and we were all tired from the incessant hum of the road. Besides our debate squad, sprinkled over a couple of booths, there were only a couple of other customers in the diner. It was a bleak scene, like a painting by Edward Hopper. There were six of us, male and female, crammed into one booth, talking over the remains of our meal. Josie was sitting next to me, pressing her thigh into mine. I was pressing back.

You get debaters together, you're going to get debates, and the escalating war was often a topic of conversation. So was the draft. This time it was the new law, criminalizing draft card burning and requiring young men to carry their cards on their person at all times.

"It just another encroachment on our Constitutional freedoms," I said.

"And exactly *which* freedoms would these be?" asked Paul. He was a bit older, so our debate coach put Paul in charge of driving the rented station wagon we six had been riding in. Paul smoked like a chimney, had crewcut hair, and was even more conservative than me. If there'd been ROTC at Phoenix College, Paul would've been an officer in it.

"The First Amendment guarantee of freedom of speech," I replied.

Paul tapped the ash off his cigarette into the ashtray in the middle of the table, then took another heavy drag on it. "And what does draft card burning have to do with freedom of speech?"

"It's symbolic speech. Protestors burn their draft cards to make a rhetorical point."

"Yeah, well, we have to have some way of regulating the manpower pool."

"Outlawing the burning of draft cards and requiring them to be kept on your person at all times is not needed for the proper functioning of the draft. They have their records. They know who everyone is, what our classifications are. They don't need people carrying around cards all the time, or even *having* one, for the Selective Service System to work. Congress did not outlaw draft card burning for administrative reasons. Burning cards does not hamper the proper functioning of the System. Congress outlawed draft card burning for purely political reasons. It didn't like the symbolic use to which the cards are being put by anti-war protesters."

Paul looked at me sideways through slitted eyes as he feathered smoke out of his nostrils. "You sound like you're opposed to the draft."

Josie pressed her thigh into mine more insistently. I knew she wanted me to stop right there. Instead, I plunged ahead.

"I *am* opposed to the draft. It's another violation of our Constitutional liberties."

"How do you get *that?*"

"Paul, read the Constitution sometime. The 13th Amendment to the Constitution forbids involuntary servitude, and that exactly describes the draft. Military service ought to be voluntary."

Paul took another heavy drag. "Damn, you sound just like a Commie."

"I'm no Commie and I don't sound like one. What I sound like is a patriotic American who cherishes the Constitution. A Commie would be *in favor* of involuntary servitude."

"Well, I never heard of anyone calling the draft involuntary servitude."

"You have now."

"Listen, it's just like requiring people to have a driver's license and to carry it."

"There's no law which says you have to carry a driver's license on your person at all times. Only when you're actually driving a vehicle. Requiring an identification card, like a driver's license or a draft card, to be on your person at all times is tantamount to a Big Brother dictatorship. Paul, any patriotic American who cherishes American freedom should be opposed to such a law."

This time Paul exhaled his smoke in my direction. "Well, if you're so opposed to the new law, why do you obey it?"

"For the same reason I carry my driver's license when I drive. For the same reason Socrates drank his hemlock. It's the law, and you should obey the law until it's changed."

Paul smirked at me. "But, isn't that hypocritical of you? You're obeying a law you think is unjust, is un-American. Would a so-called 'patriotic American' obey an unjust law?"

Paul was baiting me. And I took the bait. "You're right. If I think the law is a violation of our Constitutional liberties, I shouldn't obey it. So I won't."

I leaned over so I could reach into my back pocket. I pulled out my wallet.

"What are you doing?" Josie asked. "Don't do anything foolish."

"It's OK," I said. I searched through my wallet until I found my draft card. I showed it to Paul, Josie, and the others around the table. "Here it is, in my possession as mandated by Congress. But I don't agree with that law. And I don't agree with the law banning the burning of this piece of paper, because I think that's in infringement on freedom of speech. And so, to demonstrate my opposition to both laws, as a patriotic American I will now burn my draft card."

Josie placed her hand on my wrist to stop me. "Eric, no, don't do it." Concern covered her face like a veil.

I removed her hand from my wrist. "If I didn't, I'd be a hypocrite, just like Paul said. Paul, give me your match book."

Paul handed it over. I tore out a match and scraped it lit. I touched the flame to a corner of the draft card. It quickly caught fire and flared up. Everyone watched it burn. No one said a word. I dropped the curled piece of ash which had been my draft card into the ashtray in the center of the table. "Well, there it is. I just committed a crime under the new law. I did so as an American patriot in the name of American freedom. You all witnessed it."

Then I looked straight at Paul. "And, as Patrick Henry said, 'If this be treason, make the most of it.'"

But no one did. Not even Paul.

One Fine Day

Sometimes you know when it happens and you know there's no going back. So it was at the beginning of January, 1966.

I went looking for an interesting teacher.

I found Annie instead.

The spring semester was about to begin at Phoenix College. I'd asked around and heard about Vern. He taught philosophy and a history of religion course. Students said he was provocative, different, unusual. And he was Harvard-educated. Phoenix College didn't have too many teachers from Harvard. And I wanted to learn more about the history of religion, not just Judeo-Christianity, but *all* religions. I especially wanted to learn about the non-Western religions: Islam, Buddhism, Hinduism, Shintoism, Zoroastrianism, animism, what have you. Vern sounded like the teacher I wanted. But, before I registered for his course, I wanted to meet him.

So Josie and I went to the second floor Philosophy Department office. Phoenix College was so low-budget that teachers didn't have individual offices. When I visited Dr. Mary Maher in the English Department, I found her at her desk in a big common room she shared with the rest of the English faculty. That room was, in turn, in a temporary wooden building constructed as an after thought between two long, two-story, more permanent rows of cinderblock classrooms. Those cinderblock classrooms were, in turn, supplementary to the ones built by the WPA in 1939. At least the Philosophy Department was in one of these original WPA buildings.

But it was just as communal. As we stepped into the office, noise swirled around us like cloudy water. Sitting at a battered metal desk by the door was a young beauty with the body of Kate Winslet lounging nude in the hold of the Titanic, waiting for Leonardo to come for her. Unfortunately, she wasn't nude. Her Titian hair cascaded in a bohemian stream over her shoulders and down to her breasts. It was so unlike the bouffant beehives sported by virtually every other girl on campus, including Josie. She looked up from her desk with vivid green eyes. I asked if Vern was somewhere around the crowded office.

"Not right now, but when the student is ready, the master will appear. In the meantime, perhaps I can help you?"

"I doubt it. I'd like to talk to him about his history of religion course."

"Ah, you are seeking. You are on a quest."

"Perhaps. Are you?"

"Aren't we all?"

"What kind of quest are you on?"

"The seeker is himself that which is sought. But, sit and we will speak of such things."

Josie and I sat on hard wooden chairs near the desk. The Titian-haired beauty spoke. I listened. I asked questions. I objected. Never in my life had I heard *anyone,* much less a woman, talk about the things she talked about.

"If the doors of perception were cleansed, everything would appear as it is, infinite."

"Yes," I replied, "William Blake, the mystic poet, who saw infinity in a grain of sand."

"Because the doors of perception had been opened for him, as they may be for you."

And so it went. It seemed the doors of perception had also been opened for her, but I had no idea what she was talking about. Her language was vague, obscure, florid. She seemed to see infinity in grains of sand, eternity in tear drops. And yet, although it sounded profoundly important, I couldn't grasp anything specific in what she said.

"Could you repeat that?"

And she said: Cosmic consciousness when the Moon is in the seventh house and Jupiter and Mars align, the sound of one hand clapping, the universal Oversoul, the collective unconscious, a tree falling alone in the forest, no matter where you go: there you are, the Kingdom of God is within, be the change you seek, Mana: the immanent power, the Great Mandala, the Great Chain of Being, the eternal return, the Hero with a Thousand Faces, when the archer shoots for nothing he has all his skills, the realm of the senses and the kingdom of desires, those who seek will not find, those who find did not seek, if you strive to save your life you will lose it, those who abandon their lives will save them, desiderata, karma, satori, dharma, nirvana, consider the lilies of the field, wholeness, mindfulness, soulfulness, do not ask for whom the bell tolls, to every thing there is a season and a time to every purpose under heaven, return home and know it for the first time, and know that today is the first day of the rest of your life.

As I sat there in the philosophy office, listening to her, with Josie next to me, I heard the song the sirens sang, and I heard it before I was able to lash myself to a mast. It seemed we'd been speaking for only a few minutes. Josie had said nothing the entire time. Now she pointed to the wall clock. It'd been an hour. We had to catch our next classes. We stood up.

"What's your name?" I asked the siren.

"Annie."

"I'll see you around, Annie."

Josie and I walked out of the office and down the stairs. But, while my body was descending the stairs with Josie, my thoughts were back in the philosophy office with Annie. All I knew of her was her name. That was all I needed to know. I didn't need or want to know anything about her background or parentage or birthplace or age or closest friends or astrological sign. None of that mattered. I just knew that she was the most fascinating woman I'd ever met and I'd move heaven and earth to see her again.

Outside, Josie and I walked across campus to her class hand-in-hand, but already I'd slipped away from her grasp.

Strangers in the Night

I next saw Annie a few days later. I walked into Vern's class and sat at a desk in about the middle of the room, not in the front row, not in the back. I glanced around and there, in the very last row, back against the wall, was Annie. I smiled, patted the seat of the empty desk next to me, and motioned for her to join me. I was pleased when she did. I learned later that she was flattered that I'd remembered her and wanted her to sit next to me.

Then Vern entered. He wore a sport coat and a tie. He stood in front of the class until we grew quiet. He did not hand out a syllabus, he did not give reading assignments. In fact, we never opened the "required" textbooks for the course that whole semester. We didn't know what would happen that day, nor did we ever for any day thereafter. Nor did we ever learn anything about the history of religion or anything specific about Islam, Buddhism, Hinduism, Shintoism, Zoroastrianism, animism, or what have you. Every class was a new encounter with the enigma of Vernism, of which Vern was the sole High Priest and we his unwitting acolytes.

Vern began speaking slowly, deliberately. And, as Yogi Berra would say, it was deja vu all over again. As when I listened to Annie a few days before, Vern seemed to make no sense at all -- and yet one had the impression one was listening to ancient wisdom, that Vern held in his possession the Philosopher's Stone and the secrets of the universe would be revealed if only one could interpret the Delphic declamations of the Oracle who stood before us.

All of us have experienced that Aha! moment when we've had a flash of insight and suddenly *understood* something, perhaps a complicated problem over which we'd struggled. But listening to Vern was the exact opposite. Instead of experiencing Aha!, and understanding, I actually experienced *presque vu,* "almost seen," the mistaken impression one sometimes reached in a drug high or a deep dream of total understanding of everything -- but I actually understood nothing.

Vern spoke in vague, obscure, portentous sentences full of deep thoughts and heavy meanings and I felt I was having flashes of insight after insight in which everything suddenly made sense -- but I later realized that I had actually comprehended *nothing*, and ultimately, *nothing* made sense. From his Delphic words and demeanor, I knew he must be very wise. Therefore, he *must* be making great sense, I told myself, and I felt I *did* understand what he was saying, I *did* understand the Oracle, I *did,* finally!, understand the universe.

And then my insights dissolved as fast as they came and I was left grabbing smoke. Of course, I blamed my own denseness for not fully grasping exactly what the Wise One was saying.

So I vowed to pay closer attention to the Avatar next time.

Impressed and mystified by Vern's High Priest performance as I was, I was even more impressed and mystified by the girl sitting next to me. As class ended, the other students quickly got up and shuffled out of class. Vern glanced at us as he, too, left. I turned to the girl and I smiled at her. "So, Annie, let me buy you a Coke in the student union."

"You remembered my name."

"Of course I remembered your name. Did you remember mine?"

"No, I'm sorry I didn't."

"It's Eric. But, even though you didn't remember my name, I'd still like to buy you that Coke. How 'bout it?"

Annie glanced at the door which Vern had just closed behind him. "Yes, that'd be nice."

As we walked to the cafeteria in the student union, I asked Annie's last name.

"I don't know my last name."

"How can that be?"

"I have no memory of the past. I don't know where or when I was born, I don't know who my parents were, I know nothing about my background."

It seemed my disdain for knowing such mundane things about Annie was being mocked by the gods. "Were you in an accident?"

"I don't know."

"So, what's your relationship with Vern?"

"He found me and took me in. He gave me shelter from the storm."

"That's very generous of him."

"He's a very generous man."

I didn't believe any of this. But I wasn't going to push Annie on it. She obviously had her own reasons for being so mysterious. Besides, it didn't matter to me who she was or where she came from. I just wanted to spend time with her.

I bought her a cherry Coke in the student union and we talked about life, the universe, time and space and the nature of things. And if the conversation edged too closely to personal information, Annie's mantra was always, "I don't know, I have no memory." At least her response served to maintain the aura of mystery about her.

We talked that way all afternoon. Finally Annie said, "I have to go now. Vern is giving me a ride home."

"I'll walk with you to meet him."

We walked to a nearby parking lot where Vern was standing beside a red Italian Vespa motorscooter nestled in amongst all the larger Hondas, Kawasakis, and Suzukis. Vern smiled cryptically at us as we approached. I touched Annie lightly on her upper arm and said, "I'll see you in class."

"See you in class," she said.

Then Vern kicked the Vespa to life and Annie climbed on it behind him. I watched them as Vern scooted out of the parking lot and off toward Thomas Road. It was intriguing that he drove a motorscooter. Every other teacher at Phoenix College drove a car.

But I'd noticed something as Annie stood next to Vern, just before climbing onto the back of the Vespa. Her nose had the same curve to it as Vern's.

****

After that day, Annie always sat next to me in class. And we always went somewhere to talk afterwards. And I always walked her to the parking lot where Vern was waiting for her with his red Vespa. And when I wasn't with her, I was thinking about her.

I told my brother Rick, the only one in the family I could talk to, all about Annie: The long honey blonde hair, her mysterious background, her intriguing ideas…and how she rode behind the ramrod straight Vern on his red Vespa.

"She drives by here every day," Rick said. "She lives right down the street."

What?! Are you sure?"

"How many young blondes on the back of a red Vespa driven by an older man could there be in this town?"

My heart thudded in my chest. Annie? Here? On this obscure dirt road backwater of Phoenix? I felt like Bogey in *Casablanca*. Of all the lousy dives in all the world, Ingrid Bergman just happened to walk into the one lousy dive he owned and operated. And of all the neighborhoods in all of Phoenix, one of the largest cities in America, the girl I was pursuing at

Phoenix College just happened to live in my neighborhood, just down the street, a few houses away. How could such a miracle be?

"Where does she live?"

"At the faggot's house."

"You mean 1849? The Forty-Niner's house?"

"That's the one. The red Vespa is parked in the yard."

It'd been six years since the Forty-Niner had been forced out of the neighborhood, out of that house, because of his attempted seduction of me when I was 12. I'd been the paperboy for the entire neighborhood and the Forty-Niner -- we called him that because of his address and the 1849 California Gold Rush settlers -- had been one of my customers. One evening, as I turned to leave after collecting for the paper, he stopped me, placing his hands on my shoulders. He began massaging them, telling me how nice a full body massage felt, especially a genital massage. Wouldn't I like to see how one felt? His hands began moving down my body.

I twisted away and told him I had to get home, I was expected for supper.

I told Mom about this, and she told the cops. I was interviewed by a female cop who asked me about boners, hard-ons, erections. Did he have one?

And then the cops talked to him. And so did the neighbors, threatening him with bodily harm if he didn't disappear.

The Forty-Niner disappeared.

After he left, the house became a revolving door of short-term tenants. No one stayed there long. Two months, three months, six months. Just recently, a young black man had moved into the house. He rode a motorbike with a tall conga drum strapped to the back. He attracted our attention because he was the first and only black who'd ever lived in the neighborhood. Now Rick was telling me he'd moved out and Vern and Annie had moved in. I could hardly believe it. I had to be sure.

It was early on a late January night when Rick told me this. We immediately walked down the dusty road toward 1849. I didn't feel I could just walk up to the door, knock on it, and ask if Annie lived there. It'd be awkward if she didn't. It'd be even more awkward if she did. Like I'd come looking for her. Which I *was*. But it shouldn't *look* that way.

So I told Rick we'd create a diversion to draw out whoever lived in the house. The Forty-Niner's house, like most houses on 51st Street, had a lot of citrus trees in the front yard, heavy with fruit, even in frosty January. We'd start picking the grapefruit off of the trees in the yard, making a lot of noise calling to each other as we did so. Whoever lived there would come to investigate. If they were strangers, we'd just take off running. If it was Vern and Annie, we'd come forward and comment on what a surprise it was to find them on this street.

And that's the way we worked it. We hopped over the low cinderblock wall which separated the Forty-Niner's yard from the street and began picking grapefruit. We dropped the fruit and said damn! We called to each other. We were as brazen in our theft as we could be.

Two people hurried to the screendoor of the house and called out, "Who's there?" It was Vern, with Annie behind him.

I stepped forward into the light so that they could see me, my arms filled with stolen fruit. "It's me, your student, Eric." I gestured with my laden arms. "I live just down the street and I've come to steal your fruit. But now that I know this is your house, I'll let you keep it. Hi, Annie. What a pleasant surprise!"

I walked up to the screendoor. "If you let me and my brother come in, we'll take these grapefruit to your kitchen."

Vern smiled at us and opened the screendoor. "Sure, bring'em in."

Rick and I took our stolen fruit inside. It was the first time I'd been entirely inside the Forty-Niner's house...which, I reminded myself, was now *Vern's* house.

And Annie's house.

I'd found the fruit I'd come for.

A Fine and Private Place
Circe

       It is not your glance,
            It is not your walk,
                 It is not your word
                       That unleashes the beast.
              It is the sorcery of your touch.
You touch me,
       And I am no longer human.
You touch me,
       And I am an animal
             Straining at my leash.
You touch me,
       And I am a monster,
             Raging in my lust.
You touch me,
       And I am Ariel in love,
             Grendel in pain.
You touch me,
       And I howl in the dust.
You touch me...
       And I am your beast.

****

    Annie and I were in a state of constant sexual arousal around each other. We were teenagers and we were insane for each other. We made love anywhere and everywhere, day or night, every day, every night, and we didn't care who knew. During the day, Annie went with me to all my Phoenix College classes. Between classes, we made out. Once we were lying on top of one of the outdoor picnic tables which were sprinkled across the campus. I was leaning over Annie, kissing her, when a female teacher yelled from a nearby second floor window, "Annie! You get off of that table right now, or I'm telling your father!"

    We looked up at the window and saw the woman frowning down at us. "Annie!" she yelled again, "I see what you're doing! Stop it right this instant!"

    I looked at Annie. "Who's that?"

    "I have no idea."

    "What's she mean, 'tell your father'?" Annie was an amnesiac orphan, so far as I was supposed to know.

    "I have no idea."

    Because the teacher continued to glower at us, we got off the table and walked away, hand-in-hand.

    After school, when we got back to 51st Street, we spent all of our time together. We walked down that dusty road thigh-to-thigh with Annie's thigh brushing mine as we walked. As we did so, I could think of nothing but the fact that her thigh was brushing mine. It made me want to throw her down right there in the middle of that dirt road, tear off her jeans, and make love to her. Neither of us gave a good God-damn about the neighbors who, as far as we were concerned, did not exist. In fact, hardly anyone anywhere in the world existed. It was just us.

We didn't do it right there in the middle of that dusty road. It would have frightened the horses and the chickens and the geese, not to mention the neighbors. But we did it everywhere else. Late at night, after we were sure Vern was asleep, I climbed in through her bedroom window. Annie had the front bedroom of the house at 1849 and the screenless windows were at waist level. Annie was waiting for me to come and whisper her name. Then she opened her window and I stepped into her room and into her arms. We made love until the first dawn birds began to chirp. Then I climbed back out the window and went home briefly to prepare for Phoenix College...where I would soon see Annie once more.

We made love in the missionary position, with me on top. We made love with Annie on top. We made love doggie style. We made love upside down, sliding off the two mattresses piled on top of each other that Annie used for a bed and onto the floor. We made love standing, with Annie up against a wall. We made love with me standing, holding Annie, her legs wrapped around my waist and me inside her. We made love softly, quietly, lingering over the feel of each other's body, coming to know every centimeter of each other.

And on afternoons when Vern wasn't home, we made hard love, loudly and violently, screaming, yelling, rolling off the bed and thrashing around on the floor, first me on top, then Annie, then me, then Annie. We made love until we were completely spent, drenched in sweat, exhausted. Then we'd lie in each other's arms for awhile and then make love again. And then again. And then again.

Yes, we used rubbers when we made love. Annie didn't have access to the pill. The Supremes had made it clear in *Griswold vs. Connecticut*, in 1965, that the pill had to be made available to all married women in all states. But Annie and I weren't married. Even single women didn't universally have a right to the pill, or even other methods of birth control, until 1972 when the Supremes ruled in *Eisenstadt vs. Baird* that all adult women, married *or* single, had a right to possess contraception. But Annie wasn't an adult, so she had no right to the pill or the diaphragm or any other means of birth control.

So we used rubbers, which I could get at the drugstore. And we used the rhythm method, unprotected sex up to five days after her period ended -- and after that rubbers. And we even made love *during* her period, with a towel under her, we didn't care. Then we hopped in the shower together and lathered each other up and made out under the steaming water pouring over us.

Sometimes it was coitus interruptus, with me coming on her belly, my thigh between her legs rubbing her clit so she came as I came. And then we'd lie there silently holding each other, my cum the sticky glue binding us together.

But the best means of birth control was oral sex. I ate her, she ate me, and we ate each other in the 69 position.

"What's the speed limit on Highway 69?" I asked her one night.

"I don't know."

I grinned, "Lickety split!" Then I went down on her and she squealed. "You have a mellifluous pussy," I told her, coming up for breath from between her thighs.

"What does *that* mean?"

"It means it is sweetly flowing with honey."

She laughed and pushed my head back down toward her pussy. "Then have another taste of sweet honey!"

And I did.

The first time Annie ate me was one night as we slept out under the stars and the grapefruit trees on a blanket in her front yard. After that, it was anywhere, anytime.

Then one day Annie told me she'd never seen the Grand Canyon. Neither had I, really. I'd only seen it in the darkness, the night I'd ridden up to it with Gerald. I had no more idea what it looked like during the day than Annie did.

So I said I'd take her to see the Grand Canyon. I didn't own a car, so early one Saturday morning we packed two knapsacks and stuck out our thumbs. By that afternoon we were standing on the South Rim of the Grand Canyon. We didn't hike down into it that time. Instead, we walked along the Rim, in awe of the marvel before us.

Night came and we had no money to rent a room. We crawled under an overturned wooden river boat, a huge canoe, which was dry docked near the beginning of the Bright Angel Trail. We unrolled our blankets and lay down. All around us we could hear people coming and going, even as night deepened, but no one knew we were mere feet away, under the boat at the mouth of the Bright Angel Trail. Annie was having her period and there were no showers for us to hop into, but we were insane for each other. So I found Annie's clit with my moistened fingers as she ate me and we came together there under the river boat on the South Rim of the Grand Canyon.

Once I asked to borrow Dan the Man's car for some errand which would take most of the day. He'd traded in his Olds 88 for a cherry red convertible. Annie and I put down the top and roared out into the desert toward the Superstition Mountains. We just wanted to get out into the distant desert far, far away from everyone. As we roared down a desert dirt road in the hot Arizona sun, throwing up dust in our wake and surrounded only by cactus and sagebrush, Annie unbuckled my belt and unzipped my pants. Her mouth found my prick, already hard. Annie had the tongue of an angel and, as she ate me, I put the pedal to the metal. I was hitting a hundred down that desert road, dust devils swirling up behind me, the wind whipping at my face, by the time I came. It was suicidally stupid, like rubbing sparks off each other in a powder keg, but we were insane for each other and we didn't give a damn. We'd reached the heroin level of obsession with each other.

Beyond 52nd Street, McDowell Road becomes the boundary between the Papago desert to the right and the fenced-off Papago Military Reservation to the left. McDowell climbs in elevation as it heads toward a cleft between the two hills then known as Barnes' Buttes. Now these two buttes are more often called "Papago Buttes." All visitors to Phoenix see them as their planes land at the nearby Sky Harbor Airport.

Once it crests the ridge at the cleft between these two buttes, McDowell heads down into neighboring Scottsdale. It is a main route from Phoenix to Scottsdale, heavily travelled. The butte on the Papago desert side is smaller and accessible to the public. The butte on the left is larger, but it is inaccessible to the public, being fenced inside the military reservation.

But this was my neighborhood and I grew up along that fence. I knew every chink in the perimeter. One late afternoon, as the day headed toward dusk, Annie and I slipped through a section of the fence which ran right up to the side of the large butte. At that point the butte slanted away from the fence at a 45-degree angle, and the fence-makers didn't slant the fence to make it flush with the butte. So, it was no problem at all to slip through the resulting gap between the last fence pole and the butte face.

Then we began climbing. We reached the summit just as the sun was setting. We tossed down our blanket and fell on it. The lights of Phoenix began to twinkle in the dusk and a river of car lights flowed over the ridge between the two buttes on McDowell beneath us. In the evening sky itself the lights of planes constantly landing at nearby Sky Harbor were like the trails of giant fireflies in the night.

And we made love there on the summit of Papago Butte, burning for each other as Phoenix burned beneath us in the lingering desert heat.

We made love at night on a blanket in a gritty gully of the Papago desert, surrounded by jackrabbits and cacti and lizards.

We made love at night on the grounds of the golf course at the intersection of Thomas and 56th Street, with the sprinklers falling on us like rain.

We made love at night underwater in the demonstration swimming pools at a dealership further along Thomas on the road to Scottsdale. We climbed over the fence, stripped, and plunged into one of their kidney shaped pools. Then we climbed out and ran stark naked to the next pool as cars whizzed by on Thomas just beyond the fence. The dealership was bathed in lights, but we didn't care. We plunged into the next pool and splashed around in the cold night-time waters and made love again. And then we ran to the next pool and made love again until we could make love no more.

Just as I had once roamed my neighborhood at night with Jerry Campbell, exploring every inch of it, so I now roamed the neighborhood at night with Annie, taking her to the places that only I knew.

I took her to the corner of 56th Street and Oak, just at the boundary there between Phoenix and Scottsdale. On the other side of 56th Street was the Sherwood Heights Estates housing development, in Scottsdale. In the other direction, across Oak Street, was the Papago Military Reservation, the complete opposite side of the reservation from Papago Buttes. And, just at that corner, just inside the Phoenix city limit on an acre of desert, was an Episcopalian church. In that long ago age, when crime was less rampant, churches throughout our neighborhood left their doors unlocked at all times, even at night. The congregations subscribed to the belief that the House of the Lord should always be open, so as to provide a constant sanctuary for the spiritually seeking. For Annie and me, this church provided constant sanctuary for the sexually seeking.

We opened the unlocked doors and stepped inside. We could have then found any shadowed alcove. Instead, we walked up the center aisle to the dais upon which stood the altar and priest's podium. We mounted the dais, stripped, and performed our own Black Sabbath ritual in front of the altar. The doors were open and anyone -- an insomniac member of the congregation, a prowling cop -- could have walked in at any moment and found us engaged in sacrilegious sex before the very altar from which the priest would officiate in the morning. But the quasi-public nature of our love making on that dais was an aphrodisiac which drove us to even greater passion and we clung to each other's sweaty body and howled in our sexual hunger. We were insane for each other and we didn't give a damn. Forbidden fruit always tastes the sweetest.

But the place in which we most often made love was the sprawling Catholic St. Francis Cemetery at 48th and Oak Streets. It was huge even then. Now it is even bigger, having engulfed much of my old neighborhood, including my own home. At night it was peaceful, secluded, and beautiful in the moonlight. A old stone wall topped by a spiked iron fence enclosed it. Ghosts of the dead also protected it from superstitious intruders. In all my nights of wandering among the tombstones, I never once met anyone else walking those haunted grounds. It was a private park, reserved just for us, a sanctuary of our own where no one dared come after dark.

The center of the cemetery was a long rectangular mall shielded on all four sides from the distant streets by 15-foot-tall walls of crypts. Running the length of this interior mall was a pool, a miniature version of Washington, D.C.'s Reflecting Pool which connects the Lincoln Memorial and the Washington Monument. At one end of this pool was a set of large statues and a splashing fountain which never stopped splashing, day or night.

The first night I took Annie to the cemetery, night birds were twittering and rustling in the many trees which dotted the grounds and an owl hooted from somewhere. I spread our blanket beside the splashing pool and we lay down among the tombstones in the warm Arizona night. Then we undressed each other and we made love there, teenagers insane for each other in the quiet darkness among the dead. "The grave's a fine and private place," wrote the poet Andrew Marvell to his coy mistress, "but none, I think, do there embrace."

He was wrong.

Then, exhausted, Annie and I rolled over and looked up at the brilliant stars over Phoenix. There seemed to be a billion of them sprinkled across the clear sky. A cool breeze flowed through the dark cemetery, past the cold tombstones, and chilled the sweat on our nude bodies. Annie shivered and pressed her body harder into mine for warmth, cushioning her bare breasts on my chest. I put both arms around her. I kissed her on the cheek, cradled her close, and gazed at the stars blazing above us.

I would have been happy to have died then and there.

The Great Fear

I awoke to screeching. It was dawn, and Mom was standing in the dirt road in front of Annie's house, just on the other side of the low wall which ran along the front of the yard. She refused to step into the yard. But that didn't stop her from screeching. "Eric, you come home with me right this instant! Get up! Come home with me, right now!"

Annie and I had spent another night together. We'd tossed a blanket on her front yard, under the grapefruit trees, and lain out on the grass. The yard was relatively secluded. One side was screened by a tall oleander hedge, while a knee-high cinderblock wall ran along the entire front of the yard.

We hadn't made love that night, so we were fully clothed under a light second blanket with which we covered ourselves. We'd looked up at the stars through the tree leaves and talked about nothing in particular, just happy to be together. Eventually we'd drifted off in each other's arms.

Until Mom's shrill screeching abruptly woke us. "Eric! Get up and come home with me, right this instant!"

I sat up, groggy, and looked at Mom. Her face was contorted with anger and her shrieking was at full volume. If the neighbors had not arisen with the dawn, they were certainly up now, peering out from behind their curtained windows to seek the source of the commotion.

Annie sat up beside me. Seeing her beside me, the pitch of Mom's angry screaming crescendoed to an even higher volume. "You get up from there right now! You come home with me right now!" She screamed all of this from the street, as if afraid to come into the yard.

I looked at Annie and shook my head in resignation. "She's probably going to keep on screaming like that. When she gets hysterical she just goes on and on. I'll go home with her and calm her down. I'll take a shower and be back later."

Annie nodded, sleep still in her eyes. Her long blonde hair was tangled and disheveled from a night outdoors in my arms. She looked wonderful. I leaned over and kissed her on the cheek. That sent Mom into greater paroxysms of rage. "You stop that, young man! You stop that right now and you get up from there and you come home with me right now!"

I sighed and tossed off the blanket. Mom continued to wail non-stop as I pulled on my cowboy boots. She'd worked herself up into full-blown hysteria. No doubt she'd stoked her fires of rage all the way down the road as she stalked toward Vern's house. I squeezed Annie's hand and walked out to join Mom on the dirt road.

Mom continued to howl as we walked back home. It was the same thing, over and over. "What will the neighbors think? What will the neighbors say? How could you do such a thing? What will the neighbors think when they see you sleeping out in public with that girl?"

"Who cares what the neighbors think?"

"I care what the neighbors think, and so should you!"

"I don't give a damn what the neighbors think. They can all go to hell, for all I care."

"If you don't care what the neighbors think, I certainly do. And I'll not have you dragging my good name through the mud by having all the neighbors talk about me."

And that was the heart of the matter. Mom's greatest fear was being talked about, while I didn't give a rat's ass what anyone, neighbor or not, said about me and Annie. I felt I was surrounded by a village of hypocrites for whom I had no respect, so anything they may have said about me was simply water off a duck's back. I gave it absolutely zero consideration and I had no sympathy at all for Mom's great concern for her neighborhood reputation. Indeed, it was difficult for me to even comprehend why Mom cared about what the neighbors said. Mom's great fear of neighborhood gossip seemed to be just one more example of the parochialism from which I wanted so badly to escape. I felt that Mom had become an unwitting collaborator in the preservation and perpetuation of the same system of social control that had domesticated her.

So, because I audaciously did what I wanted and had not the slightest regard for what neighbors said about me, I did not understand, until much later, what powerful controlling forces gossip and being talked about were for Mom.

When Mom went to grade school and high school in the 1930s and early 1940s in the South, religion -- *Protestantism* -- was taught in all the public schools. I'd thought this was due to the intense religiosity of the South. Instead, as I later discovered, this was the case in public schools all across America. At that time, every public school, North and South, East and West, indoctrinated students in Protestant Christianity. They got Sunday School every day of the week.

And everyone thought it was right, no one objected.

Until, finally, during World War II, a family in Champaign, Illinois, objected. A fifth grade boy there named James McCollum, the son of a horticulture professor at the University of Illinois, was required, like everyone else in the school, to take a religion class taught by a returned Protestant missionary to China. He objected and his mother, Vashti McCollum, visited the school superintendent to get him excused. The superintendent said schooling in Protestantism was an educational requirement of the Illinois public schools which could not be waived for any student under any circumstances whatsoever.

So, in July, 1945, backed by a local Unitarian minister and financially supported by a group of Chicago Jewish businessmen, Vashti McCollum sued the Champaign school district. In January, 1946, a three-judge circuit court panel upheld the legality of Illinois' Protestant religious educational requirement for all students. So did the Illinois Supreme Court in 1947. But on March 9, 1948, the U.S. Supreme Court overruled the Illinois Supreme Court and, in an 8-1 decision, ruled that the religious education classes in Champaign's public schools violated the Constitutional mandate of the separation of church and state.

Because this was a U.S. Supreme Court ruling, this decision also banned similar religious education classes everywhere in America, including in the high schools of the South and in Chattanooga, Tennessee, where Mom was raised and lived. By then, however, Mom had already graduated from Chattanooga's Central High School.

Protestant Christianity was Mom's greatest passion. She never missed church services or Sunday School. Indeed, beginning in 1941, when she started her junior year at Central High, she had been given a Sunday School class to teach at her family's church. Her weekends were entirely devoted to religion, because she spent Saturdays preparing her lessons for her Sunday School class.

Meanwhile, at Central High, Mom majored in the Bible and always made A-plusses in her Bible classes, as she planned to devote herself to missionary work in Catholic Brazil after high school. In fact, she became recognized as the most devout student at Chattanooga Central High. She often delivered the devotionals and said the public prayers in her school assembly hall in front of hundreds of her fellow students.

As a result, upon graduation Mom was given a full-tuition scholarship to Ben Lippin Bible College in Asheville, North Carolina. Ben Lippin Bible College gave one such scholarship to each high school across the South for the best religion student graduating from that school. Mom was the most outstanding Christian student of Chattanooga's Central High School graduating class of 1943, so Mom got the scholarship for Central High.

In the fall of 1943, Mom went off to Ben Lippin Bible College in Ashville to prepare for her missionary work in Catholic Brazil. She was there only a few days before she got into trouble. Ben Lippin was 10 miles outside of Asheville and a bus took students into the town to purchase personal necessities only once a week, on Saturdays. For that trip students had to request written permission. The first Saturday she was there, Mom didn't need anything, so didn't request permission to go to Asheville on the bus.

After the bus left, however, Mom and four of her fellow students, both boys and girls, decided to slip off to Asheville on their own. They walked the 10 miles into Asheville and played miniature golf all day.

Then they walked back to school, arriving just before five o'clock. All the other students were in the dining room, eating. Mom went to her table and sat down. The dining room monitor told her to get back up and to report to the lobby. She went. The other students that she had played hookey with were already there. They were all ordered to kneel in a circle while the teachers prayed over their erring ways.

Then the Sinful Five were told to go to vespers. At vespers the Sinful Five were ordered to sit in the front row where the entire student body could see them while their teachers berated them for their sinful natures. Thereafter, the Sinful Five were shunned for two days by their fellow students. Mom said it was "like being forced to wear the Scarlet Letter."

Protestant Christianity may have been Mom's greatest love, but transgressing the social code and being talked about was her greatest fear. Nothing was more horrible than being the subject of gossip and reproach. And, as it turned out, this fear was greater than her love.

Mom wrote to her father asking for money to return home. And so, because she could not stand being talked about, Mom, the most outstanding Christian student at Chattanooga's Central High, returned to Chattanooga after just one week at Ben Lippin Bible College. And she did not become the Baptist missionary to Catholic Brazil which she had worked so hard to become over the previous four years at Central High.

Her Central High religion teacher was greatly disappointed to learn of Mom's return to Chattanooga, so Mom never went to see her beloved teacher to explain what had happened.

Mom wouldn't have been able to stand the shame.

The Superstitions

I jumped off the rock outcropping and landed smack in the middle of a band of javelina, wild desert pigs. The sows and piglets squealed in fright and scattered for the scrub brush. The grizzled big-shouldered boars flattened their ears, stood their ground, and grunted at me. A two-foot tall boar, no doubt the band leader, clattered his tusks in warning, preparing to charge.

Javelina are vicious creatures and their name comes from their razor-sharp tusks, "javelin" in Spanish. Every January, javelina hunting season, Arizona hunters go after these huge brutes with bows and arrows. But sometimes the hunted become the hunters and turn on their pursuers. An entire band has been known to attack mounted hunters, slashing legs to the bone and goring horses in the belly.

And this was most likely to happen if the boars felt they were protecting their brood from an attacking predator. Such as me. Right now. Plunging from the sky to land on top of them. Visions of slashed legs and gored bellies flashed through my mind. I knew I was long desert miles away from help of any kind. I was scared. I began yelling at the boars, making more noise than the whole band of them.

Annie and I were out in the Lost Dutchman country of the Superstition Mountains. The Superstitions are jaggedly beautiful 5,000-foot-high mountains jutting up out of the desert east of Phoenix. They're about 30 miles straight out from the city on the Superstition Freeway, past Mesa, just on the other side of Apache Junction. They dominate a huge 160,000 acre tract of cholla and saguaro and ocotillo and prickly pear cacti and desert saltbush and creosote scrub known collectively as the Superstition Wilderness Area. In the summer, the rocks out there are so hot you can't sit on them and you are wise to find the shade of a saguaro cactus at high noon.

Fact and legend mingle in the Supersitions. That's why they're called the Superstitions, although I always called them the "Stupidstitions," because of my disdain for religion. The whole area, like much of the desert Southwest, used to belong to the Apache. Supposedly, their Thunderbird god made its home in the mountain fastness. Spanish conquistadores wandered through the area, followed by Christianizing Jesuits.

Later, when the region became part of Mexico, the Peralta family of Mexican ranchers are said to have struck gold in the mountains. One legend has it that, sometime before the Civil War, Apache raiders ambushed a mule train bringing gold out of the fabulously rich Peralta mine. The Apaches massacred all the Mexican miners and loaded the bulging gold satchels into a cave. Then they closed up the cave with boulders. Sometime after this, the whereabouts of the Peralta mine, along with the gold-stuffed cave, were lost.

Then, sometime in the 1870s or 1880s, the Dutchman Jacob Waltz appeared on the scene. Actually, Waltz was no more Dutch than are the Pennsylvania Dutch. Both were and are German. It's just that Americans have never been good at understanding other languages. Waltz is supposed to have wandered around asking newcomers if they spoke German. "Sprechen zie Deutsch?" he asked. They thought he was asking if they spoke Dutch. So, he became known as the Dutchman.

According to legend, Waltz saved the life of one of the Peralta sons, or grandsons, and was given directions to the Peralta mine out of gratitude. Or perhaps he stumbled on the mine and murdered the Mexican miners for its possession. In any case, legend says, he began appearing in pioneer Phoenix with his pockets stuffed with gold nuggets. However, he never registered his mine's location, if he ever had a mine, and never told anyone where it was.

Then, in 1891, Jacob Waltz died. And the Dutchman took the secret of his mine's location with him to the grave. And so the Dutchman's gold mine was lost. And people have been searching this desert wilderness for the Lost Dutchman Mine ever since.

From time to time when I was growing up in Phoenix in the 1950s and early 1960s, the morning newspaper I delivered carried stories of gnarly old prospectors, fearful of claim jumping, shooting it out and sometimes killing each other in the Superstition Wilderness. But, by the time Annie and I were clambering around in those mountains, no one had been killed for prospecting for a long time. Even so, there were still some of the old desert rats wandering around. The government didn't close the area to legal prospecting until 1984. Even today, there are still hikers trekking through the mountains hoping they'll fall into some hidden pit where they can just pick up chunks of gold from the dusty ground.

But we weren't out in the Supersitions in the spring of 1966 hunting gold. Annie and I had gone into the Superstitions for the sole purpose of making love on the summit of the highest, most desolate mountain peak in the region. We thought it'd be romantic.

We didn't have a car, so we drove into the desert with Dan the Man in his new-to-him cherry red convertible. For him, it was just a desert hiking and climbing adventure. We didn't tell him that, for us, it was something more. Dan the Man was a teenager, like us, and so was obsessed with sex. So we didn't want to arouse his prurient interest in what we planned to do. Knowing Dan, I felt there was a good chance he'd just say, "OK, you guys fuck, I'll watch!"

We told him we wanted to spend the night on the mountain. We wanted the experience of complete desert solitude. We had our canteens of water, we had food, we had an old Army blanket to sleep on, and we'd trek out of the desert the next day and hitchhike back into Phoenix. Dan thought this was weird, but he bought it. Annie and I were always doing weird things.

Of course, we had no intention of doing any of that. Our plan was to have him take pictures of us on the mountain top, bid him a fond farewell, and then get down to some serious fucking as soon as he was out of sight. As soon as we'd made love, we'd quickly dress and yell down to Dan from the mountain top, telling him to wait for us, that we'd realized how stupid our idea was, that we'd changed our minds.

We left Phoenix before dawn, to have as much daylight as possible for the day of desert mountaineering. By the time the sun was creeping up over the eastern horizon, we were already past Apache Junction and deep into the desert along rutted dirt roads. The higher, interior portion of the Superstitions can't be reached with a frontal assault. Climbing the face of the mountains would just reward you with a slanted mesa top still well below the highest peak. We wanted that highest peak, which meant driving deeper into the desert, skirting the Superstition ridgeline until we found some accessible side canyon into the interior.

We spotted a likely canyon. It created a valley leading up toward the highest peak, which we could see in the distance. Even better, at its center was a ribbon of green. That meant there were mesquite and Palo Verde trees along some small mountain stream. Of course, we'd brought canteens filled with water, but it wouldn't hurt to have more water along the trail.

We left the car at the mouth of the canyon, with no fear that someone would trash it. We'd seen no other humans anywhere in the desert.

We climbed steadily upward all morning. A few times, off in the distance, we glimpsed desert deer bounding away from us. Sometimes we flushed cactus wren or other small birds. Jackrabbits hopped across our paths from time to time, as did a roadrunner or two. The desert looks empty from a distance but it is filled with life, from tiny horned toads and the ants they feed on up right to coyote and cougar.

We found the stream, fed by spring rains. Saltbush, creosote and late-blooming popcorn flowers, mariposa lilies, and Mexican gold poppies blossomed along its sides. We were hot from the morning climb, but the hottest and hardest part of the climb was still ahead. We plopped down beside the stream and splashed frigid water into our faces. Because it was gushing down the side of the mountain, and not some stagnant pool, we felt it was safe to drink. We gulped down huge mouthfuls and filled our canteens. The stream was as clear as tap water, but tasted better than any tap water you will ever taste. We savored the water, as we were unlikely to find another stream once we left this one. Water is scarce and precious in that land, where even the sky is thirsty and people still die of heat stroke and dehydration.

It doesn't help if humans connive with the elements to destroy you. One summer, for example, my youngest brother Brad, then a teenager, was wandering around lost without a canteen in this Superstition Wilderness. Of course, Brad never prepared for anything, so not having a canteen was typical. Also typical was his luck. He stumbled across a dark and cool cave, in which he took shelter from the blistering sun. Inside, on a ledge, was a tightly sealed small Mason jar filled with water. No doubt some prospector or habitual hiker had left the precious cache there as a potential life preserver in the dry wasteland.

Brad gulped down all the water. No doubt the person who stashed the water was bitterly disappointed to find his water gone when next he entered the cave. But Brad's action was forgivable, given his circumstances. The water was stored there to save someone's life, and the life saved turned out to be Brad's.

What was not forgivable, however, was how Brad repaid his savior.

"I pissed in the jar," he told me. "I filled it up with stinking piss, screwed the lid on tight, and put it back on the ledge." He giggled like a maniac as he thought of the shock and anger of the possible prospector when he found his water turned to piss. That his action might possibly have been life threatening wasn't important to him. Now, Brad would also lie to Christ on the Cross, so this could all be a lie, but I'm inclined to believe it, because Brad doesn't give a shit about anyone and I've known him to do things like this.

Just before noon we reached the crest of the mountain. We looked over into the innards of the mountain range and saw a small bowl-shaped valley. It obviously retained some of the sparse rain which fell in the desert, as it was green with vegetation. Even more surprising was the sight of palm trees. Sure, we had palm trees in Phoenix. Lots of them. But they were well-watered with irrigation, while these palms depended on nothing but the rain.

We turned to our right and tramped along the crest of the ridge until we came to what we were sure was the highest peak of the Superstitions. Below us, in the distance, we could see the tilted mesa which dominates the outer face of the mountain range. We were now behind that tilted mesa. Even further out in the haze of distance we could see Apache Junction and, to the right, heading north, the old Apache Trail. Thirty miles of desert beyond Apache Junction was Phoenix. All three of us whooped and hollered and jumped around laughing.

We found the cairn of rocks we knew would be at the summit. Inside the cairn was a rusted tin can, crammed with slips of paper. Previous climbers had left their names and the dates of their climbs on the slips. I pulled out my small notebook and a pen and all three of us wrote our names and the date on a page. Then I tore out the page, folded it up tight, and jammed it into the can with the rest of the slips. I then covered the can with rocks once again. Someday someone else would do the same thing, but, for now, the mountain belonged to us.

I pulled out my Kodak Instamatic and began taking pictures. I snapped Annie standing on a boulder jutting out over nothing, hands on hips, in the stance of a conqueror. Then Dan took a picture of Annie and me, arms around each other, me stripped to the waist in the hot sun, with the tilted mesa in the background.

We spread out the green woolen Army blanket I'd carried up the mountain and the three of us shared a small lunch of dates, raisins, granola bars, and lots of water from our canteens.

Then Dan the Man got up to go. "I'm giving you weirdos one last chance to come down the mountain with me."

"Thanks, Dan," I told him. "But we'll be OK. We have food, we have canteens, we know the road back to the freeway. We'll start at dawn and be down the mountain before it gets too hot. We'll be fine."

We sat on a boulder, watching Dan trudge away. As he reached the crest where we'd come up, he turned to us and waved. We waved back. Then he was gone over the crest.

We stripped. I pulled Annie down to the blanket. We made love like rabid rabbits in the hot desert sun on that lonely mountain summit in the middle of the Superstition Wilderness. We were teenagers and we were insane for each other. And it was wonderful.

Afterward, we threw on our clothes and boots and I gathered up the blanket, flinging it across my shoulder. We strapped on our canteens and began jogging down to the crest over which Dan had disappeared.

When we reached it, we could see Dan making his way slowly and carefully through the rocks far below us. He'd almost reached the little stream. We yelled to him, our voices carrying far in the desert stillness. He turned and saw us waving far above him. We yelled down the mountain cleft for him to wait for us and he understood. He sat down by the stream and waited.

And then we began running and stumbling and jumping down the side of the mountain to catch up with him. I was ahead of Annie, leaping in big strides, gravity pulling me down faster and faster. Just ahead of me was a small outcropping of rock. The ground beyond it seemed to be about five or six feet below. I was now running fast and I decided to just keep on running, jump off the rock like a diving board, and land solidly on the ground below, rolling if I had to.

I hit the rock and jumped out into the air.

And landed smack in the middle of the javelina.

I whipped the blanket off my shoulder and began flapping it wildly up and down, yelling and hollering as loudly as I could. I hoped I'd scare the javelina into flight. For two or three seconds the boars grunted at this flapping, yelling creature which had appeared suddenly in their midst. Then they turned abruptly and fled in the same direction as their sows and piglets.

And I turned also, but in the opposite direction. I began running back up the slope towards Annie, who was still coming down. "Go back, go back! Javelina!"

I joined her and we both clambered back up the hillside for a bit before pausing to look down. Annie said she saw the javelina running off, but now there wasn't a javelina in sight. There was nothing except the rocks and the desert cacti. Everything was completely silent. It was as if the desert was totally empty.

When we reached the stream, I told Dan about landing in the middle of the javelina.

He shook his head at my carelessness. "You're damn lucky to be alive."

I put my arm around Annie and pulled her close. We smiled at each other. "Yeah," I agreed, "I'm damn lucky."

Damsel in Distress

I don't know why Annie finally decided to tell me the truth about herself. Perhaps because it was becoming harder and harder to carry off the charade of her mysterious origins. She was constantly patching up holes in her story. One of them came when we hitchhiked to the Grand Canyon. We were trying to get a ride north out of Flagstaff when a cop pulled up to where we were standing. He asked for I.D. and I gave him my driver's license. Annie didn't have any I.D., so he asked her birth date.

"February 17, 1950," she quickly replied. That date meant she'd just turned 16.

I assured the cop we weren't runaways. We were both from Phoenix and we were just going to the Grand Canyon for the weekend. He got back in his car and drove off.

"That was quick thinking on my part," Annie said. "I just snapped off a date. I don't really know how old I am."

"Yeah, quick thinking. Oops, here comes a car. Stick out your thumb!"

I never challenged Annie on any of her statements. I didn't care one way or the other. Besides, I assumed she had her reasons for the subterfuge and she'd tell me the truth in her own sweet time. Or not. It didn't really matter.

One night, in her bedroom, she finally confessed. We were lying on her mattress after making love and she was nestled in my shoulder. "Actually, I *do* know how old I am," she said.

"Uh-huh. And how old is that?"

I felt her tense in my arms. "That day we met in the Philosophy Department? I was 15."

"Uh-huh. And your birthday really *is* February 17th, right? So now you're 16, right?"

"Right."

"Anything else?"

"Vern is my father."

"Uh-huh. Anything else?"

"I'm a high school drop-out."

"Uh-huh. Anything else?"

"Isn't that enough?"

"Just giving you a chance to get it all out on the table."

"Are you angry?"

"Why should I be?"

"Because I lied to you."

"I knew you were lying. I didn't care."

"But you're so much older than me. You're 19."

"By a few months. Besides, that's only three years difference, no big deal."

"But you're in college and I haven't even graduated from high school."

"It doesn't matter. Annie, you could have told me all this from the beginning."

"I was afraid you'd leave me."

I drew a little apart from her so that I could look at her directly. "What kind of a superficial asshole do you think I am? You think any of this makes any difference to me? That first day I met you I thought, 'She's the most fascinating girl I've ever met. I don't need to know anything else about her. I want her!' None of this changes how I feel about you...about us." I kissed her gently on her lips. I felt her relax in my arms.

"In fact," I continued, "I think it's *great!*"

"Why's that?"

"Because we're going to send you to college right away!"

"But I haven't graduated from high school."

"You don't need to. You can skip high school altogether. While you were talking, an idea came to me. Summer school is coming up at Phoenix College. They don't ask for transcripts or *anything* to enroll in the summer. You just show up and pay your tuition. I have to take a math course this summer to meet my math requirement for the Associate degree. And I was planning on taking an elective music appreciation course. You can sign up for both of them with me. We'll go to class together. I know you can ace both courses.

"Then, based on your grades, in September you apply to enter Phoenix College full-time. You submit your Phoenix College transcript and say, 'Look, I've proven I can do the work at this school. Admit me.' Whaddya say?"

Annie hugged me close and kissed me on the cheek. "Well, I never wanted to go back to high school, anyway!"

I kissed her on the lips, hard. "At least *now* I know who I'm fucking!"

Annie laughed. "I thought you said it didn't matter?"

"It didn't matter, and it *doesn't* matter. All that matters is that I love you, I love you, I love you, I love you, I love you!" Each time I said, "I love you," I kissed Annie, down the side of her neck, down her chest, down her breast, until I reached her nipple. Then I stopped. And lingered.

Annie giggled. "And all that matters is that I love *you!*" She pulled me close.

And then we made love, with no secrets, laughing all the while.

****

After telling the truth about herself, Annie then told me the truth about Vern, her father. I had a lot of questions. Why was someone with a Harvard degree teaching at Phoenix College? Why was a college teacher living in my run-down neighborhood on this dirt road? Why was there no furniture in Vern's house? Where was Annie's mother? Where was the rest of the family? And why was the daughter of a Harvard-trained college teacher a high school drop-out?

"Well, dad may be Harvard-trained, but he doesn't have a Harvard degree. He's a drop-out, too. He's ABD."

"I never heard of that degree."

"It's not a degree. It just means, 'All But Dissertation.' He finished his course work for his Ph.D. at the Harvard Graduate School of Education, but he didn't finish the dissertation and actually get the degree. So he's a graduate school drop-out."

"Why didn't he finish?"

"Because his committee wanted him to make revisions. He refused. He felt the dissertation was perfect as it was. So they refused him the degree."

"So that's why he's teaching at a community college?"

Annie sighed. "No, that's *not* why he's at Phoenix College. He actually got a tenured position teaching philosophy at Arizona State. But, he was fired, despite having tenure."

"I thought you *couldn't* be fired if you had tenure. That's what tenure's all about."

"Tenure won't save you if your offense if bad enough. It's a long sad story..."

It seems in those golden days of yore it was easy for even a graduate student -- which is essentially what Vern was -- to get a tenured university position because there wasn't as much competition. So, even someone who had only a Master's degree and course work beyond it,

Vern's situation, could get a comfy university berth. Which Vern did, at Arizona State University.

So Vern moved his family from Cambridge to Tempe and taught for many years in ASU's Philosophy Department. That family consisted of Harriet, who Vern married at age 19 because he impregnated her, and five children -- three girls and two boys. The girls were Jackie (the reason Vern married Harriet), Annie, and Suzanne. The boys, younger than the girls, were Tony and Victor.

And, Annie said, everything was fine and dandy until Vern seduced Ruth, one of his students. Or maybe Ruth seduced Vern and Vern, filled with hope, let himself be seduced. In any case, one night a janitor caught them fucking in Vern's ASU office. And that was the end of Vern's career at ASU, tenure or no.

It was also the end of Vern and Harriet's marriage. After being fired, Vern divorced Harriet so he could be with Ruth. Except that Ruth, who was a year older than Vern, was already married to a Jewish physician in ritzy Paradise Valley and had several children of her own. That marriage, too, however, was now essentially over. But, said Annie, Ruth had not yet divorced her husband and broken up her family. It was in the works.

In the meantime, Annie's family broke up. Harriet was distraught at the loss of Vern's love and went into a downward spiral of rage and hysteria. She took the kids and moved to Ventura, a suburb north of Los Angeles.

Vern decided to not look for another job. He said he was a "mendicant" faithfully awaiting the next thing that God had planned for him. So, he just sat at the old family home in Tempe typing endless sheets of poetry. He'd wait and see what the future brought.

The future brought the president of Phoenix College knocking on his door. Vern had a reputation as a good teacher at Arizona State. And he had a small fame as the host of a televised philosophy course on Phoenix's primitive educational TV station based at ASU. The Phoenix College president wanted the Harvard-trained, locally famous, philosophy teacher to teach at Phoenix College.

So that was what God had planned next for Vern. And because Vern had alimony requirements, and child support, and took these obligations seriously, he began teaching at Phoenix College. And almost his entire monthly paycheck went to these obligations, leaving little for himself.

Which was why he rode a red Vespa motorscooter instead of driving a car. J. Lee Thompson, a petty Mormon bureaucrat who soon became the new head of Phoenix College, objected to Vern driving up to the faculty parking lot on a red Vespa motorscooter. He didn't think it was dignified.

"Pay me more money," Vern told him. "Then I'll buy a car."

Or perhaps not. Maybe he'd have given the extra money to his family.

In any case, that was why this Harvard almost-Ph.D. who taught at Phoenix College came to live in my run-down neighborhood on my dirt road. The conga-playing black musician who'd lived in the Forty-Niner's house previously had been a student of Vern's at Phoenix College. He was moving out of 1849, the rent was super cheap, and he told Vern the place was available.

So Vern moved into 1849 N. 51st Street, just down the dirt road from me, and began living a bachelor life, with Ruth occasionally visiting. Which was why Vern's house was an empty shell, completely lacking in furniture, barren from wall to wall. A bachelor doesn't need furniture. Besides, he didn't have any money for furniture.

Meanwhile, Annie was attending Buena High School in Ventura…until she dropped out. Annie just didn't care anymore, so stopped going. The family had fallen apart. She felt her beloved father had abandoned them. Her mother was emotionally distant from her children when she wasn't physically abusing them. Harriet became unpredictably violent in her inconsolable despair over losing Vern's love. She whacked the younger children, she destroyed the furniture. One time she just stood facing a wall in the house beating it fiercely over and over with the bottoms of her fists while screaming "Jesus! Jesus! Jesus!"

Harriet's violence frightened Annie. She wanted out of the house, and school seemed pointless. Desperate for love, like her mother, Annie began looking for it in all the wrong places. One night a sailor picked her up as she was lounging on a Ventura street. He drove her to some dark secluded place and tried to rape her. As she was fighting him off, a cop drove up and shined a light into the car. "Everything all right?"

Annie was 15 and did not yet know about men. She thought that, if she did the sailor a "favor" and told the cop everything was OK, the sailor would take her home. "Yes," she told the cop. "Everything is OK."

The cop switched off his light and drove away. The sailor leered at her. "I guess ya really want it, huh, baby?" He began tearing at her clothes once.

Suddenly, Annie's door swung open and the cop pulled her out of the car, out of the sailor's grasp. "Awright, bud," he told the sailor. "Hit the road."

As the sailor drove off, the cop put Annie in his patrol car and drove her to the Ventura Police Department. He called Harriet, waking her, and Harriet drove to the station in her nightgown and bathrobe to bring Annie home. She was upset, but she didn't yell at Annie.

And she didn't yell even when Annie began fucking her first boyfriend, Paul Snodgrass, a hoodlum on a motorcycle. Vern didn't like Paul, not least because of his name. Vern put much symbolic import in names, and "Paul" means "small." He thought Paul was small in morals and small in future prospects. He thought Annie should come live with him.

Harriet agreed. "Annie's really a handful. I can't do anything with her. Maybe you can get her to go back to school."

And so Annie came to live with her father, who was living alone in an empty house in my run-down neighborhood on my dirt road. And, because she had nothing else to do, she rode to Phoenix College with her father every morning on the back of Vern's red Vespa and hung out in his office.

And then, that January, I walked in with Josie, looking for Vern. And then I smiled at her the first day of her father's class and motioned for her to come sit by me. And then I asked her to come have a Coke with me. And then I showed up one night in her front yard, hungry for her. She was desperate for love...and I had come to give her my love.

I pulled her close and kissed her. "I guess you finally looked in the right place."

"It was meant to be. It was destiny."

We lay in each other's arms until the dawn came.

Mojo Man

"If the trumpet gives an uncertain sound, who shall prepare himself for the battle? So likewise you, except you utter...words easy to be understood, how shall it be known what is spoken? For you shall speak to the air."

-- St. Paul, I Corinthians, 8-9.

****

Vern's home at 1849 was a barren monk's cell. He had a small radio in his room on which he played classical music, very softly, as almost indiscernible ambient background. You weren't sure whether you heard something or not. And it was always on, even when no one was home. But there was no TV. There was no sofa. There were no easy chairs or end tables. There was no carpet on the cold cement floor. There was nothing on the walls. The house was just an empty shell. It went with his mendicant philosopher persona.

Annie's bedroom was the same. Nothing on the walls. No dresser, no bureau, no closet. Her clothes were strewn across the room. Her bed was two mattresses piled on top of each other and tossed on the floor. She felt there was a mystic union between her and Bob Dylan, so she owned three Dylan LPs, *The Freewheelin' Bob Dylan, Bringing it All Back Home,* and *Highway 61 Revisited,* all highly scratched, as she cared nothing for possessions. But she had no turntable on which to play them. The only thing which caught the eye in Annie's room was her Martin acoustic guitar and a dulcimer with no strings.

Music came easy to Annie and she had a powerful singing style reminiscent of Odetta. I'd never heard of Odetta before I met Annie. Odetta is a burly black folk singer with a theatrical awareness of performance few other musicians possess. Years after Annie introduced me to her, I finally got to see Odetta perform. The small stage had stairs in the back going into the basement. When the lights dimmed and the concert began, all one heard as the audience simmered down was Odetta's un-amped big voice, coming from nowhere, but seeming to come from everywhere, anywhere. Slowly, singing all the while, Odetta rose at the back of the stage, climbing those stairs from the basement until she had fully emerged on stage. Once on stage, she moved with elegant gravitas down to the center front, still singing. It was the most theatrical, the most dramatic stage entrance I'd ever seen. I don't remember what Odetta sang in that concert, but her entrance is burned into my memory.

Shortly after we became lovers, Annie took me to a coffeehouse on Tempe's Mill Avenue which featured acoustic folk singers. She was known there and the manager put her in the line-up of singers. She sang songs I'd never heard on the radio, folk songs of love, betrayal, and death: "Long Black Veil," "Lily of the West," "Silver Dagger." The spotlight glowed on her in the darkened smoke-filled bistro like a light from heaven and I was bewitched by her performer's charisma. Annie could have made it as a singer but, as with so many people with talents of various kinds, she wasn't interested in her gifts. She later confessed that she used her musical charms that night just to ensorcel me. It worked.

Vern's room, toward the back of the house, was just as much a mess as Annie's. He mostly kept his door closed. When it was open, I could see that his bed, too, was merely a mattress tossed on the cement. The room was a rat's nest of loose papers, books, and newspapers covering the floor, pushed into stacks, piled in corners and toppling over. You couldn't actually see the cement floor, or even walk on it. Instead, you walked on a carpet of scattered and dusty papers and magazines.

Somewhere in the chaos was a desk, also piled high with loose papers. This was an age before computers, so on the desk was a small blue Smith-Corona portable electric typewriter, one of the first portable electrics ever made. Vern was always and forever typing away on this typewriter. He wrote a lot of poetry, but he never published any. What else he wrote, I never knew. He did publish one short article in an obscure education journal. He was very proud of this trifle and showed it to me when it was published, perhaps for my appreciation and approval which, according to his own philosophy, he should not have needed. To my knowledge, he never published anything else.

The kitchen looked like a derelict's kitchen. There was almost no food in the cupboards or the fridge. The sink and counter were heaped with filth-encrusted dishes. Zillions of cockroaches crawled over everything, making the food-caked dishes seem to undulate with glistening carapaces as the intrusion of roaches searched them for food. These roaches did not run when you flicked on the light, as they did not associate light with incipient death. Instead, they continued to placidly dine on the unwashed dishes. This was because Vern refused to kill them. He said he was conducting an experiment in co-habitation. When he wanted a dish, pot, or cup, he simply pulled it out of the sink, constantly heaving with hordes of roaches, and brushed off the vermin.

Annie was filled with revulsion at the roaches covering the floor, the fridge, the counters, the cupboards, and sink. But, she tried to live with them, because it was her father's house, and she tried to respect his wishes. But one day she could stand the vermin no longer and attacked the roach intrusion with can after can of roach spray. The kitchen was filled with noxious vapors and she stumbled out every few minutes, choking, to catch her breath. Then she returned to the fray. When she finished, the kitchen counters and linoleum floor were covered with a carpet of roach carcasses, which she swept up and dumped in the trash. Then she washed the dishes and every flat surface with scalding soapy water. Thereafter, she killed any roach she saw.

Vern may have disapproved, but he did not object to Annie's termination of his co-habitation experiment. After all, he also had to co-habit with Annie, and Annie refused to co-habit any longer with roaches. So ended Vern's roach experiment. Besides, he didn't really think of the house at 1849 as a home. It was just a place to crash. It was cheap, it kept out the elements, it was warm, it was a place to sleep. And he didn't plan on being there long. He was merely passing through, on his way to bigger and better things.

It's doubtful that Vern had more than a few conversations in his life, if by "conversation" we mean speaking with others without any objective other than social exchange and enjoyment. Vern was certain of the truth and confident of his vision. He believed he possessed the wisdom to live the "right" life, and he wanted everyone else, especially the young, and most especially young males, to receive his wisdom.

Therefore, when he spoke, it was always didactic. He was constantly channelling cosmic knowledge and had a lesson and a moral to impart in every social encounter, no matter how trivial. And, if you saw life differently from him, if you made choices other than the ones he approved of as "spiritually fulfilling," he was highly critical and judgmental.

And yet, for all his teaching and preaching, for all his incessant pushing of his views and values on others, he seldom communicated; he seldom actually transmitted his cosmic knowledge and wisdom. This was because -- although he always insisted he spoke simply and clearly -- he was incapable of speaking simply and clearly. Thus, understanding Vern's florid and lapidarian language was more difficult than solving an algebra problem. His words were pregnant with celestial fire, but his stubbornly opaque Delphic pronouncements befuddled everyone. Therefore his insights, whatever they might have been, flitted away in any listener's consciousness with gnat-like evasiveness, like the secret to the universe which come in dreams, only to dissolve in the light of dawn. Listening to Vern left me feeling inadequate because I could not decipher the oracle before me who always insisted that he spoke simply and clearly.

Vern was born and raised in Minnesota when that state still had a strong socialist tradition. In Vern's case, that tradition was embodied in Daniel DeLeon's Socialist Labor Party (SLP), America's oldest socialist party, which may still be in existence. Indeed, I think that, somewhere in his genealogy, one of his ancestors was the SLP's vice presidential candidate. He told me once that he'd visited the party's head honcho at its national headquarters and told him that, "I was willing to totally commit myself to the party and make the Socialist Labor Party a major political force in America and lead it to power -- but they had to give me complete control of the party. They refused. Their loss."

Despite the fact that the SLP wouldn't submit to Vern's dictate, he remained interested in the party's views and I often saw the latest copies of the party's newspaper, *The Weekly People,* lying around his house. The SLP was a Marxist party and Vern had been immersed in that intellectual tradition since childhood. When he wrote his doctoral dissertation at Harvard -- the one his committee rejected because Vern refused to revise it to comply with their recommendations -- it was on a Marxist approach to education. He'd also visited the Soviet Union and, appalled by the poverty he found there, gravely informed me that, "The Soviet Union is no longer a model to be followed."

Vern was the first person I ever met who thought there was anything worthwhile in Marxism. For myself, I knew next to nothing about Marxist theory, nor was I aware of the long tradition of American Marxism, so my response to his statement was simply surprise. I wondered, who could have ever thought the Soviet Union was any sort of model to be followed? Everyone knew the Soviet Union was a bloody-handed dictatorship, which imprisoned and impoverished its people.

Vern often expressed views which surprised me. He was, for instance, a firm advocate of capital punishment and believed in the vengeful Old Testament mandate of an eye for an eye, a tooth for a tooth, and a life for a life. I respected Vern, but the idea of state-mandated killing made me uneasy. Society, I felt, should be more humane than the murderers it judges.

Besides, judicial mistakes are made under even the most flawless legal system -- and our legal system, I believed, was deeply flawed. America has certainly executed innocent men. To this day no one knows who threw the bomb in Chicago's Haymarket in 1887. Convicted of "inspiring" that act, America hanged the Haymarket Martyrs for the crime of expressing dangerous ideas.

And are we sure Sacco and Vanzetti were justly executed? Are we sure Julius and Ethel Rosenberg were justly executed? Someone mistakenly sentenced to life imprisonment can later be exonerated and compensated if developments like DNA testing prove their innocence. But there is no reprieve from death.

Vern made the most amazing statements with the utmost conviction. For example, he thought glasses were a sign of a character weakness, a lack of moral vision manifested in imperfect physical vision.

Nor did he believe in germs and accidents. All illness and "accidents" were moral failings, brought on by the person's imperfect moral character. And, because disease was caused by moral failings, not germs, he scoffed at the warning that one shouldn't eat meat that had been around for days unrefrigerated. It's perfectly OK to eat such meat, he insisted to me.

One day, as we were discussing politics, he told me in complete seriousness that, "Someday, I'll run for president" -- although not, evidently, as the SLP candidate. And I wondered, how can you do that, Vern? Even then I realized that politics is a full-time career and that one had to be involved in it all of one's life to work one's way up to the presidential candidate level. Vern was engaged in no political activity with any organization, he was in his late thirties, and time was running out for him to get involved in the political life.

It also helps to be a millionaire, or the son of a senator or a president. In the 2000 presidential election, the Democratic candidate, Al Gore, was a millionaire Harvard grad and the son of the U.S. Senator from Tennessee. The Republican candidate, George W. Bush, was a millionaire Yale grad and the son of a former President of the United States. If you didn't feel like voting for either of them, you could vote for third-party candidate Ralph Nader -- who was also a millionaire Harvard graduate. The entire election was a Harvard-Yale game!

Yet Vern -- an impoverished Vespa-riding community college teacher living in an empty house on a backwater dirt road -- spoke with the utmost confidence of his presidential plans.

Actually, politics was of only passing interest for Vern. He had long since progressed into an obsessive concern with his spiritual life, and the spiritual lives of others, especially the young, and most especially young males. This was because, he said, some years earlier he'd suffered a heart attack and had died. As his soul was floating toward the light, he realized that his "dharma," his religious mission on earth, was not finished, and so he decided to return to life and lead others to enlightenment. At least his death and rebirth got him jogging and playing tennis with Ruth, his ex-student and new love, which he did on a regular basis.

The enlightenment to which Vern wished to lead the world consisted, he told me, in "doing the right thing, in the right place, at the right time, in the right way in the moment of need. That requires one to say the right thing, make the right gesture, approach people correctly, pray, sit down, make love, eat, even laugh at the right time, in the right way," all of which he was certain he did rightly at all the right times.

I began to recognize elements of all the Eastern religions -- Buddhism, Hinduism, Taoism, even animism. Vern mixed them with Native American rituals and Haitian voodoo practices to form the blurry spiritual amalgam we students called "Vernism." Vernism was what we studied in his religion class, with Vern as the High Priest claiming for himself the mystic powers of the shaman. I watched Vern hypnotize my fellow students and lead them back, back, back through their lives until they regressed into the womb -- and then into former lives. I can't vouch for the reality of these past life experiences, but the hypnotism was real enough. Watching Vern, I also learned how to hypnotize. Vern's demonstrations lent credibility to his more unbelievable claims of shamanistic power, but having done it myself, I know one doesn't have to be a shaman to mesmerize.

Vern also performed classroom rituals with voodoo dolls. The student subjects of such rituals seemed to react in tandem with the dolls, but I attributed their reactions to Vern's power of suggestion more than to the mystic power of voodoo.

He led us in rituals to call forth the elements. "I stood atop Barnes Buttes in Papago Park," Vern said, "and, out of a clear sky, with my mana [mystic power] I conjured up a monsoon rainstorm." When he said this, I had a mental image of Mickey Mouse who, in "The Sorcerer's Apprentice" segment of Walt Disney's *Fantasia*, also conjured up a fierce storm with his magic.

To impress us with his shamanistic powers, Vern took the class out to the nearby Encanto municipal park to perform Hopi rain calling ceremonies. After much chanting and dancing and shaking of gourd rattles by the class, no rain fell. But, the shaman always has a good excuse for why his mojo doesn't work. The reason, Vern said, was because we, his students and would-be acolytes, had questioned his mana and did not have enough faith that rain would be called down from the desert sky above us.

Faith, you see, was the crucial component of Vernism, as it is to all religions, since none of their claims can be proven. You must not question, you must not doubt, you must not use logic, reason, and rationality, you must simply believe, for faith is a way of knowing beyond logic and reason and rationality. "Faith is essential and eternal," he said. "It means the complete membership in that which is our devotion."

And, because faith is an essential and eternal manifestation of the sacred, it should not be denigrated by the likes of Harlem Congressman and minister, the Rev. Adam Clayton Powell, Jr. "Keep the faith, baby!" Powell told his followers, after he was expelled from Congress for corruption. Such phrases trivialize "the deeper reaches of belief," Vern said.

Vern asserted that he was a guru, a spiritual teacher, "an anointer," a mojo man with much mana. But, he said with deep humbleness, "I do not ask for such powers, neither do I prate their importance. Rather, I accept what is to happen. The sea does not bespeak its cause, does not declaim its strength, even in highest crashing tide. Only its beauty. In calm. In riotous waves. In tsunami terror. As it is with me.

"And," he continued, "there is a contrail of 'this person's doings', me, as I go along. Why, I do not know. It has happened many times: I would be driving along an Arizona highway in the middle of nowhere. Then I would stop at a one-tank gas station. Get a Pepsi. Sit. And, lo and behold, within five minutes, there would be five cars pulling in. They would all have a randomly different need: gas, directions, time of day. Why was I the one they sought out?" (No great mystery, I thought. You sat there, sipping a Pepsi, as if you owned the place.)

Thus, Vern avowed, the fact that he was a sought-after guru was not a role he desired or sought. Rather, it was a role the universe gave to him, which he simply accepted. In this, there was an element of the Calvinist concept of "grace," spiritual salvation, which could neither be sought, nor earned, nor even deserved. Rather, "grace" was bestowed upon one by God, and for God's own unknown reasons alone.

So it was with Vern and his mojo. He did not desire to be a shaman, an anointer with mana. He was merely a faithful mendicant, full of faith, who accepted the godhood that was bestowed upon him. In addition to the concept of "grace," there was an aspect of Buddhism here. The first of the Buddha's Four Noble Truths is that "Life is suffering." The cause of such suffering, said the Buddha, is desire.

Therefore, said Vern, we must not desire anything, we must not attempt anything. We must simply have the wisdom to accept faithfully what God bestows upon us. "If I reach," he said, "I am not given. Nothing comes from nothing. But, I wait, and lo, it is delivered. For all is from faith. The expectancy of things to be delivered, when they do not yet exist, is the root of life. *Ex nihilo, nihilo fit* is true, as is, but Faith is not nothing. It is the, *the,* substance of life. You do not have to know what faith is to have it. It is given. The opposite is the demand for objectification -- objects possessed, an image of being known, the 'know how' of a trade, the persona of a politician. Nothing we pursue in this world, just for being pursued, is real. For all is given. We need only be. For it is there. Be ye as the lilies of the field.

"Is the Kingdom of God within, per Tolstoy? Is it beyond, per Zwingli? Or Plato? How about tomorrow, per Marx and Lenin? They all reached. And in their gizzards knew they were empty handed. No. They, too, were mendicants. They, too, cared so profoundly that they opened faith, the doorway to the Infinite.

"Me? I got a gizzard that buzzes. Vibrates all of me. A small way of knowing, along with pissing, which tells me of my Truth, the Truth of Time that flows. That, Heraclitus notwithstanding, I can flow with the rivers which, 'stepping-while never are the same." Nonetheless, I stand tall. Time is not my dimension. I flow in and out. A mathematical torus. I am here and there. Part of what I am not. I need, then I am not here. I do not need, then I am here. Need is no more. Peace. Honest harmony. Bully for the pissers of the world!"

Perhaps we students did not have such similar faith in the efficacy of "pissing" in "honest harmony" with God because Vernism seemed well-nigh impossible for a fallible human being to follow, even if we did understand it. Vernism meant, most importantly of all, being perfect, doing the right thing at the right time in the right way, etc. But such spiritual perfectionism is an impossible nirvana, beyond the grasp of mortal humans. Perfection means being *inhuman*. Indeed, being a little imperfect means being a *lot* human. But, being inhumanly perfect is what Vernism required of the faithful if they wanted to live the spiritual life, as Vern felt he lived it.

A central part of Vern's concept of spiritual perfection and "honest harmony" was emotional invulnerability. "Needing anointment from on high," he told me, "we are so emotionally vulnerable." And a spiritual man, he insisted, should *never* be emotionally vulnerable. Such seeking of "daddy's approval" is, he said, emotionally infantile. Vern's advocacy of emotional invulnerability was a lonely vision, comprised of equal parts Freudian male-oriented separation-from-parents psychology (which he'd studied in graduate school at the University of Minnesota), blue collar machismo, and good ol' American individualism, with an overlay of his eclectic, garbled, and self-serving Vernist spirituality.

A rock bottom basic part of being human is exactly such emotional vulnerability, is needing other people, is needing the respect and approval of others. How can one even love another person without being emotionally vulnerable to that person? If you are invulnerable and that other person can never touch your emotions, how can it truly be said that you love that person? If you have absolutely no need for that other person's love, approval, or appreciation, are you truly in love? Or are you, instead, emotionally stunted? Or, in your heart of hearts which can never be hurt, are you perhaps completely dead? If your heart can never be hurt, do you even have a heart? Or do you have some piece of stone instead where your heart should be?

Psychologist William James said that, "The deepest principle in human nature is the craving to be appreciated." Likewise, in his much maligned classic, *How to Win Friends and Influence People,* Dale Carnegie suggested that we make a habit of expressing *sincere* (not insincere) appreciation for other people, for he recognized the fact that most of us are starving for appreciation, any appreciation at all. In other words, people need people, and those who don't, Aristotle said, "are either beasts or gods."

Vern felt that he did not need the love, approval, or the appreciation of others, nor should any enlightened person. Aristotle would have said that, in that case, since he wasn't a beast of the fields, Vern must have been a god.

And so Vern believed, for he was convinced that he was an avatar, a being which, in Hinduism, is the human incarnation of a god. And part of being an avatar, at least in Vernism, meant being completely alone, independent of all others, emotionally invulnerable, dependent upon no one for love, appreciation, approval, support, or understanding which, in any case, would not be forthcoming.

Thus, his was a philosophy of disappointment, for the fact that love and approval and appreciation would not be forthcoming was, he said, absolutely inevitable. "And so," he asked, "what if we do not get that approval and appreciation? What if the pebble drops into the well and no sound returns, what then?"

What then was to not need the love, approval and appreciation of other people, especially one's parents, in the first place. "Instead," he said, "our maturity, and strength therewith, lies in our being Father and Mother to our selves. Impossible, you say. Yet necessary. For that is precisely the genesis of the gods...and we must become as the gods, thereby attaining true maturity and the clarity of light a spiritual life requires. We must repose ourselves in acceptance beyond authorization. And therefore beyond recognition. In this we join the mystery of Truth; and being part of Truth we become the Truth Mysterious.

"None of this is mystigogical," he insisted, "it is simple."

It was our own fault, then, if we did not comprehend the simple teachings of the Truth Mysterious incarnate before us.

One day in class an incredulous student asked a question for us all. "Are you for real? Or are you just some kind of faker bullshitting us with all this mumbo-jumbo?"

We waited expectantly for Vern's answer. He paused for a moment. "The question is insufficient," he finally said, "for the answer will not bring you the reassurance you seek. The answer will be the same, regardless of who I am. If I am the real deal, then, of course, I will tell you that I speak the truth. And if I am a faker, then, of course, I will tell you that I speak the truth. Instead of asking me if I am for real, you must, yourself, out of the wisdom of your own soul, decide whether or not I speak the truth."

Poor Annie. How could any child flourish with such a perfectionist mystic mojo man as a father? No mere mortal could ever live up to Vern's standards of perfect right action and emotional isolation from others. But, she and her siblings not only had to live up to such inhuman and emotionally frigid standards of perfection, she also had to first understand, "out of the wisdom of her own soul," what the hell Vern was talking about. And, if she did not, that was yet another sign of her failure to attain the spiritual life's "clarity of light," for none of what Vern said was "mystigogical," he insisted. "It is simple."

Annie also had the spiritual handicap of being born female, for women occupied a subservient status in Vernism. Vernism was completely a male religion, a religion of the patriarchs, in which men occupied the privileged position of power. Vern disdained homosexuals because, he said, they had denied their manhood, and thus their godhood, and their privileged positions of power. They were, therefore, relegated to the inferior status of women in his spiritual hierarchy because, he said, they had decided to "become" women. Therefore, they could never be the patriarchs that real men were born to be.

I never told Vern he was living in the home of a homosexual, the home of the Forty-Niner who'd tried to seduce me years before when I was his paperboy. Perhaps the Forty-Niner engaged in debased sexual perversions in Vern's very own bedroom, right where Vern's desk with the blue portable electric Smith-Corona sat. The idea would have alarmed Vern and he'd have immediately moved out lest his soul become contaminated by proximity.

As privileged patriarchs-to-be, Vern took his sons, Tony and Victor, off into the desert at puberty to induct them into Vernistic "manhood" in secret masculine rites of passage. These mystic rituals involved blood-mingling from mutual cuts and were meant to bond young and old males together, and what transpired in them could never be revealed to any woman, not to their sisters, not to their mother, not to their future wives. This was because, in Vernism, men were on top, women on the bottom, and the two worlds should never meet in the spiritual realm, the male realm, which was the only "real" realm.

But perhaps living up to Vern's perfectionist standards was impossible, even for his sons. Tony ran as far away from Vern's world as he could and became an auto mechanic in Virginia. And Victor, Vern's youngest son, eventually put a shotgun under his chin and blew his head off. In their own ways, both rejected Vern's passage into the patriarchy.

Meanwhile, there were no similar female rites of passage to be performed for the avatar's women, his daughters, when they came of age at puberty. There was no need for them, for only men could be fully spiritual, fully human. Thus, if Annie accepted the spiritual values taught by her father, she had to also accept the subordinate role those values entailed.

Part of being subordinate meant, Vern said, that women had to be kept always emotionally off balance so they could never take you, the man, the master, for granted. They must always be kept in limbo about the relationship, so that they would always be seeking to please you. They must always be kept seeking the love, approval, and appreciation that a spiritual person -- i.e., a man -- did not require.

For instance, one day we were talking in his living room and, unbidden, Ruth brought him a cup of his favorite tea. Vern thanked her, but did not immediately drink it. Instead, he very deliberately -- perhaps, I thought, it was a "right" action at the "right" moment, in "honest harmony" with God -- sat it down on the floor beside his chair, and then seemed to forget it.

After Ruth returned to the kitchen, Vern instructed me in manly action by telling me that his act had been conscious and purposeful, it had been a spiritually "right act." A man, he said, should never let his woman think that she completely knows his desires and needs. Women had to be kept constantly guessing about their men. And that was why he did not immediately drink the tea Ruth brought him. In actions like this he thus deliberately guaranteed that Ruth (or Annie) would never obtain from him the unconditional approval and appreciation Vernism taught would never be forthcoming to anyone, in any case. For Ruth, for Annie, and all other women in Vern's life, it was a self-fulfilling prophecy. They never received Vern's unconditional approval.

Before I met him, Vern had created a one-man entity to further his projects which he awkwardly entitled the "Greatest Of-all Design." According to him, the Greatest Of-all Design (the initials for which, in his reading, spelled G.O.D.), the Master Plan of the Universe, was "to be a Man," by which he meant the spiritually enlightened mendicant he claimed to be.

But, if God's Master Plan for us, avataric godhood, meant becoming "a Man," what role was there in Vernism for women? What was a *woman's* Great Design? Women were precluded from the manhood rites, precluded from becoming men, precluded, therefore, from attaining perfect spiritual lives. What, then, was their nirvana? To anxiously wait upon their men, seeking the approval which never came?

On another day, Vern told me that Annie had the voluptuous body of a woman meant by God to have many children. Was that Annie's role in Vernism, I wondered? To be, like Ruth, the man's helpmeet, cheerleader and the bearer of the man's children? To me, this just sounded like traditional patriarchy. No wonder Harriet, Vern's discarded wife, observed that Vern had left one of the words out of his Greatest Of-all Design acronym. It does not spell "GOD," she said. It spells "GOAD." Vern, Annie told me, was angered by Harriet's observation.

My feeling that Vern was a stereotypical patriarch who was blind to the sexism of his personal religion appeared to be confirmed one day when he and Annie happened to discuss Betty Friedan's 1963 feminist classic, *The Feminine Mystique*. Friedan argued that, in 1950s America, there existed a female "problem that had no name," but which all suburban housewives experienced. This was society's expectation that they should be simply housewives, mothers, and ancillary helpmeets to their husbands, with no aspirations of their own beyond these roles. This social expectation, Friedan said, was "the feminine mystique."

Vern asked Annie if she agreed that such a "feminine mystique" existed. "Of course," Annie answered. "We all feel it."

Vern scoffed. "It doesn't exist. It's just cultural obfuscation by a false prophet."

It was clear to me, however, that the feminine mystique *did* exist, that everything Vern preached reinforced that very mystique.

And finally, when you really understood what Vern preached, you also realized that the perfectionism he advocated was a level of "spiritual clarity" that even he, avatar that he was, could not attain. Like so many prophets, if you pointed out that he had fallen short of his own standards, he not only refused to acknowledge it, he then said you were morally petty and spiritually fallen to have even made such an observation.

For example, for all his avowals of his emotional invulnerability and his mystic powers, it seems his soul, unlike his emotions, was not invulnerable and impervious to the actions of others. His soul -- indeed, everyone's soul -- was an extremely fragile entity, constantly being damaged by the immoral "un-right" actions of others.

Thus, he told me that "It diminishes one's soul to be occluded from another's memory." But when I fought Nick Nolte that semester in his classroom -- I'll tell you about that -- he not only later had trouble remembering the particulars of the event, but he also completely forgot that Annie, his daughter, was present in class at the time, sitting right next to me, and witnessed the whole affair. Did the avatar's occluded memory therefore diminish his daughter's soul?

When I pointed out to him that he'd forgotten that Annie was there that day, which Annie also confirmed to him, his only reaction was an angry, "Is it your habit to stick it to someone? One upmanship is a sign of what?"

No doubt it was a sign of my moral imperfection, unlike his diminution of Annie's soul by occluding her from his memory. Vern was a verbal genius at deflecting any criticism of himself into yet more evidence of the imperfect spirituality of his accuser.

It seemed to me there was also yet another way in which the avatar was less than spiritually perfect. I asked him how a Harvard-trained and tenured ASU professor had come to teach at a lowly community college.

"My life flow had been dammed," he said. "I was young, impatient, and uptight. I did not want to merely make a difference, I wanted to change the world. I shuddered daily as I heard and read of our leaders thinking the unthinkable -- entering an atomic war. I felt drained listening to the drones of my fellow committee members. I took a sabbatical; then I took a position at Phoenix College."

No, I thought to myself, Annie has already told me the truth. ASU fired you because a janitor caught you fucking Ruth, your student, in your office one night. It seemed the pissing avatar who was the incarnation of the "Truth Mysterious" had difficulty telling the truth when it came to his personal life.

No doubt I further diminished his already diminished soul by even noticing how far Vern had strayed from the "Truth Mysterious."

Vision Quest

As far as I could see the lights of Phoenix were spread out below me like a vast bed of glowing embers. I sat alone, cross-legged and nude, on a rough boulder at the very peak of the camel's hump. Nightfall had brought a chill, but the rock beneath me still retained some of the heat from the day's fierce sun. I was grateful for that.

The rain began to fall. Then came the wind. I shivered as the storm swept in from the desert. I made no move to find my clothes which were stashed somewhere on the mountain peak. I let the cold and the rain pour over my nude body as I sat in the Lotus Position high above Phoenix. This is good, I thought. This is the way it's supposed to be.

I thought of all the many thousands of Phoenicians going about their myriad ways in the city below, unaware that I was sitting above them in the rain. But I was sitting on top of Camelback Mountain in the middle of the storm for only one of them. I was there for Annie.

****

Annie's Vernistic mysticism was hard for me to accept. It violated everything I believed. All my life I'd fought a long lonely battle against the religious superstition in which I was raised. I disdained the hypocritical mumbo-jumbo of my traditional religious upbringing. Only reason and science, I felt, could explain the mysteries of existence.

But Annie, like her father, saw the world, the universe, existence itself, quite differently. For her, logic and rationality were not the gateways to understanding they had always been for me. For her, there was some nebulous higher spiritual plane which was the true reality. Thus, this intangible spiritual realm was far more important to her than tangible reality could ever be.

And the hippies, who I was hearing about more and more, agreed with her and Vern. The hippies also rejected rationalism and were always prattling on about energy focal points like Stonehenge, about mystic crystals, about Native American shamans, mandalas, and Atlantis. All of these were mixed up in a heady woo-woo brew which proclaimed that we were entering a new "Aquarian Age" in which peace, love, and understanding would reign supreme over the forces of darkness, evil, and the military madness which seemed, "deceptively," triumphant all around us. "Just chant 'Om,' everybody, and we'll levitate the Pentagon!"

Much about the emerging hippie movement attracted me. Its revolt against traditional social constraints and its "do your own thing" ethos appealed to my anarcho-libertarian sensibilities. I'd never been a social conservative and I'd always believed in absolute individual liberty. I'd always been against "the Establishment." So I began to grow my hair long and I began to look like a hippie and I considered myself a hippie. But there was always some distance between me and hippies in general.

When I was in the church there had been a saying we used to express our attitude toward the spiritual corruption in which we were immersed. We were "*in* the world, but not *of* the world." Physically, we were necessarily *in* the corrupt material world, but we were not *of* that world, for our values were different.

Likewise with the hippies. I was increasingly *in* the hippie world, but I was not *of* the hippie world. There were important elements of hippiedom I could never accept. Too often "do your own thing" did not mean genuine personal eccentricity. It meant wearing the scruffy hippie uniform and acting "different" in exactly the same way as all the other hippie clones.

It also meant pledging allegiance to New Age mysticism. Being a Vernist, Annie didn't recite all of the New Age mantras, but she preached enough of them. I was just as skeptical of New Age mysticism, with its shamans and crystals, as I was of the Ol' Timey Religion, with its Holy Ghosts and glow-in-the-dark crucifixes. Both seemed equally irrational. I did not believe in astrology, crystals, mandalas, pyramids of power, the mystic wisdom of the ancient Egyptian pyramids, or the cryptic teachings of Carlos Castenada's Don Juan. I did not believe in geographic sacred sites, Erich von Daniken's chariots of the gods, reincarnation, visions, vibes, cosmic consciousness, Donovan's Atlantis, Hindu karma, John Lennon's Instant Karma, or the Dawning of the Age of Aquarius. It was all just old wine in new bottles, more superstitious nonsense dressed in granny dresses and love beads. New Age gurus like Timothy Leary and Baba Ram Dass were as bogus as Baptist preachers like Billy Sunday and Billy Graham. At a very basic level, I could no more be a comfortable denizen of hippiedom than I could be a happy and mindless believer of my mother's traditional religious worldview. Psychedelic cosmic consciousness was just another kind of anti-intellectualism, as was Vernism.

But I loved Annie, so I bit my tongue and listened respectfully as she and Vern preached incessantly and tirelessly about living the "right" spiritual life.

Besides, perhaps they knew something I didn't know. I knew Christianity and all organized religions were the sources of most human evils. But perhaps I was overreacting. Perhaps my revulsion toward the stupidity, cruelty, and hypocrisy of institutional Christianity was blinding me to a larger spiritual truth. Perhaps all organized religions -- Christianity, Judaism, Islam, Hinduism, Buddhism -- were merely flawed attempts to access and express a transcendent reality. Indeed, hippies were flirting with exotic Eastern religions for exactly that reason. Perhaps these various religions were all avenues to the same universal cosmic truth. It seemed possible.

Which is why I was sitting in the nude in the midst of a storm on top of Camelback Mountain. It was my "vision quest." Among the American Indians of old, the young men were sent into the wilderness on a vision quest when they came of age. The purpose was to undergo privations in order to become receptive to a vision from the Great Spirit. Each such vision was a personal vision, unique to each seeker. The vision not only revealed the true and hidden nature of the seeker, but also gave the seeker his appropriate adult name. It was in such a vision, for example, that Crazy Horse got his name.

Although the Indians used the wilderness experience to find their personal visions, mystics had sometimes also used hallucinogenic drugs to bring on visions. The Christian Mexican Penitentes of New Mexico, for example, used peyote in their rituals. Aldous Huxley had done much the same. His 1954 book, *The Doors of Perception,* described how he'd experimented with mescalin as a means of reaching a higher state of consciousness.

And certainly a lot of hippies were having visions on their acid trips. Even Timothy Leary, the newly notorious LSD guru, had started something he called the "League for Spiritual Discovery," which used lysergic acid to open devotees to the spiritual realm of cosmic consciousness. "Turn on, tune in, and drop out," he advised. At least in the beginning, "mind expanding" drugs and New Age mysticism went hand-in-hand. Drugs were supposed to be the superhighway to expanded consciousness.

I believed in trying to "expand one's consciousness," but I wasn't going to turn on in order to tune in. This was because drugs were another important identifying element of hippiedom I did not accept. It wasn't a morality issue and had nothing to do with my Baptist and Mormon upbringing, although it was certainly compatible with that upbringing. It was an intelligence issue. Tobacco and alcohol, the most dangerous drugs in America, were organic poisons. Deliberately poisoning oneself with them had always seemed stupid to me. It was a form of slow suicide. And it was even more stupid to *pay* to kill yourself. And just because hippies were now raving about the awesome visions acid brought them didn't make drug use seem any more intelligent.

But, there was a road to spiritual enlightenment other than drugs, perhaps an even more ancient one. This was asceticism, which hermits and flagellants had practiced since before the time of Christ. In fact, though they used peyote, the Penitentes also flagellated themselves, whipping themselves with cactus spine whips until the flesh was flensed from their bare backs. And they also literally nailed a Chosen One from amongst themselves to a cross in imitation of the Passion of the Christ. All of this contributed to either a hallucinatory or a spiritual vision, depending on your point of view. I was willing to accept that such visions might be authentic.

I wasn't about to pound nails into my palms or whip my back raw in search of a spiritual experience. But I was willing to endure some amount of pain and deprivation if it might alter my consciousness and make me more receptive to a spiritual vision. From what I'd read, since time immemorial mystics had always gone to mountain tops for their visions. Camelback Mountain, therefore, seemed the ideal place of self-torture.

Camelback is a desolate 1,200-foot high mountain dominating the north-eastern border of Phoenix, with the entire metropolis at its base. On the far side of it is the appropriately named Paradise Valley, home of the very rich. Republican U.S. Senator Barry Goldwater lived there.

Camelback got its name from the simple fact that it looks exactly like a resting single-humped camel. Unlike constellation patterns in the night time sky, it requires no stretch of the imagination at all to see this camel. It is no Rorschach test nor a nebulous cloud image. The camel is right before your eyes. Its head faces west, a long neck climbs to a tall peak, which is its hump, and its rump is to the east. No matter where you are in Phoenix, you can see the camel. And, because it is exactly on a west-east axis, you can never get lost in Phoenix. You always know the four directions just by looking at the mountain which dominates the north.

I'd climbed Camelback many times when I was younger. The lower stretches of the mountain have typical cactus and desert shrub. These thin out as one climbs until there is just bare desert rock at the small apex of the hump. And from this hump there is a dramatic view of the entire urban grid below. You can see Phoenix all the way to the horizon.

So, I arose at dawn and took my brother Rick with me on my blue Suzuki 90cc motorcycle out to the camel's rump. I'd gotten the Suzuki by coordinating the first computerized dating program at Arizona State. I'd seen an ad in the *State Press*, the ASU student newspaper, asking for someone to be the field rep for the program. I was still attending Phoenix College, but one didn't have to be an ASU student to run the program. All it entailed was putting flyers and information forms under the windshields of all the gazillion cars in the ASU student parking lots. I also put up holders with the forms on every campus bulletin board. For extra coverage, I also did this at Phoenix College.

I then rented a mail box at the Tempe post office, because the people who organized the operation at colleges across the nation wanted it to appear to be local. Why, I don't know. Interested students filled out the forms and mailed them to the local mail box. I collected the forms at my Tempe post office box and forwarded them to an out-of-state center. Programmers there ran the forms through a computer and matched up male and female respondents based on their interests. They then sent every respondent a list of possible dates. As it happened, two people I knew separately at Phoenix College actually hooked up with each other in this fashion. So, they got each other...and I got enough money to buy my Suzuki.

The border between Phoenix and Scottsdale in my old neighborhood is 56th Street, which also runs straight as an arrow north into the side of the camel's hump. But I was familiar enough with Camelback to know that it was easier to climb to the hump from the rump than to attempt a frontal assault straight up the side, so that's where I headed with Rick.

Once we reached the camel's rump I handed Rick the Suzuki's key. He thought my plan was pretty damn weird, but he didn't care. I was letting him ride my bike anywhere he wanted for a day and a night, so long as he didn't wreck it and was waiting for me when I came down. He gave me a shit eating grin and roared off on my Suzuki.

Then I began climbing. It was hot and it was tiring. I hadn't eaten breakfast and I'd brought neither trail mix nor water. Nutritional deprivation would be a good thing, I decided, as it'd put more strain on my body. I welcomed my hunger and my thirst. My low blood sugar levels meant it was all that much harder to slog my way up the mountain. But, that's good, I thought, as I panted and climbed.

Night was falling by the time I reached the top of the camel's hump, but there was still some lingering light. I stripped off my boots and all my clothes and stashed them in a hollow formed by two rocks. Stripping off such raiments of civilization went with the physical isolation from civilization. I needed to make it physically hard on myself to prove myself worthy of a vision. I walked around the peak, the rocks digging into my tender soles, in full view of the city below. I didn't care if anyone down there saw me bare-assed naked.

The sunset was beautiful. Urban pollution was already a problem in Phoenix and the smoggy haze gilded the fading light with a luminous glow. A good beginning, to a long dark night of the soul. As the twilight settled in, the lights of Phoenix came on and brightened beneath me. I found a prominent boulder, jutting up like a throne, and climbed on top of it. The Christian Syrian ascetic Saint Simeon Stylites, who died at about age 70 in 459 A.D., spent the last 30 years of his life sitting on top of a pillar -- *stylos* in Greek -- about 60 feet high. I could sit on this boulder in a similar fashion for at least one night.

And then, in the distance, I saw the flash of lightning. And then, a few seconds later, I heard the thunder come rolling in. One of those monster desert monsoons was sweeping in toward Phoenix. My first impulse was to seek shelter. My boots and clothes were somewhere, perhaps I could find them. But I'd brought no flashlight and there was no way I could stumble down the side of the mountain in the darkness. It was too dangerous. I was stranded on Camelback as the storm came on.

Then I thought, this is good! In fact, this is perfect! Now it's going to be an even greater trial by ordeal than I'd planned. Maybe this is some kind of mystic coincidence. Maybe this was *meant* to happen, to test me, to see if I'm worthy of a vision. I decided to sit out the storm and thus find my personal vision.

Then the storm front hit me. I shivered in the cold rain and the strain of sitting in the Lotus Position became more and more painful. As exhaustion pulled me down, I slowly curled over, still cross-legged, until my forehead rested on my ankles, arms limp at my sides. The rain speared down on my naked back. This was how ancient societies killed off unwanted baby girls. They exposed them to the elements. Perhaps, I thought, I'll catch pneumonia from hypothermia.

Or I'll be struck by lightning. I was on a boulder on top of Camelback Mountain. I was higher than the mountain! I was higher than anything in Phoenix! Lightning is bound to strike me first, because my body is the highest thing in the vicinity. This is completely insane.

But that's good, I instantly reminded myself. The spiritual *is* irrational! It's not *supposed* to make sense! This is good. And that became my mantra, which I repeated over and over, hypnotizing myself into oblivion to shut out the storm.

Humbly and patiently, as a faithful mendicant endlessly repeating "This is good, this is good!" I awaited the personal vision the universe would bestow upon me.

The storm lashed me for hours.

Finally, like the grace of God, my vision came to me. I was granted hard-earned esoteric knowledge. Exhausted, with the storm still raging around me, I faded into the nothingness of blessed sleep.

I awoke before dawn. I was still sitting cross-legged, forehead on my ankles, and my legs were asleep from nerve compression and the loss of blood circulation. I yelled in pain as I uncrossed my crossed legs and rolled over and then rolled off the boulder. I lay on the ground where I fell, trying not to move even microscopically, as the pins and needles of returning circulation slowly subsided. As they receded, I massaged my legs to help the circulation.

Light gathered strength with the returning dawn. The desert mountain side smelled fresh from the storm. A desert wren chirped loudly from a nearby rock to greet the morning sun. Even Phoenix, below me, seemed to be washed clean of its pollution. All was right with the world.

Eventually, I was able to stand. I found my boots and clothes, damp from the night's rain. I dressed and started down the mountain. My clothes dried as I descended and the sun climbed.

To my mild surprise, Rick was waiting for me when I finally reached our rendezvous. And, even more surprising, he hadn't wrecked my Suzuki.

He smirked when I reached him. "Did you find your vision?"

I took my Suzuki key from him. "Yes, I found my vision."

"And what cosmic wisdom did you learn, O, Enlightened One?"

"I learned that only a Goddamned fool spends the night nude on a mountain top in the middle of an Arizona storm."

Final Exam

Nick Nolte gave me the finger. "Why don't you suck on this?"

I bolted out of my seat and advanced on him, glowering, fists clenched. He did the same. Vern moved to intervene. As the three of us met in the middle of the room, it exploded. Male students poured out of their seats to join the fray. What was meant to be a minor altercation between me and Nick turned into a general melee. Blows landed indiscriminately, mostly on me. People grabbed my arms, Nick's arms, pulling us apart. Someone kicked Vern in the balls, and he doubled over. One rabid bystander began jumping around outside the ball of confusion screaming, "Lynch him! Lynch him!" The girls sat transfixed in their seats, staring with horror at the swirling mass of flailing bodies. Some ran from the room.

Eventually the students pulled Nick and me apart. We stood glowering at each other. Things began to cool down. The madness passed. Eyes turned to Vern.

Calmly, Vern said to the class, "This was your final exam."

****

It was April of 1966 and Vern had chosen me as his fight collaborator because I had black hair and he thought I looked like a stereotypical street punk. I would be a believable troublemaker. He chose Nick as the good guy because Nick was the local Golden Boy. He looked the part. He had been a football player and was 6'1," over 200 lbs., and had beautiful blond hair. Everyone felt he belonged in Hollywood. Eventually, he did go to Hollywood and became an Oscar nominated millionaire actor.

Because he looked the part, Nick was typecast as Biff in the school's production of "Death of a Salesman." But, Nick was far more than Biff. Already in his early thirties, he was older than the rest of us, old enough to have absorbed some lingering Beatnik hipness. Nick was born and raised in Omaha, but he'd bummed around a lot, had a lot of jobs, taken classes at a lot of schools here and there. Now he was a fellow student in Vern's religion course at Phoenix College. He exuded an air of cool detachment, listening, soaking things up, evaluating them. Perhaps that, along with his looks, was why Nick was cast as King Creon in the local professional theater company's modern dress production of "Antigone."

Sophocles wrote "Antigone" almost 2,500 years ago, probably in 441 B.C. The action takes place in the chaotic aftermath of the Theban civil war. It'd been a vicious war of succession between Eteocles and Polyneices, the sons of King Oedipus and Queen Jocasta. Brother had slaughtered brother. As Antigone says to her sister, "We were two sisters of two brothers robbed/ Killed on one day each by the other's hand." Eteocles and Polyneices had killed each other in single combat. The wounds to the body politic remained deep. Because hands had been drenched in fraternal blood, the hatreds smoldered, ready to re-ignite in an instant.

Out of the chaos and confusion emerges Creon, a strong man with an iron fist, to become the new king. He is determined to bring an end to the bloodshed and peace to Thebes. To demonstrate that he will not tolerate further violence, from any side, Creon orders that all slain combatants will remain where they had fallen on the field of battle. They will not have the honor of proper burial, but will become a feast for vultures and carrion crows. The souls of the slain will wander in the afterlife forever, never to find peace. Any *new* disturber of the peace will pay the same price.

Antigone defies Creon's edict. In Greek thought, it is clear that she has an absolute family obligation to bury her brothers. In the night she goes out to the battlefield to gather up and bury the bloody corpse of Polyneices, her most beloved brother, left where he had fallen, and is caught. Brought before King Creon, he tells her why Polyneices must remain a feast for the crows. And Antigone tells him why she must bury Polyneices, come what may. Even so, Creon warns her, upon pain of death, not to attempt the burial of her brother again. He then releases her.

Antigone, fully aware it means her death, returns to the battlefield to bury her slain brother, is captured again, and by King Creon orders buried alive. Antigone, knowing this fate awaited her, chose to act as her conscience dictated.

Sophocles presents a clash of political pragmatism and unalterable moral principle. Antigone lives in a world of moral absolutes and nothing can dissuade her from doing the right thing; audience sympathies are on Antigone's side, but it is not clear that the sympathies of Sophocles are on her side. Sophocles' complex Creon understands and sympathizes with Antigone's reasons burying her dead brother. But Antigone does not understand the conscience of the king, nor Creon's responsibility to the greater good. Because of this clash of rival principles, both Antigone and Creon are doomed to bring about tragedy. In the end, Creon emerges just as much the hero as Antigone. And it remains for the audience to determine who is ultimately right.

In the lobby after the play, women had crowded around Nick, still magnificent in King Creon's tuxedo. His blonde head towered over them as he soaked happily in the sea of female adulation. It was clear to me where the sympathies of the female audience members resided.

It was natural that Vern would cast Nick as his defender in the upcoming "Final Exam" of the philosophy course. Before class time, the three of us met in the empty classroom next door and rehearsed. I was to let Vern begin and make his main point before I began interrupting, asking rudely for clarification of his always nebulous thoughts. Nick would then tell me to shut up and let the professor talk. This would lead to words between me and Nick, culminating in an exchange of blows. We rehearsed the fight scene, planning how to throw real-seeming punches which never landed. Crouch over, fist to the solar plexus, check it before the blow, the recipient reacting as if hit. Audience expectation does the rest.

And then to class.

The chairs were arranged in the usual circle, leaving an open space in the center. That would be the arena of my and Nick's combat. Vern stood calmly before his desk waiting for the students to settle into their seats. Then he began.

"I was riding on a Greyhound bus from Los Angeles to Phoenix," he said. "It's a long ride, as those of you who have taken it know. It's 500 miles and takes about ten hours or more. Night came and, as the bus droned on into the dark empty desert, people settled into their seats.

"In the metal luggage rack overhead, there was a loose marble. And, because of the way people had piled in their luggage, there was a free aisle all the way down the length of the luggage rack. As the bus rocked and swayed on the highway, this marble rolled noisily all the way down the rack, from the front to the back, and then from the back to the front. And it went on like this, mile after mile after mile. It was not a soft sound, the marble made. It bounced and banged as it rolled down the rack, from the front to the back, and then back again.

"And around me people tried to sleep. They were restless. They turned this way and that in their seats. But, above the hum of the bus tires on the highway, there was the noise of this marble, filling the entire interior of the dark quite bus with its rolling. And, as the bus rolled on through the night, the marble also rolled on inside the bus.

"And I waited to see what would happen. I wondered how long it would be before someone put an end to the problem which vexed us all; before someone could take the noise and the irritation no longer; how long before someone stood up and captured the marble as it rolled past in order to stop its horrible noise.

"No one did. The bus rolled on through the night, and the marble rolled on through the bus, and none of those who heard it ever stopped it.

"Every time the marble rolled down the long length of the luggage rack, I said to myself, 'There goes another Jew into the ovens. People saw. People knew. But no one did a thing to stop the burning of the Jews.'"

I interrupted. "And did *you* stop the marble?"

Vern smiled at me patiently. "Yes, I finally stood up and stopped the marble and put it in my pocket. I'd learned what I wanted to learn."

"And what did you learn, professor?"

"I learned that, when faced with something that is wrong, most people will do nothing to stop it. Most people will just let it be. And that is the final ethical question each of us must face in the end, isn't it? When you *know* something is wrong, what do you do about it? Do you do the right thing, regardless of consequences? Or do you do the easy thing, which is to do nothing?"

"And which do you suggest, professor?"

Nick butted in. "Will you just shut up and let the professor talk."

I glared at Nick. "You know, Pretty Boy, I've had a semester full of you and I'm getting pretty damn tired of you. Why don't you just shut the fuck up and let me ask my questions?"

That's when Nick gave me the finger. "Why don't you suck on this?"

And that's when I advanced on Nick. He rose from his seat to meet me in the circular arena of the desks and the class erupted.

As passions cooled, students slowly returned to their seats. Others returned from the hallway where they'd sought safety. Eyes turned to Vern, leaning silently against his desk at the front of the room, bent slightly over, as if he'd been hit in the fracas.

Finally, he straightened up and spoke. "This was your final exam. Nick and Eric were not really angry with each other, nor really fighting with each other. The three of us staged everything. The point was to create a crisis. To create something which was obviously very wrong.

"And the test was a test of your own reaction, in the moment of crisis, to something which was very wrong. You must now ask yourself, 'What did I do?' Some of you ran away. Some of you sat and watched. Some of you tried to stop the fight. Some of you began beating up on Eric. One of you wanted to lynch him. Some of you came to help me when you saw I was injured. What did *you* do when you saw something was wrong? It is an ethical question. It is a sacred question. It is the only question.

"That was the Final Exam of this course. Think about what happened in this class today, and how you reacted to it. As far as the administration is concerned, everyone gets an 'A.' But you have to decide for yourself the grade you think you really deserve, in this course and in your life. What did *you* do about the rolling marble which confronted you today in class?"

And what did Nick Nolte do about the rolling marble? Nick was convicted of counterfeiting draft cards with fake deferment classifications and was sentenced to five years probation.

Rite of Passage

Besides the mattresses tossed on the floor on which Annie and Vern slept in their respective bedrooms, and the desk which held Vern's blue Smith-Corona portable electric, the only furniture in Vern's entire house at 1849 was in the living room. This comprised a low Japanese bamboo table coming up to shin level and four low bamboo chairs grouped around the table. These chairs were so low that one almost collapsed into them and, once down, one's butt was only millimeters above the painted cement floor. It was a struggle getting up out of them. You had to scoot forward so that you were almost squatting, and then stand straight up. Either that or roll over to put your hands on the floor beside the chair with your butt in the air and then straighten up. This was ungainly and unattractive, so it was better to squat first, then stand up.

One day toward twilight the three of us, me, Annie, and Vern, were squatting in these low Japanese bamboo chairs sipping tea. Annie had prepared it, so I knew that the cups were clean and the tea free of roach debris. Vern was preaching about something, as he always was, and kept using the word "organic" in a way I'd never heard.

"Let me stop you one moment," I said. "I know what the word 'organic' means when talking about a chair made out of bamboo." I tapped the arm of the chair in which I was sitting. "It means something is related to or derived from a living organism, a plant or an animal. But you keep using the word in a way that can't possibly mean that. What do you mean when you use 'organic' the way you do?"

Vern placed his teacup deliberately on the Japanese bamboo table between us. "When I use the word 'organic' in the sense I'm using it, I mean that something is an integral element of a whole and arises out of that whole smoothly, as if growing from it naturally."

"Ah. I understand. A natural development or evolution."

"Exactly."

Just then there was a loud *bam, bam, bam!* on the screen door and I jerked, spilling some of my tea. Then I heard my mother's voice, her familiar screech reverberating throughout the empty hollow house. "Eric! You come out of there right now! You hear me? Come out of there right now!"

All three of us rushed to the screen door on the porch, me in the lead. Mom was standing outside the door, kicking it and banging on it with her fist, *bam, bam, bam!* Her face was contorted with rage. At the end of the driveway I saw Mom's friend Mary Goldenkoff sitting in her car with the engine running. Mom saw me coming and screamed at me through the screen, "You come home with me right this instant, you hear?"

I stood just inside the screen door. "Mom, what are you doing?"

"I'm bringing you home, right this instant, you come out of that house!"

Vern stood well back, in the living room, letting me handle this. It was *my* crisis, not his. Annie was to my right and just behind me. Both of them were waiting expectantly to see what I would do. Both of them, I knew, saw this as my personal final exam in Freudian male-separation-from-parent maturation, overlaid with Vernism. I resented their expectations of me, but I was also tired of Mom's neverending anger toward me. I was tired of her neverending screaming.

An image flashed through my mind of me, years before as a boy, standing at this very same screen door, looking out. The Forty-Niner had his hands on my shoulders, massaging them. "I have to get home to my mother," I told him. "She's expecting me. I have to go." And I hurried out of this house and back to my mother's house. And it was what happened *that* night, I realized, which had, *organically,* brought about *this* night.

But I was not going to hurry out of this house and hurry back to my mother's house this time. I was no longer that little boy. And so I said, "No, Mom, I'm *not* coming home with you. I'll come home when I *want* to come home, not before. We're going to stop all this right now."

Mom kicked the screen door as hard as she could, *bam!* "I'm not going to stop *anything!* You're going to come out of that house and come home with me *right now!"*

"No, I'm not. And I want you to stop screaming and I want you to leave."

"I'm not going home until you come home with me!"

"Mom, why are you doing this? Go home."

Mom kicked Vern's door again, *bam!* "I told you, I'm not leaving here without you."

Standing there, with Annie beside me, Vern behind me, Mom raging in front of me, it felt as if things had suddenly become much larger than just whether or not I'd go home with Mom that instant. It felt as if I were at a crossroads, a fundamental point in my life when it was one or the other. It was either Annie or Mom, I had to make a choice. If I went with Mom, screaming and banging on Vern's door in front of me, then it would mean turning my back on Annie, leaving her. It would mean remaining a little boy, Mom's little boy, going home with her, instead of becoming a man with a woman by his side.

And if I stayed there, at that moment, with Annie by my side, it felt as if I were saying good-bye to Mom, good-bye to my childhood, good-bye to my entire life up to that moment. I felt I was being torn in two. It was either one or the other. It was my sudden bar mitzvah. But would I become a man, or would I remain a boy?

It was clear to me, however, who I loved, and it was clear to me what I had to say, no matter how much it hurt. "Mom, you *are* leaving here without me, right now, because I'm *not* coming home with you, now or at any time in the future. *I'm never coming home again!"*

Mom let out a long quavering wail and began to spin around and around, screaming all the while, like she'd suddenly lost her mind. "I can't stand it any more!" she screeched, tearing at her hair, "I can't stand it any more!"

Mary came up behind her and put her hands on Mom's shoulders. "Kathy. Get in the car, c'mon, get in the car." Mary led Mom, screaming and thrashing all the way, down the driveway and stuffed her, still struggling and screaming, into the passenger side of her car. I opened the screen door and walked toward the road, Annie behind me. Vern stayed in the house, silently watching it all.

As I reached the end of the driveway, Mary began to drive away. Suddenly, the passenger side door flew open and Mom threw herself, screeching and flailing, out onto the dirt road. Instantly she was up and running down the road toward McDowell. "I can't take it any more!" she continued screaming. "I'm going to throw myself in front of a car and end it all right now! I can't take it any more!"

Mary had slammed on her brakes as soon as Mom fell out of the car. Now she jumped out and ran after Mom, chasing her up the road toward McDowell. "Kathy! Get back in the car! Get back in the car!"

Tears began to trickle down my cheeks as I watched Mom run screaming up the road, threatening to kill herself, with Mary in pursuit. I didn't understand why Mom was doing all this. It seemed so excessive. It hurt to see Mom and Mary disappearing up the road in the twilight, running for McDowell, but I didn't run after them. I didn't believe Mom would really throw herself in front of a car. I believed she was playing her favorite role, that of martyr, so that I would come running after her. I felt I was being emotionally manipulated yet again by a past mistress of the mind fuck, as I'd been manipulated so often by her in the past.

And I refused to be mind fucked by Mom any more.

I put my arm around Annie. "She's not going to kill herself. Let's go back in the house." Together, arms around each other, we walked back up the driveway.

That night Annie and I decided to live together. I had a little money, enough to pay the first month's rent on a cheap studio apartment. The future was uncertain, but we had each other. We knew we'd be OK. We knew it was the right thing to do.

Vern didn't object when Annie said she was moving out to be with me.

Later that night, I walked down to my house -- my former house, now only my mother's house -- to get a few important belongings. Mom was there, prowling from the living room to the kitchen and back again. Her hair was disheveled, her face streaked with tears.

"I knew you weren't going to kill yourself," I said as I came in.

"And I knew you'd come home."

"I'm just here to get my stuff. I'm moving out to live with Annie."

Instantly, her look of vindication at seeing me was transformed into a rictus of rage. "You mean that *whore!*"

"Annie is not a whore. Please don't call her that. She's the woman I love."

"You're going to live with that *whore!*" Mom grabbed the first thing which came to hand, as she often did when her beating rage seized her. It was her broom. She held it by the handle and whacked me over the head with it as hard as she could, almost doubling over to bring it down on me with all her strength. "That *whore!* That *whore!* That *whore!*" she screamed, hitting me hard with each *whore*, whack! whack! whack!

Habits of submission die hard, and so I lifted my arms, hunched up my shoulders, ducked my head as if I were a turtle withdrawing into my shell, and just took it. Mom continued to hit me with the broom, screeching all the while, consumed with anger like an insane person. "You're going to live in sin with that *slut!* That *slut!* That *slut!*" And with each screeched *slut* she brought the broom down on me again, as hard as she could.

And then I decided I'd had enough. I grabbed the broom in mid-swing, twisting it out of her hands.

The word *slut!* died in her mouth. Instantly Mom cowered against the wall, hands raised protectively over her head, face white with fear, still screaming, but now with terror: "You'd better not hit me! You'd better not hit me!" She was creeping fearfully away from me along the wall, half begging, half threatening that I'd better not hit her with the broom in my hands.

"I'm not going to hit you. I just don't want *you* hitting *me* any more. I've had enough and it's going to stop. You will never hit me again."

And then I threw down the broom and walked out, leaving my mother behind.

Part Five
Decline and Fall

Against the Wind

Annie and I found a hovel at 733 W. Pierce Street in downtown Phoenix, a decayed residential section of town much closer to both my old North High and to Phoenix College. Technically, it was a studio apartment, although that suggests a more modern abode. It was the rear section of a rundown larger wooden building. At one time it had perhaps been a single house before renovations turned it into two apartments. Our smaller rear apartment had the back yard of that once-upon-a-time house as our front yard. You approached it by driving up a gravel alley and turning into our driveway.

The "living room" had a sofa with a back which ratcheted down to form a bed. It was ratty and the center crevice, where the sofa seat met the back, was ripping and becoming a crevasse. The old landlady promised to replace it soon. She never did.

There was a built-in desk with some built-in bookshelves above it. The room also had a closet with sliding doors. It was long enough for a person to lie down in. The previous tenant had splashed and streaked the walls with red and black paint. When Vern saw it sometime later he termed it "evil" and asserted that to live in such a place would diminish one's soul. For him, almost everything did.

The landlady said the tenant who'd created the soul-diminishing red and black decor had moved out without paying the last month's rent. He was a student at Phoenix College and, when she learned that I also attended PC, she offered me a percentage of the take if I'd track him down at the school and get the money. I wasn't tempted.

Off to one end of this main room was a tiny bathroom with a tin shower just large enough for one person. Because there was no air conditioning and Annie and I didn't even have a fan, we both often crowded into this shower that hot Arizona summer of 1966 and just let cold water run over us. After we stepped out of the shower we wouldn't bother to dry off. We let the stifling arid air evaporate the water from our skins.

At the other end of the main room was the small kitchen-dining room with tin cupboards and linoleum counters. There was a round wooden breakfast table and a built-in bench on two sides in what might be called a "breakfast nook." The stove and refrigerator were leftovers from the 1930s. I opened the doors to look under the sink and I saw a hole in the back wall into which the drain pipe disappeared. Through this hole I could see into the front apartment. I heard the tenants talking in that apartment. I closed the doors and kept them closed.

The landlady said it was $75 a month, utilities included. No security deposit. We were in a hurry to find a place. I handed over the money and we had a hovel.

Neither of us had that many belongings and a friend with a car helped us quickly move Annie's stuff into our new home. I still had to get my clothes, books, and other stuff from 51st Street. Dan the Man agreed to drive me back to the old family homestead in his convertible and help me move out. Elmer, my step-father, was waiting for me when we got there. He said Mom told him I'd hit her with the broom. I had to fight him to get my stuff. It was messy.

Shortly after Annie and I moved into the Hovel, Vern moved out of the house at 1849. He'd become uncomfortable with his proximity to Mom, just up the street. He moved into a nice, fully-furnished rental house on a pleasant street just off Central Avenue and not far from both North High and Phoenix College. As it turned out, it also wasn't that far from our Hovel, although he didn't know that at the time. We hadn't told him where we lived at that point. We were trying to break away from *both* families.

I severed all contact with Mom. She didn't know where I lived with Annie, Phoenix College only had a post office box for my address, I didn't have a phone so there was no phone book listing for me, I never called her, and I never went by the house on 51st Street. There was no contact at all between us.

And that was fine with me.

I did, however, run into her by accident once at the Thomas Mall shopping center near the old neighborhood. I rounded an aisle corner in Sears and there she was. As soon as she saw me her face contorted into a mask of rage and hatred and she began screaming, "Are you still living with that *whore?* Are you still living with that *slut?*" Other shoppers turned and stared. Mom ignored them. She advanced on me, screeching, "Are you still living in sin with that *Jezebel?*"

I turned and walked out of the store. Mom followed me to the parking lot, screaming all the way. I never said a word to her. I just got on my blue Suzuki 90 and rode off. I saw Mom in my rearview mirror continuing to scream hatred and abuse at me as I drove away.

And that was the last I saw of Mom for some time. After that, I stopped even going to east Phoenix so I'd never again accidentally encounter her. I wanted to have nothing more to do with her, with Elmer, or with the family. As far as I was concerned, I had no family. I'd finally escaped from that hopeless entanglement and, from now on, there was only me and Annie.

Meanwhile, at our Hovel, Annie and I were evolving into teenaged hippies. In many ways, however, we were still very traditional. Perhaps the most traditional aspect of our life at the Hovel was the belief that it was up to me to pay the bills. We never even discussed finances. We just assumed and accepted the traditional gender roles. Besides, Annie was just 16 with no particular skills and couldn't have found much of a job, anyway. I was 19, and equally unskilled, but I was the man. It was up to me to support us, to pay the rent and to put food on the table, while still attending Phoenix College. I never thought twice about it. I accepted the responsibility.

I had a deep resonant voice and had studied speech at both North High and Phoenix College. I thought I might have a future in radio announcing. I had a friend who was a DJ on one of the local FM rock stations. I asked him how I might get a foot in the door. He said I should just ask for an interview and tell the interviewer I was "heavy," the current slang for "hot" or "cool," as the case might be.

So, I went around to all the local stations in Phoenix and told them I was "heavy." I deepened my voice in the interviews so they'd know that I was, indeed, heeaavvyyy. Evidently, I wasn't heavy enough. No one put me on the air.

So I looked for other ways to get on board. I studied for and passed the Federal Communications Commission's test for a Third Class FCC license. It wasn't that hard. I did it with the aid of a booklet. Then I put an ad in *The Arizona Republic* listing my qualifications: College student, resonate voice, expert typist, Third Class FCC license. The last item brought in a few dollars when I got a job at KEFN, the local Spanish language station.

I couldn't speak Spanish and I had no idea what the Spanish songs that station played were all about. They were all trumpets and accordions. "It's just love songs and corridas," one of the Mexican announcers told me. "Traditional mariachi music."

But, I wasn't hired to be on-air talent, anyway. The announcers at KEFN had a problem. All of them were Mexican nationals who'd come up from Guadalajara. None were American citizens. And only American citizens can obtain an FCC license. And someone with at least a Third Class FCC license was needed to flip the switch turning on the station's power in the morning and turning off the power at night. So that became my job.

This meant I had to be at the station in South Phoenix every morning at six to flip the switch. The Mexican announcers stood around me and watched as I flipped the switch. Then they went to their mikes and drive time began. I hung around for a bit after flipping the switch, then left for school. I returned at one in the morning to flip the switch again, taking the station off the air.

This paid only a few bucks and wasn't going to cover the $75-a-month rent. I had to find something else. What I found was a 20-hour-a-week night job, from eight to midnight, Monday through Friday, as a record gofer at KUPD-FM. KUPD (pronounced "Cupid") was an easy listening station and every night it aired a call-in request show called the "Johnny McKinney Mish-Mash." It was hosted by a hotshot Army vet named, of course, Johnny McKinney.

The KUPD broadcast studio was a small wooden building out in the middle of nowhere. There were only three of us at the station, McKinney, me, and a goofy doofus with an even heavier voice than mine who read the news every half-hour. My job was answering the request line and getting the records for the Mish-Mash.

I sat in an office chair with casters at a beat up metal desk which held nothing but the phone, a notepad, and a pencil. To my right was an entire wall of alphabetically-shelved vinyl LPs. Beginning at eight o'clock the phone began ringing and it didn't stop until midnight. I answered, took the request, and wrote down the dedication, if there was one. In the seconds between calls I kicked the desk and rolled my chair over to the wall where I quickly found the album with the requested song and pulled it down. I placed it face down on the desk with the request slip. When I had four or five piled up, I flipped them over so the earliest was on top and took them into the next room, where McKinney was on the air. I placed them on the control board in front of him and, eventually, he played them and read the dedications on the air.

McKinney had a warm and friendly on-air persona. He wasn't so warm and friendly off the air. He was a clean-cut Army type and I was obviously a hippie. He didn't like my long hair and my beard. "Why cultivate on your face what grows wild around your asshole?"

I just smiled. "Speak for yourself, Johnny. My asshole is as smooth as a baby's bottom."

I endured his harassment for hours each night. When the show went off the air at midnight, I filed all of the albums I'd pulled back into the wall of records, ready for the next night. Then I drove to KEFN, where I flipped the switch to take that station off the air at 1:00 A.M. Then I'd buy pizza-to-go on the way home and get to the Hovel around one-thirty or so. Annie and I ate the late pizza dinner, then we crashed and I caught a few hours of stingy sleep. I had to be back at KEFN at 6:00 A.M. to flip the switch again and listen to more mariachi music. And from there I went to school.

I hated being away from Annie so much. I knew she listened to McKinney's Mish-Mash, so I did my best to let her know I was thinking of her. Only about half the callers actually dedicated their requested songs to someone. When they didn't, I supplied a dedication to Annie. I began with the dedication "To Annie, with love." Then I dedicated a song to Mimi, the cat we bought to keep Annie company while I was away. Then I began dedicating songs to Annie and Mimi under all the nicknames I had for them. I never said who these dedications came from, because Annie knew our codes. Also, McKinney wouldn't have made the on-air dedications if he'd known they came from his hippie record gofer. The anonymous listeners who supposedly made these dedications thus became the most regular listeners to the Mish-Mash. They never missed a night as long as I worked there.

The easy-listening music McKinney played on KUPD wasn't my type, but it was a job in radio. I hoped it might lead to something. I took the requests, wrote the dedications, and pulled the records. Listeners requested the same songs and artists over and over, show after show, so I got to know them all too well: "Tara's Theme" from *Gone With the Wind*, "Somewhere, My Love," "Stanyon Street," "Baby, The Rain Must Fall," "Green Dolphin Street," "Ballad of a Sad Cafe," "Theme From 'A Summer Place'," Percy Faith, the Roy Conniff Singers, Ferrante and Teicher, Cal Tjader, Les Brown and his Band of Renown. If I never hear this music again for the rest of my life, I still won't forget it. At least I became very fast at finding the same ol' albums with the same ol' requested songs.

That summer Annie and I attended classes together at Phoenix College. I took her down to the campus and walked her through the registration process, just as Terry Lee had done for me. No one asked for a transcript. She paid her tuition and officially became a Phoenix College student, even though she was just 16 and a high school drop-out. Annie enrolled with me in a math course I had to take for graduation, as well as an intro psychology course. As in that first history of religion course that I'd taken from Vern, Annie sat next to me in both classes. This time, however, she was a legit student.

Between classes we lingered over sandwiches in the shade of a campus tree. After classes we ambled through nearby Encanto Park, or perhaps we caught a movie matinee. I couldn't imagine a better way of spending a summer day than spending it with Annie at my side. And so, even though I spent my nights with Johnny McKinney instead of with her, I spent my days with Annie, all summer long.

And, as planned, Annie earned an "A" in both classes. We knew she would. She was smart. She applied to Phoenix College that fall. She submitted her Phoenix College transcript to demonstrate that she could perform academically at the level Phoenix College desired.

It didn't matter. Her chances of skipping high school and going directly to college had always been slim to anorexic, but it was worth a try. But the Phoenix College bureaucrats simply refused to admit her. They told us that her proven academic ability was irrelevant. Annie had to genuflect at each and every Station of the Academic Cross. None could be omitted. She had to graduate from high school before she could go to college.

So, instead of Phoenix College, that fall Annie enrolled at North High, my alma mater, which was in our neighborhood. She was back in high school after all, as a junior. At least she *was* back in school, she was no longer a drop-out.

Meanwhile, I began my third year at Phoenix College. Between work and life and love, it was taking me longer than anticipated to accumulate the 60 hours of credits -- 20 courses -- needed to graduate.

Halfway through that fall semester of 1966, I decided to take over the Phoenix College student government. The times they were a changing and I thought running the student government would be a way of shaking things up. Staging a coup was simplicity itself, because most students at Phoenix College, like most students everywhere, didn't give a damn about student government and didn't any pay attention to it. They disdained it, rightfully, as "sandbox politics." In a sense, Phoenix College was just a high school with ashtrays and student government there was just as infantile and irrelevant as student government at any high school.

But, I thought, it didn't *have* to be that way. It was that way only because the kind of students who ran for the offices were twerps who didn't give a damn about the larger world. They were just Goody Two-Shoes who wanted to be in student government so they could put it on their resumes when they applied for jobs or graduate school.

But, with a vision of things larger than the sandbox, I could push the envelope and enlarge the sphere of student government activities. Most importantly, I would have control of the student activity fund and could decide to use that money for better things than paying for the usual parties.

At that time there were four elected student government officers -- president, vice-president, secretary, and treasurer -- elected on a semester basis, as well as a lot of competition for these offices when school began in the fall. Almost all that interest dissipated by the time it came to electing officers for the spring semester. When the candidates for the spring term were announced in the student newspaper, I noticed that there was only one candidate. The guy who'd been elected president for the fall semester was running for re-election for the spring semester. But there were no candidates for the other three offices! I realized that, in the absence of any competition, any group of three students could get elected with a handful of votes and their three-out-of-four votes would then control the student government.

I did some quick research and discovered that it only took the signatures of 25 registered students to get on the ballot. I rounded up two friends to be candidates for secretary and treasurer and I ran for vice-president. If I'd wanted to, I could've found a third friend to be the vice-presidential candidate and I could've run for president, but, why bother? Control of the student government was what I wanted and it was a sure thing with our three unopposed candidacies.

We stood outside the cafeteria for one day and, in an hour, collected the signatures of 25 students on our nomination papers. To be safe, we then doubled the number, to 50 signatures. Students signed up willingly when we asked. No one cared, anyway.

In the election later that semester, perhaps a hundred students bothered to vote. We four unopposed candidates were elected in a landslide. We were scheduled to take office in January of 1967. Until then, I and my co-conspirators bided our time. Our cabal had engineered a student government coup and no one had even noticed. That's the best kind of guerrilla politics.

I quit my job as Johnny McKinney's gofer when KUPD honchos decided the hippie record gofer was making too much money slashed my minimal pay to sub-minimum levels. I told them I couldn't make it on my new salary. I was barely paying my bills, as it was.

"Tough," they said.

"Then shove it up your hairy ass," I said, and walked out the door.

Luckily, Dan the Man was also leaving his night job at a South Phoenix soft drink plant. He said I could have it. He took me down to the plant one night and introduced me to his supervisor. "Here's the guy I want to take over my job."

"OK, have him fill out this form and you teach him."

I filled out the form and Dan taught me his job that night. Dan worked alone in a section of the plant that contained huge open vats of soft drink mix. These were stainless steel kettles with large paddles swirling eternally through the orange or cola-colored liquids. That night Dan confirmed my suspicions of what went on in such plants. As we walked past a gleaming neck-high vat of orange drink, Dan hawked a big gob of snot into it. The snot was quickly stirred into the mixture.

"Dan, that's repulsive!"

"Yeah, ain't it?"

"Someone's going to drink that."

"But it won't be me. C'mon. I'll show ya what ya have to do."

What I had to do was simple, and a couple hours of instruction was all it took to learn it. A line of delivery trucks sat in the outdoor parking yard. During the day the drivers had delivered cases of bottled drinks and pressurized canisters of soft drink mixture to stores on their routes. The canisters were tall cylinders stashed under a soda fountain counter and hooked up to a dispenser. When a customer ordered a drink, the soda jerk jerked a handle and filled a glass with the mixture from one of these silver cylinders. When they were empty, the delivery man picked them up and returned them to the plant.

Which is where I unloaded them from the truck. I opened the tops and lined them up on a conveyor belt which then conveyed them into a washer. This sprayed them, inside and out, with high pressure jets of hot water. Then I filled the canisters with new mix, according to a list each driver left for me. I closed the lids, pressurized and labelled them, put them on a wooden flat until the flat was full, and fork lifted the flats up and out into the parking yard where, the next morning, each driver retrieved his own canisters.

Minimum wage hourly work, boring as hell, the good thing was that it didn't take all that long and I was the only one in that section of the plant, so I was my own supervisor. I punched a time clock on and off the job and I stretched my time as much as I could. I opened and loaded the cannisters onto the conveyer belt through the washing machine, then went into the vat room and hunkered down behind one of the huge steel vats and read a school book for half an hour as the steel blades swished through the syrup beside me.

When the cannisters finished their trips through the washing machine, I filled about half of them, and then took another half hour reading break. Then I'd fill the rest and take another half hour reading break. Then I'd move all the flats out into the parking yard. Then I'd hunker down behind a vat again for another final half hour of reading before I punched out and went home. This way I got in about two hours of paid reading time each night. It helped cover the rent and I finished my required reading at the same time.

So it went, night after night, day after day, all that fall of 1966. I went to Phoenix College during the day and worked at night while Annie went to North High. It didn't leave much time for us to spend with each other, but what time we stole from the world we treasured. We were together and that was all that mattered. Our faces were against the wind and we had the confidence of the young.

The Happening

Wet white fog filled the entire house, limiting visibility to inches in front of my face. Dim shapes flickered around me in silent movie motions as the flashing strobe light lit the billowing clouds with lightning strokes. An incessant and discordant pounding of kitchen spoons on pots and pans filled my ears as the dim shapes writhed and twisted, chanting as they danced. Above the din, Frank Zappa and the Mothers of Invention intoned "Suzy Creamcheese, Suzy Creamcheese, Suzy Creamcheese." The Mothers' recent album, *Freak Out!*, was the soundtrack for this happening.

Annie and I danced and chanted too, enveloped in the flashing fog, the chanting, the pounding noise, Suzy Creamcheese, and waited for the blaze of enlightenment to surge over us as our consciousness suddenly expanded.

Though we danced and chanted in the fog until we were exhausted, my mind, at least, never expanded. Instead of being spiritually expansive, the happening seemed primitive, barbaric, elemental. As I danced and chanted with Annie in the flickering fog, holding her tight as the shadows leaped and howled around us, I felt I'd reverted to some primeval past. The only part of me that expanded was in my jeans. In the midst of the dim fog and pulsating drumming I was burning for Annie and I wondered if anyone would even notice if I pulled her down right there in Vern's living room and made love to her on the fog shrouded floor in the middle of the gyrating tribe. Perhaps, if I'd done so, that would have been perfectly in keeping with the expectations of a happening. It would've been performance art.

****

Happenings, like so many other aspects of the Sixties, originated in the Fifties, or even earlier, and owed an inspirational debt to the absurdist juxtapositions of post-Great War dada and surrealist art. By the early 1950s artist-musician John Cale was staging chaotic art performances at Black Mountain College. One of Cale's students was New York artist Allan Kaprow, who adopted the word, "happening," to describe these performances and created the concept as it came to be known with his proto-performance art presentation *18 Happenings in 6 Parts*. Kaprow's 18 "happenings" took place over six days, October 4-10, 1959, at Manhattan's Reuben Gallery.

Like Kaprow's initial presentations, subsequent happenings staged by avant-garde artists involved lights, surround sound, slide projections, and spontaneous audience participation. The audience might sing, dance, play music, read poetry, or speak in tongues, all simultaneously. The event itself, whatever "happened," was the work of art. Its ephemeral and evanescent nature, unrepeatable in exact details from happening to happening, was one of its major attractions.

The other great attraction was the hope that, as a result of this unpredictable mixture, you would, in some fashion, transcend your own consciousness and expand your awareness in unforeseen directions. The hippies' hope was that the event would "blow your mind."

But what really exploded happenings out of the bohemian avant-garde art world into popular culture was Ken Kesey's notorious Acid Tests in San Francisco in 1965, culminating in the great Trips Festival of January, 1966. Kesey's Acid Tests were centered around lysergic acid diethylamide, more commonly known as LSD -- or just plain acid.

I once knew a local garage band called Sandoz Liquid Blues Band because Sandoz Pharmaceutical, a Swiss company, first synthesized acid just before World War II. By the mid-

Sixties the drug was still so new and unknown that it was completely legal and would remain so until Congress outlawed it on October 6, 1966. Sandoz was the sole legitimate distributor of the hallucinogen until it ceased manufacturing acid in April, 1966. At that time, a Sandoz representative said, "I would not be surprised if at any one of a number of campuses there is more LSD than we have ever made."

By the spring of 1966, he was probably right. And it was the United States Army which was responsible for that. The Army thought the psychotropic drug might be of use in breaking POWs or captured spies because it induced delusional states. In February, 1958, Army labs in Maryland secretly dosed unsuspecting soldiers with LSD to test the effect. One GI volunteer, dosed four times, didn't learn of the true nature of the mind experiments until 1975 when the Army contacted him to do a follow-up study.

Ken Kesey volunteered to be dosed with acid by the Army. In 1959 he was a graduate student in creative writing at Stanford University working part-time at the nearby Menlo Park Veterans Hospital. There he agreed to become a human guinea pig for a study on the effects of psychoactive drugs, including mescaline, psilocybin -- and LSD. Kesey admits it was a weird trip, and warped his mind permanently, rather than "expanding his consciousness."

Kesey's experience working in the Vets' hospital as a drugged-out guinea pig, and with the patients, found its way into his 1962 novel, *One Flew Over the Cuckoo's Nest*. The book was a big commercial success, which allowed Kesey to stop working at the V.A. hospital and purchase a secluded ranch in La Honda, California. The 1975 movie of the book, with the same name, won five of the top Academy Awards for that year, including Best Adapted Screenplay, Best Director (Milos Forman), Best Picture (with the Oscar going to producer Michael Douglas), Best Actress (Louise Fletcher), and -- marking his break-through into the big leagues -- Best Actor for Jack Nicholson.

Kesey dropped out of grad school at Stanford and began dispensing acid -- still legal and mostly manufactured by San Francisco Bay Area hip chemist Oswald Stanley III -- to friends at parties he threw at La Honda. He called these parties "Acid Tests." They featured rock by Bay Area bands like The Warlocks (later known as The Grateful Dead), strobe lights, fluorescent paints, and, of course, liberal amounts of acid for everyone. Essentially, the Acid Tests were old beatnik happenings -- taken into new mental territory by the addition of acid. People turned on to acid at these Acid Tests became known as "acid heads," or just plain "heads." Tom Wolfe described these acid happenings in his book *The Electric Kool-Aid Acid Test,* and a 1964 cross-country trip in a gaudily painted psychedelic bus by Kesey and his Merry Prankster friends also helped spread the acid gospel.

On January 3, 1966, The Psychedelic Shop, the first "head shop," opened at the intersection of Haight and Ashbury Streets in San Francisco. "The Haight," as the neighborhood around that intersection was called, soon became the capitol of hippiedom. Among other things, The Psychedelic Shop sold tickets to the first Fillmore Auditorium Acid Test five days later on January 8th. As with earlier, smaller, acid tests, the first Fillmore Acid Test featured Ken Kesey and his Merry Pranksters, the Grateful Dead, strobe lights, and a bathtub filled with acid-laced Kool-Aid. Almost 2,500 "acid heads" tripped out on the punch, the Dead, and the scene, thus passing the Acid Test and becoming missionaries of the resulting expanded consciousness.

Stewart Brand, who later created the famous *Whole Earth Catalog,* then organized an even bigger "Trips Festival" to be held over three nights shortly thereafter, January 21-23, at San Francisco's Longshoremen's Hall. Thousands showed up, the Dead played, lights flashed, people tripped, and acid, the new and entirely legal hippie high, was the happening thing. And so "happenings" evolved from esoteric Beat performance art to mass participation acid fueled hippie head trips.

And they began happening across the country -- even in Phoenix.

The first happenings I participated in were held that fall of 1966 at Vern's newly rented house just off Central Avenue and were attended entirely by Vern's male students from Phoenix College. Except for Vern, there were no adults on hand. Indeed, except for a medical doctor named Walt Emory, Vern seemed to have no adult friends. All he had were young acolytes. Even Walt seemed to be more of an acquaintance than a friend.

Walt had taken a philosophy course from Vern when Vern still taught at ASU and had then stayed in touch with Vern afterward. The fact that Walt was a medical doctor was incidental to their acquaintanceship. What was more important was that Walt was also an artist. His medium was welded metal, from which he created gigantic sculptures, and he'd gained a small reputation around Phoenix for such creations.

Annie seemed to be more friendly with Walt than Vern was. One time I drove her to Walt's house on my blue Suzuki to see Walt's latest creation, a detailed metal sculpture of a nude man looking as if the skin had been peeled away, leaving only the musculature and skeleton. No doubt Walt's medical training helped make it so anatomically detailed. Massive, 18-feet tall, with uplifted arms extending perhaps another six feet into the air, the figure's head was thrown back, as if he were staring at something in the sky. Walt called it "The Sun Worshipper." It stood in Walt's driveway and he took us up onto the roof of his house to get a closer look at it. He later sold it to a shopping mall in downtown Phoenix, just off Center Avenue near Thomas, where it greeted shoppers for many years. Perhaps it stands there now.

Walt took us down into his garage, where he was working on a new piece, picked up his acetylene torch, pulled on his goggles, and began burning small strips of metal to it as sparks spattered all over. Annie and I stood well back as he worked. The sculpture was composed of the interlinked metal vertebrae of a human spine arching up from a pedestal until it ended in a convoluted human brain. Sitting crosslegged on top of the brain was a small gnomic man in a business suit. His arms were folded over his chest and a glowering frown disfigured his face.

Over the noise and sparks I yelled to Walt, "What do you call this piece?"

Walt stopped welding and turned to me, a big grin on his goggled face. "'The Bureaucrat'. You like it?"

"I like it."

"Don't ever become one." Walt snapped his torch on again and turned back to his welding. The flame played over the sculpture and Walt's face flickered amid the flying sparks like a modern Vulcan at work at his forge.

Walt, Vern's only "friend," never attended any of Vern's happenings.

Nor were there any female students. The only female around was Annie.

Nor was there booze or munchies.

Nor was there any grass, speed, or acid. Vern was a product of the Beat Fifties rather than the hippie Sixties, so it was drugless psychedelic experience, a Beatnik throwback.

At first that first happening was relatively sedate and artistic. Guys read poems. One student guitarist sang a song he'd composed in honor of Vern's Greatest Of-all Design and Vern's teachings. It was entitled "The Great Design." It was all about the "Master Plan, to be a Man, to be a Man...." Vern beamed on him beatifically as he sang. As people loosened up, they began supplying their own music, banging on kitchen pots and pans with spoons, drumming on the furniture, chanting in unison.

And then one of the students turned on a fog machine he'd brought. Quickly filling Vern's living room, the mist began seeping into other rooms of the house. Someone turned on a strobe light. Someone else cranked up Frank Zappa and the Mothers real loud. We all began freaking out as we howled and danced and gyrated through the lightning fog. It turned out you didn't need drugs to get high. You could get a contact high just from the energy of the crowd, just from the dancing and chanting and drumming and ear-piercing music and the sensory distortion of the lightning flickering through the fog -- just from what was happening.

Which was, of course, the whole idea of the original happenings. You got a natural high and your mind expanded in unexpected directions.

Unfortunately, I never had a singular aha! moment of revelation at that happening or any other...but I later realized that my consciousness was changing anyway, slowly, subtly, by what was happening around me over the course of the mid-Sixties. All the time I thought I was the same person, but I wasn't. I was becoming more and more "radicalized" by the spirit of the times, by the zeitgeist, by what was happening around me.

When Jimi Hendrix came to ASU in the fall of 1968 on his first American tour to perform in the ASU gymnasium, I had a small shock of awareness about how much I'd changed. We could get right up close because Jimi had not yet become a mega rock star. His warm-up act was a British band he'd brought over from London called The Soft Machine. They played while a psychedelic bubble and light show splashed over them. Then Jimi blew our minds into a Purple Haze and, when he distorted the printed lyrics by singing, "'Scuse me, while I kiss this guy!," he pointed dramatically at his bassist, Noel Redding, so we were sure to understand the words he actually sang. A few years earlier, I would've been offended by Jimi's homosexual reference. By then, I just thought it was cool.

Such changes seemed glacial to me at the time. In '66, as I danced and yelled amid the howling hippies at that first of my many Happenings, there was just arson in my heart for Annie, burning and weaving in front of me as we freaked out in the flickering fog.

Paranoia Strikes Deep

"Stop right there, or I'll blow your fucking head off!"

I stopped. Later, I wished I'd jumped off the fence and ran.

It was Saturday night, November 12, 1966. That morning Annie and I had awakened in the Ventura, California, home of Harriet, Annie's mother. We'd spent a slow, lazy day getting ready for our trip back to Phoenix. Now we were running for our lives down a dark alley off bloody Sunset Strip in Los Angeles.

Behind us the LAPD -- the Los Angeles Police Department -- was going crazy, beating the hell out of any hippies they caught. We were teenagers and I had long hair so, as far as the cops were concerned, that meant we were hippies.

So we ran.

Straight into a gang of cops waiting for us at the other end of the alley.

It wasn't supposed to be this way.

****

Annie and I had decided to take a long break from our classes so that we could go to L.A. and I could meet her mother for the first time. Being a high school student, it was harder for her to just take off, but good ol' Dr. Walt Emory, the sculptor, wrote a letter to North High saying Annie needed to be hospitalized for a battery of medical tests. Meanwhile, I'd trained a friend to work my job at the bottling plant temporarily. The deal was that, when I got my paycheck, I'd turn over to him my pay for the hours he worked. I'd never seen anyone but other workers going about their jobs in the distance since the first night Dan the Man had told his supervisor I was taking over his job. I was my own supervisor, so I figured as long as the job was done, as long as the canisters were washed and filled, there'd be no problem.

Annie and I took the Greyhound bus from Phoenix to Los Angeles. Harriet picked us up at the L.A. Greyhound station and drove us to her home in Ventura, just north of Los Angeles.

As she drove, we listened to "Radio Free Oz" on KPFK-FM, the L.A. listener supported radio station. The show was hosted by someone claiming to be the Wizard of Oz. He was allowing these outrageous local comedians called the Firesign Theater to run amok over the airwaves. But, they were beyond funny. They were *hippies*. Hippie comedians mocking the straight world! Nothing like *that* in Phoenix.

Indeed, it seemed like *everything* in Los Angeles was more exotic and exciting than in Phoenix. The Byrds, the first rock band to make it really big after the British Invasion of 1964, had come out of L.A. They'd made it big by rockifying Dylan. In July, 1965, Bob Dylan had played the legendary Newport Folk Festival, backed by the Paul Butterfield Band. They played electric and the folkies supposedly hated it. But Dylan had already given Roger McGuinn of the Byrds, an L.A. folky group, his song, "Mr. Tambourine Man." The Byrds released an electrified version of it that same month, and it went huge. In September, '65, the Byrds released another electrified Dylan song, "All I Really Want To Do." It also went huge. The Byrds were number one in America and local heroes in L.A. By the summer of 1966, every remaining folky group -- or even duo, like Simon and Garfunkle -- had also gone electric. The folk music boom was dead. Now it was "folk rock."

Then there was the avant-garde multi-racial hippie band, Love, which had a gigantic cult following in L.A. And there were the Doors, dark and dangerous, like the city itself. They'd not yet released their first album, that would come in two months, but they played in the local clubs and everyone was talking about them. And then there was Frank Zappa and the Mothers of Invention, the Happening freaks who were so bizarre they seemed to come from another dimension entirely.

These groups played at funky places like Bido Lito's, the Whisky-A-Go-Go, London Fog, and even Pandora's Box, all on Sunset Strip. The Strip was the hippie heart of L.A. It was where the action was, where the hippie head shops were, where the music happened. The Strip was the happening Scene.

Cops harassed hippies at the Scene. There was constant low-level tension on the Strip, as the cops routinely arrested kids for loitering, littering, or being a general nuisance. There were mass arrests at GeeGee's and other Strip joints. Confrontations were a nightly occurrence. Los Angles was trying to domesticate the Strip, and the first step was to close down Pandora's Box and demolish it.

Pandora's Box was located at 8118 Sunset Strip, not far from where the Strip crossed the line into Los Angeles County on a traffic island in the intersection of the Strip and Crescent Heights. The city said it just wanted to widen the road, and Pandora's Box was in the way. No one believed them.

Pandora's Box wasn't actually a rock club, like the Whisky and other places. It was a throwback, an old Beatnik coffee house which still had poetry readings and acoustic folk music. When it was ordered to close, it became the focus of all the hostility that had been building between the kids and the city for a long time.

Kids began demonstrating around Pandora's Box, Sonny and Cher joined them in a sit-down protest which blocked traffic on the Strip, and more and more kids came down to the Strip every night to join the growing crowds.

The cops ramped up their harassment.

Into this tinder box that Annie and I stepped on the night of November 12th.

That afternoon Harriet had driven us down into L.A. to the Greyhound station. We had several hours before our bus left, so we decided to visit the Strip and see what was going down for ourselves.

The Strip was jammed with people and cars. We wandered from store to store, entranced by it all: Bead curtains, incense, black lights, psychedelic posters, hippies. Lots and lots of hippies. I'd never seen such hordes of long hairs in fringe jackets, beads, and face paint. In Phoenix we were a despised and fugitive minority. Here there were thousands of us! We had our own stores, our own lingo, our own dress, our own newspapers. I picked up a copy of the *Los Angeles Free Press* and read about an entirely new world. Annie and I discovered that the counter-culture was alive and thriving on Sunset Strip. No wonder the cops were trying to shut it down.

And no wonder the kids were fighting back.

Suddenly, down the Strip toward the west, we saw a line of cops outfitted for war marching toward us. Behind them, row upon row, were other cops dressed just like them: Black uniforms, black gloves, shiny black boots, white helmets with face shields, clubs in their hands. The line of armored cops stretched from one side of the Strip to the other, from storefront to storefront. They were clearing the street of kids, who melted back eastward along the Strip toward the county line. The cops were shoving, pushing, jabbing with their clubs any kid who didn't move fast enough. If a kid fell, a relay of cops kicked or clubbed him along the street until he could get up and run. Annie and I moved with the crowd, away from the cops, down the Strip toward the county line.

But the Los Angeles County line was barred by a cordon of county cops, also in battle armor, also stretching across the street from storefront to storefront. It seems L. A. County didn't want any hippies on its end of the Strip, either.

The fleeing tide of kids came up against the line of county cops and recoiled from their clubs. Front and rear, kids were going down under flailing police clubs. The crowd became more and more compressed, more and more frantic. Kids were running back and forth, trapped between the unmoving line of county cops and the advancing line of city cops. The Strip was littered with beaten kids holding bloody heads. Some were screaming in pain, others screaming curses. Some began throwing rocks at the cops. We heard glass breaking. A car was burning. The cops were getting closer.

I grabbed Annie's hand and we began running down a dark alley away from the hysteria. Shit, I thought. Every time I come to L.A. I run into trouble. Last time it was the Commies chasing me and Jerry at the time of the Tonkin Gulf. Now it's the cops.

We came to a tall chain link fence across the alley, cutting us off. I jumped on it and began climbing. Annie was right behind me. That's when I heard the cop.

"Stop right there, or I'll blow your fucking head off!"

I'd just reached the top of the fence when I saw the gang of cops in battle armor waiting on other side. I yelled, "Annie! Run!" She jumped down and ran back up the alley.

"Get your fucking ass down here or I'll blow your fucking head off!" one of the cops repeated. Stranded on the top of the fence, fearing I'd be shot, I climbed down the other side into the arms of the waiting cops.

One rammed his club into my belly. I went down, gasping for breath. They began kicking me. One pulled me up by my shirt, shoved me against a brick wall, and hit me in the stomach again. Another punched me in the mouth and my head banged against the wall from the blow.

Then they hauled me out of the alley to a waiting police bus. It was surrounded by hordes of cops in battle armor and filled with arrested kids peering out through barred windows. A cop pushed me up against the side of the bus and held me by my torn shirt as a photo was taken of the two of us, arrester and arrestee, hunter and hunted. I was dizzy and gasping for breath and could hardly stand. When I staggered, the cop grabbed me by my long hair and held me up.

A superior officer walked over and asked the cop holding me why I was being arrested. It was just a formality. "Public intoxication," the arresting cop told him.

The superior officer asked to smell my breath. I exhaled in his face.

"Phew! He's drunk as a skunk! Throw him in the bus!"

I may have had bad breath, but there wasn't a whiff of alcohol on it. Jack Mormon I was, but I still didn't drink.

The arresting cop threw me into the bus with the other kids. I plunged frantically from one side of the bus to the other, looking out the windows, searching for Annie over the heads of the encircling cops. She was nowhere to be seen. I didn't know if she'd also been beaten and arrested or had, somehow, escaped back up the alley. And, if she'd escaped, where was she? And how was I going to find her in all this chaos and confusion?

The police bus became more and more crowded as bleeding kids in torn clothes were tossed in among us. We stared out the windows at the police rioting around us. The LAPD was running berserk, beating kids all over the streets, wherever they caught them. And, each time we saw yet another gang of battle-armored cops pile onto yet another running and falling kid, we erupted in impotent fury, yelling and screaming at the cops.

That's when I began calling cops "pigs." "You fucking pigs!" we yelled, rocking the bus from side to side. "You fucking shit eating pigs!" The turmoiling inside of that bus seethed with our rage and hatred. If I'd had a gun, that night I'd have become a teenage cop killer.

After what seemed like hours of watching this baptism in blood, we were driven to a police station. I had no idea where I was. I was stripped of my belongings and fingerprinted. Then I was photographed again. I wondered if I would be able to introduce the picture of me, bleeding and bruised in my torn shirt, at my trial. Then I was shoved into a cell already packed with beaten and bleeding kids. Hundreds were arrested that night on Sunset Strip. One of them, I learned later, was Peter Fonda. I didn't see *him* in my cell.

Hours later I called to a cop patrolling the jail corridor, asking when I could be released on my own recognizance.

"When you sober up!" He laughed at his own wit.

In the morning, I guess I'd sobered up. In any case, the cops released me on my own recognizance. I still didn't know where I was, or how I'd begin searching for Annie in a huge and strange city where I knew absolutely no one.

But, when I walked out of the jail that Sunday morning, I walked into a miracle. Annie was there, waiting for me. Somehow, she had escaped a beating or arrest. Somehow, she had found a cellar and had hidden in it until dawn had cleared the Strip of cops. And, somehow, she had traced me to a police cell in West Hollywood.

I collapsed into her arms and we hugged for a long, long time.

Here Comes the Night

Troubles come to the poor like piss-ants to a picnic and it seemed Annie and I had an infestation after we got back to Phoenix.

Despite the fact that I spent the Saturday night of the Sunset Strip police riot in a West Hollywood jail cell, Annie and I still made it to Phoenix on a Greyhound by Sunday night. Monday morning, November 14th, we both went to school, same as always, Annie to North High, me to Phoenix College. It felt strange sitting in a Phoenix classroom as if nothing had happened, when just over 24 hours earlier I'd been sitting in a crowded California cell. No doubt it felt even more bizarre for Annie, in her North High classes. Instead of going to a movie the previous Saturday night, like her classmates, she'd spent it hiding in a strange Los Angeles basement while the LAPD ran amok out in the streets, beating and arresting kids just like her. How could such things be happening, I wondered, and people around us still go about their daily lives as if nothing was amiss in America?

By this time, I'd quit my switch flipping job at KEFN. It was just too much trouble for too little pay. But I still had to get to the bottling plant that night to wash and fill soda canisters.

I parked in the plant's yard and walked over to the line of delivery trucks. There was already some guy running the empty canisters through the washers. And it wasn't my buddy.

"So who are you and why are you doing my job?"

"I'm the guy who does this job now. Go see the super."

I went looking for the supervisor, the same guy who'd hired me that first night when I came in with Dan the Man. I asked around the yard and finally found him yelling at some Mexicans loading trucks. "Andalay, pronto, Goddamn it!"

I interrupted his yelling and introduced myself. "What's with the guy doing my job?"

"It ain't your job no more."

"So I took a couple of nights off. I made sure I had a replacement who knew how to do the work. Where's the problem?"

"That wasn't your call. We don't want people we don't know wandering around the place. You should've cleared him with me.

"I didn't know I had to. I brought in a temporary replacement to do the job just like Dan brought me in to do the job."

"Yeah, well, you did yourself out of a job. You don't work here no more. Your last check will be in the mail."

It's one thing to quit a job, as I'd done at KUPD and KEFN. I felt in control of the situation. It was quite different to be fired unexpectedly, told to turn around and leave as I was now, that I didn't have a job any more. That was a real kick in the balls. I felt like a failure. Beaten by a gang of cops, falsely arrested and jailed, and fired from my job, all in three days. And I still had a court date on the public drunkenness charge for which I had to return to L.A. I felt like a super failure. If I'd actually been a drinker, I'd have driven straight to a bar and gotten drunk.

Instead, I drove home and told Annie I no longer had a job. It felt like a confession of sin. I felt guilty and ashamed. I didn't qualify for unemployment compensation because I'd been fired. Besides, I was a full-time student, which also disqualified me. The state didn't pay you unemployment so you could go to school. You had to be willing and able to work full-time at a moment's notice to collect benefits.

I tried desperately to find a quick job. Asked everyone I knew. Pored over the want ads and made hundreds of calls. I just didn't have qualifications for anything in particular and there were plenty of others out there looking for the same minimum wage jobs. I couldn't buy groceries, it looked like I wouldn't be able to pay the rent, and it was getting so bad that I even had to scrounge to put gas in my bike, and gas was then only 25-cents a gallon.

Then it got worse.

My brother Rick found me and asked if he could crash with me and Annie. He was the next oldest of the brothers and, with me gone, he was the one fighting the big battles with Mom. Annie and I had only a studio apartment. There was no place for Rick. It was just one big room, and we were sleeping on a pallet thrown on the floor of that room. We'd tossed out the folding couch, as it was falling apart and we were falling into the center crevasse.

Annie suggested that she move back home. I'd burned my bridges more thoroughly than the Luftwaffe ever did in Poland and France and there was no going back for me. But she'd not left her home in bitterness and violence. Vern would welcome her back. Then Rick could move in with me. He'd dropped out of high school and had a shit job, so he'd be able to help with the bills.

Besides, Vern lived just a few blocks away from us, although he still didn't know it. Annie could continue going to North High without interruption and I'd come over to see her every day after I finished my classes. It'd be like before we moved into the Hovel. And, it'd only be temporary. Until I could find another job.

I agreed. I didn't know what else we could do.

So Annie moved out and Rick moved in. He claimed the huge closet with the sliding doors as his bed. It was long enough for him to stretch out in and gave him a small element of privacy. We ran an extension cord into it so he could plug in a small lamp.

And I felt more like a failure than ever.

I finally found a job with a crew of Mexican janitors for a few hours late every night cleaning a department store in a shopping mall. With Rick's contribution, it brought in enough to pay the rent and utilities and buy some few groceries.

But not enough for Rick to move out and Annie to move back in.

I felt exhausted all the time. I worked cleaning shitty bathroom stalls and piss stained urinals until three in the morning. Then I drove the Suzuki home for a few hours of comatose sleep on my floor pallet. Then to classes at Phoenix College. Study and homework in the school library for a few hours before heading over to see Annie. Then off to vacuum rugs, polish floors, and clean toilets in the department store. Then home for a few hours on my pallet before getting up to do it again. And again. And again. It seemed endless. It was the worst of all possible worlds.

Then it got worse.

One night in the department store, I was vacuuming the rug in an executive's office, maybe the head honcho. I sat down on the executive's plush leather sofa to rest for a moment. The next moment I jerked suddenly awake to find early morning light flooding the room. Outside the office I could hear bustle of store employees preparing to open for the day.

I jumped up and stashed the vacuum in a closet. Then I walked out of the office and onto the main floor of the store. There were employees going about their business all around me. Despite the fact that the store had not yet opened and I was a stranger in their midst, no one stopped me, no one seemed to even notice me. I walked to the exit, walked outside, climbed on the Suzuki, kicked over the engine and roared off.

The next night I showed up for work, same as always. Perhaps no one had noticed that I'd fallen asleep on the head honcho's couch.

As soon as I turned off the Suzuki's engine, my boss climbed out of his car and came over. "You don't work for me any more. I got a spick to replace you. They don't sleep on the job."

I nodded and said nothing. What was there to say? That I'd flog myself harder? That I promised not to be exhausted and sleepy in the future as I cleaned shitty toilets and piss stained urinals and vacuumed rugs?

I wasn't going to beg. I just kicked the Suzuki into life and rode home for a bit more sleep than usual on my floor pallet before heading off to my morning classes. I sat glumly through them.

So I was fired again. Scrambling to pay the rent again. A failure again. A pattern was emerging which I didn't like.

Then it got worse.

Paint it Black

It was Ruth who told Annie what was wrong.

Annie was nauseous all the time. The smell of food repulsed her. What she ate she threw up. She began each morning before school worshipping the toilet bowl, heaving her guts out as she knelt before it.

Ruth questioned Annie about how long she'd been sick in the morning, how long since her last period, she looked at Annie's belly. "You're pregnant," she said. "You've been pregnant for a few months." Indeed, it appeared that, even as she was running and hiding from the LAPD on Sunset Strip, Annie was already pregnant.

And then, fearfully, Annie told me.

I hugged her close. "Marry me," I said. "We're going to spend our lives together and, at some point, we'll marry anyway. This only moves up the date."

"And what will we live on?"

I took her hand and smiled at her. "We'll live on a hippie commune in New Mexico. I've heard about one up around Taos called New Buffalo. Anyone is welcome. And you don't need money. You just have to be willing to work. We can make it, Annie. So, will you marry me?"

"We'll have to talk to my father. He'll know what we should do."

And so we spoke to Vern. And he did, indeed, know what we should do. "An abortion is the only right thing to do," he said.

I was shocked. It felt like he'd just told us to murder someone. But then I remembered that he also believed in capital punishment. "We can't do that, Vern. Abortion is illegal. It's a crime, everywhere. No one does abortions."

"Just because it's illegal doesn't mean it's wrong. Sometimes a crime is the right thing to do. And I have contacts who can provide us with the service."

"What do you mean, *us*? It's not *your* baby!"

"Eric, think about what's best for Annie. Think about her future. She's only 16. She has her whole life ahead of her. She's only a junior in high school. It would mean an end to her education. It would mean an end to her hopes for a better life."

"I can take care of her. And she can finish her education. She kept going to school even when we lived together."

"But she's not living with you *now*, because you *couldn't* take care of her. Eric, you're only 19. You have no skills or education. You're an unemployed janitor, living in a hellhole that I wouldn't want my daughter or grandchild living in."

"I'm going to school, I'm getting an education so I can get a better job."

"You're in your third year at a two-year junior college. *That's* not encouraging. And even when you get your Associate of Arts degree, it won't mean anything in the real world. It's just an advanced high school diploma. It won't change anything. It won't get you a better job. You'll still have to go to a four-year college, perhaps ASU, and get a bachelor's degree. And even *that* won't change anything. It won't get you a better job, either. A bachelor's degree in history, your major, will just mean you'll be an educated janitor.

"But, with a child and wife to support, the chances of you even getting that bachelor's degree are slim. You're going to be trapped in a minimum wage job for the rest of your life, Eric. And you're asking Annie to share that impoverished minimum wage life with you. Think about what's best for Annie, Eric. You're not being fair to her."

Vern painted a bleak picture of my future. And of Annie's future with me. And of the child we would have together. We were caught in a biological trap which guaranteed dead-end lives for all three of us.

Then Annie interrupted. "But we *love* each other. We're going to raise a family together *anyway,* at some point. We'll just start earlier than we planned."

Vern looked at Annie for a moment. "Love won't pay the rent. Love won't pay the doctor bills. Love won't send your child to college. And, believe me, love won't survive the future you'll have together if you have this baby now. You'll end up hating each other for ruining each others' lives."

"You married Harriet when she was pregnant with Jackie," I said, "and you were *exactly* my age. You managed to make it."

"Most do not. Wait to start a family until *after* you both have educations. That will make it possible for you to give your children the lives of hope and promise you want for them. Don't repeat my mistakes. Get an education first. *Then* get married and start a family. That will make it possible for you to give your children the best lives they could possibly have."

"But, Vern, even if what you say is right, there's a *reason* abortion is illegal. It's a crime because it's *murder!*"

"Is it, Eric? Is it, *really?*"

"Well, of *course* it is! It's taking a human life!"

"Is it?" Vern asked again, using his teacher's voice. "When does human life begin, Eric? A two-week-old fertilized human egg is a blastocyst the size of the dot in the letter 'i.' This blastocyst does not yet even have a brain. Biological life has already begun, but is it *human* life at that point? That's hard to accept. But, if it *isn't* human, then when does it *become* human? At four weeks? Eight weeks? Twelve weeks? Sixteen weeks? Twenty? As it develops, the fetus is not viable, is not able to live outside the womb, until at least 23 weeks, almost six months, which Annie has not yet reached. Perhaps at that point, when it is capable of life on its own, we might easily say it is human life. But, did it actually become 'human' before that? If so, Eric, at what point on this continuum did the brainless dot-sized blastocyst become definitively human?"

"I don't know."

"Then you can't say, *really,* that we're talking about a human life here, can you?"

The logical answer was 'no,' but I didn't want to say that. It seemed to be a gray area, with no definitive answer. I didn't know what to say. I looked in agony at Annie. She looked back in silence. She squeezed my hand. I smiled weakly at her and squeezed back.

The discussions went on, night after night. Vern was adamant that there would be an abortion. He seemed sure in his knowledge of what was right, and he seemed to be right about everything he said. Annie and I *were* both teenagers. We *didn't* have educations. Annie was still in high school and I was an unemployed janitor in my third year at a two-year junior college. I had no money and I seemed to have a dark future with little promise; and I was condemning Annie and our child to live that dark future with me.

Annie and I also wanted to do what was right, what was best for everyone, even the blastocyst in her belly which may or may not have been human. But there was no clear choice, no obviously right decision. Maybe there *was* no right decision. All we were sure of was that we loved each other, we wanted to be together, and we wanted what was best....but that no matter what we decided, it was going to be wrong.

And it was going to hurt.

The Sharpest Thorn

Abortion had not been our first choice, but it was our last choice. Given the little knowledge we had, given the little experience we had, given the little wisdom we had, it seemed, finally, to be the right decision. But how could we know for sure? We only live once. We only get one chance to decide in a situation like this. How do we ever know we've made the right decision? We can't see the future and we don't get a chance to come back and make a second, a third, a fourth decision and play out our lives all over again to see what the future consequences of those other decisions might be. We're given only one chance to get it right.

So we do the best we can in an uncertain world...and we hope we got it right.

Annie and I decided to go forward with the abortion that Vern insisted was the only right decision. He contacted Walt Emory and Walt said he'd make discreet queries among his medical colleagues.

And Vern took me aside and told me I'd pay for Annie's abortion, whatever it cost, every penny of it. It was my responsibility.

"I know that. I'll pay for the abortion. I don't have the money at present. But eventually I'll pay for it. Every penny."

"And you will not say a word of this to Annie."

"Why?"

"It's just between you and me. It's between men."

"Alright, I won't say a word to Annie. It's between you and me."

I was thinking about my pledge of silence when I rode over to Annie's that night. It was one of Vern's "man" things. I didn't understand it, but that's the way he wanted it. So, I would keep my word. I'd pay for the abortion, every penny, and I'd say nothing to Annie of it.

Annie had insisted that I come over as soon after class as possible that day. I was late. I'd gone to the library and begun scribbling a rough draft of an essay in a yellow legal pad for my English history class with Mr. Goldberg, my favorite history teacher. I'd lost track of time and it was suddenly dark outside. I quickly packed up and ran down the steps of the library to my Suzuki in the parking lot. I turned on the ignition and kicked it over. I roared out of the lot and down Thomas toward Central Avenue. I knew I'd have some apologizing to do when I saw Annie.

I pulled into her driveway and turned off the engine. Annie heard me drive up and opened the front door. There was a frown on her face. I was feeling apologetic already. She came out onto the porch and pulled the door shut behind her.

I grinned as I reached the top of the porch steps. "I know, I'm late. I'm sorry, I lost track of time."

I stepped forward to hug her. She pushed me forcefully back with both hands, hard on my chest. I was surprised and puzzled. She'd never before pushed me away like that. "Annie, I'm sorry, I was working on a paper for Mr. Goldberg. I didn't realize how late it was."

"We have to talk. Come to the backyard."

It's never good when a woman says, "We have to talk." It always means trouble. "What's wrong? Did something happen?"

"Just come to the backyard."

I followed Annie down the driveway to the backyard. There were no lights in back and the yard waited in deep darkness. There was no moon, but some faint reflected light came from the tall office building on Central Avenue which towered over her back yard. Floodlights splashed the building in brilliance and it looked like the edifice soared upward forever until lost in the blackness of the night sky. The lit building looming above us just accentuated the darkness of the yard.

Annie sat in one of the two lawn chairs. I sat in the other. I began to remove my backpack.

"Don't take it off," Annie said. "You won't be here long."

I stopped and looked at her. Her face was hard to see in the gloom. "What do you mean?"

"There's no sense pussyfooting around this. I don't want to see you any more."

"What!?"

"Our relationship is over. I never want to see you again."

I felt like I'd been hit between the eyes with a sledge hammer. I didn't know what to say. It came out of nowhere. When I'd left Annie the previous night, we'd kissed good-night and I'd sensed nothing diffident in her kiss. We'd not argued. We'd had no disagreements about anything. I didn't believe her. "Why are you saying this? Are you testing me somehow?"

"I'm not testing you. I'm breaking up with you. It's over."

"But why? What have I done?"

"Nothing. It's us. It's the relationship. It's not good for me."

"I don't understand."

"I want to be strong. Being with you makes me weak. So it's over."

I just wasn't following Annie at all. None of it was making sense. I reached for her hand in the darkness. She pulled it away quickly.

"Annie, you *are* strong. Think of all the things we've been through recently, what *you've* been through. Annie, you're the strongest person I've ever known. But you can't go through this abortion alone, no matter *how* strong you are. We're going to go through this *together*."

"No, I have to go through the abortion *alone*. I have to be strong, *alone*. As long as I'm with you, I'm weak. Relationships make you weak."

"No, relationships make you *human*."

"Relationships are for weak people."

"Then all of us are weak, because we all need relationships. There's nothing wrong with needing other people, Annie. No one gets through life alone."

"I do. I don't need other people."

"That's just crazy talk. Of course you do. Everybody does. Annie, how long have you been feeling like this? I've never heard you say *anything* like this before."

"I've been thinking about it for a long time."

"And you never told me? You never even *whispered* a doubt about us before. You should've *told* me so we could've talked about it."

"There's nothing to talk about. It's over."

I reached for her hand again.

"Don't touch me."

"But, Annie, you're not giving me a chance. I'm hearing all this for the first time. It's hard for me to take it all in. Tell me what bothers you about me. I'll change it. Whatever it is, I'll change it. We can work it out."

"There's nothing to work out. It's the relationship. Being with you makes me weak."

"Annie, stop saying that! Think of all the things we've been through together. We've had some bad times, but we got through them *together!* Being together doesn't make us *weak!* Being together makes us *strong!* Annie, you can't just toss our relationship in the trash just like *that!*

And for something I don't even understand! You're not talking like Annie would talk. You're talking like someone I don't even *know*. Annie, something happened. What is it? Tell me."

"Nothing happened. I just have to think about what's best for me."

"Of course you do. But what about what's also best for *us?*"

Annie nodded at the glowing office building which soared over the yard. "There is no 'us.' There's just me, and I want to be as strong as that building. Being being dependent on a lover is a weakness. I can't be as strong as that tower as long as I'm with you."

I felt like Annie had just ripped my heart out of my chest. I felt like my lover had betrayed and murdered me. I felt like my world was all in ashes. I couldn't believe what she was saying. It just didn't make sense. I tried again.

"Annie, what do you *mean,* being with someone else makes you weak? Being together has *always* made us stronger than either of us has ever been alone. We're more than lovers. We're a team. We're partners. We *depend* on each other. That makes us *strong -- together.* Two are stronger than one. It's always been us against the world, right? We're going to spend our *lives* together, right? We're going to raise a family together, right? I'm going to be at your side through this entire abortion, *right?* And, *damn,* you *know* I'd walk barefoot through hell for you, Annie. You know I'd put out the sun with my bare hands for you. Annie, you know I'd *die* for you. How can having someone like that by your side at a time like this make you *weak!?"*

"I don't want you to die for me. I just want you to leave me."

I felt like I was just beating my face into a stone wall, over and over, and getting nowhere. "Annie, you know I'd do anything for you. If you really, *really* want me to leave, I will."

"I *really* want you to leave. It's over between us. I never want to see you again."

She couldn't have said anything worse. My life was over. An hour before I'd been a happy man, on my way to see the woman I loved. Now I was a dead man. What else could I say?

"Annie, it's the abortion, isn't it? I understand how scary it is. But you don't have to go through with it. We'll tell Vern we've changed our minds. We'll take care of this baby, somehow. And we'll do it *together."*

"It has nothing to do with the abortion."

"I don't believe you."

"It's about me being strong, and I can't be strong with you."

"I don't believe you. That just doesn't make sense."

"Then believe that I just want you to go. It's over between us."

"I don't believe you."

"It's *over* between us." Annie stood up. "Please leave *now."*

I also stood up and I faced her. "Annie, how can love just turn off like a faucet?"

"Sometimes it just does. Please leave. I don't want to see you again."

I nodded. I turned and stumbled toward the driveway. I looked back and Annie was watching me go, grim-faced. I tried again. "Annie, that tower is just a building. It's not a human being. Human beings *need* each other. *Please* don't do this."

I waited for a response. Annie said nothing. I'd said all I could.

I turned and walked like a zombie to the Suzuki. I straddled it and kicked the engine over. I could hardly see the end of the driveway because of the film across my eyes. I rolled out into the street and turned toward home. I don't remember anything after that.

Part Six
Resurrection

The Lower Depths

As the New Year of 1967 began, it seemed to be the end of my world. It was the nadir of winter, and the nadir of my spirits.

It was also my last semester at Phoenix College. I went to school, I sat in class, I wrote papers, but my heart wasn't in it. I was flying on automatic pilot, coasting toward graduation. Graduation, when it came, would be pointless.

At night Rick crawled off to his closet and pulled the sliding door closed. He had a light inside. Perhaps he read. Perhaps he just lay in the darkness listening to me as I stayed up into the wee hours, until exhaustion finally drove me to collapse on my pallet. If he was listening, what he heard, over and over, was Brahms' Lullaby, played by a small windup angel. As the music played, the angel rotated. It was Annie's. Harriet had given it to her. In the move back home, it had been left behind. Now it was all I had of Annie. I played it over and over. Perhaps its faint tinkly tune, made even more faint by the closed door, lulled Rick to sleep in his closet.

It did not lull me to sleep. It helped keep the memory of Annie foremost in my mind. It reminded me of what I'd lost. And therefore I treasured it. I wound it up, again and again, and it played for me as I wrote page after page of poetry. We know that poetry is a distillation of language, the essence of emotion, and so in times of turmoil we instinctively scribble line after line in an attempt to somehow express, for our eyes only, our hearts only, what we feel. If we feel joy, perhaps those lines will help up preserve the memory of that joy. If we feel sadness, perhaps those lines will help us come to some reconciliation with our sadness. And sometimes we write just to discover what it is we feel.

Much of what I wrote were haikus, dozens and dozens of them. Haiku is a form of Japanese poetry. It is perhaps the most compressed of all poetic forms, and one specifically designed to express a single thought or feeling or discovery in a single instant. Haiku is rigid in format. The poem can be only three lines and must be of 17 syllables, no more, no less. The first line must be five syllables, the second seven, and the third five again.

Haiku

Japanese poem
    Seventeen syllables long,
        Three lines: An insight.

Even so, within this rigidity there is much freedom of expression. And so, as I'd written haikus about Hiromi, so now I wrote haikus about Annie, trying, and failing, and trying again to express in three lines and 17 syllables all I felt about her. I wrote haikus about every aspect of her, and so I wrote about....

Her Angel

A windup angel
    Playing Brahms' Lullaby
        Left after she left.

Most of us don't spend our lives writing poetry, becoming more proficient with practice, so what we write when we turn to poetry during times of turmoil is, from a professional view, unpublishable. That's irrelevant. At such times, we don't write for critical approval. We write for ourselves and ourselves alone.

Eden Remembered

I still hear the call:
>Paradise, before the Fall.
A chain 'round my heart.

And so it went, poem after poem, page after page, night after night, as I listened to the angel and tried to describe what I'd lost when I lost Annie. In such a black period, everything around me was black. I hated coming home from school to the dark and dreary hovel splashed with streaks of red and black paint that I now shared with Rick. That hovel had seemed a cheerful place when Annie brightened it. Now that she was gone, every corner of it was dark because it reminded me of her. Every morning when I stepped into the tiny tin shower, I remembered the showers we shared in the long hot summer of '66, holding each other tight as the cold water dribbled over us. When I ate at the wooden table in the breakfast nook, I tasted the pizzas I'd brought home for Annie after leaving KUPD at midnight. I began thinking of our apartment as a hell hole hovel.

Nights were the worst. When I finally tired of writing poem after poem at my desk and lay down alone on my floor pallet, I stared up for long hours at the shadowy ceiling recalling the times we'd made love on that pallet. No doubt Annie had conceived right there on that pallet. And when I finally fell into exhausted sleep, I dreamed of making love to Annie again on that pallet.

Eventually, the nights in that hell hole hovel became just too painful to endure, so I auditioned for a play. Perhaps, more than anything, it was an effort to wrench myself up out of my well of loneliness and spend as little night time in the hell hole hovel as possible. As it chanced, the play I auditioned for seemed to mirror my life at that moment. It was *The Lower Depths* by Alexei Maximovich Peshkov, who wrote under the name of Maxim Gorki ("Maxim the Bitter"). It was staged by the semi-pro Arizona Repertory Theater (ART, of *course*). Although I'd taken speech classes at North High and Phoenix College and had been on the Phoenix College debate squad, I'd never acted. I hadn't been a member of the Drama Club at North High and I'd never taken a drama class or been in a play. I didn't think of myself as an actor and I didn't expect to be cast. It was just a stab in the dark. Something to do to escape the hell hole hovel.

Not thinking of myself as an actor turned out to be an advantage. I wasn't saddled with actorly mannerisms. In the audition I just portrayed myself, and that was exactly what the director was looking for. I was cast and went on to be cast in every play I auditioned for, became a sometime actor and, in doing so, paid my rent. I attribute my good fortune to the big fish in a small pond phenomenon. I've never auditioned in America's two acting meccas, Los Angeles and New York.

And so I began to learn about the acting world...and I learned about Maxim Gorki. He soared to fame in 1898 with a collection of short stories about the impoverished and homeless of Czarist Russia. He'd followed the classic advice to would-be writers and he wrote about what he knew, as he was, himself, impoverished and homeless much of his life. Born into a poor family and orphaned as a young child, he was raised by his equally poor maternal grandparents until the age of ten. Then his brutal maternal grandfather kicked him out to live on the streets. With no education or skills, he drifted through an incredible variety of marginal jobs, voraciously reading and scribbling all the while. He published his first short story, based on his life among the lowly, in 1892. More followed, which he eventually assembled into the 1898 collection which made his reputation. Gorki's eyewitness stories of the misery and oppression endured by the derelicts, bums, day laborers, thieves, and whores who swarmed Russia's slum tenements were a revelation to the bourgeoisie and to the artistic set.

Anton Chekov, already famous, became Gorki's mentor and patron and introduced him to Konstantin Stanislavski, who founded the Moscow Art Theater in 1898, the same year Gorki burst upon the scene. Stanislavski, seeking new plays for his new acting company, asked Gorki to write a play for him. Gorki did so, producing *Philistines*, which Stanislavski's company performed in 1901. It was an angry attack on bourgeois luxury bought by the sweat of others' labor. Its hero was a mechanic who became the first of the proletarian heroes so familiar in later Marxist literature.

Gorki's second, and most famous, play for Stanislavski, *The Lower Depths*, dealt more specifically with the "creatures who once were men." It is a grim portrayal of the *bosyak* inhabitants of a fetid St. Petersburg flophouse. The Russian term *bosyak* literally means "a bare foot," and it was applied to the those in Czarist Russia who did occasional menial odd jobs, but who lived mostly by their wits. The lives of such schemers are always dark and blighted. And so Gorki's play does not contain a glint of optimism.

Konstantin Stanislavski is perhaps the greatest theorist in the history of drama. He developed a unique acting "Method" by which actors did not just strut the stage and recite their lines, but actually felt the emotions they portrayed. They did so by dredging up memories of such emotions from their own pasts and reliving them on stage. It was Stanislavski's Method which Stella Adler and Lee Strasberg famously taught at New York's Actor's Studio in the 1940s and 1950s to such proponents of the new realistic acting style as Marlon Brando. Thus, in preparation for *The Lower Depths*, Stanislavski sent his actors, all from genteel homes, into the slums of Moscow to see and smell and feel the lives of the *bosyaks*, the barefooted ones they would portray on stage.

I didn't feel I needed to do such similar research. Because I'd roamed the streets at night with Jerry Campbell, I already knew what it was like to live in a chicken coop and work at the Midnight Auto Supply, where you lifted what you could, anywhere you could find it. I already knew what it was like to walk on cardboard soles stuffed into my shoes and eat mustard sandwiches, because that was how I was raised. Indeed, the director told me in my audition that my performance seemed so real he was waiting for me to spit on the stage.

But, although their futures were all equally bleak, not all the characters in *The Lower Depths* were completely barefoot. Two longshoremen, characters named simply "the Goiter" and "the Tartar," retained vestiges of decency amid the crime, deceit, and poverty surrounding them, and together they represented the conscientious upright working man doing his best to live an honest and moral life in a degraded and immoral world.

I was cast as the Tartar. It was a small role, but I felt as if I'd been cast to type. Although the odds seemed against me, I was doing my best, as was the Tartar, to put some shoes on my bare feet. And I discovered one advantage of being the Tartar. At the beginning of every performance the props manager ensured that a long baguette of coarse black bread that I got to eat on stage was on the common table the characters shared. It was a strange type of bread I'd never come across before, but it was filling, which was important to me. As part of the stage business we representatives of the hungry poor were allowed to pull off hunks of this bread and chew on it while the other actors orated. It wasn't Method acting for me to act hungry, because I really was, and every night I eagerly chewed the black bread while my compatriots chewed the scenery.

However, while I merged right into the character of the Tartar, I hoped I wouldn't end as he did. Between the second and third acts, his arm is mangled in a workplace accident. Afterward, the Tartar is truly just a *bosyak* beggar like all those around him, with a future as barren as theirs. At the play's conclusion, the Tartar cries in defeat to a fellow creature of the abyss, "Well, devil Bubnov, now we have some of your vodka. Drink we will, play we will, death will come, die, we will!" Seconds later, death does come for "the Actor," as he hangs himself in despair and the play suddenly ends, suggesting a similar fate for all those on stage.

When *The Lower Depths* premiered in 1902, the squalor and hopelessness portrayed on the stage of the Moscow Art Theater was seen as a condemnation of Czarist Russia. Indeed, Stanislavski wrote that Czarist secret police swarmed the final dress rehearsal. Nevertheless, the play was allowed to open.

Three years later, the hopelessness Gorki portrayed lifted briefly with the 1905 Revolution, which nearly toppled the Czar. However, the Czar recovered and ruthlessly crushed the revolution. Gorki, along with thousands of other perceived enemies of the state, was imprisoned. Many were executed. But Gorki was too famous to put up against a wall and shoot, so he was expelled into exile. The following year, in New York City, Gorki wrote *Mother,* the prototype of the proletarian revolutionary novels which soon began to appear so profusely.

Gorki remained in exile until the 1917 Revolution, after which he returned to Mother Russia. After the Bolsheviks consolidated their own revolution in the 1920s, Stanislavski's Moscow Art Theater was renamed the Gorki Art Theater. Following Gorki's death in 1936, Nizhni Novgorod, the town where he was born, was renamed Gorki, in his honor.

The Lower Depths introduced me to the tradition that "the show must go on," no matter what happens. At the end of the third act there is a mass fight scene where bodies are flailing about wildly hither and yon. The costume designer had shod me in soft leather Eskimo mukluks, no protection at all in a gang fight. In a melee, you have to be booted, as every cowboy knows. But I may as well have been barefoot, like a true *bosyak*. And I paid the price. A local TV news anchor, who weighed around 250 lbs., was one of the actors and his heel came down hard on my right big toe one night as we fought.

Incredible pain seared through me and it felt as if my toe had been crushed. I didn't have to fake the pain the Tartar felt in the next act, after the lights briefly dimmed and then came up again. Between those two acts the Tartar's arm had been mangled at work and he spends most of act four groaning and writhing in pain on his bunk. And I certainly groaned and writhed realistically. After the night's performance, the director congratulated me on my Method acting. I wasn't acting at all. I was hurting, I was hurting bad. But it didn't matter how much you hurt. You went stolidly on. You did what you had to do.

That night when I pulled off my mukluk I saw that my big toe was swollen and bloody and completely black. The entire toenail was smashed and dangled loose. It soon fell off completely and it took months for a new toenail to grow in.

Meanwhile, the show went on. And I fought in the third act melee night after night. However, the costume designer kindly replaced my luckless mukluks with a pair of sturdy black Wellington boots. To make them seem more "Cossack," she stitched thick tan leather extensions to the tops, which made them about five inches taller and gave them a buccaneer boot appearance. I liked them so much I liberated them after the play's run ended and wore them long thereafter. *Bosyaks* must seize the day, or truly go barefooted. Besides, the boots didn't fit anyone else.

The other aspect of theatrical life I discovered was that a significant percentage of actors are gay. It's just another case of the cliche being true. At first I was baffled by some of the mannerisms and actions of the guys I encountered. I didn't know what to make of them. Except for my passing encounter with the Forty-Niner, I'd never come across guys who acted like girls, guys who "liked" guys. If any of my friends or classmates had been gay, they'd wisely concealed it. My blue collar world was intensely homophobic and no overtly gay classmate would have long survived in my neighborhood or in any school I attended.

But, if I wanted to be part of the theatrical world, I had to accept gays.

And so I did.

And, before long, in addition to being my fellow actors, they became my friends.

I was changing. I kept changing.

Sandbox Politics

Yet Still I Try

I don't know why
    I still carry these scars
        And howl in pain
            Beneath the distant stars.
I don't know why
    I still beat my hands
        Against the dark
            And angry sky,
Why I still raise my fist
    To the fiery angels
        And the shadows in the mist,
            Still shake my chains
        And dance stark naked
            In the midnight flames.
I don't know why.
        Yet still I try.

****

It was a time when every white kid in America seemed to suffer from multiple personality disorder. We fervently and simultaneously held two wildly divergent beliefs about the period. On the one hand, we believed it was the dawning of the Age of Aquarius, when peace, love, and understanding would soon end all wars and hatreds.

On the other hand, we believed it was an age of incipient fascism, when military madness was sweeping the land and Amerika had become a Moloch monster devouring its own children. It was thus the best of times and the worst of times, and it wasn't clear which tendency was in the ascendant. We would readily acknowledge either one as dominant, depending on the day, our mood, or who we were talking to.

So, on the one hand, 1967 was "The Year of the Hippie." That was the year the "San Francisco Sound" went national. It was the year of Jefferson Airplane's *Surrealistic Pillow*. It was the year Janis Joplin and Big Brother and the Holding Co. exploded out of the Bay Area after the Monterey Pop Festival made them stars. Monterey Pop was the first big rock concert, drawing 50,000 fans to that small California coastal town. The Monterey Pop Festival also introduced Jimi Hendrix to America, while, in London, the Beatles released *Sgt. Pepper* and the Stones released *Their Satanic Majesties Request,* both as psychedelic as those two bands would ever be.

More than anyplace else, San Francisco's Haight-Ashbury district was the home of the hippie. At the beginning of 1967 the Haight community began making plans for a gigantic hippie party to celebrate the dawning of the new age of peace and love. *The Berkeley Barb,* a local radical rag, burbled with typical apocalyptic joy about the upcoming event: "The spiritual age will be manifest and proven. In unity we shall shower the country with waves of ecstasy and purification. Fear will be washed away; ignorance will be exposed to sunlight; profits and empire will lie dying on deserted beaches; violence will be submerged and transmuted in rhythm and dancing." The only thing the *Barb* omitted was that pigs would fly.

On January 14th over 30,000 colorfully dressed flower children, many with, yes, flowers in their hair, congregated in San Francisco's Golden Gate Park for the promised "Gathering of the Tribes for a Human Be-In." It was the first, and greatest, of the hippie festivals. Dozens of local bands played, including Janis Joplin and Big Brother, Jefferson Airplane, the Grateful Dead, Moby Grape, and Sopwith Camel. Timothy Leary was there to play LSD guru and Jerry Rubin, not yet a yippie, was there to play Berkeley radical.

Meanwhile, 'Frisco Beat holdovers Gary Snyder read poetry and blew a conch shell while Allen Ginsberg, dressed in white Indian pajamas, played his finger cymbals and tried to lead the hippies in "Om" chants. Mostly, however, these would-be leaders were ignored. The kids were there in their peacock finery to see and be seen and to just have fun with each other. As the sun set in the Pacific, thousands of the revelers walked to the nearby Ocean Beach strand to watch it set and celebrate the dawning of the Aquarian Age.

The Gathering of the Tribes was considered such a success that the coming summer was soon dubbed "The Summer of Love," during which there would be further such Be-Ins in the Bay Area. Meanwhile, hippies in dozens of other cities staged similar large Be-Ins, most notably in Los Angeles and, on March 26th, Easter Sunday, in New York's Central Park.

So much life, so much hope.

At the same time, and in glaring contrast, the war in Vietnam was intensifying. On January 6th, just a week before 'Frisco's hippie festival, the American military launched Operation Cedar Falls, the biggest offensive yet of the war. Over 30,000 American troops swept through the Iron Triangle, a guerrilla stronghold northwest of Saigon. In a scorched earth campaign, they burned 500 buildings and evicted thousands of villagers from their ancestral lands. These peasants were transported to camps south of Saigon where they could be tightly supervised.

Army honchos declared Operation Cedar Falls a huge success and initiated even larger so-called "search and destroy" campaigns in the months which followed. To carry out such tactics, American military strength would be increased to almost half a million soldiers -- 474,300 -- by the end of the year, exceeding the total American troop level in the Korean War. This meant increasing levels of young Americans being drafted for that war in the jungle. And, as troop levels in the jungle escalated, so did the dying. That year, 9,353 American soldiers would die in Vietnam, more than in all previous years combined.

But, their deaths would not bring victory any closer. To be effective, America would have had to occupy and hold every hostile square foot of Vietnam after every search and destroy campaign like Cedar Falls. But even half a million American soldiers slogging through the jungle wasn't enough to do that. So, as soon as the Americans left the Iron Triangle to search and destroy some other Vietnamese peasant province, the guerrillas returned and were welcomed with even more support than before from the embittered villagers who had not been forcibly displaced. Such escalating American incursions simply created more and more enemies in an ever-growing spiral.

The air war against North Vietnam was no more successful, despite a similar escalation. *New York Times* reporter Harrison Salisbury had been reporting from Hanoi, the North Vietnamese capitol, that the American bombing campaign was mostly killing civilians, and only incidentally hitting military targets. On January 21th the Defense Department conceded that aerial photos had confirmed that American planes were bombing civilian residential areas. That same month a CIA study estimated that civilians comprised 80% of the victims of the American bombing campaign against North Vietnam. By the end of the year we'd dropped 1,630,000 tons of bombs on Vietnam, exceeding the total bomb tonnage dropped on Germany in World War II, and the vast majority of those bombs missed military targets and killed civilians.

This growing air war was becoming increasingly expensive, as the operational costs of the bombing had almost tripled, from $460 million when it began in 1965 to $1.2 billion in 1966. At the same time, the number of American planes shot down over North Vietnam almost doubled, from 171 in 1965 to 318 in 1966. Every month, every week, every day brought similar news. More search and destroy operations, more air raids, more civilian deaths.

So much death, so much despair. More and more the war seemed a horrendous nightmare from which there was no waking.

And I, too, felt increasingly mired in this nightmare. I realized that I was kept from being drafted to help meet the voracious manpower needs of the jungle war only because of my student deferment. And that alone would have insured that what happened every day in Vietnam caught my attention. Within months I would graduate from Phoenix College -- and only going on to Arizona State in Tempe, after finding the money to do so, would keep me from the killing fields.

But, even more, I felt somehow personally responsible for the war. True, I had no political importance or influence of any kind. I was just an American *bosyak*, an impoverished kid still below voting age attending a junior college in Phoenix. I hadn't planned the war, I didn't start it, and I wasn't prosecuting it.

But I'd once supported it. I'd once been gung-ho for the war. Now, with no social life and plenty of time on my hands, I was spending all my free hours in the Phoenix College library. I became a news junkie and read everything reported on the war. I discovered the news magazines, *Time, Newsweek, U.S. News & World Report,* and devoured them. I read the reports from the field published in *The New York Times,* which contradicted everything the government said about the war.

I didn't stop with current news. I read Arkansas Senator William Fulbright's highly critical 1966 anti-war book, *The Arrogance of Power.* As I began reading more about the history of the war and the history of Vietnam, what I learned appalled me.

I'd gone to the Westward Ho Hotel in 1963 to cheer the Dragon Lady. Now I discovered that she was a monster who made Marie Antoinette look like a saint. At the time of her Westward Ho appearance her husband headed the Can Lao, President Diem's barbaric secret police, which viciously repressed any hint of dissent. Vietnam was a devoutly Buddhist society, but French-educated Catholic Madam Nhu had laughed when the first Buddhist monk immolated himself in protest against her brother-in-law's dictatorship. She called it a "barbecue" and offered to provide the gasoline and matches for the next Buddhist monk who planned to burn himself to death.

In 1964 I'd rallied for Goldwater's anti-Communist crusade. Three years later I realized our crusade was a crusade against Vietnamese independence. The Vietnamese had fought a succession of imperialist conquerors, the Chinese, the Japanese, the French. We were the latest. Ho Chi Minh, I belatedly realized, was the George Washington of Vietnam, and we were the British fighting for King George. We weren't the good guys. We were the bad guys.

In 1964 I'd tangled with Commies on a beach in California when they dared to challenge the Gulf of Tonkin Resolution. Now I learned that the Gulf of Tonkin Incident was a lie. Our destroyers weren't in international waters, they were well inside the North Vietnamese territorial limit. And the attacks never happened, as least not as described. My president had lied to me and all Americans. In fact, the entire war was a war of aggression concocted out of lies. Our entire government, I realized from my reading, was run by liars and hypocrites who preached freedom and supported dictatorship, who preached peace and promoted war, who preached justice and dispensed injustice. And, more than anything, I hated liars and hypocrites who preached love and practiced hate. They reminded me too much of the Christians among whom I'd been raised.

And I felt angry that, by believing my government and by supporting the war, I'd also compromised my integrity, at least within my own mind. I believed that one had to always do the right thing. And I'd done the wrong thing. I'd become one of the bad guys.

So I had to make it right -- I had to help make *America* right -- by becoming one of the good guys. I agreed with Edmund Burke's contention that, "All that is necessary for the triumph of evil is that good men do nothing." He may have been a conservative political theorist, but he was absolutely right about morality.

But, what could I do? I was just an American *bosyak,* with no influence whatsoever. I didn't belong to any anti-war group, as there were none at Phoenix College. For all I knew, there wasn't a single anti-war group anywhere in Phoenix. At least I never heard of any in the news. But surely, I thought, there was *something* I could do to help end the military madness and get right with my conscience.

As it happened, I and my friends controlled the sophomore student government at Phoenix College. We'd unobtrusively taken control in the elections at the end of the previous semester. As the highest elected representatives of the students, we felt we could do something, we didn't know what, about the war.

The only thing we could think of doing was using the student activity funds for good works; something other than the usual parties or the usual token class gift to the college upon graduation, upon which previous student governments squandered student funds. Knowing of no other worthy project, I invited Vern to appear at one of our student government meetings and describe the Greatest Of-all Design, and what he hoped to accomplish through it. Although Annie had broken up with me, I still believed in Vern and his work and I wanted to help him and it however I could. A small symbolic donation from the Phoenix College student government to further his work seemed appropriate, especially since he was a Phoenix College faculty member.

Vern readily accepted my invitation. In the hallway, just before the student government meeting, I asked about Annie and the abortion. "She's being strong," he said. "The procedure to induce a miscarriage has been initiated. It will take time to come about. In the meantime, she's going to classes at North High every day and going about life as usual. It's what I would do if I were in her place."

Which you'll never be, I thought. Instead, I just nodded. "My thoughts are with her." I didn't ask Vern to pass anything on to Annie. I didn't know that he would. And, if he did, anything I said would have been an unwelcome imposition on Annie, who just wanted to forget about me.

"How much did it cost?" I asked.

"$150."

"I'll pay it. I don't have it right now. But I'll pay it."

Vern nodded.

Then I introduced Vern to the meeting and invited him to describe his work and goals. I don't remember the specifics of what he said, I just remember the impression he made. Powerful, ethical, persuasive. He asked for a $100 donation to the Greatest Of-all Design. The money itself was not as important, he said, as the student government endorsement which the donation represented. It would be a vote of confidence in his work.

Immediately after his presentation, Vern left the meeting so that we could discuss his request and vote on it in private. Only the four student government officers and Louis Polichino, our Faculty Adviser, were present. The presidential twerp voted against Vern's request. I'd expected that, but felt he was irrelevant. The remaining student government officers -- the vice president, the treasurer, and the secretary, meaning me and my buddies -- voted for it. We then authorized John Nash, our treasurer, to cut a check for $100.

"I won't allow it," Mr. Polichino said. Mr. Polichino taught in the Political Science Department. Like Vern and everyone else who taught at Phoenix College -- except for Mary Maher, who prided herself on being the only Ph.D. in the English Department -- he had only a Master's degree, and therefore was only a "Mister." In those days, you could go a lot further as a college teacher with very little education.

I was stunned. "Excuse me, Mr. Polichino, but the Student Government officers just voted three-to-one to authorize this check."

"I don't care, I won't allow it."

"Why don't you think this is a valid authorization?"

"I don't think the Greatest Of-all Design is a worthy cause. I don't have to give any reason beyond that to keep you from misusing student activity funds."

I suddenly suspected there was a history between Vern and Mr. Polichino of which I was unaware. What other reason could there be for Mr. Polichino's opposition? Vern's presentation had been impressive.

But, that secret history didn't matter to me. Nor did what he thought about the Greatest Of-all Design. What mattered to me was his annulment of a legal and democratic vote. "Well, it doesn't matter that you think the cause is unworthy. A majority of the Student Government officers has made a decision and we expect that decision to be carried out."

"It won't be. I control the checkbook, and I won't let you write the check."

"Mr. Polichino, you don't have veto power over our decisions. There is nothing in the constitution of the Phoenix College Student Government which gives you the authority to override a legitimate and democratically arrived at vote by the duly elected officers."

"I don't care. I won't allow this check to be written."

His adament disregard of the democratic process angered me. "Mr. Polichino, you're just the Faculty Adviser. Your role is simply to 'advise.' You have no constitutional authority to vote, to veto, or to decide in any way what the Student Government will do."

"I have the power of the checkbook, and that's all the authority I need. I won't allow it."

And with that, Mr. Polichino stood up and sauntered out of the room. The presidential twerp, who I realized now was his toady, quickly followed. The rest of the Student Government officers -- meaning we three -- remained where we were.

"Well, I guess that's that," John said. "He has the checkbook. Unless I wrestle it away from him, I'm not going to be able to write that check."

"This was just a measly little $100 check to support the good work of a faculty member," I said. "If we just sit back and let Mr. Polichino overrule us on *this,* we won't be able to do *anything.* He'll veto every vote we make on any important issue. Student government is completely meaningless if he's the one who really runs things, all by his lonesome, and not a majority of the elected student representatives. And he doesn't even have the *right!* He's just the *Faculty Adviser!"*

"Faculty Dictator, more like," Geof, our secretary, said. "We should change the wording of the constitution to make that fact clear. 'Faculty Dictator,' it should say. What does the constitution actually say about the powers of the Faculty Adviser?"

I banged my fist on a copy of the student government constitution which lay on the table before me. "It doesn't say *anything!* I've read it. It just says he's the *adviser.* It doesn't give him a vote or veto power or any powers whatsoever!"

"Which means it's just our interpretation against his interpretation of his powers."

"Damn! It's just not *right!*"

"Might makes right, and he's got the power. He's got the checkbook."

"Then we'll just get rid of him."

John laughed. "How do we do that? Assassinate him?"

"No, unlike Mr. Polichino, we do things democratically." I grabbed the copy of the constitution which lay on the table and flipped through the pages. I found the passage I wanted and pounced on it. "Here! The constitution says the elected student government officers will number four: president, vice-president, treasurer, and secretary. It then says the elected officers will appoint the appointive officers. And then it says that the Faculty Adviser is an appointive officer. According to the constitution, Mr. Polichino is an appointive officer who serves at *our* discretion. Since we have the constitutional power to appoint the Faculty Adviser, we can dis-appoint him and appoint someone else in his place."

"Can we really do that?" Geof asked. "He was here before we were."

"The constitution doesn't say anything about tenure or term of office. It says he is appointed by us, period. It's clear we can't work with this Faculty Adviser. Acting on our legitimate constitutional authority, and this being a legitimate Student Government meeting with a quorum present, I move that we appoint a new Faculty Adviser. Who seconds?"

Geof and John grinned at me. "I second," said John.

"All those in favor, raise your hand." We three raised our hands.

"Geof, let the secretary record that a majority of the elected officers of the Phoenix College Student Government voted to appoint a new Faculty Adviser."

"It is so noted."

"I now move that we appoint Vern as our new Faculty Adviser. Who seconds?"

"I second this one," Geof said.

"All those in favor, raise your hand." We three raised our hands again.

"Geof, let the secretary record that a majority of the elected officers of the Phoenix College Student Government voted to appoint Vern as our new Faculty Adviser."

"It is so noted."

The next day, the three of us visited Mr. Polichino during his office hours and informed him that we had removed him as our Faculty Adviser and replaced him with Vern.

"I won't allow it," he said. "I'm Faculty Adviser for as long as I want to be. You don't have the authority to remove me."

"Yes, actually we do," I said. "The Student Government constitution defines your position as that of an appointive officer. It also says that the elected officers, which mean *us,* choose the appointive officers. So, we've chosen someone else."

"I won't allow it."

So the majority officers of the Phoenix College Student Government made an appointment with Mr. J. Lee Thompson, President of Phoenix College. Although Phoenix College was founded in 1920, Thompson was only the second president of the college in all that time. He was new to the job, having been appointed only in 1965.

Today, the President of Phoenix College has a Ph.D. But, like everyone else in the Phoenix College administration in 1967, President J. Lee Thompson had only a Master's, so, like Mr. Polichino, he was a "Mister." In those days, not only could you be a college teacher with very little education, you could also be a college president with very little education. One semester we students organized a festival we called "The Festival of Dionysus." Mr. Thompson walked about the campus glowing with pride because the students were celebrating something he vaguely suspected was classical -- more than that, he hadn't a clue. And neither students nor faculty enlightened him, as both considered our president a joke.

In those days you could also be a college president with very little dedication to education. Mary Maher told me that Mr. Thompson had instructed the faculty not to teach anything "controversial." Evidently, a college education wasn't meant to be challenging to a student's mental horizons. And, Mary said, he also instructed the faculty not to tell the students anything about their rights. "It just stirs them up," he said. God forbid! Better the students should remain ignorant, not only about their rights, but also about anything beyond what they already knew.

Mr. Thompson was also, like many in the Phoenix College administration, a good Mormon, unlike the Jack Mormon who now stood in his office with his two fellow Student Government officers. So, for all these reasons, we had no great hopes for redress from President J. Lee Thompson. But, we had to try.

Mr. Thompson knew why we were there. I'd told him when I made the 1:00 P.M. appointment. Democracy had been overthrown in the Student Government by a Faculty Adviser coup and we wanted to restore it. Perhaps that's why he kept us waiting for Godot with his secretary until 3:00 P.M. When he felt we'd cooled our heels and passions enough, he asked his secretary to usher us in.

Mr. Thompson didn't rise from his polished mahogany desk or offer to shake our hands as we entered. Instead, he remained barricaded behind the desk, drawing authority and security from its imposing bulk. He leaned back in his creaking wooden chair and surveyed us with distaste. "Please be seated," he finally said.

We sat arrayed in the front of his desk. The chairs were straight backs and uncomfortable. No doubt they were meant to be.

"Which one of you is John Nash?" he asked.

Startled, John replied, "Why, I am."

Mr. Thompson zeroed in on him. "You just signed a petition to establish a Young Socialist Alliance chapter on campus, did you not?"

"Why, yes, I did."

"Are you a socialist?"

"No, I'm not."

"Then why did you sign the petition?"

"Because I believe in the First Amendment rights of freedom of speech and freedom of association. The Young Socialists have as much right to be a campus organization as the Rodeo Club or the 4-H Club."

It seemed clear that Mr. Thompson thought John was the trouble-making ringleader and was singling him out for special attention. I wasn't aware that John had signed a petition to allow the YSA on campus, but the fact that he had both surprised and delighted me. John was just about as straight as they come.

I also realized that Mr. Thompson had thrown us off balance and had seized control of the agenda. I decided to intervene. "Excuse me, Mr. Thompson. Perhaps you can schedule an appointment to pursue this line of questioning further at some other time. We asked for this particular appointment to discuss the fact that we have dismissed Mr. Polichino as our Faculty Adviser and we have appointed a new one."

Mr. Thompson swiveled toward me in surprise. It seemed he'd been blindsided. He'd been prepared to focus on and intimidate John. Now it appeared that someone else was the trouble-making ring leader.

"And you are?"

"I'm Eric Davin, the Student Government Vice President. I scheduled this meeting with you, remember?"

"Well, Eric, I won't allow you to replace Mr. Polichino."

I won't allow that seemed to be the mantra of the Phoenix College administration when it came to student democracy. I pushed on. I placed a copy of the Student Government constitution on Mr. Thompson's desk, open to the appropriate page with the pertinent paragraph circled in red ink. I tapped it with my finger. "Mr. Thompson, we have a constitutional right to appoint the Faculty Adviser. It says so right here in the student government constitution. I ask that you read the section of the constitution I've indicated. Does it not say that the Faculty Adviser is an appointive officer? And does it not say that the elected officers, which means *us*, are the ones who appoint the appointive officers? And, by a vote of three-to-one, we have done what the constitution gives us the right to do."

Mr. Thompson scanned the circled section of the constitution. It took awhile, as it seemed to be the first time he'd ever encountered the Student Government constitution and he was trying to think of an appropriate response. He finished reading and then leaned back in his chair. It squeaked as he did so. He peered at me. "Yes, the student government constitution does seem to give you that authority."

I stifled a grin. I didn't want to seem triumphant, but it appeared we'd won!

"But we've never interpreted it that way," Mr. Thompson continued. "Nor are we going to interpret it that way this time. I appoint the Faculty Adviser, and Mr. Polichino will remain the Faculty Adviser, with complete veto power over your decisions, as long as he desires to stay in that position."

I was stunned. "The constitution doesn't give you the authority to appoint the Faculty Adviser. It gives *us* that right. Nor does it give him any veto power over our decisions."

"That's an oversight. We will rewrite the Student Government constitution so that this ambiguity is cleared up in the future."

I was appalled. Where was the rule of law? Where was the respect for the will of the people? Where was the respect for democracy? "There's no 'ambiguity,' Mr. Thompson. The constitution is quite clear on this matter. And if you unilaterally rewrite the constitution to strip us of our power, then there's no difference between you and any Banana Republic dictator in sunglasses. It's a mockery of democracy and it makes you a hypocrite."

The President of Phoenix College stared grimly at me. "You're not going to change my mind by calling me names, young man."

"I'm just telling it like it is, Mr. Thompson. You're a hypocrite who has no more respect for democracy than Joseph Stalin."

Abruptly, J. Lee Thompson stood up behind his desk. His chair jiggled as he did so. He placed his hands, fingers spread, on the shiny mahogany surface of his desk. "I think I've heard all I need to hear. Mr. Polichino and I are saving you from your own irresponsible actions. It doesn't matter what the constitution says. What matters is the way I interpret it. And I say Mr. Polichino stays as your Faculty Adviser to make sure you don't do anything foolish. This meeting is over."

And so it was. There was nothing more we could do. We were defeated.

After we left Mr. Thompson's office, we huddled. We didn't have any good ideas. We considered appealing to the Phoenix College Board of Trustees. They would, of course, back their president and faculty adviser. We considered taking our case to the students at large by doing a group interview with the student newspaper.

"Naw, that won't work," Geof said. "Everyone on the student newspaper is a fuckin' toady, just like our student government president. And even if we found a reporter or editor with any balls, the newspaper has a Faculty Dictator, too. He'd never allow it to publish the interview. Phoenix College is just a God damned high school with ashtrays. The fuckers control everything. There's no way to fight them."

"Then getting elected was just a joke," John said. "It doesn't give you any real power. You can't do anything that matters. It's all just sandbox politics. It doesn't mean shit."

"Yeah," I agreed. "It's a joke, but it's a joke on us. All those apathetic students we ridiculed for not voting were absolutely right to be apathetic. Student government is a farce."

"It doesn't mean shit," John repeated.

"It doesn't mean shit," I agreed.

The Call to Resist

"The mass of men serve the State thus, not as men mainly, but as machines, with their bodies. They are the standing army, and the militia, jailers, constables, *posse comitatus,* etc. In most cases there is no free exercise whatever of the judgment or of the moral sense; but they put themselves on a level with wood and earth and stones; and wooden men can perhaps be manufactured that will serve the purpose as well. Such command no more respect than men of straw, or a lump of dirt. They have the same sort of worth only as horses and dogs. Yet such as these even are commonly esteemed good citizens.

"Others, as most legislators, politicians, lawyers, ministers, and office holders, serve the State chiefly with their heads; and, as they rarely make any moral distinctions, they are as likely to serve the devil, without *intending* it, as God.

"A very few, as heroes, patriots, martyrs, reformers in the great sense, and *men,* serve the State with their consciences also, and so necessarily resist it for the most part; and they are commonly treated by it as enemies."

-- Henry David Thoreau
On the Duty of Civil Disobedience

****

Eating the Tartar's black bread wasn't a long-term solution to hunger. Nor was acting a secure means of paying the rent. I'd soon graduate from Phoenix College and I knew the Associate's degree I'd then have was useless. All it qualified me to do was be a janitor or a soft drink mixer. I'd just turned 20. I wasn't a teenager any more and I knew I had to develop some kind of a career. And that meant obtaining some form of credentials above and beyond the Associate's degree. I had to get more schooling. Only that would get me out of my hell hole hovel, only that would get me out of Phoenix, which was just as much of a hell hole without Annie.

I began haunting the Phoenix College careers office. It was there that I discovered student loans. Tuition at Phoenix College was still just $27 per semester, $54 a year. If I wanted to transfer as a junior into Arizona State over in Tempe, which it seemed everyone at Phoenix College planned to do, I'd have to find some way of paying the much higher tuition. And some way to support myself while going to school. A student loan promised to do both.

So, at the same time I applied to Arizona State for the fall, I also applied for a National Defense Student Loan (NDSL). These were loans the federal government had instituted in the wake of Sputnik in 1957, when it seem the Russkies had a lot more on the ball scientifically than did America. Frantic to catch up, Congress decided to make it easier for more people, including impoverished *bosyaks* like me, to go to college. I hadn't known of the existence of NDSLs when I'd first started at Phoenix College. I paid for everything out of my own raggedy-ass pocket.

I was admitted to Arizona State for the fall and I also got the National Defense loan for the 1967-68 school year at ASU. Both were pretty much routine. You qualified for admission to ASU and the loan if you were a student in good academic standing.

It has since become the accepted wisdom that those who were affluent in the Sixties went to college, while the working class *bosyaks*, too poor for college, went to Vietnam. The Vietnam War, like all wars, was indeed a rich man's war, but a poor man's fight. The privileged elites who ran things launched the war, and the working class fought it. But this wasn't because it was impossible, or even difficult, for a working class kid to go to college and thus obtain a student deferment. Any poor boy in America, like me, who had $54, or thereabouts, could pay for a year at a community college, and thus be deferred from the draft. After he graduated from the community college, he could easily get a federally subsidized loan to pay his tuition at a four-year college. If he was drafted, it wasn't because he was too poor for college, it was because he decided *not* to go to college, it was because he *let* himself be drafted.

I knew where I'd be come September of 1967. The National Defense Student Loan paid my tuition and gave me $500 per semester on which to live. That $500 would pay the rent on a better apartment than my hell hole hovel for the four-month semester, with a few shekels left over for luxuries -- like food.

My gig with the Arizona Repertory Theater was ending, and I had to think about the long term. I thought again about radio. I had the Third Class FCC license, which qualified me for flipping switches at sub-minimum pay. Perhaps, I thought, if I had a First Class license, it might give me more of an edge. In the careers office I discovered a school in Sarasota, Florida, which offered a summer course of study in preparation for the First Class license exam. Classes began in June. If I left immediately after graduation, I'd be able to take the course and still be back in Phoenix in time for September classes at ASU. Tuition at the school cost $150. I didn't have $150. If I had, I'd have given it to Vern to pay for Annie's abortion. But I was desperate and I decided on a leap of faith. As soon as the semester ended, I would hitchhike to Sarasota and, somehow, find a job there which would support me and cover my tuition. I had nothing to lose, as my life was at a dead end and I had no other alternative.

Rick decided to go with me. His alternatives were just as meager. He couldn't pay the rent on the hell hole hovel by himself, so it was hitchhike across America with me or move back home to Mom. He wasn't eager to crawl back to Mom. Besides, Chattanooga was on the way to Florida. We'd go there first. He'd stay with Grandfather Frank, Mom's father, while I went on to Sarasota. And I thought it'd be good to reconnect with some part of the family I hadn't completely written off or alienated.

Meanwhile, more and more of my peers were protesting against the war. There were now almost half a million American soldiers fighting in Vietnam, and the war machine's voracious hunger kept crying out for more. When John F. Kennedy had taken office in 1961, he'd supposedly brought in "the best and the brightest" from among his classmates at Harvard to manage the escalating conflict in Vietnam. By the spring of 1967 it seemed to me that "the best and the brightest" among my peers were choosing to go to jail rather than fight a war of aggression and oppression for the American Empire on the other side of the world.

Among the best and brightest who were opposing the war was the Rev. Martin Luther King. In 1966 he'd helped found Clergy and Laity Concerned about Vietnam. In February, 1967, during my last semester at Phoenix College, he issued a call for all "creative dissenters to combine the *fervor* of the civil rights movement with the peace movement...until the very foundations of our nation are shaken." In March he led a peace procession of 8,000 in Chicago in protest against the jungle war.

The month after that, on April 4th, 1967, Rev. King delivered a speech at the Riverside Church in New York City in which he called America "the greatest purveyor of violence in the world today." There was "no doubt in my mind," he said, "that we have no honorable intentions in Vietnam....our minimal expectation is to occupy it as an American colony....it should be incandescently clear that no one who has any concern for the integrity and life of America today can ignore the present war. If America's soul becomes totally poisoned, part of the autopsy must read 'Vietnam.' It can never be saved so long as it destroys the deepest hopes of men the world

over....A nation that continues year after year to spend more money on military defense than on programs of social uplift is approaching spiritual death."

Then Rev. King called for those who loved America, as I did, to become Conscientious Objectors to the draft. "We are at a moment when our lives must be placed on the line if our nation is to survive. Every man of humane convictions must decide on the protest that best suits his convictions -- but we must all protest....As we counsel young men concerning military service we must clarify for them our nation's role in Vietnam and challenge them with the alternative of conscientious objection....I recommend it to all who find the American course in Vietnam a dishonorable and unjust one."

Here, it seemed to me, was a way in which I could take a stand against the demonic and destructive vampire war which was draining America's soul. For me, it wasn't a political issue, it was a moral issue. It was what I had to do, the *only* thing I could do, to oppose the greatest evil of my time. The war machine wanted me to become a part of it. I was potential cannon fodder, enmeshed in the Selective Service System, kept from participating in the war only because of my student deferment. If I cooperated with the draft, then I was complicit with evil and I'd lose all respect for myself. The most direct thing I could do to oppose the war was to refuse at the most personal level to be part of the evil I increasingly condemned. I decided that I would apply to my draft board for Conscientious Objector status.

I didn't know anyone who was a Conscientious Objector. Once, briefly, I'd had a conversation with an old Phoenix College janitor who'd been a Conscientious Objector during World War I. I don't remember how the subject came up. At the time, I didn't fully understand what a Conscientious Objector was. Nor did I realize how much courage it had taken to be one during the Great War, when patriotic hysteria gripped America.

At another point I was hanging out in the Phoenix College Humanities Department, where the Philosophy teachers had their desks, when two FBI agents came looking for Vern during his office hours. As late as 1967, the FBI automatically investigated all who applied for Conscientious Objector status to determine if they were sincere. This procedure was dropped with the passage of the Selective Service Act of 1967, as it was beginning to eat up too much of the FBI's time. One of Vern's students, someone I didn't know, had applied for Conscientious Objector status and had given Vern as a reference.

The FBI agents found Richard Goldberg, my history professor, who was also a referent for the student, but not Vern. Vern viewed office hours as irksome infringements upon his valuable time and so was never in his office during his posted office hours. That was why I'd found Annie instead of Vern when I'd gone looking for him the previous fall. Later, in the hallway, I overheard the agents refer to the always well-dressed Mr. Goldberg and to the elusive Vern as "Dapper Dan and Slippery Sam."

That was as close as I ever came to knowing anyone who was a Conscientious Objector. But, I knew they were out there. The same month, April, '67, that Rev. King issued his call to resist the war, a group of Bay Area draft resisters formed an organization to oppose the draft called "The Resistance." The Resistance adopted as its symbol the Greek letter omega. The reason for this was that the omega is also used in electrical engineering to signify the amount of resistance to an electrical current in a conductor. I found a button with the Resistance omega symbol and I began wearing it constantly. When people asked me what it meant, it gave me a chance to explain my reasons for opposing the Vietnam War.

On April 15th, 1967, the largest anti-war demonstrations yet -- the Spring Mobilization Against the War -- took place. Martin Luther King marched with 200,000 war resisters in New York City while his wife, Coretta Scott King, addressed 50,000 war resisters in San Francisco. At

Sheep's Meadow in New York's Central Park about 175 resisters burned their draft cards while protestors chanted, "Hell No, We Won't Go!" I'd long since burned my draft card. Now I knew there was a name for what I did. It was called Resistance.

    The next month, May, 1967, General William Westmoreland, the supreme commander of U.S. forces in Vietnam, privately requested that President Johnson authorize another 200,000 troops for combat in the jungles of Vietnam. Johnson agreed, but, in order to meet Westmoreland's request, draft calls would have to be ramped up.

Dark Lady

When I looked up, I saw Annie striding confidently along on the other side of the atrium. I was reading in the Phoenix College library. The library was a recent construction, begun during my first year at Phoenix College. It was three stories high and, instead of being dismal gray, like all the Great Depression buildings around it, it was red brick. Since the campus was running out of room, it'd been plopped right down in the middle of the central yard where the flag pole would've been, had Phoenix College been North High. Inside the new library was a covered atrium extending the entire height of the building. If you peered over the railing on the third floor, you could spit down on a student sitting on the first -- if you wished.

And there, on the other side, was Annie. My heart pounded. What's Annie doing here? Is she with Vern? I leapt up from the solid wooden table where I was reading, toppling my chair. It thudded dully on the carpet and students around me turned to look. Forgetting my books and papers, I ran in the direction Annie was walking to intercept her. She turned the opposite corner of the atrium just as I turned mine. She stopped, suddenly, alarmed by me running toward her.

I jerked to a stop also. It wasn't Annie at all. It was just a girl who, from a distance, looked like Annie, who walked like Annie. "Sorry," I said. "I thought you were someone else."

The girl nodded and continued on toward the stairs. She threw a wary glance over her shoulder at me as she began descending them. I smiled at her sheepishly and turned back toward my table. I lifted the fallen chair and sat down, conscious of everyone staring at me. I ignored them and peered down at my open book, pretending to read, as if nothing had happened. The other students returned to their reading. Soon, it was indeed as if nothing had happened.

Except that my eyes and my mind had betrayed me...again. I'd been seeing Annie a lot on campus: The places where I'd first met her, the hallways we'd walked hand-in-hand as students the summer before. I saw her going into classrooms, coming out of classrooms, in the cafeteria...in the library. In each case, her appearance was just a mirage, an illusion, a waking dream. I should've gotten used to it. There was no reason Annie would've been walking around the Phoenix College campus, even though Vern was teaching there. She was walking around the North High campus, a mile or so down Thomas Road.

But every time I saw someone who looked like Annie, my heart colluded with my eyes to betray me. My heart began to stutter and it told me that, this time, it really *was* Annie, that she was here to see Vern for some unknown reason. And, burning hot and cold with eagerness and fear, I hurried to catch up to her. I couldn't take the chance that it *wasn't* her.

And, each time, I discovered that it was someone else. It was *always* someone else.

In February, 1967, Buffalo Springfield's "For What It's Worth" reached No. 7 on the pop charts. Its inspiration was the Sunset Strip police riot the previous November of '66. Every time I heard it on the radio I thought about me and Annie running from the cops on the Strip.

February 17th came. It was Annie's birthday. She turned 17. I thought about her all day. Did she have the abortion? How was she? What was she doing? Was she still going to North High every day? If I'd owned a phone, I'd have called her and risked having it slammed down on me. Instead, that night I wrote a poem for her, a birthday gift she'd never see:

Abu-Annie:
A Tale of Ancient Splendor

Abu-Annie
    Rises above all.
Below this great and mighty head
Ten thousand slaves sweat
To finish before sunfall.
Abu-Annie
    Will view the work at dusk.
The colossal bust
Must
    Be finished, lest Abu-Annie be displeased.
Abu-Annie:
    A behemoth of stone
Towering a mile above the desert sands.
A monument built
With blood and bone.
Abu-Annie
    Stares silently toward the horizon.
The scream of a falling slave
Breaks the monotony of
Cracking whips and bellowed curses.
The work goes on.
Abu-Annie:
    Ten thousand slaves labored
For seventeen years to complete this
Monolithic statue.
The last stone is fitted into place.
The work ceases.
Abu-Annie
    Is finished.
For the first time in seventeen years
The slaves, their drivers, their overseers, and
The planners rest.
Abu-Annie
    Looks upon herself
And decides.
She strides to her chariot and,
With a last arrogant look back
Gives the command:
"Abu-Annie
    Is pleased with your work.
It is a noble and magnificent monument
    To myself.
However -- it is in the wrong position.
It catches my mood better over there.

>Move it."
>>Abu-Annie
>>>Motions to her driver
>>>>And is gone over the sands.

****

One day in March I heard someone on campus playing a guitar and singing "Long Black Veil." It sounded like Annie, it was a song I'd heard her sing dozens of times, it *had* to be Annie!

I followed the sound and rounded the corner of one of the cinderblock rows of classrooms. It was Annie's song...but it wasn't Annie. It was a slim raven-haired siren sitting at one of the campus picnic tables in the shade of an orange tree. She was strumming on a Martin and singing about a forbidden lover visiting the singer's grave when the night winds wail. She shook her dark mane as she sang. It rippled and shimmered like sunlight on a crow's wing. It was dangerous to look at her, but the danger was exciting. I listened to her play the old song of steadfast love and tragic death. She ended with a flourish on the Martin and the last chords hummed in the hot air.

I clapped lightly. "That was beautiful. Do you know 'Lily of the West'?" It was another song Annie had sung myriad times.

"Of course." And the siren plunged into another old song of love and death, only this one was of faithful love rewarded by betrayal. She wore a silky magenta blouse with a low-cut neck. Peeking above the neck of the blouse, curving over her suntanned right breast, was the filigree of her bra. It was bright blue. Less really is more, and although I dared give it only the barest glimpse, that slim strip of frilly blue against her brown beast seemed incredibly sexy. As she sang I felt drawn to her. I knew my attraction was a moth-to-the-flame fascination, but I couldn't help it.

As she finished singing, I sat down beside her. She picked at the Martin lightly, her fingers flying over the strings. I recognized the tune. It was Paul Simon's instrumental from *Sounds of Silence*. It was technically difficult. I was impressed. "What's your name?"

"Shana. It means 'Beautiful.'"

"Then you are truly named."

Shana smiled at me. "Flattery will get you everywhere. And you are...?"

"Eric. It means 'kingly.'"

Do you play, Kingly Eric?"

"No, I just appreciate the music. And the ones who play it."

"I could teach you."

"I doubt it. I played drums in high school because I didn't have the fingers for the guitar."

"I can teach anyone to play *something*. Watch closely." She stopped playing the Simon tune and began a very simple chord progression. The fingers of her right hand picked delicately at the strings as her left hand fingers danced over the neck. She stopped and did it again. It was simple, but beautiful. Then she handed the guitar to me. I cradled it in my lap, right hand on the body, left hand on the neck. She took my left hand and placed my fingers over the correct frets. "OK, start picking."

I began stumbling slowly and awkwardly through the chord changes I'd seen her do. She lifted the fingers of my left hand and moved them to fret after fret. "You're doing great."

I wasn't doing great. I was doing awful. But it was fun. Shana laughed at my clumsy fingering and kept telling me I was doing great. I kept at it because she was laughing and telling me I was doing great. And, after awhile, I began to sound...okay. It wasn't virtuosity, but the simple chords sounded more complex than they were. I kept repeating them over and over. If I didn't have to play anything else but these chords, it actually sounded like I knew what I was doing.

"See? I told you I could teach you. And if we had two guitars, you could just play that theme over and over while I played variations on it and we'd make beautiful music together."

"Then I'll have to find another guitar so we can make beautiful music together. What else can you teach me?"

Shana glanced sideways at me. "I could probably teach you a lot. Are you flirting with me, Kingly Eric?"

I smiled. "Of course I am, Shana the Beautiful. Are you flirting with *me?*"

Shana smiled back. "Of *course* I am. Don't you know that music is the language of love?"

"I know that I'm going to buy a Martin this very day."

Shana threw back her head and laughed. Her flowing black hair rippled as if a wild horse had shook its mane.

Her full name was Shana Schwartz. It was a nice Jewish name for a nice Jewish girl.

Except her parents didn't think she was so nice. They didn't like her music, they didn't like the tight black jeans she wore, and -- when she finally took me home to meet them -- they didn't like me. And they didn't hide it. I was a hippie. Even worse, I was a goy, a gentile. Shana should be dating nice Jewish boys, they said. Instead, she hung out with hippie goyim. And now she'd brought another one home. Oy!

"He's a mensch," Shana said.

"Fie!" her mother answered. "A meshugganah mensch, maybe. You wouldn't know a real mensch if he walked through the door."

Shana cranked up the volume on the radio. "Listen to this song." It was Aretha Franklin singing her new hit, about how she needed some *respect*. "That's what I need from you," Shana yelled at her mother. "R-E-S-P-E-C-T! Find out what it means to me!"

Her mother clapped her hands over her ears. "Turn it down! I can't stand it! It's *me* who needs respect. And if you respected me you wouldn't bring home another hippie *goy!*"

"It's my life, and I'll do what I want and I'll bring home who I want!"

I liked Shana's fire and I liked her defiance. Anyone who defied her parents with her vehemence was a kindred soul.

And I liked her passion as we made love in my hell hole hovel with the walls splashed red and black. We were nude on the pallet and Shana was in my arms. It was hot in the hell hole hovel and her skin was hot and feverish to my touch. My right hand was tangled in her mane and I pulled her head back to expose her neck. I bit her neck like a vampire and sucked, careful not to give her a hickey by sucking too hard. She moaned and I moved down to her nipples, running my tongue over them. She howled and thrashed under me and dug her nails into my back, and neither of us gave a fuck that brother Rick was lying in his closet just a few feet away, listening to us. To hell with him. To hell with everyone except Shana the Beautiful, dark and dangerous in my arms.

****

Shana

Your diamond talons,
  Sharper than a panther's claws,

Leave scarlet trails down my back,
    A cicatrix of fire
        To mark your passion and desire.

Thou Art the Man

"A wise man will not leave the right to the mercy of chance, nor wish it to prevail through the power of the majority. There is but little virtue in the action of masses of men. When the majority shall at length vote for the abolition of slavery, it will be because...there is but little slavery left to be abolished by their vote....

"I do not hesitate to say, that those who call themselves abolitionists should at once effectually withdraw their support, both in person and in property, from the government of Massachusetts, and not wait till they constitute a majority of one before they suffer the right to prevail through them. I think that it is enough if they have God on their side, without waiting for that other one. Moreover, any man more right than his neighbors constitutes a majority of one already."

-- Henry David Thoreau
On the Duty of Civil Disobedience

****

Spring came. I'd be graduating from Phoenix College simply because I'd kept plodding along out of sheer momentum. I was looking forward to escaping from Phoenix, if only for the summer to attend the FCC school in Sarasota. My only regret was that I'd be leaving Shana. I liked her more each day. I wondered if she'd still be there for me once summer ended and I returned...or would she discard me, as Annie had done? I'd just have to find out.

One day Mr. Polichino informed me that the college required my services as a student government officer. It seemed the dweeb student government president would not be graduating. He didn't have enough credits. And the student government constitution mandated that the *highest graduating* student government officer would deliver a farewell address to the graduates at the graduation convocation and, as the representative of the students, present the class gift to college president J. Lee Thompson. As I was the vice president and I *was* graduating, I was the one the constitution anointed as the man of the hour. And it appeared this was one aspect of the constitution Polichino and Thompson decided to respect.

I could tell Mr. Polichino did not relish inviting me to share the auditorium stage with him and President Thompson. He'd been unremittingly hostile toward me and my fellow plotters ever since we'd attempted to remove him from office. I savored his discomfort and made it worse for him by cheerfully agreeing to fulfill my constitutionally mandated duty.

The graduation convocation for the Class of 1967 took place in the Phoenix College auditorium on the morning of May 26. The hall was filled with the Class of '67, a dark mass of black gowns and mortar boards speckled with mostly white faces. Three years before, when I'd graduated from North High, I'd been sitting with Hiromi in a similar anonymous mass. This time I was not among them. Instead, I was sitting above them, on stage, flanked by my arch-foes, Louis Polichino and President J. Lee Thompson, making nice to each other, pretending that we didn't despise each other. All three of us wore the scholarly caps and gowns, although Polichino and Thompson had some strips of color denoting their Masters' degrees added to the tassels dangling from their mortar boards.

President J. Lee Thompson rose and approached the podium. He tapped the microphone to make sure it worked. The din of massed conversations among the students faded and died. Thompson made some innocuous remarks welcoming the prospective graduates. And then he began to warn them of the dangers which they must avoid in the turbulent times we all faced in the hostile outside world. "There is turmoil and dissent in these troubled times," President Thompson said. "There is temptation and disaster for the unwary. We have become a society awash in trendy mind-altering drugs, such as marijuana and LDS."

There was a murmur of confusion among the students. They weren't sure they heard President Thompson right. Nor was I. Was this a joke? As most of us knew, "LDS" was how Mormons, the Latter-Day Saints, usually referred to themselves. Surely President Thompson meant to warn us against the dangers of LSD?

No doubt he did. But it was only the second graduation convocation he'd presided over since his appointment as president in the fall of 1965, and he was unused to the ritual. He was easily befuddled by his new responsibilities and, besides, he was a devout Mormon, and so habitually referred to his church and his fellow Mormons with the shorthand "LDS." Now he was using those same initials ingrained in the furrows of his brain. "Beware of LDS," he repeated. "Its seductive lure promises heaven, but it will deliver only the torments of hell."

The students began to laugh outright. Sitting behind President Thompson on the stage, I smiled. Mr. Polichino, next to me, grimaced and twisted in his seat. Like me, like the entire auditorium of students, Polichino realized what President Thompson was saying. Thompson, alone, was unaware and, being unaware, misinterpreted the student laughter.

"Do not laugh," he implored, his quavering voice rising. "I'm speaking of a serious matter. The danger is real. LDS will blast your soul and destroy your mind. It is everywhere around you. The people you meet on the street could well be high on LDS. Your closest friends might be using LDS and urge it upon you. But you must avoid LDS at the peril of your immortal soul."

The student laughter swelled as more joined in. This was better than they could have hoped for. It wasn't going to be a boring old convocation ritual, after all. And the louder the students laughed, the more flustered President Thompson became, confused by their mockery of his dire warnings against the soul destroying LDS. It wasn't going as it was supposed to go. Where was the respect and decorum the occasion demanded? He became more and more shrill, more and more desperate to make his point. And the more he warned the students against LDS, the more they laughed at his botched warnings.

At last, in despair, not know what else to do, President J. Lee Thompson gave up and turned to me, sitting behind him and smiling at his distress. "And now, I would like to introduce the vice president of the Class of 1967 who, as the representative of the graduating students, will have the honor of presenting the class gift."

I rose and approached the podium as President Thompson returned to his seat. I waited, smiling, as the laughter of my fellow students died down. Then I thanked President J. Lee Thompson for his insightful comments about the dangers of LDS. There was a renewed ripple of laughter at that. I then welcomed my fellow students to their final event in the Phoenix College auditorium before they left for their lives beyond the college.

And then I said that I would like to tell them a story, a Bible story, which was pertinent to their lives, not only as students, but, more importantly, to their lives as American citizens. It was the story of David and Bathsheba from Second Samuel, Chapters 11 and 12. I figured Mr. Polichino and President Thompson would let me tell a Bible story long enough to make the point I'd come that day to make.

At that time in ancient Israel, I told the assembly, there was war in the land and King David had sent his great general, Joab, to besiege the city of Rabbah and destroy the children of Ammon. But David, himself, remained behind in Jerusalem while the battles raged.

One hot summer night, unable to sleep, David rose and sought the cool breezes on the roof of his palace. And, as he enjoyed the night breeze, cooling the sweat of his brow, he gazed out over the buildings of Jerusalem spread below him. And there, on the roof of one of them, was a young woman also suffering from the heat of the night. And, to cool herself, she was on her rooftop alone, bathing, nude in the moonlight. She was Bathsheba, the wife of Uriah, the Hittite, one of David's most loyal and bravest warriors, who was away, at the siege of Rabbah, fighting for the king. And, the Bible tells us, David saw that Bathsheba "was very beautiful to look upon."

Now King David had a large harem filled with many beautiful women, but he was seized with lust for Bathsheba, bathing in the silver moonlight, and he sent his soldiers for her. They brought her to him and he took her immediately to his bed and made love to her in the hot summer night while her husband was away, fighting his enemies. And, when he'd finished with her, King David summoned his soldiers and sent Bathsheba with them back to her husband's house, while he slept the sleep of the contented.

But that night of hot summer lust was not without consequence, for as the siege of Rabbah continued week after week, Bathsheba sent word to King David that she now was with child. And everyone knew that her husband was away, fighting the king's battles. And everyone knew that David's soldiers had brought her to him that hot summer night. And so everyone would know that her child was his.

Hoping to conceal his night of lust, King David recalled Bathsheba's husband, Uriah, from the siege of Rabbah. His excuse for calling Uriah home was that he wanted news of the siege from his best warrior. After Uriah briefed his king on the siege, David thanked him and sent him home to be with his wife. Uriah had long been absent from the beautiful young Bathsheba, and he was eager to see her. David was certain there would be a lustful homecoming, and the child who would arrive thereafter would be taken for Uriah's.

And, had Uriah been less loyal and less honorable, that surely would have happened. But Uriah refused to go home that night and sleep with his beautiful young wife. Instead, he slept in the doorway of King David's palace, among the king's servants.

Puzzled, and irritated that his plan to conceal his sin against Uriah was thus frustrated, David asked Uriah why he had not gone home to be with his waiting wife. Uriah replied that he was a soldier of the king and Israel was at war. Uriah said that he had just come from the long and bloody siege of Rabbah, where his comrades and his commander, Joab, were encamped in tents in the open fields. "Shall I then go into mine own house to eat and to drink, and to lie with my wife" while his comrades continued to suffer the privations of the long siege? "As my soul liveth," he said, "I will not do this thing."

Desperate, now, to hide his adultery with Uriah's wife, King David concocted a further, more heinous plan. He sent Uriah back to the siege at Rabbah with sealed orders to be delivered to Joab, his general. Uriah returned and delivered the orders to his commander. Joab read the orders and was, no doubt, appalled, for what Uriah had faithfully delivered was his own death warrant. In the document, King David ordered Joab to put Uriah "in the forefront of the hottest battle." And, as the enemy surged forward, Joab was to order his men to retreat in such a way that Uriah would be abandoned and surrounded, fighting the king's enemies alone, certain of death.

And so it was done, and the loyal and faithful Uriah was killed in battle just as King David had commanded him to be. When the news reached King David that Uriah was dead, killed fighting the king's enemies, David shrugged it off, saying to his court, "The sword devoureth one as well as another. Let not this thing displease thee."

After a suitable period of mourning, King David took Uriah's young and beautiful widow, Bathsheba, for his wife, adding her to his harem. And they named the son who was soon born to them, "Solomon."

But the Lord then sent the Prophet Nathan to David and the Prophet Nathan told King David a story. "There were two men in one city," said Nathan, "the one rich, and the other poor. The rich man had exceeding many flocks and herds. But the poor man had nothing, save one little ewe lamb, which he had bought and nourished up; and it grew up together with him, and with his children; it did eat of his own meat, and drank of his own cup, and lay in his bosom, and was unto him as a daughter.

"And there came a traveler unto the rich man, and he spared to take of his own flock and of his own herd, to dress for the wayfaring man, but took the poor man's lamb, and dressed it for the man that was come to him."

And the Bible tells us that David's anger was greatly kindled against the rich man and he said to Nathan, "As the Lord liveth, the man that hath done this thing shall surely die! And he shall restore the lamb fourfold, because he had no pity."

And then Nathan said unto David, "Thou art the man."

"*Thou* art the man," I repeated to my listening fellow students, "for you have taken the poor man's lamb and you have murdered Uriah. We are *all* 'the rich man,' we are *all* King David, the one who had no pity and used his power to murder the powerless. Only now Uriah goes by the name of Vietnam, and the conspiracy against him continues even today, as we are murdering him on the battlefield each and every day." There was a stir among the students and I could tell that Mr. Polichino, behind me, was becoming agitated.

"Like King David of old, we must recognize the evil that we do," I continued. "We must recognize that, like him, we are using our power unjustly, that we are killing the innocent, and that we are plundering the land that belongs to another." The stir among the students became a babel of voices as they leaned toward each other, questioning what they heard. I leaned into the mike and raised my voice.

"And we must atone for our sin. We must renounce the evil that we do daily and we must make it right. I, for one, cannot continue to murder Uriah on the battlefields of Vietnam. I, for one, cannot proceed with the theft of the poor man's lamb and the poor man's land. And therefore I, for one, say today that I intend to file for Conscientious Objector status with my local draft board."

There were scattered boos from the begowned students before me. I pressed on. "And I urge all good men of conscience to do the same..."

That was as far as I got. Mr. Polichino lunged out of his seat behind me and shouldered me away from the dais. My mortar board cap fell off as I stumbled aside. "The vice president is not authorized to make these statements," he yelled into the mike.

"Let me speak!" I said. "I am the representative of the students. Let me speak!"

Polichino covered the mike with one hand and glared at me. "You have no authority to make these statements."

"I have the authority of the student government! I am the representative of the students! Let me speak!"

"You represent no one but yourself," Polichino replied, still covering the mike. "You're a disgrace to student government. Get off the stage!"

I surged forward and shouldered Polichino aside, just as he had done to me. I grabbed the mike and shouted into it, "Let me speak! I represent the students!"

Again Polichino shoved me away from the mike and also yelled into the mike, "The vice president has no right to speak against the war at this event. This is a structured event with a recognized agenda."

Then he turned to me, barring me from access to the mike, and pointed toward the wings. "Get off the stage!"

A howl rose from the assembled students. There were cries of "Get off the stage!" mixed with "Let him speak! Let him speak!"

I glowered at Polichino guarding the rostrum. I can take down this academic wimp, I thought. One swift kick in the balls and Polichino goes down. And all eyes are on me, waiting to see what I'll do next. All I have to do is push it and, one way or another, things will explode.

There was a pause for an instant as the deafening clamor from the students poured over us and Polichino and I glared at each other. Polichino again jerked his pointing finger toward the stage wings like the angel at the Gates of Eden pointing Adam the way into exile.

I decided not to push it. In a quick overhead sweep I pulled my gown off and threw it in a clump at Polichino's feet. "Fuck you in the ass, Polichino!" The students roared. I pointed a straight-armed finger back at him. "You are nothing but a lying hypocrite! *Thou* art the man!"

Then I turned and strode off the stage into the curtained wings. I parted them with a flourish and passed through. The student bedlam receded as the curtains furled behind me.

It doesn't matter, I told myself. I didn't need to kick Polichino in the balls to make my point. I'm already a majority of one.

A Rose From the Ashes

That night Shana took the mirror which hung in my tiny bathroom and placed it on the table in the kitchen breakfast nook. She slid out of her tattered jean jacket and tossed it on the alcove bench. She sat down next to it and took a baggie out of the jean jacket breast pocket. From the baggie she sprinkled a pile of white powder onto the mirror. She used one of my kitchen knives to shape the pile into two long narrow lines. I sat down across from her. "What's this?"

"Coke."

"Cocaine?"

"Right. You ever done it?"

"No, and I don't want to start now."

"Sure you do. We'll get high to celebrate your graduation and then we'll fuck like crazy."

"We fuck like crazy, anyway."

"We'll be even more fuck crazy when we're high." She pulled a dollar bill out of her shirt's breast pocket and rolled it into a tube.

"You've done this before?"

"Sure. It's why I'm such a great crazy fuck and come fast as hell."

I reached across the table to touch her hand. "Shana, I didn't know you did this. I can't. I'm not into drugs."

"Oh, c'mon, don't fuck with me, man. You're a hippie, right?"

"I'm a *weird* hippie. I'm not into drugs. I've never even been drunk. I'm always sober as a judge. I get high naturally." Then I smiled at her and squeezed her hand. "I get high on you!"

Shana looked askance at me. "Don't fuck with my head, man. There's no such thing as a hippie who isn't into drugs. So, c'mon, take a snort." She held out the dollar bill tube.

I pushed it back toward her. "Shana, believe me, no matter how freaky I look, I'm completely straight when it comes to drugs."

"Wow, man. What a bummer! And I thought you were a stone head. Well, if you're not gonna take a snort, I certainly am." She stuck the dollar tube in her left nostril and leaned down toward the powdery lines on the mirror.

I placed my hand over the end of the tube, stopping her. "Shana, don't do this. You don't need to get high to have crazy sex."

"I need to get high to feel good about myself, man." She was almost crying. "Coke is my only hope. I'm like Aretha. I don't get no respect!"

"I respect you! You're smart, you're a great musician, and you're Shana the Beautiful!" I shook her shoulder to drive home my points. "And you're a crazy fuck even without the coke. You don't need coke to feel good about yourself. All you need is love."

"Why are you saying all this shit, man?"

"Because it's true. And because snorting coke is just plain stupid. It'll fuck you up, and then you'll just prove everything your parents said about you was true. You don't want to prove them *right*, do you?"

"Man, you're really bringing me down. You sound just like my fuckin' father."

"No, I sound just like the mensch you *told* him I was. Shana, please don't do this. You're breaking my heart. If you're into drugs, we can't stay together. I mean it."

Shana shrugged my hand off her shoulder. "Well, fuck you, man. Pricks like you are a dime a dozen. I don't need you. But I sure as hell need this coke. Now, back off!"

I stared into Shana's eyes. She glared back. "OK, Shana, I guess you made your choice. Snort your coke."

I rose from the table and walked over to my pallet. I sat on it crosslegged and looked back at Shana. She was still glaring at me. Defiantly, she again put the dollar tube in her nostril and leaned down toward the mirror.

"Shana," tried once more. "Please don't do it! I mean it. It's either me or the coke."

Shana gave me the finger at the same time she snorted an entire line of coke. It vanished into her nose. She gagged and rocked back as if splashed in the face with a glass of cold water. She placed the dollar tube in her other nostril and snorted the other line. It, too, disappeared into her nose. She choked, gagged...and then sighed. There were scattered grains of coke still on the mirror. Shana licked her birdie finger and sponged them up with it. Then she stuck her birdie finger in her mouth and sucked on it. She leered over at me as she slowly pumped her birdie finger in and out, fucking her mouth with her finger. Coke flecked her wet lips.

Then she rose and came over to me. She knelt and placed her arms on both my shoulders, touching her forehead to mine. She was smiling now, stoned and mellow as she looked into my eyes. "Don't be mad at me, Eric. Make love to me now, and I'll be your baby tonight." She unbuttoned her blouse and slipped it off.

I put my arms around her and pulled her down beside me. "Shana, oh, Shana," I said as we lay together on my pallet and I hugged her close and rocked her gently until she fell asleep.

****

She came with the dawn, long after I'd given her up. I awoke to her shaking me. I opened my eyes to a brilliant sunrise streaming in through the window above my pallet. I squinted against the light and saw Annie squatting beside the pallet. I'd left the door unlocked and she'd walked right into the apartment she'd once shared with me. She stopped shaking me when she saw I was awake. I lay there, looking up at her, my heart pounding, with Shana still asleep on my chest.

"Annie, what are you doing here?"

"I wanted to talk to you."

"Your timing is amazing. But I'm glad to see you." And I *was* glad.

Shana stirred next to me. She sat up quickly, eyes wide and holding her hands crossed over her bare breasts. "What's going on?"

"I have no idea," I answered, also sitting up. I handed Shana her blouse and she quickly slipped it on. As she did so, I said, "Shana, this is Annie. She and I used to be lovers. But she broke up with me and told me it was over between us.

"And Annie, this is Shana. She and I have been seeing each other for awhile. But Shana made a decision about us last night." I looked at Shana as I said that. "And this is certainly an embarrassing situation. Or it *would* be, if Annie and I were still together and she had just caught me cheating on her. But," I said, looking pointedly at Annie, "we're *not* together. So, Shana, it's not as embarrassing as it might be, and you have no reason to be alarmed."

Shana shook her dark mane. "Who said I was?" She began calmly buttoning her blouse.

I looked at Annie, who remained squatting beside the pallet. "So, Annie, let me ask again. What are you doing here?"

"I wanted to talk to you. Can we?"

"Of course you can," Shana said. "I'm going to the bathroom." She got up and walked the few steps to my tiny bathroom. She shut the door and I heard her turn on the water in the sink and splash her face.

I looked at Annie. "Would you like some coffee?" I asked. She nodded. I rose and walked to the kitchen. Annie rose and followed me. I ran water into my dented kettle and put it back on the stove. I turned on the burner and reached for three cups from my cupboard. My hands shook slightly. I put the cups on the counter and then turned to Annie, standing behind me, watching me. "I'm *really* glad to see you."

Annie looked into my eyes. And then we stepped into each other's arms and hugged tightly. Her face buried in my chest, Annie began crying softly. I squeezed her more tightly.

The kettle began to whistle. I released her and motioned her toward the breakfast nook. "Annie, sit down."

She did, wiping tears from her cheeks. She noticed the bathroom mirror on the table. "What's this doing here?"

"I'll tell you some other time."

I put the three cups on the table and dumped a spoonful of instant coffee crystals into each. I poured in steaming water until they were almost full and then quickly stirred each cup with the same spoon. I put the kettle back on the stove and it whistled a last dying breath as the cooling burner heated it briefly. I brought over the sugar bowl and then pulled a small carton of cream out of the fridge. I put it on the table next to the sugar. I plucked Shana's coke baggie off the table and stuffed it in her jean jacket breast pocket. Then I hung the jacket up on the edge of the bench.

Shana came out of the bathroom. She'd washed her face and combed her wild hair. She looked great. You'd never guess she was a cokehead and you'd never guess she'd said good-bye to me last night. I handed her one of the cups of coffee, black and bitter as the grave, the way she liked it.

She took it and, standing there, sipped at it. "Ahh, thanks. I needed that." She looked at Annie over the steaming rim of the cup, analyzing her. Then she handed it back to me, still half full, and scooped up her jean jacket from where I'd hung it. "I'll be going. You two should talk. I can see this girl needs to speak with you alone."

"Shana, I'll call you later."

Shana looked at me as she shrugged her shoulders into her jean jacket. "OK, call me."

She opened the door and stood there for an instant, framed by the golden sunrise flooding the doorway. She smiled at me. "You really are a mensch," she said.

Then she was gone.

Blood Nativity

Hold My Heart Gently

I am here.
    Seek me.
        Hear me.
           Draw near me
               In the darkness.
Hold my heart gently
    in your healing hands.
        My heart
    Is far from home,
        For I have been
           Swimming with the Sharks,
              Running with the Wolves,
                  Sleeping with the Enemy.
And now
    My heart hunts alone
        Through the dark
           And wounded lands.
Draw near me
    In the darkness.
        Hold my heart gently
           in your healing hands.

****

    Despite what John Donne wrote, the bell never tolled for Vern. He was not part of the human continent. He felt he was an island. He needed no one for anything. Needing people was a weakness, and Vern was not needy and weak.

    Except that he did need someone for Annie's abortion. It was 1967 and abortion was illegal in America, a criminal act which Vern could not arrange on his own. But such a crime could be arranged if one had the right contacts. And Vern did. His contact was Walt Emory, the only adult "friend" Vern had. Luckily, Walt was a doctor.

    Walt couldn't perform the abortion himself in any of the hospitals with which he was associated, so he made discreet inquiries. He discovered there was no doctor in Arizona who was willing to commit the crime. Annie would have to leave the state. Indeed, she would have to leave the country. That year, 1967, Janis Joplin went to Mexico for an abortion. So did Annie. It didn't matter if you were famous or unknown. There was no place else to go.

    Walt found a doctor just over the border in Nogales, Mexico, who would abort Annie's fetus. He wanted $150 to do it. Vern agreed. It didn't matter what it cost. He wasn't paying for it, I was.

    In January of '67, shortly after she broke up with me, Vern drove Annie across the border into Mexico. The Mexican doctor's office was a small one-man clinic which looked, Annie told me, like a veterinarian's office. She wondered if he was a real doctor. Nevertheless, she climbed on his table and spread her legs.

The Mexican doctor clamped a wad of sterile gauze with a forceps and shoved it up inside her vagina. He moved the forceps around, searching, and then shoved it further up inside her, into her uterus. Annie screamed with the pain which shot through her belly and the Mexican doctor stopped for a moment. Then he pulled the bloody forceps out of her vagina and picked up another wad of gauze with it. He shoved the new wad of gauze up inside her vagina, up inside her uterus. And then he did it again. And again. And again. And each time he did it, the pain flamed through Annie's belly and she clenched her teeth to hold back her screams. Finally he felt he'd packed her uterus with enough gauze, 15-feet of it, to induce a miscarriage. Then he sent Annie and Vern back across the border to America and told her to wait. Her body would do the rest.

Despite constant pain, Annie returned to her classes at North High. It's what Vern would have done, and she wanted to do what Vern would have done. And she waited. And she waited. But Annie's body was strong, and it did its best to save the fetus. Annie did not miscarry.

So Vern drove Annie across the border into Mexico a second time.

Again the Mexican doctor shoved his forceps up inside her and packed her uterus with wad after wad of cotton gauze. And again he sent her home and told her to wait. And again Annie returned to her classes at North High.

This time her body could not save the fetus. She miscarried. Just as Janis Joplin had complications following her Mexican abortion, so did Annie. It wasn't uncommon following a Mexican abortion in 1967. On the morning of her 17th birthday, February 17th, the same day I wrote "Abu Annie" for her, Annie suddenly woke from a few short hours of uneasy sleep to a world of pain. She said it felt like a ruptured appendix. She said it felt like razor blades cutting their way out of her belly from the inside, like the last agonized stages of stomach cancer with no morphine. She curled into a fetal position in her bed and moaned and screamed and writhed in the worst pain she'd ever felt in her short life.

Walt had given Vern a powerful pain killer for Annie. But Vern didn't give it to her. It was good and right that she feel the torment of the damned writhing in hell for their sins. Instead, Vern turned up the volume of the classical music he always had on the radio, loud enough to cover Annie's moans and screams coming from her room, loud enough to keep the sound of Annie's pain from his ears.

And then, like a gigantic bowl movement, Annie's insides fell out through her vagina and there was blood everywhere. Blood covered her thighs, blood drenched the sheets, blood soaked the mattress. And, mixed with her insides, covered with dark sticky blood and glistening mucus, was the fetus. It was small, but perfectly formed because it was five-and-a-half months old. Annie saw that it was a boy, several inches long. And she saw that it had a long gash across its head. It was dead from that gash long before her body flushed it from her insides. The Mexican doctor had killed it with his forceps, shoving it up inside her, up inside her uterus.

Annie picked up the bloody and mucus covered fetus and looked at it, small and perfect in her hands. And then she wept over her dead son, my dead son, cupped in her gore smeared hands, she wept great wracking sobs as the tears streamed down her cheeks. And then, still crying, she placed our son in an Igloo cooler she had standing by, for just that purpose. And then she called for her father, listening to his classical music in the living room, to phone Walt and tell him it had happened. Vern did so as Annie collected her bloody bedclothes and washed the blood from herself as best she could, washed the blood from her hands as best she could.

Walt's wife came for Annie. She told Annie to lie down in the back seat. After Annie did so, Walt's wife placed the Igloo cooler with the body of our son on the floor of the car next to Annie. She drove Annie to Walt's office. There she hurried Annie inside, frightened that someone might see them, for everything they did was a crime. Walt examined Annie and cleaned her up some more and said she would be okay. And Annie gave Walt the Igloo cooler with our dead son inside. Walt took the Igloo away and Annie never saw it again, nor did she ever ask about her son, my son, our son.

And the next day, Annie returned to North High, as if nothing had happened. She sat in class, as if nothing had happened. She acted -- as if nothing had happened. She acted strong, like she needed no one, like she was an island, and she did not cry. It was what her father felt she should do. "Life goes on," Vern told her. There was a death, but the bell had not tolled for him.

At night, alone in her bed, where Vern could not see her, Annie was not strong. Alone, in her bed, staring up at her dark ceiling, Annie cried for herself and for our dead son, quietly, silently, so that her father would not hear her and condemn her for being a weak girl who had just turned 17 and had lost her baby on her birthday and who needed someone.

And then, one morning, three months later, Annie rose before dawn and, in the pre-dawn chill, slipped out of her house. She walked the dark Phoenix streets back to the apartment where our son had been conceived. She walked back to the hovel she had shared with me and where I still lived. She walked down the alley to the hovel, the gravel crunching loudly beneath her feet. She climbed the cement steps to the hovel just as the sun was creeping above the horizon. She didn't bother to knock. She turned the knob instead. She knew the door wouldn't be locked.

She opened the door and stepped inside. And she saw me asleep on my pallet, our pallet, with Shana asleep in my arms. She paused for a moment, looking at us holding each other in sleep. A feeling of great betrayal swept over her, making her weak in her knees. She could have turned and left once more, closing the door softly, careful not to wake us. But, she'd been strong and alone for too long. She walked over and squatted down beside me. She shook me gently. I opened my eyes and looked up at her.

"Annie, what are you doing here?"

"I wanted to talk to you."

****

I asked Annie why she came back after breaking up with me. We were still sitting at the wooden table in the breakfast nook. We'd gone through several cups of coffee and only cold dregs remained at the bottom of our cups. The radio was playing a new song just released by Scott McKenzie, some singer I'd never heard of, "San Francisco (Be Sure to Wear Flowers in Your Hair)." You'll meet gentle people in San Francisco, he sang, with flowers in their hair. This summer there'll be a love-in there. Come to San Francisco for a summer of love. I wondered if I'd made a mistake in planning to go to Sarasota instead.

"Because I never broke up with you," Annie answered.

"It certainly felt like it to me."

"I was simply following orders the night I told you I didn't want to see you again."

"Vern's orders?"

"Yes, he chose the time, he chose the place, he told me exactly what to say. Everything I said came from him, it didn't come from me. It didn't come from my heart."

"That seems like such a perversion to me."

"A perversion by me?"

"No, a perversion by Vern. I felt you were terribly wrong about our relationship when you broke up with me. But I did think you were saying what you truly believed. Now, to learn that Vern forced you to say what you did, forced you to speak against your own heart -- that seems perverted. Vern is always condemning those who 'diminish the souls' of others. I thought that respect for the 'soul' was some bedrock of his ethics. I guess I was wrong about him. There is a holiness to the heart's affections, Annie. And surely it wounded your heart and diminished your soul to force you to renounce the affections of your own heart that night. That's just bedrock evil. Vern's just another Goddamn hypocrite with feet of clay. We're drowning in a sea of hypocrisy, Annie. I can't stand it."

"You don't usually speak so spiritually. I'm touched."

I waved my hand disparagingly. "Oh, I don't want to be another hypocrite and pretend I'm being spiritual when I'm not. Or perhaps I am and I don't know it. I've been reading and writing a lot of poetry. I was quoting John Keats. He said 'the holiness of the heart's affections' was one of the few things of which he was certain in this world. When I read that, it seemed true to me, also."

"I did feel I was speaking against my heart's affections that night. I felt I was not only hurting you, I was betraying myself."

"Then why did you do it?"

"Vern can be very forceful. He said, 'This is the way it's going to be.' He gave me no choice. I had to completely sever our relationship, a clean sharp break."

"But, why?"

"Because he doesn't like you, Eric. He has big plans for me. I'm going to go to an elite college. I'm going to have a high-powered career. I going to marry someone with prospects. I'm going to *be* someone and do important things. But he said none of that would happen if I stayed with you. You're poor, Eric. He said you're just a slunky street punk from a dirt road slum. You're nobody from nowhere. You'll never amount to anything. And you got me pregnant and almost trapped me in your poverty. He'd ensure I'd abort our child and escape your trap. But you might yet pull me down into your weakness. You might get me pregnant again. So I had to be strong and tell you that you had to go."

"Then why did you come back?"

"Because Keats was right. There is a holiness to the heart's affections. And I told you, in my heart, I never broke up with you. I never stopped loving you. And I want to be with you. I want whatever life we will have together."

"What about Vern?"

"I *can* be strong, and I *can* stand up to Vern. I'll tell him we're going to be together, if you want, and *this* is the way it's going to be. He will have to accept it and accept you, even though he doesn't like you. And if he doesn't accept you and he doesn't accept our relationship, then I will completely sever my relationship with *him*. There will be a clean sharp break. And Vern will never see me again. He will no longer be my father."

I smiled at her and squeezed her hand. "You're the strongest woman I've ever met, Annie. And I love you madly. And we *will* have other children together."

"I know. And I know we are destined to be together. Always. My heart tells me that."

Freedom Road

For some, the summer of 1967 was the Summer of Love. Scott McKenzie was all over the radio singing about wearing flowers in your hair if you were going to San Francisco. And tens of thousands of runaway kids were indeed descending on 'Frisco's Haight-Ashbury for the promised love-in. In retrospect, the Haight's Summer of Love turned out to be a hellacious drug-addled mess, but we inhabitants of the rest of America didn't know that at the time. We just knew that the Haight was the Promised Land.

So it felt like we should be heading for San Francisco in the summer of '67, like every other footloose kid in America. Instead, Rick and I were headed east. He wanted to get to Chattanooga and I wanted to get to Florida. He wanted to visit Mom's family and I still hoped that a miracle would happen and I'd be able to attend the FCC school in Sarasota. I didn't have the money for tuition, but I believed that if I just had faith and showed up at the school, lightning would strike. I didn't know what else to do. I was desperate to change my life.

We couldn't stay around Phoenix, in any case. I didn't have a job and we couldn't pay the rent on the hell hole hovel. I parked the blue Suzuki in Vern's garage and we stacked our meager possessions in cardboard boxes beside it. Vern wasn't happy to see me back and he wasn't happy about this use of his garage, but Annie told him this was the way it was going to be and he'd best get used to the new order of things.

Annie, meanwhile, was not happy to see me leave. She didn't understand why I wanted to go to Chattanooga and Sarasota. She'd just come back to me, and now I was leaving town. "You're going on the road to look for a girl," she said.

I was stunned she could think something as crazy as that. I realized it was because she was insecure about our relationship. She'd found me with Shana in my arms. "Annie," I said, "there are so many things wrong with that idea. First, if I was setting out on a girl hunt, I wouldn't be wandering hither and yon across America. I'd stay right here. The best place to find someone is in your own backyard, on your own dirt road. Or maybe Haight-Ashbury. But not in Chattanooga, where I'm headed.

"Second, I never even *looked* at another girl in all the time we were together. I was totally focussed on you. The only reason I was with Shana was because I *wasn't* with you, because I believed everything was over between us. And, in fact, the only reason I found Shana was because I was looking *for you.*"

What I said was true, but some deep part of Annie's heart never believed me. She'd found me in bed with another woman. It affected her more strongly than I realized. The wonder was that, instead of turning and leaving when she found me with Shana, she ignored the woman in my arms and shook me awake instead.

But, no matter what the mitigating circumstances, she never again felt entirely secure about us. Any time we were apart, she felt I was hunting for another woman. Any new discovery of mine was evidence of a new woman in my life. Some time after this I stumbled across *Imitations,* Robert Lowell's 1961 book of poetry which, even now, remains one of my favorite poetry collections. It is a volume of original poems by Lowell, each one written in a different style unique to a different poet, from Sappho to Frost. It's a tour de force exhibition of Lowell's ability to mimic the styles of others and an excellent primer in the personal peculiarities of poets.

In imitation of *Imitations* I began writing poems in the styles of different poets, Emily Dickinson, Walt Whitman, Edgar Allan Poe, Lowell himself. Filled with excitement, I showed the book and my own poor attempts at imitation to Annie.

She looked upon them with a cold eye and spurned my lyric poetry. It was a new interest of mine, something she was unfamiliar with, and therefore it was suspicious. I could not have come upon Robert Lowell's book by myself. It had to have been given to me by a new lover. What woman was I seeing? My praises of Lowell died in my mouth and my enthusiasm for his poetry shrivelled in my heart.

No matter what I said, no matter what I did, I could never alleviate this entrenched insecurity. It was a fear Annie would never be able to shake off. For my part, I felt I now bore the Mark of Cain, and there was nothing I could do about it. If I wanted to be with Annie, I just had to live with it.

If I'd been more perceptive at the time, I'd have realized that Annie's insecurity was not entirely, or even mostly, of my own making. She was the Avatar's Daughter, destined for greatness, and she felt she could never live up to her father's expectations. She felt she wasn't that smart and that capable. She was just a normal teenage girl. Physically, because she was not emaciated, like Twiggy, she felt she was unattractive. As a person, she felt she was unlovable. By some miracle, she had attracted my attention and my love. But someday soon the scales would fall from my eyes, and I would see her as she really was -- and then I would leave her. And she would not blame me for leaving her. I *deserved* a woman better than her. A woman, perhaps, like Shana.

In an effort to make it clear to Annie that I was always thinking of her, even if absent, I prepared surprises for her. I dropped by the Phoenix College Humanities Department before I left. At Vern's desk, the one he never used, the one where I'd first met Annie, I concealed tiny treasures in various drawers, in the back, behind staplers and various supplies, under envelopes and stationery. Other small things I secreted on book shelves behind certain volumes. Then, over the course of the summer, from the road, from Chattanooga, from Sarasota, I dropped Annie postcards. Each one had explicit directions for finding yet another gift I'd left somewhere in Vern's office for her. About once a week Annie went to the office and found some new treat from me. It was a way of being there, with her, even when I wasn't.

And then Rick and I stuck out our thumbs for Chattanooga. We each carried a huge backpack stuffed with supplies. I wore the faux fur Tartar cap I'd worn in *The Lower Depths*. I also wore my Tartar Wellington boots with the tan leather extension reaching up almost to my knee. They had flat heels and so were better for hiking than my cowboy boots.

And Rick wore a big Bowie knife strapped to his belt. He wore it ostentatiously on his waist because he didn't want some redneck cop picking him up on the way for carrying a concealed weapon. In clear sight, dangling down his thigh, it was completely legal. But, with the monster blade clearly visible, the wonder is that anyone picked us up at all. Perhaps America was a more trusting place in 1967.

The Bowie was only one reason I began to see Rick in a new light on that trip. Ever since Mom had kidnapped him back from Albert, our bio-dad, at age eight, Rick had been retiring to the point of invisibility. So much so that, in later life, Mike, one of our younger brothers, couldn't even remember Rick as a part of the family. But now, like a butterfly emerging from its cocoon, Rick began making a transition from Invisible Boy to Macho Man. It was his own way of compensating for the feeling of inferiority which seems almost universal in all of us. Thrown together 24/7 on that marathon trek across the continent, Rick and I became closer than we'd ever been. We talked about things and feelings we'd never talked about before. He called me his "mentor." He said I'd shown him how to be a rebel.

We hitched north to Flagstaff and Route 66. Then we headed east, riding day and night, down the long slanting decline into the Albuquerque valley, across the Rio Grande, then up again on the other side. We hitched at night across the rain lashed and lightning streaked Great Plains through Amarillo and the Texas Panhandle, then into and out of Oklahoma City.

Somewhere in eastern Oklahoma the farmer who'd picked us up turned off the main highway and roared off into the countryside on a two-lane blacktop. We had our maps and we knew that wasn't the way to Fort Smith, Arkansas, where we were headed. "Don't worry," he assured us, "the road curves around. We'll hit the highway again up the road here a piece."

Eventually, the farmer turned off the blacktop onto a dirt road and stopped. He turned to us. "This here's as far as I go. I'm heading on up to the farm from now on."

"So," I asked, "where's the highway?"

He jerked his thumb up the road. "Just up the road there a piece. You'll hit it 'fore long."

We climbed out with our packs and the farmer left us choking on his dust. Then we started hiking up that lonesome road a piece. The only vehicles on that two-lane blacktop were tractors pulling flatbeds of hay and battered pickups which veered away from us when we stuck out our thumbs. No one stopped for us all day, and we never did hit the highway up the road there a piece.

We walked that ribbon of highway all day, because at least when we walked we put a few miles behind us. We trudged on through the bucolic countryside until I felt like a plodding beast of burden with the pack on my back growing heavier with each step and the June heat sapping my energy. At last I told Rick I just couldn't go on and had to stop. He wouldn't hear of it. "C'mon, you wimp, let's go. Just follow me, big brother." Scrawny Rick took the lead and set a grueling Marine Corps pace as he chanted "Hup, hup, hup, one, two, three. Hup, hup..." I stared at his marching boots in front of me and just followed along mechanically to the sound of his drill instructor voice.

Dusk came on, and then the complete darkness of Oklahoma farmland where no lights shone. We couldn't see the road in front of us. We found a thick tree by the roadside and sat down under it, Rick on one side of the trunk, me on the other. We were both so tired we didn't even shrug off our packs. We just leaned back against the tree and we were both instantly asleep. If any car passed us in the night, we weren't aware of it.

We slept straight through to sunrise. When the dawn sun woke us, we simply stood up and started walking. Our packs were already on our backs.

Somewhere along that road we passed a farm house and a dog charged out, barking fiercely as his racing claws threw up dust in his eagerness to get at me. He was lightning fast and I didn't have an eighth of a second to run. He sank his teeth into my calf just above the top of the black part of the Wellington boot. Luckily, his jaws locked on the thick tan leather extension which the costume mistress for *The Lower Depths* had sown onto the boots to make them more Tartaresque. Perhaps the dog thought the tan color indicated vulnerable flesh. His bite was powerful, but his teeth didn't pierce the leather.

I swung my right fist down in a powerful overhand arc and smashed the dog hard on the side of his skull with the bottom of my fist. I put all my strength into it and followed through the arc. The force of my blow spun the dog around 180-degrees and he raced, yelping in pain, back toward his house as fast as he'd ran out. I felt great about that blow and I hope I broke the dog's jaw, I hit him hard enough. No doubt it was a big surprise to the mutt that, when he bit into my leg just above the black part of the boot, he tasted leather instead of blood squirting into his mouth.

The leather was indented and thereafter permanently bore the teeth marks of the dog but, because it wasn't punctured, my skin wasn't broken. Even so, a large and painful bump soon appeared on my calf where the dog had chomped down. If not for having my big toe smashed on the stage of the Arizona Repertory Theater, requiring the replacement of my Eskimo mukluks with the modified Wellingtons, I'd have had my calf torn open on some back road in the Oklahoma boondocks. I felt I got the better of the deal.

As morning became noon became afternoon we abandoned hope of getting a ride and began standing in the middle of the road as cars or pickups came on. To get around us, the farmers had to swerve all the way into the other lane and almost off into the ditch on the other side. And as the farmers disappeared up the road, we gave them the finger and cursed their Goddamned redneck Okie souls to burn in eternal hellfire.

Eventually, a police car came along and stopped, as we knew it eventually would. The cop asked for identification. We showed him. We were both over 18. He saw Rick's Bowie dangling from his belt. "You better be careful with that Bowie, these Okie boys around here will take that pig sticker away from you."

"Yeah, well," Rick answered in his best John Wayne drawl, "I used this pig sticker to carve my initials in the back of the last Okie hayseed who tried that." Macho Man had eclipsed the Invisible Boy.

The cop looked at Rick, perhaps considering the information, and then said he'd gotten complaints about us. He asked us what the hell we thought we were doing, standing in the middle of the road, running people off into the ditch and then cursing them and giving them the finger?

"Officer," I said, "we're just trying to get a ride back to the main highway. Can you give us a lift?

"Sorry, boys, can't do that. Now stay outta the road and don't cause any more trouble." Then he got back in his cop car and left us in the back end of nowhere.

We marched up that road all the rest of that day and, as dusk came on, we ambled off into a weed choked field. We unrolled our blankets and threw ourselves down on them. It didn't take long for us to fall asleep. The next morning we woke to red welts all over our bodies and horrible itching at the site of every welt. We scratched ourselves bloody for the rest of the way to Chattanooga. Only there did we discover that we were infested with chiggers, bugs we'd never heard of because they don't exist in Arizona. Chiggers are tiny critters which bore into your skin and suck your blood. The only way to get them out is to wash your body with alcohol soaked cloths. When we got to Chattanooga, we *bathed* in alcohol.

Until then, we itched, we scratched, we bled, and we marched. We marched all that day, too, because no one gave us a ride. It took us three days to slog all the way out of Oklahoma and into Arkansas. And, as we stood on roads near swampy Arkansas bogs all night long, mosquitoes joined the chiggers in sucking our blood. Those two vampire bugs continued to suck on us all the way across Arkansas and into Memphis. By that time, I'd long since wished that we'd headed for San Francisco instead of the Deep South. I doubted San Francisco had mosquitoes, and I was damn sure it didn't have chiggers.

Then we crossed the Mighty Mississippi into Memphis. It was the biggest damn river we'd ever seen. The Colorado was a little stream in comparison, and even the Rio Grande in New Mexico was a tiny trickle next to it. It was a huge natural barrier, and crossing the Mississippi into Memphis, into Tennessee, seemed like crossing a national frontier into a foreign country. We didn't know what to expect of the natives and we were suspicious of everyone, but it was in Memphis that we had our best ride. A middle-aged man picked us up and treated us to a meal at a diner. When he dropped us off on the other side of Memphis, he handed me a $20 bill. "You'll need this," he said.

The further east we went on that trip, the more the accents of the people around us became strange and difficult to understand. And the further east we went, the more lush and primitive the land seemed to us. We went from Southwestern desert to Great Plains prairie to Arkansas swamps. It was as if, by travelling deeper into the Southland, we were also travelling deeper into some alien time. We were not only hitching and hiking into Dixie, we were also hitching and hiking into some forgotten past.

That seemed especially true beyond Memphis as we hitched our way along Route 64 across southern Tennessee toward Chattanooga. Tennessee is a long state, and Route 64, which is not a major Interstate, seemed to wind its way through green fields forever. About midway between Memphis and Chattanooga is the small town of Pulaski, where Confederate General Nathan Bedford Forrest founded the Ku Klux Klan just after the Civil War. It's a benighted place, although when we passed through the day was hot, bright, and steamy humid. I reminded Rick that everything we saw around us was actually our native land. We were both born in Tennessee, and all our ancestors during the Civil War were Confederates. Some had died fighting for slavery. And I also reminded Rick that we had a relative by marriage on Mom's side who'd been a big mucky-muck in the Klan. And then I reminded him that I'd been born just north of Memphis when Albert, our father, was working in Dyersburg.

"You know," Rick said, "Albert isn't really your father."

"What're you talking about?"

"Every time it came up, Albert always told me he wasn't your father. He was insistent and consistent on that."

I'd never had any reason to doubt that Albert was my father. Mom had always told me he was. I had no memory of him, as Mom had left him in 1951, when I was just four. Rick, though, had spent years with him. Albert drove up to our yard in Chattanooga one day in 1951, while Mom was at work and a babysitter was watching Rick and me play, and he snatched up three-year-old Rick and drove off with him, while I ran screaming for the babysitter.

It was after Rick's kidnapping that Mom decided she had to escape from Chattanooga and left for Phoenix with me and Bruce, the two remaining sons of Albert. It was in Phoenix that Mom met and married Elmer, our step-father. Then, in 1957, Mom had kidnapped Rick back from our father, Albert.

But now Rick was telling me that Albert had always denied his paternity. "Then who *was* my father?"

"I don't know. Albert never said. He just said you were no kid of *his.*"

And hearing Rick say this, on that road outside Pulaski in southern Tennessee, I didn't doubt that I was hearing the truth. It explained, for instance, why Albert sent Christmas gifts to Rick and Bruce when we were younger, but never to me, supposedly his first-born son.

And I also realized why Albert had only seized Rick when he came for us in Chattanooga all those years ago, and why I escaped his reach. It wasn't by chance. It wasn't luck. It wasn't an accident. Albert had come for his son.

And I was not his son.

Chattanooga Stonewall

Grandfather Frank's home on Kelly's Ferry Road, the home in Chattanooga's Lookout Valley where Mom grew up, was a modest little two-story wood frame house. It was also the end of the trail for Rick. He intended to hang out there until he wore out his welcome, while I went on after a few days to Sarasota.

Grandfather Frank gave us the attic bedroom which had once been Mom's. He was in the process of remodelling it, but he'd wait until we left to finish the job. Pristine white drywall panels had been newly installed on the slanting ceiling. Paint cans of various colors, red, yellow, black, some half-empty, some not even opened, were scattered around the floor. There was a large metal trash can half-filled with debris. Light came from two bare light bulbs.

Behind the house was Grandfather Frank's one-room print shop where he puttered around doing odd jobs for friends and neighbors. Above it was the small apartment he'd built for Mom and Albert shortly after their marriage. That apartment was one of the places where Albert, who I now realized was not my father at all, had often beaten me savagely only a little more than 15 years before. It didn't look like a horror chamber. It was just a very small and very normal apartment.

And Grandfather Frank was a very normal looking grandfather. Only he wasn't small. He was tall, well over six feet, and completely bald. From the pictures I'd seen of him in his youth, it appeared he'd always been bald. He told us news about Mom. "Your mother is divorcing your father. Didn't you know that?"

No, we didn't know that. Both of us had cut ourselves off from the family after moving out. I was a bit surprised. Elmer was a vicious brute, but I never thought Mom would divorce him. She feared what the neighbors might say about a divorce. It wasn't proper. So I thought she'd be his little punching bag until the day either she or Elmer died.

"Well, no great tragedy," I said.

"Doesn't it bother you that your mother and father are divorcing?"

"Absolutely not. Kathy should've done it long ago. And Elmer isn't our father."

Grandfather Frank seemed disturbed by what I said, especially by me calling Mom "Kathy," but he said nothing more. Ever since moving out of 51st Street and in with Annie, I'd called Mom "Kathy." I wanted to separate myself from her and this was a way of distancing myself. I could tell Grandfather Frank didn't like it. He looked pained every time he heard me call her "Kathy." It wasn't proper. He thought it was disrespectful. I didn't care.

Once we were settled in at Kelly's Ferry Road, all the relatives had to come and take a gander at us. So Mom's younger sisters, my aunts Frances and Carol, came over. Cousins came over. Mom's older brother, Uncle Harold, visited. He was pudgy and he was balding, just like his father. Damn, I thought. If that runs in the family, I'm glad I'm flying my freak flag now!

I explained to Uncle Harold that I was on my way to Sarasota to enroll in an FCC school for the summer, but I didn't have the $150 tuition. Could he loan it to me?

"Let me get back to you on that," he said.

That was the last time we ever spoke, as he didn't get back to me before I left Chattanooga.

After a few days, I realized Harold wasn't going to get back to me, so I asked Grandfather Frank the same question. Could he loan me the tuition money?

"I don't think I can. I have expenses right now. I'm remodelling your mother's old bedroom, as you know."

"Yes, I know."

I then decided to ask him about Albert. What could I lose? "Rick and I spent a week on the road," I said. "We talked about a lot of things."

Grandfather Frank nodded, puzzled by my change of direction. "I suppose you did."

"One of the things Rick told me was that Albert always denied he was my father. That means Kathy always lied to me about my birth. So, I want you to tell me: Who was my father?"

Grandfather Frank seemed startled. He stared at me in confusion, trying to think of what to say. "I won't tell you *anything* so long as you refer to your mother as 'Kathy.' You have to show more respect for your mother."

He response just confirmed that what Rick said was true. If it hadn't been, he'd have reacted to the charge as absurd. Now he was just weaseling, trying to avoid answering. "Respect is something you earn," I said. "You don't deserve it just because of biology."

Grandfather Frank stood up from the table. "Your mother deserves respect simply because she's your mother. And if you respected her, you wouldn't call her 'Kathy.'"

I realized he wasn't going to tell me anything. "You're just using that as an excuse to avoid answering my question. The truth is, you don't want to *tell* me the truth. You're *afraid* to tell me the truth."

"You'll have to ask your mother about this. I have nothing more to say." He turned and headed for the door.

I raised my voice at his retreating back. "You're a moral coward, *Frank*. And I have no respect for cowards...*Frank!*"

Frank didn't look back. And that was the last I ever saw of him. And those were the last words I ever spoke to him. Between then and the day he died, I never spoke to my grandfather again. Ever since I was a kid, Kathy had complained that I was as stubborn as a mule. She was right. And I never had any regrets.

As soon as Frank was out the door, I rose from the table and stomped up the stairs to my attic bedroom, the room which had once been Kathy's. Coming up I woke Rick, who was sleeping on one of the two mattresses which had been placed on the floor for us.

"'Sup?" he asked.

"Frank is a Goddamned coward."

"You mean Grandfather Frank?"

"I mean *Frank*. He won't tell me about Albert. He won't tell me who my father was."

"Whaddya gonna do?"

I was prowling angrily back and forth, kicking the construction material which littered the floor. I looked at the garbage can, overflowing with debris, its lid leaning by its side. "This is what I'm going to do. Gimme your fuckin' Bowie knife."

Rick tossed it over. I caught it and unsheathed the razor sharp blade. Then I picked up the metal garbage can lid by its handle and clapped it to the pristine white drywall of the slanting ceiling. Then I stabbed the Bowie deep into the drywall at the top edge of the lid.

"What the fuck are you doing?" Rick asked.

"You'll see."

I cut around the edge of the lid with the Bowie, sawing an outline in the ceiling. When I finished I dropped the lid. I'd dug an almost perfect circle as big in diameter as the lid into the drywall. Then I dug the Bowie into the drywall again, digging straight parallel lines about two inches apart down from the top. Small bits of drywall crumbled out of the grooves, dusting me and the floor. When I was half-way to the center of the circle I veered off to the left and right with more parallel lines at 45-degree angles. Then I carved two more parallel lines down from the center until I reached the bottom of the circle. Finally I dug the Bowie into the drywall again and followed the curve of the circle all the way around so that I had a double circle with about an inch of space between the lines. When I finished, I'd carved a deep peace symbol into the nice new drywall ceiling of Kathy's old bedroom.

"Grandfather Frank isn't going to like that," Rick said.

"Like I fuckin' care?"

I slammed the Bowie back into its sheath and tossed it to Rick. I stepped back and admired the peace sign. I felt it needed more. I picked up a paint brush from the floor and searched the paint cans. I found one of yellow and another of red. I popped the lid off the red and dipped the brush into it. Then I began painting the space between all the parallel lines. Rick watched in silence.

When I finished I had a red circle enclosing a thick red peace sign. I dropped the brush into the can of red paint and found a new one. I dipped it into the can of yellow and carefully painted the background field of the symbol. When it was done I had a blood red peace sign on a bright yellow field dominating the slanting ceiling of the room. It was beautiful.

"He won't know what it means," Rick said.

"Tell him it's the claw-footed Mark of the Beast. He'll believe it."

"Why don't you tell him?"

"Because I won't be here."

Early the next morning I called a cab to take me to the Greyhound station. I paid for my ride and gave the cabbie a tip out of the $20 our benefactor had given me in Memphis. I used most of the rest to buy a one-way ticket to Sarasota. By morning rush hour I was on a bus rolling south toward Atlanta and points beyond.

Sarasota Summer

I arrived in Sarasota filled with the audacity of hope. I had blind faith that there was magic in commitment, and that if I moved, the world would move with me. That if I asked, unanticipated aid would materialize. That if I knocked, the right doors would open to me.

But sometimes audacious hope and blind faith aren't enough. I knocked and the right doors did not open. I asked and the aid did not appear. I moved and the earth did not move beneath me.

I went straight from the Greyhound station to the FCC school. I asked to speak with whoever was in charge of admissions. The door to his office was the only door which opened when I knocked. I explained my situation. I already had a Third Class FCC license and I'd worked in radio in Phoenix, but I wanted, I *needed,* a First Class license to go any further in radio. So I'd hitchhiked across America to reach his school and get that license. Now, here I was, in his office. But I had no money. Could I have a scholarship?

I could not. One didn't exist. The school wasn't a college. It wasn't a charity. It was a private business, and the sole purpose of a private business is to make a profit. It was very impressive that I'd trekked across the continent to attend his school, but I should've brought some money with me. Sorry about that. Come back when I have the tuition in hand.

So, I was not going to attend school in Sarasota. Instead, I was destitute in Sarasota. I was 3,000 miles from home and had three dollars in my pocket. I knew no one and had no place to stay. Sarasota is on Florida's Gulf Coast, just below Tampa Bay and St. Petersburg. Unlike the dry summers of Arizona, Florida summers are sticky and muggy. But at least they're hot. I could always sleep comfortably on the beach, I thought.

But I wasn't ready to give up just yet. I found a phone booth and looked up single occupancy rooming houses. America used to have a lot of these so-called flophouses, where one could rent cheap rooms by the day or week. Now they're gone with the wind, and the derelicts and winos and *bosyaks* who used to live in them live on the streets instead. There was one just a few blocks from the FCC school. I heaved my pack to my shoulders and headed for it.

It had a vacancy, a small room barely larger than the metal frame bed which dominated it. One wooden chair took up the remaining space. There was also a communal bathroom with a bathtub at the end of the hall. It cost two bucks a day. I handed over two of my three dollars and dropped my pack on the chair in my new room. At least I could bathe and had a place to flop for one night.

When I found the flophouse I'd also noticed that there was a Royal Crown Cola bottling plant right across the street. The plant's yard was filled with sweating barebacked men grabbing cases of soft drinks off a conveyor belt and loading them onto trucks. I walked across the street and asked for the foreman. One of the workers jerked his thumb toward the yard boss. I told him I needed a job. Could he use me on the conveyor belt? I didn't ask about pay.

"When can you start?"

"Right now."

"OK, start loading."

I stepped up to the conveyor belt with the other workers and began grabbing cases off the belt and loading them onto trucks.

It was a small plant, and at five o'clock when work ended, there was no second or third shift. I followed the yard boss into his office and filled out a job application. It was minimum wage work, paid every Friday, which was two days away. That was fine, I said. But I didn't have a bank account. Could the company cash my paycheck for me? It could.

I returned to the flophouse and told the desk clerk I had a job at the plant across the street. Could he let me slide until Friday? Then I'd not only pay him for Thursday and Friday, but I'd pay for another week in advance. No problem, he said. He had plenty of empty rooms, anyway.

I asked about a place to eat. There was a hamburger joint close by. I found it and used my sole remaining dollar to buy a small vanilla milk shake and a small hamburger. No cheese, no lettuce, no tomato, just a thin patty, some shredded onions, and a splash of mustard and ketchup. It cost 49-cents. It was all I ate that day. It tasted great. And I had enough for another burger and shake the next day. I'd arrived in Sarasota that morning homeless and with three dollars to my name. Now I had a home, a job, and food in my belly. Everything was fine.

I settled into a routine. Every morning I walked across the street and, like everyone else in the yard gang, did whatever had to be done until five o'clock. Then I walked back to the flophouse and took a bath to wash off the sweat and grime. Next I walked to the hamburger joint and had my sole meal of the day, a burger and vanilla shake. Then I returned to the flophouse and flopped on my bed. I picked up my paperback copy of Boris Pasternak's *Dr. Zhivago* and read about the Russian Revolution until I fell asleep. It was a thick tome which I'd lugged all across America from Phoenix. Now I had nothing else to do but read it.

Summer nights in Sarasota are sticky and stifling, just like the days. As I lay on my bed, the sweat rolled off my nude body and soaked the sheet. I discovered there was a storage closet in the hallway filled with the abandoned detritus of former residents. The clerk said I could use anything in there. I found a small electric fan and brought it back to my room. I plugged it in, set it on the chair, and pointed it directly on me. I read that way and I slept that way and the sultry nights became bearable.

I was 20 and strong and, although I was hungry all the time, I was able do the hard physical labor of lifting and loading all day on just the burger and shake from the previous day. If I was still awake at midnight, and my stomach was hurting too much from hunger, I dressed and walked across the street to the plant. Because it was a small plant, there were no guards, and I knew the place well. I slipped through a gap in the fence around the yard where I worked during the day and picked up a few bottles of Chocolate Soldier, a soft drink with the taste and consistency of chocolate milk. I took them back to my room and chugged them as I read Pasternak. They at least filled my belly.

And the next morning I walked across the street to the bottling yard and began my routine all over again. Most of my fellow workers were Cubans. They worked stripped to the waist, the sweat rolling in rivulets off them as they lifted and heaved in the broiling Florida sun. I also stripped to the waist and I tanned quickly. Before long, I was as brown as my Cuban companeros. Two summers before, the summer of '65, when I'd picked cantaloups in Yuma, my tanned skin had caused me to be mistaken for a Mexican. Now I was mistaken for a Cuban among Cubans.

So it went, day after day, night after night. So much seemed to happen that summer, good and bad and who knows what in between. That summer Israel fought the Six-Day War and seized the Gaza Strip and the Sinai desert from Egypt, the Golan Heights from Syria, and the West Bank from Jordan.

That summer, on June 2nd, The Beatles released *Sgt. Pepper.* As I read Boris Pasternak each night, I listened to it on a radio I'd found in the storage closet down the hall. I'd never heard anything like it. It was a psychedelic smorgasbord and I was amazed that pop music could sound like that. They're revolutionaries, I thought. Two weeks later, the weekend of June 16-18th, the Monterey Pop Festival in California catapulted Janis Joplin and Jimi Hendrix to stardom.

And two days after that, on June 20th, Muhammed Ali, the boxing world champ, was convicted of violating Selective Service laws by refusing to be inducted into the military. "No Vietnamese ever called me 'nigger'," he said. So he refused to go fight people he had no problems with, on the other side of the world, for a country which *did* call him "nigger."

That summer, on July 29th, The Doors scored their first No. 1 hit with "Light My Fire." I'd not heard of The Doors before. Nor did I think a pop song on the radio could be as long as that song. It just went on and on. Later I learned that the album version was even longer. Wow! They're revolutionaries, too, I thought.

That summer Jayne Mansfield was beheaded in a horrific auto accident as her young daughter, Mariska Hargitay, watched from the back seat. That summer Detroit burned in a race riot in which 43 were killed and thousands arrested. That summer President Johnson signed an executive order making 19-year-olds the first to be drafted for his continuing war in the jungles of Vietnam. I was 20, close enough to worry.

And that summer I loaded cases on trucks, ate my one burger a day, drank Chocolate Soldier at night, read Pasternak, and saved my money. My isolated world had narrowed down to my room, the bottling plant across the street, and the burger shop. I was living in Gorki's *Lower Depths*. I was a Yanqui *bosyak* working among Cuban *bosyaks* during the day, reading about Russian *bosyaks* in revolution at night. I did nothing else. I could've afforded to spend more than the 49-cents I spent each day on a burger and shake, I could've gone to a movie, I could've bought a newspaper. But I went nowhere and I spent no more than that 49-cents for the burger and shake and the two dollars-a-day for my room. At first I thought I might be able to quickly save enough money in this way to pay the tuition at the FCC school up the street.

But the days passed faster than my money accumulated, despite my scrimping, and the summer session at the school came to an end while I still worked at the conveyor belt. Getting my First Class FCC license just wasn't going to happen. I'd trekked across the country not to go to school, but just to sweat with a *bosyak* Cuban work gang in a Royal Crown Cola bottling plant.

Then I realized that it was good that I'd gone hungry and had saved my money. I had another financial obligation I'd promised to pay. At the end of the summer I had almost $200 in my pocket. It was enough for a bus ride to Phoenix and enough to pay Vern's bill for Annie's abortion. Perhaps things worked out for the best.

As the summer drew towards its close, I bade my Cuban companeros adios, stuffed my tattered *Dr. Zhivago* in my pack, and walked to the Sarasota Greyhound station. I'd thought about Annie every day, all day, as I worked at the conveyor belt. It'd been a long summer. I'd missed her terribly and I was eager to see her again.

And I had questions that Kathy was going to answer.

Misbegotten

"I was going to tell you the truth when you were an adult," Kathy said.

"I don't believe you," I told her. "You thought I was an adult three years ago when I graduated from North High and I left with Jerry Campbell for L.A. That's why you were crying when you packed my clothes. You thought I was leaving home for good. But you didn't tell me the truth then, did you? And you didn't tell me the truth when I really *did* leave for good, to be with Annie. And we wouldn't be having this conversation right now if it was up to you. We're having this conversation because I'm *demanding* that we have it. And so I want you to do the right thing by me, which you *haven't* done and *wouldn't* have done if I hadn't found out on my own. I want you to stop your lies and I want you to tell me the truth. Albert wasn't my father. Who was?"

"Alright, I'll tell you the truth."

And this is what my mother told me about my birth.

****

Raymond Pope did not come home from the war.

That caused everything which followed.

It was 1945 and all over America, brothers and lovers and the boy next door were coming home from World War II.

Harold, Kathy's older brother, came home to Chattanooga from fighting with Patton's Third Army artillery at the Battle of the Bulge in the Ardennes Forest.

And Kenneth Bryant, the boy who lived in the log cabin next door on Kelly's Ferry Road, who'd been stationed in England with the "Mighty Eighth" Army Air Force, he came home from the skies over Europe.

But Raymond Pope did not come home.

Raymond was Kathy's lover, from somewhere up North. Like Kenneth, Raymond had also been a pilot, but in the Marine Corps. He'd flown in the Pacific in the war which swept across that ocean closer and closer to Japan. Raymond and Kathy had met when Kathy and her father, Frank, had taken the train to visit Harold when he was stationed at Fort Dix, New Jersey. Harold was Frank's precious only son and was being shipped off to England to invade Hitler's Festung Europa on D-Day. They might never see him again, so they had to see him now.

On the train to Fort Dix, a train packed with soldiers, Raymond bumped into Kathy and began flirting. "What's your name?" he asked.

Kathy flushed and smiled back. "Tootsie," she said, which was her nickname.

And Raymond was smitten with the cute dark-haired Southern belle with the pixie nose.

And Kathy was smitten with the tall and handsome Marine Corps officer.

Once at Fort Dix there was no room to be found anywhere for the horde of visiting relatives. But Raymond found Frank and Kathy rooms. And Raymond took Kathy to dinner. And he took her to a movie. And then he kissed her. "There was magic in his kiss," Kathy said. "My toes just curled up when he kissed me." And Kathy, a teenager who had just graduated from high school and was ready for love, fell truly and deeply in love then and there with the handsome Marine Corps officer.

Two days after Kathy returned to Chattanooga, she received her first letter from Raymond. He must have written it immediately after she left Fort Dix. After that, she received a letter from him every day without fail. He called her on the weekends in an era when long distance phone calls were rare and expensive. Like many in the military during the war, he was being moved all over the East Coast. But it didn't matter where he was, the letters and calls from him kept coming.

Finally, Raymond came to Chattanooga and proposed. Kathy had already given her heart to him and she readily agreed to marry him, the sooner the better. For her, it was a fairy tale come true. Raymond was her prince, and Kathy was ready to go wherever he led.

But Kathy's father, Frank, disapproved. He said she was too young for marriage. And in Tennessee at that time one had to be 21 to marry without parental approval. Kathy was only 19.

So Raymond and Kathy planned to elope and marry in Georgia, just a few miles away, where the age of consent was lower. As they were coming down the stairs from Kathy's attic bedroom in the house on Kelly's Ferry Road, suitcases in hand, Frank was waiting for them. "Son," he said to Raymond, "don't do this to Tootsie. You'll be leaving soon to fight in this horrible war. There's a good chance you won't come back. And then you'd leave Tootsie a widow. That's no way for her to start her life, son. Think of what you're doing to her."

And Raymond thought of what he was doing to Kathy, of the chance that he would leave her a widow. And he agreed that Kathy's father was right. It wasn't a good way for Kathy to start her life. So he led her back upstairs to her attic bedroom and helped her unpack her suitcases and he left her in her Frank's house as he walked out the front door and into the Pacific war.

Ever after Kathy mourned the decision made in the early morning hours on those stairs in the house on Kelly's Ferry Road. She wished Raymond had taken her by the hand and led her out to his car standing by the curb and driven away with her. Two husbands and seven sons later, Kathy was still waiting for the only man she ever loved to come for her. "If Raymond came for me today, I wouldn't think twice, I'd not look back. I'd leave everything and everyone, including my home, my children, *everything*, and go with Raymond, wherever he led, into whatever life he wanted."

But the war ended and Raymond did not come for her. Nor were there letters. Raymond, it seemed, was among America's honored war dead, lost somewhere over the Pacific. Kathy was devastated -- but at least she wasn't a widow.

Kenneth, however, the boy who lived in the log cabin next door on Kelly's Ferry Road, did come back. Kenneth was a high school football hero, active in the Baptist church, and Hollywood handsome. Kathy thought he looked like Brian Donlevy, a tough guy actor of the Thirties and Forties.

Kathy and Kenneth had gone to high school together and hung out in the same crowd of kids who packed the malt shop after classes and danced to Glenn Miller all night on the weekends. Kenneth often showed up on her doorstep with his bicycle and asked Kathy to come riding with him. And then he'd pedal off at high speed, Kathy lagging behind. "C'mon, Tootsie!" the football hero yelled back at her. "C'mon, I gotta sweat! I gotta sweat!" In the normal course of events, Kathy thought she'd have ended up marrying Kenneth.

Until she met Raymond, handsome and gallant, on the train to Fort Dix.

But Raymond didn't come home, and Kenneth did. And Kenneth, like Raymond, had been a pilot. The day Kenneth came home from the war, some time in March, 1946, he came next door to see Kathy. She answered his knock and went out on the porch to meet him. He was still in his pilot's uniform, a uniform so like Raymond's, and he was Hollywood handsome, looking just like Brian Donlevy. He took off his officer's hat as Kathy came out and said, "I heard about your Marine fly-boy, Tootsie. I'm real sorry."

And Kathy collapsed into Kenneth's embrace, sobbing violently on his shoulder, her tears soaking into his uniform jacket as he rocked her gently and said, "There, there. There, there."

They got in his car, the car his parents had kept tuned for him while he was away at the war, and they drove. Kathy doesn't remember where they drove. They just drove, as Kathy wept for Raymond, who would never return, and Kenneth held her to his side. Somewhere in the night, they stopped driving. Sometime in the night Kenneth began kissing her tears away. Somehow in the night Kathy lost her virginity to Kenneth, the boy next door, who wore a uniform so much like Raymond's.

Not long after, Kathy realized she was pregnant with me.

****

At least this was the story Kathy first told me when I asked about my birth, soon after I returned from Sarasota. But, later, when I asked for more details, Kathy said, "No, that's not the way it happened. It wasn't like that."

"Then how *did* it happen?"

This was the way it really happened, she said:

Raymond did not come home from the war in the Pacific.

And Kenneth did come home from England and the skies over Europe.

That much was true.

But she didn't collapse into his arms on the day of his return and she didn't lose her virginity to him on the night of his return.

She lost her virginity to him much later.

And in a different way.

Kenneth was out of uniform and getting back into the swing of civilian life. He was still the boy next door and she was still living at home. Kathy's brother, Harold, had been shot in the neck by a German sniper hiding in a barn in the Ardennes Forest. He had married the Army nurse he'd met while healing, and so had moved out. So Kathy was living alone at the house on Kelly's Ferry Road with Frank and Estelle, Frank's his new wife. And, though she was now 20, for a while it was like Kathy was a teenager back in high school. She found a job in a hosiery mill and at night hung out with her old high school crowd at the malt shop and they still danced to the music of the Big Bands.

And Kenneth was also part of that ol' gang which got together once more after the war and once more danced to the music of the Big Bands.

One night Kenneth and Kathy went to a party at Chattanooga's Road House Tavern to bid farewell to Kenneth's cousin, who was leaving town. "It was a blast," Kathy said. "I'd never drank before, but I drank that night. Everyone was getting really drunk, including me." Kathy was dog sick as Kenneth drove her home and she told Kenneth he'd better pull over to the side of the road, quick, or she'd puke all over his front seat.

Kenneth pulled over, quick. Kathy opened the passenger door, leaned out, and began heaving. Kenneth rubbed her back in sympathy as she vomited, saying gently, "There, there. There, there." His endearments became more rote, his caresses more insistent, his fingers fumbling at her buttons, hands pulling at her skirt. "No," she said, "don't, Kenneth, don't."

The next morning Kathy woke up feeling awful. Her head pounded, her mouth felt like the bottom of a bird cage, and the blood on her clothes reminded her that she was no longer a virgin.

They didn't call it date rape back then and Kathy wasn't even sure she thought of it as rape. But, she knew it was dirty and rotten and wrong and she knew she would never, ever, forgive Kenneth for what he'd done to her. In the normal course of events, Kathy thought she'd have ended up marrying Kenneth. But this was not a normal event and she was certain now that she could never marry him.

She was still certain of that when she discovered, not long after, that she was pregnant.

****

"No, that's not the way it happened either," Kathy told me later. "It wasn't like that."

"Well, Kathy, how *did* it happen? What *is* the truth?"

Finally, reluctantly, Kathy told me. *This* was the real truth, she said. This was how it really, *really* happened:

It was Kenneth who was drunk, stinking drunk, from the party at the Road House Tavern. Kathy was afraid to ride home with him. But she had no other way to get home, so she got in the car. On the way home, Kenneth pulled his car off the road and began mauling her, tearing at her clothes. "It's about time you got that Goddamned Marine out of your mind," he snarled at her, "and I'm just the man to do it!"

Kenneth pushed Kathy down on the seat. He shoved his hand up under her skirt, grabbed her panties, and pulled them down and off her, ripping and tearing them as he did so. He grabbed the front of Kathy's blouse in both hands and ripped it apart, the buttons popping and flying. He shoved up her bra and seized her breasts, one in each hand. He squeezed them both, viciously, as he held her down. "Don't, Kenneth, don't!," Kathy pleaded. "Please, you're hurting me!"

But then he was on top of her, pushing himself between her legs. Then his hard prick was inside her, ripping and tearing her like he'd ripped and torn her panties and her blouse. "Please don't," Kathy begged. "Please, Kenneth, don't."

Kenneth ignored her. He pounded his prick into her, hurting her because she was a virgin, and the blood flowed from between her legs. It drenched her dress, it soaked the front seat of Kenneth's car, it covered Kenneth's prick, wet and sticky, as he pulled it out of her.

Kenneth took the hem of Kathy's skirt and wiped his bloody prick with it. It left wet smears on her dress. "Jesus Christ, you fucking bitch! I didn't know you were a Goddamned virgin. Look what you've done to my fucking car!"

He drove Kathy home in silence but for Kathy's weeping. As soon as his car stopped, Kathy ran into her house on Kelly's Ferry Road. Kenneth parked next door and went into his own house. Frank did not wake up as Kathy came in, but Estelle, her step-mother, did. "She came into the bathroom and saw the mess I was in," Kathy said. "She took my clothes outside and hid them in the backyard and burned them in the morning."

Kathy quit work at the hosiery mill and kept to herself, holed up in her attic bedroom, filled with the shame of what Kenneth had done to her.

And then she discovered she was pregnant.

It was Chattanooga, 1946. Good Southern girls didn't get pregnant before they were wives, even against their will. Only whores and sluts got pregnant before they married. Kathy was a good girl of good family, but she knew no one would think so as soon as it became obvious that someone had done to her what just wasn't done to good girls, what was only done to whores and sluts in the back seats of cars.

Now Kathy was living a dark and sordid nightmare. She knew no one who might be able to help her. Indeed, the help she wanted most she dared not even mention, to anyone, as it was against the law, it was a crime. What she wanted most was an abortion, or a miscarriage, as quickly and as quietly as possible. No one must ever know that she was damaged goods, no one must ever know that she was a whore and a slut.

So Kathy resorted to dark and sordid methods to save herself. She drank various secret potions which were whispered to kill the fetus that grew within her like a cancerous tumor, but they just made her sick. She jumped off heights high enough to perhaps do the job, but not high enough to seriously injure herself. That didn't work, either. And at night she lay awake in her bed, staring at her dark slanting attic ceiling in unending panic, beating her blossoming belly with her fists as the incriminating fetus within continued to grow like some malignant alien seed.

Albert, a local boy Kathy knew and had sometimes dated, came back to town. He, also, had been a soldier. But, before that, he'd been a member of that ol' gang at the malt shop and had also dated Kathy's best friend. Now he began pestering Kathy to marry him. She didn't love him, wasn't even attracted to him, certainly had no intention of marrying him. Desperate though she was, she wasn't desperate enough to marry Albert.

But one night, after Albert had brought her home from a date, her emotional control dissolved. "I went into hysterics," she said, "and told Albert what Kenneth had done to me. Daddy heard the commotion and came in and all hell broke loose. Daddy said, 'You're probably pregnant now and you'll ruin my good name here in the Valley.'

"I felt awful and unclean and filthy when Daddy said that. But Albert quickly told Daddy that he'd be willing to marry me and take me off his hands. Daddy didn't even ask me if that was OK. He just waved his hand at Albert and said, 'Good. Take her. Get her out of my sight.'" Kathy was too young to marry without her father's consent. This time he consented. "He was just glad to wash his hands of me so he could save his good name," Kathy said.

And so, that very night, to save the good name Frank had in Chattanooga, Albert stuffed Kathy in his car and drove her away from her father's home on Kelly's Ferry Road. Albert stopped driving only after he reached Dyersburg, a small town just north of Memphis.

But then Kathy discovered there was a problem. Albert couldn't marry her because he was already married, and even had a daughter. He'd kicked his wife and daughter to the curb and abandoned them, but that still meant he couldn't legally remarry. At least not right away.

So Kathy lived in sin in Dyersburg with the man she didn't even like and pretended she was married to him in order to protect her father's good name. Albert finally divorced his abandoned wife, the mother of his daughter, in September of '46. But, he was in no hurry to then marry Kathy, despite his promise to Frank.

A growing fetus, however, does not wait.

I was born a bastard just before Christmas, 1946.

Just after the New Year of 1947, my still unwed mother took me back to Chattanooga to show her friends and family. Somehow, word had gotten out, at least to some, about what Kenneth had done to her in the front seat of his car after the wild party at the Road House Tavern. Kenneth's father and mother and other relatives came to see me and all agreed that I was, indeed, one of theirs.

Then Kenneth came to see if what his relatives told him was true. He took me up from my crib and looked me over carefully, turning me this way and that to catch the light. He decided it was true, the bastard was his, and he put me back down.

"You've ruined my life by getting pregnant," he said to Kathy. "But I know you're not married to Albert and I'm willing to make an honest woman out of you by marrying you."

Angered, Kathy replied, "The child is yours, but I'd never marry you. It's you who ruined *my* life by raping me. I'll never forgive you."

"I don't give a damn. I don't want to marry you, either, but my family said I had to make the offer. I'm glad you don't want to marry me. I'm off the hook. You can keep this shitty little bastard, I don't want him."

Then my father walked out the door. Kathy heard news of him from time to time thereafter through that ol' gang of theirs. Kenneth became a salesman, married, raised a family, became an alcoholic, divorced, became estranged from his adult children.

But Kathy never saw him again.

"Did Elmer know about all this?" I asked. "Did he know about me?"

"Of course. I couldn't keep a secret like this from my husband."

"But you could keep it a secret from the shitty little bastard, right? Well, it explains a lot."

****

In the spring of 1947 -- not dead but wounded, shot in the testicles in some air battle over the Pacific and fearing he'd never father a child, convalescing slowly in a V.A. hospital, too ashamed to contact the woman with whom he could never have children and a proper family -- the only man Kathy ever loved walked through her front door in Chattanooga.

Raymond Pope had finally come home from World War II.

And it didn't matter to him what Kenneth had done to her. And it didn't matter to him that Kathy now had a baby son. Raymond still loved her and begged Kathy to marry him. He would raise her son as his own.

But, by then, Albert had finally deigned to make Kathy an honest woman and had married her. And it was Chattanooga in 1947, and good girls did not divorce their husbands in Chattanooga in 1947. Even if they did not love their husbands. Even to marry their first and only true loves. People would talk about them and they would loose their good names.

And Kathy was a good girl with a good name.

And being talked about and losing her good name was her greatest fear.

And her greatest fear was greater than her greatest love.

So Kathy remained a good girl with a good name.

Blood Money

Vern was finishing up a summer course at Phoenix College. I called the school and found out when and where he was teaching. I was waiting for him as he came out of his classroom. I pulled out the $150 I'd saved for this purpose from my summer at the Sarasota bottling plant, the $150 I owed him for arranging my son's death. I handed him the wad of seven twenties and a ten.

Vern glanced around the hallway, took the wad, and then, without counting it, stashed it quickly in his pocket. It felt like a Mafia payoff. "This is between you and me," he said. "It's not to be mentioned to Annie."

"Another secret, eh? Like the abortion itself. We mustn't talk about it."

Vern looked closely at me. "It was the right thing to do."

Was it? I looked at Vern. It was one of those moments when time seemed to stretch out in slow motion. Easy for you to make that call, I thought. It wasn't *your* son you killed.

But when I finally found my voice, I realized I had nothing to say to Vern.

I turned and walked away.

Part Seven
Smoke From a Distant Fire

Ho Chi Minh at Versailles

In a way, the Vietnam War began at Versailles, France, in 1919 when the victors of World War I met to design the peace treaty ending the war. A major goal of the American effort in that war had been self-determination for the people of Europe who had for centuries been subjected against their wills to the political domination of one nation or another. One of the Fourteen Points President Woodrow Wilson claimed America was fighting to implement was that every oppressed people should have their own independent nation. Thus, Austria, Poland, Hungary, Czechoslovakia, Rumania, Bulgaria, Yugoslavia, and other nations came into existence in Eastern Europe as the ancient Hohenzollern, Hapsburg, and Romanov Empires were broken up. At the same time, the modern Muslim nations of the Middle East were created out of the ashes of the Ottoman Empire.

At that time Vietnam was a French colony, part of a larger colony called French Indochina. Ho Chi Minh, who later came to lead the Vietnamese independence movement, was living in Paris at the time. He took Wilson at his word and felt that Wilson would be sympathetic to Vietnamese aspirations to be free of French colonial rule. In his 1967 book, *Last Reflections on a War,* p. 71, Bernard Fall recounts how Ho bought a pinstriped suit, derby, and overcoat, all secondhand, so that he would appear "respectable" to the peace conference delegates at Versailles. He then went to Versailles and spent some weeks seeking an audience with Wilson. Ho wanted to present a petition to Wilson for Vietnamese independence and plead with him to support Vietnamese independence for the same reason he supported Eastern European independence.

But Wilson was not sympathetic. Wilson, a Virginian, was a white supremacist who believed in the subordination of inferior blacks back home in America. Freedom was not for them. Likewise, freedom internationally was not for Asians. Wilson refused to meet with Ho and Ho went away from Versailles empty handed.

The Communists, on the other hand, who had just achieved a successful revolution in Russia, *were* sympathetic to the aspirations of Third World people, like the Vietnamese, who sought to throw off the yoke of Western imperialism. Thus, Ho became more and more immersed in Communist theory and practice. The fact that he became a Communist later blinded the American government to the fact that he was, first and foremost, a Vietnamese patriot dedicated to Vietnamese independence from *all* external powers.

Ho Chi Minh went on to become a leader of guerrilla forces which fought brutal Japanese occupation armies in Vietnam during World War II. Ho and the Vietnamese felt that Vietnam had earned the right to freedom by fighting for it against an Axis foe for eight long years. They also felt that, when they proclaimed Vietnamese independence in 1945, following the defeat of Japan, they were living up to the ideals of freedom proclaimed by the Americans and French themselves in their own revolutions. Thus, they believed that America and France would support Vietnamese freedom because it was the right thing to do.

This expectation can be seen in the Vietnamese Declaration of Independence proclaimed on Sept. 2, 1945: "'All men are created equal,'" begins the Vietnamese Declaration of Independence, quoting the words from the American Declaration of Independence from British colonial rule. "'They are endowed by their Creator with certain inalienable rights; among these are Life, Liberty, and the pursuit of Happiness.' This immortal statement was made in the Declaration of Independence of the United States of America in 1776. In a broader sense, this means: All the peoples of the earth are equal from birth, all the peoples have a right to live, to be happy and free.

"The Declaration of the French Revolution," the Vietnamese Declaration continued, "made in 1791 on the Rights of Man and the Citizen also states: 'All men are born free and with equal rights, and must always remain free and have equal rights.'

"Those are undeniable truths. Nevertheless, for more than 80 years, the French imperialists, abusing the standard of Liberty, Equality, and Fraternity, have violated our Fatherland and oppressed our fellow-citizens. They have acted contrary to the ideals of humanity and justice.

"For these reasons, we, members of the Provisional Government, representing the whole Vietnamese people, declare that from now on we break off all relations of a colonial character with France....We are convinced that the Allied nations...[which] have acknowledged the principles of self-determination and equality of nations, will not refuse to acknowledge the independence of Vietnam. A people who have courageously opposed French domination for more than eight years, a people who have fought side by side with the Allies against the Fascists during these last years, such a people must be free and independent."

The French, however, did not agree, and like the Dutch and other European powers, sought to re-impose colonial status on their former Asian colonies following World War II. Fighting between the French and the Vietnamese, led by Ho, began on Dec. 19, 1946.

The war to re-conquer Vietnam drained the fragile and weak post-war economy of France, so, beginning in 1948, President Harry Truman began financing the French war effort. You could say, then, that America's Vietnam War began in 1948 when we started picking up the bill for it.

Despite massive American financing, the Vietnamese defeated the French army in 1954 at the climactic battle at Dien Bien Phu. The formal agreement ending French efforts to re-conquer Vietnam were the Accords signed in Geneva that year. These Geneva Accords *temporarily* divided Vietnam into two zones, one controlled by the guerrilla armies in the North, another zone controlled by French forces in the South. The truce line between the opposing armies was the 17th parallel. The Accords further provided for nation-wide elections in 1956, in both north and south, to determine the future government of Vietnam.

The United States government, however, which had become the principal backer of French interests now concentrated in the south, refused to abide by the Geneva Accords because it feared Ho Chi Minh would be elected president of Vietnam in any free election. Which is true. Therefore, the United States blocked the scheduled 1956 election which was to determine the future status and government of Vietnam.

Instead, the United States began pouring in massive amounts of funding to turn the French-controlled zone in the south into a de facto nation controlled by the United States, called South Vietnam, or the Republic of Vietnam. Thus, the truce lines between the competing armies along the 17th parallel solidified into ad hoc national borders dividing South Vietnam and North Vietnam.

Even before Dien Bien Phu, in 1953, the CIA had become interested in the Dragon Lady's brother-in-law, Ngo Dinh Diem, who was then living in exile. They viewed him as a possible surrogate for American interests should French power in Indochina falter. This was made clear in the February 12, 1968 *New York Times* (p. 9), which observed that, "This new information makes a monkey of the Johnson Administration's claim that we have come to the aid of our allies in Vietnam. In reality we have come to the aid of our...puppets." After the French pulled out, the CIA installed puppet-Diem as the dictator of the so-called "Republic of Vietnam."

The guerrillas never accepted this foreign division of their country or the American puppet-government and they continued a war which now became not only a war for independence, but also a war for national unification.

In May, 1961, U.S. involvement in Vietnam made a quantum leap when puppet-Diem told JFK he was on the verge of defeat unless the United States stepped up its aid. President Kennedy sent in Green Beret military advisors and much more military hardware.

The problem with puppet-Diem, however, was that he was brutal, corrupt, and unpopular. It didn't look so good that we backed this guy against the patriotic Ho and his guerrillas. So, President Kennedy decided to get rid of puppet-Diem. In early November, 1963, an American-backed military coup -- to which Kennedy had given his blessing -- overthrew puppet-Diem and murdered him and his right-hand-brother, the Dragon Lady's husband. Puppet-Diem was replaced by sequential puppet military dictators approved by the United States, who lasted up until the end of the war in 1975.

Meanwhile, American military involvement increased even more as Johnson, assuming his role as the new president after JFK was assassinated in 1963, began a massive bombing campaign designed to "pacify" the countryside by bombing it into oblivion. At the same time, Johnson introduced the "strategic hamlets" program, a massive re-location of the rural population into newly-created villages controlled by United States military forces. Anyone, or anything, outside these "strategic hamlets" was in "free fire zones," which meant they were fair game to be blow away. The strategy was intended to undercut guerrilla support among the rural population; all it succeeded in doing was driving more people into the guerrilla armies.

Then, in the summer of 1964, came the Gulf of Tonkin Incident, which never happened, at least not the way the American government described it as happening. American warships, led by the destroyer *Maddox*, were sent into the Gulf of Tonkin well within the territorial waters of North Vietnam to support South Vietnamese commando raids along the North Vietnamese coast. North Vietnam sent out its only defense, small torpedo boats, in an attempt to drive off the American warships. At least one of the Vietnamese torpedo boats seems to have fired on the *Maddox*. President Johnson went before Congress and lied, claiming that Vietnamese torpedo boats had repeatedly attacked innocent American ships in international waters without provocation.

In virtuous outrage, Congress quickly and overwhelmingly passed a resolution giving Johnson a free hand to respond to North Vietnam's "Communist aggression." Johnson sent massive numbers of ground troops to South Vietnam in January, 1965. This invasion is commonly considered the starting point of our "Vietnam War."

Only one senator, Senator Mike Gravel of Alaska, voted against the Tonkin Resolution. The Constitution says only Congress can declare war. Congress, however, never declared war on Vietnam so, in a sense, it was an illegal war. Instead, this Resolution became the "substitute" for the legally required declaration of war. It was war through the back door. Congress abdicated its watch-dog function, giving the president a blank check to do whatever he wanted. This set the precedent for the way America has conducted its wars ever since.

What followed over the next four years, from 1965 to 1969, was escalation of U.S. ground troops until more than half a million were fighting in the jungles of Vietnam, as well as the biggest air war since World War II.

From Protest to Resistance

"These are the times that try men's souls: The summer soldier and the sunshine patriot will, in this crisis, shrink from the service of their country, but he that stands it now deserves the thanks of man and woman."

-- Thomas Paine, 1776
The American Crisis

****

The 1967 Summer of Love was followed by an angry autumn. "Hippie," devoted son of Mass Media, died on October 6, 1967. His close friends carried his coffin through the Haight and bid him a fond farewell with songs, bells, and whistles. The Summer of Love had been too much for him. He'd overdosed on media attention and the spirit had gone out of him.

Two days later, on October 8, guerrilla leader Che Guevara was executed by Bolivian soldiers following his capture in a jungle fire fight.

But the spirits of both "Hippie" and Che lived on -- at least for a while.

A week later the shape of things to come appeared in the streets of Oakland, across San Francisco Bay from the Haight. The longer a social movement goes on, the more radical it tends to become. Such was the case with the antiwar movement. After innumerable marches, vigils, petitions, rallies and speeches, the Movement, at least in the Bay Area, decided to up the ante. It decided to shift from endless and ineffectual symbolic protest against the Vietnam War, which seemed to accomplish nothing, to active resistance. It would at the very least become a public nuisance. Perhaps, if large enough, that nuisance might cause enough chaos to actually hinder the workings of the war machine. The week beginning with Tuesday, October 16, was declared "Stop the Draft Week" in the Bay Area. One activist declared there would be a "draft holiday;" the Oakland army induction center, to which army inductees were bussed from all over Northern California, would be closed down by the Movement.

The week's resistance activities began that Tuesday with a peaceful sit-in in downtown Oakland at which 124 resisters, including Joan Baez, were arrested. At the same time, "The Resistance," as the Movement began to call itself, turned in 400 draft cards at the San Francisco Federal Building. It was a peaceful enough beginning to what became known as "Bloody Tuesday."

Independent of the above actions, thousands of activists marched on the Oakland induction center, where they were met by an angry army of cops. What followed was the Sunset Strip all over. The cops went on a rampage of rage. The next day, *The San Francisco Chronicle* reported that, "Police swinging clubs like scythes cut a bloody path through 2,500 antiwar demonstrators who had closed down the Oakland Armed Forces Examining Station yesterday for three hours....[the cops beat the demonstrators with] their hard wooden sticks mechanically flailing up and down, like peasants mowing down wheat."

That same day, in Madison, SDS students at the University of Wisconsin picketed recruiters from Dow Chemical Company, the manufacturer of napalm, the jellied gasoline U.S. planes dropped on the people of Vietnam daily. The recruiters in Madison kept on recruiting. The next day, Wednesday, October 17, the students blocked the recruiters from entering the campus. They were attacked by club wielding cops, who felled the students "like peasants mowing down wheat." Thousands more University of Wisconsin students then attacked the police and freed the beaten and arrested protestors. Seven cops and 65 Madison students were hospitalized for injuries following the battle.

On Friday, October 19, the battle resumed in Oakland. Antiwar demonstrators, perhaps as many as 10,000, returned to the Oakland induction center ready and eager for combat. Outnumbering the 2,000 cops who faced them, they pushed the cops back block by block in bloody street battles until they sealed off ten square blocks around the induction center. They declared the blocks they'd won "liberated territory" and spray painted "Che Lives in Oakland!" across storefronts. At noon the demonstrators marched back to Berkeley singing antiwar songs. The draft had not been stopped...but at least it had been delayed for a few hours. And in the future, there would be more such delays. Weatherman leader Bernardine Dohrn later said that Oakland's Stop the Draft Week battles convinced her that the time had come for fighting in the streets.

Meanwhile, hippie flower power was not entirely dead. The "March on the Pentagon," organized by the National Mobilization Committee to End the War in Vietnam (the "Mobe"), was its last dying spasm. On Sunday, October 21, the armies of the night confronted the Pentagon a continent away from Berkeley in Washington, D.C. It was the largest antiwar demonstration America had yet witnessed, with over 100,000 participating. The Mobe's chief organizer for the March on the Pentagon was Berkeley radical Jerry Rubin. Rubin had joined Abbie Hoffman and other hippies the previous summer when they'd tossed hundreds of dollar bills from a balcony onto the floor of the New York Stock Exchange, laughing as the stock brokers scrambled wildly for the money. Rubin invited Hoffman to join him as the co-organizer of the Pentagon march. It seems to have been Hoffman's idea for the march to culminate in a levitation of the Pentagon and an exorcism of the demons inside by assembled hippie witches, warlocks, and wizards.

The March on the Pentagon attracted a new cross-section of Americans. SDS and unaffiliated student activists were there, but so were hippies, civil rights leaders, and Black Power militants such as H. Rap Brown, in addition to middle class liberals like Dr. Benjamin Spock, Paul Goodman, and Norman Mailer, who would write about the march in his book *Armies of the Night,* published the following year. The marchers were overwhelmingly nonviolent. The vast majority marched to the Lincoln Memorial, where Phil Ochs and Peter, Paul, and Mary serenaded them and where they listened to speeches. One of the speakers, however, pacifist David Dellinger, told the throng that "This is the beginning of a new stage in the American peace movement in which the cutting edge becomes active resistance."

A few thousand of the demonstrators then marched two miles to the Pentagon, which was ringed by thousands of military policemen. There was a brief confrontation as some of the demonstrators tried to force their way past the soldiers. Then the demonstrators sat down in the Pentagon parking lot and began singing songs. Some placed flowers in the rifle barrels the soldiers pointed at them. As night came on, the hippies among them built campfires and smoked dope while their seers and sorcerers chanted "om" in order to levitate the Pentagon and exorcise the demons within. The Pentagon, it seems, did not levitate, nor, unfortunately, were demons exorcised.

Around midnight, paratroopers of the army's 82nd Infantry Division assembled at the edge of the hippie encampment in the parking lot and replaced the MPs. Then the troopers of the 82nd attacked, clubbing down the hippies "like peasants mowing down wheat." Federal marshals, following in the wake of the paratroopers, arrested over 700 of those who'd placed flowers in the barrels of rifles that day. As dawn came, the remaining hippies slipped away.

Flower Power died that night under the flailing clubs of the paratroopers in the Pentagon parking lot. From then on, it was war against the war.

A few days after the rout of the hippies in the Pentagon parking lot, Jesuit Father Philip Berrigan and three fellow antiwar Catholics entered a draft board, opened the file drawers of draft records, and poured red paint over the files. Radical priests and nuns, including Philip's brother, Father Daniel Berrigan, subsequently destroyed records, sometimes with homemade napalm, at other draft boards.

Meanwhile, support for the war declined among Americans at large. In July, 1967, a Harris poll reported that 72% of Americans supported the war. By October, only 58% supported the war. By November, those who thought the war was a mistake equalled those who did not, and a *New York Times* poll revealed that half of Americans had no idea why we were fighting in Vietnam.

That month Minnesota Senator Eugene McCarthy announced that he would challenge President Johnson in the upcoming 1968 Democratic Party presidential primaries, beginning in New Hampshire, on an antiwar platform.

That same November, Signet Books published John Kenneth Galbraith's booklet, *How To Get Out of Vietnam*. It wasn't just a plan for getting out of Vietnam, it was a history of the war which, when I read it, made it even more clear to me than ever before that the war was based on the government's massive ignorance of why the Vietnamese were fighting. The government assumed that Third World revolutionary and nationalist movements were the creatures of Moscow. As such, anti-imperialist movements had to be fought everywhere they appeared. After the Korean conflict, America became increasingly entangled with often corrupt and autocratic anti-Communist proxies, such as Diem and the Nhus. America became the principal bastion of reaction in a revolutionary world. The U.S. government felt that it could indulge in and control limited wars against revolutionary movements as a means of bringing about a congenial international socioeconomic environment.

Galbraith's arguments had a profound impact on my understanding of the Vietnam War and made it imperative for me to resist that increasingly deadly and evil war by immediately filing for Conscientious Objector status. Vietnam had become carnage incarnate. I could not be a "good German" who, without protest, placidly went along with an evil holocaust of monstrous proportions. I had to resist.

Meanwhile, that same November, Johnson told his advisers that, "The clock is ticking...the main front of the war is here in the United States." Accordingly, he launched a PR campaign in support of the war. Vice President Hubert Humphrey spoke at a convention of military suppliers, accusing the Pentagon marchers of giving aid and comfort to the enemy. Ellsworth Bunker, the American ambassador to Vietnam, was recalled from Saigon to tell the American media that, "We are making steady progress in Vietnam." General William Westmoreland, the commander of American forces in Vietnam, told the media that, "It is significant that the enemy has not won a major battle in more than a year." Ambassador Bunker and General Westmoreland (ridiculed by the marchers as "General Wastemoreland") appeared on *Meet the Press* and declared that America was "winning a war of attrition" and that there was "light at the end of the tunnel," as the war had entered its last stages.

But Johnson was not content to simply have his minions lie to the media about the war. He also unleashed the CIA to engage in domestic spying, something specifically forbidden by its mandate. He also instructed the FBI to infiltrate and disrupt Left and antiwar organizations, such as SDS and the Socialist Workers Party, in a program known as COINTELPRO, the Counter Intelligence Program.

Then, in December, Dr. Benjamin Spock, Yale chaplain Rev. William Sloan Coffin, Marcus Raskin, Mitchell Goodman, and Michael Ferber were indicted for "counselling, aiding and abetting" draft resistance. The killing and dying went on. By the end of December the media announced that 15,000 American soldiers had died in the war, 60% of them in 1967 alone.

Fighting in the streets between the police and antiwar demonstrators became more prevalent after this, but there was no place for a street fighting man in sleepy Phoenix. While there were protests against Dow recruiters at campuses nation-wide, there were none at Arizona State, where I was enrolled. I knew of no antiwar demonstrations or levitations in Phoenix, I was still too young to vote; all I could do was register with the Selective Service System as a Conscientious Objector to the war.

Then I discovered that I couldn't even do that. My draft board informed me that I didn't qualify for Conscientious Objector status. To be a C.O. one had to be, first of all, a pacifist. I was not a pacifist. I hadn't been raised in a pacifist tradition. I wasn't raised as a Quaker or a Jehovah's Witness. I was raised as a Baptist and a Mormon. Neither Baptists nor Mormons had any problem fighting wars and killing people.

Further, as a working class kid, I was raised to not take shit from anybody. And if anybody *did* give you any shit, you did not turn the other cheek. You kicked his fucking ass. At the level of international relations, that meant that if your country was attacked, then you defended yourself and you kicked the aggressor's ass. The Japs attacked us at Pearl Harbor, Hitler had declared war *on us* first, so I felt World War II was certainly what Studs Terkel called "The Good War," and I certainly would have fought for my country against the Axis powers in that war.

And if there were ever a just war in United States history, it was the Civil War, in which my relatives in the South attempted to destroy the United States of America by shattering the Union. So, I believed the North was justified in fighting to preserve the Union and, along the way, destroying slavery, and I thought the Revolutionary War was justified to gain our independence from Great Britain. Not only had I not been raised in a religiously pacifist tradition, I, personally, was *not* a pacifist, and freely confessed that fact.

While I was not a pacifist, I believed that, just as you don't take shit from anybody, you don't give other people shit, either. If you do, you are the bad guy, and you deserve to have your ass kicked by whoever you are giving shit to. At the level of international relations, my reasoning led me to conclude that, if you attacked, invaded, and occupied another country, then you were an aggressor who deserved to be defeated, because you were the bad guy.

And that's exactly what was going on in Vietnam. We were a Goliath nation -- in fact, the biggest Goliath on the planet -- and we'd attacked, invaded, and occupied a small David of a nation on the other side of the world which had never harmed or threatened us, nor even had any ability to do so.

This David, it turned out, had a sling, a belief in freedom and independence, and this David was using that sling to kick our ass in the jungles of Vietnam. And we deserved to have our ass kicked, because we were the bad guy shoveling out the shit to others. The war was the Vietnamese War of Independence and Ho Chi Minh was the Vietnamese George Washington, while we were the British determined to make sure Vietnam never became free.

It was clear to me that justice was on the side of the Vietnamese people. I couldn't jump in and help America continue to do evil, just because I was an American. I was a man before I was an American, and as I understood it, a man always did the right thing, the moral, ethical, and just thing, to the best of his understanding and ability. I was opposed to fighting in the Vietnam

War in any way, shape, form, or fashion, not because I was a pacifist, but simply because the war was *wrong*.

The law and the Selective Service System told me my argument was unacceptable. I couldn't pick and choose which wars I thought were just and unjust, good and bad, ethical and unethical. I had to be morally opposed to *all* wars. I had to be a pacifist.

Since I was not, I wasn't eligible for C.O. status.

There was another, perhaps even more important, reason why my local draft board would never give me C.O. status: I didn't believe in God. I was an atheist. And the law said you had to believe in God if you wanted to be a Conscientious Objector. More specifically, the Selective Service questionnaire asked me to explain how my "belief in a Supreme Being involves duties which...are superior to those arising from any human relation." Evidently, according to the Selective Service System, only someone who believed in a Supreme Being could have any moral or ethical duties "superior to those arising from any human relation."

Of course, I didn't believe in a Supreme Being, no matter how you defined It. As far as the draft law was concerned, therefore, I had no moral or ethical beliefs which qualified me as an objector to the Vietnam War on grounds of conscience. As far as the Selective Service System was concerned, I was shit out of luck. No way on God's green Earth that an atheist who just objected to *this particular war* for moral reasons was going to be classified as a Conscientious Objector.

I could not answer Rev. Martin Luther King's call to resist the war by registering as a Conscientious Objector. He was a minister. He could claim a religious objection. I was an atheist, and there was no such thing, I was told, as an atheistic objection to war. I could protest all I wanted, but I could not resist the war as a Conscientious Objector.

The Acid Vat

    Phoenix was out of the mainstream not only of the antiwar movement but also of the counter-culture. It wasn't until the autumn of 1967, after "Hippie" had already been declared dead and buried in the Haight, that the first hippie head shops blossomed in Phoenix along one block of Eighth Street between Thomas and McDowell. They had exotic names like The Purple Bag, Electric Banana, and the Liquid Giraffe. They didn't seem to actually sell anything, but nevertheless attracted huge crowds, perhaps drawn by the allure of their reputations.

    Looming over these hippie havens was a huge billboard which made clear the hostility such places elicited from the straights. It portrayed a hippie in a Dylanesque Afro, sideburns, and beads next to the admonition: "Beautify America. Get a haircut." A conservative businessman had paid to have this billboard appear all across America that angry autumn and, by chance or design, there it was in the midst of Phoenix's hippie strip.

    The Liquid Giraffe was a small shop with walls completely covered with psychedelic posters, an art form new to us. Strobe lights continually flickered, incense burned, and rock blared from ear-damaging speakers. It was jammed all the time with lonely hippies desperate for communion with each other.

    I wandered through the Liquid Giraffe and the other head shops, but the one I frequented the most was the Acid Vat, where I became friends with the owner. The Acid Vat was a huge old house which this hippie entrepreneur had bought and transformed into a mysterious counter-cultural enclave. He covered the windows with aluminum foil facing outward to totally block out the harsh Arizona sun and heat, a common Arizona tactic to make interiors cooler. The resulting dark interior was made even darker by black silk parachutes which billowed from the ceilings and concealed the walls. The wall-to-wall carpeting was composed of multi-hued squares of carpet samples. Huge puffy pillows were strewn everywhere, tempting visitors to linger and lounge. Acid rock blasted from hidden stereo speakers at even higher decibels than at the Liquid Giraffe. It was a psychedelic Aladdin's cave lit only by blue ultra-violet lights. To walk from the blazing hot Arizona daylight into this hippie cave was to enter a different plane of existence, far from the hostile mundane world we knew.

    The cops continually patrolled the street outside, looking for trouble. As far as they were concerned, all of these places along Eighth Street were drug dens and all the denizens of the dens were of dubious humanity. All of us were "scum" and "maggots" to them. One night some cops pulled up in front of the Acid Vat and began checking everyone's I.D. I told them I was a student at Arizona State; they laughed and demanded proof. When I showed them my student I.D., they looked at it and me in disbelief.

    Vern, too, thought the Acid Vat was a cauldron of drug dealing and a sump of licentiousness. It was yet one more of the world's myriad ways to diminish one's soul. He didn't want Annie anywhere near it. So, when I hung out there, I did so without her. And I never saw any drug dealing or drug taking while I was there.

    Which is not to say I didn't have drug-like experiences at the Acid Vat. But my consciousness was altered simply by the ambience of the place. And it was this ambience which was crucial in turning me into a Doors devotee.

    The Doors had released their first, self-titled, album on New Year's Eve, 1966, and it began to get air play in January of 1967. It was revolutionary. "Break On Through," their first single, failed to break on through to the charts, but by the end of July their "Light My Fire" was number one in America. Somehow I had missed Dylan's "Like A Rolling Stone" when it was big in September of 1965 and I picked up on it only later. The first rock song I was aware of which violated the sacred three-minute radio limit on pop songs was "Light My Fire." Their entire album seemed to alter the parameters of what rock music could be. With the Doors, rock became a mystic invocation of some kind of cosmic consciousness hitherto beyond the ken of mortals. At least that's how I felt in the Acid Vat one day that fall after listening to this album all the way through for the first time.

It was a typically hot Arizona day, with the brazen desert sun baking everything, but the interior of the Acid Vat was cool and dark. Some of us lounged on the huge pillows thrown across the carpeted floor, rapping about nothing in particular. In a private room next to ours, the Vat's owner was balling some hippie chick. From his room he put on the Doors and cranked the volume up to eleven. Jim Morrison's shamanistic incantations flooded the UV-lit interior of the Vat and we all fell silent and just listened. His voice sounded surreal, prophetic, delivering on what he promised, the opening of the doors of perception into another dimension.

Not a word was said as we listened to both sides of the LP, ending with the long, hypnotic "The End." "This is the end," Morrison sang, "My only friend, the end." The end, not only of the album, but of elaborate schemes, dreams, hopes and illusions. It was an apocalyptic autumn and we'd long felt ourselves on the eve of destruction, near the end of *everything*.

Finally, after a long period of silence, some hippie said, "Wow!" No further comment was needed. We all knew what he meant. It was the nearest I'd ever come to a mystic vision, and I didn't have to spend the night nude on top of Camelback Mountain in the middle of a storm to experience it. I didn't know the meaning of the experience, but I felt that I had, in some way, transcended myself. I felt preternaturally aware of everything which surrounded me. I'd have to be a priest or a shrink to adequately describe my feelings at that moment.

Just then the Vat's owner and the hippie chick he'd been balling ambled into the room. The hippie chick was Shana, wild and wonderful Shana, *my* Shana, who I could still taste on my lips. My heart pounded at the sight of her. And I suddenly hated the man standing with his arm thrown possessively over her shoulder, the man who had been my friend. I knew *exactly* what they'd been doing in the next room as they, like me, listened to Jim Morrison open the doors of perception. With vivid intensity, I knew every move Shana had made in her passion, every sound she'd made immersed in the ecstasy of the music and the moment and the coke I knew she used when fucking.

Our eyes caught. Neither of us said a word, but we both lived a lifetime together in that instant. There was no reason for me to feel jealous. Shana and I had gone our separate ways. Even so, irrationally, I felt Shana had betrayed me. And Shana's place in my heart turned to ashes.

I got up and walked out of the darkness of the Acid Vat into the blinding Phoenix sun.

And I never went back.

Famous for Fifteen Minutes

No matter how much I lashed into Andy Warhol -- calling him a fake, a charlatan, a fraud, a pretender, an impostor, and, repeatedly, an artistic hypocrite -- he wouldn't defend himself. He just took my abuse silently from behind his dark shades. And all the while Viva, at his side, smirked at me, as if privy to some arcane knowledge. The longer Warhol stood there in silence, the more frustrated I became with his lack of response. I felt like punching him out, right there on the Grady Gammage stage. Perhaps Valerie Solanas felt a similar frustration when she put a bullet in him the next year. Perhaps she shot Andy Warhol just to get a response.

In the end, though, I neither plugged him nor punched his fixed nose. I told Warhol and Viva to go back to New York City, where they seemed to love phonies. Then I walked on the backs of the audience seats to where Annie waited for me and I sat down beside her. As usual, I was a minority of one.

Neither Annie nor I had set out for the Warhol presentation with any idea that I'd be telling Warhol up close and personal that he was a fake and a fraud. I'd just wanted to broaden our cultural horizons with another free event for students at Arizona State University's Grady Gammage Auditorium.

The Grady Gammage, as ASU officials like to boast, is the last building that architect Frank Lloyd Wright designed. It looks like a big birthday cake with icing flowing over the sides. Supporting the cake are two long pedestrian ramps like flying buttresses, topped for their entire length by large metal hoops. Grady Gammage Auditorium is the cultural heart of the ASU campus. And so it was also the fall of 1967, when I began my first semester there.

Since I was a student, I got tickets to a certain number of events for me and a guest as part of my student activity fees. I took advantage of these tickets and frequently took Annie with me over to Tempe on the blue Suzuki. It was at the Grady Gammage that we saw the tiny, frail, white-haired, and stooped Igor Stravinsky, present for the world premiere of his new three-act opera, *The Rake's Progress.* There was much whoop-dee-do over the fact that it was a multi-media production. The composer of the revolutionary *Rites of Spring,* we were told, was still pushing the envelope. What this actually meant was that large closed-circuit TV sets were installed on either side of the proscenium and the singers often appeared on the screens, singing from somewhere backstage. It was much ado about nothing, as was the opera itself, Stravinsky's last neoclassical work and a minor effort. The old man had lost it.

I later learned that a librettist had sympathized with Stravinsky over a particularly bad review he'd received for a performance he conducted of *The Rake's Progress.* Stravinsky took out a check he'd received for conducting the performance and said, "This is the only review I read." No doubt Stravinsky also received a nice review of that very nature from the ASU administration for deigning us with his presence at the Grady Gammage premiere.

Much more enjoyable was renowned French mime Marcel Marceau. Annie had never heard of him or of mime.

"He's a famous French performer," I told her. "They'll be selling his albums in the lobby and I'll buy you his greatest hits collection."

"Save your money until I decide I like his music. What? Why are grinning like an idiot?"

"I'll be saving my money, because he's not actually a singer or a musician. In fact, no one has ever heard his voice on stage. He's a silent performer who acts out -- 'mimes' -- things. I'm sorry, I couldn't resist."

Annie punched me in the shoulder. "Resist this!"

Marceau was the first and the best mime I've ever seen. He was the master original. He did all the routines which, by now, have become standard for all street mimes -- walking the dog, trapped in a box, leaning on a non-existent ledge. For your edification and enjoyment, I pass on to you here a Marcel Marceau gesture you can easily and realistically replicate for the astonishment of your friends and small children. It's his imitation of a butterfly. Put your thumb and forefinger together as if making the OK sign. Your other three fingers should be rigidly straight and firmly together. Now quickly and repeatedly flick your rigid fingers up and down from the wrist, while moving your hand around erratically as if it is a flying butterfly. It's OK if your forearm jiggles. If you can do this in front of a mirror, all the better. And as the butterfly flits around in front of you, watch it in awe and wonderment. There it is, a master mime move, straight from Marcel Marceau to you, via moi.

I also expected to watch the film snippet by Andy Warhol in awe and wonderment. I was eager to see the latest from the hippest icon of the New York avant-garde in person. Warhol was touring college campuses, bringing hip culture to the hinterlands. He'd just come down from Salt Lake City, where he'd confused, bewildered, and bothered the Mormon students. I made sure Annie and I got to Grady Gammage early so we could be up front in the first few rows.

I confess I didn't know much about Warhol's art. Based on his famous images of Campbell's soup cans, which he first began exhibiting in 1962, I had some vague idea that his art was a pastiche of popular culture. I wasn't entirely convinced it was "art," but I was *willing* to be convinced. I especially wanted to see what he did in film, which was the subject of the evening's discussion. If I'd known about his 1964 film, *Empire,* I wouldn't have been so quite so eager to see Warhol's cinematic offering. *Empire* is an eight-hour long static image of the Empire State Building. That's it. Nothing else. Just the camera staring at the Empire State Building for eight hours. Nothing happens for those eight hours except that clouds pass and lights come on.

Sorry, but I don't call that art. For me, art involves a combination of technical mastery and creative imagination in the production of an aesthetic object in some medium. It takes no skill or creative imagination to turn a camera on and film an immobile building for eight hours. You can just set it up and walk away, which Warhol did. The camera does all the work.

Each artistic medium has its own requirements. Painting and photography, for example, work with the static image, and the artist's skill and imagination make that static image come alive, in some way, and say something to the viewer. Even if the painting is a Jackson Pollock dribble of color, the artist makes it come alive, in some fashion, in the mind of the viewer.

Film, however, works with the moving image. That's why it's called "motion pictures." The movies *move,* and they move forward toward some destination. To work, they must have *profluence,* a sense that they are "going somewhere," that it all adds up and will eventually mean something. That something can simply be entertainment, and that's fine. Or it can have some meaning beneath the entertainment, some truth about our lives. And that's even better. Then the movie becomes a lie which tells the truth, and the artist becomes a liar who is a truth-teller. But the basic requirement of the film medium, above all others, is that the movie has to move and *arrive* somewhere. If it doesn't, then the artist should work in some other medium, such as photography, or painting, as Warhol did, and stop pretending to be a filmmaker.

The film fragment Warhol showed that night did not arrive anywhere. We were told it was a "work in progress." I don't remember its title, or if we were even told the title, assuming it had one. It was about 30-minutes long and could have been a preview of Warhol's 25-hour-long film known as ****, which he released a couple of months later in December of that year. The very fact that **** has no pronounceable title indicates its lack of theme and meaning, and so what we were shown that night could well have been part of that monstrosity.

Whatever it was, the film had no profluence, it didn't go anywhere, it didn't say anything. It was just a chaotic jumble. And because of that, I can't remember much about the film itself. There wasn't much the memory could latch onto. It had no plot, no narrative line, no coherent images, and no discernable point. The soundtrack was composed of music by The Doors, with Jim Morrison singing about how the killer awoke before dawn, he put his boots on, and he walked on down the hall to murder his father and rape his mother. The camera may have walked on down a hall at that point. We, the audience, attempted to read some significance into those lyrics as they applied to Warhol's film, but it was hard slogging and I, for one, failed.

I became more and more pissed off viewing the chaotic hodgepodge. There was no content, no substance. Warhol seemed to be putting his audience on. If this was Warhol's "art," then he was just pretending to be an artist. There was no artistry involved in what we were shown, there was no discernable creative imagination at work. It all seemed fundamentally fraudulent. Warhol was a liar who was only *pretending* to give us the truth. He was a liar who was simply lying.

In my eyes, Warhol was a hypocrite. He was pretending to be an "artist," but he wasn't. I could not stand hypocrites. The fact that everyone in the audience seemed to be in awe of the crap on the screen irritated me. I may have been a know-nothing in the hinterland, and Warhol may have been the celebrated guru of coolness from the Big Apple, but if Warhol had some kind of question and answer session in the talk after the film, I was certainly going to question his artistic credentials.

As the lights came up, Warhol and "Viva," his latest "superstar," came on stage from a slit in the curtains. *Everyone* in Warhol's entourage was called a "superstar," which just seemed to be another example of Warhol's complete lack of aesthetic standards. If *everyone's* a "superstar," then the designation is meaningless. Viva was tall, thin, and had a huge head of frizzy blonde hair. Her real name was Janet Susan Mary Hoffman and she'd met Warhol just that August at a party. There she told Warhol she wanted to be in one of his movies. He agreed, but said she'd have to take off her clothes. She did, and he immediately put her in his movie, *Bike Boy*. But, before doing so, he gave her a new name, "Viva," after the Viva brand of paper towels. The Warhol aesthetic, I suppose.

Now Viva was on the road with Warhol, showing a snippet of his latest film. And, as it turned out, she was also Warhol's mouthpiece. Warhol would give no talk, Viva said. He would just answer questions. Actually, however, only Viva answered questions. Warhol remained totally mute and skulked behind Viva in his usual uniform of black T-shirt, black leather jacket, dark shades and his signature wild white wig, which he wore to conceal his early hair loss. Typical behavior from the bizarre Andy Warhol.

He didn't need to say anything. The hip young audience showered The Master with all the praise he could've desired for the masterpiece we'd just seen. After listening to this adulation for awhile I could stand it no longer. I stood up and jabbed an accusing finger at the lurking figure on the stage: "This man is nothing but a fraud and a fake!"

The audience immediately erupted in hoots and hisses. Viva shushed them. She seemed vastly amused by my accusation, perhaps, I thought, because it was a dissent from the approving chorus. "Would you like to come on up on stage and tell the audience exactly why you think Andy Warhol is a fake?"

I accepted the challenge. Like Adrien Brody many years later when he climbed over the backs of seats to claim his Oscar for *The Pianist,* I climbed over the backs of rows until I reached the edge of the stage, where Viva offered me a helping hand up. Then she gave me her mike and asked me to elaborate on my charges of artistic fraud.

I proceeded to detail why Andy Warhol was a poseur, an artist-manque, a derivative, unimaginative, fraudulent non-entity who was a parasite on the celebrity of others. Warhol cowered beside me like a frightened gazelle, not saying a word as I flayed his oeuvre and lacerated his reputation.

No matter how much I blistered him, nothing provoked him to respond -- and Viva only smiled. But, they didn't need to defend themselves. The audience rose to The Master's defense and we *did* have the promised debate on Warhol's art, after all. I said everything I've written to you above and did my best to answer audience objections. I finished by saying, "Just because you don't understand it doesn't mean it's a work of genius. Trust yourself! Consider the possibility that maybe it's just a pile of crap!"

But, I was a one man band performing alone up on that stage. No one at Grady Gammage that night agreed with my views. They were all True Believers. Even so, I'd made my case and had nothing more to say. I'd done what I could. I gave the mike back to Viva.

"I like his style," Viva told the audience, "we're going to put him in Andy's next movie."

"Don't call me," I told her, "I'll call you. I don't usually hang out with phonies." Then I returned to my seat beside Annie the same way I'd come.

In February of the following year I discovered why Andy Warhol did such a good imitation of a frightened gazelle that evening on the Grady Gammage stage. It seems that Warhol never actually left New York City on that particular tour. Evidently, he thought it'd be a hoot if he sent out Viva and a look-alike to masquerade as him in the hinterlands. The Great Unwashed wouldn't know the difference, anyway. The man who stood beside me in silence that night as I accused him of being a fraud and a fake was actually Allen Midgette, one of Warhol's "superstars" who, in fact, acted in the 25-hour-long movie, ****. They'd simply put Warhol's clothes, shades, and wig on him and sent him out. He'd impersonated Warhol on stage after stage across the country and, since Viva did all the talking while he skulked in the shadows, no one realized he really *was* an impostor. After the tour ended, someone who'd taken a photo of Midgette-as-Warhol compared it to a picture of Warhol, and the truth came out.

When I stood up in the audience at Grady Gammage and denounced the skulking figure in the shades and white wig as a fake and a fraud, no doubt Viva and Midgette feared they'd been unmasked right then and there. Relief must have flooded over them when they realized I wasn't accusing the fake Warhol of being a fake -- I was accusing the *real* Warhol, back in New York City, of being a fake! So, why not play with the fool? Invite him up on stage, give him the mike, and encourage him to really go to it. What better cover for the fake Warhol than to have an angry critic stand right next to him and speak right in his face while denouncing the *real* artist as a fake? What better way to validate the fake as the Real McCoy? Viva and Midgette, who later married each other in a hippie wedding, must have laughed their asses off backstage afterward.

But, Allen Midgette was a good actor. He never broke character. He never lost his cool. And neither did Viva. So, it turns out that Warhol was right about one thing when he sent her and Midgette out on the tour. Viva later complained that "I toured 50 colleges lecturing for Andy, and he didn't pay me a penny. 'It's good practice for you,' he told me."

At least that time Andy Warhol was telling the truth.

The Most Dangerous Man in Phoenix

Be Afraid

Of the people over here
    And the people over there,
        The dark-skinned mother,
            And your own blood brother,
                Of the red
                    In your bed,
                      And people everywhere.
Be afraid
    Of your shadow
        And kids in Colorado
            Who might be packing guns,
                Of the man with the beard
                    And people looking weird,
                        Of the graveyard ghosts
                            And the people on the Coast,
                              Be afraid of the nuns!
Be afraid
    Of the short and afraid of the tall,
        Of just about any damn one at all
            Who doesn't look like you,
                And doesn't cook like you,
                    Doesn't drink like you,
                        And doesn't think like you.
        Trust only in the Lord,
And the brute in the suit
    Pointing his finger
        At the people over there,
            And the people over here
                At the straight and the queer
                    And people everywhere,
                      Telling you
                          Ya gotta,
                              Ya gotta
        Ya gotta be afraid,
            Ya gotta be afraid,
                Ya gotta be very, very afraid.

****

    The first members of any Leftist organization I ever met were the "California Commies" I and Jerry Campbell fought in August of '64. The second group of Lefties I met seemed just as antiquated. I met them when I began at Arizona State in the fall of '67. They were doddering old codgers who belonged to the Socialist Labor Party (SLP). The SLP is the oldest socialist party in America and, to my young eyes, these white-haired ancients might have been at the party's founding convention in 1876. I first saw them one morning after I'd parked the blue Suzuki in a student parking lot and begun walking toward campus. They stood on the sidewalk waylaying passing students. As I approached the nearest geezer, he thrust a leaflet toward me and said, "Capitalism stinks on ice. Find out about the Socialist Labor Party."

I lifted my hands as if warding off a slobbery dog and walked out into the street to get around him. "Find out the truth about capitalism," he yelled after me, waving the leaflet in the air.

I didn't know what the hell he was talking about, and I didn't want to know. I didn't trust him and his comrades any more than I had the California Commies, so I avoided them every morning thereafter on my way to class. More than anything, I think it was their age. They seemed to be from some long-gone and fading past. I couldn't imagine their having anything to say which might interest me. The other kids also avoided them. I don't think those SLP codgers ever recruited a single ASU student.

For that reason, I'd guess that the FBI never aimed their COINTEL Program, which had been created as per LBJ's orders that very year, at those old dinosaurs. As we later discovered through the Freedom of Information Act (FOIA), COINTEL was the FBI's "Counterintelligence Program" designed not only for surveillance of New Left, antiwar, and Black Power groups, but also for the disruption of those groups, no matter how legal their activities might be. The feds, as well as so-called "Red Squads" of local police departments, engaged in the systematic monitoring and harassment of dissidents and New Left, antiwar, and Black Power groups throughout the Sixties. Any challenge to the status quo could lead to police surveillance and intimidation that ranged from the photographing of peaceful and legal demonstrators, to the infiltration of nonviolent groups by agent-provocateurs hoping to foment violence, to encouraging the termination of one's employment.

One of the principal targets of such surveillance and harassment by the FBI was the Socialist Workers Party (SWP). The SWP pledged allegiance to Leon Trotsky and believed that Stalin had betrayed the Bolshevik revolution. Although Trotsky preached permanent revolution and had once commanded the Red Army, the SWP believed education and elections were the ways to socialism. Thus, everything it did was legal and peaceful. That didn't stop the FBI from spying on it, infiltrating it, and targeting its members for disruptive actions out of fear of its influence.

Which is why the FBI felt that Dr. Morris Starsky, tenured professor of philosophy at ASU, was the most dangerous man in Phoenix. Starsky was a short, pudgy, balding and bearded chain smoker. He was also a leading member of the Arizona SWP and he made no secret of his opposition to the Vietnam War, which he denounced in sometimes foul language at campus rallies. Many students listened to him and admired him.

That was the problem, as far as the feds were concerned. When Starsky later got parts of his own COINTEL file through FOIA, he discovered that his popularity worried the Phoenix office of the FBI. In a May 31, 1968 letter to FBI Director J. Edgar Hoover, the Phoenix office reported that, "On the basis of developments to date, it is apparent that New Left organizations and activities in the Phoenix metropolitan area have received their inspiration and leadership almost exclusively from the members of the faculty in the Department of Philosophy at Arizona State University, chiefly Assistant Professor Morris J. Starsky. Starsky has already received considerable publicity in Phoenix papers in connection with his antiwar and anti-draft activities.

The most logical targets for potential counterintelligence action locally are therefore pretty obvious. Starsky is presently the subject of active investigation in the Selective Service category. This suggests an avenue of counterintelligence approach as well as that offered by reliable and cooperative contacts in the news media."

Professor Starsky worried the FBI even more when he and his wife began working for the SWP presidential candidate in 1968. In an October 1, 1968 letter to Hoover, the Phoenix FBI office reported that, "Morris J. Starsky, by his actions, has continued to spotlight himself as a target for counterintelligence action. He and his wife were both named as presidential electors by and for the Socialist Workers Party when the SWP in August, 1968, gained a place on the ballot in Arizona. In addition, they have signed themselves as treasurer and secretary, respectively, of the Arizona SWP.

"Professor Starsky's status at Arizona State University may be affected by the outcome of his pending trial on charges of disturbing the peace. He is alleged to have used violent, abusive and obscene language against the Assistant Managing Director of Gammage Auditorium at ASU during memorial services for Martin Luther King last April. Trial is now scheduled for 10/8/68 in Justice Court, Tempe, Arizona.

"Bureau approval is requested to mail a copy of the enclosed anonymous letter to each member of the faculty committee which is hearing the charges against Starsky."

The anonymous letter accusing Starsky of fomenting violence, which the FBI sent to the faculty committee investigating him for his actions at the Grady Gammage rally, did not succeed in getting Starsky fired that time. But the FBI may have been more successful a bit later.

In January, 1970, eight University of Arizona students in Tucson were arrested for protesting against the University of Arizona's participation in sports competitions with Brigham Young University (BYU), the Mormons' flagship college in Utah. BYU, like the Mormon church itself, discriminated against blacks. The students felt, for that reason, that BYU should be boycotted. A rally in support of the arrested students was scheduled in Tucson for January 14th. Starsky was asked to speak. He requested and was granted permission by his department chair to have his teaching assistant teach his class that day so he could attend the rally.

It was exactly the opportunity the FBI had been hoping for, as the COINTEL documents on him indicated; the FBI had been encouraging the university to "find cause to separate Professor Starsky from the public payroll." When Professor Starsky returned from Tucson, he discovered that his dismissal was in the works, despite his tenure. Although the ASU President and the Academic Freedom and Tenure Committee of the Faculty Senate supported him, the Arizona Board of Regents terminated Professor Starsky that spring. He never again found a full-time teaching position and moved from part-time teaching in California to part-time teaching in the Midwest. Thus, the FBI finally succeeded in neutralizing Professor Starsky in Phoenix.

When I met Morris Starsky in the fall of '67, this was all in the future. He was still a fully-tenured ASU professor and firebrand campus SWP activist. Perhaps because he was a professor, perhaps because he wasn't a geriatric, he didn't seem so alien to me, despite being a socialist. He often hung out with students on campus and was willing to talk about anything, from Descartes to Agent Orange. And I was often in the knot of students around him, listening to him and laughing with him as he denounced the war in colorfully obscene language.

One day, between classes, I was with a cluster of students listening to him explain the philosophy and organization of the Socialist Workers Party. It was a militant and disciplined organization, he explained, totally focussed on the class struggle.

"But is it a *democratic* organization?" I asked.

"Of *course* it's democratic. The party works on the principle of democratic centralism. It combines the best aspects of democracy with discipline."

The word "discipline" aroused my latent suspicion of Commie control. "And who thought up this principle?"

"Vladimir Lenin, the Russian revolutionary leader."

Ah! Suspicion confirmed! "And Lenin was raised under a Czarist autocracy, so what did *he* know about democracy?"

"You don't have to have been *raised* in a democracy to *believe* in democracy."

"Hmmm. Perhaps. So, how does this democratic centralism work when the party debates issues? Disciplined democracy sounds like a contradiction in terms."

"Not at all. Every member of the party is completely free to debate any position on any issue which comes up. What could be more democratic? Once a decision has been reached, however, the debate ends and every member is expected to rally around and carry out the group decision. Thus, there is a central thrust to the party's efforts. Democratic centralism."

"But, what if a member of the minority still thinks the decision the party made is completely wrong? He's supposed to just shut up and do what he's told?"

"You need a disciplined fighting organization to fight the class struggle. You can't have your troops heading off in all directions. That dissipates energy. You have to be totally focussed on the struggle."

"Even if you think the focus is wrong?"

"You had your chance to make your case during the debate. If you couldn't convince your comrades of the correctness of your position at that time, then most likely you weren't correct."

"That doesn't sound very democratic to me."

"It's disciplined democracy. A soldier has to carry out the orders he's given and you need an army to fight an army in the class war. The SWP is that army."

"Well, then, I guess I'm not joining your army. It seems I'm allergic to *all* armies."

"You can't fight the class struggle by yourself."

"The first struggle is just to *be* yourself."

"You sound like a hippie."

I smiled and flashed the peace "V" sign with my fingers. "I *am* a hippie, Professor Starsky. I believe in making love, not war."

"Yeah, well, that hippy-dippy shit won't do you much good when they smash down your door in the middle of the night and come for you while you're fucking your hippie chick girlfriend. Ya gotta stand with your comrades and fight back!"

"You can also fight by *refusing* to fight."

"Son, you turn the other cheek and all you'll get is slapped on the other cheek."

"I'm not a pacifist. I'll fight. I just prefer to do it my *own* way."

"Your own way is a losing way. Like I said, you need an army to fight an army."

"I'm a one-man army, professor."

Signs and Portents

It was around nine o'clock on a cold December night of 1967 and Vern, Annie, and I were nighthawks in a diner at the Tower Plaza shopping mall on Thomas Road. The mall was called Tower Plaza because of the giant radio towers protected by tall square walls of cinderblocks out in the parking lot. The radio towers had been there for as long as I could remember. Even before Tower Plaza existed, when that entire area was a vast expanse of cow pasture, the towers were there. When the Plaza was built, they just built around the towers.

Annie and I were sitting together on one side of the booth. Under the table, her hand was resting on the inside of my thigh, which I was pressing against her thigh. And my hand was resting on the inside of her thigh, which she was pressing against me. Across from us sat Vern. Because it was clear that Annie was determined to be with me, he'd seemed to accept me, but he hadn't given up trying to pry us apart.

Now he was talking about Annie's going away to college. She was 17 and in her senior year at North High. But, because she'd missed an entire year of school when she moved from Ventura to Phoenix to live with Vern, she didn't have enough credits to graduate. Vern dismissed that fact. He hadn't graduated from high school, either, but that hadn't stopped him from going to Harvard. Nor would it stop Annie from going to an elite private college, somewhere out of Phoenix. There were no schools good enough for Annie in Phoenix, or even in Arizona. Vern expected great things from Annie. And Annie was anxious to live up to her father's great expectations.

So how could either Annie or I object? Didn't we want what was best for Annie's future? So we both accepted as inevitable that Annie would go somewhere else for college and a bright shining future. Annie and I were sure that our love was strong enough to withstand any separation. We would stay together, no matter what.

"Why do you think Annie can be admitted to one of these elite schools without graduating from high school?" I asked Vern.

"The best schools aren't bound by rules and regulations. Those are just for the lower ranking schools, like Phoenix College and Arizona State, which have no imagination and do things in lockstep. The best schools judge applicants by other standards."

"Like?"

"Like whether or not the applicant is interesting and shows passion and initiative. And, of course, a good academic record. Annie has that, not only in high school, but also at Phoenix College. She's already *gone* to college."

"I know. It was my idea."

"And a lot depends upon the personal essay she'll write. And her interviews. But she'll do fine in both." Vern smiled confidently at Annie.

"So what schools do you suggest I apply to?" Annie asked.

"Radcliffe, Smith, Swarthmore. Pitzer College is also good. It's part of the Claremont College complex in California."

"What about Prescott College?" I suggested. It was an elite liberal arts private college recently established in that small northern Arizona town amid the pine covered mountains. It also wasn't all that far away.

"Yesss," Vern answered slowly. "She could apply there, also. It's good, and if she wants to have a wide-open future, it's important for her to have a degree from a top-ranked school."

"Well, perhaps that's true, but that doesn't seem like a guarantee. You went to Harvard and here you are teaching at a community college in Phoenix."

Vern pressed his lips together and glared at me. "There are many reasons for that. Not least is the fact that I did not get a *degree* from Harvard."

"Why didn't you get your degree?"

Vern sighed and was silent. Annie and I looked at him expectantly. "My committee wanted me to make unacceptable changes to my dissertation," he finally said.

"And, if you'd made those changes, they would have given you a Ph.D.?"

"Yes, they would have given me a Ph.D."

"So, you finished all your course work at Harvard for the Ph.D."

"Yes, I finished all my course work at Harvard."

"And you wrote your dissertation."

"And I wrote my dissertation."

"And all that stopped you from getting a Harvard Ph.D. was a few changes to your dissertation? Vern, everyone keeps telling me *I'm* stubborn, but that just sounds *stupid* and stubborn!"

"The changes would have completely altered the thrust of the dissertation."

"Vern, who *cares?* No one outside your committee members would've ever *seen* the dissertation, and you'd have had a Harvard Ph.D. And you wouldn't be teaching at a community college, which we know you think is beneath you. You headed down the wrong road that day."

"Well, it's done. It was years ago."

"If it was years ago, then those guys on your committee have probably moved on. You've done all your course work. You just have to knock off an acceptable dissertation. Vern, it's not too late! Why don't you go back and get that Harvard Ph.D.?"

Vern looked at me as if the idea had never occurred to him. I pushed on, appalled at what I perceived as Vern's stubborn foolishness. "You wouldn't have to quit P.C., they'd give you a sabbatical. I don't know, but I'd guess they might even give you a percentage of your salary while you return to school for professional development. If Annie's leaving Phoenix for college, what's keeping you here?"

Vern nodded his head. "You know, Eric, you have a point. Nothing's keeping me here. I just might do that."

And so Vern decided to apply to the Harvard Graduate School of Education for re-admission to its doctoral program. And then, as Annie wrote her own personal essays explaining why various elite colleges should admit her, despite not graduating from high school, he began writing his personal essay explaining why Harvard should take him back. As they did so, I felt that both Vern and Annie would probably succeed. But, if both left Phoenix for the schools of their choice, only one would leave a hole in my heart.

****

School year 1967-68, as every year, I was living hand-to-mouth. After paying tuition at Arizona State, my student loan gave me just enough for rent. The loan came in semester installments, so I paid four months' rent at one whack. That way, the money was out of my hands and I had a guaranteed roof over my head each semester.

I found an unfurnished studio apartment at the end of a row of cinderblock apartments. It was even closer to Annie's house than the hell-hole hovel had been, but we both kept the location secret from Vern. We didn't want him to know how quick and easy it was for us to reach each other. The less he knew about us, the better. I even gave Annie a key so she could come over any time, even if I wasn't there.

The apartment had a small bathroom with a shower. When I moved in, I discovered a large spider in an even larger web in one corner near the ceiling. I left him alone. He was there before I was, and he was doing me no harm. I named him "Ahimsa," a word I'd gotten from reading Gandhi's autobiography, *The Story of My Experiments With Truth*. "Ahimsa" is the Buddhist and Hindu doctrine of refraining from harming any living being. Each morning I greeted Ahimsa and sometimes sang to him as I showered. He never sang back. Other than that, he was a great roomie. He was quiet and never kept me awake at night.

There was formica-topped table in the tiny kitchen off the main room, along with two 1950s vinyl-covered chairs. Other than that, the apartment was completely empty. But, I didn't care. The apartment seemed a couple of decades newer than the hell-hole hovel, so it was fine with me. I had nothing but books, a typewriter, a small radio, a portable turntable with some LPs, and some clothes, which I stored in an old blue wooden steamer trunk. I salvaged a one-person mattress someone had thrown in the trash. Once it was covered with sheets, a blanket, and a pillow, with my trunk at the foot, it looked fine. I lined my books up along the baseboard of the main room, going around the entire periphery. They were out of the way and completely accessible. I had everything I wanted.

The apartment complex was surrounded by tall oleander bushes. I parked the blue Suzuki in back of my apartment, just under the window of my tiny kitchen annex. Shielded by the bushes, it was completely out of sight, and also within hearing distance. Should anyone wish to steal my faithful blue Suzuki, I'd be right there. I couldn't afford to have it stolen. Given the wide open distances of Phoenix, and the lack of a decent public transit system, anyone without wheels was crippled. With gas at 25-cents a gallon, my 90-cc blue Suzuki cheaply took me everywhere I needed to go.

After paying a semester's worth of rent out of my student loan, I had nothing left to live on, so I got by on part-time work-study jobs provided by ASU. I bussed tables early every morning at an off-campus Catholic student dining room. I was paid five dollars a week for this, plus anything I wanted for breakfast at the end of my shift. I ate a big breakfast, as it was often my only meal of the day. When it wasn't, I'd buy some el cheapo bean burritos from a Taco Bell near the campus.

In addition, I did clerical work in the library. They were surprised to discover I could type. I looked like a scruffy hippie from the streets. I didn't look like someone who could type. This seeming contradiction especially fascinated Jan Pinkoski, one of my fellow student-workers. He'd been wary around me when I first started working with him. It turned out I could type faster and better than him, that I seemed to know a lot more about the books than he did, and I became an endless revelation to him.

I liked working in the ASU library. It meant I had access to the forbidden books room. These were books kept under lock and key because they were too dangerous for college students to read. Over the course of the fall semester of '67, a few pages at a time when I was sent to the forbidden books room on various errands, I read all of *Naked Lunch* by William Burroughs. I didn't think it was all that dangerous.

My birthday came on a Tuesday that December, '67. I turned 21 and could finally vote. I planned to register right away. I'd long since cast off my Republican loyalties, so I would register as a Democrat, but there was no way I'd vote for that war criminal, Lyndon Johnson, in the next year's election. I didn't know who I'd vote for. Maybe I'd write-in my own name. I'd cross that ballot when I came to it, but it was the first presidential election since '64, when I'd paraded for Goldwater, and I sure as hell intended to exercise my franchise.

I'd ridden the blue Suzuki into Tempe that morning and bussed tables at the Catholic dining hall and then gone to classes. After putting in my time clerking in the library, I headed over to Annie's. I went to Annie's every afternoon. It was the high point of every day. We'd talk, we'd laugh, and we'd rehearse the two-person production of Edgar Lee Master's *Spoon River Anthology* we were putting together. We combined the poems, enacted by both of us, with Annie's singing and guitar-playing. We had no idea what we'd do with our production, but it was fun to work together.

That day Annie fixed me a chocolate cake, my favorite. After we finished rehearsing, I blew out the forest fire on top of the cake as Annie laughed and called me an old man. Then Vern joined us for cake and ice cream. We joked and laughed, and I had seconds of my birthday cake. Then Annie followed me out to the blue Suzuki, parked in the driveway. Night had fallen and darkness threatened to swallow the small pools of light cast by the old-fashioned street lamps lining the tree-shrouded street. I straddled the Suzuki and pulled Annie close. She leaned over and kissed me. We kissed for a long time. "Happy birthday, my love," she whispered in my ear.

"It's a perfect birthday," I whispered back. "You made it perfect."

I kissed her again, a quick peck on the lips. Then she stepped back and I kicked the Suzuki into life. "I'll see you tomorrow," I said. Annie smiled a big Cheshire Cat grin and waved. I smiled back and rolled out of the driveway.

After I got home I sat at the kitchen table and read. I never cooked at home, so there was no food or cooking utensils in the kitchen. The kitchen table, therefore, was my work desk. It was where I had my typewriter and my textbooks.

I'd been reading for about an hour when someone knocked loudly at my door. I jumped, dropping my book. No one *ever* visited me, especially at night. "Who is it?" I yelled.

"It's me, Tom!"

I recognized the voice. It was Tom Wagers.

In her second year at North High, Annie had made the first friends I'd ever known her to have. One was a girl named Jan Sownie, who she met in the library during lunch hour. Annie saw Jan reading Albert Camus' *The Plague* and figured anyone who read Camus must have something on the ball. They began talking and immediately connected. Jan had just transferred into North High as a senior and her parents were in the midst of a bitter and blaming divorce. She was lonely and hurting and seeking and Annie became a bright spot in her life.

They both ended up in the closed Humanities course taught by Mr. Ferris which I'd taken and which I'd recommended for Annie. The administration wouldn't let her in, as the course had a full enrollment. Vern did nothing about it, but Walt Emory took it upon himself to get her enrolled. He visited the principal and discussed it with him. I don't know if the principal was more impressed by Walt's arguments, or the fact that Walt was a medical doctor, but he allowed Annie into the course. Then Jan and Annie both enrolled in a speech class in the same classroom where I had taken my speech class. They took as many classes together as they could and spent their lunches with each other. They became best friends.

The other one of Annie's friends was Tom Wagers, a junior who also read Camus and was in that same Humanities class. As it happened, Tom and Annie had been classmates years before, at Tempe High School, when Vern and his family lived in Tempe while he taught at ASU. Now time and chance had thrown Tom and Annie together once more.

Tom was a odd and bitter loner, but he was intelligent, and intelligent students were rare at North High. Consequently, Tom, Jan, and Annie became good friends and, shortly after, Jan and Tom became my friends, as well. Tom may have been a junior in high school and I may have been a junior at ASU, but we spoke as intellectual equals.

It helped that we were both militant atheists and we both liked esoteric rock. It was Tom who introduced me to The Fugs, a group even weirder than Frank Zappa and the Mothers of Invention. The only thing which bothered me about him was his ever present cynicism. Everything about the world was, to him, shitty and getting shittier. For that reason, he vowed never to bring any children of his own into this Vale of Tears.

Tom himself was an only child. His parents owned a huge old apartment complex in downtown Phoenix close to the Westward Ho Hotel. It may have been a hotel itself, before it'd been converted into apartments, as it was a multi-storied labyrinth of corridors. His parents lived there, in their own apartment. But Tom also had an apartment all to himself. He also owned a blue VW bus-like van, the like of which I'd never before seen. It had an open back, like a pickup truck, which could be completely covered with a canvas top when desired. He seemed and lived more like an adult than a high school kid.

I swung open the door and saw blonde Tom smiling broadly at me. "Happy birthday, old man! I came to treat you to a birthday dessert. Wanna come?"

"How can I refuse someone who's come out on a dark, cold, December night just to spend money on me? Let me grab my coat."

We walked out front to Tom's blue VW van and he drove us to a nearby restaurant we'd come to favor. In 1964 that same space had been a Goldwater campaign office, but no one seemed to remember that but me.

I ordered a sundae and Tom ordered a small bowl of ice cream. He asked me about my day. I told him about *Spoon River* and the cake that Annie had made for me. We chatted for a half hour and then he said he had to get on home.

As we parked in front of my apartment complex, I asked if he wanted to come in and just chat for a bit more. I had some sodas in the fridge and I was reluctant to see him go.

"Sure, just for a little while."

We walked down to my darkened apartment and I unlocked the door. We stepped inside and I flicked on the lights. And I stared in shock at a bookcase against one wall where no bookcase should've been. It was made out of cinderblock bricks as supports and planks as shelves. It reached to the ceiling and every book of mine which had encircled the baseboard periphery was stuffed in it. Then Annie walked out of the bathroom with the same Cheshire Cat grin I'd seen on her when I'd kissed her goodnight.

"Happy birthday, my love. I wanted to make it special for you."

"Oh, Annie! You did!" I embraced her and kissed her on her neck, her cheek, her lips.

Then I turned back to Tom, standing in the open door and smiling. "How did all this happen?"

"We had the bricks and lumber loaded already. After you came home, I drove Annie over here and we parked in back. We quietly unloaded everything and stacked it next to your apartment. Then I knocked on your door and lured you away with the promise of ice cream. As soon as we left, Annie unlocked your door and moved everything in. We figured half an hour would be enough time. Then she just waited."

"Tom, you're a good friend."

"And a good friend knows when he's no longer needed. I'll be going now." Still smiling, Tom shut the door and disappeared into the night.

And I turned off the lights and pulled Annie down onto my mattress. "It's the best birthday present anyone *ever* gave me," I said.

"I wanted your 21st birthday to be perfect. If I go away to college, and if Dad goes to Cambridge, I might not be here for your next birthday."

"It was perfect before. You made perfection even *more* perfect."

And then we made love, long into the night.

Which made that cold December night yet even more perfect.

Arrogant Ignorance

Tempe, where ASU is located, lies on the southeastern border of Phoenix. The dry bed of the Salt River separates it from Phoenix and Papago Park. The bed was entirely dry when I was growing up and then attending ASU. Since then part of the bed has been dammed to form Tempe Town Lake, upon which people go boating.

Adjacent to this artificial Town Lake is Sun Devil Stadium, home of ASU football. It is called the Sun Devil Stadium because the Sun Devil, a mythical imp with a pitchfork, is the ASU mascot. In 1996, Super Bowl XXX was played at Sun Devil Stadium and it was also the long-time home of the Fiesta Bowl games.

Looming over Sun Devil Stadium, indeed, looming over the ASU campus and Tempe's main street, Mill Avenue, is 300-foot tall Tempe Butte. Atop the Butte is a 50-foot radio tower, erected in 1962. The east side of the Butte was partially excavated in 1958 to build Sun Devil Stadium. At the foot of the western side is a series of tall white silos which were part of the old Hayden Flour Mill. Mill Avenue, which runs past the silos, was named after the Hayden Flour Mill and runs over a Salt River bridge into Phoenix. Where the bridge starts, and the surrounding area, used to be called Hayden's Ferry, named after pioneer businessman Charles Trumbull Hayden, the father of Carl Hayden. As U.S. Senator Carl Hayden, the son pushed through the Central Arizona Project, bringing Colorado River water to Phoenix and Tucson. Charles Trumbull Hayden began a ferry service across the Salt River at that spot in 1871. And the Butte was at that time known as Hayden Butte.

However, it seems Hayden felt the area should have a more poetic name. Educated in the classics, he'd read about the Vale of Tempe, near Mount Olympus in Greece, and renamed the place, "Tempe," and thereafter Hayden Butte became Tempe Butte.

No doubt the Hohokam (pronounced Ho-ho-com), the ancient Indians who once lived on the Butte, called it something different. We know they lived there because traces of their habitation -- petroglyphs (rock art), pottery shards, and scrapers -- have been found on the Butte.

Traces of the Hohokam, including ruins and hundreds of miles of their irrigation canals, have been found all over the metropolitan Phoenix area. Phoenix is named Phoenix because, just after the Civil War, when the first white men began to settle the region, they found the remains of the Hohokam, who we now know occupied the area from the time of Christ to about 1450. The white settlers expanded the ancient Hohokam irrigation system, taking water from the Salt River, and built their own community on the ruins. By 1868 about 50 settlers lived there, among them an Englishman named Darrell Duppa, who had arrived in December, 1867, and who was familiar with the classics. The emerging community did not yet have a name, so in 1868 he proposed that the new community be called "Phoenix," arguing that it was like the mythological phoenix bird rising anew from the ashes of a previous civilization.

At least that's one story. The other story, equally possible, is that a Confederate soldier named John Swilling, who arrived in the area a month before Duppa and who was equally familiar with the classics, dubbed the place Phoenix. I've seen a photo of Swilling taken in 1870. He looked like an outlaw, with a drooping mustache, long "hippie" hair, and a Colt revolver in his hand. Swilling had deserted from the Confederate Army, perhaps Sibley's Brigade, which had briefly occupied New Mexico and Tucson in 1861, to become a U. S. Army scout and teamster. When he arrived in the Salt River area, he noticed the Hohokam irrigation system and realized the place had agricultural possibilities.

Swilling quickly created the Swilling Irrigating and Canal Co. (of which Darrell Duppa became a stockholder) and began deepening and expanding the old Hohokam canals, digging new ones, and planting crops. His major market was nearby Ft. McDowell, a U.S. Army outpost built to protect the region from marauding Apaches. Settlers quickly poured into the area. Swilling, the Confederate deserter, is thus recognized as the "father of Phoenix," whether or not he or Duppa actually named it.

Unfortunately, Founding Father Swilling did not prosper for long. He seems to have been an alcoholic, and perhaps also an opium addict, and he lost his business and fell into poverty. And perhaps there was a *reason* John Swilling looked like an outlaw. He died of "natural" causes while being held in the Yuma Territorial Prison awaiting trial for robbing a stage coach.

We know what eventually happened to Founding Father John Swilling, but no idea what happened to the ancient Hohokam who preceded him. Perhaps it was an extended drought which drove them away, perhaps something else. But, after one-and-a-half thousand years of living along the banks of the Salt River, the Hohokam disappeared from the region about half a century before Columbus set sail. Of course, we have no idea what the Hohokam called themselves. Their very name is taken from the modern Pima Indians, who live in the area, and it means, "those who have disappeared." All they left were their canals and their adobe ruins.

One of the largest of their ruins, Pueblo Grande, is located inside the Phoenix city limits at 4619 E. Washington Street, near 46th Street and not far from where I was raised on 51st and 52nd Streets. Pueblo Grande belongs to the city of Phoenix, which pretty much ignored it until the Great Depression of the 1930s when the New Deal poured a lot of money into Phoenix and FDR's Works Progress Administration (WPA) built North High and Phoenix College. The WPA also developed Pueblo Grande. It built a small museum and office facility of adobe bricks made right on the site, stabilized the ruin, and constructed trails. Today the Pueblo Grande museum is a new building, built in 1974, and has perhaps the best exhibits on the Hohokam in existence. And you have to pay to get in. For all the time I was in Phoenix, however, the museum was the old adobe one built in 1933-34 by the WPA, and getting into the museum and walking around the ruin were still free.

In January, 1968, as a new year and a new semester at ASU began, I drove the blue Suzuki over to Pueblo Grande. I wanted to write. I wanted to write history. And I'd always been interested in Indian history. When I was in elementary school, I gave an oral report to my class on the Navajo Indians of Arizona and New Mexico. I read a lot about them and was sure of my facts. But, since everything I knew about them came from my reading, and I'd never heard anyone talk about them, I got one major detail wrong. I called them the "Navajoe." My teacher corrected me.

I was fascinated by Indians and their history not just because they were close at hand but also because they were the underdogs of American history, and I always sided with the underdogs. And what could be more historic than Indian prehistory? And there was Pueblo Grande, right there in my own neighborhood.

So I went to Pueblo Grande that January looking for something I could write about, some tiny historical niche into which I could fit. I wanted to make some small contribution. It was a fit of arrogant ignorance, for I knew virtually nothing about the Hohokam. Sure, being raised in Phoenix, I'd acquired a small bit of knowledge about them just by osmosis, and I'd been to Pueblo Grande as a kid. But I'd never paid much attention to them; I'd never seriously studied the Hohokam or any other prehistoric Indians of the Southwest.

But, here they were, and I wanted to "do history." The Hohokam seemed the obvious choice. In my ignorant arrogance, I felt something might leap out at me at Pueblo Grande, that I might discern a pattern, or see something interesting, simply because I wasn't inured to archaeology's traditions and the known facts about the Hohokam.

I studied the Hohokam exhibits in the Pueblo Grande museum minutely. I stared at their pottery shards, their reconstructed pots, their beautiful jewelry made from turquoise and sea shells traded into the region from the Sea of Cortez. I looked at their manos and metates and reconstructed villages. I read all the plaques on the walls next to the exhibits. I tried to think of questions to ask of the artifacts which had not already been asked. I tried to think of what had been omitted from all the exhibits. I spent an entire afternoon moving slowly from exhibit to exhibit and walking slowly around the crumbling adobe ruin staring at the ballcourt.

The ballcourt was sunken and oval shaped, with an embankment around the edges for spectators. There were entrances at both ends. It most likely was an example of cultural diffusion from central Mexico, as the Olmecs and Toltecs, as well as the later Aztecs, all had similar ballcourts. In central Mexican Indian cultures, the ball game played in the court was associated with the worship of Quetzalcoatl, the Plumed Serpent god reputed to have brought civilization to pre-Hispanic societies. Supposedly, at least the captain of the losing team, on some ritual occasions, was sacrificed to Quetzalcoatl after the game. That probably didn't happen at the Pueblo Grande ballcourt, but the Horned Rattlesnake figure associated with the Plumed Serpent is found on prehistoric petroglyphs throughout the Southwest, including in Hohokam country. It was a fascinating story, but I didn't see what I could do with it.

By the time the museum prepared to close, nothing had leapt out at me as a possible research and writing subject. Why should it have? I really didn't know enough to even ask appropriate questions. I bought some books on the Hohokam from the museum gift shop, climbed on my Suzuki, and drove home to my cinderblock studio apartment to read my books.

Even after I read the books, nothing came to me, so I decided to try something else. Many National Parks and Monuments in Arizona contain ruins of the prehistoric Hohokam, Salado, Sinagua, and Anasazi cultures. Surely they needed additional workers for the upcoming summer tourist season. Come the end of May, ASU would be out, my student loan for the year would be gone, and I'd have nothing with which to pay my rent. I had to find a job, anyway. Why not work for the National Park Service? Why not be a Park Ranger and wear a Smokey the Bear hat? It'd be fun. It'd also be a sudden immersion in prehistory and I'd learn stuff fast -- and maybe even find something to write about.

Arrogant ignorance.

Nevertheless, I wrote to every National Park and Monument in Arizona which contained Indian ruins. I wrote to Canyon de Chelly, Casa Grande, the Grand Canyon, Montezuma's Castle, Montezuma's Well, Navajo, Tonto, Tuzigoot, Walnut Canyon, and Wupatki National Monuments asking for summer employment.

And waited.

And waited.

And none of them replied.

Except one.

Wupatki, a Sinagua/Anasazi ruin about 40 miles northeast of Flagstaff, asked me to come up for an interview.

I was elated. One interview is all I need, I thought.

I called Wupatki and arranged an interview date as soon as possible. Then I cut my hair short and shaved. I was willing to sacrifice my freak flag to become a Ranger. I, Annie, and Tom Wagers all skipped school and took off in Tom's VW van for Northern Arizona. Straight north out of Phoenix, up the Mogollon Rim, to Cordes Junction. There we turned northeast toward

Flagstaff, past Tuzigoot off to the left of us, and Montezuma's Castle and Montezuma's Well to our right, none of which had deigned to answer my letters.

Through Flagstaff and still north on Route 89 we drove. Flagstaff is pine tree country and the nearby San Francisco Peaks are the highest in Arizona. But, after the turnoff to Sunset Crater, the remains of a volcano which erupted about the time of the Norman Conquest of England, the land falls quickly in elevation. It becomes dry rangeland and, eventually, by the time you reach Tuba City beyond the Gray Mountain trading post, even dryer desert.

Ten miles beyond the turnoff to Sunset Crater, we reached the entrance to Wupatki, a 55-square-mile National Monument containing around 3,000 prehistoric ruins, most quite small. As soon as we turned off Route 89 we saw the first one. There was a small parking lot on the right, with a one-person Ranger shack, which was empty. Just beyond it was an excavated ruin, low on the ground, with the half-walls of the rooms making the ruin look like a giant beehive. Then, above us on a volcanic outcropping, were the stones of a much larger ruin. There was a footpath to the higher ruin, so we climbed up to it.

The ruin, which I later learned was called the Citadel, turned out to be unexcavated. Behind it was a deep cleft of solidified black lava looking like it had been gouged out of the land with a hot iron. All around was a grassy rangeland, which I also later learned was called Antelope Prairie. We stood on the butte topped by the Citadel and looked out over the grassland. And there, in the distance, beyond the volcanic cleft, we indeed saw a herd of antelope bounding away from us. In the even further distance, we saw flat-topped mesas, volcanic buttes, and, beyond them, the San Francisco Peaks, still capped with winter snow. It was huge and silent and beautiful, and I began falling in love with the place.

We drove for another 15 miles, falling in elevation from rangeland to desert, before we came to the Visitor Center, behind which was the main ruin of Wupatki. The Wupatki ruin was composed of tan flat stones and looked like it grew out of, rather than was built on, the tan rock which was its base. Everywhere the land was covered in black volcanic cinders and ash, in some places blown by time and wind into deep drifts. I later learned that it came from the thousand-year-old eruption of Sunset Crater.

Tom turned his van into the Visitor Center's parking lot. Except for gray Park Service pickup trucks, the lot was otherwise empty. Tom and Annie decided to walk around the parking lot -- the vista was gorgeous -- while I went inside.

There was a Ranger behind the counter to my right as I walked in. I introduced myself and said I was there for an interview. He shook my hand and told me to come around the counter. Behind the counter were the offices, one after another. He introduced me to a crewcut Ranger named George Chambers. He also shook my hand, then picked up his desk phone and called for the Superintendent. "He's just up at his house," Ranger Chambers said, gesturing out the window. I glanced out the window and saw a large isolated house a little up the side of the mesa which overlooked the Visitor Center. To the right of it was a line of attached apartments which looked just like the Alzona Park apartment rows I lived in when we first moved to Phoenix in 1952. The Alzona Park apartments were built during World War II and perhaps the Wupatki apartments dated from the same period.

The Super came down from his large isolated house on the side of the mesa. He was a large grandfather type who seemed deliberately gruff and macho, as if this was how a manly man acted. But, both he and Ranger Chambers were friendly. I told them I was a junior and a history major at Arizona State. And I was 21. That was essential, as a Park Ranger, even a summer one, is also a federal law officer, at least at the level for which I was being considered. And I said I was eager to work at Wupatki, as I was passionate about the prehistory of the Southwest.

That seemed to be all they needed to hear. Superintendent Gruff shook my hand. "Welcome to Wupatki, you're our new Ranger." Ranger Chambers also shook my hand and told me I'd live in facilities at Wupatki for the summer. I wondered if it would be in one of the Alzona Park apartments. I was given an address to send a check to for my Ranger uniform, which I was to bring with me when I reported for duty on June 2nd.

And that was it.

I walked, beaming, out to the parking lot. I told Tom and Annie I was going to be a Park Ranger. Annie hugged me and Tom slapped me on the back, a big grin on his face.

We drove out of the lot and turned right, in the opposite direction from which we'd come. We wanted to see the rest of Wupatki and drive through the separate Sunset Crater National Monument. We climbed in elevation and were shortly in snow-covered pine tree country once again, all so strange to desert rats like us, who never saw the snow. Tom pulled over and we jumped out to have a snowball fight. We were soon happily exhausted. I looked out over the snow forest and began singing, "This is Eric's country, land that he loooves!"

Tom and Annie laughed and joined in, "This is Eric's country, land that he loooves!"

And so I became a Park Ranger at Wupatki, the most beautiful prehistoric ruin in Arizona.

Arrogant ignorance.

The Tet Offensive

"It is not desirable to cultivate a respect for the law, so much as for the right....Law never made men a whit more just; and, by means of their respect for it, even the well-disposed are daily made the agents of injustice. A common and natural result of an undue respect for the law is that you may see a file of soldiers, colonel, captain, corporal, privates, powder monkeys and all, marching in admirable order over hill and dale to the wars, against their wills, aye, against their common sense and consciences, which makes it very steep marching indeed, and produces a palpitation of the heart. They have no doubt that it is a damnable business in which they are concerned; they are all peaceably inclined. Now, what are they? Men at all? Or small moveable forts and magazines, at the service of some unscrupulous man in power?"

-- Henry David Thoreau
On the Duty of Civil Disobedience

****

Ever since the Gulf of Tonkin Incident in 1964, Johnson and his generals had been telling us that Vietnamese resistance to American aggression had been crippled, almost crushed. It'd soon be over. We could see the light at the end of the tunnel.

Meanwhile, troop levels climbed steadily. By January 5, 1968, we had almost half a million soldiers fighting in Vietnam and almost 16,000 had been killed. More were being drafted daily. That very day, in Boston, pediatrician Benjamin Spock was indicted for counseling all men of good conscience to engage in draft resistance.

Then, on January 30, came Tet, the Asian New Year. On that day the guerrillas launched a coordinated offensive along the entire length and breath of South Vietnam. The supposedly broken and crippled guerrillas *simultaneously* attacked hundreds of villages, 60 district capitals, 36 of 44 provincial capitals, and five of six major cities, as well as 12 big American military bases. Hue, the ancient imperial capitol, was completely overrun. They even penetrated the American Embassy in Saigon, despite a massive U.S. Marine presence around it, and held it for six hours.

The fighting to dislodge the guerrillas from the cities they had taken was a long and bloody struggle covering many weeks. It continued on through the entire month of February and into March. The city of Hue was almost completely destroyed in the fighting to retake it. Over 7,500 civilians died in the fighting, as well as 4,000 South Vietnamese soldiers and 1,100 American G.I.s. The number of guerrilla casualties is unknown. Over 400,000 civilians were turned into homeless refugees. In the end, you could say it was a military defeat for the guerrillas, because they were beaten back everywhere.

But military defeat is irrelevant in an insurgency or a guerrilla war. What matters the most in such a war is the political dimension, and in that dimension Tet was a great victory for the guerrillas. For years the American military had been lulling us into a false sense of security by saying the guerrillas were on the ropes, they were almost defeated, give us a little more time and just trust us with this a little bit longer.

The Tet Offensive made it evident that none of this was true. The guerrillas were not on the ropes, we were not on the verge of victory, and the light at the end of the tunnel was the headlight of an on-rushing locomotive. There was no end to the war in sight. Indeed, on March

10 *The New York Times* reported that General Westmoreland, the American commander in Vietnam, had requested another 206,000 troops for Vietnam, which would've raised the troop level to almost three-quarters of a million.

But there was no reason to believe that even this massive troop surge would make any difference. It became ever more evident after Tet that the war simply could not be won. And from then on, until the war finally ended years later, every public opinion poll revealed that a majority of Americans opposed continuation of the war. A March 31, 1968, Gallup Poll revealed that only 36% of Americans still supported the war.

Tet was thus the political turning point of the war. It not only convinced a majority of Americans that the war could not be won, it also undermined Johnson's will to continue as president. He had been elected in 1964 with the largest vote total since FDR's historic landslide victory in 1936. In less than four years his popularity had plummeted into the basement and many saw him as a war criminal. Realizing this, he denied Westmoreland's request for yet more troops and, on March 22, recalled him from his command in Vietnam, signalling his decision against a major escalation.

Less than a year earlier, in the spring of 1967, I'd told my classmates at the Phoenix College graduation ceremony that I was a Conscientious Objector to the war, and that I was going to apply to the Selective Service System for that status. I'd later discovered, however, that, as an atheist, I was not eligible for C.O. status. I didn't believe in a "Supreme Being." And the law recognized only religious reasons, not simply moral and ethical ones, for opposing war.

I also was not a pacifist, which wasn't acceptable to my local board. I believed in the use of force. In some situations, in some circumstances. But, with the draft board, it was all or nothing at all. Under the law, one couldn't pick and choose in which situations and circumstances you approved or disapproved of the use of force, as I did.

Since graduation from Phoenix College in 1967, however, I'd become more and more vocal in my opposition to the war. Watching the fierce fighting in Vietnam every night on TV through February and into March, I felt I had to do something more than just talk. I felt I to put my body on the line. I still had my II-S student deferment. I didn't have to worry about being drafted. But I *was* a Conscientious Objector, and I felt that was how I should be classified. I didn't care what the law said. I didn't care how the law defined a Conscientious Objector. I *was* a Conscientious Objector, on my own terms, and on those terms, regardless of what the law said, I was going to make my stand.

On March 20th, two days before LBJ recalled Westmoreland, I wrote to my local draft board, Board No. 29, requesting a Conscientious Objector application.

The board secretary quickly responded, sending me the Special Form for Conscientious Objectors, Form I-50, to complete and return. So, as March trailed toward an end and soldiers in Hue fought their last battles with the Vietnamese resistance in that devastated city, I began composing essays in which I argued grounds for my opposition to the Vietnam War and my rationale for Local Board No. 29 classifying me as a Conscientious Objector, despite what the law said. I had to articulate my secular and particular opposition to the war, and to military service, as convincingly as I could, given the odds against my ever gaining C.O. status. I ignored my school work and obsessively thought and wrote about the war and the military. I felt I was fighting in the Tet Offensive, in my own way, just as much as anyone in Vietnam.

The language of the C.O. application was couched in religious terms. It asked me to describe how the nature of my belief in a Supreme Being involved duties superior to those arising from human relations; it asked me to explain how, when, and from whom I received my religious training and belief which led to my conscientious objection; it asked for the name and address of the person upon whom I relied most for spiritual guidance.

Within the confines of the language of the Selective Service System, I wrote a long essay trying to explain my secular and ethical objections to the war and military service. Whom did I rely on for spiritual guidance? "I believe," I wrote, "that true spiritual convictions have the attribute of being the deep and abiding guidelines of conduct which are always and simply there....Therefore, I am in a large degree my own source of spiritual guidance and, like Thomas Paine, I can say that 'My mind is my church.'"

How, when, and from whom did I receive my religious training and belief which led to my conscientious objection? My convictions were largely "a product of my own thinking, feeling, reading, and experience," I answered. "The first external influence I am conscious of is the Bible. I remember being repelled at the seemingly senseless slaughter and wars perpetuated by the Children of Israel....Thus, the Bible was the first source from which my sense of justice began to grow. These feelings...were further encouraged when I read *The War Prayer* by Mark Twain. From there, I went to Twain's books *Letters From the Earth* and *The Mysterious Stranger*."

Then I recorded and elaborated upon all the other readings which led to my beliefs: *The Will to Doubt* and *Why I Am Not a Christian* by Bertrand Russell; the writings of Julian Huxley; *The Rights of Man* and *The Age of Reason* by Thomas Paine; *Walden* and *Civil Disobedience* by Henry David Thoreau; *The Story of My Experiences with Truth* by Mohandas K. Gandhi; and *The Moral Equivalent of War* and other writings by William James. As I wrote, I doubted that anyone on my draft board, "respectable" citizens drawn from the local community, would have the faintest familiarity with any of the books I mentioned. Nevertheless, I persevered.

Then I tackled the Biggie: "Describe the nature of your belief...and state whether or not your belief in a Supreme Being involves duties which are superior...." I referred to my favorite among the Founders. "Like Thomas Paine, I state that, 'To do good is my religion.' In his *Age of Reason,* Paine stated his religious creed, which I also subscribe to: 'I believe in the equality of man, and I believe that religious duties consist in doing justice, loving mercy, and endeavoring to make our fellow creatures happy.'"

Then I cited Thoreau and William James. In a lecture at Edinburgh University, James said that he believed true religion should be characterized by "a temperament of peace, and in relation to others, a preponderance of loving affections." And in *Civil Disobedience*, Thoreau described how soldiers cease to be men, that they abdicate their reason and individuality and become merely "small movable forts and magazines, at the service of some unscrupulous man in power."

"A soldier is taught to unthinkingly obey an order," I wrote, "not to use his reason. A soldier is taught to immediately obey an order, not to submit that order to his conscience. What are reason and conscience for, but to be ceaselessly used? Through the use of one's reason and conscience, a man can determine his own choices, his own life, his own destiny. It is that which defines a man: The ability to shape his own life, to make his own choices.

"A soldier is no longer a man, a being of reason, conscience, and will, but, rather, a thing of clay to be shaped and moulded to the specifications of the Armed Forces. I don't believe that I could be faithful to myself or my convictions by being a member of a totalitarian system whose sole purpose, whose sole argument for existence, is to kill."

As I wrote, I discovered what I fundamentally thought about the war and military service. I had no great hope that my secular appeals to reason and conscience would make any impression on the members of my draft board, but there it was. It was what I believed. In the process of trying to articulate my beliefs, I discovered and described why I was a Conscientious Objector to the war and to military service. Whether or not the Selective Service System agreed with me was irrelevant. I would serve my conscience and my country by refusing to serve.

That very month, March, the first presidential primary of 1968 was taking place in New Hampshire. In late 1967, an obscure Democratic Minnesota Senator named Eugene McCarthy had announced that he was challenging Lyndon Johnson, the sitting president of McCarthy's own party, for the presidential nomination. He was doing so on a peace platform calling for an immediate withdrawal of American troops from Vietnam. At the time, no one took him seriously and the media ignored him.

But Tet changed the dynamics of McCarthy's primary challenge. As the fighting raged in the cities of Vietnam, and as American soldiers died by the hundreds day after day, week after week, the media began to take McCarthy seriously. At the same time, hordes of liberal college kids got "Clean for Gene" and cut their hair, put on ties, and flooded into New Hampshire to canvas door-to-door for McCarthy.

When the primary votes were tallied at the end of the day on March 12, McCarthy didn't win, but he stunned the nation by gaining 42% of the vote against President Johnson's 48%, almost beating the incumbent president who was seeking the renomination of his own party. It revealed the depths of dissatisfaction with Johnson, even within his own party.

Sensing Johnson's vulnerability, four days later, on March 16, New York Senator Bobby Kennedy, JFK's brother, announced that he, too, was entering the race for the Democratic nomination on an antiwar platform. He called for an immediate end to the bombing of North Vietnam and a revival, instead, of Johnson's War on Poverty.

Johnson saw the writing on the wall. He realized that the Vietnam War had destroyed his presidency. It was over. Neither he nor the war was popular enough to win in November. Indeed, he wasn't popular enough even to win his own party's renomination in Chicago that summer. It was clear that the charismatic Kennedy would trounce him for the nomination and then go on to win the White House.

On March 31, the same day Gallup announced that only 36% of Americans supported Johnson's War, LBJ announced to the nation on TV that he would not continue his campaign to seek his party's nomination for the presidency. Further, Johnson declared that he was calling a halt to his massive bombing campaign against North Vietnam, which was exactly what Bobby and Gene McCarthy were demanding.

My spirits soared. Adrenalin surged thorough me. I was ecstatic. I'd already sent in my C.O. application, but now, perhaps, that wouldn't even be necessary. That night I roared over on my Suzuki to see Annie at Vern's. I pounded on her door.

Annie threw it open in alarm. "What's wrong?"

"Nothing's wrong! We've won! Bobby will be president and the war will soon be over!"

"I know. Isn't it wonderful?"

We hugged in the open doorway for a long time, squeezing and rocking each other in our happiness as the living room light cast our shadows out onto the lawn.

The next day was April 1, April Fool's Day. I sincerely hoped that I wouldn't wake up from my walking dream to discover that it was all a cruel cosmic April Fool joke. It wasn't. Johnson, who I'd come to regard as a war criminal, really was leaving. It was like a revolution had taken place and we, the people, had overthrown a monster and stopped a criminal war.

A few days later, on April 4, my euphoria was shattered by the news from Memphis. The Rev. Martin Luther King had gone to Memphis to support a bitter two-month-old strike by the city's mostly black sanitation workers. Martin realized that civil rights, crucial as they were for political justice, were not enough to bring about a more egalitarian America. Blacks, and poor whites, as well, now had to fight for economic justice. Indeed, he had already launched a racially integrated Poor People's Campaign, which was planning to march on Washington to demand a renewed commitment to Johnson's stalled War on Poverty.

Just hours before he was to lead a mass march on the Memphis City Hall, as King stood on the second floor balcony of the Lorrain Motel, someone shot Martin with a long-range rifle. He was killed instantly. To me, it was the JFK assassination of five years earlier all over. Only worse. Because when Martin died on that Memphis balcony, the Civil Rights Era died with him. The Poor People's Campaign died with him. The possibility of blacks and whites going forward together for economic justice died with him. For me, JFK's death had just been a massive shock. Unlike so many of my generation, I'd had no hopes tied to JFK. But Martin's death felt like the death of hope itself.

I wasn't alone in that feeling. More than a hundred black ghettoes all across America, even in Phoenix, erupted in flames and bloody riots. Over 20,000 U.S. Army troops and 34,000 National Guard troops were mobilized and moved in to pacify the ghettoes. They killed 46, injured 2,600, and arrested 21,000 black citizens. America's cities were pacified, the same way we were pacifying Vietnam. And it was clear to everyone that Martin's dream of non-violent change died with him. The Black Panthers, in their military berets and hard leather jackets looped with ammunition belts, stepped to the fore. Now for black Americans, and many others, it was the hour of the gun.

On April 10th, my draft board met and read my antiwar essays. On April 12th the board's executive secretary wrote informing me of their decision. "They were not convinced," she said, "of your qualifications for the I-O [Conscientious Objector] classification." My application was denied. They gave no specific reasons. They just "were not convinced." I would remain classified II-S, the student deferment.

But I didn't care. Bobby would soon be president. The war would soon be over. Hope had completely died with Martin. Bobby kept the dream alive.

As did my fellow students all across the nation. It was the springtime of rebellion. At the end of April, Columbia University erupted. A thousand Columbia students barricaded themselves in five campus buildings to protest Columbia's ties to the Pentagon-funded Institute for Defense Analysis, as well as the university's plans to build a gym in an area needed for low-cost housing. New York cops attacked them viciously on April 30, injuring 150, arresting 700, and ejecting the students from all campus buildings. In response, the entire student body went out on strike, with considerable faculty support, effectively shutting down Columbia until June.

The Columbia revolt triggered student demonstrations around the country, as students everywhere began demanding a voice in the administration of their schools. The National Student Association reported that between January 1 and June 15 of that year, 39,000 students participated in 221 major demonstrations at 101 colleges and universities. There were even rallies and marches at ASU. At one point, I watched a crowd of angry students march toward the campus flagpole, determined to pull down and perhaps burn the American flag. Campus cops ringed the flagpole, as determined to stop them as if they were G.I.s fighting the Viet Cong in 'Nam. Perhaps, in their minds, that was exactly what they were doing. The radical students ringed the cops ringing the flagpole and there was a shouting stand-off before the students finally gave up, not willing to physically attack the cops.

I understood the student anger. I was angry myself. The American flag represented a country which was Evil Incarnate in Vietnam. We were not protecting the people of Vietnam; we were murdering the people of Vietnam. This is not rhetoric. It is fact.

The murdering had been going on for a long time. Even before the American invasion following the Gulf of Tonkin Incident, American air and ground forces had been aiding ARVN (Army of the Republic of Viet-Nam) forces in committing atrocities. In his 1967 book, *The New Legions,* pp. 163ff., Green Beret officer Donald Duncan recounted one such attack on a hamlet by American air forces and ARVN troops he and other Green Berets advised. American helicopter gunships devastated the village, after which ARVN units moved in.

"English and Vietnamese commands mingle with a bugle call," Duncan wrote, "and a ragged line of screaming men are half running toward the trees, shooting wildly. The choppers, rockets unloaded and machine guns empty, turn toward home.... The tiger-suited line swarms into the treeline.... Thatched roofs burn on most of the houses.... The area is an inferno.... Torn and broken bodies litter the area, their clothes blown off by rocket explosions. A brown leg with a dirty foot lies by a well... From a smouldering ruin two soldiers carry a skinny girl of eight or nine, a hand under each arm to keep her frantically flailing feet off the ground; her child voice screams in fear and anger, her matchstick arms try to break free.... She twists free and scurries on her stem legs...toward her baby brother and dead mother. She picks the protesting child from the dirt and blood, and clutches it to her.... Ignoring the soldiers she walks a short distance and sits down, rocking her little brother and crooning a squeaky song.

"Soldiers ransack the houses that aren't burning, collecting trophies of little value.... Women, children, and old men dragged from the houses are herded into the center of the village, and as each house yields its last souvenir it is put to the torch.... An old man dressed in pajama bottoms is dragged forward. An old woman claws at a soldier, a torrent of words pouring from her pink-stained lips.... A burst from a carbine sits her abruptly in the dust.... Another woman starts to run back into her burning house and a soldier clubs her with the stock of his carbine; there is a sickening crunch and he kicks her in rage when he finds the wood is broken.... There is a commotion behind the assembled villagers, who give way as four soldiers drag a young man in black shorts by his feet into the center. His arms are tied behind his back.... One shoulder is raw as a result of the dragging and one leg has been broken below the knee by a bullet.

"The company commander bends over him brandishing his .45 automatic and barking questions. The youth is silent." The young man is subjected to water-boarding -- near drowning -- to make him talk. It doesn't work. "One of the soldiers, irritated by the prisoner's stubbornness, gives the broken leg one kick, another. The prisoner -- his face twisted...with pain, streaming with tears -- still refuses to talk.

"The little [ARVN] exec [officer in charge] whips a knife from his belt and kneels beside the young man, grabbing a handful of hair and yanking up his head. He...passes the blade back and forth before the pain-filled eyes. The blade traces a thin line down the bony chest to a point just above the navel. The knife is pressed deep against the bare gut while the question is screeched. Blood around the young man's mouth indicates he has bitten his tongue or through his lip. The question is screeched again -- silence. The mustached exec is livid with anger.... Slowly his weight shifts to his knife arm...the blade disappears into the man as if he were soft butter. A wail of pure agony [erupts from the young man] as the blade continues into the ground.... The senior American NCO [apparently Duncan] turns away.... 'My God, what's he doing?'

"Mon, the tall Vietnamese platoon leader, straddles the...youth and drives a large knife into the bloody gut, extending the opening in one upward slash. The prisoner rises off the ground, rigid and arched from the waist, face distorted, eyes bulging, screaming. Mon's face flashes annoyance and he slams a backhanded fist into the unhuman face, knocking the body flat, and continues his butchering. The body gives a few jerks...and is still. Mon shoves his hand [in] and brings out the gall bladder, [holding] his gory trophy overhead for all to see."

Duncan is shocked, but his lieutenant confronts him. "Jesus Christ...what's wrong with you? We didn't do it, they did. We're not animals, but you have to be practical.... Hell, man, cheer up; this is a big victory.... We have a kill ratio of five to one."

Within a short time, however, American troops were doing much the same. During the Tet Offensive the guerrillas occupied the Mekong River delta village of Ben Tre. American forces responded by completely obliterating the village, along with all its inhabitants. Afterward, an American officer said to reporter Peter Arnett, "We had to destroy the village in order to save the village." What the officer admitted to Arnett was, I and my fellow students felt, standard operating procedure, even if we didn't know the details at the time.

And, it turned out that it *was* SOP. After the fact, details on what Americans were actually doing in Vietnam, details on the atrocities we suspected at the time, slowly emerged. The most notorious atrocity committed by American troops was, of course, My Lai.

On the morning of March 16, 1968, after the Tet Offensive had been beaten back and the very day that Bobby Kennedy declared he was in the race, American soldiers commanded by 24-year-old Second Lt. William C. Calley from C ("Charlie") Company, 1st Battalion, 20th Infantry, an element of the 11th Light Infantry Brigade of the 23rd "Americal" Division, entered the village of My Lai 4 in the Son Tinh district of Quang Ngai province.

Quang Ngai is a few hundred miles north of Saigon and is composed of mountains and a coastal plain through which runs the main north-south highway, Route 1. On March 9th, a week before Charlie Company entered My Lai, Jonathan Schell's account of riding with American troops in Quang Ngai appeared in *The New Yorker* ("A Reporter at Large: Quang Ngai and Quang Tin"). Schell estimated that 70% of the villages in the province had already been destroyed and carefully explained how he arrived at that estimate and what the ruined villages looked like. Almost the only area left intact, he wrote, was a string of settlements "standing in a long belt of a few kilometers wide bordering Route 1, a partly paved two-lane road running the full length of the coastal strip." Beyond that, little remained, and it seemed only a matter of time until that little was blown away. The countryside was a moonscape of bomb craters, napalm-scorched fields, and pitted mountain sides defoliated and burned bare.

American artillery fire continually raked Quang Ngai, Schell wrote, sometimes pinpointed as called for from the field, sometimes on a saturation basis. "Just as often," an officer told Schell, "they'll give us a block five or ten kilometers on a side. At one time or another we've had these blocks just about everywhere in the district." Certain blocks were continual free-fire zones. Schell reported that in three and a half months, "the batteries at Duc Pho alone had fired 64,044 shells into the populated flatlands" nearby, a figure which "does not include shells fired by the Navy from the South China Sea, or shells fired from batteries taken out into the field to supply direct support to operations." Nor, of course, does it include bombs dropped by the Air Force. One of the American officers Schell interviewed in the field told him, "When I got here, some of the villages were wiped out, but quite a lot were still there.... Then every time I went out there were a few less, and now the whole place is wiped out."

The ARVN commanders in the district approved of the American destruction of Quang Ngai province, Schell said. "General Hoang Xuan Lam, Commander of the I Corps, came down to look...and when he saw how the place was torn up, he just said, 'Good, good! They are all V.C. Kill them!'"

Which was exactly what the men of Charlie Company did in one of the few remaining villages in Quang Ngai a week after Schell's report on the province was published. The average age of the soldiers in Charlie Company was 20. They were not soldiers brutalized by combat. They'd been in Vietnam for only a few weeks, having recently completed their training with high marks back home in America. At My Lai they found a village of women, children, and old men, many still cooking their breakfast rice over open fires.

A search of the village found no guerrillas. Nevertheless, Lt. Calley ordered his soldiers to round up all the villagers and kill them. His men herded the villagers together and then opened fire on them with their automatic rifles, killing most of the villagers instantly. Others they drove into nearby ditches. There the Americans raped the women and young girls, some just 14-years-old, before shooting them. Other soldiers gathered about 20 women and children near the village temple. There, as the women and children knelt and prayed and cried and begged for their lives, the Americans shot them. The soldiers later told an army investigator that, "Various soldiers...walked by and executed these women and children by shooting them in the head."

While they were shooting these crying and begging women and children in the head, other Americans were throwing grenades into huts, then firing into them, then setting them on fire. In a 1969 interview with CBS-TV reporter Mike Wallace, Private Paul Meadlo, who participated in the killings, was asked how many he killed at My Lai. "I fired on automatic," he answered, "you just spray the area, so you can't know how many you killed...So I might have killed ten or fifteen of them."

"Men, women, and children?" Wallace asked.

"Men, women, and children," Meadlo answered.

"And babies?"

"And babies."

"Why did you do it?"

"Because I was ordered to do it, and it seemed that, at the time, I felt like I was doing the right thing."

A Charlie Company sergeant who also killed villagers that morning and who was also interviewed on the PBS *Frontline* program agreed with Private Meadlo. "We carried out our orders," he said, "and I feel that we did not violate any moral standards."

Another soldier who killed at My Lai that day was interviewed for the "Remember My Lai" episode of the PBS *Frontline* series broadcast on May 23, 1989. He said he killed 25 villagers, shooting them, cutting their throats, scalping them, slicing out their tongues and chopping off their hands as he mutilated his victims in an orgy of blood lust. His explanation for his actions? "Once you start," the highly-trained soldier said, "it's very easy to go on."

We don't know, for sure, how many women, children, babies, and old men the young Americans of Charlie Company murdered that morning in My Lai. At least 350, perhaps as high as 567. No official body count exists. No one on the American side was counting. The soldiers of Charlie Company were too busy following their orders to kill everyone. Well before noon they'd finished their work. The village of My Lai had been obliterated, and most of the people who'd awakened in it that morning were dead.

Lt. Calley's superior officer, Captain Ernest Medina, was present on the ground in My Lai during the killing of the old men, women, children -- and babies. Colonel Oran Henderson, commander of the 11th Infantry Brigade, of which Charlie Company was a part, hovered over My Lai watching everything from his command helicopter as the slaughter progressed. Other officers up the chain of command -- including the division commander, Major General Samuel W. Koster -- all knew of the massacre soon after it happened. None of them did anything about it. When some soldiers reported what happened at My Lai, they were told to shut up -- and so the My Lai massacre was covered up.

Eventually, through the grapevine, another soldier, chopper gunner Ron Ridenhour, who had not been at My Lai, heard about it. His observation chopper flew over My Lai a few days after the massacre and he saw the aftermath. He nosed around, asked more questions, and -- feeling safe enough to do so only after he left the military -- wrote the details of the massacre in 30 letters to various politicians, including Secretary of the Army Stanley Resor, who ordered an investigation. Ridenhour's account reported details such as one soldier of Charlie Company coming upon a three- or four-year-old boy in My Lai who was desperately trying to stop the bleeding from his wounded arm. The soldier shot the boy as he begged for his life.

Private Meadlo, who told reporter Mike Wallace that he killed perhaps "ten or fifteen" villagers, was also in Ridenhour's account. According to Ridenhour, Meadlo said he and another soldier were guarding about 80 huddled villagers when Lt. Calley ordered him and his fellow soldier to "Waste them!" The two soldiers fired their automatic rifles into the cowering mass of villagers until they ran out of ammunition. Then they slapped in more ammo clips and continued firing until they ran out of ammunition again. And then they loaded in more ammo clips -- perhaps five in all -- and continued firing until no more movement came from the 80 crying and begging villagers in front of them. It was like a Nazi SS massacre of a Jewish village on the Eastern Front during World War II.

In the subsequent court martial, only four men were tried and only Lt. Calley was convicted. He was finally sentenced to two years of house arrest, and then Nixon's Secretary of the Army, Howard Callaway, paroled him from even that.

The murders which American troops committed at My Lai are well-known; furthermore, they were not an aberration. As the Tet battles raged on the morning of February 8, one group of soldiers was ordered to sweep the rice paddies along Vietnam's central coast. They entered a nondescript village in Quang Nam province which offered no resistance. Then Jamie Henry, the 20-year-old medic with the company, heard his lieutenant report on the radio that he'd just rounded up 19 civilians. He wanted to know what to do with them. Henry heard his company commander reply, "Kill anything that moves."

Henry stepped outside the hut in which he was resting and saw his fellow soldiers surrounding a huddled mass of women and children. There were no men in the small group. And then he saw his fellow G.I.s of B ("Baker") Company begin shooting into the group of women and children. Within seconds, all the women and children were dead.

When Jamie Henry left the military upon returning home to California, he held a news conference to publicize the massacre, and he published an account of it. Like other G.I.s who publicized similar massacres, he was denounced as a liar and a traitor. No one was ever prosecuted for murdering the 19 frightened women and children in the Quang Nam village on the morning of February 8, 1968.

Eventually, years later, the U.S. Army declassified records showing that Jamie Henry told the truth about the February 8th massacre, and other mass murders of innocent civilians by the men of Baker Company. But, in Vietnam, women, children, babies, and old men and old women were often the victims of American soldiers like those in Baker and Charlie Companies. The declassified Army files revealed that Army investigators substantiated 320 such massacres of innocent civilians -- families in their homes, farmers in rice paddies, kids out fishing -- not including My Lai. Hundreds of soldiers in interviews and letters to their commanders, described the actions of fellow soldiers who raped, tortured, and murdered their way across Vietnam with impunity.

On the night of February 25, 1969, for instance, 25-year-old Lt. Bob Kerrey -- later governor of Nebraska and U.S. Senator from that state -- led a group of six Navy SEAL commandos into the village of Thanh Phong in the Mekong Delta. As with the soldiers at My Lai, Kerrey had not been brutalized by combat in Vietnam. Kerrey had been in Vietnam for only one month, and it was his very first combat mission. According to one of those SEALs, Gerhard Klann, once in Thanh Phong, Lt. Kerrey ordered his men to round up all the women and children, the only villagers they found, and huddle them in the center of the village. There were about 13 to 20 of the unarmed villagers. Kerrey then ordered his men to kill them all. And so they did. Two of Kerrey's men say Lt. Bob Kerrey did his part in the killing that night. Kerrey later reported that his seven-man team killed 21 Viet Cong guerrillas in a "firefight" at Thanh Phong.

In 2001, when accounts of the Thanh Phong massacre finally surfaced, a reporter pointed out to Kerrey that all the dead at Thanh Phong were women and children -- and that their corpses were found clumped together in the middle of the tiny village in a manner suggesting an execution. The reporter asked Kerrey if the grouping of the bodies didn't contradict Kerrey's account of a "firefight."

"I do not have an explanation for that," Kerrey replied. And, in a *New York Times* interview, Kerrey confessed that he was unsure his men were ever fired upon that night. Perhaps they merely heard a "noise," he said, and overreacted. Even so, he reported 21 dead Viet Cong guerrillas after he returned to his base.

No one was ever prosecuted for what happened in the village of Thanh Phong. Instead, Kerrey was awarded the Bronze Star for the 21 guerrillas he and his men supposedly killed in the fictitious firefight in Thanh Phong on the night of February 25, 1969.

Such atrocities were not confined to a few rogue units, like Bob Kerrey's Navy SEALs or Lt. Calley's Charlie Company of the U.S. Army. According to the Army investigators, these atrocities and other abuses were committed by the soldiers of every division which served in Vietnam, without a single exception. Included among the substantiated abuses cited by the Army investigators were seven massacres from 1967 through 1971 in which at least 137 civilians were murdered; 78 other attacks on noncombatants in which at least 57 were murdered, 56 wounded, and 15 raped; and 141 instances where U.S. soldiers tortured captured civilian noncombatants with clubs, bats, or electric shocks.

Army investigators also determined that the allegations against 203 American soldiers were strong enough to warrant formal charges. Of these 203, only 57 were tried and only 22 were convicted. Of the 22 soldiers found guilty of abuses against Vietnamese civilians during the war, only 14 were given prison sentences. None of these 14 served more than a few months. A pedophile military intelligence interrogator who raped a 13-year-old girl he was questioning served the longest. He spent seven months in the stockade.

All of this is fact, as reported by official U.S. Army investigators. Ben Tre and My Lai and Thanh Phong and Jamie Henry's village in Quang Nam were not anomalies. They were routine. We were raping, torturing, and murdering the people of Vietnam. It was Standard Operating Procedure.

But even in the absence of such deliberate face-to-face atrocities, every routine aerial search-and-destroy operation in Vietnam was an atrocity because of the sheer firepower of American weapons. C-47 helicopter gunships carried Gatling guns with rotating barrels which, according to the official description, could put "a round in every square inch of a football field in less than a minute." Thus, any attack in or near a village by such gunships -- also firing rockets -- was likely to shred villagers along with their village.

Not that American pilots made careful distinctions. A correspondent for *The New Yorker* who flew with pilots on a number of missions in Vietnam reported pilots singing "atrocity songs" at their base camp, one of which went like this:

  Strafe the town and kill the people,
  Drop your napalm in the square,

>Get out early in the morning,
>Catch them at their Sunday prayer.

Given such firepower and such attitudes, every village and hamlet in Vietnam may as well have been named "Guernica." How could anyone have thought we could win the hearts and minds of the people we were murdering in such fashion? All we did was turn the survivors against us, survivors who had nothing left to lose, as their lives were already forfeit.

American officers told Jonathan Schell that, "The reprisals against the villages [of Quang Ngai] had impelled a number of women, old people and children to take up arms against our troops. Many Vietnamese of the district threw their lives away in desperate impossible attacks on our troops.... I heard one officer tell wonderingly of two old men who had rushed a tank column, carrying only rifles.... A G.I. told me he had discovered an old woman trying -- and failing -- to fire a machine gun at his unit while two small children attempted to guide the ammunition belt.... In the mountain valleys, there had been several cases of attacks with bows and arrows."

That was the American war in Vietnam: The highly-trained well-equipped soldiers of the most powerful military machine in the history of humanity against old men, old women, children, people armed with bows and arrows, willing to throw their lives away in "desperate impossible attacks." Short of the genocidal massacre of every man, woman, and child in Vietnam -- which it seemed we were attempting -- why did anyone think we could win at all?

And why didn't any of the 20-year-old highly-trained soldiers of Charlie Company at My Lai -- fresh from the nice, clean, safe suburbs of America -- who raped, mutilated, and murdered the old men, women, girls, and babies as young as seven months -- why didn't any of them have the moral courage to disobey their orders? Why didn't they try to stop the slaughter? It was clear to everyone there that a great evil was being committed that morning in the village of My Lai. Why didn't at least *one* of the men in Charlie Company say, "No, I won't do it"?

Only three Americans exhibited moral courage that day in My Lai. The three were chopper pilot Hugh Thompson, then 24, flying at tree level over My Lai that day with his two-man crew, door gunner Lawrence Colburn and crew chief Glenn Andreotta. Their mission was to draw fire so that following choppers could then destroy the revealed enemy positions with machine guns and rockets.

Only they never drew fire. There were no enemy positions beneath them.

Instead, they saw below them a young girl lying wounded on the road leading out of My Lai. Thompson dropped a smoke grenade near her to mark the spot and radioed for someone to help the girl. He then hovered above as he watched an American officer walk up to the girl that Thompson had marked with his smoke grenade, kick her over onto her back, and shred her with fire from his M-16.

Thompson then noticed the bodies of Vietnamese children, women, and old men piled into a nearby irrigation ditch, with American soldiers lounging nearby. He landed his chopper in the dirt road to investigate. He found that some of the villagers in the ditch were still alive and he called to the nearby soldiers to come help the wounded. The soldiers sauntered over and raked the bodies in the ditch with automatic weapons fire until there was no more movement. Later, 102 bodies were counted in that ditch.

Thompson and his buddies in the chopper were confused by what they saw and couldn't understand why their fellow Americans were massacring unarmed civilians. Then Thompson noticed an old woman standing in the doorway of a nearby hut with a baby in her arms and a child clutching her leg. Other villagers were crowded fearfully into the hut behind her. American soldiers were advancing on the hut. Thompson asked the officer commanding the soldiers approaching the hut to help him fly the villagers out of what looked like a combat zone.

The officer replied that the only help the villagers in the hut were going to get was a hand grenade tossed in among them.

Thompson realized he wasn't standing in a combat zone. He was standing in the midst of a massacre. He ran to his chopper, powered it up, and sat it down between the villagers in the hut and the approaching soldiers of Charlie Company. He told Colburn, his door gunner, to train his M-60 machine gun on the advancing soldiers of Charlie Company and to open up on them if they continued to advance. Colburn took aim at the advancing soldiers, who stopped advancing. Thompson then radioed two chopper gun ships which had been following him to sit down beside his chopper. They did so and Thompson herded about a dozen villagers from the hut into the waiting choppers.

Next, Thompson flew back to the irrigation ditch where he'd first landed. He hovered low over it, searching for signs of life. Glenn Andreotta, his crew chief, saw something move. Andreotta jumped out of the chopper and waded through the bloody bodies until he found a two-year-old boy clinging to his dead mother in the ditch. Andreotta picked the boy up and carried him back to the chopper, where he handed him to Colburn, waiting in the door beside his M-60 machine gun. "You've never seen shock like that," Colburn later said. "Such a blank stare."

Colburn cradled the boy in his arms as they flew the rescued villagers to a field hospital far from My Lai. The rescue took about 15-minutes. Thompson recalled thinking at the time that his fellow American soldiers "were the enemy," and he was willing to machine gun them if he had to in order to save the lives of the innocent.

But the moral courage that Hugh Thompson, Glenn Andreotta, and Lawrence Colburn displayed in My Lai that day was exceptional. Most American soldiers in Vietnam obeyed orders -- and when they were ordered to slaughter, they slaughtered. Rare is the hero with the courage to disobey orders -- it takes no courage at all to pull the trigger on crying babies and screaming children and begging women.

If it was easy for a combat soldier like Hugh Thompson to view his fellow soldiers at My Lai as "the enemy," how much more so for those back home, also appalled by the war, to also view American armed forces in Vietnam, even America itself, as "the enemy"?

I understood why people I knew wanted to burn the flag of the country which was committing such atrocities. And such burnings were happening frequently enough that, on July 5th, LBJ signed a bill rushed through Congress making it a federal offense to "cast contempt" on the U.S. flag "by publicly mutilating, defacing, or trampling upon it." The new law imposed a $1,000 fine and/or one year in jail.

While I understood and shared the anger of the flag burners, I also felt it was a political mistake to attack the flag. The flag is like a religious icon to most Americans. To burn it or "cast contempt" on it is viewed as an unforgivable desecration by most Americans. Anyone doing it is automatically, by that very act, the enemy. And the inflamed passions unleased by the act will prevent the average American from ever listening to any justifications for the act. In the minds of most Americans, there can be no possible justifications. The flag is untouchable. It is beyond rational discourse. Perhaps I understood this so well because I had been such an American believer, myself. Just four years before, I'd denounced Commies in California and had proudly carried an American flag as I rallied for Goldwater.

Instead of *burning* the flag, I felt a more powerful symbolic act would have been to *wash the flag*. We could have a demo, I argued to anyone who would listen, in which the flag was dipped into a bowl of water dyed red. And then, after we had purified the flag by washing out the red dye, the blood-red water would be poured out on the ground in a dramatic gesture. Instead of "casting contempt" upon the flag, we'd be *honoring* the flag much more than America, itself, was honoring the flag by its murderous actions in Vietnam.

My fellow students were too angry, too alienated from America, to listen. Casting contempt on the flag was exactly what they *wanted* to do. This was a mistake the Movement made, a mistake which severely handicapped it. Every dissident movement in American history before the Movement -- the Populists, workers, the Civil Rights Movement -- had marched behind the American flag and argued that they represented the "true" ideals of America. In the Thirties, even the Communist Party's official slogan was that "Communism is twentieth-century Americanism."

But not the Vietnam antiwar movement. Instead, it marched under the banner of the Viet Cong, abdicating its legitimate claim to represent the best of American ideals, and then handed the flag over to those who truly cast contempt on American ideals. Richard Nixon began wearing an American flag pin in his lapel and every right-wing Neanderthal who has come after him has done the same. Today, only nationalistic reactionaries wear American flag pins in their lapels. It is an immediate identifier, a gang color. It says we Neanderthals are the only *true* Americans, and you liberals are traitors who represent something America doesn't believe in. If a liberal sees you wearing the other gang's colors, an American flag pin, as I sometimes do, he immediately assumes you are his enemy. Passions ruled reason in 1968, and we lost the flag under which we should have been marching. Un-Americans have marched under our flag ever since.

The antiwar movement on the ASU campus wasn't completely stupid and politically inept. From noon to one every Wednesday afternoon protestors stood mutely in a single line on the mall in front of the library as a "silent witness" against the war. That spring semester I joined them at every Wednesday vigil and stood with them for an hour, silently protesting the war. I paid for it with a poor grade in my Mexican history course, which was also from noon to one every Monday, Wednesday, and Friday. I was very interested in Mexican history, but I was more committed to protesting the war. So, I missed a third of the course. It was hard to stay interested in school that spring. School seemed so irrelevant. It was an apocalyptic time, and revolution seemed imminent.

It was also the springtime of revolt in Europe. On May 3, 1968, at the Sorbonne, in Paris, the police brutally dispersed a student demonstration against the antiquated state-run university system. The next day, in response, students threw up barricades all over the university and called for a general strike. Students poured into the streets all across France. The student revolt spread to Italy and Germany. By May 26, an estimated ten million workers had also gone out on strike, paralyzing the nation. It appeared that the government of President Charles de Gaulle would fall.

Meanwhile, back in America, draft resistance was moving beyond words and individual draft card burnings. On May 17 a group of nine Catholic antiwar activists, led by priests Philip and Daniel Berrigan, raided a draft board in Catonsville, Maryland, seized over 900 draft files, and burned them in the board's parking lot. Tried and sentenced to prison, many of them, including the Rev. Daniel Berrigan, disappeared into an underground of resisters, where they carried on their anti-draft agitation.

People were in motion everywhere. History seemed to have speeded up and things were changing rapidly. Presidents from France to America were falling. Revolution was in the air.

And soon, Bobby would be our president. Soon, the horrible genocidal war in Vietnam would be over.

One of the graffito scrawled on the walls of Paris by the revolutionary students was "Demand the impossible!" And, in the spring of 1968, nothing seemed impossible.

Disappearances

In the midst of the Revolution, normal life went on. That spring Annie was enrolled in a speech class held in the same auditorium annex classroom where I'd had my own speech class at North High. She told her teacher about the version of *Spoon River Anthology* she and I'd perfected as a two-person performance piece, and we were invited to perform it in her class.

Returning to North High, returning to that same classroom to perform *Spoon River Anthology*, wasn't exactly a case of deja vu. It was more like Janis Joplin returning to her hometown of Port Arthur, Texas, after she made it big. I wasn't big, but I was an invited guest and there is a certain "performer's charisma" that any performer has, no matter how penny-ante. That people are focussing their attention on him gives him an aura. And just as Annie had the same teacher I had in her Humanities class, she also had my same speech teacher. I'd done OK in his class, but now I was a "star." Time changes everything.

Annie was also a "star," in her own way. She'd been admitted to a number of the private women's colleges to which she'd applied. She'd decided to go to Pitzer College, in Claremont, California. They'd given her a scholarship. But she still didn't have enough high school credits to graduate. In fact, she hadn't even submitted her North High transcript. Pitzer asked her to send it along, for the sake of formality, so I accompanied Annie as she went to North High's administrative office.

"I'd like to have my transcript sent to a college," Annie asked the blue-haired biddy behind the counter.

The blue-haired biddy knew her. "You *know* you can't go to college until you graduate."

Annie smiled. "So you say, but I've already been admitted to Pitzer College, and they'd like to see my transcript. Please send it to them. Here's the address."

So, it turned out that Vern was right. You *don't* have to go through life in lockstep. And, like her father, Annie never did graduate from high school. But, she went on to graduate from Pitzer College, so who cares?

Vern was also right about something else. He was sure Harvard would accept him back so he could get his Ph.D. And Harvard did. Come September, he'd be in Cambridge, on the East Coast, and Annie would be in California, on the West Coast. Only I would be in Phoenix.

But Vern was leaving even before September, as he had to find a place to live and settle in before his Harvard year began. So, he planned to leave at the beginning of summer. Tom Wagers sold Vern his blue VW van for $300 and Vern intended to load it up and amble at his leisure across America to Massachusetts. If I'd had the money, I'd have bought Tom's van. Tom kept it in excellent condition, and I had no means of moving to Wupatki for the summer. I'd not be able to take much up there on my 90cc Suzuki. Just what I'd be able to stuff into a backpack.

Since Vern was moving out and moving on as of June, Annie would be on her own in Phoenix for the summer. She couldn't move in with me, as I wouldn't be there. I'd be at Wupatki, one way or another.

So she moved into the Wagers' hotel. There were always available apartments in that labyrinthine maze and Tom's parents offered her one free for the summer. It was just a studio apartment, with a big brass bed, but it was all she needed.

Then Tom Wagers disappeared. One day he was there, the next he was gone. His belongings were still in his apartment in the Wagers' hotel, but he wasn't. He was mature beyond his years, and his parents weren't worried at first. But, as the days became a week, then two weeks, and they'd heard nothing from him, nor had any of his friends, they began to worry. They reported him to the police as a missing person. The police couldn't find him, not that they tried very hard. There was no sign of foul play. Tom was 17 and a lot of teenagers were running away from home in the Age of Aquarius. The police said he'd turn up in a hippie commune somewhere.

They were almost right. When Tom's parents queried the North High administration, they discovered that Tom's transcript had been sent, at Tom's request, to a high school in San Francisco. They followed the paper trail and eventually discovered Tom in 'Frisco. He'd rented an apartment not far from the Haight and he'd already enrolled in a local high school for his upcoming senior year. He'd told everyone his family had just moved to the city. No one asked any questions. Who'd expect a teenager to transfer to a new high school in a strange city on his own?

Tom was OK. He just wanted to escape from Phoenix to a more happening place. His mother continued to worry, but his father was proud that Tom had pulled off the transplantation so competently and so secretly. And so Tom Wagers disappeared into the drift of the years.

Jan Sownie, Annie's best friend, who *was* graduating from North High, said she was going to Northern Arizona University in Flagstaff.

But come the fall, I'd still be in Phoenix. The city increasingly felt like a prison. Phoenix was already a big city, and was growing bigger by the day. By 1980 it'd be the ninth largest city in America. But it felt like a small town to me. Everywhere I looked, I saw walls around me. I was suffocating. I was desperate to get out.

At least I'd escape for the summer. I was going to Wupatki, the land of prehistoric ruins and wide open spaces. Jan Pinkoski, my fellow student clerk in the ASU library, asked what I was doing for the summer. "I'm going to be a United States Park Ranger, Pink. I'm going to guide turistas around ancient Indian ruins."

"Wow! Wish I could do that."

"Actually, Pink, you can. When I was up there for my interview I learned that they were still looking for one more Ranger."

"Should I write to them?"

"No, you need to be more assertive. You need to get on the phone and call them. Ask for an interview. You need to do it today. In fact, you need to do it right now."

I pulled our supervisor's desk phone over and handed it to him. "Call, Pink. This instant. Tomorrow might be too late. Here's the number. Tell'em you're a student at ASU. You're a history major. You're excited about working at Wupatki. Do they have an opening?"

I watched while Pink dialed. I nodded encouragement as he stumbled his way through the conversation with Ranger Chambers. Interview, I mouthed at him.

"So," Pink said, "would it be possible to drive up for an interview? This Saturday?" Pink looked at me. I nodded. "I'll be there. Thanks, see you soon."

Pink hung up and smiled at me. "That went well."

"It was excellent. And I'm sure you'll do well in the interview. Here's what you say..."

So Pink drove up to Wupatki that weekend. And Pink did, indeed, do well in the interview. Come summer, the two of us would be Rangers together at Wupatki. And we'd drive up to Wupatki with all our stuff in his car.

Pink sent off a check for his uniforms. We had to purchase three gray short sleeved shirts with the Department of the Interior - Park Service arrowhead patch on the left sleeves, two pairs of brown pants, a pair of black patent leather shoes which I referred to as "foot coffins," a brown leather belt with oak leaves and acorns incised into it, and, because it was for the summer, a straw Smokey the Bear hat with a black leather hat band, also incised with oak leaves and acorns.

Cost was about $150. I simply didn't have it, so I went to the Valley National Bank and took out a $150 short-term loan. Then I, too, sent off for my straw Smokey the Bear hat and accoutrements.

I don't remember if Annie went to her senior class farewell assembly in the North High auditorium. Of course, she didn't attend the graduation ceremony, as she wasn't graduating. No loss there. Nor did we go to her senior prom. Neither of us were the kind of people who went to proms. She found a summer job as a soda jerk at a drug store lunch counter not far from the Wagers' hotel. Then I helped her move into her hotel apartment. She didn't own much. She wasn't allowed to keep her cat, Mimi, so I said I'd take Mimi with me and Pink to Wupatki.

And then we christened her big brass bed. Two old ladies who lived in the apartment below later complained to Tom's father that we made too much noise. They demanded peace and quiet. Mr. Wagers smiled and said he'd talk to Annie about keeping it down.

The last thing I did before Pink and I took off was sell my beloved blue Suzuki 90 to Brother Rick. He'd returned from Chattanooga sometime during the school year, but I wasn't in contact with the family, so I didn't know when. He was again living at the cinderblock house on 51st Street, which was now just Mom's house, and had begun his reign of terror over our younger brothers. I'd moved out, Mom had divorced Elmer, and Rick was the oldest male in the house. Mom worked every day and Rick was an unemployed high school drop-out, so he was around 24/7. He took full advantage of his newfound power and roostered around like the cock o' the walk. Brother Mike's memory of Rick kicks in with the fall of 1967, as Mike was a principal target of Rick's tortures. The victim always remembers.

But, I didn't know that Rick had morphed into Caligua. I just knew that he was back and that he probably needed some cheap wheels. I called the house and asked if he wanted to buy my blue Suzuki.

"Shit, yeah! How much?"

"$100."

"I don't have $100."

"Do you have $25?"

"Yeah."

"OK, I'll sell it to you for $25 up front and you send me $25 a month for the three months I'm at Wupatki. Think you could swing that?"

"Yeah, I could swing that."

"Then it's a done deal."

We met, Rick handed over $25, and I gave him the signed title to my beloved blue Suzuki. What I eventually learned from this transaction is that you never *ever* sign over the title of your vehicle until you have the cash in hand. Not even to your brother. Because, when it comes to money, you can't trust anyone. Not even your brother.

Ancient Fire

For weeks the land trembled. Great cracks split the earth and choking gasses spewed forth. Then, in the snow-clad pine tree country, molten rock tore through the surface and burning cinders burst into the sky. The land was angry and it was best to leave.

In small groups, families gathered their belongings. They dismantled their pit houses, even digging up the poles supporting the brush-covered roofs. And then, carrying everything they could, they left the land of their fathers, trekking far, far away from the burning earth.

In the winter of 1064 A.D., two years before William the Conqueror and his Norman knights invaded England, the most recent volcano in the vast San Francisco volcanic field in northern Arizona erupted. And it continued erupting ceaselessly over the next 25 years. It sent tongues of lava flowing over the land. It coughed up millions of tons of cinders, which then rained down in all directions for over 20 miles. Indeed, three-quarters of the material ejected from the volcano was cinders, deposited in nearly equal amounts over the surrounding land and on the cone which the volcano constantly built up.

After the initial quarter century of constant eruption, the volcano fell silent for years at a time, only to then belch forth lava and cinders yet again for more years. Indeed, for almost 200 years, until about 1250 or later, the volcano, about 15 miles northeast of present-day Flagstaff, continued to erupt intermittently, building up the yellow and rust colored, 1,000-foot high, one-mile-wide cinder cone which is now known as Sunset Crater.

Today, the land seems quiet, but in the long geologic history of the Flagstaff area there have been many such volcanic eruptions. Indeed, the entire San Francisco Peaks mountain range in northern Arizona is composed of extinct volcanoes, with Mt. Humphreys, the tallest mountain in the state, simply the most prominent of these dead volcanoes. The Peaks, in turn, are surrounded by a 3,000-square-mile volcanic field composed of at least 600 lesser volcanic cones and vents. This field stretches from the Little Colorado River in the east to Ash Fork in the west, and from Cameron in the north to the Mogollon Rim in the south.

Humanity is very young, and the earth is very old. It is estimated that this volcanic field took over eight million years to develop to its present size, beginning with eruptions around the Mogollon Rim and then moving north. If only the 600 or so known extinct volcanoes in the area are considered, the average time between eruptions was over 13,000 years. The most recent evidence indicates that Native Americans came over the Bering Strait land bridge no more than 15,000 years ago. It is likely that the Sunset Crater eruption was the first in the region that humans ever witnessed in the thousands of years they may have lived in the area. Today, Northern Arizona is quiet. But, because the land is now quiet does not mean that the volcanoes have ceased erupting. Someday, in hundreds or thousands of years, this land will burn again.

Ten thousand years before Sunset Crater began erupting in 1064, a nomadic paleo-hunter crossed the limestone rangeland of Antelope Prairie, the present-day entrance to Wupatki National Monument about 15 miles north of Sunset Crater. As he did so, he dropped a Clovis spearpoint. It remained where it fell for 11,000 years, until it was found in the 1980s. No doubt, over the years, hunters just like him continued to hunt the pronghorn antelope which still roam that prairie.

By the time of the eruption, however, the people in the region were no longer nomadic hunters, but lived in pit houses dug in the ground and covered with brush. They are now known as the Sinagua (sin-naw-wah), "those without water." They are the same people who built the cliff dwellings at Walnut Canyon, just east of Flagstaff, and Montezuma's Castle south of

Flagstaff and Tuzigoot in the Verde Valley. The initial eruption drove them away from the area and covered their pit houses.

They soon returned. The region was not only their ancestral homeland but, as the volcano subsided into intermittent eruptions and grumblings, it became better farmland than ever before. Not only did the blanket of cinders covering the land act as an insulating mulch, helping to retain more rainwater, but there was more rain. The continued eruptions of Sunset Crater happened to coincide with a 200-year period of increased precipitation throughout the prehistoric Southwest. Pueblos began to rise across Antelope Prairie and even in the more arid lowland desert of Wupatki Basin below the prairie.

The largest of these pueblos, with about 100 rooms, is the ruin known as Wupatki. It is a Hopi word meaning, the Rangers will tell you, "tall house." However, there is good reason to believe the word actually means "long valley," and the ruin is, indeed, on a hill crest inside a long valley. It is the largest prehistoric dwelling for at least 50-miles and could support its large population because of a permanent spring nearby.

Near it is a ballcourt similar to the ballcourts at Pueblo Grande, in Phoenix, suggesting a Hohokam influence. In fact, Hohokam artifacts were actually found inside the Wupatki ballcourt. This ballcourt is the northernmost such ballcourt yet discovered, linking Wupatki to a pattern of cultural diffusion emanating not only from the Hohokam, but even further south, from the Olmecs and Toltecs of central Mexico, and therefore perhaps with the Quetzalcoatl cult of the Plumed Serpent which, in the desert Southwest, became the Horned Rattlesnake.

On the cliff overlooking Wupatki pueblo is the Monument's Visitor Center. One parks in front of the Visitor Center and walks through it and out the back doors to the cliff overlooking the Wupatki ruins.

About a mile or so on the other side of the Visitor Center's parking lot, in the direction of the Little Colorado River and the Navajo Reservation beyond it, is the beautiful Wukoki pueblo. Wukoki is perhaps the most photographed of all Southwestern Indian ruins. It stands tall and majestically alone on a bare rock surrounded by the ash-covered desert of Wupatki Basin. It is the ruin which should bear the name "Wupatki," signifying its tallness.

On Antelope Prairie above Wupatki Basin is the unexcavated Citadel ruin, which Tom, Annie, and I had climbed to view when we first visited Wupatki. At the base of the Citadel is the excavated Nalakihu ruin. Not far away is the lovely Lomaki ruin, on the edge of Box Canyon. In the back country, with no paved road and off limits to all visitors, is the Crack-in-the-Rock ruin with its thousands of petroglyphs. In addition to these major ruins, there are perhaps 3,000 other, smaller, ruins sprinkled all over the 55-square-miles of Wupatki National Monument.

Eight hundred years ago this desolate land was a heavily populated and even cosmopolitan farming region. Most of the pottery debris, called shards, found at Wupatki are the undecorated reddish-brown ware of the Sinagua. In addition to the Sinagua, however, perhaps half of the people living there were Kayenta Anasazi (ann-ah-saw-zi), from the northeast, who brought their tradition of building multi-storied stone dwellings. Indeed, the T-shaped doorways of the Wupatki pueblo are typically Anasazi.

Some of the 78 different kinds of pottery found at Wupatki also include Cohonina types from the west. In addition, southern Hohokam stone and shell jewelry has been found all over Wupatki. This evidence, as well as seashells from the Pacific and the Sea of Cortez and parrot and macaw feathers and skeletons and copper bells from deep in Mexico, indicate that the people of Wupatki were part of an extensive trade network. It is unclear, however, what the Sinagua and Anasazi of Wupatki may have traded for these items; perhaps cotton grown along the floodplain of the Little Colorado River, which runs through the area.

The Little Colorado River begins as streams in the White Mountain Apache region of eastern Arizona. It then flows, when it flows at all, northwest until it meets the Colorado River north of the Grand Canyon. It is the biggest river in northeastern Arizona and drains the Painted Desert region and the area north of the Mogollon Rim.

It is also an ephemeral river, sometimes there, sometimes not. In the spring, fed by snowmelt from the White Mountains, it is strong enough to have carved a deep canyon, the Little Colorado River Gorge, about 12 miles northwest of Cameron just before its confluence with the Colorado River. But, by the time I arrived at Wupatki, at the beginning of June, it was completely dry and it remained dry all that summer and beyond. That dry bed was the northeastern border between Wupatki and the Navajo Nation.

We know from dendrochronology (tree ring dating) that Wupatki pueblo's first roof beam was cut in 1106, only 42 years after Sunset Crater first erupted. More beams were cut for more rooms in 1137, 1160, and 1192. Some of these beams can still be seen sticking out of the pueblo walls. The nearby ballcourt dates from sometime after 1150. By then, perhaps 3,000 people lived in the Wupatki area.

By the end of the 1100s, however, the climate all over the Southwest turned arid, as a drought which may have endured for a century or more desiccated the region. Ancient peoples from Mesa Verde to Chaco Canyon to Wupatki abandoned their homes seeking water. The last roof beam for Wupatki pueblo was cut in 1215, the same year King John attached his seal to the Magna Carta at Runnymede in England. By 1225 or so, Wupatki and nearby pueblos were probably abandoned. Some people from Wupatki may have moved south, to join the Sinagua at Tuzigoot, near the Verde River. Others may have moved east, toward the Zuni villages, already settled by that time. Still others may have moved to the Hopi Mesas, as the Hopi village of Shungopavi dates from the 1200s.

And, as the Sinagua-Anasazi of Wupatki abandoned the region to ghosts and ruins, Sunset Crater continued to grumble and, sometimes, erupt, lighting the dark night sky with flames and adding its clouds of cinders to a day-time sky devoid of clouds bringing rain. The volcano would not fall finally silent for another half-century or so.

And perhaps, sometime after that, a lonely hunter, crossing Antelope Prairie like his paleo predecessor, noticed that the cinders no longer fell.

Petroglyphs of Wupatki

Pink and I didn't live with the other Rangers in the row of World War II-era apartments just above the Visitor Center. We were quarantined way down the road, in a small tin trailer hidden behind some hills. There were about a half dozen such trailers there for the Navajo laborers who did all the maintenance work at Wupatki. We were the only Rangers among them.

The trailer was about ten-feet wide and perhaps 24-feet long. Despite the small size, it had a small bathroom, a combination living room-kitchen, and two tiny bedrooms. About the only thing the bedrooms had room for were beds. Pink took the one in mid-trailer, next to the bathroom, I took the one in the rear. The bed stretched from one side of the trailer to the other, with enough space for me to stand up beside it. We piled our belongings in that teensy space beside our beds.

The sole door to the trailer opened right into the living room. Cinderblocks were our steps up into the living room. There was a small formica-top table, upon which I placed my clunky manual typewriter. The trailer had running water and electricity, so I was able to plug in my portable stereo record player. I had LPs, the newest of which was Pete Seeger singing about his sloop Clearwater and cleaning up the Hudson River, along which he lived. We listened to a lot of Pete Seeger that summer.

We'd driven up from Phoenix in Pink's car, which was parked outside. Also outside was the gray Park Service pickup we took turns driving. Each door of the truck had a large arrowhead Park Service logo on it, the same logo we wore as patches on the short sleeves of our uniform shirts. We worked different shifts, so Pink or I always drove back to the tin trailer and turned the truck over to the other at the end of our shifts. It was a 40-hour week, with two days off, in the middle of the week.

Our jobs consisted of four responsibilities, two of which were at the Visitor Center. The most boring of these was simply standing behind the counter just to the right of the main entrance and clicking off the number of turistas who walked through the door. If they asked questions, like where the restrooms were, or how far to Sunset Crater, we answered them. If they bought slides of Wupatki, or postcards, we took their money. At that time, the parks and monuments were free. It didn't cost anything to go to the Grand Canyon or to Montezuma's Castle or to Wupatki. Now, you pay, so I suppose the Ranger at the counter also collects entrance fees.

Better than standing at the counter was standing out back of the Visitor Center on the cliff overlooking the Wupatki ruin. As turistas walked out and saw the ruin, they invariably had more questions, this time perhaps more pertinent to the history of Wupatki. Sometimes, if a busload of turistas came in, I'd lead the group on a guided tour of the ruin. That was fun, as I could give a capsule history of the site.

Even better was being assigned to the lonely Ranger station at the Citadel ruin out on Antelope Prairie, near the entrance to the Monument. This was the first ruin turistas came upon and they usually stopped to take a look, just as I had when I came to Wupatki with Annie and Tom Wagers for my job interview. But, there weren't many turistas. Most of the time I was out there alone. I had plenty of time to read the book on the Grand Canyon by Joseph Wood Krutch which I always carried with me. If I looked up at the call of a raptor, I sometimes saw pronghorn antelope grazing far off in the distance. I noted their number and the date I saw them in a log book. And then I just listened to the silence and savored the cooling breeze on my face as the antelope bounded out of sight.

But the best job of all was driving the pickup around to the various ruins, "showing the flag" and making sure all was well. When I did this, I was free to explore. I was expected to remain on the paved roads and the well-travelled dirt roads to the primary ruins. Pink was a well-behaved boy and did as he was told, so he stayed on the main roads. Sometimes, however, I went on "unauthorized back country patrols." The permanent Rangers at Wupatki saw no reason to teach or show Pink or I much about Wupatki, so the only time I saw the big back country Crack-in-the-Rock ruin, which Pink never saw, was when I drove the pickup on the bouncy dirt road out to it on my own. So long as I was back at the Visitor Center when my shift was over, no one was the wiser and all was well.

Once, though, I was caught. I'd driven off onto an obscure and rutted dirt road behind the Citadel, having no idea where it led. I found myself driving up the long valley to the main Wupatki ruin, coming on it from behind, with the Visitor Center on the other side. I decided it was best to turn around and retrace my path. But, in attempting to turn, my back wheels became buried in the deep cinder blanket of the valley. I could get no traction and all I did was bury myself deeper and deeper into the cinders as I tried to rock myself out. Eventually I had to abandon the truck and trek up to the Visitor Center and ask for help.

All the Rangers eagerly jumped to the task of retrieving my truck. It was a diversion from the boring routine of daily life. Four Rangers stood on the back bumper to add their weight to the rear wheels as another Ranger slowly drove the truck out of the cinders. I was considered incompetent to drive the truck out, as I was the one who'd gotten it stuck. Perhaps unwisely, I took photos of the rescue. That did not endear me to the permanent staff.

Whether driving the roads of Wupatki or standing my lonely vigil at the Citadel, I kept searching for something to write about. I'd not abandoned my desire to write a scholarly article about the Southwest's prehistoric past. I'd not found anything to write about Pueblo Grande, but perhaps there was something new I could say about Wupatki, despite my limited training and knowledge about the region's history.

The permanent Rangers at Wupatki were no help at all. Even though Ranger Chambers had studied anthropology under Margaret Mead at Columbia, he had no interest in Wupatki's Indian past. He spent all his free time at the honky-tonk at the Gray Mountain Trading Post on Route 89, drinking beer, playing the jukebox, and trying to pick up Navajo girls in their ass-hugging jeans. The other Rangers were just as uninterested about Wupatki's past. Sunset Crater had a camp site that turistas were allowed to stay at overnight. Pink and I suggested that we present talks on Wupatki to the turistas staying there. Ranger Chambers vetoed that. "No. You start something like that and we'll just have to continue it after you're gone. Don't make more work for us."

There was also a storage room adjacent to the Visitor Center in which artifacts found at Wupatki, including intact pots of all types, were kept. Not once were I and Pink invited even to look inside that room at the treasures hidden therein, although I once caught a brief glimpse as another Ranger came out of it.

Nor were we given anything to read on the history or geology of Wupatki, although there was a small library of books and articles on the Monument in Ranger Chambers' office. He didn't offer them to us as resources, but he had no objection to my reading them, so I made my way through everything he had. It didn't take long, because, at that point, not much had been written about Wupatki.

Actually, the first idea I had for a research topic didn't result from reading the material in Ranger Chambers' office. It came from something I'd read about World War II. Early in that war, as the Japanese empire spread over Southeast Asia, it cut off American access to natural rubber sources in that region. This was potentially crippling to America's war effort, so there was an all-out drive to find or fabricate some kind of alternative rubber source. Eventually, synthetic rubber was manufactured from oil, but there were many possibilities explored before that was hit upon. One of the possibilities the scientists investigated was guyale.

Guyale is a bushy desert weed indigenous to the Southwest. During the war, researchers actually discovered that a kind of "rubber" could be made from the milky sap of the weed. It wasn't much, and it wasn't ideal, so that research was abandoned once oil-based synthetic rubber began to be developed.

But I remembered this research one day as I was standing on the cliff behind the Visitor Center looking down on the Wupatki ruin and its nearby ball court. Some kind of ball game was played in that court, and in the ones further south in the Hohokam region. But, no one knew where the Indians got the bounce for their balls. Obviously, it had to come from somewhere locally. What could be the rubber source for their balls? Perhaps, I thought, it might be guyale.

So, in my free time, I began walking out in the desert with a plastic trash bag, collecting guyale. I didn't know how to make rubber, and there was nothing on rubber-making anywhere on the Monument. And there was no way of researching it elsewhere as, in that age before the Internet, we were completely isolated at Wupatki. But, I guessed that the first step was pulverizing the guyale. So, I found a large flat rock, I found a round rock I could use as a hammer, and, with my makeshift mano and metate, I began pulverizing guyale plants into a sticky mass of pulp outside our trailer.

I figured the next step was boiling it. But, I had nothing to boil it in, nor did I have any idea what after-boiling product I was looking for. I was stymied, so I abandoned my hunt for a native rubber source. To my knowledge, no one has yet identified an indigenous source for the prehistoric Indian balls and I think guyale still remains a prime suspect. I just didn't have the proper skills or equipment to carry out my investigations. All I proved by my efforts was that I could make a yucky mess with mashed plants.

But I didn't give up. I continued reading and searching for something to write about Wupatki. There had never been an intensive archaeological inventory survey of Wupatki, nor would there be until the mid-1980s. Many major ruins, such as the 51-room Citadel, have yet to be excavated. Much about Wupatki therefore remained a mystery. There seemed to be the possibility of *something* I could investigate.

That's when I hit upon the idea of writing about the petroglyphs of Wupatki. Petroglyphs are prehistoric rock art, pecked into rocks all over the Southwest by the ancient inhabitants. Despite all the decades of research on the subject, no one to this day, including the current Indians of the Southwest, really know what this rock art means. Was it intended as astronomical records? Magical or ritual symbols? Works of art? Doodles? Graffiti? The equivalent of the notes Annie and I left in a tin can on top of the Superstitions saying, "We passed this way?"

And, despite the wealth of petroglyphs at Wupatki (the mid-1980s archaeological survey identified 450 rock art sites), I discovered from my reading that summer that no one had written a full article on the area's petroglyphs. The most I could find in 1968 was a few lines on Inscription Point, a large petroglyph site on the Navajo Reservation just across the Little Colorado River from Wupatki. In his 1960 book about the region, *Black Sand: Prehistory in Northern Arizona*, pioneering archaeologist Harold S. Colton had simply said it existed. And in his 1946 article in *Plateau*, "Fools' Names Like Fools' Faces," Colton wrote, "Inscription Point...appears to be a...registration book....At the western end of a small mesa the rocks are covered with dozens of drawings which we assume were made between 1000-1300 A.D."

That was it.

So, one day on patrol, I drove out on the seldom used dirt road past the Wukoki ruin and down to the Little Colorado River. I bounced across the dry bed of the river and drove parallel to the river course until I came to Inscription Point. There was a windmill nearby, pumping up ground water, and a large metal tank of water the windmill had filled. Near it an unsaddled Navajo horse grazed on the grasses which flourished on the spilled water around the windmill's tank. I left the pickup and climbed up into the rocks. They were covered with hundreds of petroglyphs: spirals, zigzags, labyrinthine squares, anthropomorphic figures with enlarged extremities and genitals sporting elaborate headdresses, snake spirals, giant feet, stalks of corn, and even a realistic figure of two copulating antelopes. I photographed every petroglyph there, from many angles.

And then I stood on top of the rocks, in the complete silence of the desert with only the horse grazing below me at the water tank. I looked at all the petroglyphs around me and wondered what I, who had no credentials or training in the subject at all, could possibly say about this amazing collection of prehistoric rock art. I didn't think of anything I could say as I stood there amid the petroglyphs in the desert. In fact, I didn't think of anything for a long time. But I continued reading, learning more and more about prehistoric rock art.

And, eventually, I *did* think of something to say. I described the petroglyphs, I correlated their age with known age markers developed by archaeologist Christy Turner in his work on Glen Canyon petroglyphs, I discussed the incidence of fertility symbols (such as corn, snakes, the anthropomorphs with enlarged genitals, the copulating antelope, and another antelope with an erect phallus), and the possible cultural origin of the petroglyphs. I concluded that "the cultural origin of many of the petroglyphs at Inscription Point was located in central Mexico, being transmitted northward through the Hohokam into the Anasazi area. Inscription Point could well be the first site in the Kayenta-Anasazi cultural area where these designs, in particular the snake and flute player symbols, made their appearance."

After drafting the article, I gave it to Annie to critique and revise. I'd never written an academic paper like that and wasn't sure of my ability. After she rewrote it, we sent it off. The article, "Petroglyphs of Wupatki," with our joint by-lines and along with my photographs, was accepted and published in *Southwestern Lore,* the journal of the Colorado Archaeological Society. It has since been cited in several scholarly publications. In addition, my photos are the only remaining records of some of the petroglyphs, such as the copulating antelope, as they were obliterated when Inscription Point was vandalized many years later.

And so I did, after all, end up producing something of value and adding, in my small way, to the knowledge of the prehistoric Southwest. And the product did not come about because Annie and I knew the most about Wupatki's petroglyphs. Perhaps Ranger Chambers, or someone else, knew more. It came about because I was the only one at Wupatki who *wanted* to write about Wupatki. And the desire to write finally found a subject about which to write.

Passing as a Pig

The People stood at our open door in silence. They didn't like to be called "Indians." They preferred to be called "Navajo." Even better, they preferred to be called "Dine," which they pronounced "Dee-nay" and which, in their own language, meant "The People." And so the two young men of The People stood at our open trailer door in silence.

They were from the Navajo work crew who lived near us in our isolated trailer park. When we were in the trailer, we left the door open all the time. During the day we needed the ventilation, as the trailer had no air conditioner. At night we left it open so that Mimi, Annie's cat we brought with us, could hunt. She prowled all night and, in the morning, we found the tails and hindquarters of desert mice that she left on the linoleum floor for us, as if to say, "See what I brought for you?"

And so, when I looked up at the crunch of gravel, I saw the two standing at the open door. Like all Navajo males, and even Navajo girls, they were dressed like cowboys: Levis, cowboy belts and buckles, cowboy boots, cowboy hats. There was much more of an Indian presence in Flagstaff than there was in Phoenix. Northern Arizona University has the largest population of Indian students in the country and I saw lots of sexy Navajo girls in cowboy boots and tight-ass jeans walking the streets of Flagstaff. During the annual summer Pow-wow, or Indian festival, Indians came from all over the Southwest and Flagstaff almost became an Indian town, most of them, excepting the old women in their long-sleeved velvet shirts and "squaw dresses," looking just like cowboys.

I went to the door and invited the The People in. They said nothing, but they came in and sat on the built-in padded bench which ran the width of that end of the trailer. Just as they had when standing at the door, they sat in silence. I returned to typing the letter I was composing on my battered manual typewriter at the kitchen table.

When the Navajo had first begun visiting us, I'd asked them why they'd come. They didn't answer. They just sat in silence. I eventually learned that it did no good to ask why they came. They would not be rushed. It didn't matter if I sat and tried to talk with them or got up and went about my business, ignoring them. They sat in silence. Eventually, when they'd sat for what they considered a polite or appropriate amount of time, they spoke. So I learned to continue whatever I was doing while they sat in silence. It must be very hard on Anglo teachers at NAU, I thought, to have a classroom full of silent Navajos. But, perhaps it wasn't all that different from having a classroom full of white students. Brick walls, in either case.

And so the Navajo cowboys sat in silence. About ten minutes after they sat down, one of them spoke. I stopped typing and turned to them. "Yes?"

"Can we borrow your record player?" he repeated.

And so I knew why they'd come. I unplugged my portable stereo, which I'd brought from Phoenix, closed it up, and handed it over to the Navajo. They grunted and left with it. I never worried about getting back anything I loaned them. They always returned what they borrowed.

Had Pink and I not lived in the isolated trailer camp with the Navajo work crew, we'd not have had any contact at all with the Navajo at Wupatki. They and the Anglo Rangers lived entirely separate lives. When the Rangers had a picnic or a party, the Navajo workers were never invited. And, I discovered, it was not solely because the cultures were so different. It was also because the Rangers hated the Indians. They routinely disparaged them. "Blanket butts," they called them. "Injuns."

Ranger Chambers was the source of much of the anti-Indian sentiment at Wupatki. He didn't have a good word to say about any of them, especially the ones who still lived at Wupatki. There was a family of Navajos who still lived and grazed cattle in the Wupatki Basin. They had a legal right to do so. This was the family of Clyde Peshlakai. Peshlakai means "silver" and is pronounced "Beesh-lagai," which translates as "white metal." Peshlakai can also simply mean "silversmith." About half of all Indian silversmiths are Navajo and the Peshlakai name is a venerable one among these Navajo silversmiths.

The Peshlakai name and Navajo silversmithing both began at Bosque Redondo (Fort Sumner) New Mexico. In 1864, the famous Indian fighter Kit Carson forced most of the Navajo out of their ancestral lands in northern Arizona and New Mexico on a notorious "Long Walk" of 470-miles to Bosque Redondo in southern New Mexico. By 1865, 9,022 Navajo were imprisoned there. One of the imprisoned Navajo, Atsidi Sani, asked the soldiers overseeing them at the fort for metalsmithing tools so he could teach his people that trade. He became the first known Navajo metalsmith of iron and silver, reputedly learning his craft from a Mexican teacher.

In 1868 the Navajo survivors at Bosque Redondo were allowed to return to their ancestral homes and Atsidi Sani took his tools, and newly-acquired skills, with him. Atsidi Sani, also known as Atsidi Peshlakai ("Atsidi the Silversmith"), settled at Black Point, where his wife's family lived, along the Little Colorado River north of today's Wupatki National Monument. Over the next half century, silverwork among the Navajo blossomed, with the sons of Atsidi Peshlakai foremost among the silversmiths.

Besides doing silversmithing, Atsidi Peshlakai also ran sheep and cattle on Antelope Prairie. In the 1880s, Anglo ranchers, wanting that lush grazing land for themselves, forced him off Antelope Prairie, and he moved his sheep and cattle down into the much less desirable Wupatki Basin. Atsidi Peshlakai, now a weathered old man, was still there in 1924 when President Calvin Coolidge created Wupatki National Monument. Not many tourists visited Wupatki in the Twenties and Thirties and the place was completely closed in the winter. When that happened, the Peshlakai family acted as winter custodians of the Monument.

In 1937 President Franklin D. Roosevelt added 34,000 acres to the Monument, including Wupatki Basin, where four branches of the Peshlakai family lived. Those four branches were allowed to remain at Wupatki, and the head of each family received a grazing permit for their cattle, for the life of the family head. When he died, the family could no longer graze cattle at Wupatki and, indeed, had to leave Wupatki. In 1937, Clyde Peshlakai, Atsidi's son, was the winter custodian. Thirty years later, in 1968, Clyde was still there, and his family was the last Navajo family still living at Wupatki.

The first time I saw Clyde Peshlakai was one day while I was standing at the Visitor Center counter and gazing out the window. I saw an old Navajo ambling slowly across the desert on his tired horse. I asked Ranger Chambers who he was. "That's Clyde Peshlakai. All his brothers are good Indians, but Clyde is a bad Indian. Soon, though, he'll be a good Indian, too."

"He doesn't look like he could cause much harm."

"Oh, he's harmless."

"But you said he was a bad Indian."

"Only because he's not dead yet. The only good Indian is a dead Indian."

I said nothing and turned to watch Clyde Peshlakai and his horse slowly disappear into the desert vastness. Northern Arizona has large tracts of endless land and sky. Sometimes it seems you can look all the way across the continent to the Appalachians. When I took my turn standing at the Visitor Center's counter, I could look out the tall window and there, 60-miles straight across the featureless desert, I could see the massive mesas known as the "Hopi Buttes."

They are the remains of sediment laid down in an ancient lake six to twelve million years ago, then capped by solidified lava from volcanoes erupting into the lake. This long-gone lake, dating from the Miocene and Pliocene eras, is called "Hopi Lake" by archaeologists. It covered perhaps a 7,500-square mile area north of the present I-40 Interstate near Winslow.

The lake's demise, however, was not due to volcanoes pouring lava into it. It was due to erosion caused by the Colorado River as it ate its way headward toward the northwest. Once the river worked its way through the highlands on the western side of the ancient lake, the lake quickly drained into the Colorado and made its way to the sea. Over the eons, the winds eroded the softer sediment under the hard lava covering until only the eroded buttes remained. When I first noticed these spectacular mesas while standing at the Visitor Center counter and gazing out the window, I asked Ranger Chambers what they were called.

"Hoppy Butts," he told me. I learned their true names later. I also learned it was a mistake to ask Ranger Chambers anything concerning the Navajos, the Hopis, or the land.

I was also standing at that Visitor Center counter one day when I heard a noise out in the parking lot. I looked out the same window through which I could see the Hopi Buttes and I saw a drunken member of our Navajo work crew trying to get into one of our pickup trucks. It's not a myth that Indians are easily affected by alcohol. It doesn't take much to get them drunk and the young Navajos at our trailer park were frequently drunk and boisterous at night. But this was the middle of the day, and the one outside was so drunk he could hardly stand up. He certainly couldn't manage to get into the truck cab. He opened the door, but he couldn't get his foot up in order to climb in. Every time he lifted his foot, he lost his balance and fell down. And he kept getting right back up to try again. I was concerned, as we always left the keys in the ignitions of all trucks. That way, any Ranger could get into any truck without hunting down the key.

I called to Ranger Chambers in his back office. He came and stood beside me. He didn't seem concerned at the drunken Navajo struggling to get into our truck. "I'd better stop him," I said.

"No, leave him alone."

"If he starts the truck, he could crash it."

"If he starts the truck, we can get him for grand auto theft."

I looked at Ranger Chambers. Why, I wondered, would he want to get the drunken Navajo, who had no idea what he was doing and who, more over, was one of "our own," for grand auto theft? "He could smash into one of our other trucks," I said. "Or he could hit a tourist. I'd better stop him."

"Leave him alone," Ranger Chambers told me, but I was already out the door. The Navajo was just climbing to his feet after having fallen to the pavement once more. I grabbed him by the upper arm and pulled him away from the truck. I slammed the door and began walking him back toward the Visitor Center. He staggered and I held him up by his arm.

Just then a work truck filled with his buddies pulled into the lot. "Yah-tah-hey!" I yelled to them. They stopped and took their friend off my hands, manhandling him into the back of their truck. Then they drove off without saying a word. I went back inside the Visitor Center.

"I told you to leave him alone!" Ranger Chambers said as I entered.

"He was a danger to others."

Ranger Chambers glared at me, then stalked back into his office. Yet another action which has not endeared me to Ranger Chambers, I thought. I probably don't have a future in the Park Service, at least not at Wupatki.

But, there were also other reasons it seemed I didn't have a future in the Park Service. I just didn't share the worldview of the Rangers. They seemed to hate everybody. In addition to the

Navajos, they hated the turistas, who were just a pain in the butt. And they passionately hated the Sierra Club. The Sierra Club is America's largest environmental organization and its members proudly announced their membership when they came in, as if that would make them welcome to presumably fellow-minded Rangers. It didn't, although the Rangers forced themselves to be polite. The Rangers hated Sierra Club members because Sierra Club members actually *cared* about the ruins and the land, which the Rangers did not. To the Rangers, working at Wupatki was just another Government Service Administration job.

And the Rangers hated hippies. That summer rumor had it that there was going to be a giant hippie love-in at the Grand Canyon. Thousands of hippies were supposed to descend on the Canyon and fuck and do drugs and run amok. Like Rangers at other National Parks and Monuments all over the Southwest, we were notified to be ready to fly at a moment's notice to the Grand Canyon in order to beat hippie heads. The permanent Rangers were excited at the prospect of kicking hippie ass. I said nothing, but I realized I'd have to refuse to go. Or, if I went, I'd have to refuse to take any action against the hippies, because I was still a hippie myself, underneath my Park Service uniform. And refusing to kick hippie ass would certainly kill any future I might have with the Park Service.

And I wondered how the hell I managed to end up on the other side of the Sunset Strip divide. I was a hippie who'd shaved and cut my hair and now I was passing as a pig. Now I was the one who was expected to swing a club. I hadn't signed up for this at all, but how easy it'd been to become a pig.

I was still just a college kid, but I was always aware that I was also an authority figure. The Park Service badge I wore above my left breast pocket seemed to weigh about five pounds and I felt I listed to the left as I walked because of it. Some things about being an authority figure I didn't mind. Sometimes on patrol I'd drive up to the lonely Ranger station at the Citadel ruin and I'd see a family of turistas out on Antelope Prairie, heads down, collecting some of the pottery shards which littered the ground by the thousands. I'd stop and walk out to them.

"I'm going to have to ask you to toss those pottery pieces back," I'd tell them.

"Why," the father always asked. "There's thousands of them."

"There won't be if every family takes a bag full. Besides, we still haven't done a full archaeological inventory of the Monument. It's very possible that you've just picked up the only pottery shard on the Monument which proves that the people here had trade contact with some distant culture. And, because you removed it, we'll never know that." And what I said was true. It was on Antelope Prairie, for example, that the 11,000-year-old Clovis spearpoint was found. If a turista family had picked up that one spearpoint first, that history would have been lost forever.

And so the father told his kids to toss their shards back on the ground. And I'd done what I thought I'd signed on to do, I'd protected some of Wupatki's history.

But there were other aspects of being an authority figure I didn't like. I remember once walking through a grade school parking lot in Phoenix just as school was letting out. Of course, it was a school zone with a 15-mph speed limit. A motorcycle cop was parked out of sight by the side of the building. As I passed him I jokingly said, "So, trying to catch someone, eh?"

He looked at me, his mirror shades hiding his eyes. "No, I'm trying to save a life."

In those days I angered easily, especially at hypocrisy, and what I felt to be the cop's hypocrisy enraged me. "No you're not," I said. "If you were trying to save a life, you'd be out where drivers could see you and slow down. Hiding back here you'll get'em only *after* they've run down a kid. You're just trying to make your ticket quota."

"You'd best keep moving," the cop said.

As a Park Ranger, however, I found myself doing the same thing as that cop. Antelope Prairie was wide and flat and the road coming off Highway 89 was long and straight. Having driven at high speed on the highway, it was usually difficult for turistas to slow down to park speed on that stretch, even though there was a sign at the Citadel telling them the speed limit was now 45-mph. Often they'd not bother stopping at the Citadel, but drive right past it at full tilt, pedal to the metal, eager to get wherever it was they were going. Antelope Prairie was just a big empty space, so why not?

Just down the road from the Citadel station was a turn-off to a dirt road. As it met the paved road the dirt road forked. And in that fork was a huge bush, more than large enough to hide a pickup truck. So, like the other Rangers, I sometimes parked behind that bush out on Antelope Prairie, facing the pavement. Like as not, a turista would fly past me going flat out. When that happened, I fired up my engine, turned on my flashers, and roared out from behind that huge bush in a cloud of dust. I floored it and soon was right on the ass of the speeding turista.

What happened next was always the same. The turista pulled over and I parked behind him, engine running and flashers blinking. I took my time pulling out my ticket book, putting on my Smokey the Bear hat, and climbing out of the truck. I walked slowly up to the driver's side, conscious of the heavy weight of my badge above my left breast pocket, the turista's kids staring wide-eyed out the rear window at me. I stood a little behind the turista's open window, so he'd have to twist awkwardly to his left a little to see me and I could easily see everything he was doing. "Sir, do you know how fast you were going?" I asked.

"About 65?"

"About 75. Do you know what the speed limit is?"

"No, I don't." They never knew what the speed limit was.

"You passed a sign just a quarter mile back which told you the speed limit is 45-mph."

"I didn't see it." They never saw it.

"Sir, if I write you a speeding ticket, you'll have to return to district court in Flagstaff to deal with it. If you don't, you'll be fined and the government *will* get its money. I know you're on vacation with your family and you want to have a good time. But we also want you to arrive alive. I'm not going to write you a ticket this time, but I *do* want you to slow down and drive safely. Will you do that for your family, sir?"

"Yes, officer, I will."

"Thank you, sir. Enjoy your visit...and drive safely."

"Thank you, officer."

And then I walked slowly back to my truck, flashers still blinking, while the turista just as slowly drove away.

I never wrote a single speeding ticket, but I realized I *was* that motorcycle cop I'd berated for his hypocrisy. Like him, I was hiding from speedsters in order to catch them. I was doing it because I'd been told to do it. But, if I'd *really* been concerned about safety, I'd have parked on the *other* side of that big bush, so the speeding turistas could see my Ranger truck far in advance and slow down well before they reached me. It would have served the same purpose. But, I wouldn't have been displaying my authority. I realized I'd become a pig. And I'd become one so easily. And I didn't like it.

And I didn't like living and working in a military encampment. That's what Wupatki was. Every permanent Ranger there but one, from the Super on down, was a military vet. Even the female secretary who never left the office was a military vet. The Park Service was clotted with military vets because it was part of the federal government, and the federal government gave priority in hiring to military vets over civilians. And the one young permanent Ranger who wasn't a vet was eagerly biding his time until the fall, when he planned to join up and volunteer for Vietnam. No wonder they all were so eager to beat hippie heads.

    And I was not only a hippie passing as a pig, I was a Conscientious Objector trapped behind enemy lines. I kept my mouth shut and I continued to pass -- but I knew for sure there was no future for me in the Park Service.

The War at Home

"Let us have faith that right makes might, and in that faith, let us, to the end, dare to do our duty as we understand it."

-- Abraham Lincoln
The Cooper Union Speech
February, 1860

****

On June 6th, 1968, four days after Pink and I arrived at Wupatki, Bobby Kennedy was murdered in Los Angeles. A Palestinian, Sirhan Sirhan, put a .22 bullet in the back of his head because he thought Bobby was too friendly toward Israel. Any friend of the Jews had to die. Sirhan wanted to kill Bobby on June 5th, the one-year anniversary of the outbreak of the Six-Day War. He missed his target date by one day, but did not miss his target.

Bobby had just won the California Democratic Party primary. His last words to his supporters had been, "Now it's on to Chicago, and let's win there." Earlier, he'd won in Indiana. Despite jumping into the primaries late and having no real campaign organization, he'd beaten Eugene McCarthy time and again and it was clear he was going to beat the Hump -- Vice President Hubert Humphrey, LBJ's heir apparent -- at the August Democratic Party convention in Chicago. Then he was going to beat Nixon, become president, and end the war in Vietnam.

As of June 6th, none of that was going to happen. McCarthy remained in the race, but it was doubtful he'd be able to dump the Hump. Hubie would be the Democratic nominee and it really didn't matter whether he or Nixon was elected in November. The war would go on, more Vietnamese would die, more Americans would die.

My war against the war would go on, as well. I had not given up my fight to win Conscientious Objector status, regardless of what my local draft Board said, and now that struggle took on more urgency.

Even before leaving Phoenix for Wupatki, I'd launched the next phase of my battle against the S.S. System (I always referred to the Selective Service System as the S.S. System in letters to my Board), which entailed garnering support for my C.O. application from as many different sources as possible, letters attesting to my sterling character and the sincerity of my beliefs. As the Navajo cowboys had sat silently in my trailer, waiting until the appropriate time to speak, I'd been typing my next letter to my local draft Board. That July 15th letter to Mrs. Alice Dimmick, the Executive Secretary of my board and the one who handled all matters, said, "In your [April 12] letter, you stated that the Board was 'not convinced' of my qualifications for the I-O [Conscientious Objector] classification. As your letter was very vague as to the reasons for their doubt, I should like to ask you for the *specific* grounds upon which their decision was based.

"I should also like you to place...the enclosed letters in my file. The enclosed evaluative letters cover a wide area due to the fact that I do not know which exact area of my C.O. application the Board found inadequate. The enclosed letters are from:

"Bruce Smith, Chairman, Psychology Dept., Phoenix College; Steve Carson, Dean of Students, Phoenix College; Dr. Mary Maher, Chairman, English Dept., Phoenix College; the Rev. Raymond G. Manker, Minister, First Unitarian-Universalist Church of Phoenix; and the Phoenix Police Department."

I then cited U.S. Attorney General Ramsey Clark, from the July 12th issue of *Time*. "When the state itself kills," Clark said, "the mandate 'Thou shalt not kill' loses the force of the absolute...state-inflicted death chiefly serves to remind us how close we remain to the jungle."

I no longer have copies of the other letters, but the one from Rev. Ray Manker, dated June 20th, said in part, "I have found Eric to be unusually perceptive, very sensitive to the monitions of conscience and to his duties and responsibilities to his fellow man, society and to himself as a moral and ethical being....His ideas and mine in the area of religion, war, and the use of force are very similar....I am a conscientious objector and have maintained this position publicly and from the pulpit consistently through the years."

I'd met Rev. Manker because of Minnie Jack, one of my American literature teachers at Phoenix College. Minnie was a Unitarian and she maintained that my beliefs were compatible with Unitarianism. At her urging, I'd attended a few Sunday services at her church, the First Unitarian Universalist Church of Phoenix, out on Lincoln Drive in (how appropriate!) Paradise Valley, and gotten to know Rev. Manker. He was sympathetic to my fight for C.O. status. One Sunday morning he turned the entire church over to me and Annie and the two of us, Annie on guitar and me in the pulpit, presented antiwar poetry and song at that Sunday's service.

Ray had been raised as a Quaker before converting to Unitarianism. Understandably, he was a complete pacifist. This made it easy for him to obtain Conscientious Objector status when he first registered with the S.S. System in the 1940s. At that time the number of registrants applying for C.O. status was still quite small, so the FBI opened a file on every such registrant and sent two of its agents out to interview those who might know the registrant for the resulting dossier. By the late 1960s, the number of young men applying for C.O. status had increased to such numbers that the standard FBI background investigation had become too onerous a drain on the Bureau's manpower, so the Selective Service Act of 1967 eliminated the requisite FBI investigation of everyone who applied for C.O. status.

Once the FBI opens a file on someone, that file never closes. Especially if the someone is liberal, and Ray was liberal. After the Freedom of Information Act passed, Ray, like Professor Starsky at ASU, requested a copy of his FBI file. He discovered that the FBI had continued adding to his file throughout the Forties, the Fifties, the Sixties, the Seventies, and the Eighties. At his first church in Massachusetts during the McCarthyite Red Scare of the Fifties, Ray had been investigated for suspected solicitude toward Communists. Later, his Civil Rights activities kept him under surveillance. After he came to the First Unitarian Church of Phoenix in 1963, he was investigated for his opposition to the Vietnam War. When Ray Manker stands before St. Peter at the Pearly Gates, all he'll have to do to gain admission to heaven is submit a copy of his FBI file.

If he believed in heaven, that is. In his letter to my draft Board, a copy of which probably also ended up in his own FBI file, Ray stated that his and my ideas on religion were very similar. What he did not tell them but did tell me was that he was an atheist. How one can be an avowed atheist and also an ordained minister, I don't know, but it seems Unitarianism is extremely liberal. If I ever felt the need to join a church, I suppose it would be a Unitarian church. Ray certainly made his Unitarian congregation a welcoming community, unlike the Baptist and Mormon churches with which I was familiar.

However, the letters from Rev. Manker and the others made no impression on my Board, nor was it interested in giving a reason for rejecting my C.O. application. Mrs. Dimmick covered the Board's failure to articulate its rationale for rejecting my application by falling back on Standard Operating Procedure: "The Local Board does not make a practice of stating its specific reasons for disapproving a claim of conscientious objection." The struggle to get my draft Board to give specific reasons for rejecting my claim would thereafter take on increasing prominence in my war with the Board.

In that same letter, July 23, 1968, Mrs. Dimmick enclosed S.S. Form No. 127, a current information questionnaire similar to the one I filled out at age 18 in order to be properly classified by the S.S. System. One of the questions on it was whether I had any "physical or mental condition which, in your opinion, will disqualify you for service in the Armed Forces."

I did have a mental condition which disqualified me. In capital letters I explained it: "I am antagonistic towards the Armed Forces." No doubt this was not a diplomatic thing to write.

On July 29th I returned the questionnaire to Mrs. Dimmick, along with a new letter to her in which I wrote, "Although as a member of the Armed Forces I perhaps would not be put in a situation where I must kill a man, by becoming a part of an organization that kills I am lessening my own soul by co-operating in the eventual killing of a man."

Evidently my Board did not take my mental condition or my letter seriously. It again refused to re-classify me as a Conscientious Objector.

I remained immersed in the prehistoric past at Wupatki, but echoes from the outside world filtered in to my desert hermitage. The Republican convention came in early August, and Nixon was, indeed, the One. In late August came Chicago, and the whole world was watching as Hizzoner Mayor Richard Daley's cops rioted and beat the holy shit out of anyone who dared protest the war on the streets of the Windy City.

Meanwhile, inside the convention hall, the combined forces of Daley and the Hump rolled over McCarthy's antiwar delegates. The Hump became the Democratic nominee. What a choice! The Hump or Nixon for president in '68! No choice at all.

The only man who had a real chance to make a difference in 1968 was Bobby Kennedy and, shot from behind, he died in a pool of his own blood on the floor of the kitchen in L.A.'s Ambassador Hotel. Cities across the land did not burn when Bobby was killed, as they had when Martin had been murdered two months earlier. But hope burned and hope died with Bobby. There was a war going on in Vietnam...but there was also a war going on in America.

And it seemed every time we put our hope in some leader, that leader was shot down.

Finger on the Trigger

Things didn't look good when I walked into the dark garage. Then things went from bad to hell. Rick pointed his gun at me and said, "I'm going to give you a bullet in your Goddamn fuckin' head." He sounded like he meant it. One way or another, I figured this was probably the end of our relationship.

Rick was threatening to kill me because I'd come to collect the $75 he still owed me for my blue Suzuki. I'd sold the bike to him for $100 when I'd left for Wupatki. He gave me $25 at that time and said he'd send the remaining $75 to me in three installments over the course of the summer. So, I'd signed the title over to him. That turned out to be a mistake. Either he couldn't come up with the $75, or it wasn't important to him. After all, why bother? He already had the title. In any case, he never sent another penny to me.

Rick had changed greatly since the previous summer, the summer of '67, when we'd hitchhiked together across the country from Phoenix to Chattanooga. We'd never been closer. After that, we'd never be close again.

Rick had stayed behind at our Grandfather Frank's when I left Chattanooga for Sarasota. I don't know how long he stayed in Tennessee, but he was still there at the end of that summer when I returned to Phoenix from Sarasota. When he finally came back to Phoenix he had no money and no job, so he went back to Mom and the 51st Street house. Which meant he returned to battling Mom. He was 19 and, like me at 19, was trying to break free of her death grip. But she had her fingers around his throat and refused to let go.

When I returned from Wupatki in early September, I learned that the summer of '68 had been an eventful one for Rick. His struggle with Mom had come to a head during my absence. He'd finally moved out for good. But he still had no money and no job. So Marie Goldenkoff, Mom's good friend, now ex-friend, had taken him in.

Something had also changed between Mom and Marie. Two years before, Marie had been a stalwart support for Mom in her battle with me during my own fight to be free of her grip. Now Marie was giving aid and comfort to the enemy, Rick in this case. I thought at the time that this was perhaps because Marie had come to see that Rick and I had good cause to battle free of Mom's grip. Many years later, when I asked Mom about this rift, she said it was because she'd begun dating a Mexican, who became her husband (and thus, my new step-father), soon after she divorced Elmer. Marie, Mom said, despised Mexicans and was appalled at Mom's miscegenation.

Attached to her house, Marie had a garage with electrical connections for her freezer. A lot of Phoenix homes had freezers in their garages or on their covered car ports. The weather was warm in Phoenix, even in the fall, so the garage didn't need to be heated, and Rick could come into the house to use her bathroom. So Marie offered it as a place Rick could crash until he could find a place of his own. They moved in a cot and some blankets and Rick's radio, and Rick had a new home.

But he no longer had my blue Suzuki. Seems he'd become a hellion on wheels over the summer and had run it into the ground. Before he destroyed it completely, he used it in trade as part of his payment for a pickup truck. Which he also no longer had.

Even though he no longer owned my bike, nor even the truck he'd gotten for it, he still owed me $75, so I wanted to talk to him about when he planned to pay me.

I'd bought a new and larger bike with my Wupatki earnings. I paid for it in full, with cash. It was a gray 160cc Honda Scrambler with a cherry red gas tank, purchased right off the showroom floor in Flagstaff. Pink had dropped me off at the bike dealership and then driven my belongings down to Annie in Phoenix. I followed soon after on the Scrambler.

I'd also gotten my student loan and had paid a semester's worth of rent on a new apartment, a one-bedroom with a kitchen and a living room, for the same price as my previous cinderblock studio. And I'd paid for the upcoming semester at ASU, so I was broke once again.

Annie still lived next to the Westward Ho at the hotel owned by the parents of Tom Wagers. That day I rode the Scrambler over to pick Annie up and take her with me to see Rick. I thought I'd get at least some of the money Rick owed me and perhaps take Annie out to a fancy dinner. She'd soon be leaving for Pitzer College and I treasured every moment I could spend with her. Annie hopped on behind me and I drove to Marie's place on 51st Street, looking for Rick in his garage.

I roared up Marie's gravel driveway and stopped the Scrambler behind her house near the back entrance to her garage. Annie and I walked up to the garage door, which looked like a kitchen door, and I knocked. "Rick! You here?" I opened the unlocked door and we stepped into the interior gloom.

Rick rolled up off his cot, his gun in his hand. He pointed it at my face. "What the fuckin' shit do *you* want?"

"Well, nice to see *you,* too."

"Don't get cute with me. What the fuck do you want?"

"I think you *know* what I want, Rick. You promised to send the $75 you owed me for the Suzuki over the summer. You never did."

"I don't have the fucking Suzuki anymore."

"I know. But you still owe me the $75."

"I don't owe you shit. All I'm going to give you is a bullet in your Goddamn fuckin' head."

Rick was making me mad. I didn't like his attitude and I didn't like him pointing his Goddamn gun at my face. "Well, Rick, you've just dug a crawl space beneath your all-time low. What the fuck's wrong with you? I just came over to talk about the $75. Why are you pointing a gun at your own Goddamn brother?"

"As far as I'm concerned, we're no longer brothers. Now get the fuck out of here before I pull this trigger and blow your fuckin' ass to hell."

I thought about rushing Rick. The garage was dark, I could duck, I could reach him in a couple of steps and grab that gun out of his fist and slap him in the face with it. My body tensed and I bent over the slightest bit into a crouch, ready to jump and grab.

And then I felt Annie's hand gently touch my spine right between the shoulder blades. Shit! In my anger at Rick, I'd forgotten about Annie, standing right behind me. And I realized how stupid it would be to rush Rick. I was so fucking mad at Rick I was ready to risk my life in a rush at him. But I wasn't ready to risk hers. Rick was a fucking crazy asshole and he just might pull the trigger. He might hit Annie. Her life was worth more than a fucking $75. Hell, *my* life was worth more than a fucking $75!

I began to relax. I straightened up. Annie's hand left my back.

"Alright, Rick," I said slowly and with deliberate emphasis. "If that's the way you want it. It's *your* choice. If $75 is more important to you than being my brother, then that's the way it's going to be. We. Are. No. Longer. Brothers."

And then I turned, not caring if the fucker shot me in the back. I nodded for Annie to leave, and I followed her out of the garage into the bright sunlight. We got on my Scrambler and we left Rick in his dark garage with his gun and his grudge against me.

And I never saw Rick again before I left Phoenix for good. Why should I have? We were no longer brothers.

Fender Benders

I'm sitting in a Harvard Square cafe named "As You Like It" with my back to the wall and my eye on the door. In a restaurant or cafe, it makes me nervous to sit with my back to the door. I always sit so I can see who's coming in. If possible, I also sit where I can look out the window. I don't want to be taken by surprise.

If I'm with people and they happen to sit down first, taking the chairs facing the door, I ask if I might exchange places with them. If they ask why, I make a joke about it. "Jesse James was shot in the back," I say. "Wild Bill Hickock got it in the back of the head while playing poker by someone who had a grudge against him. I just don't want someone with a gun and a grudge against me sneaking up from behind and shooting me in the back."

And then we all laugh. And they let me have the chair facing the door. I know I'm being melodramatic and I don't really expect to be shot in the back. I'm not that important. But it still makes me nervous to sit with my back to the door.

So I'm sitting at a window table in "As You Like It" where I can watch the door and also watch the hordes jamming the Square outside. Directly across Mass. Ave. from me is the brick wall enclosing Harvard Yard, sheltering it from the chaos of the Square. To the left is the Out of Town News on its island in the middle of the Square. Heavy traffic parts at that island, some of it flowing up toward Cambridge Common, another stream flowing down onto Brattle Street.

"As You Like It" is indeed as I like it. I've gotten to know the waitresses on the mid-day shift and they let me sit here as long as I like, sipping my hot tea, reading the paper, glancing out the window now and then. It's low-key, casual, friendly. Named after Shakespeare's play, the decor is Elizabethan. The paper place mat on the table before me is filled with quotes from the Bard's plays. I've memorized some of them. "Blow, blow, thou winter wind," howls King Lear. "Thou art not so unkind as Man's ingratitude."

Suddenly there's the loud hard bang of smashed metal, followed by tinkling glass. I jerk my head up and look out the window. Right before me, out in the Square, some unwary driver in a nice Mercedes has plowed into the rear of a old Ford stopped at the light. It's not too bad as fender benders go, but it's possible the driver in the old Ford has suffered some whiplash.

The driver of the Mercedes is nicely dressed, white shirt, tie, jacket -- some kind of professional. A businessman, perhaps. He opens the door and gets out of his car, looking concerned, and starts walking toward the Ford. *Aw, Jeez,* I think. *What a moron.* I know what's going to happen next.

The driver of the Ford swings open his door and jumps out: jeans, tank top, beer belly - Joe Six-Pack. He runs toward Businessman, "You stupid fuck!" Then Pow! Pow! Pow! Joe Six-Pack punches Businessman in the face three times fast with a hard right.

Businessman reels back, surprised, startled. Pow! Pow! Pow! Three more fast and hard punches to the face, again with Joe's right. He grabs Businessman by the throat and begins bouncing Businessman's head on the hood of the Mercedes. Businessman's blood splatters his windshield. Joe's screaming all the time, "You Goddamn stupid fuck!"

If there'd been time, I could've told the Mercedes moron what was going to happen, but he wouldn't have believed me: morons like him think everyone's nicey-nice like them. They have to learn how the real world works in the school of fast and hard knocks. And the moron sure as hell was taking some fast and hard knocks out there in the Square. As traffic backed up behind his Mercedes, a police siren wailed in the distance and a crowd gathered to catch the action.

I knew what was going to happen to the Mercedes moron because it wasn't the first time I'd witnessed such a scene. The first time had been a continent and years away from Cambridge and Harvard Square in 1960 while I lounged on my Schwinn Black Phantom bicycle at the gas station across from the National Guard Armory at 52nd Street and McDowell in Phoenix. I was 14-years-old, a paperboy, and I picked up my newspapers in the pre-dawn darkness at that gas station, only it wasn't early morning when I saw the accident. It was around noon and traffic was moderate. Cars were stopped at the red light.

Then, Bam!, right in front of me a car plowed into one of the stopped cars. The impact made a lot of noise, but the accident wasn't too serious. The offending car was driven by a single male. The car he hit contained a middle-aged couple and, driving it, their adult son. It was an era before seat belts or air cushions, and the collision's impact had thrown the older man forward into the dashboard. Blood covered his face.

The driver who'd hit the parked car got out and began walking toward the parked car. The adult son leaped out of the parked car and ran to meet him, screaming "You hurt my father!"

"I'm so sorry," the other driver said, spreading his hands. "It was an accident."

Then the adult son was on him, smashing him in the face, screaming all the while, "You hurt my father, you Goddamn fucking bastard!"

Dazed by the attack, the offending driver staggered back, shock and surprise on his face. "I'm so sorry," he cried, as his assailant continued punching him. "I didn't mean to hurt him! I'm so sorry." His apologies didn't stop the beating, which ceased only when his assailant ran out of energy. He gave a final hard and fast kick to the stomach of the offending driver, lying bleeding on the pavement, and then went back to see about his own bloody father. This all took place about ten feet in front of me. There was nothing I could do about it except stand there with my bike and watch in amazement.

But I learned something the Mercedes moron hadn't, at least until his turn came in Harvard Square: You never know what's waiting for you down the road. One moment you're coasting down the road, not a care in the world. A moment later, a raging maniac is banging your head on the hood of your own car and splattering your blood all over your own windshield. The future's uncertain and death is always near.

And that's why I always sit with my back to the wall and my eye on the door.

Across the Mojave

Mile after mile the flat desert highway sped beneath the wheels of the Scrambler. Perhaps only Nevada's salt flats are more barren than Southern California's Mojave Desert. It's 100-miles of dry desolation from Indio to the Colorado River and the Arizona line. Despite my thick shades, I squinted against the harsh desert glare. Even at a steady 65-mph the wind was hot on my bare arms. L.A.'s wet dawn mist had long since evaporated from my clothes. Along with the steady rhythm of the engine pistons beneath me, the heat had a lulling effect. The only point of interest was the funhouse reflection of my distorted body visible in the cherry glaze of the gas tank nestled between my legs. There was nothing to my left and right, no twists or turns in the road, no changes in elevation, just flatness and desolation straight ahead into the blazing desert. It was easy to lapse into automatic pilot and drift off into thoughts of Annie as I drove, alone, deeper and deeper into the burning hell of the Mojave.

Annie had to get to Pitzer College, the elite private women's college to which she'd been admitted. It was in Claremont, California, part of the urban Los Angeles sprawl which stretched from the Pacific inland 100-miles to Indio. Tom Wagers, who might have driven her, had fled to San Francisco. And Vern had escaped to Cambridge, driving Tom's VW van. So I offered to drive her to Pitzer on my Scrambler.

That meant she couldn't take much. You can't carry much riding on the back of a motorcycle. But, that didn't bother Annie. She owned very little and she didn't care for possessions, anyway. She had a backpack. She stuffed it with some clothes, some personal items, her journals. That was all she needed.

She'd wear the new hiking boots I'd just bought her with my Wupatki earnings, the first she'd ever owned. I'd also bought a new pair for myself, the first I'd ever owned. We'd broken them in a few days before by hiking down into the Grand Canyon. It was the first time we'd actually made it *into* the Canyon. The first time we'd gone to the Canyon, we only got to the Rim, where we'd spent the night making love under an overturned river boat. This time we hiked down into it, all the way past Indian Gardens, down to the pea green river's edge, then back up.

It was a long, hot, tiring climb back up. Annie reached the Rim before me. She just kept plodding along while I rested and gasped for breath. Female endurance. Then she sat on the edge of the Rim and watched me climbing slowly far below on the trail. By the time I reached the top, she was waiting for me with an ice cold vanilla milkshake she'd bought from the Fred Harvey canteen at the trailhead.

We sat next to each other on the Rim, holding hands and sharing the milkshake. The sun set over the Grand Canyon in a golden blaze and then dusk slowly bled onto the horizon. The witchery of the fading light deepened the shadowy depths and heightened the spires. We sat rapt in revery as the darkness gathered around us. I noticed that Annie had a milkshake mustache and I kissed her, kissing away the mustache as she laughed, her laughter echoing out into the dark and empty Canyon.

And she'd laughed as we tumbled into her big brass bed back in her apartment on our last night together in Phoenix. The old ladies downstairs thumped on their ceiling as we made noisy love in the big brass bed. We ignored them and, when we at last lay sweating in each other's arms, the old ladies ceased thumping. Annie kissed me. "I'm going to miss you so much."

I smiled. "Not half as much as I'll miss you." I nuzzled her and whispered in her ear and we held each other close as we drifted into sleep.

We rose and left Phoenix at three the next morning. We had three hundred miles of desert highway and a hundred miles of L.A. sprawl ahead of us. We wanted to get as much of it behind us as we could before the heat of the day began to take its toll. We headed straight west on Highway 10, Annie hunched behind me out of the blast of pre-dawn cold. The sun rose behind us as we passed the Big Horn Mountains and then the Eagle Tail Mountains. It was desert all the way. About eight o'clock we suddenly came upon a long ribbon of green bisecting the road. We roared across the Colorado River and stopped for gas in Blythe, on the far side. Orchards of date palms grow along the river and I bought us date milkshakes for breakfast.

Then it was into the bleakness of the Mojave as the sun climbed toward noon. Fifty miles into the Mojave is a widening of the road called Desert Center. We stopped in the center of the desert and filled up on gas again. We stretched out the kinks and then climbed back on the Scrambler. Fifty miles more of burning desert and we pulled into Indio. We found a Denny's restaurant and shared our last meal together.

After that it was a maze of freeways, increasingly jammed, as we drove deeper and deeper into the heart of L.A. Eventually we found the turnoff for Claremont. Eventually we found Pitzer College. I took Annie's backpack with all her earthly possessions and carried it as we found the administration office. It took hours as we hiked in our new hiking boots from office to office.

Finally, Annie was assigned a dorm room. We found the dorm. Her roommate was already there. Annie asked if I could spend the night. The roommate looked uncomfortable. Annie didn't care. "I guess that'd be OK," the roommate said.

We shed our boots, collapsed into Annie's bed, and soon lapsed into exhausted sleep. I awoke in darkness at three in the morning. Annie was breathing quietly next to me. I kissed her cheek and she stirred. She opened her eyes, recognized me, and then hugged me close. "I'm going to miss you so much," I whispered.

Annie smiled. "Not half as much as I'll miss you."

I pulled on my boots as silently as I could, careful not to wake Annie's roommate. Annie walked me to her door. We clung to each other fiercely. I kissed her gently on her lips. She opened the door and I slipped out. Annie watched at the open door as I walked down the hallway. At the hallway's end I turned and waved. Annie blew me a kiss. Then I opened the door and walked out into the dark dawn.

A damp fog veiled everything. The Scrambler was pearled with dew, but it fired up instantly as I kicked it over. I headed out onto the L.A. freeway and turned east, eager to make as much distance as I could before the sun turned the Mojave into a furnace. The dawn mist coated my face with moisture until it rolled down my cheeks in tiny rivulets, like tears.

And then, once more, I was out in the barren and empty desert, heading back to Phoenix, a city even more barren and empty than the desert itself.

Part Eight
Children of the Revolution

The Grovel-In

Mark raised his clenched fist and, from the balcony of the seized ROTC building, shouted "End the militarization of the campus!" We applauded and cheered, but it was pro forma, and Mark knew it. Mark was the main revolutionary rabble rouser on the ASU campus. Some of us had become connoisseurs of Mark's rhetoric and critiqued his technique after each rally. We agreed he was improving his communication skills and was getting better at rousing the rabble. Which meant us. But this slogan wasn't making it, so Mark knew he'd have to do better to fire us up. He changed to something simpler for the rabble.

"ROT-C must go!" he began chanting, punching the sky with his fist. "ROT-C must go!" "ROT-C must go!"

That was more like it. The crowd of students standing in front of the ROTC building, of whom I was one, picked up his chant. "ROT-C must go! ROT-C must go!" And as we chanted, we also punched the sky with our fists. In high school, I'd been an ROTC cadet. Now I was demanding an end to the militarization of the ASU campus. Now I was demanding that ROTC be eliminated. Standing in the midst of the chanting students, following the lead of Mark on the balcony, it was hard to believe that I'd ever felt any other way.

Mark jumped to the podium to harangue the crowd at every antiwar rally, but this time I think he'd been trapped in his role of revolutionary leader. Across from the library, on the central mall of the campus, was the permanent Hyde Park soapbox, a concrete speaker's podium. Mark had been firing up the rabble with anti-ROTC rhetoric from it when one of the rabble yelled "Seize the ROTC building!" Immediately the rabble, us, began chanting "Do it! Do it! Do it!" Mark either had to do it or lose his leadership role. So he and about a dozen of the hottest firebrands did it. They led the rabble, *us,* down the mall toward the ROTC building and then they charged inside while the rabble, *us,* hesitated outside.

Moments later Mark appeared on the second floor balcony, surrounded by his revolutionary cadre, and continued his political theater for our benefit, with the entire ROTC building for his soapbox. "ROT-C must go!" he chanted, "ROT-C must go!" And we followed his lead, punching the sky with a hundred fists and echoing "ROT-C must go! ROT-C must go!"

Then the fat lady sang. The police appeared, the inevitable finale to the show. Paddy wagons and cop cars rolled up on the grassy sward behind the building and disgorged platoons of Tempe's finest. It was their turn to charge into the building. They suddenly appeared on the balcony behind Mark and his cohorts and a brief tussle ensued before Mark & Co. were dragged out of sight. The rabble, meaning *us,* surged around to the back of the building just in time to see the struggling revolutionaries hustled out a back door and into the waiting paddy wagons. Rings of cops surrounded the wagons, and rings of the rabble, *us,* surrounded the cops. "Pigs off campus!" we began shouting, "Pigs off campus! Pigs off campus!"

The wagons began to leave and some of us sat down, crosslegged, in front of them. The cops on foot cleared a path for the slowly moving wagons, pulling and tossing us aside. And then the wagons were gone and only the police occupied the ROTC building. The entire action, from the first rousing of the rabble to the arrest of our leaders, had taken about an hour. Mark and his comrades were charged with trespassing, but he was not expelled and was soon back on campus rousing the rabble. And ROT-C also remained on campus.

Even so, there were more antiwar actions than ever on the ASU campus that fall of 1968. The silent Wednesday noon vigils, in which I always stood, continued. Mark and Professor Starsky and others continued to rant against the war. There was no SDS chapter, so the Vietnam

Day Committee, the main radical group at ASU, led antiwar marches down Mill Avenue, Tempe's main street. The Committee also became more imaginative. For instance, instead of attempting to tear down the American flag on campus, the Committee surrounded it with a vast field of small white wooden crosses.

The best activity the Committee ever sponsored was Freak Week. Fraternities and sororities were big on campus and every year they took over the main mall for a five day celebration called "Greek Week." In the name of fairness and balance, the Committee argued that the ASU powers should also allow the Committee to put on a five day celebration of music and political discussion. The Committee also promised there would be no building seizures. So the administration agreed. The result was Freak Week.

There were two big oppositional cultural groupings on campus: Politicos, represented by the Vietnam Day Committee, who were obsessed with radical politics; and "freaks," representing the counter-culture, hippies, the long hairs into dope and rock who wanted nothing to do with the politicos, because the politicos were straights, mainstream society. For one week though, Freak Week, the Committee bridged the cultural divide and brought the freaks and the politicos together to celebrate both radical politics and the counter-culture. The freaks jumped at the possibility because it was a legitimation of their existence. The politicos liked it because the hippies were a helluva lot more colorful and fun than they were. The hippies brought in rock bands, every day the mall was a vast concert arena, and there was dancing in the streets -- or at least on the mall.

Whenever the hippie bands didn't rattle the windows of the surrounding buildings with their speakers turned up to eleven, the politicos held teach-ins about the history of the Vietnam War and the concept of imperialism. Far more students danced to the blasting bands than listened to the politicos, but even so more students were exposed to alternative interpretations of the war than would have otherwise been.

Around this time I discovered the ASU Civil Liberties Union (ASU-CLU), a student club affiliated with the Arizona chapter of the American Civil Liberties Union (ACLU). While it was recognized by the university and had a faculty advisor, the ASU-CLU was completely dormant. It had no members, nor had there been any for almost a year. According to university regulations, within a few days it was slated to go out of existence.

I decided not to let that happen. My student government experience at Phoenix College had taught me how to do this. I quickly rounded up enough friends to fill all of the club's official positions, with me as president. We visited the faculty advisor and, after we introduced ourselves, he notified the ASU administration that the ASU-CLU was back in business. We made it just under the wire.

The club's new vice president was Richard Jones, a poet philosopher I'd met at one of Vern's happenings. Richard had been a favored student in one of Vern's philosophy classes at Phoenix College and was now at ASU.

Richard had been at a friend's house playing wiffleball in the backyard. They worked up a sweat and, since everyone was in cutoff jeans, Richard ran toward the friend's sunken swimming pool to cool off. He executed a beautiful dive into the pool -- which had only a few feet of water. Richard's head smacked into the concrete bottom. His neck was broken instantly and he was almost completely paralyzed from the blow. Able to move only his hands, and then just barely, he paddled on his back to the pool's ladder and grasped it with a single finger to keep himself afloat. He called for help and his friends came running. "Don't touch me!" he yelled. "My neck's broken. Call an ambulance."

Richard was lucky. He was in the hospital for a long time but the spinal cord injury wasn't as bad as it could have been. The spinal cord had not been severed. And, with extensive physical therapy, he was eventually able to walk again, although with a jerky shambling gait. Vern never visited Richard in the hospital during all that time. Because Vern said he considered hospitals places of moral pollution, and he did not want to diminish his soul by visiting Richard in such an environment. Vern also said he considered Richard's broken neck a case of instant karma. In Vern's worldview, there was no such thing as an accident, and sickness was a matter of morality, not microbes. In some fashion, Vern felt, Richard had brought his broken neck upon himself. Vern's blame-the-victim attitude didn't seem to bother Richard. He said he understood where Vern was coming from. I understood too, but I didn't like it.

Richard was determined to live a normal life. When he finished his therapy he got his own small apartment and bought a Japanese motorcycle. It was bigger than my Scrambler, so it had an electric starter. Once he was on it, you couldn't tell there was anything wrong with him.

The most treasured books in Richard's small paperback library were his philosophy tomes and his poetry collections. He could explain the Romantic Movement and Friedrich Nietzsche's Apollonian and Dionysian values. He could discuss with equal fluency Hermann Hesse's *Siddhartha* and his *Steppenwolf*. He could deconstruct the poetry of Goethe and the poetry of Shelley. I learned more just sitting around chatting with him than I've learned from most of my professors. Richard wrote page after page of poetry himself, much better than any of my pathetic attempts. I admired his guts and I admired his mind. He was the first real intellectual I ever met who was my own age.

As officers of the ASU-CLU, Richard and I attended all the meetings of student organizations on campus. As leader of the ASU-CLU, I also got to know the officers of the Arizona chapter of the ACLU and, because we were an official student organization, we were allowed to post announcements and leaflets on various campus kiosks.

We used that license to display a large poster every Monday on the main kiosk at the entrance to the mall. In huge black letters the poster said, "THE WAR IS OVER!" In much smaller letters underneath, it said, "...for 30,000 G.I.s," or whatever the number of dead G.I.s had climbed to that week. We kept track of the casualty figures and each Monday we updated the number with the new body count. Every week the total number of U.S. soldiers killed in Vietnam rose by at least another hundred. The war had dragged on for over four years since the Gulf of Tonkin and the dead kept piling up. In the first half of 1968, from January to the end of June, 9,557 G.I.s were killed, more than in all of 1967. In the more than 100,000 air missions over North Vietnam since February, 1965, the U.S. had lost 900 planes and 1,500 airmen killed, captured, or missing. It seemed there would be no end to the climbing casualties, as the war had become a permanent part of our lives.

Both Richard and I depended on government financial aid to attend ASU, so we were appalled when the Arizona legislature passed a measure declaring that any student who participated in a protest rally of any kind, not just antiwar, would be stripped of any aid that student received from the state. This seemed like a blatantly un-American violation of every citizen's Constitutional right to freedom of assembly and freedom of speech. As the leaders of the campus Civil Liberties Union we felt we had to do confront the Arizona legislature on this decision.

We decided to hold a "Grovel-In" on the grounds of the state capitol building. It would be a protest rally in which we begged the Arizona legislature not to rescind our financial aid for publicly grovelling before them. We made posters announcing the Grovel-In for noon on an upcoming Saturday. One of the other club members was a good artist and he drew a cartoon for the poster which depicted a student grovelling pathetically in the dust. We tacked the posters up all over campus. We didn't know how many students might show up, but Richard and I would certainly be there.

That Saturday I reached the capitol grounds just before noon. I parked the Scrambler and walked toward the front lawn of the capitol building. No one was there except two older men sitting under two trees on opposite sides of the lawn. Both wore shades and both had cameras with telephoto lenses strapped around their necks. We hadn't notified the media, more out of ignorance than anything else, so I figured they had to be pigs. I stopped well before reaching them and also sat down under a tree. It was a typical sunny and beautiful Arizona day. It was pleasant sitting in the shade and feeling a cool breeze on my bare arms.

Noon came, but no one else came. Then 12:30 came and the two pigs with the cameras decided no one would be grovelling that day. They rose, met each other, talked for a minute or two, and walked away, their cameras swinging from their necks.

About 15 minutes later Richard pulled up on his bike. He parked next to the Scrambler and shuffled over to where I sat under my tree. "Sorry I'm late, got here as soon as I could."

"No problem. You saved us from having our pictures end up in some Red Squad file. Two pigs were waiting to take fotos of the grovelers, but they left when no one showed to grovel."

"Well, I'm here to grovel."

"Then let's do it!"

Richard and I walked out from under my tree to a clear sunny space on the capitol building lawn. We kneeled facing the building, Richard with some difficulty, and then we performed three salaams with our hands high above our heads. We bowed low, touching our hands to the ground before us. And each time we bowed we begged the state legislature, "Please don't take away our student aid! Please don't take away our student aid! O, pleeeze don't take away our student aid!" We grovelled before the Arizona state legislature as we promised to do, even though we were the only ones to grovel. After the last salaam we collapsed laughing on the lush lawn of the state capitol building.

And we learned something important. ASU students could not be counted on to read our posters and come to our protests. But we could depend on the pigs to do both.

Carlo the Magnificent

I was late getting to the Vietnam Day Committee meeting that night. When I arrived at the large hall on the ASU campus, I could barely get inside. It was jammed with hundreds of radicals and I was stuck in the rear behind a wall of backs. The hall was hot and stank of sweat. Far in the distance I could see the Committee leaders on the stage. With them was Carlo. I was pleased. He'd gotten there first and, somehow, had been invited up on stage. Perhaps the Committee had already agreed to sponsor a performance of our acting troupe.

But something was strange. Except for Carlo, saying something from the stage, the hall was absolutely quiet. All those hundreds of Lefties in front of me were listening with rapt attention to Carlo. And Carlo sounded different. He was speaking with a thick and lilting accent which sounded vaguely Middle Eastern. And he was making cryptic comments on the Committee's antiwar strategy and tactics. Every time someone on stage said something, they waited, expectantly, for Carlo to respond. And Carlo did, saying something right out of Kahlil Gibran. And I suddenly realized that, somehow, before I'd arrived, Carlo had convinced them he was some exotic mystic who brought them the esoteric wisdom of the East.

Carlo looked the part. He was large and muscular, with a head shaven as smooth as a billiard ball. Today, such hairless male heads are common. At that time, except for Telly Savalas and certain black militants, no guys shaved their heads. In addition, Carlo's shining bare head made his dark Van Dyke beard even more prominent. And his accent was damn convincing. If I hadn't known him, I'd have been fooled too. Carlo Mancini was the best damn actor I ever knew.

Carlo had almost no social awareness at all. As an actor he knew how to dramatize himself. His looks, his actions, his voice, everything about him was theatrical. But he was often completely unaware of how he affected people.

And that was the case now. I realized that almost every radical at ASU was there and Carlo had beguiled them all. He was not an ASU student, they'd never seen him before, he simply appeared in their midst, a paragon of arcane wisdom spouting opaque aphorisms they didn't understand because, they assumed, they lacked the insight. I cringed and hoped that Carlo would keep up the subterfuge until he'd persuaded them to sponsor our performance. If he dropped the pose, if he dropped the accent, all of them would feel like fools for having been taken in by the charlatan before them, the imposter who had wasted their precious time with his charade. Please, Carlo, I begged him silently, keep it going!

But, as I said, Carlo lacked social awareness. As I cringed in the back of the hall, praying that Carlo would keep it going, he suddenly dropped the accent and the pose. He began talking just like them. And then he sat revealed as someone just as befuddled as them. His ancient aphorisms, his mystic insights which they had struggled to decipher, were all just a sham. He'd fooled them completely. And no one likes to be made a fool.

Carlo explained who we were. He explained that we, the Universal Players, wanted the Committee to sponsor us in an antiwar theatrical performance. And he justified his Carlos Castanada act as a demonstration of what good actors we were.

It was all hopeless. The crowd hardly listened to him. They were too busy booing him. "Get the fuck off the stage!" they yelled. "Get the hell outta here, you Goddamned fraud!"

Carlo sat on the stage, paralyzed like a deer in the headlights. He had no idea why the hundreds who had been so riveted on his every word were now hurling abuse at him. I just wanted to silently slip unnoticed out the back and abandon Carlo to his fate. It seemed suicidal to cast my lot in with his and share in the abuse. But he was my buddy and my comrade, and I had to rescue him if I could.

I stood on my chair, spread my arms wide, lifted my booming voice, and called from the back of the room. "Let me speak! Let me speak! I'm with that man on stage and I'd like to explain. Let me speak!"

I continued yelling, eventually making myself heard. The angry crowd quietened and, necks craning, turned toward me on my chair in the back. "Perhaps my friend was mistaken in misleading you as he did," I said. "But he did not do so in order to make fools of you. He meant well. He merely wanted to demonstrate the acting ability of our troupe in hopes that you would sponsor our antiwar performance."

"Like hell we will," one of the Committee leaders yelled from the stage. "Whether he meant to or not, he's wasted enough of this meeting's valuable time and I advise you to leave now while you still can!"

The assembled radicals echoed that sentiment with howls of rage even louder than before. I motioned for Carlo to come down from the stage to the rear of the hall where I stood on my chair. Carlo stepped down and walked nervously up the aisle toward me. The radicals continued to heap insults on him in wave after wave of anger, but no one moved toward him. I was relieved when he reached me and I climbed down from my chair to put my hand on his shoulder. Together, as if I were his escort, we walked through the doors and out into the night, leaving the still-shouting radicals behind us. When we were safely away from the hall I turned to Carlo.

"That was one of the stupidest things I've ever seen. We both could've been beaten badly by that crowd. You made'em crazy with anger."

"I just wanted to show'em we could act."

"But they didn't *know* you were acting. You made'em feel like fools."

"So, I blew it."

"You blew it, Carlo. Let me handle these things in the future."

"I'm sorry, Eric."

"Me too, but what's done is done. Forget it. Case closed."

****

As with Richard Jones, I'd met Carlo at one of Vern's happenings. Vern routinely gathered around himself those of his Phoenix College students who seemed gifted in one way or another. Thus, there were always student musicians, poets, actors, and those with special skills of one kind or another revolving around him. I always thought Carlo was a better actor than Nick Nolte, another of Vern's actor students, but Carlo didn't have the local stardom of Nick. So, while Nick played King Creon, Carlo was cast as just another spear carrier, or another Conquistador in *The Royal Hunt of the Sun*. While Nick was Biff in *Death of a Salesman*, Carlo was just a walk-on. He was always undervalued in dramatic plays.

But when Carlo did the nose scene from Edmund Rostand's *Cyrano de Bergerac*, everyone in the audience roared with laughter. He could look and play mean if the role called for it, but he was a big pussycat who always kept us laughing. Once, when he was touring the country with a traveling troupe while I thought he was in Hollywood, I got the following letter from him:

"Dear Eric: Believe it or not this 30th day of October I'm in Columbus, Ohio. Yeah, I know, 'What the hell is that idiot doing in Columbus?' Well, it's like this. I met this girl in a Los Angeles tavern who looked lonely and weary. She poured out her soul and troubles to me saying that her lover had left her. She said they had a house and kids in the East. Now the rent was just about due and the landlord demanded the money or he would tie her to the subway tracks. So, like a chump, I forsook my dreams in the great palaces of Plastic City and followed her East.

"No sooner did we arrive at a modest little shack on the outskirts of Columbus but a man bearing a striking resemblance to Akim Tamirov clomped me on the head with a lead pipe. When I awoke two days later, I discovered my fate. I was a prisoner gigolo in a cheap red light district gigolohouse which secretly caters to the rich old ladies of Haversten Heights. They work us long hours giving us only the sparest portions of potato gruel and compressed balls of horse fat. Giant gnomes with whips and cans of Mace guard the exits against escape.

"Eric, it's hell! The poor girl I met in the California tavern owns the place and every couple of hours she pulls a Joan Crawford on us, yanking a whip from a shivering gnome and, screaming hysterically, flails it on the privates of the more well-endowed of us. Needless to say, I suffer the most from her wrath. If you can't save me, Eric, at least send some younger business!"

And so it continued, page after page of Marx Brothers craziness. I never did find out from that letter what the hell Carlo was doing in Columbus, Ohio.

The idea of working with Carlo came to me when I discovered a new club called the "Vaudeville" on North Miller Road in the upscale Phoenix suburb of Scottsdale. Jay, the owner, had opened the Vaudeville with a grand vision. He wanted to provide improv theater and comedy along the lines of 16th century Italian Commedia dell'arte, a form of street theater with stock characters, such as Pantalone, Arlecchino, and Dottore, stereotypes recognized by their exaggerated quirks: crankiness, foolishness, and pomposity. There was a standard script, but it was acceptable to incorporate into it whatever happened on stage (or off) in an improvisational manner. Thus, no two performances were ever the same. It was loosely structured chaos.

Jay's vision was a nice idea -- but there wasn't anyone around to provide the requisite talent. Meanwhile, acoustic folk singers were still to be had for the asking in Phoenix, so he put folkies up on the stage to fill the time and space. But Jay was still looking for actors who were slightly crazy and willing to try Commedia dell'arte. I thought Carlo good enough to fit the bill.

It also occurred to me that the Vaudeville gig might be a way to insure that Annie and I stayed together. Vern still felt that I was too lower class for his daughter, and he was sure that Annie and I would grow apart once Annie was out of town. Away at college, she'd find someone more appropriate for her, a fellow student at the private colleges in the Claremont College complex. Or perhaps I would find someone else. The "infatuation" we had for each other would wither and die a normal death due to the distance between us. I was determined not to let that happen, and the Vaudeville was a means of preventing it.

Annie and I had perfected a two-person rendition of *Spoon River Anthology,* which we'd already performed in her speech class at North High. I asked Carlo to join us in expanding the production and adding more variety. He readily agreed. Then I approached Jay and told him I belonged to a small theatrical troupe called, um, "The Universal Players." We had a three-person production of *Spoon River,* with music, running about 45-minutes. Would he be interested?

Desperate, Jay readily agreed. He said he'd pay us $100 for one performance, just to see how it went. If Carlo and I didn't take any of the $100 -- and neither of us wanted any of it -- that'd be just enough to fly Annie in from L.A., round-trip, for a long weekend.

So Annie flew in the Friday of the last weekend of September. I picked her up at Phoenix's Sky Harbor Airport and drove her on the Scrambler directly to my empty new apartment. As I drove, Annie reached around my waist, as if she were holding on, and clung to my crotch, squeezing. I drove all the way home with my prick straining against my jeans. There we frantically tore off each other's clothes. We fell onto the one-man U.S. Army bed I'd bought at the Army-Navy store and we made love like we hadn't see each other for years.

Afterward, as we lay exhausted in each other's arms, soaked in our sweat, Carlo banged on my door. His pounding boomed through my empty apartment. "Eric, Annie, open up! It's Carlo! I know you're in there fucking! The Scrambler's out here."

I slid out of bed and pushed up the bedroom window. Still nude, I stuck out my head and yelled to Carlo. "Hold your pecker, will ya? I gotta get dressed."

As I pulled my head back in, the window slid smoothly down, trapping both my hands which I'd rested on the window sill. I was surprised more than hurt, but I couldn't move. Annie hopped out of bed and whapped the window with the heel of her hand. It slid up and then down again, giving me just enough time to jerk my hands out of the way before it slammed closed.

And then Annie and I began giggling like two silly kids. Carlo kicked the door again, loudly. "I hear ya in there laughing! Open up, will ya? I can't hold my pecker much longer!"

I wrapped a towel around my waist while Annie, still nude, slid back under the sheet. When I opened the door, Carlo saw me nude but for the towel and said, "Well butter my buns and call me a biscuit! You started without me! I was looking forward to a *menage a trois*."

"Well you can just keep holding your pecker. It's a private party."

"Damn, just my luck! The way this day's been going, if it were a fish I'd throw it back. Can we at least rehearse? Or are you two just gonna fuck all night?"

"Of course we're gonna rehearse. Will that make you happy?"

"As happy as a sissy in Boys' Town." Carlo stepped inside and walked to the open door of the bedroom. "Hey, Annie, any room for me under that sheet?"

"O, Carlo," Annie cooed. "You're just so big and muscular that there's just no room at all for you in this teeny tiny little bed. I'm sooo sorry."

"Well, I guess that's the way the Mercedes Benz. Just as well. I get these terrible muscle cramps in my legs when I fuck. Last night my ol' lady was on top of me and I was buckin' like a bronc when my leg cramped up. God, it hurt, and I began yelling, 'Oh, God! Oh, Jesus! Oh, fuck! Oh, God!'

"And then Amy, bouncing on me like a buckeroo, began yelling, 'Oh, yes! Yes! Yes!'

"'Amy,' I yelled, 'Get off! Get off!'

"'I'm tryin'!' she yelled, 'I'm tryin'! I'm tryin'!'

"Meanwhile, I'm screaming in pain like a banshee. Then Amy gets off…and then she gets off. She said it was the best sex we had in a long time, but I'm thinking about a vow of chastity. Anywho, ya better get up and get dressed so we can rehearse. We have our first performance as a threesome tomorrow night. On stage, that is."

"It's good to see you, too, Carlo."

We rehearsed until dawn. Carlo was familiar with *Spoon River* and picked up his parts quickly. Each poem in the play stands alone as an autobiographical monologue. They fit together in a montage which, collectively, presents a powerful impression of life in the small Illinois town of Spoon River in the last days of the 19th century. I acted as director, mixing and matching the poetry collage with Annie's music.

Besides Mimi, her cat, who'd lived with Pink and me at Wupatki, Annie had left her guitar with me when we rode the Scrambler across the Mojave to Pitzer. The guitar sat in a corner of my bedroom, a constant reminder of how much I missed Annie. Sometimes Mimi, brushing up against it in the middle of the night, knocked it over, startling me out of my sleep. Then I'd pick it up and strum it awkwardly, pretending I was listening to Annie play. Now I didn't have to pretend. Annie was there, in my living room, playing and singing with us all night long.

Carlo left at dawn and Annie and I crashed. She'd not slept since leaving Pitzer almost 24 hours before. We woke in the early afternoon and shared some Afternoon Delight. We showered, dressed in our show clothes, and climbed on the Scrambler, Annie clutching her guitar.

It was a Saturday night and the Vaudeville was jammed. Jay had a procession of folkies, all pretty good. Then he introduced us. "Ladies and gents. From the beginning here at the Vaudeville, we desired to present theatrical, as well as musical performances. Tonight, we are pleased to present our debut theatrical performance. Put your hands together and give it up for the very talented Universal Players in their version of the popular *Spoon River Anthology.*"

Jay didn't know if we were talented or not. He'd just taken my word for it. It was all an experiment and he was nervous.

He need not have worried. We got a standing O. And afterward, I introduced Carlo as a master of improvisation who would entertain the audience with impersonations of any one or any thing they cared to shout out. And shout out they did, eagerly, excitedly, laughingly. Cary Grant. John Wayne. Richard Burton. A flushing toilet. A talentless opera soloist. A Christmas tree shedding its needles. The audience quietened, listening, and heard the needles drop from Carlo's tree. And then erupted in applause. We were a success.

And Jay was happy. "Can you come back next weekend?"

Annie and I looked at each other. "No," I said. "Not next weekend." Still looking at Annie I continued, "How 'bout the weekend after that?" Annie nodded.

"Great! You're booked."

After that, Annie flew in from Pitzer every other weekend. We made love, we rehearsed with Carlo, we laughed, we played, we sang, and we began to build a small reputation.

And Annie and I stayed together, despite the distance.

Civics Lesson

In 2004, with a 56% majority, Arizona voters passed the anti-immigrant Proposition 200. The referendum denied certain state and local benefits to illegal immigrants. It also required state-issued photo identification proving citizenship in order to register to vote. The following year, 2005, over a third of those attempting to register -- 35% -- were rejected for insufficient proof of citizenship in Phoenix's Maricopa County, the state's largest county in population.

But Proposition 200, touted as a means of keeping illegal immigrants off the voter rolls, actually had nothing to do with keeping illegals from voting. By 2006, of Arizona's 2.7 million registered voters, only 238 were believed to have been non-citizens in the years 1996-2006. Of those 238, only four actually voted during that decade. Both numbers are so low they approach invisibility. Illegals, who are not likely to be integrated enough into the American political universe to care who is elected, are also not likely to risk a felony and then deportation in order to vote illegally. In fact, most don't want to interact with government officials -- even people staffing a poll -- in any capacity whatsoever. They, too, wish to remain invisible.

The new law, therefore, was aimed at a problem which did not exist. But, the ostensible problem was but a smoke screen. As it happens, the driving force behind the measure was the Arizona Republican Party, and the new law was actually aimed at disenfranchising those legitimate American citizens most likely to lack proof of citizenship: Mexican-Americans, blacks, and Indians. These particular citizens are also the ones most likely to vote Democratic. Together, blacks, Indians, and Mexican-Americans constitute a majority of the people living in Phoenix. Because so many of them have been disenfranchised, political power in this "minority majority" city is still controlled by the minority whites, just as in South Africa under apartheid. As it also happens, most white voters in Phoenix are Republican. Proposition 200, then, was merely a means to ensure continued minority white-Republican power in Phoenix and in Arizona.

There was nothing new about this power grab. Arizona Republicans have a long history of disenfranchising new Democratic voters. Indeed, they did it to me.

November 5, 1968, was the first Tuesday after the first Monday in November of that year, Election Day. The 26th Amendment to the Constitution, lowering the voting age to 18, would not become law until 1971; you had to be 21 to vote in 1968, the last presidential election limited to those 21 and older. I'd turned 21 the previous December, so I was able to vote in 1968.

I'd travelled a long way in my understanding of the Vietnam War. At the time of the Gulf of Tonkin Incident in '64, I'd been gung-ho for the war. But I'd come to realize that, at the time of the Gulf of Tonkin, I didn't know shit about what was really going on in Vietnam. I'd come to realize the war was a criminal war, that we were the aggressor. Therefore I understood that not only was it a war we could not win, it was a war we *should not* win. The president and all his men called anyone who opposed our war of aggression a "traitor." But it was the president, and all his men, who were the traitors. They had betrayed the best principles of democracy and humanity for which America supposedly stood. They had unleashed a whirlwind of death and destruction on a poor people on the other side of the world who were fighting for their freedom and independence.

Everything our leaders told us about the war was a lie, and everything they represented was wrong. And when you see something that's wrong, you have to do something about it; you have to do what you believe is right -- even if your leaders and people around you call you a traitor.

I had done what I could. I applied for Conscientious Objector status, and registered to vote as a Democrat. At the time of the previous presidential election in 1964, I'd been a member of Youth for Goldwater and had rallied for Goldwater as the Republican candidate. But the Democratic Party seemed to be the best electoral hope of stopping the war. To me the most significant event of the 1968 election was the revolt within the Democratic Party against Johnson and the Vietnam War by Minnesota Senator Eugene McCarthy and Bobby Kennedy. I wanted to be a part of that revolt. The Democrat I supported when I registered was McCarthy who, as an explicitly antiwar candidate, challenged LBJ for the party's nomination.

Then Bobby jumped into the race, and it no longer seemed that toppling Johnson, and then his hand-picked successor, Hubert Humphrey, was an impossible dream.

When Bobby, like Martin before him, was shot down, Mayor Richard Daley and the Democratic Party machine rolled over McCarthy and the antiwar forces at the party's Chicago convention in August. Instead of a New Hope as the Democratic candidate, we got the Hump, tired old Hubert Humphrey, representing the tired old politics of the past.

I had no enthusiasm for the Hump, but I had a responsibility to vote, to use any means available to resist the war, no matter how insignificant my resistance seemed. Since his nomination in August, the Hump had begun distancing himself from LBJ's war policy, so he seemed to be the lesser of two evils.

The greater evil was the Republican candidate, Richard Nixon. He had begun trying to capitalize on the war's unpopularity by claiming that he, too, was antiwar and that he had a plan to end the war soon. He couldn't tell us what that plan was, however, because it entailed delicate negotiations and premature publicity would spoil it. We just had to trust him and his "secret plan" and vote for him if we were truly antiwar.

But I didn't trust that Nixon had a secret plan to end the war. I hadn't trusted him when I'd been a Goldwater Republican in high school and I trusted him even less now that I was a Democrat in college. I intended to step into the voting booth, hold my nose, and pull the Democratic lever for the Hump.

But I knew something was wrong when I walked up to the table just inside the polling station and gave the man sitting there my name. He began flipping the pages of the large ledger filled with names and addresses on the table before him. "What did you say your name was?"

"Eric Davin."

A young man dressed in a suit and holding a clipboard stacked with sheets of paper was standing just behind him. The young man, who was about my age, began riffling quickly through his sheets. He found what he was looking for and whispered in the ear of the man with the ledger. He showed ledger man something on his clipboard and ledger man nodded. "I'm sorry," ledger man said, "you can't vote."

"And why not?"

"Because you no longer reside in this voting district."

I'd registered while living at the cinderblock apartment. After returning from Wupatki, I rented a new apartment. But I hadn't changed my voting address. I thought I'd just go back to the polling station for my cinderblock apartment and vote there. I didn't think there'd be any problem with that, as I wasn't registered anywhere else. I'd thought wrong.

But, how could they know I'd moved? I thought I'd push it. "Why do you say that?"

The well-dressed young man with the clipboard spoke up. "Because we sent a registered letter to you at your voting address. It was returned to us marked 'Undeliverable. Addressee unknown.' You no longer reside there."

"And who the hell are *you* and who is 'we'?"

"I'm a poll watcher for the Republican Party. That's who I am and who 'we' are."

"But I'm not registered anywhere else," I said to ledger man. "I'm not trying to vote twice. If I can't vote here, I can't vote *anywhere.*"

"I'm sorry," he said. "It's the law. You have to be an actual resident at the address where you are registered. It seems you are not. Therefore, you cannot vote at this polling station."

I glared at the poll watcher. "Do you have any newly registered *Republicans* on your list?"

He didn't even bother to look. "Not on *my* list."

I clenched my fists. A real man doesn't take shit from *anyone.* "Well, *fuck you in the ass*, you Goddamned Republican asshole!"

The Republican asshole smiled at me serenely. "No, I think *you're* the one fucked in the ass, just like all the other new Democrats on my list."

I felt like tossing the table in front of me aside and punching the smirking Republican asshole behind it in his smirk. But that would've just gotten me thrown in jail for assaulting a poll watcher, and it would've been good publicity for the Republicans. There was nothing I could do except swallow my anger and leave before they called the cops.

I gave the Republican asshole the finger. "Eat shit and die you shit-eating maggot!" Then I spun and stalked out of the polling station. The smirking Republican asshole was probably still smirking at me as I left, but I didn't give him the small satisfaction of me glancing back to see. He had the law on his side and I did not. I just had to accept it.

But I have never forgiven the Republicans for barring me from voting in my first election. And I've never voted for a Republican since. The only consolation I have is that the Republican asshole kept me from voting for the Hump.

Not that it made any difference to anyone but me. Arizona Republicans didn't need to keep me and who knows how many other newly registered Democrats from voting in the '68 election. Nixon carried Arizona easily.

But that's how Republicans are. It's in their nature.

I know.

I used to be one of them.

Hearts and Minds

Annie liked flying into Sky Harbor from L.A. every other weekend. It made her feel like a star on tour, flying into yet another town for yet another performance. As the daughter of an avatar, she was expected by Vern to become a Very Important Person doing Very Important things, and Annie had internalized Vern's expectations. Now, in a small way, she *was* a Very Important Person and she *was* often flying into a city to do something Very Important. It was surely a foretaste of things to come.

For myself, I was happy to have Annie with me every other weekend, even if there was still a war going on, even if I was still fighting my own war against the war. The crowds loved us when we performed *Spoon River Anthology* at the Vaudeville, and there were a couple of antiwar poems in it, but it seemed irrelevant to my war against the war. I wanted to do something more explicitly antiwar and contemporary.

Then I stumbled across *Where Is Vietnam?*, an anthology of anti-Vietnam War poems edited by Walter Lowenfels. The title was taken from the Allen Ginsburg poem of the same name in the collection. The Lowenfels anthology held many poems which were written in a style which could be easily adapted to the same monologue format in which we did *Spoon River*. It seemed possible, then, to assemble a play about the same length as *Spoon River* from them and present it as the second part of our performance.

I selected a number of the poems and the three of us began rehearsing them. Some didn't work, and we dropped them. Each of us performed each poem and we decided by consensus which of us performed which poem best. We added Annie's music, either pure instrumental, a song, or her just humming with guitar. The production grew under our fingers like a living thing.

Performing our new two-parter for the Vaudeville audience, we thought we were too close to it, that the two pieces would seem too disjunctive. *Spoon River* was bittersweet nostalgia for a world we had lost. *Where Is Vietnam?* was the present, controversial and completely bitter.

But the two parts meshed. After a ten minute intermission, the Universal Players were back on stage with another set of poetry monologues. People cried and stomped and cheered and stood to applaud us. We discovered that poetry does not have to be a moribund art form, rarified almost out of existence by ambiguity and preciousness. When poetry speaks simply and clearly to the emotions about matters of utmost importance, it still retains the power to touch the hearts, as well as the minds, of ordinary people. That night at the Vaudeville, we touched the hearts and minds of people in a way no one in the Vietnam Day Committee or Professor Starsky ever had ranting from the concrete podium on the ASU campus mall.

****

We weren't content to perform only at the Vaudeville. Performances there paid Annie's air fare, but we wanted to reach a larger audience. We decided to present a performance at the ASU campus, and the Vietnam Day Committee seemed the ideal student organization to sponsor us. Meanwhile, Annie approached the Academic and Cultural Events Committee at Pitzer and Pomona Colleges for performances in Claremont. And Jan Sownie, Annie's best friend from North High, who was attending Northern Arizona University in Flagstaff, began to work on scheduling us for a performance. Another friend began working on a play date at Prescott College.

We'd chosen "Universal Players" as our troupe's name because we didn't want to limit ourselves to *Spoon River* or *Where Is Vietnam?* We felt we had the potential to do anything and we had ambitious dreams. We therefore needed a logo or an image to represent our universal aspirations, especially if we were going to be plastering ASU and Pitzer and other colleges with posters. We settled on Leonardo da Vinci's famous Vitruvian man sketch.

Leonardo's Vitruvian man is his best known image after the Last Supper. It's a frontal portrait of a nude long-haired man splayed out in an encircled square. He has two sets of arms and two sets of legs, with his horizontal arms touching the edges of the square and his diagonal arms and legs touching the rim of the circle. Leonardo intended the drawing to illustrate the ideal of regular proportions. To the three of us, the drawing illustrated the infinity of human potential. I found a good but inexpensive print shop on Mill Avenue next to the Valley Art Theater and had them print posters for our performances with the Vitruvian man, in all his glory, prominently displayed.

The ASU Vietnam Day Committee decided not to sponsor us for a performance on the ASU campus, but Richard Jones and I controlled the ASU Civil Liberties Union. We used the imprimatur of that student organization to reserve a student union ballroom for December 2, 1968. We covered the campus with posters advertising the event, our first college performance, which we scheduled in conjunction with another performance at the Vaudeville, so we'd have the money to fly Annie back and forth yet again.

That ASU performance was "sold out" and SRO, as was every subsequent college performance. Students seemed to be starved for theater demonstrating a social consciousness. I began to believe the theater really could be a means of social change.

In the December 6th issue of the *State Press,* the ASU student newspaper, a reviewer gushed, "The Universal Players have only been in existence three months, yet Monday night's performance in the MU ballroom of Edgar Lee Masters' *Spoon River Anthology* and selections from *Where Is Vietnam?* embodied a power, force, and excitement usually found only in long-standing professional groups.

"Carlo Mancini struck an imposing figure on stage Monday night. Large in stature, head shaven bald, with mustache and goatee, Mancini mastered a variety of characters, dialects, and emotions. Shouting or weeping, Mancini created moods that filled the ballroom and enveloped the audience.

"The sole female member of the group demonstrated a musical as well as dramatic talent. Playing the guitar, the harmonica, and singing songs which ranged from "The Battle Hymn of the Republic" to those of Simon and Garfunkel, she added a subtle and poignant background of continuity to the performance.

"The Universal Players say there is symbolism to their initials - UP. And after their performance, it must be agreed that is how they are moving."

A few days later we were in Claremont, California, in a December 13th performance at Pomona College's Smudge Pot on a double bill with "This Way Out," a local jazz band. Incongruous double bill it may have been, but we blew the audience away.

On December 14th, we presented what the fine arts editor of the student newspaper, *The Claremont Collegian,* called "an electrifying performance to a large audience" at Pitzer College. In the December 18th issue of the *Collegian,* the reviewer began her review by saying, "There comes a time when a reviewer at some particular event can no longer remain a detached observer, and, despite all efforts, she finds herself participating in the mood. Such was the feeling I experienced last Saturday night as I sat crosslegged on the floor of the Founder's Room of Pitzer's McConnell Center watching three young people, two men and one woman, equipped with only two guitars and three chairs, present a blending of dramatic poetry and songs accompanied by guitar.

"More a series of dramatic monologues than a poetry reading, the three each in turn would sit, stand, or pound on the podium, speaking for the dead of Spoon River. First a Swedish farm girl mourning her illegitimate child, an old man cursing his grey hair as he scowls at his image in the mirror, a frightened young boy pierced through the heart with a bullet while fighting.

"Their movements were powerful, both physically and verbally, and the people they spoke for became very real. The emotions evoked from the audience were also very real as I watched the audience tense and relax in unison. Throughout the readings a deep sense of timelessness was felt.

"The second selection, *Where Is Vietnam?*, was equally powerful and moving. Most of the poems dealt with people somehow touched by the war in Vietnam. Soldiers describing the horror of the reality of war, a pregnant wife questioning the morality of war, a war resister recounting blowing up an ROTC building. The war was brought very close to the audience that night, as I observed many lowered heads among the audience.

"Though they do not like to call themselves actors, these three have achieved the art of drama. To them it is a means of asking, "Where is America?" I was impressed with their fresh enthusiasm, both while performing and when I conversed with them. It was an enthusiasm of the young who have discovered that they just might have the power to communicate to many people that there is a common bond of humanity despite the wars and the civil strife. This newly formed group call themselves the Universal Players, and, as their initials suggest, they are on the way UP."

We'd discovered *our* own way to fight a war against the war. Our antiwar message touched the hearts and minds of others. We dared believe our theater company could play its small role in stopping the slaughter.

If the FBI had only known, they'd have monitored us instead of Professor Starsky and Rev. Manker.

Peace on Earth

The Mayfly's Love Song

Our love is eternal,
        As we flit among the flowers,
'Til the seconds become minutes,
        And the minutes become hours,
'Til the sun ends its flight
        And settles in the West,
'Til the day becomes the night.
        Our love will stand the test.

****

Meanwhile I wrote and sent my local draft board essay after essay for inclusion in my file, each one expressing, in a different fashion, my opposition to the war. On October 28th, 1968, I sent my board a letter from Dr. Arch Egbert, from whom I'd taken two courses at ASU, American history and Survey of Christian Denominations. When I'd signed up for them, I hadn't known that Dr. Egbert was also an officer in the Arizona National Guard, but I did know that he was the Director of the Mormon Institute of Religion at ASU. Indeed, I took the latter course at the off-campus LDS Institute of Religion in a class filled with Mormon students. I wanted to learn as much as I could about religion, and I wasn't afraid to beard the Mormon lion in his own den. Walking into his class on the first day of the semester I'd felt like a lion stalking into a den of Daniels and was eagerly anticipating the coming theological combat.

But Dr. Egbert wasn't the antagonist I expected. He was knowledgeable about other Christian denominations and, for the first time ever, I encountered a Christian, indeed, a *Mormon,* who wasn't intolerant of dissenting opinion. He shushed my snarking Mormon classmates and let me say my piece in class. I took a chance and gave him a copy of "An Objector's Search," one of the essays I'd sent my draft board. I'd spent some time on it, elaborating on my original statement written when first requesting Conscientious Objector status. Dr. Egbert wrote a favorable response which he allowed me to forward to my draft board.

"The credibility of your essay is excellent," he wrote. "I think your sincerity is well expressed. Obviously, you are speaking from deep, well-founded feelings.

"Style: Well-written, persuasive, and shows a well-read background of the writer. The ideas are thought-provoking and impressive.

"Content: The examples and quotes are very illustrative and show good variety. Gandhi's comments are well used. The material from Thomas Paine shows ingenuity and a real search through many men's views to really achieve your concepts....

"Conclusion: I am convinced you deserve C.O. status and hope you may achieve it."

No such luck. Endorsement from a Mormon religious leader and military officer carried no more weight with my draft board than the endorsement from a Unitarian minister had previously. On December 11th, 1968, my draft board notified me that my student deferment had been revoked. I was reclassified I-A, grade-A prime beef, the highest draft classification. Young men so classified were those most likely to be drafted next and sent out as fresh cannon fodder.

The reason given by my board was that I'd not earned enough college credits -- a required 30 semester hours -- the previous year at ASU to retain my Selective Service student status. Which was true. I'd been too busy fighting the war. I was still at ASU, but my classes were an after thought if I thought of them at all.

As Christmas of 1968 approached, while I performed in the Universal Players, finished up the fall semester at ASU, and planned my courses for the spring term -- the military had other plans for me -- a spring vacation in Vietnam.

I didn't worry about being I-A and changed my daily routine not in the slightest. I was never going to be shipped off to Vietnam, or anywhere else the Empire had a military base, because I was never going to allow the Empire to draft me. If that meant prison instead, then so be it.

Annie came home from Pitzer College for the holidays. Home was not in Cambridge, with her father. Home was in Phoenix, with me. On December 19th, I turned 22. The two of us celebrated my birthday alone in my Spartan apartment. I had way too much space in that apartment. There was nothing in my bedroom but the single-person Army cot I'd bought and the bricks-and-lumber bookcase Annie had built for me. A closet held my few articles of clothing. On the floor was the old portable LP turntable I'd had since I was a kid. Lined up next to it and leaning against the wall were my albums. Next to my cot I had a radio with a built-in alarm clock.

My kitchen was bare except for a refrigerator and a stove I seldom used. Some friends had raided a citrus grove and dumped about a hundred grapefruit on my kitchen floor, as there was no place elsewhere to put them. I tried to keep them segregated to one side of the room, but they tended to roll all over the floor and had to be kicked out of the way. I had a grapefruit every morning before heading off for school, but their number did not seem to diminish.

I used the kitchen table as my desk in the living room. My clunky manual typewriter and my school books took up all the space on it. There was nothing else in my living room but the chair at my desk. From the ceiling hung a handmade Alexander Calder mobile made of string and balsa wood which a Phoenix College friend had laboriously constructed and given to me.

Between the kitchen and the living room was a short hallway with built-in shelves and sliding doors hiding the shelves. They were for linen, but I had almost no linen, so I used them for more books, including my extensive collection of science fiction magazines, mostly *Astounding-Analog*, the first SF magazine I ever bought, in March, 1960. I purchased that first issue at the Bayless supermarket on Thomas at 56th Street, on the border with Scottsdale. I bought a subscription then and I'd never missed or discarded an issue, so by 1968 they were taking up a lot of space.

Annie had no money to buy me a birthday present, and I had no money to buy myself a birthday cake. But I had enough to buy a small pound cake from the local Circle K convenience store. I stuck a single candle in it, and placed it on my living room floor right under the swinging Calder mobile. Annie and I pretended we were Japanese and sat on the floor on either side of the pound cake and held hands over it. Annie sang "Happy Birthday" to me and said she loved me, and that was my birthday present. It was enough.

I made a silent wish and blew out the candle. I sliced some pound cake for both of us, and we ate with our fingers off of small paper plates, carelessly scattering crumbs on the floor as we munched and laughed. "We've been through so much together," I told Annie. "I feel like I've loved you forever."

"I know, I can't remember when I *didn't* love you!"

"And you're not bored with me yet?"

"Are you bored with me?"

I smiled at her. "Actually, I think I need a teenager right now."

"I *am* a teenager!"

I reached for her over the pound cake. "Then I think I need *you!* Right now!"

We kissed and I pulled her down, crushing the pound cake under us, and we made mad hard love on the bare hardwood floor under the swinging Calder mobile. That was a wonderful birthday, because I was rich. I had everything I wanted. I had Annie.

My work-study job at ASU that semester was in the biology department. It entailed feeding chimpanzees and cats used for experiments by the professors and their grad students. I never knew the details of these experiments. I also cleaned the the rooftop cages of these chimps and cats with a high-pressure hose which I sprayed over the cage floors. The bars in the back of the cages stopped about an inch or so above the floor. Using the hose I swept the animals' crap out the back of the cages and into a gutter which went who knows where. Both the chimps and the cats were vicious, and who could blame them? Their cages were crowded and the cats, at least, died in droves from highly contagious cat distemper. Every workday I removed dead cats from the cages.

In my ignorance, I passed the disease along to Mimi, Annie's cat, the one she'd left with me to care for when she went to Pitzer. Shortly after my birthday, Mimi began exhibiting all the signs of cat distemper, which I knew well enough from my job. Mimi and I lived alone in that big bare apartment and I never let her out. She could only have gotten cat distemper from me, bringing it home on my clothes. Annie and I took Mimi to a vet and begged him to save her. He said it was too late. Once contracted, there is no cure. At my insistence, he gave her distemper shots anyway. As predicted, they did no good.

Mimi died over several days, wasting away on the red velvet pillow trimmed with gold I'd given her for her bed. We gave her water with an eye dropper and watched as she panted and gasped and became weaker and weaker. When she finally died we placed her, still on the red velvet pillow, in a box. That night Annie carried the box as we rode on the Scrambler out to Papago Park. I chopped a hole in the hard desert ground and we placed Mimi, still on her pillow, in the hole. Annie covered her with a towel and then I covered her with dirt. Annie said a prayer for Mimi and we left her under the hard desert soil. So the season of birth also became a season of death.

The next day, Christmas Eve, Annie and I went to a Woolworth's and took our pictures in a photo booth where you got a strip of four small black-and-white shots for a buck. All the department stores had these booths in those days. In one of the photos, which I still have, Annie is looking directly into the camera with a gaze so fierce and intent it seems she can see right through the camera and into the eyes of the viewer. When Annie saw it, she said she looked that way because the soul of Mimi had entered into her.

And so the season of death became a season of rebirth.

That night we invited Richard Jones, also living alone in a bare and echoing apartment, to come over and share Christmas Eve with us. After he arrived, he and I slipped out to a nearby Christmas tree lot and liberated a tree from the back of the lot. They weren't going to sell many more trees by the morning, anyway. We carried it back to my apartment, laughing all the way. I'd scraped together a little money since my birthday and the three of us had a nice supper by candlelight on my living room floor under the swinging Calder mobile. Annie played her guitar and led us in Christmas carols. Then she just picked and hummed tunes of her own making as we told each other stories and talked about our futures.

"You're I-A," Richard said. "You're going to be drafted soon. What're you going to do?"

"I'll fight the S. S. System for C.O. status with every legal means I can muster. I'll exhaust every appeal so that, in my own small way, I become a pain in the ass for them. I know I'm going to lose at the end of the day. I'm not a religious pacifist so, under their rules, as they see them, I don't qualify for Conscientious Objector status. But, you know me. I'm stubborn. I refuse to fight for the Empire."

"He's as stubborn as a mule," Annie said, "and he'll argue with a sign post."

I smiled at her. "That's what my mother used to say about me."

"I know. It's the only thing she and I agree on."

"Then you'll spend the next five years in prison," Richard said.

"That'll be OK, so long as you both promise to visit me."

"I promise to visit you in prison," Richard replied.

"And you know I'll be there," Annie said.

"Then everything will be fine."

Richard raised his cup of hot chocolate to me in a toast. "Peace on Earth," he said. Annie and I raised our cups of hot chocolate to meet his. "Peace on Earth," we answered.

Richard wrote me years later about that Christmas Eve night. Here's his letter:

"Yesterday," he said, "I was sweeping the floor of the new car dealer where I work and my eyes fixed on some red tags that had spilled on the floor. Ordinary tags, the type used to identify cars coming back for repairs or cars new and leaving. Red, surrounded by a steel rim with a red string going through a little hole at the edge of the paper. Ordinary red paper tags, but my mind went back to a Christmas when we had stolen a tree and decorated it with red, red, paper out of a box of chocolate cherry-filled candies. We gave each other our used paperback books as gifts. We shared our food. Annie's cat had died the night before and we were still flushed with that death. I thought all that in a moment, without stopping or breaking stride, and I said to myself, that was the best Christmas I have ever had."

My silent wish, as I'd blown out the single candle on my birthday pound cake, had been that, no matter what the future did to us, Annie and I would always be together, would always be able to hold each other in our arms. That Christmas Eve night, as we three -- lovers and friends -- toasted each other with our hot chocolate and wished for peace on Earth, we had no way of knowing that it was my last Christmas in Phoenix and we would not celebrate another like it.

Endless War

A new year began, and on April 3, 1969, U.S. combat fatalities in Vietnam surpassed the number of Americans killed in the Korean War: 33,629 in Korea vs. 33,641 in Vietnam. On April 3, 1969, the Vietnam War became the fourth bloodiest war in American history, after the Civil War, World War I, and World War II. By the end of that April, U.S. troop levels in Vietnam -- which had continued to climb after Nixon took office -- reached their all-time peak of 543,482, more than half a million.

In the 1968 presidential campaign, Richard Nixon ran as an antiwar peace candidate with a "secret plan" to end the war in Vietnam. His "secret plan," which he called "Vietnamization," wasn't a plan to end the war. Instead, it was a way to continue the war by shifting the human burden of it onto the shoulders of the hated Saigon dictatorship.

"Vietnamization" had two aspects. First, increase the capacity of the Saigon dictatorship's military to "step up to the plate" and fight through increased training and the supplying of more military hardware, thus making it possible to decrease American troop levels in the country. Since the increasing American casualties were undermining domestic support for the war, lower troop levels would mean lower casualties. After reaching that end-of-April peak, U.S. troop levels in Vietnam did, finally, begin to decline, after having steadily increased ever since the Gulf of Tonkin non-Incident.

The second aspect of "Vietnamization" was to ramp up the air war. Since a ground war involved too many politically unacceptable casualties, Nixon turned to an ever higher escalation of the massive air war against the north, as well as intensified bombing in the south. Over the next two years Nixon dropped twice the tonnage of bombs on Southeast Asia that we dropped on all enemies in World War II.

Nixon also held the nuclear option open. As early as the Kennedy Administration of the early 1960s, MIT's Walt Rostow, the most blood-thirsty of JFK's warhawks, had urged Kennedy either to invade North Vietnam or to annihilate it in a nuclear holocaust. In 1969, Nixon told his Secretary of State, Henry Kissinger, to make it known to the North Vietnamese leaders that he was willing to push the nuclear button. Kissinger did not believe that a "fourth-rate country," as he called North Vietnam, didn't have a breaking point. He didn't believe North Vietnam would fight endlessly for freedom and independence.

I certainly wasn't one of what David Halberstam later termed "the best and the brightest," MIT and Harvard men like Walt Rostow and Henry Kissinger, who initiated and prosecuted the war, but I felt "Vietnamization" was doomed to failure. I didn't know the extent of damage the air war was doing to the north, but indiscriminate bombing of the south had already turned a quarter of the South Vietnamese population into refugees. How could homeless fugitives be expected to display any kind of loyalty to America and the Saigon dictatorship which destroyed their homes and forced them into urban slums? America had the power to destroy the people of Vietnam -- but America could not win their hearts and minds through bombing them into oblivion.

Nor, I felt, could the other aspect of "Vietnamization" work -- having the Saigon dictatorship's military replace American troops -- no matter how many advisers and how much military hardware we sent. The Saigon dictatorship was completely venal, corrupt, cowardly, and incompetent. Its soldiers ran from the battlefield and its field commanders used their positions for financial extortion. American advisers had been training the dictatorship's troops since the 1950s, with no success because the Saigon dictatorship's troops had little desire to fight and die for the regime. LBJ had to send half a million ignorant American troops to fight and die for a dictatorship the South Vietnamese themselves would not fight to save.

Meanwhile, the Americans were told, and believed, they were fighting and dying for democracy. A million American boots marched through a jungle hell, in the longest war we've ever fought, as our soldiers fought and died for a bright and shining lie. There was nothing in Saigon on which to build "Vietnamization." Only American boots on the ground kept the war going. Once American boots stopped stomping the people of Vietnam into the jungle mud, the Saigon dictatorship, propped up solely by American money and military power, would collapse.

Which would be all to the good, so far as I was concerned. We were fighting to defend a brutal military dictatorship and to keep Vietnam part of the Empire's imperial system. It was the other side which was motivated by the ideals, beliefs, and values Americans claimed to hold dear. It was the other side which fought and died selflessly and bravely for freedom and independence, while we died for lies and tyrants. It was the other side that all men and women of good will, all freedom-loving Americans, should properly have supported.

But, until the blessed day came when the bloody-handed Saigon dictatorship collapsed, the endless war dragged on year after year. Political campaigns came and went, presidents took and left office, leaders rose and fell, but nothing seemed to stop the deadly juggernaut. It seemed to be a permanent part of our lives.

And I was now I-A, Prime Beef, soon to be drafted for the Empire's eternal war on the other side of the world. In Vietnam, the fight against the American war machine was a life or death struggle for the Vietnamese. In America, my fight against that same war machine, and my fight to retain my freedom, was much more mundane. It was a long slog through the S.S. System, fighting with every bureaucratic weapon I had, even though I knew I'd lose in the end.

But I was as serious in making that long march as any guerrilla fighting in the jungles of Vietnam. I was determined my boots would never be on his neck. In my mind, we were comrades in arms, even though we'd never meet. We were fighting the same war. Only the battlefield was different.

When facing inevitable defeat, one must delay the inevitable defeat as long as possible, create as much friction as possible, throw as much sand in the gears as possible. I began fighting the long legal battle with the S.S. System which eventually became an obsession. I became more and more like the comedian Lenny Bruce who, before his death in 1966, became so obsessed with the court case against him for public obscenity that he began reading transcripts of court testimony to his audience in his night club act. And that wasn't any fun for them at all. It was a drag. Lenny just wasn't funny any more after he became ensnared in America's legal morass.

Nor was I much of a fun guy as I spent more and more time researching the legal cases involving the draft and conscientious objection. I began speaking in the tongues of bureaucratic legalese and draft classifications levels. I knew it didn't mean anything to those around me, but my freedom literally depended on mastering such arcane legal technicalities.

The more I obsessed about my personal battle against the S.S. System, the more boring and irritating I became to those around me, including Annie. I always seemed to be in a permanent state of sexual arousal when I was around her, but Great Pan was not with me on the night of December 27th, 1968, just a week after we'd mushed the pound cake beneath us and two weeks after my draft board revoked my student deferment, reclassifying me I-A, Prime Beef. There was precious little time for us before she returned to Pitzer, but as Annie called for me to come to bed with her, I obsessed at my bulky manual typewriter. I was writing a long appeal letter to my draft board.

"Eric, come to bed right now!" she yelled down the entire length of my apartment from the darkness of my bedroom.

"Annie, I can't! I have to write this appeal letter to my draft board."

"You can write that damn letter after I leave!"

"Annie, please, I'm under the gun here!"

"Eric, stop being so *stubborn!* You make me so damn mad that I *hate* you with a passion!"

I stopped typing, sighed, and just looked at my fingers on the keys. Boy, I thought, that sounded like she really *meant* it. This isn't good. I got up and slowly walked the entire length of the apartment back to the dark bedroom where Annie sat amid the crumpled sheets on my bed. I sat down on the bed's edge, put my arm around her shoulders, and pulled her close in the darkness.

"Annie, sweetie, I know you don't hate me. You're just mad because I'm typing in the other room and you want me here, with you, because we have so little time together. I understand. But, honey, I'm I-A and I'm going to be drafted soon. That means I have very little time to put the entire appeal process in motion. I have to get it out, OK?"

"But I want you *here,* with me. I have to go back to Pitzer soon."

"I know. Tell you what. Let me write for just another half hour and then I'll come to bed and snuggle up with you, OK?"

Annie sighed. "OK. If I'm asleep, wake me."

"I will."

I kissed Annie on the cheek and walked the length of my apartment back to my empty living room and began typing once more on my dinosaur typewriter. To this day I feel I made the wrong decision that night. Annie was right. The damn letter could've waited. I should've crawled into bed with Annie right that moment and made soft and slow love with her. We *both* would've felt better. But my obsession made me stupid, and so I continued writing the letter.

The next day, December 28th, 1968, I hand-delivered my appeal letter to Alice Dimmick, the Executive Secretary for Local Board 29 and my contact with the S.S. System, at her office in Room 215 of the Post Office Building, 522 N. Central Avenue in downtown Phoenix.

Richard rode his bike over early that morning and went with me in a show of solidarity. Together we climbed the steps to the second floor of the Post Office Building, found Room 215, and he stood with me as I introduced myself to Mrs. Dimmick and handed her my appeal letter. After getting a receipt from her, we walked across the hall to visit the Executive Secretary at Local Board No. 7, Richard's own draft board.

When he broke his neck, Richard was told he'd never walk again. But, he did walk again. Even so, he'd never pass an Armed Forces physical, and so Local Board No. 7 had classified him I-Y, what used to be called "4-F" during World War II. He was physically unacceptable for military service. He introduced himself to his own Executive Secretary and asked her for S. S. Form 150, the form used to apply for Conscientious Objector status. I'd not pressured Richard in any way to do this. It was his own idea, his own decision, which he'd come to after our Christmas Eve together. A real man does the right thing, and it didn't matter to Richard that the S. S. System had given him a medical deferment. He wanted to stand and be counted among the dissenters and resisters. Richard Jones was a real man, what Shana had called a "mensch."

The woman was puzzled. "Why do you want that? You've already been taken care of." He was not in danger of being drafted, and she could not imagine why anyone would otherwise apply for C.O. status.

"Because I'm a Conscientious Objector to the Armed Forces and to this current war," Richard told her. "I want the Selective Service System to know that. I also have moral objections to any classification other than that of Conscientious Objector. I want to be classified as I should be properly classified. Please give me the appropriate form."

The woman prowled around until she found the form and gave it to Richard. It was clear that his request was completely incomprehensible to her. Outside, in the second floor hallway of the Phoenix Post Office Building, with draft boards lining the hall on both sides of us, I shook Richard's hand and congratulated him for doing the right thing. Who knows? Richard may have been the only I-Y registrant during the entire war who protested his medical deferment and demanded to be reclassified as a Conscientious Objector. Pink, who'd served at Wupatki with me and who was a devout Catholic, had also applied for Conscientious Objector status. I wasn't alone anymore. Now there were three of us. The FBI should have been watching me.

My own hand-delivered letter to Mrs. Dimmick, dated December 28, 1968, and written instead of going to bed with Annie, stated that I was simultaneously appealing my I-A classification for I-O (Conscientious Objector), I-S and II-S, the latter two being student deferments. "As I am anticipating eventually taking my case into court in an effort to be classified I-O," I wrote, "I would appreciate you clearing up some of the foggy areas in my understanding of my case. I should like to ask you once more for the *specific* points in my I-O application form that the Board found 'not convincing.' In my letter of July 15, 1968, I asked this question so I might know which area of my application the Board found inadequate. Your letter of July 23, 1968, in response, simply stated, 'The Local Board does not make a practice of stating its specific reasons for disapproving a claim of Conscientious Objection.'

"Please allow me to explain why I'm asking you this question once more. *U.S. vs. St. Clair* (E.D.N.Y., November 20, 1968) involved a pantheist who was not a member of an organized religious group. Judge Weinstein, who presided over the case, ruled in favor of the pantheist and held there was in fact no basis for St. Clairs' I-A classification.

"In a section of his ruling entitled 'Lack of Specificity in Record,' Judge Weinstein wrote that the local board alleged insincerity on St. Clair's part, but the record indicated 'no hint of what part of his claim was believed to be untrue.'

"The Court next observed, in a statement with Sixth Amendment overtones (i.e., the right to be informed of the nature and cause of an accusation): 'A registrant is at least entitled to be told in what way his case is defective so that he has a reasonable opportunity to obtain evidence to support it.' The Court suggested that it was more prone to protect the registrant who has no record to argue against because the 1967 Selective Service Act has dispensed with the Justice Department [FBI] investigation of registrants who applied for Conscientious Objector status.

"Another section of the Court's opinion, 'Right to Appeal on Questions of Sincerity', observed that the registrant's right to rebut incorrect local board conclusions before an appeal board is meaningless 'where no facts or inferences upon which the Local Board's conclusion is based are stated....' In effect, the Court held the local board was required to build a record or to state the specific reasons for denying a requested I-O classification.

"When my case is brought into court, it will bear a remarkable similarity to the above case if it remains as it is. Since you have refused to state the specific reasons for disapproving of my claim for Conscientious Objector status, I am in the exact position of the acquitted Conscientious Objector St. Clair, who had 'no hint of what part of his claim was believed to be untrue.' In the light of this decision, it now seems that you should either grant me I-O classification or explain to me the specific reasons you doubt my sincerity."

My draft board never did give me any specific reasons for doubting my sincerity. This became a point to which I returned again and again in subsequent correspondence.

In that same December letter I also noted that the U. S. Supreme Court itself, and recent federal court decisions based upon the Supreme Court's rulings, had upheld the right of registrants with beliefs similar to mine to be granted Conscientious Objector status. In the Supreme Court case of *U.S. vs. Seeger,* the Court handed down a legal definition of what beliefs might qualify a registrant for Conscientious Objector status. "The test might be stated in these words," the Supremes wrote. "A sincere and meaningful belief which occupies in the life of its possessor a place parallel to that filled by the God of those admittedly qualifying for the exemption comes within the statutory definition."

I then mentioned the case of Michael Shacter. "Earlier this month, a federal judge in Baltimore, Maryland, declared that Shacter was eligible for I-O classification, even though Shacter stated on his C.O. application that he was an atheist. He went on to say that, 'I do not believe in any being superior to man in the universe. Man's mortal [sic] soul is the most perfect element in the cosmos.'

"Acquitting Shacter of his draft delinquency," I continued, "Judge Alexander Harvey II declared that, in the light of *U.S. vs. Seeger,* Shacter's beliefs were clearly 'a product of faith.'" Thus, I concluded, beliefs of an atheist, similar to my own beliefs, have been held legally valid grounds for granting Conscientious Objector status. These two legal cases, *Seeger* and *St. Clair,* were ignored by my board in all subsequent actions, and so became the twin pillars of my legal battle against them.

Mrs. Dimmick ignored everything I wrote and, in a December 30, 1968 letter said, "You are hereby requested to come before the local board for a personal interview at 3:00 p.m., January 8, 1969 at this office. The primary purpose of the interview will be to develop further facts on which the Conscientious Objector claim is based, and the sincerity of such claim."

Meanwhile, in the midst of my war against the war, I went on with other aspects of my life. I went to classes, although they seemed completely irrelevant to not only my life but to the war and everything else that was going on around me. I went back to the Newman Catholic Student Center just off the ASU campus. There I bussed tables every morning for a big breakfast and five bucks. I also stopped tending the cats and monkeys for the Biology Dept. and found a new work-study job as a cartographer with the U. S. Forest Service's Rocky Mountain Forest and Range Experimental Station, which was located on the ASU campus. There I learned a lot about riparian vegetation, that is, river bank flora. And I scheduled further college appearances for the Universal Players at Prescott College and Northern Arizona University (NAU) in Flagstaff. Jan Sownie had made the arrangements for a March appearance there and began publicity for it.

Because Annie came home for the holidays to be with me, not him, Vern seemed to accept that Annie and I were determined to stay together, no matter what he did, and he decided to make the best of it. From Cambridge he sent me, and Carlo as well, applications for a summer drama program at Harvard University. Carlo and I laughed at the idea of either of us going to Harvard, but we filled out the applications. Carlo had a long theatrical career that he was able to synopsize. I had no such track record, as I'd only acted in "The Lower Depths" at the Arizona Repertory Theater before founding the Universal Players. I'd never even studied acting. Nevertheless, I wrote an account of what the group was doing on college campuses in Arizona and California and sent it off, along with copies of our reviews from student newspapers. Come summer, though, I expected to be either in prison or on my way there.

I certainly wasn't going to be at Wupatki again. I was pretty sure I was *persona non grata* there. Pink wouldn't be returning either. I knew Wupatki would have vacancies and I told Annie to apply. The Park Service accepted women as Rangers, although they didn't go out on road patrol as law officers. At Wupatki they stayed in the Visitor Center and sometimes conducted tours of the big ruin out back. I coached Annie on what to say and what not to say. What she should definitely *not* say was that she knew me.

Nor did they know her. When we'd driven up with Tom Wagers in the spring of '68 for my job interview, she and Tom had wandered around parking lot and then through the Visitor Center's exhibit on the prehistory of Wupatki while I was interviewed. I'd never introduced them to the Rangers.

Annie was accepted as a Ranger at Wupatki for the summer of '69 and sent off for her Rangerette uniform. Today, female Park Service Rangers wear pants and a uniform much like what the men wear. At that time they were required to wear brown skirts down to their knees and little brown caps which they precariously perched on their heads. They looked like airline stewardesses from the Fifties.

On January 6, 1969, I borrowed Richard's larger bike to drive up to Prescott College. There I delivered a presentation on the archaeology of Wupatki to the Prescott Chapter of the Arizona Archaeological Society. The chapter's president had been in a group I'd led on a guided tour of the Wupatki Ruin the summer before and asked me to give a similar presentation to his chapter.

There was a huge turnout of amateur archaeologists for my presentation at Prescott College, the largest showing of chapter members for many a long moon, they said. I brought slides I'd taken of Wupatki during the summer, and I did the best job of being an archaeologist that I possibly could.

In the subsequent January, 1969 issue of the chapter's newsletter, *The Yavapai Drum Beat,* the chapter's president, Ron Brown, commented that, "Our January 6th meeting was *quite!* an experience. It is seldom that we have the opportunity to enjoy such a fresh and delightful lecture (if that is the word for it) as that presented to our group by Mr. Eric Davin. When one considers that this young man is not an archaeology major, and that what he knows must be primarily from his reading in preparation for a summer as a Ranger at Wupatki, the program was all the more amazing." And I wasn't even paid for that Prescott lecture (if that is the word for it)!

The actual account on my presentation was recorded under the headline, "Eric Davin's Report on Wupatki Enthusiastically Received." It ended by saying, "Eric's skill as a photographer is to be seen in his fine slides; his love of nature in his pictures of beautiful small animals; and a kindly sense of humor in his telling of the lighter side of a Ranger's life. Eric loved the Ranger's life and hopes to return to it. We, too, hope to find him again helping to guide and guard in our National Park Service."

That was not to be. I wasn't the kind of Ranger the Park Service wanted. At least I wasn't the kind of Ranger those at Wupatki wanted. Too curious. Too enthusiastic. Too sympathetic toward the Navajos.

The night ride back to Phoenix on Richard's motorcycle was torture. I wore thick insulated leather gauntlets, but as the snow covered terrain sped past me, my hands and fingers were freezing and painful. At Cordes Junction I pulled off the road, turned off the engine, squatted beside the bike, and placed my gloved hands on the bike's hot engine as it pinged and slowly cooled. As the heat seeped through the gloves a bit, I turned my hands over and laid the back of them on the engine. I continued turning my hands like this, as if cooking meat, until the frost had been driven out and I was finally able to flex my fingers. Then I climbed back on Richard's bike and began the descent into the Sonora Desert, but even that desert below the Mogollon Rim was cold.

When I finally pulled up to Richard's home in Phoenix, I was so stiff with the cold that I could barely climb off his bike. I was almost frozen in a crouched riding position. My feet didn't bend and I climbed the stairs to Richard's second floor apartment like a clumsy Frankenstein monster. Every step was painful.

Richard opened a can of Campbell's and put it on the stove. As I sipped the steaming hot soup and basked in his warm apartment, my chattering and shivering diminished and life slowly returned to my frigid body. I told him all about my lecture (if that was the word for it!) at Prescott College and we talked about my upcoming appearance before my draft board. Richard was a mega Bob Dylan fan and so played Dylan's recently released *John Wesley Harding* as I thawed. We listened to it and wondered if Dylan was going country on us, or if this was just another one of his many phases. That was the coldest ride, the best soup, and the most pleasant Dylan-listening session I've ever experienced.

The Long March

"He whose heart is firm, and whose conscience approves his conduct, will pursue his principles unto death."

-- Thomas Paine

****

The rest of 1969 became, for me, a long march toward the war. The January issue of *Fortune*, the magazine for capitalists, was dedicated to "American Youth: Its Outlook Is Changing the World" -- and that wasn't good for capitalism. Among other things, *Fortune* reported a Daniel Yankelovich survey of college students conducted the previous October which found that 42% were "unconcerned about college's practical benefits."

I wasn't surveyed, but I would've said the same. I couldn't see any "practical benefits" to college. It all seemed so trivial, so disconnected from the real world, and I could see no future in which college would help me. Besides, I had more important things -- actual matters of life and death -- to attend to.

Two days after returning from Prescott College, on January 8th, I appeared at the appointed hour before my local draft board for my first meeting with the members. There were only two of them present, besides Mrs. Dimmick. I was told that the other members were ill with the flu. Neither of the board members were introduced to me, and one never spoke. The one who did speak proved to be completely ignorant of both my case and S. S. classifications so, since I don't know his name, I'll call him Mr. Ignoramus.

Mr. Ignoramus asked me what my "trouble" was. I explained I was seeking the I-O classification of Conscientious Objector status.

"Why is that?" he asked.

"Well, I've written reams of essays and letters presenting my reasons, all of which are in my file. But, I'll summarize: I believe in justice, and I believe that doing justice is the highest moral obligation of any person. I am not a pacifist, but I believe there are just and unjust wars. A just war is a necessary war. A necessary war is a war that is forced upon you, in which you have to defend yourself. An unjust war is an unnecessary war which is not forced upon you, but one which you choose and in which you are the aggressor. The Vietnam War is an unnecessary war in which America is the aggressor. Therefore, the Vietnam War is an unjust war. Thus, it is a violation of my principles of justice to support this war.

"Further, I've come to believe that it is a violation of human dignity to even serve in the Armed Forces. The military is a hierarchical, anti-democratic institution. In it, a soldier is expected simply to follow orders, even if they violate his conscience. But using one's conscience to decide what is right and what is wrong is the very essence of what it means to be a human being. Because the military in inherently hostile to the exercise of the human conscience, I am also opposed to military service, per se."

"Then why didn't you apply for I-O status earlier than a year ago?," Mr. Ignoramus asked.

"Three reasons. I was still evolving into my beliefs; I was informed that I didn't qualify for I-O status because one had to be a religious pacifist, which I am not; and because Mrs. Dimmick wrote me that one is given the lowest classification for which one qualifies. For me, that meant the II-S, student deferment. I've asked for clarification on this last point, but I've never received it. I wrote Mrs. Dimmick that I was especially puzzled by this, as a fellow student I know at ASU was given C.O. status last August, even though he is still a student at ASU."

"What board has him?" Mrs. Dimmick asked.

"As I informed you in my most recent letter, Mrs. Dimmick, Local Board No. 35."

"There is no Board No. 35. There's a Board No. 34 and a Board No. 36, but no 35."

"I apologize for getting his Board number wrong. But the facts of his case are as I stated."

"There are probably other reasons for him being reclassified I-O."

"But he *is* a student, and isn't II-S a lower classification than I-O?"

Mrs. Dimmick did not answer. Instead, Mr. Ignoramus broke in. "Why was your II-S classification revoked?"

"It's in my file. Mrs. Dimmick wrote me that I did not complete the required 30 semester hours of credit last year. However, I *am* currently qualified for the I-S temporary student deferment, which is lower than I-A, as I am presently enrolled as a full-time student at ASU."

"That's not true," Mr. Ignoramus replied. "You're not qualified for a I-S classification."

Mrs. Dimmick interrupted. "Actually, he *is* qualified for the I-S classification."

"Well, what the hell is this I-S classification? I never heard of it."

"The I-S classification is a temporary student deferment for currently enrolled students. It consists of the classification I-SH for high school students and I-SC for college students."

"Well, then, why the hell didn't he say I-SC?"

"Because the notice of classification sent to registrants only lists the I-S description, so he didn't know he was supposed to say I-SC. Besides, the II-S classification is only given if the registrant requests it on the proper forms obtained at the student's college, and Mr. Davin did not request II-S classification on the appropriate forms."

The entire discussion bogged down in explaining draft classifications to Mr. Ignoramus, so I attempted to steer the discussion back toward its ostensible purpose. "I realize I'm not qualified for the II-S classification at this time and, although the I-S classification does, in fact, exist and I am, in fact, qualified for it, I will appeal even that status. I should be given I-O Conscientious Objector status, for which I legitimately qualify. In your letter of April 12, 1968, you stated that you were not convinced of my C. O. qualifications. May I ask the specific areas of my application you find unacceptable?"

"The Board does not answer questions of that type," Mr. Ignoramus replied, speaking in the third person.

"Well, then, all I can do is repeat what I have written and what you have in my file. I believe I am qualified for Conscientious Objector status. If I remain classified I-A and I am ordered to appear for induction, I will refuse to be inducted, thus committing a felony. If my case thereafter goes to court, I will seek to be defended by the Arizona branch of the American Civil Liberties Union."

"We understand and respect your feelings," Mr. Ignoramus replied. "But there are regulations issued in Washington by which we must abide."

"And there are legal rulings handed down by federal courts and the United States Supreme Court, by which you must also abide. And they say I am qualified for Conscientious Objector status according to your own regulations."

"Well, that is for us to decide, not you."

"It's not I who made those decisions. It's the courts, including the United States Supreme Court, who made the decisions. And you must abide by *their* decisions."

"Well, Mr. Davin, this Board has no further questions of you. We will put your case under advisement and consideration."

I thanked Mr. Ignoramus and the silent one beside him for their time and left.

But, Mr. Ignoramus and his fellow missing and silent board members didn't consider my case for too long. On January 13th, Mrs. Dimmick wrote me saying, "This is to inform you of the local board's decision not to reopen your I-A classification." Which meant I was still Grade-A Prime Beef. It seemed they were determined to put me on a Midnight Special toward induction.

On January 20th, I replied to Mrs. Dimmick's letter. My reply was not designed to win friends and influence people. I felt there was no possibility of that, in any case. I was certain my Local Board would never give me C.O. status, no matter what I said. My letter, then, was more for myself than Mrs. Dimmick or the members of my Local Board, who didn't read my letters and essays, in any case.

Of course, I appealed the board's retention of me as I-A, requesting, as was my right, a meeting with the Government Appeal Agent assigned to my draft board.

Then I continued, saying, "I was heavy of heart after leaving my January 8th interview with my Local Board members. The Board members gave the impression of being totally ignorant of my case. They did not know the reason I was at the meeting and they did not know the reason my student deferment had been revoked. I had to explain both to them. I was asked elementary questions pertaining to my I-O application which could have been answered by simply reading my C.O. application or any one of the essays and letters I have written to my Local Board over the past year. When you, Mrs. Dimmick, had to explain the I-S classification to the Board, my depression deepened. As a meeting to 'develop further facts on which the Conscientious Objector claim is based, and the sincerity of such claim,' the meeting was a singular failure.

"Everything that I go through in relation to the S. S. System is just empty procedure. My appearance before the board was mere procedure having absolutely no meaning outside of procedure. I feel that my upcoming meeting with the Government Appeal Agent will be mere procedure. I expect no help from him. And my personal appeal appearance before the Board to appeal their recent decision, now scheduled for February 12th, will be, I fear, more empty procedure. I am convinced my Board is totally unresponsive to whatever I say.

"The temptation is very strong, Mrs. Dimmick, to become a complete non-cooperator with the draft. However, I will continue. I do not intend to drop out of an alienating situation. If the System is ever to be reformed and corrected, it can only be done by staying in the System and fighting it. I would sincerely like to see an end to the draft system. I will fight all my life to put an end to the draft, as I see it as an illegal and monstrously evil manifestation of dictatorship. It is against my nature to accept a situation I feel is immoral. It is my nature to oppose that situation. I believe I do not have to accept America as I see it. I believe that I can change America into something better.

"I do not understand why you will not freely give C.O. classifications. Is it because you think we who apply are cowards? My mother once told me of a C.O. in her town during World War II. While some draftees shot off their toes at that time to avoid service, this C.O. refused service with his conscience. The towns people accepted the ones who shot off their toes, cowards though they were. It was even considered something to laugh about. But they did not similarly accept the C.O., and he eventually left town to escape their harassment. No, in a society which persecutes C.O.s, the coward does not choose to be a C.O. In light of the fact that one is safer in the Army than on our streets; that the C.O. is and always has been a pariah in our society; and that we live in the era of the G.I. Bills and other forms of financial advantages to serving in the military, it is not the self-seeking coward who seeks C.O. classification. Instead, the coward goes into the Army.

"Whatever your reasons for refusing to grant me C.O. status, I shall continue to fight for that status. I shall also continue to do everything in my power to end the draft as a blatant moral evil and an institution of illegal existence in violation of the American Constitution's prohibition of involuntary servitude. Yesterday, a friend of mine [Richard Jones] told me that an age of reaction, such as the present, tests what one is made of, tests one's strength. I agree. Only when we are tested do we truly know what we believe, and what we will do to fight for our beliefs. Viewed in this light, no battle is ever a futile battle, nor is any battle ever really lost. And, viewed in this light, I will not lose this battle."

On January 22, Mrs. Dimmick replied. Letters between us seemed to travel quickly, perhaps because I mailed all my letters from the Post Office Building on North Central Avenue in downtown Phoenix. Expecting to someday go to trial, I wanted to prove that my local draft board received everything I sent it. Therefore, I sent everything to it via registered mail, with a return receipt requested, and so I had to go to the counter every time. And from that Post Office counter my letters merely went up one flight of stairs to the second floor of that same building to reach Room 215 and my draft board. Likewise, I received all my mail at a mailbox on the same building's first floor, so all return letters merely went downstairs.

In that January 22 letter, Mrs. Dimmick began by writing, "Dear Sir: Would you please indicate your Selective Service Number on future correspondence? It saves some time looking it up every time. Thank you." (I never did include my S.S. number on *any* of my future correspondence with her. I refused to be reduced to a number. In her reply to my *next* letter she underlined my S.S. number in red pencil. When I didn't take the hint and still refused to include my inmate number on correspondence, she gave up.)

Shortly after that, on January 27th, I received a confirmation from Mrs. Dimmick of my February 12th personal appearance before my Local Board to appeal their decision denying me C.O. status. "Under no circumstances will you be permitted to be represented by an attorney or legal counsel," Mrs. Dimmick warned me. In other words, it would be more pro forma procedure, with no real chance on my part to accomplish anything. But, I was determined to avail myself of every administrative procedure the S.S. System offered. It was war, and in war you use every possible resource.

The meeting with the Government Appeal Agent, Osmond Burton, Jr., took place at his office in the First Federal Savings Building at 3003 N. Central Avenue at 10:00 a.m. on January 28th. To my surprise, it turned out *not* to be mere procedure. Osmond Burton was surprisingly helpful. Perhaps this was because he wasn't employed by the S.S. System. He was an attorney in private practice who'd been appointed to give independent advice to registrants. I actually don't remember that meeting, but I kept notes on everything, and so, following our meeting, I synopsized it for my records.

Osmond Burton was very friendly, I wrote to myself, and, "although he could not pass judgment on my case as to whether or not I should be given C.O. status (that not being his job), he will recommend to my board that: (1) my claim be given 'full consideration'; and (2) that, if the board does not give me I-O status, it should state its reasons for not doing so. This is what I contended they *had* to do under the *St. Clair* decision. He told me that he has himself told the board for some time that an appeal from their decisions without knowing what their decisions are based upon, is meaningless."

He also recommended that I ask the board to allow Rev. Ray Manker, the minister of the First Unitarian Church of Phoenix, which I sometimes attended out in Paradise Valley, to appear before the board at the February 12th meeting and testify on my behalf. So I requested, and received, permission for Ray to appear with me at my February 12th meeting.

Meanwhile, the express train toward the war continued down the tracks. Two days later, on January 30th, my local board ordered me to report on February 17th to the Phoenix Armed Forces Examining and Induction Station at 545 E. Moreland Street, "no earlier than 6:45 AM, or later than 7:00 AM," for my pre-induction physical exam. Evidently, the members of my board didn't anticipate changing their minds about me after my February 12th appeal meeting with them.

At that meeting, I submitted a new letter for inclusion in my dossier. In it, I synopsized my meeting of January 28th with attorney Osmond Burton. I said that Mr. Burton would submit a report recommending that the board give the "fullest consideration" to my request for C.O. status. Further, if the board did not grant me I-O status, then, "in the light of *U. S. vs. St. Clair*, the board should state the specific areas of my case the board objects to. The St. Clair decision was presented to the board in my letter of December 28, 1968. Mr. Burton also stated that he has himself raised the same objections to the local board on which the St. Clair case was decided.

"My current position has not changed from that already stated in my file," I continued. "I do not support the military murder machine. I have never hunted or fished in my life as, in our present society, I see this as unnecessary and unloving force. Yet, I love the outdoors and spend much time in it. Last summer I served as a Ranger in the National Park Service because I love the outdoors. As a Ranger, I was also a Federal law enforcement officer. At that time, I made clear to my superiors that I would not carry a weapon, nor use Mace if requested to do so. I would do all in my power to enforce the law up to that point. Force was not necessary to carry out my job, something my fellow Rangers found difficult to comprehend.

"For example, on July 4th, last, I and a fellow Ranger [Pink] successfully handled two drunken Navajos who were threatening to burn the residential quarter and kill our park Superintendent. As we were the only two Rangers on duty and our Superintendent refused to come out of his house, we had no help. Nevertheless, we successfully handled the situation without force. After we had convinced the Navajos to abandon their arson plans and after we returned them to the Navajo Reservation, two Coconino County Sheriffs and two other Rangers, all armed, showed up. They were too late. We'd handled everything, without the use or threat of force.

"I am in a strange position. I must now, at this meeting, state the sincerity of my beliefs to men who have already stated that they doubt my sincerity, while not telling me what it is about my beliefs they find insincere. Because of this position of doubt that I have been placed in, it is next to useless for me to speak at length about myself. So, I have asked another to speak for me. I am accompanied today by my minister, Reverend Ray Manker, and ask the board for the privilege of having him speak about me. As my minister is neither my attorney nor my legal counsel, I know of no legal reason for denying my request."

The board allowed Ray to appear and testify on my behalf. I don't know what he said, as I wasn't permitted to be in the room with them. When he came out, Ray smiled and placed his hand on my shoulder. "They listened very closely," he said. "I told them what I know about you and why I think you are sincere in your beliefs. I'm confident they will reclassify you as a Conscientious Objector. This should be the end of it."

I smiled at Ray. That was reassuring. He'd testified before draft boards for other young men in his congregation. He knew how these things went. I thanked him for his support.

But it turned out Ray really didn't know much about my local draft board. The next day, February 13th, my board sent me a letter again denying my appeal for Conscientious Objector status and re-confirming my I-A status. I was still Grade-A Prime Beef. And I was still scheduled to appear for my pre-induction physical exam four days later, on February 17th.

The steady stream on which I'd been drifting began to pick up more speed and force as it neared the fast-approaching precipice.

The Autocrat of the Dinner Table

Off and on through the years I was growing up, Mom worked as a prescription clerk at Bausch & Lomb Optical, the same firm for which she'd worked in Chattanooga and to which she'd transferred in moving to Phoenix in 1952. One of those times was when we moved one block away from the white stucco house on 52nd Street, which we rented, to a tan cinderblock house at 2244 N. 51st Street, which my parents decided to buy. It was almost at the corner of Oak and 51st and across the street from the Orangedale Elementary School, which I attended. Shortly after that, Mom begun to work again on a regular basis at the local office of Bausch & Lomb, the same office at which she'd worked upon arrival in Phoenix. And, for one-third of her take-home salary, Mom hired a trailer trash babysitter named Wilma.

Wilma was so huge she needed her own personal ZIP code. As soon as she waddled through the door, she turned on the TV and plopped down on the one easy chair we owned. The leather cushion farted loudly as Wilma's enormous butt hit it, and then settled as it deflated. Wilma left us alone to do as we wished and never stirred from that chair until Mom came home. At the end of the day she wrestled her bulk out of the chair, leaving behind the flattened cushion. Over time, the seams of the cushion ripped from this daily abuse and the stuffing pouffed out on all sides.

Wilma was delivered to our house and picked up by her husband in a rattle-trap jalopy. He was scruffy, raggedy, and wrinkled. He also had long greasy hair, combed back and flowing down to his shoulders. This was years before the Beatles and the British Invasion, and I'd never seen any man with long hair before. But, it didn't bother me. It was just the way he was. He also had no job. This was because, Mom said, "He was so lazy he wouldn't work in a pie factory." So his family depended on what Mom paid Wilma and whatever he could scrounge.

One Saturday morning, he drove Wilma over to our house so Wilma could pick up her weekly pay. A bar bud of my step-father's had dropped by to see Elmer before they both headed off to the tavern for the day. Elmer watched intently as Mom handed over the week's pay to Wilma, her husband standing beside her. Then Wilma and her husband left and got into his jalopy.

As soon as the living room door closed behind them, Elmer called for his buddy to come quick. They gathered at the closed living room curtains and peered out at Wilma's long-haired husband. They giggled and squealed and poked each other with delight as they mocked his sissy long hair. Standing behind them, watching them, they seemed to me like two ignorant and small-minded little boys, like all the little boys with small minds I had to deal with each day at school. I was disgusted, not only by their intolerance of what was different, but also by Elmer's hypocrisy. He'd simply stood silently in the husband's presence. But, in his absence, he laughed at and ridiculed the husband mercilessly. I always feared Elmer as a gargantuan bully. But that day was a revelation of another aspect of Elmer I didn't like. My "parent" seemed to be just a mean and immature little boy in an adult's body. I had to obey him, as he had the power of the fist over me, but I had no respect for him at all.

Meanwhile, since Wilma didn't bother us while she "babysat," we seven brothers essentially raised ourselves. We were like an assemblage of strangers thrown together in a rooming house, coming and going on our different errands. I think this lack of any real semblance of family coherence was a major reason only two of us, me and my brother Denny, managed to graduate from high school. And it was probably inertia which carried the two of us through, although Denny always seemed more committed to high school than me.

The most distant stranger in this assembly of strangers was Elmer. By this time he hardly seemed a part of the family at all. He was officially there on a daily basis, but we almost never saw him. My youngest brother Brad, who was born in 1961, once told me that he has absolutely no memory of his father at all until after 1970, when Elmer was no longer married to Mom. And that first memory of Elmer was of his father not showing up. Brad and brother Pat, the next youngest, had to sit in their best church clothes on the living room couch waiting all day for Elmer to come and pick them up on his visiting day. They had to be ready, in their best clean clothes, for their father. If their clothes were dirty, Elmer would bitch that Mom did not have them ready for him, and would storm off. Any excuse would do to avoid spending time with his sons, and Mom had learned the hard way not to give him this particular excuse.

But, it hardly mattered. Elmer usually didn't come for his sons, anyway. Once the sun went down and it was clear that Elmer would not come, Mom said it was OK for Brad and Pat to leave the couch and change out of their clean clothes.

Years later, as an adult, Brad asked Elmer why he so seldom came for them on his visiting days. Elmer thought about it and eventually replied that he just couldn't bare the heartache of seeing his sons, knowing that their precious family life together had been shattered. Brad, wanting desperately to be loved by Elmer, eagerly believed this as proof of how much he and Pat meant to their father.

But it was a lie. The truth was that spending weekend time with his sons would have meant taking weekend time away from his bar buds and his women -- and Elmer had his priorities. In the years I was growing up, Elmer always bitched that the house, the kids, and Mom were one big "ball and chain" around his neck, which he'd gladly cut loose from if he could. After the divorce, he finally *was* rid of the familial ball and chain. He wasn't eager to pick it up once more.

But, Elmer's absence after the divorce was not something new. Except for the very beginning of his marriage to Mom, Elmer had never been part of the family. He just wasn't there. He came home after the bar closed at one in the morning and we were already in bed.

If we weren't in bed, he beat the hell out of us. If I wanted to watch an old movie on the late night *Creature Feature,* it required constant alertness. I had to be ready to switch off the TV as soon as Elmer's headlights swung into the driveway. And I also never watched TV in a dark room. Not only could the glow of the TV screen be seen outside, but the screen also had a faint white spot in the center as it took its own sweet time in fading to black. In a dark room, that last white remnant of the dying tube would betray me, even though I'd switched off the TV and disappeared down the hall before Elmer walked through the door. So, I always left a small lamp lit by the living room window. The light it threw concealed both the glow of the TV when it was on, as well as the afterglow as it died. And it had the added benefit of seeming thoughtfulness on the part of Mom, so that Elmer wouldn't stumble in the darkness as he came in.

Elmer then staggered to bed and arose and left for work a few hours later in the wee hours of the pre-dawn darkness. Since this was before we awoke for school, we seldom saw our "father." He was the Invisible Man. And, for him, our home was just a mail-drop and a clothes closet.

Besides the absence of the Invisible Man, the next most noticeable absence was that of family meals. Often there was little to eat in the house, except bread and mustard, which we slapped together for mustard sandwiches. We foraged in the fridge and the pantry for what we could find and ate when we could. Then we went our separate ways.

If the Invisible Man happened to be around, on the weekend, say, no one ate. If Elmer caught any of us taking food out of the fridge, it meant a beating. That was because we were eating *his* food, the food he'd paid for. "What the fuck do you think I am," he yelled as he whacked us, "your Goddamned fucking meal ticket?"

It had not always been like this. In the early years of his marriage to Mom, before Brad was born, before he resigned from the family, we had meals together at a set time in the evening, 6:30, and Elmer presided over them as the paterfamilias. He was a stern autocrat and ruled the dinner table with a heavy hand. But at least at these times we seemed like a real family. Not surprisingly, I suppose, these early dinners of the 1950s are my fondest family memories.

And the foods we ate at these early family meals are still my favorite foods, my comfort foods. We had whole potatoes, boiled with their skins on, which we mashed up with our forks and smothered in thick brown gravy. We had pot roast cooked so long in a broth of carrots and onions that it fell apart at the touch of a fork. Each of us kids had a glass of milk straight from the fridge, so cold that moisture beaded on the outside of the glass. In the center of the table was a stack of Roman Meal whole wheat bread, which we used to sop up the gravy from our plates after we'd wolfed down our food.

We never said grace, but none of us could begin eating the food steaming on the plates under our noses until Elmer strolled in at his leisure from the living room and sat down. We looked at him expectantly. He nodded at us, and then we could eat. When we finished, if we wanted a second helping, we had to ask his permission to eat his food. "Yes, you may," he'd say, and nod again with the air of a prince granting a great boon upon his subjects.

And, once we had food on our plates, we had to clean those plates. Everything had to be eaten. Nothing could be left, even if we were full. "I'm paying for your Goddamned food," Elmer told us, "so you'll eat every bite. You're not going to waste my money."

Usually, this was no problem. We were always hungry, and we ate whatever was put in front of us. But I couldn't stand cooked spinach. I hated to see the flaccid green pile of it on my plate. Not only did it look unappetizing, it was slimy on my tongue and acrid in taste. But, we had to eat *everything,* so I always choked it down, gagging and almost retching as I did.

Until, one night, I could stand the taste of spinach no longer. I ate everything else on my plate but the spinach, which I carefully shoved off to the side with my fork. And then I just sat there, looking at it.

And I decided that I would never eat cooked spinach again.

"Eat your spinach," Elmer said, "or I'll kick your fuckin' ass."

I raised my eyes from the limp and slimy pile on my plate and looked at him. He was glowering at me, forehead creased in a frown. I knew what would come next. If he said he'd kick my ass, that meant he really would kick my ass. It wasn't a figure of speech. I knew he'd do it. I saw him kick Mom's ass after telling her that's exactly what he'd do. It was because Brother Denny was still acting like a baby.

Between June, 1955, and January, 1961, Mom was pregnant five times and produced four babies, with one miscarriage, in five-and-a-half years. It seemed she was permanently pregnant and there was always a new baby in the house. But Elmer didn't like babies and thought they should grow up as fast as possible. So, as soon as a new one was born, the one just up the line had to stop acting like a baby. This included sucking a milk bottle.

But, when Brother Pat was born in June of 1959, Brother Denny, who was then a-year-and-a-half, still wanted his bottle. He cried for it and stole Pat's bottle whenever he could. But Elmer forbade it. And he told Mom that if she let Denny suck a bottle, he'd "kick her ass."

One early afternoon Mom was in the kitchen of the stucco house on 52nd Street with Cleo, a neighbor, fixing the evening supper. Cleo had brought over some goat milk from her little farm for Pat, who was anemic and it was thought that goat milk would help him. Although Cleo stayed to help out, Mom was frazzled, because we kids were creating a chaos under their feet of fighting and bickering. And Denny was screaming for a bottle because he saw Pat sucking one in his crib. So Cleo said, "Oh, Kathy, let him have one. It won't hurt."

Elmer was in the tavern and wouldn't be home until 6:30, dinner time, if he showed up at all. So, Mom prepared a bottle of milk for Denny and gave it to him. Denny shut up, so she went back to her work and forgot about it.

And then, for some inexplicable reason, Elmer drove into the driveway. That day, he had not gone straight to the tavern from work. He walked in the door and the first thing he noticed was Denny sucking on a bottle. He scowled and, without saying a word, stalked over to where Mom was standing at a kitchen counter next to Cleo. Mom had turned to speak to Elmer as he'd come in. He grabbed both of Mom's shoulders, twirled her around so that her back was to him, and swung his foot in a wide arc into her ass with all his force. When his heavy construction boot plowed into Mom's ass, she screamed and was thrown face first up against the counter, knocking the salad she'd fixed for Elmer to the floor.

"I told you that if you let that boy have a bottle I'd kick your Goddamned ass," Elmer said.

"Elmer," Cleo broke in. "I'm the one who told her to give the boy the bottle."

Elmer whirled on Cleo. "And if you were my wife, I'd kick your Goddammed ass, too! Now you get the fuck out of my house!"

Mom couldn't sit without pain for a month after Elmer kicked her ass. He'd cracked her coccyx bone.

I'd seen Elmer do this, and I'd seen him beat Mom plenty of other times, so I knew what to expect from him. If he said he'd kick your ass, that's exactly what he'd do. He'd use his heavy work boots on you.

But, it didn't matter. No matter how hard he hit me, even if he kicked my ass, I decided I was not going to eat the spinach. "No," I said. "I'll never eat spinach again."

Elmer raised his left hand to his right shoulder, ready to smack me backhanded. I cringed, waiting for his hand to come down.

"Don't you hit the boy!" Mom said.

Elmer paused, hand still raised for a back swing. "You shut your Goddamned fuckin' mouth, Kathurn, or I'll slap you away from this table along with him!" Elmer could never get his tongue around "Katherine," Mom's name, and always called her "Kathurn." Mom hated to be called "Kathurn." She bridled every time the word came out of Elmer's mouth.

"I'm telling you, Elmer," she said, rising from her chair, "don't you dare hit the boy!"

Mom stood at the other end of the table, staring at Elmer. My bothers sat around the table in silence, staring at Elmer. I stared at Elmer, waiting for the slap which would send me flying away from the table. Elmer stared back at us.

And then, surprisingly, he lowered his hand. "Alright, you shitty little bastard," he said, pressing his face into mine. "You're going to sit right there until you eat every last bite of that Goddamned spinach."

Relief poured over me. This time, at least, I would not be beaten.

Elmer rose, shoving back his chair. "You boys," he said to my brothers, "you get to bed." In a scooting of chairs, my brothers quickly ran from the table.

"Clear the table, Kathurn," he ordered Mom. "And don't you dare touch the shitty little bastard's plate. He's going to sit there until Hell freezes over or he eats that Goddamned spinach, whichever comes first."

Then he stalked into the living room, where he snapped on the TV and fell onto the couch, which belonged to him when he was home.

"Just eat the spinach," Mom said to me as she began clearing the table.

"No. I will never eat spinach again. I will sit here until Hell freezes over."

"Why do you always have to cause trouble? Just stop being as stubborn as a mule and do as you're told. Eat your spinach and watch your mouth, or I'm the one who'll slap you."

Mom put away the leftovers in the fridge.

I said nothing and stared at the spinach on my plate.

Mom washed the dirty dishes in the sink and piled them in the drainer to dry.

I said nothing and stared at the spinach on my plate.

Mom glared at me as she left the kitchen and went to get my brothers ready for bed.

I said nothing and stared at the spinach on my plate.

In the living room, I heard the TV show Elmer was watching end and another one begin.

I said nothing and stared at the spinach on my plate.

That show ended, and another began.

That show ended, and another began.

I said nothing and stared at the spinach on my plate.

I heard Elmer turn off the TV and go into the bathroom to brush his teeth. I heard him spit into the bathroom sink. I heard him turn off the bathroom light and walk back. He stood in the doorway to the kitchen. "You think you're a smart-ass, you shitty little bastard. But you're gonna sit at that Goddamned table and eat that Goddamned spinach no matter *how* long it takes."

I said nothing and stared at the spinach on my plate.

He left me alone in the kitchen and I heard him undress and crawl into bed next to Mom, the bedsprings creaking, the covers rustling.

And I felt exhilaration, I felt euphoria. Elmer could slap me away from the table. He could beat me. He could, if he wanted, force the spinach down my throat with his fist. He could even kick my ass, like he did Mom's. He could do all that because he was bigger and stronger than me.

Or he could make me sit at the table all night and all the next day and all the next night, until I peed my pants where I sat and fell face down, asleep in my plate of spinach. He could do all that and there was nothing I could do to stop him. He was too big, he was too strong.

But one thing he could never do, no matter how hard he hit me or how long he made me sit at the table, staring at the plate of spinach, was make me willingly eat the plate of spinach. Hell would burn out and freeze over, I decided, before I would ever eat spinach again.

And, sitting there in the dark and quiet house, staring at my plate of cold spinach, I discovered something wonderful. I discovered one of the most powerful weapons of the weak. I discovered passive resistance, although I didn't know it was called that at the time. But I realized that, if you are willing to accept the consequences, then no matter how powerful the person may be who is telling you to do something, that person actually has no power over you at all. If you are willing to take the punishment, no one can make you do anything. *Anything!* You may *choose* to cooperate because you don't want to accept the consequences of non-cooperation. But, that's your *choice*. So, no matter *how* weak you are, you have complete control over your life, because you *always* have a choice over whether to cooperate or not.

For the first time in my life, I felt powerful.

And so I chose to sit there and stare at my plate of spinach. And I chose to listen to the second hand of the clock on the kitchen wall click around the clock's face. And I chose to listen to the house settle into silence around me. And I chose to sit there hour after hour, staring at my plate of spinach as the long night wore on.

And I was happy with my new-found power. And I was willing to sit there until Hell burned out and froze over, if I had to. Because, no matter how long I had to sit there, I knew I'd already won. Mom was right about me. I was as stubborn as a mule.

Sometime before dawn, Elmer appeared in the kitchen doorway. He glared at the limp and cold pile of spinach on my plate. Then he glared at me. "Alright, you shitty little bastard. Get your fuckin' ass to bed."

I rose and walked past him in silence. He towered over me as I walked past him, but I walked past Elmer like a man. As soon as I passed him and my back was to him, I expected him to kick my ass, as he'd kicked Mom's. I tensed for the coming kick.

But, the blow never came. Elmer didn't kick me. He let me walk past him and into my bedroom without a word. I'd beaten Goliath without even a slingshot. All I had was my determination to disobey his orders.

But, that was enough.

Honor

"If one *honest* man, in this state of Massachusetts, ceasing to hold slaves, were actually to withdraw from this co-partnership, and be locked up in the county jail therefor, it would be the abolition of slavery in America. For it matters not how small the beginning may seem to be: What is once well done is done forever."

-- Henry David Thoreau
On the Duty of Civil Disobedience

****

It was the morning of February 17, 1969. Dawn had not yet come to Vietnam's northern Quang Tri Province near the so-called Demilitarized Zone separating North and South Vietnam. In the darkness a small suicide assault group of Vietnamese guerrillas crawled silently toward the U. S. Marines encamped at the giant Fire Support Base (FSB) Cunningham. The Marines at FSB Cunningham were engaged in Operation Dewey Canyon. This was an invasion of the neighboring country of Laos meant to interdict the Ho Chi Minh Trail, by which North Vietnam funnelled supplies into the south. FSB Cunningham was near the Laotian border and a major support base for the invasion.

Vietnamese sappers crept up quietly on the Marines and attached explosives to the barbed wire surrounding the base. Then they set off their explosives, blowing holes in the wire. Other guerrillas then charged through, throwing grenades and satchel charges. They dashed in a suicide run toward the center of the base. They were not attempting to overrun the huge Marine base. They knew that was impossible. They were too few and they were out-gunned. Rather, they wanted to inflict as much damage as possible before they were killed, as they knew they would be.

And, in the dark and brutal firefight which followed, that's exactly what happened. The Marines rallied and repelled the attacking guerrillas, but Vietnamese managed to kill four Marines and wound 46 in the assault. Later, after the sun rose, the Marines counted 37 Vietnamese bodies in and around FSB Cunningham. "Not one of the gooks we had inside the perimeter had less than three or four holes in him," said one Marine lieutenant. "Usually it took a grenade or something to stop him completely."

The Marines at FSB Cunningham couldn't comprehend why the Vietnamese who attacked them fought so hard. What could possibly explain such outnumbered and outgunned soldiers assaulting a powerful military base like that? What could possibly explain soldiers continuing to fight even after three or four big holes had been punched in them? What could possibly explain such wounded soldiers continuing to fight until they were literally blown apart with grenades?

Certainly the Saigon dictatorship's soldiers didn't fight and die like that. The Marines themselves didn't fight and die like that. What could possibly have motivated the Vietnamese soldiers to fight and die like they did on the dark morning of February 17, 1969, at FSB Cunningham near the Laotian border?

The only explanation the Marines at FSB Cunningham could come up with was that the guerrillas who attacked them had to have been high on narcotics. Nothing else could explain why the Vietnamese fought and died as they did.

But the Marines didn't conduct an autopsy on any of the 37 Vietnamese bodies they found around FSB Cunningham to confirm their assumption. They didn't need evidence. They had an explanation which satisfied them. They just dug a hole, dumped the Vietnamese in, covered them up, and forgot about them.

And continued with the invasion of Laos.

But Operation Dewey Canyon, which the Marines at FSB Cunningham were supporting, failed to cut the Ho Chi Minh Trail. In fact, every American effort to cut the Trail during the entire war failed. American B-52s pounded the Trail daily, for years. In 1970 and again in 1971, we dropped 400,000 tons of bombs on the Trail. We dropped time-delay bombs and magnetic mines designed to leap at passing trucks. We defoliated it with herbicides, like Agent Orange. We seeded clouds in an effort to turn the Trail into impassable mud. We inserted clandestine special ops forces to ambush convoys. We repeatedly invaded Laos with full-scale assaults, the last time being the Lam Son 719 invasion in 1971, when we sent in 17,000 of the Saigon dictatorship's troops to cut the Trail. That invasion, too, was a debacle.

But all of America's hi-tech power was unable to cut the no-tech Trail. A steady stream of ancient and battered trucks, bicycles, and human beasts of burden -- men and women plodding through the jungle for months at a time with 100-pound sacks on their backs -- moved 20,000 tons of supplies per month down the Trial. Over six years, one Vietnamese porter named Nguyen Viet Sihn carried his weight in cargo on his back a distance equal to the circumference of the globe at the equator. Trinh Phi Binh travelled the Trail for nine years and was the only survivor of his 17-man platoon of transporters. American bombs killed the rest. But still he and his comrades moved their supplies down the Trail. The Vietnamese say two million men and women traversed the Trail over the course of the war. Another 75,000 men and women worked constantly to maintain the Trail. They eventually built the 12,000-mile jungle network of the Trail into an impregnable fortress, with service areas, field hospitals, and a fuel pipeline which stretched nearly to Saigon.

The American military likes to boast that, while it lost the war in Vietnam, it won every battle. That's a lie. The American military lost the Battle of the Trail, the most important battle of the war. In early 1971, a new antiwar organization, Vietnam Veterans Against the War, held its "Winter Soldier" forum about the myriad American atrocities in Vietnam. Although the forum was filmed, the film was never widely distributed. In the film, however, Gordon Stewart, who had been a forward artillery observer at a fire support base in Laos during 1969's Operation Dewey Canyon, recalled his experience during the invasion. "The whole company had set up a base camp on a hill," he remembered. "For the next three days it was pretty much hell. We ran through a lot of contact and lost a lot of men....The men became quite embittered during this operation. It became easy to kill Vietnamese. You were just animalistic....When moving through Laos, taking our dead and wounded, we took a lot of casualties."

All together, the American military lost 130 Marines dead and 920 wounded in Operation Dewey Canyon, including the four dead and 46 wounded at FSB Cunningham on February 17th. And, despite the intervention, the Trail kept pumping supplies into the south. American technology and fighting power was defeated by millions of ordinary Vietnamese men and women hacking trails out of what had been impassable jungle and lugging backbreaking loads over it to supply the war effort in the south. They endured and they died. After the war, Hanoi revealed that over one million of its soldiers were killed in the war, as compared to about 58,200 American soldiers, and another 600,000 of Hanoi's fighters were wounded. But they were never beaten into submission. They won the Battle of the Trail and this battle, more than any other, won them the war.

Our leaders and our soldiers never understood what the war was about. They thought they were fighting doped up zombies, as they assumed the outgunned and outnumbered Vietnamese guerrillas were who assaulted FSB Cunningham. But it wasn't narcotics which made the Vietnamese guerrillas fight like demons until their bodies were blown apart. It was their belief that they were fighting for their freedom, and freedom is a belief worth dying for, no matter what the odds against you. And it is because America never understood why the people of Vietnam refused to surrender, no matter what punishment they endured, never understood why they ceaselessly fought and died in myriad nameless firefights like the one at FSB Cunningham on the morning of February 17th, that America finally lost the war in Vietnam.

****

That same February 17th was also Annie's 19th birthday. I wondered what she was doing that day at Pitzer College as she entered the last year of her teens. It was probably a typical beautiful California day, full of sunshine, and Annie was going to classes. Which classes? Did she have anything special planned for later?

And that same February 17th was also the day of my Armed Forces pre-induction physical. I reported to the Armed Forces Induction Station on Moreland Avenue at 6:30 a.m. It was going to be a long day.

So far as I knew, there was nothing physically or medically wrong with me. I was a strong and healthy 22-year-old who the S.S. System was determined to draft as quickly as possible. Moloch suffered 50 Marine casualties that morning in the Vietnamese attack on FSB Cunningham. The Monster needed more young bodies to replace them. My physical was just another ritual we all had to perform before the Monster could get its hands on me.

And so the doctors poked and prodded me, along with a hundred other young men. They asked questions and listened to my heartbeat with stethoscopes. "Breath deep," they said. "Exhale. Again." They lifted up my eyelids and shined lights in my eyes. They told me to stick out my tongue and say "Ahh." They held down my tongue as I did so and looked at the back of my throat. They looked in my ears.

And then they tested my hearing. I was placed in a soundproof booth with earphones over my ears. When you first hear the tone, they told me, press this button. I listened until I heard a soft low solid tone becoming louder, first in one ear, then the other. I pressed the button when I heard the tones in my ears. My hearing was good enough for the Monster.

Looking back, I wonder why they didn't take blood samples. It was long before AIDS, but what if I had V.D.? What if I had diabetes or pre-diabetes? What if my blood cholesterol levels were so high that I was headed straight for a heart attack, even at my young age? Apparently, none of that was important. I was healthy enough to serve Moloch, and the examining doctors stamped my forms and passed me on to the next and final stage of the ritual.

That final stage was to stand in line before a seated panel of three head doctors in white coats who asked if there was any medical reason of which we knew that would disqualify us from serving Moloch. The middle doctor, shuffling papers on the table in front him like the others, was Dr. Walt Emory, the sculptor in metal, the doctor who had arranged Annie's abortion, Vern's friend -- and my buddy. I had no idea that Walt freelanced for Moloch. We looked at each other, but exchanged no signs of recognition.

The doctor to Walt's right ran down the list of names on a sheet of paper he held in his hands. When he got to my name he asked the same question he asked everyone else. To my knowledge, did I have any medical condition which would disqualify me from service?

"No," I answered.

And having writ, the Moving Finger moved on.

At the end of the list of names, the head doctor told us to be seated and wait while the three of them huddled in the next room over the results of our physicals.

As I lounged on one of the folding metal chairs, Walt came out of the inner sanctum and sat down beside me. "It's been awhile," he said.

"Yes. I was surprised to see you here this morning."

"I'm here to do what I can. And what I can do is give you a medical deferment."

"Even though I'm healthy?"

"I do it all the time. Flat feet. Hard of hearing. Whatever. I pull as many out of the draft as I can. It's what I do to oppose the war. Just say the word, and I'll exempt you."

"I've applied for Conscientious Objector status."

"Are they going to give it to you?"

"No, I'm not a religious pacifist."

"Then they're going to draft you?"

"Yeah, I'm on an express train to induction. My board seems to have it in for me."

"Well, we can derail that train right here. You want a medical deferment?"

For an instant, I thought about it. Walt was handing me a free get out of jail card. After today, I'd never have to worry about the draft again. And no one would ever know. I was home free. All I had to do was say "yes."

"No, Walt, I don't. I want my draft board to reclassify me as a Conscientious Objector."

"But, you said they aren't going to do that."

"No, they probably aren't."

"And then what?"

"Then I refuse induction."

"And then you go to prison."

"And then I go to prison."

Walt looked at me in puzzlement. "Do you *want* to go to prison?"

"No, I don't. But I don't want to go into the military, either."

"Exactly! Which is why I'm offering you a medical deferment."

"I can't do that, Walt. It wouldn't be right."

"Yes, it *would* be right. Anything that takes young men out of the draft pool is right."

"I don't agree. It wouldn't be right to accept a draft deferment to which I'm not entitled. But, I *am* entitled to a Conscientious Objector deferment, even if my draft board doesn't think so. And I'm fighting to force them to give me the proper classification for which I'm legally entitled."

"Eric, you just told me that's not going to happen. You're not a religious pacifist, so you don't qualify for C.O. status. So they're going to draft you. Don't you want to dodge the draft?"

Everyone always thought I was trying to dodge the draft. My draft board thought so. My teachers thought so when I asked them for letters attesting to my character. Now Walt thought so. Everyone thought so. I suppose it was the logical thing to think. Everyone else seemed to be trying to dodge the draft, in one way or another. It made sense to think I was, too. And, evidently, it was easy to do. Right now, all it meant was saying one word, "Yes," and I'd have dodged the bullet.

But what I was trying to do was much more difficult than dodging the draft. And, evidently, much more incomprehensible to those around me. I wasn't trying to *avoid* the draft. I was trying to *abolish* the draft. It was my moral obligation to refuse to cooperate with the draft, and so make the Empire's war that much more difficult to prosecute. It's what I had to do to respect myself.

But we live in a cynical world, and morally absolute positions seem to be hard for people, even good people like Walt, to understand and accept. They're more familiar with moral expediency. So, when you tell them you have moral obligations, that there are some things you just will not do because they're not right, they don't believe you. They look at you like you're either crazy or a liar. The way Walt was looking at me now.

"Walt, you don't understand. I don't want to *dodge* the draft. I want to *destroy* the draft. Besides, I've already been drafted. I've been drafted by my situation and by who I am. I'm *already* a soldier in a war *against* the war, and a soldier doesn't win a war by running away and avoiding combat. A soldier wins a war by standing and fighting. The draft will never be abolished so long as we conform to it and avoid confronting it. We can't slide out the back door. We can't run and hide. We have to refuse to *cooperate* with the draft. And by refusing to cooperate with it, we will *destroy* it. And, by destroying it, we'll help stop this war. They can't prosecute the war if we refuse to give them bodies for the war."

"Eric, you say 'we,' but you're just one person. You, alone, can't stop the draft and you can't stop this war. It's too big."

"You're right, Walt. One person can't do that. I'm not so egotistical to think I can. But if *enough* of us simply *refuse* to be drafted, then we can stop the draft, we can stop the war."

"Eric, be sensible. *Think* about where you are. This isn't Berkeley. This is Phoenix, Arizona. *No* one is thinking like you here in Phoenix. I work for the Selective Service System, I know. I deal with young men coming through here all the time. Most of them just go along with what's happening. Some want my help in dodging the draft with a medical deferment. But *none* of them are talking about *refusing* the draft and stopping the war. You're the only one I've ever heard talk like this."

"Well, someone has to be the first."

"Eric, you're not going to be the first. You're going to be *the only one*. What's the point in being a martyr? You can't change the world."

"Maybe not, but neither can the world change me. I have to do this."

"Eric, you're all by yourself. And all you can do by yourself is go to prison, which is certainly what will happen if you refuse to be drafted. There's no need for that. I'm offering you a way out. Don't be stubborn. Take it."

"Well, I know prison's most likely...."

"Not 'most likely.' *Certainly.*"

"OK. I'm *certainly* headed to prison if I refuse to be drafted. But, Walt, you have to do what you think is right, even if you go to prison because everyone else thinks it's wrong."

"And when you get out of prison, everyone will know *why* you were in prison and they'll call you a coward and a traitor to your face."

"I expect that's true. Nothing I can do about that. But *I'll* know the truth. *I'll* know I was a P.O.W. who went to prison for the good of my country. And *I'll* know that I didn't take the coward's way out by accepting a fake medical deferment I didn't deserve."

Walt looked at me in silence. Then he held out his hand. I took it. He held my hand firmly. "Eric, I think you're just being stubborn and stupid. But I wish you the best."

I smiled and shook Walt's hand with both of mine. "Thanks, Walt. Then I'm not all by myself, after all."

Walt squeezed my hand and then walked back through the door into the sanctum sanctorum where the doctors made their decisions. I never saw Walt again after he walked through that door. And as the door closed behind him, I knew it also closed on my last chance to just slide right out of the draft, forever. I knew I'd be judged physically fit, good soldier material, able to climb on the Midnight Special to the war.

"You're as stubborn as a mule," Mom always told me. With which Annie agreed. Now to that could be added stupid. Stubborn and stupid, just like Walt said. There it was, a medical deferment, handed to me by Walt on a silver platter. All I had to do was say, "Yes." And the S. S. System would never have known how easily I'd slipped out of its clutches.

But I turned it down.

Because it would not have been resisting the draft. It would have been working the draft, exploiting an unforeseen advantage I had to dodge the draft, to sidestep it. And the death machine would not have known that there was at least one kid in Phoenix who refused to kneel down before it and bow like one who believed. I would not be helping to destroy the draft.

So I couldn't do it. I had a moral obligation to resist evil by publicly taking a stand, even if it meant standing alone, even if it meant prison. You have to stand for something, or you stand for nothing. A cliche, perhaps, but cliches become cliches because they're true.

And I turned down Walt's offer because it would have been dishonorable. It would have been cheating. It wouldn't have been fair to every other kid in that waiting room who played by the rules and passed his physical and never had his good bud, Dr. Walt, come out and say, "Hey, you want me to defer you?" It wouldn't have been right. Even though no one would ever know but me and Walt, it wouldn't have been right.

And I'd never have been able to hold my head up again when talk of Vietnam came up. Twenty, thirty years down the road, when my son asked me what I did during the Vietnam War, I'd have to say, "Well, son, your dad cheated his way out of the draft. The examining doctor was a good friend of mine, so he gave me a medical deferment, even though I was as healthy as a horse."

I was never going to put myself in that position. I didn't care whether or not it was the smart thing to do. I wasn't going to do something I'd be ashamed of for the rest of my life. I wasn't going to cheat my way out of the draft. It just wasn't right.

And a real man does the right thing.

Even when it's stupid.

Shortly thereafter, I received a notice from my draft board, dated that same day, February 17th, stating that I'd been found "fully acceptable for induction into the armed forces."

Give Peace a Chance

John and Yoko married that March. Paparazzi fluttered around them like moths to an outdoor lightbulb. At first, the attention drove John and Yoko crazy. They were on their honeymoon and they just wanted to be alone with each other.

Then John and Yoko decided that since the attention was a fact of life and there was no way they could escape it, they would use the media's fascination for something *they* were interested in: Peace. If the paparazzi were going to send pictures of John and Yoko and everything they said around the world anyway, it may as well be for a good cause.

So John and Yoko paused on their honeymoon tour and holed up at a Montreal hotel where they invited the paparazzi into their honeymoon suite to see what they were doing in bed. Salivating salaciously at the chance to photograph the outrageous John and Yoko "doing it," the paparazzi flooded in. But, instead of finding John and Yoko doing it, they found them sitting up in bed, fully clothed in their jammies, awaiting them. John and Yoko were surrounded by homemade signs John had taped over the windows and walls saying, "Give Peace a Chance."

Puzzled, the paparazzi asked John and Yoko why they were just sitting there in their jammies. Weren't they going to "do it"?

John and Yoko said they *were* "doing it." They were "doing" a "Bed-In for Peace." They wanted the world to stop all the killing and just give peace a chance.

The paparazzi duly took their pictures and transmitted them around the world.

John and Yoko continued lolling in bed for peace and continued to generate publicity by inviting a stream of fellow celebrities into their hotel room to be filmed talking with them about world peace. Eventually, they invited anyone and everyone they knew simultaneously into the hotel suite to join them in recording John's new single, "Give Peace a Chance." That's all we're saying here in bed in our jammies, John and Yoko told the world, just give peace a chance.

It wasn't just John and Yoko. That spring antiwar students at Harvard occupied University Hall in Harvard Yard, the administration nerve center of the campus.

A year previously, students occupied several buildings at Columbia, including President Grayson Kirk's office. Kirk called in the police to clear the buildings. New York's working-class cops welcomed the Establishment's permission to beat the shit out of privileged students. In a fury of class hatred, the cops swiftly seized the buildings, leaving in their wake a bloody mess.

In response, the entire Columbia student body and faculty went on strike. That summer, Kirk was forced to resign and the student radicals won all their immediate demands, including the ending of war research on the Columbia campus. The Establishment's unleashing of police violence on students backfired at Columbia.

One would have thought the big-brain leaders of Harvard would have learned from that history. But, they must've been asleep at the wheel during the Columbia experience. So Harvard did the same thing Columbia had done and called in the working class cops of Cambridge, who also rejoiced in the permission thus given by the Establishment to kick the shit out of privileged Harvard students. Another bloody mess resulted as the Cambridge cops cleared the buildings in Harvard Yard.

And, predictably, the entire Harvard campus was soon stencilled with the now-famous Harvard Strike Fist and the student body and faculty went on strike, shutting down the university. Ivy League university administrators, it seems, Ph.D.s all, are as slow to learn as generals, who are always said to be fighting the previous war.

But, what happened at Harvard was not an isolated incident. That spring American students demonstrated at over 300 colleges attended by one-third of the nation's students. At 75 colleges there were strikes or building occupations. There was a constant drumbeat of demonstrations, picket lines, building occupations, sit-ins, police beatings, arrests, and even bombings.

But the war went on. Indeed, Operation Dewey Canyon, the U. S. invasion of Laos, also continued for most of March, ending on the 19th when the Marine invasion force retreated in defeat back across the border into South Vietnam.

And, as the endless war in Vietnam went on and, indeed, seemed to be expanding into neighboring countries like Laos, there were more demonstrations, more picket lines, more building occupations, sit-ins, police beatings, arrests, and bombings. What had originally been a student and black revolt more and more took on the aspects of a general revolt against the powers-that-be. It seemed to many, including me, to be a revolutionary time.

The Universal Players performed at Prescott College and Northern Arizona University (then called Arizona State College) in Flagstaff. Jan Sownie, Annie's best friend from North High, organized the show in Flagstaff. Annie flew into Phoenix and we had some time together before we went up north. Then I rented a VW bug, the cheapest car I could get, and we packed in the four of us. By then we'd picked up a young kid from the Vaudeville who was a fantastic guitarist, so now we had two guitars. The kid and Carlo sat in back, the kid playing his guitar and Carlo joking all the way to Flagstaff.

We performed in a huge auditorium to a capacity crowd. The standing ovation at the end of "Where Is Vietnam?" washed over us, going on and on and on. The performance in Flagstaff was the last performance of the Universal Players. At least we went out at the peak of our powers and our popularity. The spring semester of '69 was drawing to a close and it wasn't possible to pack in any more campus appearances before the end of the school year. If I wasn't in prison the next school year, we planned to recruit more actor-musicians and do even more shows. But, our first year of touring college campuses for peace had been far more successful than we imagined it could've been.

Meanwhile, on March 12th I wrote to Mrs. Dimmick and my draft board concerning their February 13th classification of me as I-A, Prime Beef. "Once more you and Local Board No. 29 have improperly classified me I-A. Again, I ask you and the local board for the reasons for your decision. What aspects of my case do you find inadequate?"

It was important to keep hammering away on the point that my board never gave a reason for their decision. It would be a major argument on which my case would pivot once I met the military in court.

"I am hereby appealing your decision," I continued. "Please set up an appointment with Osmond Burton, the Government Appeal Agent affiliated with my local board.

"I understand that it is the right of the registrant to view his file if he so wishes. I would like to do this. Either the local board is not viewing my complete file, the local board has not even opened my file, or the local board is ignorant of the fact that I am qualified under the law for Conscientious Objector status. I would like to find out if the first possibility is true by comparing your file with my own copy of my file. It truly frightens me to think the board is opting for one of the other two possibilities.

"From the very beginning of my fight with you, Mrs. Dimmick, I have not expected to be treated justly by the S.S. System. From the beginning I have prepared to refuse induction and take my case to court. Time has shown the truth of my expectations and the necessity for my preparations. I cannot foretell the decision of the State Appeal Board, but I believe I can very definitely foretell the decision of the court when I eventually reach the court.

"Mr. Burton, the Government Appeal Agent, has told me that I will win in court.

"The Rev. Ray Manker, my minister and an experienced draft counselor, believes I will win in court.

"The American Civil Liberties Union believes I will win in court.

"And I believe I will win in court.

"This, Mrs. Dimmick, is the only satisfaction I have in dealing with you people."

How to win friends and influence people, eh?

But I knew I had no friends on my draft board and there was no way I could favorably influence them, so I didn't even try. As I told them, I did not expect justice from them and I expected them to draft me. And, since I would refuse induction, I expected to face the military system in court one day soon. Thus, everything I wrote, I wrote for my day in court.

On Monday, March 17th, one month after my physical and Walt's offer of a deferment, I visited my local draft board and Mrs. Dimmick allowed me to examine my file. So far as I could tell, it was identical to mine. Everything I'd sent them was there. The board just didn't give a damn what I sent them. They had their own agenda.

I wasn't doing too well in school during all of this. It wasn't that the work was too hard, it was that I just missed too many classes. On individual assignments, I did fine. In my course on "Populism and Progressivism" I received an "A+" on an essay I wrote critiquing Eric F. Goldman's interpretation of Progressivism in his classic work, *Rendezvous with Destiny*. I didn't know an "A+" grade existed. But, I ended up with an Incomplete in that course because I just wasn't able to finish all the course work in a timely fashion.

Two of the five courses I took that semester at ASU were in "Aesthetics" and "The Oral Interpretation of Poetry." In my Aesthetics course I submitted a poem, "Wisdom," which I'd written three years before, in 1966, while at Phoenix College. The professor, Dr. Harry Wood, liked it so much that, for our Tuesday afternoon class on March 18th, he mimeographed it (Hey, gang! Remember mimeographs?) and distributed it to the class for discussion:

****

Wisdom

"We must end this senseless slaughter on the highway,"
                                                    says LBJ.
    While far away,
        We kill thousands more
            In a senseless slaughter called war.
    But killing there is no great crime,
        And so there they lay,
            With their heads blown away,
                While I listen to a man
                    With his mind blown away
        Say:
            "We must end this senseless slaughter...
                                    On the highway."

****

I surely don't claim this is great poetry. It's just an observation made by a teenager in a community college in Phoenix in 1966 who, not long before, had supported the war. I'd travelled a long road in a short time. And, three years later, in 1969, at ASU, the same poem was grist for a contentious classroom discussion of the war. I had fun reading and then defending the view expressed in the poem, which was probably more acceptable in 1969 than in 1966.

But I also received an Incomplete for that course that same semester, and for the same reason as the Incomplete in my "Populism and Progressivism" course. I didn't complete all the course work.

And I actually ended up officially withdrawing from my course on the "Oral Interpretation of Poetry." I was doing exactly that to standing ovations from SRO crowds on college campuses across Arizona and in California, but I was also missing too much course work to get a decent grade at ASU for the oral interpretation of poetry.

So I realized my academic transcript wouldn't look too good. But, the military had long since yanked my student deferment, anyway, so it hardly mattered. All that semester, as I went to classes and worked at my student work-study job with the Forest Service and fought the S.S. System and performed with the Universal Players in antiwar presentations around the state, I was I-A, on the fast track to induction. It'd now been a full year since I'd officially applied for Conscientious Objector status with my local board and the possibility of being given that status was further away than ever. My draft board was determined to put me in uniform. And I was even more determined that would never happen.

So, I was preoccupied that entire spring of 1969. My mind was elsewhere. School wasn't important. What was important was the war.

On Thursday, March 20th, I wrote another letter to my draft board requesting "Form 150 as Revised for Conscientious Objectors," as I'd discovered during my visit to their office on March 17th that the form I'd originally filled out and submitted was obsolete. Of course, I'd not been informed of that. I had to find out on my own. I also enclosed with that March 20th missive a letter from Rev. Ray Manker, dated March 17th, recounting his February 12th appearance before the board on my behalf.

"As nearly as I can recall," Ray wrote, "the following is the gist of that meeting. I related that I have known Eric for approximately two-and-a-half years, during which time we have had many conversations and much counselling. I find him to be an extremely sensitive young man, with high intelligence, morals, and ethical commitment....Asked, specifically, my appraisal of his sincerity, I answered that he is, in my opinion, an unusually sincere, honest person. Furthermore, I am convinced that he is sincerely a conscientious objector....His religious beliefs strongly parallel my own and I, too, am a conscientious objector to war in any form.

"I left feeling that there had been real communication and that the Board respected my appraisal of Mr. Davin and his convictions. As a result, I felt the Board would grant him his request for I-O classification."

Of course, that didn't happen. But the reason I wanted Ray's account of that meeting in my file was because I'd discovered during my examination of it on March 17th that there was no account of Ray's appearance on my behalf. When my day came, I wanted his account to be part of the court record.

The next month, on April 14th, I followed up with another letter from Dr. Arch Egbert, the Director of the Mormon Institute of Religion at ASU. "I have been acquainted with Eric Davin as a student in my American History and World Religion classes and through many private conversations," Dr. Egbert wrote on Institute of Religion stationery.

"I am convinced he is a very wholesome, honest man of deep integrity and warm concern for his fellow man....I have read his papers [essays] and talked at length to him about his beliefs and feel he should be allowed Conscientious Objector status. He is willing to do equivalent work instead of military service and I believe this would be more just, wise and legal rather than trying to force him to go against his convictions."

Of course, it didn't matter whether I had a Unitarian minister or a Mormon religious leader going to bat for me. The S.S. System was determined to send me to their war and ignored everything I or anyone who championed me wrote. I knew they would. But I was fighting my own war against them and I was methodical in covering all my bases in preparation for the coming legal showdown.

Thus, preparing the new Form 150 for Conscientious Objectors was, from my perspective, another opportunity to place in the record a new, more extended, statement about my moral objections to the war and to the military system itself. I refused even to consider military service as a non-combatant. My objection to the military, I wrote, "is not that I will carry a weapon and maybe shoot somebody...but that the Armed Forces is inherently a murderous and evil system....It matters not whether I would carry a gun -- I would still be Government Issue."

I returned the completed Form 150 and my new essays with a cover letter to my draft board, dated May 4th, in which I began by saying, "Chief U.S. District Judge Charles E. Wyzanski, Jr., in Boston earlier this month, declared the Selective Service Act of 1967 unconstitutional. The American Civil Liberties Union voted in February that the draft law 'as presently administered and in present circumstances' violated civil liberties and constitutional guarantees. This has been my contention for some years now. Your authority is an illegal and immoral authority which betrays the ideals this nation was founded upon.

"It is my fervent hope that my actions in opposition to you will, in their own small way, aid in the destruction of the S.S. System. Every Man who refuses your authority and drags you into a courtroom forces the Justice Department to spend time, money, and effort on prosecuting him. My case against you will be but one of thousands. Every time we force the issue in these constructive confrontations before a judge such as Justice Wyzanski, we are forcing you and the people of this nation to take another look into your position -- another look to reassure yourselves that you are right. Every case such as mine forces you to re-evaluate the 'justice' of your crusade. President Nixon would never have suggested a volunteer army if it were not for the thousands of resisters such as myself.

"In all justice, can even you blame me for wishing your destruction? I want to be a constructive law-abiding member of my society with all my heart. And that is what I would be, were you not forcing me to oppose you and the laws of my society to the point of refusal to be inducted. I will not let you use me. I am not your property. I will not live for you. I will not let you steal two years of my life. If the old men in Congress, the S.S. System, and our other Establishments want to make the world think like us -- let them go out and do it, because I will not! I will oppose you. I am fighting you -- and I'll beat you!"

Bravado, perhaps, but that's how I felt. Although dated May 4th, I didn't send this letter and my new Form 150 until May 12th. According to the signed and stamped return receipt which accompanied it and everything else I sent my Board, they received it the next day, May 13th.

On May 19th Mrs. Dimmick wrote me saying, "At their meeting May 14th, the Local Board reviewed your new SSS Form 150 and related papers, but decided not to reopen your classification."

Of course not. Perhaps, considering the short shrift they gave my new application and essays, they never even bothered to read them. They'd already made up their minds. They were going to keep me I-A, Prime Beef, on the fast track to induction. That'd teach my ass!

On May 15th, the day after my draft board refused to reconsider my application for Conscientious Objector status, the police in Berkeley, California, seized People's Park, ejected about 75 occupants, erected an eight-foot high chainlink fence around it, and posted "No Trespassing" signs on the fence. People's Park was a vacant lot which belonged to the University of California. As the university wasn't currently doing anything with the land, local activists dug it up, planted grass and flowers and gardens, and turned it into a park for the people of Berkeley: People's Park.

The university did not approve and sent in the cops to seal off eight city blocks around the park and bulldoze the gardens. As they did so, about 2,000 angry demonstrators gathered outside the chainlink fence and denounced the police actions. The police responded with tear gas and shotguns loaded with buckshot. For hours the police fired their shotguns into the crowd, into passersby, into reporters, into people running away from them. The police wounded between 50 and 100 people. They permanently blinded an artist named Alan Blanchard with their buckshot and ripped open the belly of James Rector, killing him. It was the first time a white kid had been killed in such a confrontation. It would not be the last. It seemed the university valued property more than life and so was willing to use murderous force to protect its property.

California Governor Ronald Reagan decided there was an incipient revolution in the making and that the insurrection at Berkeley had to be completely and immediately crushed. That night he ordered his state's National Guard to seize the park, seize the University of California campus, and seize the city of Berkeley. It was the first time an American university had ever been occupied by military forces. This, too, would not be the last time. And it was also the first time a largely white American city was militarily occupied and placed under martial law. A nightly curfew was imposed and public gatherings of more than three people were banned. Travel was restricted and streets were blocked off to all except proven residents.

Over the next week police and National Guardsmen arrested more than a thousand Berkeley residents, 200 on felony charges. Those arrested were beaten and otherwise brutalized. One student, Frank Bardacke, was handcuffed and then punched as the Berkeley police forced him to sing "The Star-Spangled Banner." When students peacefully rallied on the Berkeley campus, a National Guard helicopter flew over and blanketed them and the entire campus with nausea gas to disperse them. Then National Guard troops wearing gas masks moved in to seal off the campus and beat the fleeing and vomiting students.

With People's Park it seemed the war really had come home, and students like me were now the Vietnamese, to be gassed and shot by the occupying American army. Some Berkeley radicals pointed to the whole experience as proof that it was now time to "pick up the gun" and fight back militarily. Any last lingering hope for "Flower Power" died when the police bulldozers plowed up the flowers of People's Park. Ronald Reagan was fulfilling his own prophecy of rebellion and insurrection.

On May 22nd, in the midst of People's Park, Canada broadened its immigration guidelines to accept U.S. Army deserters, along with civilian draft resisters, for which it had long been a haven. As America seemed to be descending ever more into a murderous tyranny, leaving for Canada was an attractive option. Canada did not have a military draft. Hence, refusing to be drafted was not a crime in Canada. And since, under Canadian law, draft resisters had broken no law and were not criminals, they could not be extradited back to the United States. Indeed, over the course of the Vietnam War, around 30,000 young American men took advantage of this northern refuge and fled to Canada to avoid being drafted.

Now, Canada had opened its door even to army deserters. Membership in a military organization, the Canadian government said, "is a matter to be settled between the individual and his government." It was no concern of the Canadian government.

The news made me think about Canada favorably, but I rejected the idea of fleeing America, even though I was I-A and it was clear my draft board wanted to draft me as fast as it could. If I'd simply wanted to dodge the draft, I'd have accepted Dr. Walt's easy offer of a fake medical deferment. But my real goal was destroying the draft, and by doing so help end the war, and I didn't see how running to Canada would help do that. The draft could only be abolished, I felt, by staying and fighting it in the courts, which is where I appeared to be headed.

Besides, despite the war, despite People's Park, I did not see America as irremediably evil, as most of those on the anti-imperialist New Left apparently did. To my eyes, they didn't even seem to think of themselves as Americans. They were in America by an accident of birth, but had no apparent loyalty to it. Thus, leaving America was no big trauma for them.

But I was a patriotic American who was completely wrapped up in America. I believed in the democratic and humane values for which it claimed to stand, certainly the values for which I stood and for which I was fighting. And if America increasingly seemed to have abandoned its own core values, it was my patriotic obligation to help bring America back to those basic values. So, it was my patriotic duty -- a concept seemingly alien to most student radicals -- to stay and fight for the soul of America.

Besides, I was in love with this great big wonderful country. That was one of the reasons I'd served as a Park Ranger at Wupatki. I loved America more and better, I felt, than right-wing reactionary Republican assholes like Nixon, who'd taken to wearing an American flag pin in his lapel. Now all the right-wing reactionary Republican assholes in America, like Ronald Reagan and his ilk, were doing the same, as if to say *they* were the only true Americans. That's what the Berkeley cop who beat the handcuffed Frank Bardacke while forcing him to sing "The Star-Spangled Banner" believed. *He* was an American, not Frank Bardacke, and *he* was doing what any true American would do: Beating the shit out of a handcuffed prisoner while forcing him to sing the national anthem.

But I loved America more and better than that Berkeley cop because I loved what America embodied, while that cop and Reagan and Nixon had no concept of what America stood for and had no loyalty at all to American values. Instead, they worshipped the power to beat a handcuffed prisoner while forcing him to sing the national anthem. It was the kind of thing a Latin American death squad killer would do before putting a bullet in his prisoner's head -- and, indeed, the Berkeley cop who beat Frank Bardacke had also held his pistol to Bardacke's head as the cuffed Bardacke lay on the ground beneath him. If Christ had returned to preach that peacemakers were blessed and that the meek shall inherit the earth, Reagan and Nixon and the cops who thugged for them would have crucified Christ again, while forcing Him to sing "Onward, Christian Soldiers."

So I wasn't going to abandon America, the land I loved, to the tender mercies of Neanderthal maggots like *them*. If I fled America for a Canadian exile, I could never return. Thus, leaving America, no matter how repressive and murderous it was becoming, was as unthinkable for me as leaving Annie. It just wasn't gonna happen. I was wed to both forever, through thick or thin, for better or for worse, no matter what happened. America might abandon *me* and people like me, as it appeared to be doing, and Annie might abandon me, as she'd once done, but I would never abandon either. They were both Catholic marriages.

On May 30th, while police sharpshooters targeted them from roofs along the way, 25,000 peaceful people marched peacefully through the streets of Berkeley to People's Park. There they wove flowers into the links of the chainlink fence which surrounded the park and flashed peace signs at the armed National Guardsmen who glared at them from the other side of the fence. There was no shouting, no rock-throwing, no fighting. The people of Berkeley just went to People's Park to stand unarmed before military madness and say to it, "Give Peace a Chance."

That same day, which was Memorial Day, I wrote another letter to my draft board. "Your letter of May 19th informed me that my local board has once more refused to give me my proper classification. I can find no logical reason for you to doubt the sincerity of my antiwar beliefs. You are therefore acting in an illegal, capricious, and arbitrary manner.

"You stated in your letter that my file has now been forwarded to the State Appeal Board for its consideration. The decision of that Board will not be whether or not I will go into the military. That matter has long since been decided by me. I will not serve in your military. So its decision is whether or not I will have criminal charges filed against me for refusing to be drafted.

"The procedure as I see it now is this: If ordered to appear for induction, I will appear at the induction station after writing you one more letter explaining why I will refuse induction. I will present the authorities and anyone else interested at the induction station with mimeographed statements explaining why I am refusing induction. I will sign nothing presented to me at the induction station. I will refuse to step forward, indicating my unwillingness to be drafted, and I will refuse to take an oath of allegiance to this government. Remaining a civilian, I will then return home and prepare to face the Justice Department in court. I do not wish to go to prison, but I am prepared for that, if need be. But I am confident I will prevail over the S.S. System in court."

I'm like the people at People's Park, I'm like John and Yoko, I thought, trying, in my own way, to give peace a chance.

Fork in the Road

T. S. Eliot was wrong, I thought, holding the letter from ASU and staring out at the desert scrub surrounding Sherman's house. June is the cruelest month. Already temperatures had climbed above 100. They'd climb higher and stay there until the fall. The Sonora desert is just a killer in the summer. I wasn't looking forward to baking in it, but I didn't see that I had much choice. My life seemed to be narrowing around me and I'd pretty much run out of options. As I stood there with the letter, I was thinking about buying a one-man Army surplus tent from the Army-Navy store and pitching it on empty land somewhere out in the desert. It wouldn't be for all that long. Just till the end of summer. Just till I was drafted and then went to prison for refusing to be drafted.

The spring semester at ASU had ended. The school year had also ended at Pitzer. Annie had scored a ride with a classmate who was driving home back East. The classmate had been happy to drop Annie off at Wupatki on her way. Already Annie was settling into the Wupatki routine. Unlike me and Pink, it seemed the rangers at Wupatki had not exiled Annie to the distant trailer among the Navajo workers. Annie got to live in one of the World War II apartments just above the Visitor Center. I knew Annie would come to love Wupatki as much as I had. It would've been great to have been Park Rangers together at Wupatki, but that was not to be. At least Annie would have the Wupatki experience.

Meanwhile, I had to decide how to spend the summer while I awaited my inevitable induction notice. The end of the semester meant that my work-study job as a cartographer with the Forest Service had also ended, as well as my morning gig at the campus Catholic Newman Center, where I bussed for breakfast. It also meant I'd run out of rent money. Besides paying tuition, I'd used my student loan to pay my rent. The end of the semester meant the end of the loan, as well as my student jobs, which meant the end of my apartment. So, I was broke and homeless.

But, I still had friends. One of them was Sherman, who I'd met in one of my classes. He was a geeky "nice" boy. I don't know why he liked me, but I was lucky that he did. His rich parents lived on a big desert spread out in Paradise Valley. It was so big that, like Tom Wagers, he had his own apartment on it. At least it seemed like his own apartment. It was a separate section of the sprawling compound which he had all to himself. There, Sherman's parents left him to do as he pleased. That meant he could blast Led Zep's new album as loud as he wished out of his expensive stereo with the giant speakers as his friends came and went at all hours of the day and night. Whole lotta love, baby!

There were also guest rooms in various annexes. Sherman told his parents I was going to crash in one of them. OK with them, so I moved my meager belongings into one of the rooms. I was grateful. It was as if I had my own free apartment. But I knew I couldn't depend on the kindness of Sherman -- and the tolerance of his parents -- for more than a temporary refuge. That was why I was thinking of pitching a tent out in the desert. At least I wouldn't have to pay rent on the tent and I'd not be imposing on anyone. I hated being obligated.

Meanwhile, I kept my Central Avenue Post Office mailbox and I kept up my running battle with my local draft board located just above my mailbox in the Central Avenue Post Office building. On June 13th the S. S. System's state Appeal Board voted four-to-zero to deny my petition for Conscientious Objector status and to confirm my local board's I-A, Prime Beef, classification. I had no further appeal rights.

No big deal. I'd expected them to keep me on the Midnight Special to the war. I was just exhausting my legal options so it'd be easier to fight the bastards in court after I refused to be drafted; so I could argue that I had exhausted all administrative remedies and had no other way to obtain justice but to refuse induction.

On June 15th I wrote a letter to Mrs. Dimmick, the expediter for my local board, saying, "Yes, once more the S.S. System has refused to place me in my lawful classification....While other young men my age are burning the rest of the world for America, I want only to live in peace with all men." That, however, was not to be allowed.

I then asked Mrs. Dimmick to schedule another meeting with Osmond Burton, the Appeal Agent assigned to my local board to counsel registrants. Although I had no further rights of appeal, the pamphlet I had on "Taking Appeals From Selective Service Classifications" -- my combat manual for fighting the military -- told me that, "The State Director of the State in which the Local Board of Registration is located...or the National Director [that being General Lewis B. Hersheybar]...may take an appeal to the President from the classification given by the State Appeal Board." I wanted to ask Mr. Burton's advice on doing exactly that. I certainly didn't expect the State Director to intercede with Tricky Dick Nixon on my behalf, but I was determined to fight the bastards to the last ditch.

Unknown to me, Ray Manker, the minister of Phoenix's Unitarian Church, which I still sometimes attended, was meeting at that same time with the State S.S. Director, Col. Norman Erb, in Erb's office in the Central Avenue Post Office building. Ray followed up that meeting with a June 18th letter to Erb, a copy of which he sent to me.

"Dear Col. Erb," Ray wrote, "I appreciate very much the opportunity to discuss with you the problems I have been wrestling with concerning the draft. Even more, I appreciate the consideration you showed in attempting to understand the peculiarities of the Unitarian Universalist religion as it exhibits itself when our young men apply for I-O [Conscientious Objector] classification.

"As per your suggestion to give you the names and Selective Service numbers of the young men from our church over whom I have been so concerned, I would like to refer you to Eric Davin. Eric is the young man about whom I talked with you at length and whose earlier 150 statement [my essay asking for C.O. status] I showed you. He tells me that he has refiled the new 150 Form and also that just this past week he was turned down on his appeal to the State Board by a unanimous decision. You are his only hope now. If you can help him in his efforts to get his I-O it will be greatly appreciated."

I followed this with my own letter to Col. Erb. "I am a Conscientious Objector legally entitled to a classification of I-O under the laws governing the Selective Service System," I informed him. "I have been actively seeking this classification for two years and have been repeatedly denied this classification in an illegal manner.

"The State Appeal Board rejected by appeal for a I-O classification on June 13th and I have no further rights of appeal. I am and have been I-A for the past eight months. My local board, No. 29, tells me that I will be at the top of the list for the next draft call.

"I do not intend to serve in any branch of the armed forces. If ordered for induction, I will refuse said induction. However, I would rather it never came to that. I would rather I was given my proper classification without going to court to obtain that classification.

"I ask you to investigate my case and appeal my case to the President."

Yeah, some last hope Col. Norman Erb represented. I didn't think he'd actually present my case to Tricky Dick, but I at least expected a pro forma reply. I never got even that from him.

All I got was silence. Meanwhile, I heard the ominous whistle of that Hell-Bound Train coming for me.

And then came the letter from ASU. "You have been disqualified because of low scholarship," it told me. The semester just ended had been an academic disaster. Indeed, both of the two years I'd spent at ASU had been academic disasters. My transcript was peppered with Incompletes and Withdrawals. In two years I'd earned 20 credits, the equivalent of one heavy semester of classes, about a third of what I should've earned. And my grades in even the courses I completed were not outstanding. Now I was barred from returning to ASU at all because of "low scholarship."

I didn't expect to be in Phoenix for the fall, anyway. I had no clear idea of how fast things would move, of how long the legal battle would take once I refused induction, but I felt there was a good chance I'd be in prison by the fall. So, my immediate future was in limbo. Still, to be barred from attending ASU was a big blow. It was the only four-year college in the Phoenix area. I didn't have enough money to go to NAU in Flagstaff or the U. of A. in Tucson. If I couldn't attend ASU, that meant the end of my academic career, even if I wasn't in prison.

Sometimes we know the exact moment when we reach a turning point in our lives. Reading over the ASU letter, I knew that was one. "Disqualified because of low scholarship." I realized it was the end of my college hopes.

And so it was. I never did go on to earn a Bachelor's degree. I never was able to tack B.A. after my name. I felt exactly like the loser Vern told Annie I was. Time to buy that tent and head out into the desert to await the Hell-Bound Train.

I tossed the ASU letter aside and sifted through the rest of the letters I'd brought home from the Post Office. I stopped when I came across one from the Loeb Drama Center at Harvard University. I recalled that Vern had sent Carlo and me applications for a summer drama program at Harvard. What a laugh! We'd filled out the applications and returned them, but I, at least, didn't expect anything to come of it. Now, in the same mail with the ASU rejection letter came the reply from Harvard. I didn't know that I could take another kick in the teeth just then, but I thought I may as well get it over with.

I sighed and slowly tore open the envelope. I unfolded the enclosed letter. It was from the Harvard program's director, Dr. Daniel Seltzer. I quickly scanned it. "I am delighted to inform you that you have been admitted to the 1969 session of the Harvard Summer Theater Workshop, under the auspices of the Harvard Summer School. Since you have been accepted and many other applicants remain on a waiting list, we would appreciate it greatly if you would return the enclosed form by return mail, if possible..." He went on about room accommodations, tuition bills, class schedules, other things.

Then I noticed there was another letter from Seltzer beneath that one. I looked at it. "Scholarship Award," it said in capital letters. "I am very pleased to tell you that we are able to offer you, in addition to membership in the Harvard Summer School Theater Workshop, a full tuition scholarship," Seltzer wrote. And I was also being given free housing for the summer in a Radcliffe dorm.

I found it all hard to believe. Harvard had accepted me, the loser, who'd just been kicked out of ASU because of "low scholarship"! And Harvard had given me free housing and a full tuition scholarship! I'd never had a scholarship before. Now the first one I get comes from Harvard! I read and re-read the two letters from Dan Seltzer. It was hard to focus on them. My eyes were blurry.

I looked up again at the heat-shimmering desert outside the door of Sherman's Paradise Valley guest room. It seemed I hadn't entirely run out of options, after all. I had a choice: Bake in a one-man Army surplus tent out in the Sonora desert until the Hell-Bound Train came for me -- or spend the summer instead in Cambridge attending Harvard for free and living for free in a Radcliffe dorm.

I stood there at the door holding the two letters from Harvard, thinking about this turn of fortune's wheel. I thought about Jan Sownie and Tom Wagers and Annie and Vern, all of whom had managed to escape from Phoenix. I thought about how much I also wanted to escape from Phoenix. And I remembered what baseball coach Yogi Berra said about situations like this: "When you come to a fork in the road, take it!"

I decided to take Yogi's advice.

I decided to take the fork and go to Harvard.

Love in the Ruins

"Under a government which imprisons any unjustly, the true place for a just man is also a prison."

-- Henry David Thoreau
On the Duty of Civil Disobedience

****

Far out in the desert a lone coyote called. A chill wind blew through the sage brush and into the ancient ruin as the ghosts of a thousand years gathered around us. Annie shivered and I wrapped my sheltering arms around her more closely. Outside the lonely ruin the Scrambler's hot engine pinged as it cooled. Nothing else broke the solitude of the desert night.

I was leaving for Cambridge soon. Annie was settling into her isolated summer at Wupatki. We wouldn't see each other again until summer's end, so I'd driven the Scrambler up to Wupatki to be with her once more, briefly, before I left.

Ranger George Chambers was surprised to see me when I drove into the Visitor Center parking lot just as he was locking up at five o'clock. I pulled up beside him and let the Scrambler idle. "Eric Davin," he said. "What the hell are *you* doing here?"

"I'm here to see my girlfriend."

"Who's that?"

"Annie."

His face dropped.

"Can you tell me where to find her?"

He nodded toward the line of World War II apartments just above the Visitor Center. "First on the right. She's rooming with another girl."

"Thanks."

Ranger Chambers watched as I drove up to Annie's apartment and cut the engine. Annie heard the Scrambler roar up outside her apartment. She came to the door, smiling broadly. I embraced her and lifted her as I did so. Her feet dangled as I swung her slightly back and forth. "Damn, am I happy to see you!" I said.

I set her down and kissed her all over her face. Annie laughed. "Come inside, and you can kiss me anywhere you like."

We went inside. And I kissed her where I liked. And then we set her bed on fire.

That night Annie climbed on the back of the Scrambler and we rode out into the desert. I wanted us to make love in a place which had meant so much to me, and would soon mean as much to Annie. Before I left for Harvard, I wanted us to make love in the most beautiful prehistoric Indian ruin in the Southwest. I wanted us to make love at Wukoki.

We were in no hurry and bumped slowly along the rutted dirt road until we came to the ruin, jutting into the night sky from atop its lonely isolated butte. I cut the Scrambler's engine and suddenly everything was silent. I took Annie's hand and led her up the path to the ruin. We stepped inside the walls of the main room and looked up at the sky. As with most Southwestern Indian ruins, Wukoki's wooden roof had disappeared a thousand years before and only the stone walls remained. Nothing obstructed the silvery moonlight flooding down on us.

No big deal. I'd expected them to keep me on the Midnight Special to the war. I was just exhausting my legal options so it'd be easier to fight the bastards in court after I refused to be drafted; so I could argue that I had exhausted all administrative remedies and had no other way to obtain justice but to refuse induction.

On June 15th I wrote a letter to Mrs. Dimmick, the expediter for my local board, saying, "Yes, once more the S.S. System has refused to place me in my lawful classification....While other young men my age are burning the rest of the world for America, I want only to live in peace with all men." That, however, was not to be allowed.

I then asked Mrs. Dimmick to schedule another meeting with Osmond Burton, the Appeal Agent assigned to my local board to counsel registrants. Although I had no further rights of appeal, the pamphlet I had on "Taking Appeals From Selective Service Classifications" -- my combat manual for fighting the military -- told me that, "The State Director of the State in which the Local Board of Registration is located...or the National Director [that being General Lewis B. Hersheybar]...may take an appeal to the President from the classification given by the State Appeal Board." I wanted to ask Mr. Burton's advice on doing exactly that. I certainly didn't expect the State Director to intercede with Tricky Dick Nixon on my behalf, but I was determined to fight the bastards to the last ditch.

Unknown to me, Ray Manker, the minister of Phoenix's Unitarian Church, which I still sometimes attended, was meeting at that same time with the State S.S. Director, Col. Norman Erb, in Erb's office in the Central Avenue Post Office building. Ray followed up that meeting with a June 18th letter to Erb, a copy of which he sent to me.

"Dear Col. Erb," Ray wrote, "I appreciate very much the opportunity to discuss with you the problems I have been wrestling with concerning the draft. Even more, I appreciate the consideration you showed in attempting to understand the peculiarities of the Unitarian Universalist religion as it exhibits itself when our young men apply for I-O [Conscientious Objector] classification.

"As per your suggestion to give you the names and Selective Service numbers of the young men from our church over whom I have been so concerned, I would like to refer you to Eric Davin. Eric is the young man about whom I talked with you at length and whose earlier 150 statement [my essay asking for C.O. status] I showed you. He tells me that he has refiled the new 150 Form and also that just this past week he was turned down on his appeal to the State Board by a unanimous decision. You are his only hope now. If you can help him in his efforts to get his I-O it will be greatly appreciated."

I followed this with my own letter to Col. Erb. "I am a Conscientious Objector legally entitled to a classification of I-O under the laws governing the Selective Service System," I informed him. "I have been actively seeking this classification for two years and have been repeatedly denied this classification in an illegal manner.

"The State Appeal Board rejected by appeal for a I-O classification on June 13th and I have no further rights of appeal. I am and have been I-A for the past eight months. My local board, No. 29, tells me that I will be at the top of the list for the next draft call.

"I do not intend to serve in any branch of the armed forces. If ordered for induction, I will refuse said induction. However, I would rather it never came to that. I would rather I was given my proper classification without going to court to obtain that classification.

"I ask you to investigate my case and appeal my case to the President."

Yeah, some last hope Col. Norman Erb represented. I didn't think he'd actually present my case to Tricky Dick, but I at least expected a pro forma reply. I never got even that from him.

All I got was silence. Meanwhile, I heard the ominous whistle of that Hell-Bound Train coming for me.

And then came the letter from ASU. "You have been disqualified because of low scholarship," it told me. The semester just ended had been an academic disaster. Indeed, both of the two years I'd spent at ASU had been academic disasters. My transcript was peppered with Incompletes and Withdrawals. In two years I'd earned 20 credits, the equivalent of one heavy semester of classes, about a third of what I should've earned. And my grades in even the courses I completed were not outstanding. Now I was barred from returning to ASU at all because of "low scholarship."

I didn't expect to be in Phoenix for the fall, anyway. I had no clear idea of how fast things would move, of how long the legal battle would take once I refused induction, but I felt there was a good chance I'd be in prison by the fall. So, my immediate future was in limbo. Still, to be barred from attending ASU was a big blow. It was the only four-year college in the Phoenix area. I didn't have enough money to go to NAU in Flagstaff or the U. of A. in Tucson. If I couldn't attend ASU, that meant the end of my academic career, even if I wasn't in prison.

Sometimes we know the exact moment when we reach a turning point in our lives. Reading over the ASU letter, I knew that was one. "Disqualified because of low scholarship." I realized it was the end of my college hopes.

And so it was. I never did go on to earn a Bachelor's degree. I never was able to tack B.A. after my name. I felt exactly like the loser Vern told Annie I was. Time to buy that tent and head out into the desert to await the Hell-Bound Train.

I tossed the ASU letter aside and sifted through the rest of the letters I'd brought home from the Post Office. I stopped when I came across one from the Loeb Drama Center at Harvard University. I recalled that Vern had sent Carlo and me applications for a summer drama program at Harvard. What a laugh! We'd filled out the applications and returned them, but I, at least, didn't expect anything to come of it. Now, in the same mail with the ASU rejection letter came the reply from Harvard. I didn't know that I could take another kick in the teeth just then, but I thought I may as well get it over with.

I sighed and slowly tore open the envelope. I unfolded the enclosed letter. It was from the Harvard program's director, Dr. Daniel Seltzer. I quickly scanned it. "I am delighted to inform you that you have been admitted to the 1969 session of the Harvard Summer Theater Workshop, under the auspices of the Harvard Summer School. Since you have been accepted and many other applicants remain on a waiting list, we would appreciate it greatly if you would return the enclosed form by return mail, if possible..." He went on about room accommodations, tuition bills, class schedules, other things.

Then I noticed there was another letter from Seltzer beneath that one. I looked at it. "Scholarship Award," it said in capital letters. "I am very pleased to tell you that we are able to offer you, in addition to membership in the Harvard Summer School Theater Workshop, a full tuition scholarship," Seltzer wrote. And I was also being given free housing for the summer in a Radcliffe dorm.

I found it all hard to believe. Harvard had accepted me, the loser, who'd just been kicked out of ASU because of "low scholarship"! And Harvard had given me free housing and a full tuition scholarship! I'd never had a scholarship before. Now the first one I get comes from Harvard! I read and re-read the two letters from Dan Seltzer. It was hard to focus on them. My eyes were blurry.

I looked up again at the heat-shimmering desert outside the door of Sherman's Paradise Valley guest room. It seemed I hadn't entirely run out of options, after all. I had a choice: Bake in a one-man Army surplus tent out in the Sonora desert until the Hell-Bound Train came for me -- or spend the summer instead in Cambridge attending Harvard for free and living for free in a Radcliffe dorm.

    I stood there at the door holding the two letters from Harvard, thinking about this turn of fortune's wheel. I thought about Jan Sownie and Tom Wagers and Annie and Vern, all of whom had managed to escape from Phoenix. I thought about how much I also wanted to escape from Phoenix. And I remembered what baseball coach Yogi Berra said about situations like this: "When you come to a fork in the road, take it!"

    I decided to take Yogi's advice.

    I decided to take the fork and go to Harvard.

Love in the Ruins

"Under a government which imprisons any unjustly, the true place for a just man is also a prison."

-- Henry David Thoreau
On the Duty of Civil Disobedience

****

Far out in the desert a lone coyote called. A chill wind blew through the sage brush and into the ancient ruin as the ghosts of a thousand years gathered around us. Annie shivered and I wrapped my sheltering arms around her more closely. Outside the lonely ruin the Scrambler's hot engine pinged as it cooled. Nothing else broke the solitude of the desert night.

I was leaving for Cambridge soon. Annie was settling into her isolated summer at Wupatki. We wouldn't see each other again until summer's end, so I'd driven the Scrambler up to Wupatki to be with her once more, briefly, before I left.

Ranger George Chambers was surprised to see me when I drove into the Visitor Center parking lot just as he was locking up at five o'clock. I pulled up beside him and let the Scrambler idle. "Eric Davin," he said. "What the hell are *you* doing here?"

"I'm here to see my girlfriend."

"Who's that?"

"Annie."

His face dropped.

"Can you tell me where to find her?"

He nodded toward the line of World War II apartments just above the Visitor Center. "First on the right. She's rooming with another girl."

"Thanks."

Ranger Chambers watched as I drove up to Annie's apartment and cut the engine. Annie heard the Scrambler roar up outside her apartment. She came to the door, smiling broadly. I embraced her and lifted her as I did so. Her feet dangled as I swung her slightly back and forth. "Damn, am I happy to see you!" I said.

I set her down and kissed her all over her face. Annie laughed. "Come inside, and you can kiss me anywhere you like."

We went inside. And I kissed her where I liked. And then we set her bed on fire.

That night Annie climbed on the back of the Scrambler and we rode out into the desert. I wanted us to make love in a place which had meant so much to me, and would soon mean as much to Annie. Before I left for Harvard, I wanted us to make love in the most beautiful prehistoric Indian ruin in the Southwest. I wanted us to make love at Wukoki.

We were in no hurry and bumped slowly along the rutted dirt road until we came to the ruin, jutting into the night sky from atop its lonely isolated butte. I cut the Scrambler's engine and suddenly everything was silent. I took Annie's hand and led her up the path to the ruin. We stepped inside the walls of the main room and looked up at the sky. As with most Southwestern Indian ruins, Wukoki's wooden roof had disappeared a thousand years before and only the stone walls remained. Nothing obstructed the silvery moonlight flooding down on us.

Annie handed me the rolled woollen blanket she carried and I tossed it out before me. It unrolled in mid-air and I adjusted it as it settled slowly on the ancient dust of the dirt floor. I knelt on the blanket and pulled Annie down to her knees in front of me. I kissed her lips, I kissed her neck, and I unbuttoned her blouse. We undressed each other and then Annie lay down, nude, on the blanket. The moonlight poured over her face, her breasts, her belly, her thighs, turning her into a primordial white goddess who might have lain there like Ayesha for a thousand years awaiting her lover.

A cool desert breeze blew in over the ruined walls and over the white marble of Annie's body. Her breasts dimpled with tiny goosebumps and her nipples grew erect from the cold. She held her arms out toward me and I slid into them, covering her pale body with the warmth of my own. I pressed my lips over her cold hard nipples and softened them with my hot tongue. Then I melted into her with glacial slowness -- and glaciers moved more slowly in those days.

And as we merged with each other, it seemed to me that we also merged with the thousand-year history of the ruin. Except for the coyote, calling for its mate somewhere out in the desert, we were completely alone, surrounded by the stones of a millennium. And yet it also seemed to me that our love-making was a public act. I felt that we, ourselves, had become resurrected ghosts, and the ancient ghosts of the myriad generations which had lived and made love to each other and had died in that room over the ages were there with us, surrounding us, watching us.

And, because they were watching us, our love-making was no longer private. Our love-making was a public statement, to the tribe we had thereby joined, of our union and commitment to each other. Annie arched under me. She closed her eyes and shuddered as she came. I came inside her and, at that moment, the white goddess under me was the most lovely woman in the world. I knew I wanted to spend the rest of my life with this woman and I never wanted to let her out of my arms. I wanted to freeze time, at that very instant, so that we would be united, forever, at that moment of mutual ecstasy in each other's embrace.

But, I can't freeze time. No human can. The moment passed and the eternal ghosts around us faded back into the abyss of time from whence they'd come. We were drenched with sweat and the cold night breeze chilled both of us. Annie shivered beneath me and nestled into the burrow of my arms. I covered her with my body as best I could. Where skin touched skin, our body heat warmed us.

"Annie," I said, my voice low, my face almost touching hers, "I'll soon be drafted."

"I know." She burrowed harder into my body.

"And you know I'll refuse to be drafted."

"I know." She kissed me, lightly.

"And that means I could very likely be sentenced to five years in prison."

"I know," Annie said again, looking straight into my eyes.

I paused as I looked at her, searching her face. And then I said it. "Annie, will you wait five years for me?"

"Of course I will."

"But *will* you?"

"You *know* I'll wait for you."

"Annie, what I know is how I feel about *you*. I know I want to grow old with you and die with you in my arms, just like this. But I also know you're still a teenager. You just turned nineteen, Annie, and you just finished your freshman year in college. You have three years of college still ahead of you. A lot can happen in those three years, Annie. You and I have only *known* each other for just over three years. Think of everything that's happened to us and between us in those three years.

"And then think of graduating from Pitzer and going on to graduate school for another two years and perhaps earning a Master's degree. Think of the people you'll meet in all those years of college and grad school. Think of the new interests you'll acquire, think of the new experiences you'll have, think of the new people you'll meet, think of how you'll change in those most crucial years in your life. And at the end of that time, you'll be 24 and you'll be a different person."

"And I'll still love you. I may change, but *that's* not going to change."

"But *will* you? How can you speak for that future Annie? Because during all those years of growth and change for you, we won't sharing our lives with each other. I'll be sitting in a prison cell for those five years. And when I come out, you'll be a different person because of all your years at one of the best private colleges in the land. And I'll be a different person because of all my years in some goddamned prison. Will we even *recognize* each other?"

"Eric, lover, honey, I'd recognize you *anywhere,* any *time,* till the day I die."

"Annie, I'm afraid."

"Of prison? I understand."

"No, you *don't* understand. I'm not afraid of prison. I'm afraid of time and the distance between us. I'm afraid of losing you. You're the most important thing in my life. They may as well give me a death sentence, because my spirit would die without you."

Annie clung to me in the ancient dust of that deserted ruin and whispered in my ear. "You're not going to lose me. You'll *never* lose me."

I held Annie tightly, body against body to ward off the chill of the enveloping night. And I wished I believed her.

And, again, I wished I could stop time.

And, again, far out in the desert, the lone coyote called.

Ravaged Beauty

Back in Phoenix, preparing to leave for Cambridge, I saw Shana walking down a sidewalk as I drove past on the Scrambler. I called to her, "Shana!"

Her head jerked around toward me and then she ran. I cut her off and she cowered away. I climbed off the Scrambler to speak with her. She was a mess, completely wasted.

She held out her bare arms to me to show the insides of her elbows. "Look, man," she said, a hint of hysteria in her voice. "Look, I'm not doing dope any more!" The insides of her arms were covered with the ugly bruises and needle tracks of a junkie. She was obviously shooting shit.

"Shana, it's me, Eric. Don't you remember me?"

There seemed to be a flicker of recognition in her eyes. "Oh, yeah. Eric. I thought you were a cop, man."

"Shana, what the hell happened to you?"

"It was the Acid Vat, Eric. Bad vibes, man, just bad vibes!" The hysteria crept back into her voice. "But I don't do it any more, Eric! I swear, I don't do it any more!"

Shame seemed to flood over her. She began to cry. She backed away from me, her face averted and her hands up to shield herself from my gaze.

Then she turned and ran.

This time I let her go.

That was the last time I saw Shana, the Beautiful.

Cast Your Fate to the Wind

On June 24th I met with Osmond Burton, the attorney assigned to my local draft board to counsel registrants on their appeals. We reviewed my file and he confirmed that I'd probably be called up in the next round of induction orders. He said he would write to my local board recommending that my case be appealed to Tricky Dick. Actually, he didn't call President Nixon Tricky Dick. What Burton said was that he'd recommend an appeal to the Presidential Appeal Board, the last remaining possibility of reversing my I-A, Prime Beef classification.

I told him I'd be leaving soon for Harvard and that I might not see him again. The theater workshop went for the months of July and August. Burton said I could well be drafted before the theater workshop ended, and I should be prepared for that. I told him I'd lived with that Damoclean Sword over me for quite a while, so I didn't see that anything was different. I thanked him for the advice he'd given me in my battle with the S.S. System. He'd been much more helpful than I had at first assumed he would be. And that was the last time I saw him.

Next I made the rounds saying goodbye to my friends. Since I intended to refuse my incipient induction orders, I didn't expect to see them again for a long time.

I didn't have to say goodbye to Carlo. He'd also been admitted to the Harvard Summer Theater Workshop. And he'd also been given a scholarship. It seems Dan Seltzer and the rest of the Harvard admissions committee had been impressed with what we both were doing in the Universal Players. So, I'd see Carlo in Cambridge. In fact, we'd be together in a Radcliffe dorm.

I did have to say goodbye to Richard Jones. Richard was saddened that our friendship was being curtailed by my departure for Cambridge and, likely, prison soon thereafter. So was I. Over the past year of shared struggle he'd become my best friend, as well as my comrade-in-arms. He promised that, when the fall semester began, he'd move up to the presidency of the ASU Civil Liberties Union, the moribund student organization the two of us had revived, and keep making trouble as its leader. At least I'd leave some small legacy behind at ASU.

I gave away most of what little I owned. I'd have no need of possessions in prison. I bestowed my old record player and my albums on a buddy in need of a musical life. Friends took what clothes they wanted. I gave my formica desk-table to Goodwill, as no one wanted it. I signed the title of the Scrambler over to Sherman for letting me crash in his guest room and handed him the keys. I donated my complete run of *Astounding-Analog,* going back to the first issue I'd purchased, March, 1960, to the Phoenix College library.

I distributed my books to friends left and right. What remained I piled into a battered old blue wooden trunk I owned, my only piece of furniture but for the formica desk-table. I then left the book-stuffed trunk in the carport storage closet at Mom's. It was the first time since leaving "home" I asked her to do anything for me. Even though the hostility between us had lessened with the passage of time, I hated depending on her for its safekeeping. I hated being obligated to her for anything and, besides, she had no love of books and I didn't trust her to actually keep my books safe. But, I had no choice. Today's ubiquitous rental storage units did not then exist.

My fears were justified. Mom didn't keep my books safe. Over the years, my younger brothers plundered the trunk. Bruce took my high school diaries, Mike and his buddies took the fantasy, science fiction and historical novels. Everyone ignored my history books. I didn't begrudge losing Sabatini's *Captain Blood* and the SF novels to Mike and his friends. At least someone read them and they could be replaced. My diaries could not be.

Eventually, someone in my family pulled the trunk out of the storage closet and parked it in the backyard. There it sat for years, the desert sun baking the books inside. Repeated flooding

Ravaged Beauty

Back in Phoenix, preparing to leave for Cambridge, I saw Shana walking down a sidewalk as I drove past on the Scrambler. I called to her, "Shana!"

Her head jerked around toward me and then she ran. I cut her off and she cowered away. I climbed off the Scrambler to speak with her. She was a mess, completely wasted.

She held out her bare arms to me to show the insides of her elbows. "Look, man," she said, a hint of hysteria in her voice. "Look, I'm not doing dope any more!" The insides of her arms were covered with the ugly bruises and needle tracks of a junkie. She was obviously shooting shit.

"Shana, it's me, Eric. Don't you remember me?"

There seemed to be a flicker of recognition in her eyes. "Oh, yeah. Eric. I thought you were a cop, man."

"Shana, what the hell happened to you?"

"It was the Acid Vat, Eric. Bad vibes, man, just bad vibes!" The hysteria crept back into her voice. "But I don't do it any more, Eric! I swear, I don't do it any more!"

Shame seemed to flood over her. She began to cry. She backed away from me, her face averted and her hands up to shield herself from my gaze.

Then she turned and ran.

This time I let her go.

That was the last time I saw Shana, the Beautiful.

Cast Your Fate to the Wind

On June 24th I met with Osmond Burton, the attorney assigned to my local draft board to counsel registrants on their appeals. We reviewed my file and he confirmed that I'd probably be called up in the next round of induction orders. He said he would write to my local board recommending that my case be appealed to Tricky Dick. Actually, he didn't call President Nixon Tricky Dick. What Burton said was that he'd recommend an appeal to the Presidential Appeal Board, the last remaining possibility of reversing my I-A, Prime Beef classification.

I told him I'd be leaving soon for Harvard and that I might not see him again. The theater workshop went for the months of July and August. Burton said I could well be drafted before the theater workshop ended, and I should be prepared for that. I told him I'd lived with that Damoclean Sword over me for quite a while, so I didn't see that anything was different. I thanked him for the advice he'd given me in my battle with the S.S. System. He'd been much more helpful than I had at first assumed he would be. And that was the last time I saw him.

Next I made the rounds saying goodbye to my friends. Since I intended to refuse my incipient induction orders, I didn't expect to see them again for a long time.

I didn't have to say goodbye to Carlo. He'd also been admitted to the Harvard Summer Theater Workshop. And he'd also been given a scholarship. It seems Dan Seltzer and the rest of the Harvard admissions committee had been impressed with what we both were doing in the Universal Players. So, I'd see Carlo in Cambridge. In fact, we'd be together in a Radcliffe dorm.

I did have to say goodbye to Richard Jones. Richard was saddened that our friendship was being curtailed by my departure for Cambridge and, likely, prison soon thereafter. So was I. Over the past year of shared struggle he'd become my best friend, as well as my comrade-in-arms. He promised that, when the fall semester began, he'd move up to the presidency of the ASU Civil Liberties Union, the moribund student organization the two of us had revived, and keep making trouble as its leader. At least I'd leave some small legacy behind at ASU.

I gave away most of what little I owned. I'd have no need of possessions in prison. I bestowed my old record player and my albums on a buddy in need of a musical life. Friends took what clothes they wanted. I gave my formica desk-table to Goodwill, as no one wanted it. I signed the title of the Scrambler over to Sherman for letting me crash in his guest room and handed him the keys. I donated my complete run of *Astounding-Analog,* going back to the first issue I'd purchased, March, 1960, to the Phoenix College library.

I distributed my books to friends left and right. What remained I piled into a battered old blue wooden trunk I owned, my only piece of furniture but for the formica desk-table. I then left the book-stuffed trunk in the carport storage closet at Mom's. It was the first time since leaving "home" I asked her to do anything for me. Even though the hostility between us had lessened with the passage of time, I hated depending on her for its safekeeping. I hated being obligated to her for anything and, besides, she had no love of books and I didn't trust her to actually keep my books safe. But, I had no choice. Today's ubiquitous rental storage units did not then exist.

My fears were justified. Mom didn't keep my books safe. Over the years, my younger brothers plundered the trunk. Bruce took my high school diaries, Mike and his buddies took the fantasy, science fiction and historical novels. Everyone ignored my history books. I didn't begrudge losing Sabatini's *Captain Blood* and the SF novels to Mike and his friends. At least someone read them and they could be replaced. My diaries could not be.

Eventually, someone in my family pulled the trunk out of the storage closet and parked it in the backyard. There it sat for years, the desert sun baking the books inside. Repeated flooding

Ravaged Beauty

Back in Phoenix, preparing to leave for Cambridge, I saw Shana walking down a sidewalk as I drove past on the Scrambler. I called to her, "Shana!"

Her head jerked around toward me and then she ran. I cut her off and she cowered away. I climbed off the Scrambler to speak with her. She was a mess, completely wasted.

She held out her bare arms to me to show the insides of her elbows. "Look, man," she said, a hint of hysteria in her voice. "Look, I'm not doing dope any more!" The insides of her arms were covered with the ugly bruises and needle tracks of a junkie. She was obviously shooting shit.

"Shana, it's me, Eric. Don't you remember me?"

There seemed to be a flicker of recognition in her eyes. "Oh, yeah. Eric. I thought you were a cop, man."

"Shana, what the hell happened to you?"

"It was the Acid Vat, Eric. Bad vibes, man, just bad vibes!" The hysteria crept back into her voice. "But I don't do it any more, Eric! I swear, I don't do it any more!"

Shame seemed to flood over her. She began to cry. She backed away from me, her face averted and her hands up to shield herself from my gaze.

Then she turned and ran.

This time I let her go.

That was the last time I saw Shana, the Beautiful.

Cast Your Fate to the Wind

On June 24th I met with Osmond Burton, the attorney assigned to my local draft board to counsel registrants on their appeals. We reviewed my file and he confirmed that I'd probably be called up in the next round of induction orders. He said he would write to my local board recommending that my case be appealed to Tricky Dick. Actually, he didn't call President Nixon Tricky Dick. What Burton said was that he'd recommend an appeal to the Presidential Appeal Board, the last remaining possibility of reversing my I-A, Prime Beef classification.

I told him I'd be leaving soon for Harvard and that I might not see him again. The theater workshop went for the months of July and August. Burton said I could well be drafted before the theater workshop ended, and I should be prepared for that. I told him I'd lived with that Damoclean Sword over me for quite a while, so I didn't see that anything was different. I thanked him for the advice he'd given me in my battle with the S.S. System. He'd been much more helpful than I had at first assumed he would be. And that was the last time I saw him.

Next I made the rounds saying goodbye to my friends. Since I intended to refuse my incipient induction orders, I didn't expect to see them again for a long time.

I didn't have to say goodbye to Carlo. He'd also been admitted to the Harvard Summer Theater Workshop. And he'd also been given a scholarship. It seems Dan Seltzer and the rest of the Harvard admissions committee had been impressed with what we both were doing in the Universal Players. So, I'd see Carlo in Cambridge. In fact, we'd be together in a Radcliffe dorm.

I did have to say goodbye to Richard Jones. Richard was saddened that our friendship was being curtailed by my departure for Cambridge and, likely, prison soon thereafter. So was I. Over the past year of shared struggle he'd become my best friend, as well as my comrade-in-arms. He promised that, when the fall semester began, he'd move up to the presidency of the ASU Civil Liberties Union, the moribund student organization the two of us had revived, and keep making trouble as its leader. At least I'd leave some small legacy behind at ASU.

I gave away most of what little I owned. I'd have no need of possessions in prison. I bestowed my old record player and my albums on a buddy in need of a musical life. Friends took what clothes they wanted. I gave my formica desk-table to Goodwill, as no one wanted it. I signed the title of the Scrambler over to Sherman for letting me crash in his guest room and handed him the keys. I donated my complete run of *Astounding-Analog*, going back to the first issue I'd purchased, March, 1960, to the Phoenix College library.

I distributed my books to friends left and right. What remained I piled into a battered old blue wooden trunk I owned, my only piece of furniture but for the formica desk-table. I then left the book-stuffed trunk in the carport storage closet at Mom's. It was the first time since leaving "home" I asked her to do anything for me. Even though the hostility between us had lessened with the passage of time, I hated depending on her for its safekeeping. I hated being obligated to her for anything and, besides, she had no love of books and I didn't trust her to actually keep my books safe. But, I had no choice. Today's ubiquitous rental storage units did not then exist.

My fears were justified. Mom didn't keep my books safe. Over the years, my younger brothers plundered the trunk. Bruce took my high school diaries, Mike and his buddies took the fantasy, science fiction and historical novels. Everyone ignored my history books. I didn't begrudge losing Sabatini's *Captain Blood* and the SF novels to Mike and his friends. At least someone read them and they could be replaced. My diaries could not be.

Eventually, someone in my family pulled the trunk out of the storage closet and parked it in the backyard. There it sat for years, the desert sun baking the books inside. Repeated flooding

of the yard in weekly irrigations rotted the wooded bottom of the trunk and destroyed the lowest layers of books. Few of my books remained for me to salvage when, five years later, I returned.

    I gave my big ol' clunky manual typewriter to Richard. It seemed an appropriate gift to a poet. Then, shortly before I climbed on a Trailways bus for Cambridge, my backpack crammed with my remaining worldly goods, Richard gave me a poem he wrote on the typewriter to commemorate our friendship. No one had ever written a poem for me before. I read it, carefully folded it, placed it in my shirt pocket, and took it with me. This is what Richard wrote:

Upon Your Departure

It is easy enough
to think of friendship
in the face of advancing winter,
but to shape another's
features in my memory
and set out his attributes
like a pressed suit
straight from the cleaners
is a feat that requires concentration.
So, let me begin
by saying: we're different
the eagle is cast
in your eye and
though I am predatory
our visions are distant.
My world is frozen
in hope of a blazing summer,
while your sun sits on the horizon
a monk in meditation
keeping the world free of ice,
but not warm.
So I say to you in
the tropic of this poem
that ours is the same world
in winter
cold, at different stages
of motion
but the same.
We see with our own eyes,
you, the historian,
see yourself and the rest of us
as perfectible,
while I, a poet,
with Li Po,
drink to man's constant nature.
Still, what there is
is of your treehouse

and my prison.

II

Our mouths speak
friend, both of helicon
grass beneath the lion claw,
dried leaves bleeding
between our toes.
We sing of our barefoot childhood,
you, a believer in God,
you, without a cause,
you spent years howling
your discontent
until you saw yourself, divine,
eater of fig leaves,
bathing in the central pool.
You were poor
and the poor do not rest
in the path of ambition.
You were the exception
to your rules.
You never asked.
Your brothers' keeper,
filling the dimness of their lives
with candle light.
You were the example
of a rebel made good.
Lion of faith,
Lion of love,
come closer to the fire.
The fickleness of our lives
is the tender.
We respond not to hope of salvation,
but to warmth on these cold nights.
Our shadows have danced
many cave walls.
We are not unreflective
in our lives.
The clouds shut off
even the moon,
and still we have our fire.

Part Nine
Babylon Burning

A Cowboy in Cambridge

I stepped off the Trailways bus into downtown Boston, the Hub of the Universe, as the locals modestly called it. The bus station was smaller than the one in Phoenix, with room in the rear for only a handful of busses. Compared to spread-out Phoenix, the entire city seemed crowded, with the buildings jammed up against each other. As I hefted my backpack onto my shoulders and looked around, my Frye harness boots and leather cowboy hat made me feel conspicuous, an obvious hick in the city. I should've left the hat in Arizona.

Then I heard the sliding steel guitar of Country and Western music coming from a bar just across the small alley from the station's back lot. It was called The Ram Rod Room. The music, at least, was familiar and I began to walk toward the bar. The music swelled as the door opened and two guys came out. They looked like male models. Both had short razor-cut hair neatly trimmed on the sides and the napes. Both wore tight knit shirts and tight jeans. And they were holding hands. I decided not to go into the Ram Rod Room.

"Hey, cowboy, where ya from?"

I turned at the question. A petite young woman was lounging against a wall of the station. The day was hot and sticky, but if her sprayed-on miniskirt had been any shorter she'd have died of pneumonia. "Phoenix," I answered.

"Well, Phoenix, I don't think you're looking for boy action. After coming all the way from hot and dusty Arizona, I think you're looking for a woman."

"How much?"

"$50."

"Whew! That's a bit steep."

"I'm worth every penny. I'll make you feel very welcome to the big city."

"And if I said 'yes,' where would we go?"

She nodded across the alley. "I have an apartment right there, second floor, right above the Ram Rod Room. Completely safe and private. Shall we?"

"You're a lovely lady, but I'm going to pass."

"You're making a big mistake. You won't find pussy like mine in Phoenix."

"Maybe not, but I have business to attend to." I touched the brim of my hat. "I appreciate your offer."

"OK, cowboy. You change your mind, look for me in the Combat Zone."

"I'll do that." I had no idea what she meant.

I walked to the front of the bus terminal. Across the busy street was the large green sward of the Boston Public Garden, America's oldest public botanical garden, created in 1837. I crossed the street and went up to the iron picket fence bordering the Garden. Beyond it was an ancient graveyard with weathered and leaning tombstones. I peered through the fence and made out some of the dates on the stones. They were older than the Revolution. I felt a thrill of excitement. Wow!, I'm really here, where the country began. I was in no hurry, so I decided to look around.

I walked along the sidewalk until the iron fence ended and I entered the 24-acre Garden. It was lush and blazing with floral color and crowded with people in suits, people in shorts, people on bicycles, people on blankets spread on the grass.

I strolled along broad walkways until I came to a lagoon spanned by a French-inspired pedestrian bridge. The lagoon was bordered by weeping willows and daffodils. Sunlight reflected blindingly off the water. Gliding slowly about the lagoon were several 30-foot long catamarans supporting a flat platform upon which rested what looked like park benches in rows. Each boat carried up to 20 people. Behind the floating park benches was a large, open-backed wooden cut-out of a swan. Inside each swan was a healthy young man guiding the boat and powering it by peddling with his feet as if riding a bicycle. His foot pedals turned a paddlewheel beneath him. Wow! Nothing like that at the Encanto Park lagoon in Phoenix. All we had were canoes. I later learned that these swan boats have been a Boston summer tradition since 1877.

I came to Charles Street and crossed over to Boston Common, America's oldest public park, established in 1634 as a common grazing area for cattle. Everything in Boston seemed to be an example of "America's oldest."

The Common inclined upward and as I came out on the other side I saw a large and impressive Colonial-style building. A bulging gold dome capped a pile of red brick with white colonnades out front. I looked at the map of Boston I carried. It said the building was the Massachusetts state capitol and the gold dome was designed by noted architect Charles Bulfinch. Prettier than the state capitol building in Phoenix, I thought. It actually *looked* like a state capitol.

Behind me on the sidewalk was a head-high bas relief of marching Civil War soldiers. I looked closer and discovered that it was a memorial to the 54th Massachusetts Colored Infantry, heading off to death and glory at Ft. Wagner, with Robert Gould Shaw, their white commander, leading them. Everywhere I looked it seemed I was looking at history. I loved it.

I turned to my left and began walking down the sidewalk on the periphery of the Common. According to my map, everything to my right was Beacon Hill, the crowded oldest part of Boston. I came to Arlington Street and turned left, still tracing the outline of the park. I reached yet another corner of the park, the intersection of Arlington and Boylston Streets. And right there, its spire jabbing into the blue summer sky, was the Arlington Street Church. I'd read about the Arlington Street Church in Phoenix. It was a Unitarian church where there'd been well-publicized draft card burnings. I had to go inside. Boston was the heart of draft resistance in America, and much of that resistance emerged from the Arlington Street Church.

The interior was large and, once the doors closed behind me, quiet. It was old, majestic, and impressive. I walked down the center aisle to a front pew and sat down. I was the only one in the church. I tried to imagine what the scene must've looked like during the mass draft card burnings. Probably loud, raucous, and emotional. Now, as I sat there alone in the church, with turbulent Boston swirling outside, everything was serene and peaceful. Too bad I'd come too late to burn my draft card with the others.

After awhile I rose and walked back out into noisy downtown Boston. Right across the street, in the Commons, or the Garden, I wasn't clear which, was a concrete subway entrance. It looked like a mausoleum. I'd never ridden a subway, but I had to take the subway to Harvard Square, in Cambridge, so I headed for the mausoleum. I entered it with a funnelling crowd of others. I felt like we were the doomed Eloi entering the Morlock catacombs in H. G. Wells' *The Time Machine.* As I descended, the dank smell of the underground cavern enveloped me. The Boston subway is the oldest in America, older, even, than New York's. The first tracks were laid down in 1897. But, in almost a hundred years, the dankness hadn't dissipated. When the subway car stopped to take on passengers, I wondered if the car itself dated from 1897. It looked like a battered old trolley from a Charlie Chaplin movie.

I jammed into the travelling Smithsonian Exhibit with the others and held onto a pole as the car lurched into motion with a horrendous squeal of tortured metal wheels on rails. Despite being underground, the car was not cooler than the outside. It was hot and stifling because of all the bodies and sweat soon soaked my shirt. I escaped from the crowded trolley a few stops later when I reached the junction for the line into Cambridge. The Boston subway system has a Blue

Line going here, a Green Line going there, an Orange line going somewhere else, and a Red Line going in a different direction. I needed the Red Line into Harvard Square.

I descended to yet a lower level and came to a platform with several tracks. I found the signs pointing me toward Cambridge and I waited. Soon lights appeared in the dark tunnel to my left and a long train of cars roared into the station and slowed to a stop. These cars were more modern than the museum relics above and there was more room as the Eloi crowded in. I waited my turn to enter and was the last inside.

The doors closed quickly on me, clamping onto each shoulder and holding me tight. The doors were rubber edged and they didn't hurt, but I was stuck, half in and half out of the car. Strangely, I thought about Mugwumps. They were upper-class Massachusetts and New York Republicans who broke with their party in 1884 to back Democrat Grover Cleveland for the presidency, perhaps insuring his election. One editorial cartoonist of the time pictured them as a guy sitting on a fence, his Republican mug on one side, his Democratic wump on the other. And there I was, a trapped Mugwump, with my mug inside the car and my wump still outside. This entire image flashed through my mind in an instant. Then, suddenly, the doors sprang apart and I surged forward into the car, catching myself before I fell. The doors closed again and the train began to move. People smiled at me. I felt like a doofus. But a happy doofus.

I forgot my embarrassment as the subway emerged into the light of the outdoors. Then we were skimming above the Charles River, which divides Boston from Cambridge. I starred out the windows in excitement, marvelling at an urban river which actually had water in it! Small boats with tall slim triangular sails dotted the water, heading in all directions like scattered jackstraws. I could even see small narrow canoes, sculls, I learned later, with several rowers pulling at the oars.

Then the train reached the Cambridge side and plunged into subterranean darkness once more. Stations flashed by: MIT, Central Square, then Harvard Square, the end of the Red Line. The cars emptied and I followed the crowd toward the light. We squeezed onto an ancient escalator with wooden slats for steps. It was narrow, with room for only one person at a time. I stepped onto the wooden slats behind others and we rose, single file, toward the surface. I looked up as the sky became brighter above us and I felt like a dead man moving upward through a long dark tunnel toward the light.

I emerged onto a traffic island in the middle of a busy intersection. Cars inched slowly through the throngs of pedestrians crowding the sidewalks and crossing the streets. In front of me was a tall building with pillars and a cavernous alcove. A hippie guitarist was strumming his guitar and wailing away in the alcove, which acted as an amphitheater magnifying his song. Large letters atop the building identified it as the Harvard Coop.

To the right of the Harvard Coop was the entrance to a movie theater. To the left of the Coop were stacks of newspapers on the sidewalk and magazines on racks. The newsstand was called Nini's Corner. There were also piles of newspapers and racks of magazines to my right on the traffic island and the sign over the small building told me that newsstand was called Out of Town News. Lots to read. Just what one would expect in a place called Harvard Square.

I looked around for a public phone to call Vern and tell him I'd arrived. The subway stairs had a Victorian-looking metal cupola over it with the word "Harvard" arcing over the front and "Square" in a straight line beneath it. Behind the cupola was a bank of phone booths. But also behind the cupola, opposite the Coop, was a tall brick wall ringing massive brick buildings. There was an entrance with tall wrought iron gates to the left. I realized it was Harvard Yard, right there, in front of me, and decided to visit Harvard before I called Vern.

I crossed the street and entered the iron gate, passing into the sanctum sanctorum of Harvard Yard. Walkways spread out toward all points of the compass. All of them were lined with wooden staves driven into the ground and connected with a single strand of wire to keep people off the grass. Harvard freshmen lived in the Yard, in the buildings around the edge, before they moved on to a named "House" in their sophomore year. The school year was over, but the Yard was still crowded.

To my right was a massive pile of stone with behemoth Greek pillars lining the front: Widenor Library, donated by a wealthy family in honor of their son, a Harvard grad who went down on the Titanic. There'd been a big antiwar student strike at Harvard just that spring, which had shut down the entire school. On the side of one of the stone peninsulas jutting out on either side of the library steps I could see the now-famous Harvard Strike Fist. The stencilled image had been sandblasted away, but the sandblasting had just served to stencil the fist more permanently into the stone.

I stood on the steps and looked across the grass to the chapel with its tall white spire on the opposite side. The space between the chapel and Widenor was where Harvard graduations took place. To my left was University Hall, where the Harvard President had his office. During the strike the students had occupied the hall and his office. The Cambridge cops were called in and they beat the students savagely as they arrested them. It was their merciless working class brutality against the Harvard students which escalated the occupation into a complete campus-wide walkout.

I walked over to University Hall, a gray rectangular building looking a bit newer than the freshman dorms around it. On one long side was a bronze statue of a seated John Harvard, after whom the university was named. He didn't found Harvard, he just donated his personal library to the school, but that was enough to gain him immortality. During the strike students had tied a red headband around John Harvard's brow.

I walked out of Harvard Yard and back to the Out of Town News traffic island. To my right was yet another church, right on the square. I headed over to it. It was another Unitarian church, Cambridge's First. Next to it was another old graveyard, surrounded by an iron picket fence, looking as ancient as the one in Boston Commons. And, on the other side of the graveyard, was still another church. There was a plaque on the front which said it'd been used as a barracks by Washington's troops during the 1775 siege of Boston. There was even a bullet hole in one of the walls, a remnant of the Revolution which had been preserved.

I went inside. It wasn't as large as the Arlington Street Church, and it looked much older. Several of the pews were enclosed boxes, separating the privileged congregants who sat there from their less favored brothers and sisters. We're all one in the body of Christ, but not in church.

Directly across the street from this church was Cambridge Commons. I walked over to it. Near its center was a large granite edifice enclosing a bronze statue of Abraham Lincoln. In front of the edifice was a black hippie with a bushy Afro playing an electric guitar. The sound was blasting out of a portable speaker at his feet. He wore a headband and a fringe jacket and looked like a Jimi Hendrix wannabe. He didn't sing, but he made his guitar scream just like Jimi's. There was a hat on the ground in front of him and passers-by occasionally tossed coins into it. I grooved on his music for awhile, but didn't toss any coins into his hat. I didn't have any change to spare.

Off in the distance I saw what looked like cannons, so I ambled over to investigate. They were, indeed, cannons, 200-year-old relics of the Revolutionary War. Next to them was a granite pedestal with a metal bas relief bolted to it. The bas relief depicted George Washington assuming command of the Continental Army right after his appointment by the Continental Congress. And the monument said the very spot where I was standing, on Cambridge Commons, was where Washington took command of the American army. I ran my hand along the smooth metal of a cannon barrel and felt like I was touching history. I tried to imagine what that scene must've looked like. I was falling in love with the place.

I decided to finally call Vern and wandered along uneven brick sidewalks studded with gnarly trees, their roots shoving the bricks aside as they grew, back toward Harvard Square, past the church with the bullet hole in the wall, past the Colonial graveyard, past the First Unitarian Church. Vern picked up his phone. "Vern, it's Eric. I'm here, in Harvard Square."

"Well, welcome to Cambridge. I'll come get you. It'll be about 30-minutes. Wait for me in front of the Coop."

"OK. You can't miss me. I'll be the only one wearing a cowboy hat."

Since I had some time before Vern came, I looked around for a place to grab a Coke. Just across from Nini's Corner was a hole-in-the-wall greasy spoon called The Tasty. I dodged cars and crossed over from the traffic island. The Tasty was a dump about 10-feet wide and maybe 15-feet deep. There was a curving formica-topped counter to the right with seven soda fountain stools in front. To the left was a formica-topped ledge jutting from the wall and another three stools. All the stools but one were occupied. I took that one. There was a young guy standing behind the counter with an apron around his waist spotted with grease and ketchup.

"What'll it be, cowboy?"

"Give me a cherry Coke."

"You got it."

He scooped some chipped ice into a glass, squirted in some syrup, and filled it with Coke from a nozzle. He stirred it with a spoon and set it before me. "You're a long way from Texas, cowboy. Where's your horse?"

"I'm from Arizona. And I rode a Greyhound." That sounded better than saying I came in on Trailways.

"Even further. I pity the Greyhound." He chuckled and some of the guys around the counter smiled. So did I.

There was a big plate glass window just behind me so I turned on my stool and looked out at Harvard Square. It was a solid mass of people heading in all directions with cars creeping along amongst them. "Is it always this crowded?" I asked the counter guy.

"Like they say, cowboy, Harvard Square is the crossroads of the world."

"And Boston's the Hub of the Universe, right?"

"That's right, cowboy. You've come to the right place."

"I think you're right about that."

I finished my Coke, slid two quarters across the counter, and stood up. The counter guy grabbed them and rang up the sale. He gave me a two-fingered salute and said, "Adios, Tex."

"Arizona," I said, and touched the brim of my hat.

I darted across to the Coop and stood on the corner as the wave of humanity swirled around me. Before long I spotted the blue VW van Vern had bought from Tom Wagers coming from the direction of Cambridge Commons. There was a light at that intersection and Vern hit it, stopping right in front of me. I tossed my backpack on the floor and hopped in. Vern gave me a big smile and held out his hand. "Howdy, cowboy."

I smiled back and shook his hand. It was good to see a familiar face. "I'm gonna stop wearing this hat. I'm getting a bit tired of the cowboy routine."

Vern laughed and rolled through the intersection. "How long was the ride from Phoenix?"

"Three days and three nights."

"You must be tired."

"Yep."

"Then we'll make only one stop before I take you home."

Vern had just left the Square when he pulled over and parked. We got out and climbed a short flight of steps to the door of a coffeehouse. There was a sign which said, "The Blue Parrot." I followed Vern into the dark interior. It was crowded with people sitting around tiny tables and sipping from small coffee cups. Large photos of old movie stars adorned the walls. I recognized a grizzled Humphrey Bogart from *Treasure of the Sierra Madre.* Next to him was a picture of W. C. Fields in top hat, mulling over a handful of cards. Soft guitar music came from a turntable. The air was hazy with cigarette smoke. I was in a beatnik coffeehouse for the first time in my life.

Vern spotted a table with four chairs but only two people around it, both guys. He walked over and I followed. "Do you mind if we sit here?" he asked.

"Not at all."

We sat down next to the strangers. I removed my cowboy hat and placed it on my knee under the table. A waitress came over. "Two cups of Formosa oolong," Vern said. She nodded and left.

"I noticed your hat," one of our tablemates said. "Where you from, cowboy?"

"Phoenix, Arizona."

"Wow! You're a long way from home. What brings you all the way to Cambridge?"

I smiled. "I'm going to Harvard."

Then I repeated that to myself: I'm going to Harvard.

I was beginning to believe it.

A Walk on the Moon

We Are Mistaken

We think space is finite.
    But it is infinite.
        We think our lives infinite.
            But they are finite.
And all too soon,
    Like a dying moon,
        We fade into the night,
No matter how much we rage
Against the dying of the light.

****

Brattle Street starts in Harvard Square and then heads into ritzy West Cambridge. It is lined with expensive homes. Indeed, that has been the case for over 300 years. At the time of the American Revolution, the street was called "Tory Row" because so many of the wealthy residents sided with King George against the Revolution. They fled following the battles of Lexington and Concord and the patriots occupied their mansions. In fact, George Washington, after taking command of the patriot soldiers on Cambridge Common, made the Brattle Street estate, which later became poet Henry Wadsworth Longfellow's elegant mansion, his headquarters for the 1775 siege of Boston.

Just outside Harvard Square, as Brattle Street begins, was the Brattle Street Theater, a small and ancient wooden theater which screened endless Humphrey Bogart festivals. It was the constant reruns of Bogey's films at the Brattle Theater which sparked the Bogart revival of the Sixties.

Next to the Brattle Street Theater was an old Colonial house which was the home of the Cambridge Adult Learning Center, and just beyond that, a nice little cafe called The Blacksmith Shop. This was supposedly because the spreading chestnut tree which shades its patio was *the* spreading chestnut tree under which Longfellow's village smithy once stood. This is probably myth, but it gave the place a nice mystique. The Blacksmith Shop became my first experience of al fresco dining.

And beyond the Blacksmith Shop, at 64 Brattle Street, was Harvard's Loeb Drama Center, about a five-minute walk out of Harvard Square and halfway between the Square and Longfellow's home. When I first saw it, the Loeb seemed a bit out of place amidst such antiquities. It was a new and modern two-story brick facility. It is considered to be the best theater in Cambridge, one of the best in Boston, and exceedingly better than the theater of the Arizona Repertory Theater in Phoenix where I performed in "the Lower Depths." Constructed in 1959, the Loeb would celebrate its tenth birthday in the coming fall. A big birthday bash was already being planned. Today it is the home of the American Repertory Theater, a professional company.

The Loeb is an excellent facility, having everything anyone could want in a theater. Its main auditorium is huge, as is its main stage, and the audience seats sweep in unbroken rows up to the second floor in the rear. The stage was occupied that summer by the sets for a trio of plays by a professional theater company. One of the plays was Ivan Turgenev's *A Month in the Country,* a boring title for a boring play. Mark Twain defined a classic book as one everybody wants to have read, but no one wants to read. A classic play is similar. It is one everyone wants to have seen, but no one wants to see it. And *A Month in the Country* is a classic play, a drama in which there isn't much drama. One of the stars in Turgenev's soporific play that summer was a young, tall, pretty-boy actor named Christopher Reeve. Everyone agreed he had a bright future.

Directly behind the last and highest row of audience seats was a lounge with windows overlooking Brattle Street. To the western side of the lounge were the administrative offices. Then, all along the western side of the second floor were rehearsal rooms, where Theater Workshop classes took place.

On the first floor, just to the west of the main stage and the auditorium, was a small blackbox atrium theater known as The Experimental Theater. It was an open space for the whole two floors, with catwalks and balconies above the ground floor from which could be hung spotlights. The Experimental Theater was the Workshop's theater for the summer.

The producing director of the Loeb Drama Center in the summer of 1969 was George Hamlin. He'd come to Harvard in 1961 charged with the task of developing innovative academic and professional programs at the Loeb. The Theater Workshop, of which Carlo and I were now members, was one of those programs.

Born and raised in Chicago, Hamlin had a long career in theater administration. Just after World War II he was the director of the Dock Street Theater in Charleston, South Carolina. Then he moved to New York as the executive director of the New Dramatists Committee. And then Harvard called. He left the Loeb in 1980 to return to The Big Apple as a full-time actor in New York Shakespeare Festival plays, TV mini-series, and two 1980s Woody Allen films, *The Purple Rose of Cairo* and *Zelig.* He was one of the experimental drug doctors in *Zelig* He died in 1986 after a stroke at age 65. When I met him at the Loeb, he was white-haired and seemed "old" to me, but he was only 48. He turned 49 on July 25th of that year. But I was 22, and to one of that age, perhaps most adults seem "old."

I got to know Dr. Daniel Seltzer better than I knew George Hamlin, as he was the director of the Theater Workshop itself and ran it and taught in it on a daily basis. He was the one who'd signed the letters admitting me and Carlo to this Harvard Summer School program and giving us both scholarships. Dan Seltzer was a Shakespearean scholar and left Harvard in the mid-Seventies to become an English professor at Princeton.

That, however, didn't stop him from acting. In 1976, for example, he took a five-month sabbatical from Princeton to act on Broadway in the Jules Feiffer play, *Knock, Knock.* In a February 2, 1976 review in *Time,* T. E. Kalem lauded him for his acting in the play and Dan was also nominated that year for the Tony Award for Best Actor.

Dan Seltzer looked just like Dr. Jacobs, Jill Clayburgh's shrink in *An Unmarried Woman*, who puts the make on her following her divorce in that 1978 Paul Mazursky film. In fact, that *was* Dan Seltzer. Perhaps other movie roles would have followed his film debut, but Dan, who was never over-weight, dropped dead of a heart attack on March 1, 1980. He was only 47-years-old. And he was only 33 in the summer of '69, but, like George Hamlin, he looked like a mature man to my 22-year-old eyes. Perhaps Seltzer's unexpected death led Hamlin to leave the Loeb later that same year and return to his first love, acting. Our time here is short, even at the longest, and the night soon comes wherein no one dreams.

The Theater Workshop covered every aspect of acting. It was my first and only intensive training in drama. Classes began early in the morning, broke for lunch, and then went until around five. After that, we were on our own. We were expected to hang around the theater afterward, watching, for instance, and perhaps helping on the main stage plays of the professional company.

But I couldn't afford to do that. I'd spent everything I had on my bus ticket to Harvard. I had no money at all and, although my classes were free and I was living free in a Radcliffe dorm, I had no money for food. I ran through the classifieds in *The Boston Globe* and came across an ad placed by the Becker Research Corporation, in Cambridge's Central Square, one stop away from Harvard Square on the subway, or a 15-minute walk. Becker was a polling agency and it wanted part-time telephone canvassers. The job wasn't telemarketing, it was research surveying. Politicians, for example, hired it to find out how well-known they were or which issues resonated with the electorate. I knew I had a nice sounding voice, so I answered the ad.

I was hired and became good at gaining the confidence of strangers on the phone and asking them questions. I was soon put in charge of team of more inexperienced pollsters. My boss told me the job was mine for as long as I wanted it.

But George Hamlin wanted to know why he never saw me around the Loeb at night, hanging with the other students. "I'm completely broke," I told him. "So I'm working a part-time job at night."

"Then you should've asked for more money," Hamlin said. "The *Workshop* is your full-time job."

I didn't know what to reply. I was overwhelmingly thankful that Harvard had given me a full-tuition scholarship and free housing. I had no idea that Harvard would also have given me walking-around money, had I but asked. Instead, I'd asked for just the minimum, tuition and housing, afraid of asking for too much. Money to be had just for the asking was not an easy idea for me to comprehend.

But, I *hadn't* asked, and it was too late now, so I had to continue working at night in Central Square, calling citizens in Taunton and Sudbury and Pittsfield while, during the day, acting at the Loeb like a Harvard student with no financial cares in the world. Even Carlo seemed to have more money than me, as he had no need of a pollster job at Becker, though I offered to get him one on the team I supervised. He came from a large and devoted Italian family, so perhaps they were proud enough of the Harvard student in the famiglia to subsidize him for his Cambridge summer.

Of all our Workshop teachers, I learned the most from Dan Seltzer. He was generous with advice about any theatrical problem. For example, say an accident happens on stage, another actor clumsily knocks over a chair, blocking your entrance. "Use the difficulty," Dan said. "Go with it and build on it! If the play is a comedy, trip and fall over the chair. If the play is a drama, kick and smash the chair as you enter. *Use* the difficulty!"

Good advice for life, too, I thought. Shit happens. *Use* it. Learn something from it. Use the difficulty, so that nothing is lost on you, so that you gain something from every experience, no matter how difficult it is. *Use the difficulty!*

Dan was also generous with his time outside of class. Often I walked with him on the banks of the nearby Charles River. We talked about nothing and everything. Used to the dry bed of the Salt River, I marvelled at the Charles. A river with actual water in it was a wonder to me.

"But it's dirty water," Dan said, discounting my rapture. "Completely polluted." Which explained, I realized, the title of the only hit by The Standells, a Boston band whose drummer had a hook for one hand. "Dirty Water" was their 1967 hit, and it was about the Charles River, where, at night, you could find "lovers, muggers, and thieves" along its banks. And here I was, walking along the banks of that "Dirty Water" with Dan Seltzer. The B-side of "Dirty Water" was "Riot on Sunset Strip." Now I'd covered both sides of that 45.

Befitting the fact that Dan was a Shakespearean scholar, we spent a lot of time on the Bard of Avon. One day Dan and a female Workshop teacher enthralled us with their performance of a passage from *The Taming of the Shrew* where Petruchio befuddled, enraged, and taunted Kate, the Shrew. It was a virtuoso performance by both, which we novices were expected to emulate -- or at least die in the attempt.

And so similar crucial passages from the Bard's plays were assigned to us. Dan gave Carlo and me the end of Act III, Scene 3 of Shakespeare's *Othello*. It is the scene where Iago, who has long been planting the seeds of jealousy in Othello's mind, reaches the culmination of his evil machinations and finally persuades the Moor that his beloved wife, the faithful Desdemona, has been unfaithful.

The first gift which Othello gives Desdemona, the supreme token of his love, is an exquisite silk handkerchief which once belonged to his mother. Dying, his mother gives it to Othello "And bid me," Othello tells Desdemona, "when my fate would have me wive, to give it her. I did so; and take heed on it, to lose it or give it away were such perdition as nothing else could match. There's magic in the web of it. A sibyl in her prophetic fury sewed the work. The worms were hallowed that did breed the silk, and it was dyed in mummy, which the skillful conserved of maidens' hearts."

Iago presses his own wife, Emilia, a lady-in-waiting to Desdemona, to steal this precious and mystic handkerchief. Emilia sees her chance when Desdemona drops the handkerchief and quickly snatches it up, passing it along to her husband. Iago, in turn, presents it as a trifle to Cassio, a Venetian nobleman. Then Iago tells Othello that Desdemona has given his priceless love token to Cassio, a token of her own love for that nobleman.

Carlo took the role of Othello, I was Iago, his lieutenant. Carlo said he'd come to my room in the Radcliffe dorm where we were housed to rehearse the scene as soon as he showered. He came straight from the shower, not bothering to dress, a terry cloth towel wrapped around his waist. Carlo was muscular and huge and there were still droplets glistening on his body. He'd stopped shaving his head and his thick black mane was damp. His thin and carefully trimmed Van Dyke beard seemed perfectly suited to that of a Shakespearean hero. He took one of the two scripts and curled back the pages until he got to the scene we were to rehearse. I took the other copy.

I turned to the lines where Iago was savoring the uneasiness he's already planted in Othello's mind concerning his dear Desdemona. Iago exults to himself as Othello enters, "Not poppy, nor mandragona, nor all the drowsy syrups of the world shall ever medicine thee to that sweet sleep which thou had yesterday."

"Ha! False to me?" Carlo exclaimed of Desdemona.

"Why, how now, general! No more of that," I replied.

"Avaunt! Be gone! Thou hast set me on the rack. I swear, 'tis better to be much abused than to know but little. What sense had I of her stolen hours of lust? I saw it not, thought it not, it harmed me not. I slept the next night well, free and merry. I found not Cassio's kisses on her lips. He that is robbed, not missing what is stolen, let him not know it and he's not robbed at all."

Carlo began to get into the scene. He began to open it up, taste it, roll it around on his tongue. It was a rehearsal, just the two of us in my room. He could be as extravagant, as over the top as he wished. We both let loose with the lines. It was a good way to get a feel for the piece. We could always rein it in later, once we felt the emotions seething under the surface.

"I had been happy," Carlo continued, "if the general camp had tasted her sweet body, so I had nothing known. O! Now, forever farewell the tranquil mind, farewell content!

"Villain!" he cried, turning his fury on me. "Be sure thou prove my love a whore! Be sure of it! Give me ocular proof! Or, by the worth of my eternal soul, thou hadst better been born a dog than answer my naked wrath."

Caught up in his emotions, Carlo went literal and, at "naked wrath," he whipped the towel from his waist. Dangling it in one raised fist, biceps bulging, Carlo continued reading from the booklet held in his other fist. He stood nude before me like an angry Hercules, a Greek statue come to life, threatening hell and damnation, intimidating in his single-minded fury. His unselfconscious nudity, far from making him appear vulnerable, made him all the more frightening. I was glad I was not actually Iago.

"Make me to see it," Carlo threatened, advancing on me, "or woe upon thy life! If thou dost slander her and torture me, never pray more, abandon all remorse, on horror's head horrors accumulate, for nothing canst thou do damnation add greater than that!"

I retreated before Carlo's menacing rage. I stumbled over Iago's next lines. "Heaven, forgive me! Have you a soul or sense?"

And, indeed, Carlo seemed like a madman standing nude before me. I quailed at his advance and lamented, "Take note, take note, O, world! To be direct and honest is not safe. I thank you for this profit, and from hence I'll love no friend, since love breeds such offense."

"Nay," admonished Carlo, "thou shouldst be honest."

"Nay, I should be wise, for honesty's a fool."

"I'll have some proof! Her name, that was as fresh as Dian's visage, is now begrimed and black as mine own face. If there be cords or knives, poison or fire, or suffocating streams, I'll not endure it! Would I were satisfied!"

"I see you are eaten up with passion. I do repent that I put it to you. You would be satisfied?"

"Would? Nay, I will! Death and damnation! I'll tear her all to pieces!"

"Tell me but this, have you not sometimes seen a handkerchief spotted with strawberries in your wife's hand?"

"I gave her such a one. 'Twas my first gift."

"I know not that, but such a handkerchief, I am sure it was your wife's, did I today see Cassio wipe his beard with."

"If it be that --"

"If it be that, or any that was hers, it speaks against her with the other proofs."

"O! That the slave had forty thousand lives. One is too poor, too weak for my revenge! Now do I see 'tis true! Look here, Iago, all my fond love, thus do I blow to heaven." Carlo extravagantly kissed his fingers and then released the kiss up toward the ceiling. "'Tis gone. Arise, black vengeance, from the hollow hell! Yield up, O love, thy crown and hearted throne to tyrannous hate! O, blood! Blood! Blood!"

Shakespeare's stage directions have Othello kneel at this point. So Carlo kneeled -- and then took it further. He began writhing on the floor in nude Herculean agony, booklet in hand, his towel twisted beneath him, as he bellowed Othello's murderous agony. "Like the Pontic Sea," he exclaimed, reading from the booklet, "Whose icy current and compulsive course never ebbs, even so my bloody thoughts, with violent pace, shall never look back, never ebb to humble love, till that a capable and wide revenge swallow them up. Now, by yon marble heaven," and Carlo pointed dramatically upwards, "in the due reverence of a sacred vow, I here engage my words."

Carlo rolled on the floor in a gyre of pain and betrayal, a nude Laocoon caught in the deadly coils of the green-eyed monster, swearing his vengeance till the windows of my room shook with his wrath. "Damn her, lewd minx! O, damn her!"

Suddenly he pleaded to me, holding up a hand from the floor in supplication. "Come, go with me apart. I will now withdraw to furnish me with some swift means of death for the fair devil. Now, art thou my lieutenant."

"I am your own forever," I replied, hypnotized by the misery before me as, in our own minds, the curtain fell on the scene.

Carlo's performance was extravagant, outrageous, theatrical -- and the most emotionally powerful portrayal of love turned to bloody hatred I've ever seen. And it was all for me, alone, in the privacy of my room. No one would ever see the anguished Othello, howling nakedly in his murderous pain and rage, that I had just witnessed.

And I was never to see another portrayal by any other actor as raw and heartrending as that rehearsal of Othello's final persuasion of Desdemona's betrayal. It was Shakespeare at his most shattering. It was acting at its most devastating. When we later performed the toned-down scene in class, Dan Seltzer said my Iago was "so real you expected him to spit," but for Carlo, the Magnificent, he predicted a bright future on the stage. I agreed, and told Carlo that, in years to come, when I saw his name above the title on theater marquees, I'd say, "I used to act with him."

Meanwhile, the outside world went on. On July 12th I picked up *The Boston Globe* to read that a federal court in Boston had the day before reversed Dr. Benjamin Spock's 1968 conviction for counseling young men to evade and resist the military draft. The famous baby doctor was quoted as saying that he would now "redouble his efforts" to free those young men already imprisoned for their opposition to the draft.

Damn!, I thought. Too bad my draft board isn't here in Boston. The Boston courts seemed to be far more favorable to draft resisters than I was sure my own courts back in Arizona were. I'd have a much better chance of beating Moloch here than back home. But, that was the luck of the draw. I'd have to commit my crime where I lived and take my chances.

Only Carlo knew about the draft's Damoclean Sword hanging over me. I told no one else in the Theater Workshop about it, not even Cat. Her name wasn't really "Cat." It was "Cathy," but she said to call her "Cat." And there *was* an athletic feline grace about her. She was a short and slim Canadian blonde from Toronto, Ontario, and, in addition to acting, was also a modern dancer and a skier. I'd never known a skier before. There must've been some in Phoenix, but not in my social circles.

I'd gotten to know Cat well in the short time I'd been in Cambridge because *all* the Workshop students got to know each other well in a short space of time. We spent all day working intensely with each other at the Loeb. We all lived together in the same Radcliffe dorm, the guys on the second floor, the girls on the third. And, because we were all strangers in Cambridge and knew no one else, we socialized together.

So, when *Easy Rider,* the Peter Fonda - Dennis Hopper biker movie, opened on July 18th, a group of us -- including me, Carlo, and Cat -- went to see it together in a Boston theater. It was a small-budget indie production, but *everyone* went to see the story of two bikers riding cross-country from L.A. to the Mardi Gras. If it wasn't the first, it was one of the first feature films to have a contemporary all-rock soundtrack. And it was about *us*, outlaws in America, which is how so many of us felt. "A man went looking for America," the poster said about the Fonda character, "Captain America." But what Captain America discovered was that America *really* belonged to rednecks who'd just as soon blow him away as look at him. In fact, all three of the leads -- Peter

Fonda, Dennis Hopper, and the ACLU attorney played by Jack Nicholson (in the role that made him a star) -- *were* blown away by straight America by the end of the story.

But the film had a particular resonance for me. Many of the early scenes were shot on location in Flagstaff and at Wupatki. Watching it in Boston made me homesick for Northern Arizona. I kept saying to myself, "Yeah, that's the Flagstaff restaurant with the Paul Bunyan lumberjack out front; yeah, they're gassing up their bikes at the trading post gas station just outside the Wupatki entrance; yeah, now they're riding through the Ponderosa pine forest around Sunset Crater; and, yeah, now they're making their campfire at the Lomaki Ruin. Hey! Fonda! Don't climb on that ruined wall just to outline your heroic profile against the sunset, you schmuck! It's a thousand years old! Show some respect!" The Park Ranger in me was coming out.

And yet, I identified with the biker rebels there in the ruins of Wupatki, even though they weren't as careful of the ruins as they should've been. It was schizoid. But the movie itself was schizoid, two biker rebels searching for their place in an America that had no place for them. Yeah, that felt about right. No wonder the movie was so popular.

And I thought of Annie, who was Rangering at Wupatki at that very moment. What was she doing tonight? Was she as lonely as me? Was she thinking of me? It was a Friday night. Was she dancing to "Jumpin' Jack Flash" on the jukebox at the Grey Mountain trading post, as she told me she did, and having a good ol' time without me? I was suddenly more homesick for Annie than I ever could be for the ruins of Wupatki.

Later, riding the subway back to Harvard Square, I really noticed Cat for the first time. She was wearing a puffy white peasant blouse with rainbow colored cuffs and collar. Her long blonde hair was pulled back into a loose ponytail and she wore a funky old men's felt fedora she must've picked up in a thrift shop. It looked like the one Bogie wore in *Casablanca,* only more battered, more lived in. Cat's blonde hair billowed out from under it, despite the ponytail. I'd never seen a girl wear a man's hat before. In fact, I'd never seen anyone my age wear a Bogie hat at all. Bogie's fedora and the rainbow cuffed peasant blouse made an odd and attractive combo.

"I like your hat," I told her. "It looks good on you."

Cat glanced at me. *"This?* It's just something I picked up."

"It's Bogie's hat. He must've left it for you."

Cat smiled. "Maybe he did. Ilsa will be jealous."

"But Ilsa left him."

"But gave him her heart before she left."

"Which is better than nothing."

"Which is *everything."*

"Will Ilsa ever come back?"

"She never really left."

I smiled at Cat, holding onto a post for stability in the rocking subway car, Bogie's fedora cocked over her blonde hair. "Cat, I think this is the beginning of a beautiful friendship."

"Well, that's worth more than a hill of beans in this crazy world."

I laughed. Cat laughed with me. And I wasn't quite as lonely as we rode beneath the streets of Cambridge and into Harvard Square.

Then, two days later, on Sunday, July 20th, Neil Armstrong walked on the Moon. At 4:17 p.m. that afternoon, Eastern Daylight Time, the lunar lander containing Armstrong and Edwin "Buzz" Aldrin touched down on the lunar surface and Armstrong radioed back to earth, "Houston, Tranquility Base here. [Static.] The *Eagle* has landed."

The New Left and the hippies were disdainful of the space program. It seemed they were opposed to it simply because the "Establishment" supported it. A waste of money, they said. We ought to spend that money right here on Earth. Fix our own problems before we start going off into space. As if that money -- four-cents of each tax dollar for the Apollo program, soon to fall much, much lower than that -- would've ever been spent by the Nixon White House on any of the problems *they* considered important. America was already spending 96-cents of each tax dollar funding all the *rest* of its priorities, and few of those priorities were the same as those of the Lefties. Better to have re-directed some of that *other* 96% of tax dollars, like the billions being spent on the war. But the space program wasn't keeping us from doing *anything* the nation was politically committed to doing.

But, Lefties would never have supported space exploration at any point, even if things *were* "fixed" on Earth and we were rolling in dough. They weren't interested in space exploration, even in the best of circumstances. They were completely constrained by their parochial imaginations and had no concept of how important it was, and is, for the human species to establish its presence on more than one planet. In the long term, something is bound to happen to Earth: An asteroid impact, like the one which wiped out the dinosaurs; global warming; nuclear holocaust. We better have a backup. A terraformed Mars makes a good first step in that direction.

Ignoring the long term reasons for space exploration, however, aero-space technology would soon fuel much of America's economic growth and make possible all of modern communications, from GPS guides to global TV broadcasts to cell phones and wireless communications of all kinds. Had things been left to the Lefties back in the day, Cro-Magnons would still be complaining about all the time Caveman Ugg was spending on his wheel, when there was so much stuff that needed to be dragged around.

I was a long-time science fiction fan and I'd always been supportive of space exploration. When I was a kid, almost everyone around me derided me as a kook who actually *believed* that "crazy Buck Rogers stuff," who actually *believed* that humans would one day walk on the Moon. Most people when I was growing up knew that it could never happen. Indeed, most people don't believe *anything* new can happen until it actually happens. But now America -- *humanity* -- had done it! We'd landed on the Moon! Humanity had taken the first great step beyond the cradle of the Earth.

Armstrong had not yet actually set foot on the surface of the Moon. He'd do so that night, on live TV. I was desperate to find a TV to watch it happen, as there wasn't one in the dorm, and the only Cambridge resident I knew was Vern. Like the New Lefties, he was disdainful of the space program, and I didn't think he'd be watching the Moon landing. Besides, I didn't want to ask favors of him.

The Radcliffe dorm in which Carlo and I were staying was Jordan K, at 93 Walker Street. It was a small low-rise facility in a leafy residential Cambridge neighborhood close to Radcliffe's big Schleisinger Library and Radcliffe Yard. It was like a small apartment building, despite the three stories of rooms. It had a central kitchen and a central living room. But, there was no TV in that central living room. The only ones living in the dorm were fellow Workshop students, but that night the dorm seemed deserted even of them. Carlo wasn't interested in watching Armstrong's Moon walk and had gone to bed. I didn't know where Cat or the other residents had gone. Perhaps they'd found TV sets somewhere, as 94% of American households were sitting in their darkened living rooms that night waiting for Armstrong's anticipated Moon walk.

But I wasn't in one of those darkened living rooms. I was trapped in an empty Radcliffe dorm without a TV set. I was frantic to find one before Armstrong set foot on the Moon.

I went outside and began walking around the neighborhood. I saw the green glow of a TV screen coming from the living room picture window of one dark house. There were well-trimmed bushes just below the window. The streets all around were deserted. No doubt everyone was inside watching TV. I crept up to the house and carefully pushed my way into the bushes. I got up close to the picture window and slowly peered above the sill and into the house.

There was a family, with young kids, watching the TV and the fuzzy, silvery, black and white images coming from the Moon. Over 40,000 techies in 49 countries were coordinating a complex series of satellite hookups to bring in those low-quality images from the Moon. Lurking outside in the bushes, I watched and, like the family inside, I waited for Neil Armstrong to walk on the Moon.

Sometime around 10:45 p.m., Eastern Daylight Time, Armstrong started down the steps of the lunar lander in his bulky spacesuit. As he reached the second step of the lander, he pulled a D-ring to deploy a specially hardened video camera tucked into the lander's door. It unfolded and clicked into place. Then, at 10:56:20 p.m., Armstrong stepped out from the lander stairs and placed his foot on the lunar surface. "That's one small step for [a] man," he said, "one giant leap for mankind."

The family in the living room went wild, cheering, jumping, clapping. I felt like doing the same. I wanted to join them in their excitement, but I couldn't. I had to remain quiet, hidden, peering stealthily through their picture window. Even so, watching the scene I'd imagined a thousand times, my heart was pounding and I was celebrating, silently and alone in the bushes, just as much as that joyous family in their darkened living room.

Buzz Aldrin followed Armstrong onto the lunar surface 19 minutes later. Together they tramped around, imprinting their ridged footprints into the lunar soil. They took pictures, including a famous one of Buzz Aldrin with Armstrong reflected in his gold faceplate. They set up a flagpole with a horizontal arm to support Old Glory on the windless lunar surface and one of them saluted it. Outside, in the dark bushes, I did the same. It was one of the few things America was doing right then of which I was proud.

Around midnight I slid silently away from the ghostly images coming from the TV in the darkened living room and made my way out of the bushes. I walked back to the deserted Jordan K dorm and climbed the solitary stairs to my second story room. I didn't turn on the light as I entered my room. Some moonlight came through the window by my narrow bed, and that was enough to see by. I stripped and lay down on the bed and stared out the window at the Moon, small and far away in the dark sky.

Men were up there, at last, walking on the Moon, doing something thought completely impossible for most of history; thought impossible until just the day before yesterday. When one definitely determines to do something, I thought, even something commonly believed to be impossible, the heavens themselves move unexpectedly in one's favor.

And, thinking such thoughts, I drifted off to sleep in my Radcliffe room as the men on the Moon continued their impossible walks.

The Cost of Freedom

"I should wish to be able to love my country *and* love justice."

-- Albert Camus, during France's war in Algeria.

****

I was finally drafted on August 7th, 1969, although I didn't receive my induction orders in Cambridge until August 10th. "The local board yesterday reviewed your Conscientious Objector claim," Mrs. Dimmick wrote, "including the new letters you submitted and the comments of the Government Appeal Agent, Mr. Burton." This would have been Burton's recommendation that my case be appealed to the Presidential Appeal Board, and my letter and supporting documents asking the same. "It was noted the [state] Appeal Board had reviewed the file, and classified you in I-A. The local board decided that no basis in fact exists for reopening your classification at this time."

Which meant there would be no appeal to the Presidential Appeal Board. Not that I had expected there would be. Any such appeal would have had to be made by my local board and would have meant that my local board was questioning its own wisdom. That was highly unlikely. Were *any* C.O. claims ever presented to the Presidential Appeal Board by a local board? It seems by the very nature of the process that the possibility of such an appeal was a farce.

But I had to try. I had to demonstrate, when I finally went to trial for refusing to be drafted, that I'd explored every official and legal channel of appeal without redress -- and so refusal was my last recourse.

And now I was one step closer to actually having to refuse. In the same envelope with Mrs. Dimmick's letter informing me that my local board felt "there was no basis in fact" for changing my I-A Prime Beef classification was my "Order to Report for Induction." I was to appear at 6:45 a. m. at the Moreland Street Armed Forces Examining and Induction Station in Phoenix on August 26th, just 16 days from receiving the letter. That was the same place I'd gone for my physical with Dr. Walt on February 17th, so I knew where I was expected to be. "Willful failure to report at the place and hour of the day named in this Order subjects the violator to fine and imprisonment," the Order concluded. "Bring this Order with you when you report."

So, there it was, in my hand. I at last had a schedule and a ticket for the Hell-Bound Train. The Hell-Bound Train would arrive to pick me up for delivery to the jungle in a little over two weeks. I was expected to be in Phoenix to meet it even before the Theater Workshop at Harvard ended. Indeed, if I intended to make that rendezvous with the Hell-Bound Train, I'd have to leave fairly soon, as the cross-continent bus trek back to Phoenix would take three days and nights just by itself.

And I *did* want to make that rendezvous. There'd be another, cursory, pre-induction physical exam just before the induction ceremony. Theoretically, my medical condition could have changed since my preliminary physical exam with Dr. Walt six months previously. Theoretically, something could be found by the doctors to make me physically unqualified for induction. Thus, if I didn't show up for the physical, the government could argue in court that there was no possible way to know whether or not my refusal to be drafted was warranted. Perhaps I was medically unfit for military service, and therefore would have been rejected by the pre-induction doctors.

So, for the same reason I'd made the farcical appeal to the Presidential Appeal Board, I had to be in Phoenix on August 26th to rendezvous with the Hell-Bound Train. To strengthen my legal defense against the government, I had to show that I had not "prematurely" committed a crime. I had to be able to argue that all other possibilities, including the possibility that I might have been medically unacceptable, had been exhausted. Refusing to be drafted was all that remained to me if I were to prevent an injustice from occurring.

It wasn't much of a defense. Refusing to be drafted was still a crime, no matter at what point in the process I refused. Still, it was a legal technicality by which the government could attempt to ensnare me in court and, regardless of merit, cases are won and lost on legal technicalities. Continuations aren't requested in time. Affidavits aren't filed properly. Documents aren't stapled together. Whatever. You have to jump through all the convoluted hoops in a certain sequence, in a certain way, at a certain time, or you're disqualified from even contending on the merits. That's just the way the legal system works, the way the game is played. It's one of the reasons Lenny Bruce said that the only justice in the halls of justice is in the halls.

So, since I had it in my power to eliminate that little technicality, I planned to do so. It was one small bit of control I had over my future.

I told only two people that I'd been drafted. One was Carlo.

"What're you gonna do?" he asked.

"I'm going to refuse induction. But I have to be in Phoenix in two weeks to do that."

"Why can't you just not show up?"

"A legal technicality. It'll be better for me in court if I show up, and then refuse to go."

"So you won't finish the Workshop?"

"I can't. Time won't let me."

Carlo put his arm around my shoulders. "I'm gonna miss you, amigo."

I smiled at him. "Come and visit me in prison."

The other person I told, finally, was Cat. "I'm going to refuse induction," I told her.

"In Phoenix?"

"In Phoenix."

"Then what?"

I shrugged. "I go to prison."

"Why? You going to prison won't stop the draft or the war. You're just one person."

"I know, but it always starts with one person. And if enough people refuse to cooperate, *then* we'll stop the draft and we'll stop the war."

"Please, spare me your delusions of grandeur. You *know* that's not going to happen."

I smiled. "Yeah, I know."

"Then I don't understand. If you *know* it won't make a difference, why are you doing it?"

"Because I *have* to. I owe it to my country to try to save it...because I love my country."

"I'm gonna barf. Your country will repay your love and devotion by sending you to prison. Do you *want* to go to prison?"

"No, but I don't know what else to do."

"You could go to Canada. Lots of draft resisters have gone to Canada. There are *thousands* of them in Toronto alone. I could take you."

"Cat, I can't turn my back on my country and just leave. I have to stay here and help my country do the right thing."

"Your country *never* does the right thing! That's why everybody else in the world hates it! America is the bully of the world. It goes around stomping on the hopes and dreams of all the little people of the world so that American corporations can continue to rape the earth."

"I know all that, but America isn't *always* in the wrong."

"Even when America's right, America is *wrong!* And if you stay here and refuse induction, your beloved country will call you a coward and a traitor and throw you in prison. How can you love a country that would do *that* to a man who refuses to *murder?"*

"Cat, America has a Jekyll and Hyde personality. A lot of the time it does evil in the world. Right now it's doing its best to destroy Vietnamese freedom and independence. But, compared to most of the other countries of the world, it really *is* the land of the free!"

"Oh, please, you're making me nauseous with all this 'land of the free' bullshit. Keep it up and you'll make me puke."

"OK, I'll stop. But I can't go to Canada. I have to go to Phoenix."

Cat looked at me. "Fine. Be stubborn and stupid and go to Phoenix. But I'm taking you someplace else, first."

"Where's that?"

"Woodstock."

"Where's Woodstock?"

****

Woodstock wasn't where it was supposed to be. Woodstock -- "Three days of peace and music" -- was *supposed* to be in the small upstate New York village of Woodstock, where Bob Dylan lived. It was going to be the first big outdoor rock concert in the East -- even bigger than Monterey in '67. But, as the August 15th start date drew closer, the town fathers grew ever more nervous. Like the village of Wallkill, which had refused permission for the concert before them, they didn't relish the idea of Woodstock being overrun by hordes of drug-crazed hippies. Visions of Marlon Brando's biker gang from *The Wild One* danced in their heads -- only unimaginably worse. So, in mid-July they cancelled their agreement with Michael Lang, the concert promoter.

Lang, however, had already booked almost every big name rock act in America, as well as Brit rockers such as The Who and Ten Years After. Some bands, such as Jefferson Airplane, had already been paid, so Lang would lose that money. But cancelling the concert would also mean big financial losses for those bands which hadn't been paid, as they'd already arranged their summer tours around Woodstock. They'd sue Lang for their losses. His only hope of avoiding massive lawsuits, and of perhaps still making a profit, was to somehow, somewhere, stage the concert.

So Lang scrambled and came up with 660 acres of bucolic pasture belonging to a dairy farmer named Max Yasgur just outside the village of Bethel, about 60-miles from Woodstock and 100-miles north of New York City. He signed a contract to rent the land and quickly paid Max Yasgur $50,000 right then, so the farmer couldn't back out. The concert was a "go" for Yasgur's farm outside Bethel, but it was still billed as "Woodstock," perhaps because all the tickets and the thousands of red, white, and green posters calling it that had already been printed and distributed all over the Northeast.

Construction of a huge performing stage at the bottom of a sloping 35-acre field which formed a natural amphitheater began immediately. Workers also built a six-foot tall wooden plank fence fanning out on each side of the stage to keep the audience away from backstage. The far outer rim of the 35-acre field would be surrounded by more flimsy wire hurricane fencing -- which, put up as the last task of the concert planners, proved completely useless for purposes of crowd control. Workers pitched support tents backstage and erected five 80-foot-tall towers around the stage to hold the excellent sound system. The towers also supported the many flood lights aimed at the stage. There would be continuous music, with bands playing even at night.

Water supplies, food stalls, and portable toilets called Port-o-Sans were installed for an expected crowd of 50,000 people per day. These, like the hurricane fence, the ticket booths, and everything else the planners planned, were quickly overwhelmed. The first outriders of the hippie horde, which eventually numbered 500,000, began arriving at the field on Thursday, August 14th, even before the fence and the ticket booths went up. The next day, the first official day of the concert, the fence and the booths were finally erected, but it was too late. There were too many people already in the concert field who hadn't paid, and there were too many impatiently waiting outside the fence to control. The fence went down under the numbers and the hippie hordes flooded in.

At that point Michael Lang and his partners realized it was impossible to rectify the situation, so they made the best of it and announced that it was a "free concert." Good for us that they did. Cat and I didn't have tickets. We'd planned to buy them at the concert. Perhaps most others did, also, but no one I talked to over the three days of the concert had a ticket.

Today, Woodstock is a legend. No one at the time, however, knew it was going to be one. It was just going to be a gigunza outdoor rock concert, with lots of groovy bands. But Cat and I realized something really weird was happening almost as soon as we crossed the New York border in her VW Beetle. There were breaking announcements on the radio of massive traffic jams, road closures, back-ups, and the closer we got to Bethel, the worse the traffic became. The roads were littered with abandoned cars like the discard of refugees fleeing the Wehrmacht. Was *everybody* going to Woodstock?

Eventually, a few miles from Yasgur's farm, the road became a solid mass of people and it was impossible to drive any further, so Cat and I also decided to abandon the VW. Cat pulled off the road and nosed the Beetle in amongst other cars strewn this way and that along the berm. We pulled out the two blankets we'd brought and my backpack, which we'd stuffed with munchies, heavy plastic jugs of water, and a roll of toilet paper. I put on my cowboy hat and shades and Cat pulled Bogie's fedora down over her billowing blonde hair. Then she locked the Beetle and we joined the tide of refugees flowing down the road in the stifling August heat toward Yasgur's farm.

By the time we got to Woodstock the fences were already down and the 35-acre slope was jammed with bodies as far as the eye could see. More bodies continued to pour onto the field like an endless army of South American ants on the move. It was already impossible to get close to the stage. We found some free space, tossed down our blankets, and claimed our turf. People continued to pour in behind us and, eventually, our little plot of ground turned out to be pretty much mid-way from the stage to the back of the horde.

It was late afternoon Friday, the first official day of the concert, and John Sebastian was singing down on the stage. He was so far away he looked like a little marionette. "Who'd we miss?" I asked the hippies sprawled on the grass next to us.

"Aw, not much," a freak with long bushy sideburns and Jesus hair said. "We've been sitting here forever and it just began. Richie Havens. Country Joe McDonald. Here, man, ya wanna hit?" He held out a joint.

"I'll pass."

"I won't," Cat said. "Gimme a hit of that." Cat took a long toke and held her breath as she passed the joint back. The hippie took it and toked deeply himself.

Then Cat exhaled strongly and a blue cloud billowed out of her mouth. She hacked a few times. "Damn! That's el primo shit!"

The hippie nodded and smiled. "Damn straight!" He offered it to me again.

I shook my head. "Later, not right now." It was my Mormon background coming out, the only part of it that took. I was still *in* the hippie world, but not *of* the hippie world, at least as far as dope was concerned. If anything was typical of the hippie scene, it was drugs, but I wasn't a typical hippie. I was a "straight" hippie. I didn't drop acid, smoke pot, do speed, or shoot smack. I wasn't a head. That's why Shana said I was such a downer. But maybe that's also why I still remember the Sixties.

Besides, in a crowd like this, I didn't need to toke up. If I didn't get a contact high from the people and the music, I would probably get a buzz just from all the sweet blue smoke wafting through the air all around us. Free pot! Just breathe!

I looked around at the hippie horde in amazement. Maybe I was the only Jack Mormon hippie there, but I still felt like I was a hippie, and being a hippie even in '69 meant being a member of a despised minority. Usually, there was just a small hippie community wherever you were. If you stopped at a rest stop on an Interstate, all the heads turned as you walked in. And when you sat down, you didn't know if you'd be served or told to get the hell out.

But here, there were hippies to the horizon! I felt like there was an entire hidden world of freaks and weirdos which had emerged from the underground and come together at that spot, and I was one of them. I didn't feel like a stranger. I stretched out, eased back on my elbows, watched the little puppet down on the far-away stage, and basked in the glow of acceptance. I was a member of a completely new minority group.

I glanced over at Cat, sitting cross-legged on the blanket next to me. The brim of Bogie's fedora was pulled down in front to shield her eyes from the sitting sun. The hippie on the next blanket with the Jesus hair had rolled her a joint of her own and she was bogarting it just like Bogie, the blue smoke curling up and caressing her face. She was rocking back and forth the way Orthodox Jews pray and periodically exhaling small puffs. I smiled at her. She glanced my way and smiled back. And then blew out another puff of pot. She was already getting high and mellow and grooving on the scene. I liked Cat and didn't begrudge her having fun. I'll miss her when I'm drafted, I thought.

But then I remembered that I'd *already* been drafted. I was going to be inducted in a few days. All this was just a vacation before I went off to prison. I slowly surveyed the ocean of hippies around me. Perhaps I'm the only Jack Mormon hippie here, I thought. Am I also the only hippie here who's already been drafted? And the feeling of acceptance and community I'd been basking in faded, along with the fading sunlight. I suddenly felt as lonely in that horde of hippies as I'd ever felt back home in cowboy Phoenix. Hell, I thought, watching Cat getting higher by the moment, I don't really belong here any more than I belong in Phoenix. I don't belong *anywhere.*

Darkness fell and a half-moon rode high in the sky. The night turned chill and Cat snuggled next to me. I put my arm around her and she laid her head on my shoulder. She was high and mellow and we listened quietly as Tim Hardin sang "If I Were a Carpenter." He stood on the stage alone under the bright tower lights, accompanied only by his acoustic guitar. Tim Hardin had a heroin problem and, like so many of the Woodstock performers, would die of drugs. Some later said he performed badly that night because he was smacked out even then, but he sang slow and deep and clear, and his picking was precise. He sounded as straight as me and as mellow as Cat.

He was followed by Ravi Shankar with his sitar and tabla troupe. Perhaps the Bengali took pity on the poor huddled American masses and tossed them food from the stage before he began playing. Years later I met a woman named Abbe who said she was right down front when Ravi came on and she caught an apple he tossed into the crowd. I don't remember that and I don't remember much of his performance, either, because it was just generic raga, as far as I was concerned. One raga sounds just like another to me. Then, around 10:30 or so, it began to rain and Ravi called it a night.

I wished we could've done the same, but there was no place to go. We just had to sit it out. The Jesus hippie next to us produced some clear plastic sheeting from somewhere and began passing around strips. Cat and I took one and held it over our heads. We huddled together like drowned cats while, amazingly, the music went on. Melanie came out and screeched forgettably about the "birthday of the rain." She was followed by Arlo Guthrie, who burbled happily that, "The New York State Freeway's closed, man. Far out!" A ragged cheer went up, but Cat and I didn't join in. Who the fuck cared?

Arlo was followed by another folkie, Joan Baez. She and Bob Dylan had been an item once upon a time, but now she was married to David Harris. He was a good boy who'd gone bad. He'd been the student government president at Stanford University. Then he'd become a draft resister and had been sentenced to prison for non-cooperation with the S.S. System. He was serving time at that very moment. Indeed, Joan told us that David had just been transferred in manacles from the county jail where he'd been held to a federal prison to begin serving his term. She dedicated her next song, "Joe Hill," to David. As she sang, her beautiful voice soaring effortlessly out into the night, I wondered if I, too, would soon be shuffling off in manacles to some federal prison. If so, no one would announce to half-a-million people where I was heading or dedicate a song to me.

Joanie ended her set around two in the morning. She was the last act and the stage lights went black. It'd been a long day for Cat and me and we dozed off in exhaustion on our sodden blanket shortly thereafter, wet and miserable under our plastic sheet.

Saturday morning we awoke bleery-eyed to a muddy mess. The hot morning sun was already steaming humidity off the bedraggled hippie horde and there was a steady stream of people moving toward the top of the field, where the Port-O-Sans were located. Cat headed off to take her turn, while I remained on our wet blanket, guarding our little piece of paradise from other homesteaders. When Cat eventually returned, it was my turn in the Port-O-San line. That day was probably the worst day at Woodstock. People wandered around like lost refugees until noon, hunting for food, water, and a place to pee. Sometime in the afternoon bands started playing, but I don't remember who. Certainly not The Who. Cat and I spent the day taking turns wandering around, seeing what there was to see.

Santana played that afternoon. Canned Heat came on sometime later. Some bozo from the audience managed to climb on stage and gyrate for awhile with Bob Hite, the big and bearded lead singer. Hite took it in stride and kept on singing, even when the bozo snatched Hite's pack of cigs out of his T-shirt pocket, shook one out, and lit up. Peace and love, brother. Share and share alike. What's yours is mine. We're all bozos on this bus. Bob Hite was another one who'd shortly be dead from drugs.

Sometime before midnight the Grateful Dead came on. I'd been waiting eagerly for them. But, unlike Tim Hardin, they really *must* have been stoned. They played a lackluster set and then rambled off the lit stage into the backstage darkness. Who even remembers what they played? And then nothing happened for the longest time. And then Janis Joplin was announced. The crowd cheered. Cat cheered. I cheered. Even without Big Brother and the Holding Company backing her up, Janis would give a good show.

But maybe she was also tired, who knows? It was the only time I caught Janis in concert, and it was far from a legendary performance. She was too far away to really see, but I remember her a cappella voice on "Work Me Lord" echoing in the dark. There was no echo effect in the sound system. That was just Janis, a fantastic sound system all by herself. But, there just wasn't much of her that night, and we also wouldn't have her for much longer. Another drug casualty.

But then, sometime around three in morning, Sly and the Family Stone came on. I'd never even *heard* of them, and they certainly weren't one of the reasons I'd come to Woodstock. But they just pounded out the beat, getting everyone, no matter how burned out, up and dancing. "I want to take you higher!" Sly yelled, and even Cat and I, tired and sleepy as we were, got up and danced around.

And that high-energy set was followed by The Who, keeping everyone on their feet. With his white fringed jacket open to show his muscular chest, Roger Daltry played the role of rock god better than anyone else at Woodstock. The East was growing bright by the time Pete Townshend ended their set by smashing his guitar and tossing it out into the crowd. Too bad Abbe, the woman I later met, didn't catch Townshend's ruined guitar instead of Ravi Shankar's long-gone apple.

Jefferson Airplane came on after the sun was already up. "It's a new morning," Grace Slick said, and she looked as stunning in *her* white fringed outfit as had Daltry in his. But, it was another disappointing set. It seemed all the acts which pulled us to Woodstock put on ho-hum performances, while people few had heard of, like Sly, blew us away. The Airplane's Paul Kantner later told rock critique Ben Fong-Torres that few in the band remember what they played or how they sounded. It was 7 A.M., he recalled, and "Half the crew was asleep or naked in the pond, and I remember the film cameras were pointed in the sky half the time." Paul was also up there in the sky, as he'd heavily dosed himself with acid shortly after arriving at Woodstock.

After Jefferson Airplane, there was a long pause while we all recovered. Most of that day, Sunday, the horde lined up for breakfast at the Hog Farm soup tents, used the toilets, slept, or -- a lucky few -- stripped and bathed in the pond back of the stage. Cat and I had been wise to bring food and water. We shared it with those around us, and they shared with us, and a small affinity group began to develop in our immediate vicinity.

Around two that hot August afternoon Brit rocker Joe Cocker started the new round of sets. As with many of the people who sang at Woodstock, I wasn't familiar with him. From the look of him jerking spasmodically on stage, playing his air guitar, he seemed like an epileptic going into a fit. He seemed like a hippie joke, but he had passion in his voice.

As Cocker finished, another storm front moved in. The big tarps over the stage began flapping and the announcer repeatedly warned people to climb down off the sound towers. It looked like it was going to be a big storm, and if those towers toppled a lot of people could've been hurt. For almost two hours the rain pounded down like the beginning of Noah's Flood. There was nothing to be done but just hunker down and ride it out. Cat and I huddled close, drenched in the deluge, and we stoically endured. Eventually, some of those around us decided to just make the best of things and become one with nature. Male and female alike they stripped naked and began dancing in the storm, splashing their bare bodies with mud.

Sometime around five in the afternoon the storm blew over and some in the horde turned one area of the field into a giant mud slide. They ran and threw themselves down into the mud like joyful children and slid for as far as they could. Others began banging tin cans together and chanting like some primitive tribe engaged in a communal ritual. Cat and I banged on cans and chanted with the rest, losing ourselves in the chant, which went on and on. We were just happy to have endured and survived. It couldn't get any worse. Besides, who the hell needed professional musicians on a stage? We made our own music.

I don't think anyone who was there could ever describe anything like a "definitive" Woodstock experience. Being at Woodstock was like being a soldier in battle. You saw only a small part of what was going on, the part right around you. You had no idea of anything that was going on anywhere else. People were freaking out in the Hog Farm tents on bad acid trips. Maybe *that* was Woodstock. Some babies were born at Woodstock, and at least one poor dude was run over by a tractor and killed. Maybe *that* was Woodstock. Abbe caught Ravi Shankar's tossed apple. Maybe *that* was Woodstock. After the big storm I could see, in the pond beyond the stage, some chicks and dudes skinny dipping. Maybe *that* was Woodstock, or at least a better Woodstock than I experienced. All I experienced was what happened in my very small part of the battlefield.

And, as time went on, Woodstock did take on more and more aspects of a military encampment, or a refugee holding pen. The August heat was broiling and we were hot and sweaty and thirsty, so we welcomed the rain and opened our mouths to the heavens to let it pour in. As for our clothes, we just let'em dry on our bodies.

But then, because of the rain, the encampment became a sea of mud. It never dried out, the entire time. There weren't enough Port-o-Sans, and the guys, at least, began pissing where they could. And it was impossible to escape from the sea of humanity. There were just too many damn freaks, and our car was just too far away.

And, even if we got to our car, it'd probably be blocked in by the cars abandoned by our next-blanket neighbors, who were still back at the field of mud. So, we were stuck there. The only thing we could do was hold on and wait it out. Woodstock became a test of endurance.

Down front, on the tall wooden fence separating the hippie horde from the backstage area, someone had painted, "We Are One." Certainly Woodstock felt like that at times. On Sunday afternoon, before the big storm, Max Yasgur was welcomed to the stage. He said it was wonderful that all of us had come together on his farm for three days of fun and music and we'd had nothing *but* three days of fun and music. No cops, no fights, no violence of any kind. Indeed, there *was* a feeling of camaraderie, a feeling that we were all in it together and we had to take care of one another. This was the feeling Joni Mitchell expressed later in her hit song "Woodstock," which went far in creating the Woodstock myth. Woodstock was a garden, she sang, and we all have to get back to that garden.

It certainly helped that we were encamped in a large rural pasture; that there was a nearby pond where people could skinny dip; that there were young children, perhaps belonging to the Hog Farm, running around in the buff.

But it also helped that almost everyone there was white. There were more black and brown faces on stage, among the performers, than there were in the crowd. And it helped that everyone there but Max Yasgur was young. And it helped that we all dressed and looked the same, so class differences were invisible. And it helped that there were no violence prone Hell's Angels, as there would be at the barren wasteland of Altamont Speedway four months later, where they beat to death a black dude in the crowd who was waving a gun at them while Mick Jagger was singing "Sympathy for the Devil."

So, besides the misery of the mud, it was very easy to see what we had in common and to proclaim that "We Are One." We were all white and young and we dressed the same and we all grooved on the same music. It was easy to believe we were all flower children who'd returned, for a short time, to the blessed garden, where peace, love, and harmony reigned.

But Joni Mitchell never made it to Woodstock. She just heard about it. And if it was a garden, it seemed to me less like the Garden of Eden than, increasingly, the Garden of Gethsemane, a place of trial and decision. I wouldn't be getting back to any flower child green and pleasant Aquarian garden after Woodstock. Instead, I'd be returning to the Arizona desert and prison. That made me very different from all the flower children skinny dipping and slip-sliding in the mud and grooving on their cosmic oneness all around me. None of *them* would be sharing any "oneness" with me in prison.

As dusk descended, a Brit blues band called Ten Years After took the stage. I didn't know them, either, but they rocked for two hours. They were followed by The Band, all dressed in black and, I guess, as exhausted as everyone in the crowd. When they sang "The Weight," it sounded like they were all indeed laboring under a gigantic weight and so could hardly get through their set.

Around midnight they were followed by blues rocker Johnny Winter. By then Cat was asleep on our blanket, covered by our extra one. Around three in the morning, Monday morning, a another group I knew nothing about was announced: Crosby, Stills, and Nash. They were refugees from The Byrds and The Hollies, bands which I knew. One of them said it was only their second gig together.

And then they began singing the most beautiful harmonies of the entire festival. They sang like choir boys. It may have been only their second gig, but they'd clearly rehearsed, and they were clearly stone cold sober. I sat enthralled, marvelling that rock music could sound so ethereal and beautiful. I glanced over at Cat, wisps of blonde hair covering her face, Bogie's fedora crumpled under her head for a pillow, and wondered if I should wake her for this. She looked gone to the world. I didn't have the heart to disturb her.

And then Crosby, Stills, and Nash put away their guitars and sang a cappella, their voices soaring into the night. They sang "The Cost of Freedom." I'd never heard the song before. "Find the cost of freedom...lay your burden down." They sang like angels and I began to cry as I listened to them, the tears flowing silently down my cheeks. Sitting in that dark field with half-a-million hippies around me I felt alone and frightened and, O!, how I wanted to lay my burden down! But I knew I couldn't. Because I realized that my burden was the cost of freedom. And the cost of freedom was prison.

And then Crosby, Stills, and Nash stopped singing, their echoes dying out into the darkness. But I didn't stop crying. It felt like the floodgates had been opened and I rocked back and forth in the darkness as my tears flowed. Because I truly realized the full cost of freedom. Someone has to pay the cost of freedom, and I was that someone. That was my burden.

It's scary and dangerous to be right when your government is wrong. In an unjust society, a just man must expect prison. But a real man does the right thing, even if it's scary and dangerous. *Especially* if it's scary and dangerous. *Anyone* can do the right thing when it's safe and easy. The only time it really counts is when it's *not* safe and easy. *That's* when Satan takes you to the mountain top and offers you the world, if you'll but bow down and call him "Master."

But the *real* man is the one who turns away from that last temptation in the Garden of Gethsemane. The *real* man is the one who says, "Get thee behind me, Satan." The *real* man is the one who *chooses* to pick up his cross and begin trudging with it toward his own Golgotha because he is willing to pay the cost of freedom.

And then a great sense of well-being and invincibility, of power and euphoria, flooded over me because I realized that I was free, absolutely free, and no one and no *thing* could take away my freedom. Because if you are completely willing to pay the cost of freedom, whatever that cost may be -- then Satan and his minions have no power over you. They can imprison you, they can press down on your head a crown of thorns, they can spear your flesh, they can nail you to the cross. But if you are completely willing to be nailed to the cross as the cost you must pay for freedom, they can't make you bend your knee. You may not have to pay that cost -- but you have to be willing to do so. And if you are willing, *truly willing,* to pay the cost of freedom -- then you *are* free, even if your body is in prison. It's all up to you. It's *your* choice.

And then it came to me. I had a chance to beat the devil, after all! There was nothing waiting for me back in Phoenix. I had no family, I had no job, I had no home, I had no academic future, as ASU had "disqualified" me from returning because of "low scholarship." I didn't even have Annie waiting for me back in Phoenix. She was now at Pitzer, in California. There was absolutely *nothing* waiting for me back in Phoenix except prison.

But, in Cambridge, I had a job at Becker Research. In Cambridge I had, for the time being, a place to live. In Cambridge I perhaps had a future at the Loeb. And in Cambridge I had a fighting chance to defeat the draft in court.

I would go to trial wherever I committed the crime of refusing to be inducted into the military. And if I refused induction in Boston, that's where I'd go to trial. And Boston was where federal judge Charles Wyzanski in May, just three months before, had ruled that the Selective Service Act was unconstitutional. Boston was where a federal appeals court had just the previous month overturned Dr. Ben Spock's conviction for counseling resistance to the draft.

Also, as I'd told my Local Board No. 29 back in Phoenix, the U. S. Supreme Court had already handed down a broad legal definition in *U.S. vs. Seeger* of what beliefs qualified a registrant for Conscientious Objector status. "The test might be stated in these words," the Supremes had written in their decision of that case: "A sincere and meaningful belief which occupies in the life of its possessor a place parallel to that filled by the God of those admittedly qualifying for the exemption comes within the statutory definition."

My local draft board had consistently ignored the Supreme Court definition of what secular beliefs a Conscientious Objector could legitimately hold, but the federal courts in Boston were the most liberal, the most anti-draft courts in the nation. It was unlikely that *they* would ignore the U.S. Supreme Court on this issue. Thus, there was a good chance they would rule in my favor if I went to trial for draft resistance in Boston.

So what I had to do was stay in Cambridge! I had to write my draft board as soon as I got back to Cambridge and have my induction transferred to Boston! Refusing induction in Boston would be my sling-shot, the only chance I had of bringing down the military Goliath.

I was alone and I was headed into a dark unknown future -- but I was no longer afraid.

Dawn came as I sat in that muddy field at Woodstock thinking such thoughts and planning my strategy. Cat stirred under the blanket beside me. She stretched and yawned, her blonde hair a wilderness around her face. She looked like an angel that morning. I smiled down at her. "Good morning, sleepy head. You're just in time to hear Jimi Hendrix. He's next."

Cat sat up and looked around. People were stirring and picking up their blankets. Many had already left. Where there had been humanity to the horizon, now you could see large swaths of the debris strewn field of mud in which we squatted. Scavengers were already beginning to pick over the remains of the garden.

"Where's everybody going?" Cat asked.

"Back home. It's Monday morning. They have to get back to their jobs in the real world. Just like we have to get back to Cambridge. I have a lot of work to do before my induction."

"I'm not going back to Cambridge. I'm going home to Toronto. I'm already half there."

I was surprised to hear that. "You could've told me before we left Cambridge."

"Then you wouldn't have come with me."

"Well, that's gonna make it a bit hard for me to get back."

"You don't have to go back. You can come with me to Toronto."

"We talked about this. I can't go."

"Eric, there's a whole community of American draft resisters around Baldwin Street near the University of Toronto. It's an American ghetto. They have housing co-ops, community newspapers, the whole deal. And they're politically active. There'll be more for you to do there, with them in Toronto, than rotting alone in some American prison."

"Cat, I can't do that. I don't have any money, I don't have any place to stay...."

"You can stay with me."

I looked at her. She meant it.

"Cat, I can't go with you to Toronto."

"Give me one good reason, and not just more idealistic bullshit."

"I have a girlfriend back in Arizona. Actually, she's now in California."

Cat considered that. "Eric, I'm not asking you to be my boyfriend. All I'm trying to do is save your ass from prison. If she really loves you, your girlfriend will come to Toronto. Eric, dammit, just get in the bug with me and come to Toronto!"

"Cat, if I went with you to Toronto, it'd be a permanent exile. I'd never be able to return."

"So, what's the big deal? America just wants to put you in prison."

"I know this is going to sound like more idealistic bullshit, but...my country needs me."

Jimi was on stage and was starting in on "Voodoo Child." Cat crossed her legs in a yoga position and looked at me with concern. "Yeah, your country needs you to fight in an evil war on the other side of the world. That's why it drafted you. But you said you weren't going to do that."

"No, I'm not going to do that. My country needs me to help it do the right thing."

"What's the right thing?"

"Stopping this evil war on the other side of the world."

"But one person can't stop the war! All you can do is go to prison! I'm trying to save you!"

"Cat, when you love someone, you don't abandon that person when he does something wrong, something you don't like. You tell him what he did was wrong and you try to get him to change. You *fight* for him."

"I know all that! What the fuck do you think I'm doing here?"

I looked at Cat. She was staring at me fiercely. I didn't know what she was thinking. I didn't know what she was feeling. I wasn't even sure I knew what she was saying. I took Cat's hand and held it between both of mine.

"So, Cat, then you understand that if my country is doing something wrong, I can't abandon it. I have to tell my country it's doing something wrong and it has to stop. I have to fight for my country."

A cloud passed over her face, covering it with shadow. She gazed at me in silence. I knew I was losing her. She pulled her hand from between mine. "You're going to go to prison and I just don't understand you."

Cat rose and stood over me. As I looked up at her, the cloud shadow passed and the morning sun flamed into a halo in her tousled hair. She looked like an angel. She ran her hand through her hair to pull it back out of her face and then pulled Bogie's fedora down on her head. And the angel was gone.

"Good luck in prison," she said, "you'll need it." Then she turned and walked away, her blonde hair swirling out beneath Bogie's fedora, determination in her stride.

I stood up and called to her. "Cat! I'm sorry!"

Cat paused and half turned back toward me. "I'm five minutes past caring."

On stage Jimi segued from "Voodoo Child" into a crazed and distorted "Star-Spangled Banner" on his Stratocaster. It sounded like a dying dinosaur; it sounded like rockets falling and bombs exploding; it sounded like America at war with itself.

The hippie horde swallowed Cat and she was lost from sight.

The Partisan

It was a long tiring trek hitching back to Cambridge. I reached my Radcliffe dorm room late on the night of Monday, August 18th. Even though I was exhausted, I wrote a quick letter to my draft board so I could mail it the next day. Time was short. I was due to be inducted in Phoenix on August 26th, just a week away. I informed my board that I no longer lived in Phoenix. I now lived in Cambridge. Therefore, "I would appreciate it if my induction can be transferred." I ended the letter by saying, "Your classification for me of I-A and your induction orders are illegal actions, there being no basis in fact for such classification and induction actions." And, for the record, I sent a copy to Osmond Burton, my board's Government Appeal Agent. It would take some time to transfer my induction to Boston, so at least my induction would be pushed back a bit, a few weeks, perhaps a month. I'd grabbed some breathing space.

Next, I had to find a place to live. There were only days left to the summer Theater Workshop and Carlo and I both would soon have to vacate the Radcliffe dorm. Like me, Carlo would not be returning to Phoenix, but not because he'd decided to stay in Cambridge. He'd made good connections at the Loeb. Through them, he'd auditioned for the prestigious Long Wharf Children's Theater, in New Haven. He'd been accepted as a member of the permanent troupe of actors. It was a paying gig, and so he'd soon be leaving to spend the fall, and perhaps longer, in New Haven. I wished him well when we parted. We both hoped it'd be the beginning of big things for him. "I'll see you on the silver screen," I told him.

Then I picked up a copy of the student newspaper, *The Harvard Crimson,* and turned to the classifieds. Cambridge was vastly different from Phoenix and people did things differently there. Vern, for example, had lived for free in posh West Cambridge ever since he'd arrived, first on Freshpond Lane, now on Larch Road. He "house-sat" the elegant estates of Harvard professors while they spent a year or two in Europe on sabbaticals. I had the phone surveying gig at Becker Research, but that didn't pay much, certainly not enough to cover the expensive rents of Cambridge, and I had only a few dollars in my pocket. Perhaps I could find something similar to Vern's gigs.

One ad caught my eye. Someone wanted a Harvard student to perform maintenance chores around a large West Cambridge house in exchange for a free room. No pay, no board, but it was a place to sleep and throw down my backpack. I called the listed phone number and made an appointment with the obviously old woman who answered.

The house turned out to be a huge 300-year-old Colonial Era two-story clapboard house at 8 Willard Street, just off Brattle. It was an elite neighborhood, just a five-minute walk along Brattle from the Loeb. The house next door, I later learned, towards Brattle, had once belonged to Archibald MacLeish, the former Poet Laureate of the United States. And around the corner, on Brattle, was the Longfellow House, owned and operated by the National Park Service. When Longfellow owned the house, he also owned all the land between it and the Charles River. Now a large rectangular part of that tract is the carefully manicured Longfellow Park. The park features a monument honoring the poet and his most famous subjects: Paul Revere and his midnight ride, Hiawatha and his song, the Village Smithy, Evangaline. The clapboard house I arrived at abutted the western edge of Longfellow Park.

The woman who greeted me seemed to be as old as Methuselah. She was small, frail, and stooped. Maybe she weighed 80 or 90-lbs., dripping wet. Her wispy white hair was pulled back in a bun from which stray strands waved. She had only a few yellowed teeth in her mouth. The thin and faded cotton print housedress she wore seemed as ancient as she. When I shook her wrinkled and purple-veined hand in greeting, I was careful to squeeze as gently as possible. She invited me into her living room.

As I stepped inside, it seemed my head almost brushed the lowest ceiling I'd ever seen in a house. I later learned that such low ceilings were typical of Colonial Era homes. The living room smelled musty and old. One entire side of the room was lined with a built-in bookcase stuffed with hardcover books. Every piece of furniture seemed to be an antique. I sat lightly in the chair she offered, fearful of breaking it with my weight.

I learned that the woman was Miss Harriet Peet, a Radcliffe graduate and retired teacher. I also learned that she was 100-years-old, no doubt making her the world's oldest living 'Cliffie. When she attended Radcliffe, she later told me, the female students were not allowed to sit in the same classrooms with Harvard "men." Professors like William James and George Santayana had to walk to the Radcliffe campus, not far from the Jordan K dorm where I was staying, to repeat their lectures for the benefit of the co-eds. Gender discrimination had lessened at Harvard somewhat since those days. Now we even lived together at Jordan K.

Miss Peet co-owned the large house with a retired Harvard philosophy professor, Dr. Arthur Dewing, who occupied one half of the structure. Dr. Dewing, whom I did not meet that day, was a youngster compared to Miss Peet. He was merely in his early 90s. He was comfortably well-off in his retirement. In 1923 Dr. Dewing had considered an investment proposal brought to him by a former student named Henry Luce. The student thought America needed a nationally distributed newsmagazine and asked Professor Dewing to help launch one by investing in the project. Luce proposed to call his magazine *Time*. But Dr. Dewing thought it was a sure loser and felt he had better investment options. He was wrong about *Time*, but he did fine with his other investments. Evidently, Miss Peet had, also.

Both Dr. Dewing and Miss Peet were lucid and healthy, despite their ages, but neither was up to the physical demands of caring for the house and grounds. They needed a young man to cut the grass, rake the leaves, shovel the snow, and generally look after the place in exchange for a free room. I seemed to be a nice and courteous young man and, from the moment I walked into her living room, Miss Peet accepted me. Well that she did. I was the only one who answered her ad. Perhaps I was the only poor boy who read *The Harvard Crimson*.

Miss Peet showed me to what she called the servant's quarters on the second floor at the back of the house. It was a small room which would, henceforth, be my room. It had two small windows, one looking out on Willard Street, the other on Willard Court, a cul-de-sac beside Miss Peet's house which was large enough for an attached garage and only one other house, much smaller than Miss Peet's. I learned that the garage sheltered Dr. Dewing's still-functional 1940 Packard. I would be his chauffeur and drive that Packard on his occasional jaunts to the suburbs.

Directly across from the window looking out onto Willard Court was another stately white two-story clapboard house, which faced Willard and was at 18 Willard Street. It belonged, I learned, to Miss Sarah Carlton, a retired schoolteacher in her 80s who had graduated from Smith College and who lived there alone with her cat. The house behind Miss Carlton's, the only one on the short Willard Court and directly across from Dr. Dewing's garage, belonged to Mary Ellen Preusser, a woman in her 40s who would shortly be elected to the Cambridge City Council.

The small servant's room, which was now my room, had a one-person four-poster bed under a close slanting ceiling, two small wooden bookcases at the foot of the bed, a closet so shallow that shirts had to be hung fronts out, and a Formica-topped table from the 1950s I could use as a desk. I had left one just like it behind in Phoenix, a donation to Goodwill. There was no room for anything else in the servant's quarters, and barely enough space to turn around. But, it didn't matter. All I had in my backpack were a handful of paperback books and some few clothes, as well as my cowboy hat and the Frye harness boots I wore.

Next door was a small bathroom, which would also be mine. It had a claw-footed porcelain bathtub and the first water closet I'd ever seen. The water for flushing was contained in a box at head level and was released through a pipe to the toilet bowl by a long chain ending in a wooden handle hanging down the side.

I thanked Miss Peet and told her the room was perfect. I also told her I planned to be around for awhile. I did not tell her that I'd already been drafted and that the United States military had other plans for me. No reason to cause her anxiety. I left to retrieve my backpack from my Radcliffe room and later that day moved into the ancient clapboard house at 8 Willard Street. I now had a job in Central Square with Becker Research and I had a free room of my own just around the corner from Longfellow's mansion. And, as I planned to haunt the Loeb, just down the street, my new home really was perfect.

August 26th, the day of my scheduled induction in Phoenix, came and went. And I went on about my life in Cambridge. On August 27th my draft board in Phoenix wrote saying, "You remain registered with this local board, and carry on [sic] correspondence with this office. Except, you should arrange to notify the transfer board there if you change your address while your induction is pending there. They will need to know so as to mail you the order. Local Board No. 29 will mail the transfer board only the papers necessary for your induction, and they will then be returned."

So, it seemed my local board would cooperate with my request for a transfer of my induction to Boston. The Hell-Bound Train had been delayed by an unscheduled stop, but it still planned on picking me up soon for delivery to the war in the jungle on the other side of the world from Miss Peet's genteel existence on Willard Street in West Cambridge.

In a bizarre way, however, I soon discovered that Miss Peet's genteel West Cambridge world wasn't so very far away, after all, from the war in the jungle on the other side of the world. Miss Peet had, for a time, taught at MIT when teaching at MIT didn't require the high-powered credentials it requires today. She must've had a long career, into the Fifties, because one of her close colleagues at MIT was Walt Rostow, who taught at MIT's Center for International Studies from 1950-60. After that he'd left to be JFK's principal adviser on the unfolding war in Vietnam, and continued to serve President Johnson in that capacity after Kennedy was blown away in Dallas. He finally left the halls of power in September of 1968 to become a professor at the University of Texas in Austin.

And on a visit from Austin late that August of '69, shortly after I moved in, Walt Rostow dropped by the house on Willard to say farewell to his friend and colleague, Miss Peet, before he moved to Austin. I answered the door when he knocked. He told me his name was Walt Rostow and he was there to see Miss Peet. For an instant I stared at him in shocked silence. I knew exactly who Walt Rostow was. He was an integral member of that cadre of the "best and the brightest" who sent us into the Vietnam War. Indeed, more than any single person, Walt Rostow was the "evil genius" responsible for that criminal quagmire. I recovered and invited him into the low-ceilinged living room and told him to take a seat while I went for Miss Peet.

She was flustered at the news and quickly shambled into the living room, patting at her stray wisps of hair, to say hello to her former colleague. He rose to greet her and pecked her on her wrinkled cheek. Miss Peet asked me to prepare some hot tea for our guest and I left for the kitchen to do so. As the tea kettle was heating, I wondered what I should do. I felt Rostow was a war criminal. And he, more than anyone else, was responsible for me being drafted to go fight in his criminal jungle war. Should I take this amazing opportunity to confront "the evil genius" and denounce him?

I carried a silver tray with two cups, saucers, the teapot, and a sugar bowl back into the living room. Miss Peet was fluttering with excitement at the attention Rostow was bestowing upon her. She never had visitors, and now here was a dear friend from the distant past come to spend time with her. I set the silver tray down on a small antique table between their two chairs and stepped back. They interrupted their animated conversation to reach for the tea. As they scooped tiny spoonfuls of sugar into their teacups and stirred it around, I asked myself: Did I have a moral responsibility to challenge the Warmaker-in-Chief and speak truth to power?

While still at MIT, Rostow had worked on JFK's 1960 presidential campaign and, in fact, coined the slogan "The New Frontier" to describe Kennedy's proposed presidential agenda. Kennedy, a Harvard man himself, rewarded MIT's Rostow by bringing him to Washington, along with a host of others he pulled out of Cambridge. For instance, Kennedy made McGeorge Bundy, the Dean of Harvard College, his National Security Adviser. On January 19th, 1961, shortly after being inaugurated, Kennedy appointed Rostow as Deputy Assistant for National Security Affairs, serving under Bundy.

Of all those best and brightest advisers, it was Walt Rostow who was principally responsible for Americanizing the on-going conflict in Vietnam in the early 1960s. David Halberstam placed much of the responsibility for that transformation on Secretary of Defense Robert McNamara. However, according to historian John Prados, McNamara "mostly responded to proposals brought to him by others...it was civilian strategists such as Rostow, or military commanders such as Westmoreland, who were the innovators and initiators."

Rostow was the most hawkish of all the warhawks in Kennedy's Cabinet, the one who kept pushing for escalation, even to the point of nuking the North. In the summer of 1961, Rostow became the first civilian member of Kennedy's Cabinet to advocate sending combat troops to South Vietnam. And, in a June 30th memo, he argued for bombing Hanoi, even if it threatened nuclear war with China and the Soviet Union. If nuclear war resulted, that was OK with Rostow. "We had better face it now rather than two years from now," he told Kennedy in the memo.

On July 13th, 1961, Rostow proposed to Secretary of State Dean Rusk that the United States invade North Vietnam for the purpose of seizing and holding the city of Haiphong, the north's principal seaport.

In November of 1961, Rostow submitted a report which suggested deploying up to eight thousand combat troops to South Vietnam disguised as "flood relief workers." Kennedy didn't send in the combat troops Rostow wanted, but he did expand the number of Green Beret advisors and substantially increased military hardware flowing to the Saigon dictatorship. Rostow's November report solidified America's commitment, in aid and advisers, to the Saigon dictatorship and rationalized the bombing of the North, which would come soon enough. Chester Bowles, Kennedy's Undersecretary of State, later referred to Rostow's November report as "the beginning of the end." The so-called "Rostow Thesis" of bombing North Vietnam would finally be implemented under Kennedy's successor, President Lyndon Johnson.

In March, 1965, Johnson launched Operation Rolling Thunder, the bombing campaign of North Vietnam which continued for years. In April, 1966, Johnson promoted Rostow to Bundy's job, that of National Security Adviser, and also ramped up the bombing of the North, which Rostow had advocated for years. In 1965, we dropped 33,000 tons of bombs on North Vietnam. In 1966, that increased to 128,000 tons -- and the escalation continued thereafter.

In addition to being a primary architect of the air war, Rostow was a stubborn opponent of all peace negotiations with the North. British Prime Minister Harold Wilson later blamed Rostow directly and wholly for the sabotage of his 1967 attempts to negotiate a peace settlement of the war. Rostow also advised Johnson that Secretary of State Henry Kissinger, on leave from his Harvard professorship, was too "soft" on Communism and might concede too much in peace negotiations.

In 1968, Ambassador at Large Averell Harriman attempted new peace negotiations, which Rostow opposed. Rostow urged Johnson to include terms in Harriman's negotiations which were completely unacceptable to Hanoi and urged Johnson not to halt the air war as a "goodwill gesture" during the negotiations. The Harriman peace initiative, like the earlier ones, also came to nothing. As far as Rostow was concerned, it had to be implacable war to the bitter end. Harriman later denounced Walt Rostow as "America's Rasputin" because of his hold on Johnson's mind.

The end of Walt Rostow's hold on American war policy, at least, came with the end of Johnson's own presidency. On September 16th, 1968, just six weeks before the November election, Rostow submitted his resignation as Johnson's National Security Adviser, disparaging, as he did so, any who opposed the Vietnam War. Johnson then asked Rostow to come to Austin with him to help establish the LBJ School for Public Affairs at the University of Texas. Rostow accepted, and spent the rest of his life in Austin, dying without regrets in 2003.

Except for his death date, I knew all this about Walt Rostow as I silently watched him smiling and chatting so amiably with Miss Peet. And I knew he remained a belligerent and unapologetic warhawk, quick to denounce any, like me, who opposed the war. Should I speak up? Should I tell him I'd been just been drafted to fight in his criminal war and was just awaiting my induction date?

Miss Peet was smiling and twittering with joy. She was 100-years-old. No one comes to visit people who are 100-years-old. How would she react when I ruined this rare visit? She would not understand why I was being so rude toward her dear good friend. And I would destroy the wonderful memory of this visit which she would treasure for the rest of her life, and she would have so few such wonderful memories in the little time left to her.

And so I politely excused myself, and left the two old friends alone to bask warmly in the memories of their long friendship. And I declined my only chance to personally confront the Warmaker-in-Chief and speak truth to power. Was I a moral coward for not denouncing Walt Rostow when I had the chance? I don't know. In my mind, I still debate this moment in time. To this day, I don't know if I did the right thing.

But Walt Rostow's visit made clear to me that the genteel and charming world of Miss Peet's West Cambridge neighborhood was inextricably tied by invisible threads to the mud and misery of the Empire's wars. More than any other place in America, Cambridge was where that evil war on the other side of the world was concocted and rationalized. I realized I was now living in one of the power centers of the Empire.

On September 16th, I received my new induction orders. This time the orders came from Middlesex County Local Board No. 11 in the City Hall of Cambridge, located in Central Square. They commanded me to appear at Room 211-A of the Cambridge City Hall on October 10, 1969, at 6:45 a.m. for "delivery to an induction station." The orders also told me to "Bring enough clean clothes for three days. Bring enough money to last one month for personal purchases. Willful failure to report at the place and hour of the day named in this Order subjects the violator to fine and imprisonment. Bring this Order with you when you report."

But, that was in October, three weeks away. In the meantime, as classes began at Harvard, I haunted the Loeb, the only place I really knew in Cambridge and just a five-minute walk from Miss Peet's. I learned that auditions were being held for a big November main stage production celebrating the tenth anniversary of the theater. By the time the production would open, on November 12th, I was scheduled to be in boot camp somewhere, perhaps Ft. Dix, New Jersey. To hell with that, I thought. I auditioned for the production at the Loeb.

The production was described as a "triptych." I didn't know what that word meant when I first encountered it. I had to look it up. Literally, a triptych is a picture or carving in three panels side-by-side. In this case, the triptych was three one-act plays, *Morning, Noon, and Night,* by Israel Horovitz, Terrence McNally, and Leonard Melfi. They were three young playwrights who didn't have enough cachet individually to break onto Broadway. They reasoned that, by combining their reputations, they would be able to make it to the Great White Way and collaborated on a "triptych" which featured five characters, two females and three males, all of the same general description. That way, the same five actors could perform in all three plays. And the plays would take place in the morning, at noon, and at night.

The gambit worked. The triptych premiered as the Broadway debut for the three playwrights just the year before. Because it was so new, it was mostly unknown to audiences. Now Cambridge audiences would discover it: They would discover a black family which pops some miracle pills and wakes up the next morning white in racist America; they would meet sexual perverts of all stripes meeting at noon for an explicit rendezvous with destiny; and they would meet Americans coming from all corners of the land to a cemetery at night to mourn the death of their beloved "Cock Certain."

Auditions were being conducted in one of the second floor rehearsal rooms of the Loeb. The second floor lounge was the holding pen. Audition night it was jammed with every aspiring actor and actress at Harvard and Radcliffe, desperate to grab a role in the prestigious main stage production. Summer school was over, and I was no longer officially a Harvard student, but no one ever asked my status. Perhaps there was an assumption that anyone who showed up at the Loeb tryout for a Harvard play was, in fact, a Harvard or Radcliffe student. The casting call was posted only on an upstairs bulletin board at the Loeb, so who else would even know about it? In any case, I was there to try my luck against the best and brightest actors and actresses that Harvard and Radcliffe could offer.

When my turn came, I walked into a room empty but for a table off to the side. Two older male students, obviously upperclassmen, were sitting at the table. One of them, with a prissy David Niven moustache, introduced himself as David Boorstin, the student director. The other, whose name I forget, was his student producer. Flanking them were two young girls, who never said a word. There was another actor, young, pretty, with a giant blond Afro, standing in front of the table. Evidently, he'd already been cast. I was handed a booklet of the play and asked to read a scene with the pretty boy actor.

I took the booklet and scanned the lines. The scene was from McNally's middle play, *Noon*. The entire scene was a homosexual seduction attempt. I was to be the homosexual, the pretty boy was a straight character, and I was to seduce him. I had no idea how a homosexual -- which is what they were still called at that time -- seduced a man. Nor did I even have an idea how a homosexual moved or talked. I hadn't studied them closely when I'd acted in *The Lower Depths*.

But I *did* know how a macho man tried to seduce a woman -- so that's what I did. I came on as an aggressive masculine Lothario, and the pretty boy played along, cowering before my testosterone advances. And the four people behind the table began laughing and pounding the table. So the two of us just stepped up our interpretations, making them more and more exaggerated, until we reached the end of the scene.

The laughter died down and Boorstin, still smiling, asked me to wait outside. I returned to the lounge. A few minutes later, the cute young brown-haired freshman 'Cliffie who'd been sitting next to him came out. Her name, I learned, was Susan Fiske. She was 17-years-old and had just arrived from the University High School at the University of Chicago, where her father taught psychology. There, one of her classmates had been the director, David Boorstin, whose father was Daniel J. Boorstin, a famous University of Chicago historian. David had needed a stage manager for his triptych, and so had recruited Susan as soon as she reached Cambridge that month.

Susan came over to where I was sitting, a suppressed smile on her lips. "You were the funniest who auditioned for that role," she said. "We all thought you were perfect. You have it."

I did have it, and I was cast against type. Every Harvard actor who'd read for the role had minced and swished his way through the lines, each boring stereotypical mince interchangeable with the next boring stereotypical swish.

But I didn't know how to mince and swish, so when I'd come on as a macho man, playing against all expectations for the role, every surprised person in that room laughed his or her ass off as I plied all my masculine wiles on the young pretty boy. The role also required me to strip down to a leopard skin speedo on stage during the pretty boy's seduction, so it helped that, while I no longer lifted weights routinely, I retained much of my muscular build.

I now had a leading role in Harvard's main stage fall production and we immediately began rehearsals for the mid-November opening. I told no one that I wasn't even supposed to be there come November. That I'd already been drafted. That my induction was just a couple of weeks away. That, by the time the triptych opened, instead of portraying a macho fag in a leopard skin speedo on the Harvard main stage, I was supposed to be at Ft. Dix training to be a macho killer. I told no one because, despite what the S.S. System planned for me, I did not intend to leave for boot camp. Come November, I intended to be right there at Miss Peet's, just down Brattle Street from the Loeb. I might as well star in a Harvard play as a macho fag while waiting for prison. If I really *had* been a fag, I realized I never would have been drafted at all.

Rehearsals reinforced my awareness that I was now moving among the Empire's holders of power and privilege. The student director, David Boorstin, carried himself with the confident self-assurance of one born to win. And so he had been. His father, Daniel J. Boorstin, was one of the Empire's elite apologists. David himself, like Susan, his stage manager, had graduated from the University High School at the University of Chicago, founded in 1903 as an outgrowth of progressive education theorist John Dewey's elementary Laboratory School. Dewey had established his elementary Lab School at the University of Chicago in 1896 to inculcate his enlightened educational principles. All of the professors at the University of Chicago sent their children to the University High School.

And, when they graduated from University High, many went to Harvard -- or Yale or some other Ivy League school -- helped by "legacy" admission policies through which the children of graduates are given special favorable consideration for admission. Thus, like David's father, Susan's father (as well as her 'Cliffe mother) had graduated from Harvard, as had Susan's maternal grandparents. Now Susan and David were at Harvard, like so many other students I met at Harvard who were the children of Harvard graduates.

Legacy admissions explains why someone as intellectually stunted as the second President George Bush was admitted to Yale. Not only had his father, the first President George Bush, graduated from Yale, but so had his *grandfather*. Indeed, at the very time that Grandson

Bush was applying to Yale, his Yale-graduate grandfather was serving on Yale's Board of Trustees. Grandson Bush's application was given special consideration. This is just one way that class privilege is inherited in "classless" America, from grandparents, to parents, to children, generation after generation.

During the Great Depression, David's father, Daniel J. Boorstin, briefly lost his senses, like so many others during that great crisis, and for one year, 1938-39, became a member of the Communist Party. But, by 1944, when he'd become a University of Chicago professor, eventually earning the title Preston and Sterling Morton Distinguished Service Professor of American History, Boorstin had long since repented of his youthful political sins.

His repentance included ratting on former friends and Harvard classmates who, like him, had joined the Party in the radical Thirties. In February of 1953, in the midst of the McCarthyite Red Scare, Boorstin testified before the Red-hunting House Un-American Activities Committee (HUAC) as a "friendly witness." In addition to fingering two former classmates as Commies, he also named several others, so their names could also be added to those who would be henceforth blacklisted from gainful employment.

According to HUAC's 1953 records, Boorstin didn't believe the university should be a free marketplace of ideas, nor that Commie professors should be allowed to teach in American universities. He was himself, he said, "active" in his opposition to the Party. His activism, he explained to HUAC, took the form of "discovering and explaining to my students in my teaching and my writing the unique virtues of American democracy. I have done this partly in my Jefferson book which, by the way, was bitterly attacked in *The Daily Worker* [the Communist Party newspaper] as something defending the ruling classes in America; and in a forthcoming book called *The Genius of American Politics*."

Despite telling HUAC that he used his university position to preach against Communism -- or to defend the American ruling class, depending on your viewpoint -- in his classes and in his books, despite the fact that he'd blacklisted former friends and classmates for their political views, Boorstin also told HUAC, "I am not basically a political person..."

Defense of the Empire, it seems, is never a political position. It's just simple common sense. I guess only the Empire's enemies advocate political positions, which is taken as a sign of their psychological maladjustment. This belief that defense of the Empire is never political, sometimes called the "consensus" school of American history, underlies Boorstin's popular trilogy, *The Americans,* beginning with *The Americans: The Colonial Experience* (1958). The consensus school, of which Boorstin was a major proponent, taught that there was never any serious disagreement among Americans about what the social, political, and economic structure of the United States would be. Thus, American history is characterized by a minimum of conflict over such fundamental issues, and a maximum of consensus that celebrated the status quo as the best of all possible worlds. Those who did disagree were a small minority of psychologically disturbed malcontents.

In his best-selling and award-winning *The Colonial Experience,* Boorstin claims this status quo consensus began with the supposedly non-ideological and non-theological New England Puritans who, Boorstin said, "resisted the temptation of utopia" and were "concerned less with the ends of society than with its organization and less with making the community good than with making it effective" (p. 29).

Of course, one way the Puritans created an "effective" society was by killing or exiling all those who disagreed. They may have come to America for religious freedom, but that didn't mean religious tolerance. Religious freedom meant freedom to worship their way and their way only.

They hanged Quakers on Boston Common, when Quakers were rash enough to visit Massachusetts. They expelled Roger Williams for his religious views, so he went and founded the colony of Rhode Island where he could exercise freedom of religion. Had the Boston Puritans truly believed in religious freedom, there would be no state of Rhode Island today. Such Puritan intolerance of divergent religious beliefs, Boorstin writes, was a "source of strength" (p. 9).

As for the Quakers the Boston Puritans hanged, Boorstin writes that they had it coming. In a section of his book entitled, "Quest for Martyrdom," Boorstin says the Quaker appetite for suffering was insatiable and ridicules their "bizarre and dauntless spirit." "Never before perhaps have people gone to such trouble or travelled so far for the joys of suffering for their Lord.... Never was a reward sought more eagerly than the Quakers sought out their crown of thorns (pp. 35-37)." In other words, the Quakers were sickos, and Boorstin denigrates their struggle for religious tolerance in Colonial America, a struggle in which they suffered and died at the hands of the Puritans. The Boston Puritans, Boorstin says, practiced a higher virtue than religious tolerance: social consensus and stability.

Meanwhile, Boorstin writes, in the Quaker colony of Pennsylvania, their religious tolerance was a source of *weakness* rather than of strength. Because of Quaker tolerance, non-Quakers "poured in" to Pennsylvania until Quakers were a minority, resulting in, good heavens!, diversity and dissent. Pennsylvania was thus, Boorstin sneers, a failed colony because of the "uncompromising obstinacy" with which the Quakers held to their absurd belief in religious freedom (pp. 34, 47, 63, 67, 68).

Boorstin also attacks the "unrealistic" and "inflexible" Quaker policy of friendship and fairness toward the Indians of Pennsylvania and their insistence that Indian grievances were rooted in English abuses. Unlike the Puritans, who exterminated the Indians in King Philip's War, the Quakers, he says, failed to understand "the character of these unfamiliar people" and their views of Indians were based on "false premises about human nature."

Seemingly, Boorstin's own accurate view of the Indian was that either Indian "character" was inferior or that "human nature" is inherently evil. Thus, what Boorstin writes is essentially a justification for genocide. One can see in his book the same poisonous prejudices against alien others which resulted in the Empire's war against the Vietnamese. The history profession responded to Boorstin's "non-political" book by awarding it one of the profession's most prestigious awards, the Bancroft Prize.

In the second book of this series, *The Americans: The National Experience* (1965), Boorstin lavishly praises English conservative political theorist Edmund Burke, who disdained what he called "the swinish multitude," meaning people like you and me. Boorstin also savages Thomas Paine's classic manifesto of the American Revolution, *Common Sense*. It is "crude," "hardly a profound or durable theory of government," and a propagandistic amalgam of "simples and absolutes" (p. 399). Paine is ridiculed as the archetypal maladjusted political radical, proposing utopian notions and trying to make the world over from a blueprint. It is Burke against Paine, with Boorstin backing Burke, and I knew whose side I was on. The history profession responded by awarding *this* book another of its most prestigious awards, the Francis Parkman Prize.

And so it goes. These are politically reactionary books by a man who told HUAC he wasn't "political," they are apologies for Empire and genocide passing as objective scholarly historical research. Boorstin's books are also typical of the kind of politically biased history the "non-political" Boorstin was then teaching at the elite University of Chicago and publishing for the edification of Americans. In 1969, as I was rehearsing *Morning, Noon, and Night* with his son at Harvard, Daniel Boorstin was writing the third in his politically-charged trilogy, *The*

Americans: The Democratic Experience, which would receive the 1973 Pulitzer Prize in history. America loves to be told it is great and wonderful, a land suffused with light where no shadows are to be found in any glen or valley. Boorstin was later rewarded for his celebration of the Empire with an appointment as the Librarian of Congress from 1975-1987.

It was hard for me to keep from puking in the pages of such prize-winning political propaganda when I read it, but it was also hard to avoid Boorstin and his ilk in the Sixties. Mythologies such as his were taught in every American university at the time. No wonder so many thoughtful college students disdained the falsehoods being force fed to us by tenured reactionaries like the respected and prize-winning Daniel J. Boorstin. None of these lies and distortions reflected what I and many others like me discovered when we read American history outside the classes of the tenured reactionaries. The American history we learned from our own reading revealed an America of chronic conflict and unceasing dissent over the inequities of American society, its government, and it economic structure. Like Mark Twain, we students tried to keep our schooling from interfering with our education.

Boorstin denounced in ad hominem terms people like me who disagreed with his views. He called students who differed with his interpretations "incoherent kooks" and "barbarians." He derided black studies as "racist trash." Consistent with his admiration for Edmund Burke and Burke's disdain for the "swinish multitude," Boorstin opposed open admissions to higher education as a lowering of academic standards. Daniel J. Boorstin would not have liked me, as I differed from his views in every conceivable way.

This was the record of the father, however, not of the son, and I had no idea what David Boorstin's political views were. But, while he knew nothing about me, I knew what David's family life had been like, I knew what beliefs he was exposed to as he grew up, and I knew his privileged educational background. He'd been a star at University High, having been elected President of the Student Council. Now he was determined to become a star of the Harvard theatrical scene as its premiere stage director. This was a stepping stone to his ultimate ambition, to replace Arthur Miller as America's reigning playwright.

As David directed me all that fall in the triptych he would present on Harvard's main stage in November, I couldn't help thinking about the people around me. Children of privilege, born and raised in the expectation that they would, themselves, one day occupy comfortable and influential positions of privilege in the infrastructure of the Empire. Cambridge was a seat of the Empire, and Harvard was populated with the children of the Empire's elite. I felt like a partisan behind enemy lines. This feeling was reinforced by the knowledge that I'd already been drafted to fight for an Empire which justified its war with lies from my director's father. I'd soon be heading off to prison because I refused to join the chorus of celebration and collaborate in the Empire's conquests.

I told no one of my reservations about my director. I told no one I'd been drafted. I told no one I intended to refuse induction. I went to work at Becker Research in Central Square during the day and called people in the boonies for ambitious politicians. I rehearsed seducing the pretty boy until midnight at the Loeb. And afterward I walked down Brattle Street to my narrow bed in my narrow room at Miss Peet's ancient manse.

On October 6th, four days before my scheduled induction, I wrote a letter to General Lewis B. Hershey, Director of the S. S. System, in Washington, D.C. "I am a Conscientious Objector to service in the Armed Forces of America," I said. "I have appealed my classification of I-A to the State Appeal Board of Arizona, where it was rejected unanimously. I have appealed to the State Director of the Selective Service System for Arizona, Colonel Erb, with no results. I have done everything in my power to convince my Local Board No. 29, Phoenix, Arizona, of the sincerity of my beliefs. To no avail.

"I realize I have no legal right to appeal to you, but you alone have the power to cancel my induction orders for the tenth of this month and prevent a serious injustice from being committed against me. Service in the Armed Forces would be antithetical to the beliefs upon which I base my existence....War is a cancer on the society of Man. The community of Man is larger than one nation, or even one civilization. If one is to serve the spiritual destiny of Man, one must oppose all that is detrimental to the growth of Man....I will refuse induction on my scheduled induction date. I sincerely hope that you will be able to intervene before that act becomes necessary, for I have no desire to go to prison. I will only face such a possibility as a last recourse to prevent the injustice of my illegal induction into the Armed Forces." The Hell-Bound Train might be coming for me, but I wasn't going to climb aboard.

Of course, I never received a reply from General Hershey. But, I didn't expect to. I was just exhausting all conceivable administrative remedies. And I'd made sure I sent a carbon copy to my local draft board in Phoenix. It would help in my coming court battle against the Empire. I wanted to demonstrate at my trial that I'd exhausted every conceivable avenue of redress short of induction refusal.

I thought about my upcoming induction every day. It was always in the back of my mind, whether I was on the phone for Becker Research, or rehearsing at the Loeb with David Boorstin. But I felt there was no one I could talk to about the Hell-Bound Train. The only one I felt I could talk to about it all was Annie.

But Annie was now back at Pitzer College, 3,000 miles away on America's other coast.

And so each night, after late-ending rehearsals at the Loeb, I thought about Annie until I drifted off to sleep in my lonely bed in Miss Peet's lonely house in a lonely town. Tomorrow would come soon enough.

And tomorrow would be another day behind enemy lines.

To Liberate the Oppressed

"These are the times that try men's souls: The summer soldier and the sunshine patriot will, in this crisis, shrink from the service of their country; but he that stands it now deserves the thanks of man and woman."

-- Thomas Paine
The American Crisis, 1776

****

As with every season during the Sixties, much happened that autumn, as 1969 wound down toward 1970 and I rehearsed my role at Harvard while waiting to be drafted to fight for the Empire. What was different for me was that, living in Cambridge, just a five-minute walk from Harvard Square, I seemed to be much closer to what was happening. Or perhaps more actually *was* happening, as the tail-end of the Sixties became more and more feverish.

The 5th Dimension won the Record of the Year Grammy for their album, *Aquarius-Let the Sunshine In,* an example of art trailing tardily after reality. The funeral of "Hippie" had taken place two years before in the Haight in October of '67, following the Summer of Love, and by October of '69 there was no possibility that we might have been at the Dawning of the Age of Aquarius, as their lyrics claimed. I felt that each day was either the Day Before the Revolution or the Eve of Destruction.

I was far from Chicago, where the Chicago Eight conspiracy trial began on September 24th. Defendants Tom Hayden, yippies Abbie Hoffman and Jerry Rubin, pacifist Dave Dellinger, Black Panther leader Bobby Seale, and others were accused of being in Chicago in the summer of '68 when the Chicago police ran berserk during the Democratic Party convention. When Bobby Seale protested against the trial, he was gagged and shackled to his chair in the courtroom and the case against him continued to be heard over his muffled screams. The presiding judge later sentenced the defendants and two of their attorneys to long jail terms for expressing contempt toward him during the trial. I felt the trial was a travesty and that 75-year-old Judge Julius Hoffman (no relation to Abbie) deserved whatever contempt the accused showed him.

I was nowhere near Chicago Black Panther leader Fred Hampton's apartment in the predawn hours of December 4th when the Chicago cops crept up on it, smashed down the door, and murdered Fred Hampton in his bed as he slept, as well as Panther Mark Clark. The two never knew what hit them. Four other Panthers sleeping in the apartment were wounded. I felt their only crime was "sleeping while black." A ballistics expert later reported that 199 of the 200 shots fired in the raid came from police guns. No cops were ever prosecuted for these assassinations.

Four days later, on December 8th, Los Angeles police exchanged gunfire with that city's Black Panthers for four hours before arresting 11 of them. On December 29th the American Civil Liberties Union released a statement accusing the nation's law enforcement officials of "waging a drive against the Black Panther party, resulting in serious civil liberties violations." The statement quoted top Nixon Administration officials clearly condoning the violent suppression of the Panthers. Since the beginning of the year, 28 top Panther leaders had been assassinated by the police. Others, like Huey Newton, were in jail or, like Eldridge Cleaver, in exile. The police seemed to have launched a nation-wide search and destroy operation against the Panthers and, for the Panthers, it looked like the Eve of Destruction.

On June 27th the New York police raided the Stonewall Inn. It was just another routine police raid on a fag bar to arrest those inside for partying while queer. It happened all the time. This time, however, instead of hiding their faces and meekly shuffling into the paddy wagons, the gays fought back. For the next several nights gays in the Stonewall neighborhood fought running battles with the police. These Stonewall Riots were the beginning of the Gay Liberation movement, which gathered momentum all that autumn. That December, New York's Gay Activist Alliance was founded, helping to make gays a future force in New York City politics.

I was even further from San Francisco, but I was sympathetic to Native Americans, and so I cheered when Native American activists occupied Alcatraz on November 20th. The federal prison on Alcatraz Island in San Francisco Bay had closed in 1963. Citing treaty rights to abandoned federal lands, representatives from 20 Indian tribes seized the island facility and claimed it as liberated Indian land. It was a precursor to the later 1973 American Indian Movement occupation of Wounded Knee in South Dakota.

Closer to me, the women's movement was gathering force and that autumn I witnessed my first Women's Liberation march. Thousands of angry women rallied on Cambridge Common and then, chanting and punching the sky with their fists, marched through Harvard Square and down Mass. Ave. toward Boston for a gigantic feminist gathering on Boston Common. First one group wants its freedom, then *everybody* wants freedom. Pandora's Box had been opened and it seemed *all* the Empire's oppressed were demanding liberation. For them, it was the Day Before the Revolution.

That autumn 20 members of the Weatherman faction of Harvard SDS trashed Harvard's Center for International Affairs (CIA) on the Harvard campus about a 15-minute walk from Miss Peet's house. Harvard's CIA (it later insisted that its acronym was actually "CFIA") conducted counterinsurgency research for the Empire's war machine. The Weathermen broke windows and threw documents out of them, yanked out phones, shoved around secretaries, and beat up three collaborating Harvard professors they found lurking inside. Eric Mann, a Harvard SDS leader, was later sentenced to two years at the state pen on Deer Island in Boston Harbor for this raid. It didn't shut down Harvard's CIA, and the building would be trashed again in the future, but at least it kept Eric Mann from participating in the escalating lunacy of Weatherman, part of which was a bombing campaign designed to "bring the war home." Their increasing frustration with the Empire's never-ending jungle war seemed to have driven them completely crazy.

Between that September, 1969, and May, 1970, radical groups like Weatherman carried out over 250 domestic terror bombings. The Weatherman bombing campaign culminated on March 6th, 1970, in the notorious Townhouse Explosion. In a lower Manhattan townhouse next to the home of actor Dustin Hoffman just off New York's posh Fifth Avenue, the Weathermen set up a bomb-making factory. Someone touched the wrong wires together while assembling a powerful anti-personnel bomb designed to shred human flesh, and the entire building went up. Three Weatherpeople were ripped apart in the explosion: Ted Gold, Diana Oughton, and Terry Robbins. Diana Oughton was identified from her prints on a fingertip, all that was found of her body. Not even a fingertip of Terry Robbins was found. His body simply disintegrated.

Two Weatherwomen, Cathy Wilkerson, whose parents owned the expensive townhouse, and Kathy Boudin, the daughter of prominent and wealthy liberal attorney Leonard Boudin, stumbled out of the rubble and disappeared into the Weather underground. Kathy Boudin and two other Weatherpeople, Judith Clark and Boudin's lover David Gilbert, who'd been a Columbia University SDS leader, later participated in the bloody Brinks Armored Car robbery in Nyack, New York. During that robbery, the "revolutionary" hijackers killed the county's first black police officer. All three "revolutionaries" were captured and sentenced to long prison terms for murder. Gilbert, at least, never expressed remorse for his actions. Decades later, from his jail cell, he declared, "The end justifies the means."

Some time before my scheduled October 10th induction, I was walking through Harvard Square and came across a Weatherman standing on the sidewalk at Holyoke Center, a big Harvard administration facility. He was handing out leaflets entitled, "Back to Chicago! Four Days of Rage!" I took one and asked him what it was all about.

"It's about the Chicago Conspiracy trial," he said, referring to the trial of Abbie Hoffman & Company which had begun at the end of September. "We're the Weathermen. We represent a white mother country anti-imperialist movement conceived in battle and willing to die in battle. It's not just the war which has to be ended, it's the whole goddamned imperialist system, man. We're going back to Chicago to tear the whole goddamned fuckin' city apart. Bring the war home, man!"

"And you want me to join your army, go with you to Chicago, and die in battle with you?"

"You have to surrender your white skin privilege, motherfucker. You have to put your body where your fuckin' mouth is!"

"Well, there are many battlefields in the war against the Empire, and I have my own battle to fight right here in Boston."

"You're either with us or against us, motherfucker. Like Eldridge Cleaver said, if you're not part of the solution, you're part of the goddamned fuckin' problem."

"Well, I'm certainly not with *you*, and I don't believe you're part of the solution, either. I think you're fucking crazy. And I think you need some form of therapy which doesn't hurt other people." I handed back his leaflet and walked on down the street.

The Weatherman yelled after me, "You're part of the fuckin' *problem,* you privileged chickenshit Harvard *pussy!* We'll take care of people like *you* after the Revolution! It'll be up against the wall for *you*, motherfucker!"

I stopped and turned back to him. "Then lucky for me there ain't gonna *be* no Revolution, you fuckin' moron! You can't declare war against your own people and expect them to join you!"

"They're not *my* people, motherfucker! They're *yours!*"

"That's why you're gonna *lose,* you stupid fuck!" Then I gave him the finger.

About 300 Weathermen and women just like him showed up at Lincoln Park in Chicago on October 8th for their "Four Days of Rage." It turned out to be "One Day of Rage." They charged along Chicago's ritzy Gold Coast shopping district smashing store windows, clubbing bystanders who got in their way, and fighting running battles with about 3,000 of Chicago's finest. Chicago Panther Fred Hampton, soon-to-be-but-not-yet dead, dismissed them as suicidally "Custeristic," and he was right. The Weather warriors injured 75 cops, but the cops beat the shit out of most of the Weathermen, arrested 250 of them, and shot six.

Because the Weathermen weren't the sharpest tools in the shed, they convinced themselves that this debacle was a great victory. Even so, their "great victory" was their last such public action before going underground to launch their bombing campaign. No doubt the Harvard Square Weatherman who called me a chickenshit Harvard pussy (and who perhaps came from Harvard himself) was there in Chicago breaking imperialist windows with his fellow radical nitwits. And perhaps he went underground with them shortly thereafter. But by that time their numbers had shrunk to perhaps 100 True Believers. There were fewer of these pure blood crazies every day, but still enough to hurt people.

The Weather decision to drop from sight and launch a "Custeristic" domestic terror campaign was taken at a so-called "War Council" in Flint, Michigan, Christmas of 1969. A giant cardboard machine gun hung above the large meeting room where the council took place. Strategy sessions were called "wargasms." By then, SDS had been destroyed. But, unlike the Panthers, it was not the cops who destroyed SDS. That summer in Detroit, at its annual convention on June 22nd, the fanatic Weathermen had dismantled and trashed SDS, the largest and most successful Leftist organization in America between the 1930s and the present.

Now these children of the ruling class, like Bill Ayers, son of Chicago's mega-millionaire Consolidated Edison CEO, lusted for more blood. They openly yearned for the day they would drag bleeding bodies through flaming streets. Mark Rudd, a former Columbia University SDS leader who'd taken part in the '68 Columbia Strike, and who was now a Weatherleader, rhapsodized to his sicko comrades that, "It must be a really wonderful feeling to kill a pig or blow up a building."

Another Weatherleader, Bernardine Dohrn, praised the Charles Manson gang's August 9th slaying in L.A. of 26-year-old actress Sharon Tate, along with three of her friends and a delivery boy who happened to deliver his pizza at the wrong time. Sharon Tate, wife of Polish director and Holocaust survivor Roman Polanski, was eight-and-a-half months pregnant with their child. Members of the Manson gang, comprised of three women and one man, massacred their victims in a blood frenzy.

They killed Abigail Folger, one of the victims, by stabbing her 28 times.

They stabbed her boyfriend 51 times, smashed in his head with a blunt object 13 times, and finally shot him twice.

Susan Atkins, one of Manson's women, later testified at her trial that Sharon Tate begged Atkins for mercy because she was eight-and-a-half months pregnant. "Please let my baby live," Atkins said Sharon Tate begged. But Atkins testified that she told Sharon, "I have no mercy for you." And then she rammed her knife into Sharon's hugely pregnant belly. She and her fellow butchers gathered around Sharon Tate, stabbing their knives into her 16 times. Then the attacking women rammed forks into Sharon's belly to kill the baby within. And then they smeared the word "Pig" on a wall in Sharon's blood, and the blood of her baby.

"Dig it!" child of privilege Bernardine Dohrn exulted in a wargasm to her similarly-privileged Weather comrades. "First they killed those pigs, then they ate dinner in the same room with them, then they even shoved a fork into the victim's stomach. Wild!"

Bernardine Dohrn then led her blood-crazed comrades in chants of "Fork'em! Fork'em! Fork'em!" as they waved four fingers in the air to simulate forks. The lunatics had escaped from the asylum.

It was the Day Before the Revolution.

Or the Eve of Destruction.

It was hard to tell which.

Ways of the Weak

"The greatest pleasure is to conquer your enemies, to chase them before you and kill them, to rob them of their wealth, to ride their horses, to see their loved ones bathed in tears, and sleep on the bellies of their wives and daughters."

-- Genghis Khan, Mongol Warlord
(1167-1227)

****

We all live in a world of bullies. The powerful oppress the weak. The wealthy exploit the poor. The fortunate rule the unfortunate. It is the way things are. It is the way things have always been since the beginning of recorded time.

Almost 2,500 years ago, in 416 B.C., a large Athenian fleet landed an overwhelming army on Melos, a small island state in the Aegean Sea. Democratic Athens and militaristic Sparta had been fighting the Great Peloponnesian War for 13 years. The Athenian expedition against Melos was of no military importance whatsoever in this war. Had it never occurred, the war would have turned out the same. Since it was a trivial military event, its only significance is the moral question it raises: What is the relationship between the strong and the weak?

Melos was tiny and insignificant and had taken no sides in the conflict, merely hoping neither side would trample it underfoot. Such was not to be. Athens would not accept Melian neutrality. It felt neutrality set a bad example, in that it encouraged other Greek city states to also remain neutral. So, it gave the Melians an ultimatum: Join us in our war against Sparta -- or die. Thucydides recorded the resulting "Melian Dialogue" in Book V of his history of that long war, the first reported instance we have of the weak attempting to reason with a bully.

The Melians sent ambassadors to the Athenian invasion force, objecting that they were neutral, had never acted against Athens, and that therefore the Athenian attack on them was unprovoked and morally wrong. The Athenians, being a democratic and just people, should do the right thing and leave them alone.

The Athenians readily admitted that everything the Melians said was true. Melos had never harmed Athens and the Athenians had no moral justification for attacking the island. So, it was wrong. But, they said, so what? None of that mattered. Life isn't fair and "justice" does not exist between the powerful and the weak. Fairness and "justice" exist only between equals who are able to enforce just treatment of each other in their mutual dealings.

In the case of the powerful and the weak, the powerful do what they wish, and the weak must submit or accept the consequences. That's just the way the world is. If you don't like it, too bad. "We did not lay down this law," said the Athenians, "nor are we the first to observe it; it existed already when we inherited it, and we shall bequeath it to exist forever." So, they said, accept absorption into the Athenian Empire or be destroyed. You have no other choice.

Faced with the sole choice of submission or resistance, the Melians, foolishly, resisted. The Athenian army then besieged the city and subdued it. Then the Athenians executed every last captive Melian male, man and boy, including infants. Next they deported and sold into slavery every last Melian female, woman and girl, including infants. Athenian colonists soon settled on the empty, "ethnically cleansed," island of Melos and occupied the deserted city. Melos became part of the Athenian Empire, after all.

Alcibiades, the influential Athenian orator and politician who would eventually defect to Sparta, had argued for the destruction of the peaceful and harmless Melians. After the extermination of all the Melian males, he bought a pretty Melian girl as his sex slave and soon impregnated her. Other Athenian leaders did the same with other pretty Melian girls. And so, being large and powerful, the Athenians slept at night on the bellies of their pretty Melian sex slaves.

And the Melians, being small and weak, ceased to exist as a people. It was the way of the world, the Athenians shrugged; always had been, always would be. The powerful do as they wish. The weak submit or die. Life isn't fair. Get used to it.

Almost 500 years after the Athenians destroyed Melos, the Romans destroyed Israel. In 66 A.D., the always rebellious Jews revolted against the Roman Emperor Nero. After four years of savage struggle, Titus, the local Roman commander, besieged and sacked Jerusalem in 70 A.D. He destroyed the Temple, the center of Jewish religious life. It has never been rebuilt. The present-day Wailing Wall is all that remains of it. Thousands of Jews were killed in the fighting or executed after the city's capture. Many more were sold as slaves throughout the Empire. Anyone who could claim any vague descent from the House of David was hunted down and executed.

A thousand Jewish resistance fighters, known as Zealots, held out against the Roman onslaught for three more years at the remote mountain fortress of Masada. Finally, faced with the imminent breakthrough of the surrounding Roman army, 960 of these Jewish Zealots, men and women, committed mass suicide.

The Jewish historian Josephus, who fought against the Romans in this Jewish Revolt, but survived to write a history of it, told us how this mass suicide was done. He said each husband killed his own willing wife and children. Then ten executioners, chosen by lot, killed the husbands. Finally, one executioner, again chosen by lot, executed the other nine executioners. The last executioner rammed his own sword into his belly, hara-kiri style. Only two women and five children hid and thus escaped self-slaughter. Except for these survivors, the Romans entered a fortress populated only by corpses.

The political existence of Israel ended as a result of the Jewish Revolt. The Romans abolished every aspect of Jewish self-governance, including the Council of Elders and the high priesthood. Worship in the ruins of the demolished Temple was forbidden. The land itself was ruined by the fighting. Large parts of the population had been massacred, others sold into slavery. Jews were dispersed in the Diaspora throughout the Roman Empire, where they entered into centuries of persecution as a despised minority. Non-Jewish immigrants soon settled in the depopulated land of Israel. As with the Athenians, the Romans were large and powerful, and did as they wished. Like the Melians, the Jews were small and weak and could only submit -- or die.

It was the way of the world.

Almost 2,000 years later, in 1864, General William Tecumseh Sherman stood at the gates of Atlanta with his army during the American Civil War. He had worn down and defeated the defending Confederate General John Bell Hood. Now he decided that he was going to drive every single inhabitant of the city out and burn Atlanta to the ground, leaving not one building untouched by the flames.

The surrendering Confederate General Hood was appalled when informed of Sherman's intentions. "In the name of god and humanity, I protest," he said.

Oh, please, Sherman responded, don't bullshit me. "If we must be enemies, let us be men, and fight it out as we propose to do, and not deal in such hypocritical appeals to God and humanity." You know, as well as I, Sherman said to Hood, that the powerful do what they wish, and the weak appeal to God and humanity, but would do the same, if they could. It is the way of the world. Be a fucking man and cut the bullshit.

Faced with this reality, the small and weak have sometimes retreated to the world of fantasy, where they can also become big and powerful.

Or at least their defenders can be such.

Much more than a thousand years after the Diaspora spread defeated Jews throughout the Roman Empire, in 1580, the Jews of Prague were facing a period of persecution. Walled inside their ghetto, refused the protection of the law, prohibited from owning weapons of any kind, the Prague Jews faced extermination. Praying for the deliverance of his people, it is said that Rabbi Judah Loew ben Bezalel, chief rabbi of the Prague Jews, had a vision from God. In it, God offered a way of salvation: The creation of a Golem, a giant of living clay, animated through the knowledge of the Kabala, the body of Jewish mystic wisdom.

And so the rabbi shaped a giant out of clay. Then, chanting spells of creation from the Kabala, the rabbi unleashed the power of life, which flowed from him into the lifeless clay. The giant awoke and rose from the ground. Over the days and weeks which followed, Rabbi Loew taught Golem the ways of the world, while Golem protected the Prague Jews from the rampaging gentiles who surrounded them. When a howling mob finally stormed the ghetto, Golem -- towering over them -- slaughtered and scattered them with his superhuman strength.

With the danger passed, Rabbi Loew then returned Golem to the lifeless clay from which he had been shaped. But, the legend says, should the Jews ever be so threatened again, the superhuman Golem will return to defend them against the powerful who would destroy them.

Almost exactly 350 years later, in the 1930s, it seemed that such a time had come again. The rise of Adolf Hitler and his Nazis to power in Germany brought into existence an almost invincible force dedicated to the destruction of all Jews. The Jews therefore needed an invincible new Golem to protect them against such overwhelming power. And so, as predicted, Golem returned to life. But, instead of being created by a rabbi, this time Golem was created by two Jewish teenagers in Cleveland, Jerome ("Jerry") Siegel, a writer, and Joseph ("Joe") Shuster, an artist. And, instead of chanting mystic spells from the Kabala, Siegel and Shuster used the new medium of comic books to bring Golem back to life. And, this time, Golem protected *all* who were weak and oppressed.

Siegel and Shuster were avid readers of the new science fiction magazines and in October, 1932, while still in high school, had launched *Science Fiction,* perhaps the second science fiction fanzine ever to be created. In a 1933 issue of their fanzine, which appeared as Adolf Hitler was coming to power in Germany, Siegel said he was working on "a scientific fiction cartoon strip" which would soon become the legendary comic "Superman."

The Superman character, an invincible defender of the weak and powerless against the strong and powerful, was a direct descendant of the mythic Golem and part of the chain of Jewish tradition. Indeed, like Moses in the bullrushes, Superman was a child survivor sent to Earth from his about-to-be destroyed home planet, Krypton. And on Krypton, said Superman's Jewish creators, his birth name had been "Kal-El," Hebrew for "All that is God."

In fact, God *is* much like Superman, although much more super. Indeed, God is the Greatest Golem in the universe, a supreme fantasy being created by a tiny, weak, and powerless people to protect them from all the bullies of antiquity. The Jews were a handful of small tribes surrounded by vast empires -- Assyrians, Babylonians, Hittites, Egyptians -- who threatened to extinguish them entirely in an instant. It was impossible for such an insignificant people to successfully defend themselves against such mighty empires.

And so they created God, the Greatest Golem, who said that they, the small and insignificant Jews, were His favorites of all humanity, His Chosen People. And, while the Jews could not defeat the mighty kings and pharaohs, God, the Greatest Golem, could bring the mighty oppressors low with his outstretched hand.

God, the Greatest Golem, could kill the Egyptian first born and part the waters of the Red Sea so that, later, he could drown Pharaoh and his army in its returning waters. And thus He could free the Jews from Egyptian slavery, which the Jews could not do on their own.

God, the Greatest Golem, could give Joshua more time to slay the Canaanites in battle by stopping the sun in its course, which Joshua could not do on his own.

God, the Greatest Golem, could send a plague or famine upon armies besieging Jerusalem, and thus save Jerusalem from the Assyrians, which the Jews could not do on their own.

God, the Greatest Golem, could free the Jews from their Babylonian Captivity and bring them back to the Promised Land, which the Jews could not do on their own.

God, the Greatest Golem, was the fantasy wish fulfillment of a weak and bullied people, by which they vicariously saved themselves from and revenged themselves upon all the bullies who preyed upon them in real life.

On the other hand, Jesus, the Jewish carpenter who founded a Jewish heretical sect composed, initially, only of other Jews, entered directly into a fantasy world wherein he, unlike the Zealots, could defeat the mighty Roman Empire. Jesus was as concerned as the Zealots with preserving Jewish identity and freedom. However, he believed that armed resistance to the Roman bullies by the small and weak Jewish people was suicidal -- which it eventually proved to be for the Zealots at Masada and Israel as a nation.

It is true that Jesus said, "I come not to bring peace, but the sword," but in this he was speaking metaphorically. He was not preaching acceptance of the Romans ("peace"), but resistance ("the sword"). But, his was not the actual sword of the Zealots. Rather, it was an other-worldly sword. This was why, when Peter drew his sword to defend Jesus from being seized in the Garden of Gethsemane, Jesus rebuked him and told him to put it away. "All they that take the sword shall perish with the sword (Matthew 26:51)," Jesus told Peter, a passage actually addressed to the Zealots.

Instead, Jesus said that, while we are in the world, we should not be of the world. Our bodies are unavoidably here, in the Roman reality, but our minds and our souls should be somewhere else, in a disembodied alternate reality. What he proposed was a clinically psychotic retreat from reality into an invisible fantasy world -- the "Kingdom of God" -- which he claimed was all around us.

And this invisible fantasy world, he said, was the "real" reality, the only world which mattered, not the reality ruled by the Roman bullies. So, he said, implicitly opposing the Zealots, "Render unto Caesar that which is Caesar's." That is, obey the Roman bullies, pay their taxes, don't fight them. "And render unto God that which is God's (Matthew 22:21)." That is, Jesus was saying that we should ignore a brutal reality we can't change, and turn inward, retreat into the fantasy world of our own minds -- where we are all the Chosen of God. And, in this fantasy world of the mind, the Roman bullies would be defeated.

An unsympathetic interpretation of his message might be that Jesus' retreat into a fantasy world was simply insane, that the times in which he lived had driven Jesus psychotic. This is because a mental retreat from reality into fantasy is the very definition of psychosis, a mental derangement resulting in a defective or lost contact with reality.

But, perhaps this was a positive illusion, as there is a more sympathetic way of looking at what Jesus was trying to do in his opposition both to Rome and to Zealotry. This is to say that Jesus wanted to redefine resistance to Rome as a personal and spiritual, rather than a political, struggle. What really mattered, he was saying, at least in the situation in which the Jews found themselves vis-a-vis Rome, was how one lived one's personal life and how one lived one's spiritual life. Who controlled the machinery of the state was irrelevant to what really mattered.

As it happened, Jewish Zealotry eventually resulted in suicide and the destruction of Israel, while the teachings of Jesus went on to conquer the Roman Empire and become the dominant religion of Western civilization. Perhaps, after all, and in the context of the times, it was the *real politic* Zealots who were delusional and Jesus, the spiritual idealist, who was most realistic.

Besides retreating into mental and spiritual worlds to escape from powerful bullies, the weak and powerless have sometimes tried to convert bullies into allies. They have tried to convince bullies that they should actually be *protecting* them, the weak and powerless, instead of *oppressing* them. Such was the case with the medieval invention of the code of chivalry.

During the so-called Dark Ages, knights were not the saintly defenders of the weak and powerless we today think of them as being. Indeed, that image was a medieval creation of the weak and powerless -- the Catholic Church, mostly -- and was *prescriptive* rather than *descriptive*. In other words, it prescribed what knights *should do*, rather than faithfully described what they *actually did*. What they actually did was what powerful bullies have always done. Knights killed, plundered, burned, and raped the weak and defenseless.

In Western Europe before the Year 1000 there was virtually no central government and even at the county level public authority crumbled. Charlemagne's enfeebled successors had been unable to hold the Carolingian state together and Vikings raided at will, sailing their longboats even up the Seine to loot and burn Paris. In the resulting chaos, there was a proliferation of castle-building by local warrior elites, knights and those a later age would call "Robber Barons." Each count, baron, and warlord, seizing as his own land that which the kings had originally given only as a temporary fiefdom, carved out his own little "kingdom" with his sword.

Then, from the security of their castles, these petty warlords made war on their neighbors, their neighbor's serfs, passing merchant caravans, and the local monastery as well, which had its own extensive and desirable lands and treasures. "The man on horseback," the historian Richard Erdoes tells us in his book on the Year 1000, "protected by helmet and chain mail, armed with lance and sword, could defend himself, but against him there was no defense. He took what he liked. Taking was his only work, the one he did not despise."

The cleric Gerbert of Aurillac, later Pope Sylvester II, speaking from first-hand knowledge, said, "We live in a world of recklessness. Divine and human laws are violated due to the greed of wicked men and only what passion and force extorts is deemed right, after the manner of wild beasts."

It was a state of perpetual war of knights against knights, and of all knights against the poor and the weak. After all, knights were the only ones around with warhorses, armor, swords, and training in how to use them. Everyone else was a peasant in filthy rags riding on a donkey and armed only with a pitchfork. Knights in their shining armor were faithful to human nature and laughed as they slaughtered the pathetic peasants, looted their crops, and slept at night on the bellies of their young daughters.

As the advocate of the weak and oppressed -- and as a fellow victim of the marauding knights -- the Catholic Church, and popes like Sylvester II, responded to this situation in various ways. First, the Church tried to change the nature of the knights by convincing them that killing was wrong. It did this through something called "The Peace of God." At huge outdoor convocations, all the people of a region, under the leadership of the local priests and bishops, met to pressure the local knights to stop killing and plundering and burning and raping the young daughters of peasants. "Christians should not kill Christians," the Church said. "For are we not all one in the Body of Christ? Did not Jesus say that whatever you do to the least among you, you do to me? Therefore, when you kill a Christian, you kill Christ."

But, knights disdained hard sweaty manual labor. It was ignoble, literally something a noble should not do, lest he lose honor. A powerful warrior simply took what he wanted, he did not work for it. People who worked with their hands were despicable, repulsive people, lacking in all honor due to the mere fact that they worked instead of robbed for a living. Indeed, the word "villein," meaning a hard-working inhabitant of a peasant village, entered into our language as the word "villain," meaning a low, evil, dishonorable person. Our language has a long tradition of expressing such disdain for common hard-working people. The word "vulgar," as another example, comes from the Latin word "vulgus," meaning "the populace, ordinary people." The phrase, "Vulgar Latin," simply means the Latin spoken by ordinary people.

So a knight could never, therefore, become a "villein," a peasant, and engage in "vulgar" manual labor. He would lose honor and become a "villain," that is, a low and dishonorable person. And the only other things knights knew were killing and plundering and burning and raping the young daughters of peasants, all of which were honorable, because that's what the powerful did. So, rather than become "vulgar villains," knights soon returned to killing and plundering and burning and sleeping at night on the bellies of the young peasant girls they'd seized and taken to their castles. It was the right thing to do.

So next the Church tried "The Truce of God." OK, the Church said. We realize it's your honorable knightly nature to kill and plunder and burn and rape peasant girls in your castles at night. A knight's gotta do what a knight's gotta do. Nothing's going to change that. But, you shouldn't do it *all* the time. So, we're calling a Truce of God on God's Holy Day, Sunday. You can't kill any villeins and rape their daughters on that day.

That seemed to work. Knights seemed to be able to restrain themselves at least once a week. So, soon the Church expanded the Truce. Next, the Church said knights couldn't kill, plunder, burn, and rape peasant girls during the three days that Christ was in the Tomb, from dawn on Friday to dusk on Sunday. Then the Church said knights couldn't kill, plunder, rape peasant girls, and so on, during the 40 days of Lent. And then they couldn't kill, and so on, during the various saints' days. Since the Church had a multitude of saints, virtually every other day was a Truce day.

Before long knights had to consult complex calendars to figure out if they could go out and kill, plunder, burn, and rape peasant girls that day. It just wasn't workable. So knights began to say, "To Hell with it!," and returned to killing and plundering and burning and raping peasant girls any time they felt like it.

So next the Church said, "OK, we understand that the only honorable knightly occupation is killing and plundering and burning and raping peasant girls, and that shouldn't be restrained. But, you still shouldn't do that to Christians and villeins are, after all, Christians, no matter how much you despise them for doing productive manual labor. So, be true to your nature by going somewhere else and killing. Go kill Muslims. They aren't Christians, so it's OK to kill them."

Killing others "outside the tribe," so to speak, had a long lineage in the Judeo-Christian tradition. When Moses came down from atop Mt. Sinai with "Thou Shalt Not Kill" inscribed on his Ten Commandments tablets, it was understood that God's words in this regard weren't to be taken literally. Indeed, as God's Chosen People later entered into the Promised Land that God had chosen for them, they genocidally slaughtered Midianites, Edomites, Philistines, and everyone at Jericho, all upon God's orders, and then slept on the bellies of their enemies' daughters at night.

So, if God didn't mean His commandment in this regard to be taken literally, what, exactly, did "Thou Shalt Not Kill" mean? Obviously, God meant "Thou Shalt Not Kill the Members of Your Own Tribe." But, it's OK to kill anyone who doesn't belong to your tribe. Indeed, it is this distinction which leads us to honor soldiers who slaughter the enemy during war-time, but condemn them as pathological mass murderers if they do the same thing back home.

In Christianity, this distinction developed into the crusading tradition. As far back as Charlemagne, 200 years before, knights were encouraged to work out their aggressions abroad, instead of at home. During Charlemagne's day, this meant crossing the Pyrenees to fight the Muslims in Spain. Now the knights were encouraged to go even further afield. "Get on a boat," the Church said, "and go far, far away. Go to the Holy Land and kill Muslims over there. Even better, you'll be doing God's work by liberating Jerusalem, the Holy City, from the infidel, and so we will absolve you of all your sins. You can do good by continuing to be bad."

It is no accident that, in 1095 A.D., when Pope Urban II called for the very First Crusade to kill Muslims and liberate the Holy Land, he did so at a huge open-air Peace of God convocation in Clermont, France. And, at the same time that he called for all knights to go the Holy Land and kill people over there, Pope Urban II also declared that the entire land of France was under the protection of a Peace of God. So, since you can't kill anyone *anywhere* over here, you may as well go over *there* and kill people.

"God wills it!" the knights joyously cried, and set off to the Holy Land to kill, plunder, burn, and rape Muslim daughters in the name of God. When they finally seized Jerusalem four years later, in 1099, they massacred everyone in the city, the remaining Jews as well as the Muslims, before sitting to work pillaging everything in sight. One ancient chronicle reported that the Christian knights rode in mingled Jewish and Muslim blood up to the stirrups of their horses. Entering the City of God must have been like entering Heaven for them, a paradise of blood and slaughter, all in the name of God.

And after the Crusaders had raped and murdered everyone they could, they went to the Church of the Holy Sepulcher, built over the tomb where Christ was buried, and knelt and prayed.

And God blessed them for their bloody work.

So, the Church had found a way to put the bullying nature of the knights to good use. And, for hundreds of years, Crusades such as this first one seemed to work pretty well. There was an endless supply of Muslims who needed to be slaughtered in the name of God, so there was always a need for a new Crusade to the Holy Land. And so Europe got rid of hundreds of thousands of murderous thugs -- knights and barons and princes and kings, like Richard the Lion-Heart.

And, if the Holy Land was too far away, there were closer non-Christians the knights could also kill. The Teutonic Knights, a crusading order of German knights, steadily expanded the borders of Christendom eastward as they slaughtered the people of Lithuania and other pagan Eastern European lands.

And, if even Eastern Europe was too far away, there were others who were not members of our tribe even closer to home who could be slaughtered in the name of God: Jews. The first recorded pogroms against European Jews were conducted by knights of the First Crusade in 1095 as they marched through the German Rhineland on their way to the Holy Land. They viewed it as getting a head-start on the work of God's slaughter of those who didn't belong to the tribe.

For the knights still at home, the Church launched a massive re-education campaign to domesticate the bullying nature of the knight. They prescribed a code of "true" knightly conduct which came to be known as the code of chivalry, and which troubadours sang about up and down the countryside.

A "true" knight, the Church said, should not use his weapons and fighting skill to kill the weak and rob the defenseless. A "true" knight *protects* the weak and defenseless -- against all those *other* knights who have not yet seen the light. And a "true" knight should not kidnap and rape innocent maidens, the Church said. A "true" knight *defends* innocent maidens -- against dragons, perhaps, or against all those *other* knights who have not yet seen the light and who were much more real than dragons.

And, in time, the very word "knight," which had originally simply meant a warrior on horseback, came to mean a pure-hearted warrior who used his skills to defend the very ones he had, heretofore, spent all his time killing and robbing and raping. Whether this new code of chivalry actually changed the hearts and minds of the murderous knights is debatable. But the new code did enter into mythology and the idealized image of the knight -- not the thuggish reality -- is now what we think of when we hear the word "knight."

Today, however, our modern knights do not ride around in armor and with sword in hand, like the antiquated Don Quixote, seeking damsels to rescue and evil giants to slay. Instead, our modern knights carry a gun and wear the garb of a policeman or a soldier.

Or a cowboy. Certainly, when I was a boy in the Fifties, the cowboy was the foremost modern knight and both television and the movies offered us a wealth of such cowboy knights. Two early Fifties movies, *High Noon* and *Shane,* are outstanding examples of this tradition.

Some critics claim that the first "adult" Western film was *High Noon.* This 1952 movie starred Grace Kelly as a Quaker bride and Gary Cooper as her lawman husband who stood alone against a band of outlaws in a terrorized town. An outlaw Cooper had put in jail had finally been released and was coming back, with his henchmen, on the Noon train. He wanted revenge against the town and the sheriff who had sent him to jail. As the town sheriff, Cooper tried to rally his fellow townsmen to face the outlaw band. Every one of the townsmen gave him a good reason to make themselves scarce.

Cooper had a good reason to disappear, too. He had just married the gorgeous Grace Kelly. As a Quaker, she disapproved of violence. And she gave him an ultimatum: Leave town with me now, or I leave town without you.

Despite the fact that Cooper loved her deeply, he refused to leave with her. He was a true knight and a real man. He'd never run from danger in his life, and he wasn't going to start running now. He had to stay and do the right thing. So, she left him.

And then, at High Noon, he stood alone against the outlaw thugs and faced them down. And, when the smoke settled, he was the last real man left standing.

And then he threw his badge into the dust in disgust and left the town of cowards forever, as he joined his bride who was, after all, waiting for him on the edge of town.

I did not see *High Noon* when it opened. I was only five. But, when I was a bit older and saw it on TV, Gary Cooper became one of my heroes. That is what it means to be a real man, I thought. You do the right thing. You stand up to bullies, even if it means you stand alone.

Then, years later, as an adult, I saw old 1950s news footage of Gary Cooper testifying as a friendly witness before the anti-Communist witch-hunters of the House Un-American Activities Committee (HUAC) at the very time he was portraying a true knight on screen. His answers to their questions revealed not only that he was a complete political ignoramus, but also that there was absolutely nothing heroic about Gary Cooper. His heroism was all just an act. In real life, as opposed to reel life, Gary Cooper cowered and quailed before the thuggish witch-hunters and did his best to ingratiate himself with the bullies. When faced with his own real life High Noon, Gary Cooper was not a true knight. Gary Cooper was not a real man. Instead, Gary Cooper was a complete moral coward who kneeled before the HUAC bullies and said, "I'm your bitch." I felt personally betrayed when I saw Gary Cooper's HUAC testimony, but I was not the first to discover that heroes often have feet of clay.

At least Alan Ladd never disappointed me in that way. In 1953, a year after *High Noon*, Ladd starred as "Shane," a gunman, a cowboy knight, a real man who wanders into a small Western village. He discovers that a local Robber (Cattle) Baron is attempting to drive all the weak and defenseless villeins (homesteading farmers) off their land. Ladd joins with the villeins against the Baron. And, as he takes a young boy from among the villagers to train as his page in the ways of knightly combat and real manhood, there was someone in the movie, the boy, with whom I could closely identify.

The chief henchman of the Baron is a rogue knight (gunslinger) played by Jack Palance at his most evil. The "true" knight, Ladd, fights the "bad" knight, Palance, and kills him. Of course, he won't stick around afterward and become a farmer. After all, he is a *knight,* not a *villein,* and such lowly manual labor is not in his nature. So, he rides off into the sunset, no doubt seeking a dragon to slay and a fair maiden to rescue somewhere in Arizona or New Mexico.

If this sounds like *The Lone Ranger,* that's because the "true" knight's code of chivalry has become a powerful cultural myth which is endlessly repeated in different guises. I liked *The Lone Ranger,* but my favorite TV cowboy knights were those of *Zorro* and *Have Gun Will Travel,* both of which debuted in the fall of 1957.

"Zorro" was played by Guy Williams, who later became the father on the popular science fiction TV show, *Lost in Space.* The action takes place in Spanish California before 1820, when Spain still rules Mexico, of which California was a province. Don Diego de la Vega, played by Williams, returns from schooling in Spain. He discovers that the local Robber Baron...that is, Army Commandant...is tyrannizing the local landowners and their peons. While posing as a cowardly fop, he creates a secret identity as "Zorro" (Spanish for "Fox"), a master swordsman, who, like a "true" knight, uses his sword skills to defend the weak and oppressed. For a short time, in the fall of 1957 and the spring of 1958, Zorro was almost as popular as Davy Crockett had been in 1955. Indeed, the theme song, which I still remember, even made the Top 40 in 1958.

Have Gun Will Travel starred Richard Boone as a gunfighter who was both named "Paladin" and *was* a paladin. Originally, a "paladin" was the champion of a medieval prince, and the Emperor Charlemagne's paladins included such nobles as Roland, who died for his king fighting the Moors in Spain while on crusade. Now, however, the word has come to mean simply someone who defends someone else.

The TV Paladin was literate and sophisticated. A West Point graduate, he had fought in the Civil War. Afterward, he headed west to San Francisco, where he took up residence in the elegant Hotel Carlton. He then became a fast gun for hire -- but only by the oppressed, for whom this "true" knight became their paladin.

Once Paladin took on a cause, he left his cultured San Francisco lifestyle, donned all-black clothes, strapped on his gun, and became the avenger of the weak. Sometimes this meant turning on the very people who had hired him, if he discovered that *they* were the guilty oppressors. At the end of each show, Paladin freely passed around his business card, which featured the knight chess piece. In its first season, the show was among the nation's top five TV programs and, from 1958-61, it was the third highest-rated show on TV, just behind *Gunsmoke* and *Wagon Train*. Like Zorro's, Paladin's theme song also became a top radio hit in the early Sixties. I still remember Paladin's song, too, which described Paladin as "A knight without armor in a savage land."

In virtually all cases, the cowboy knights acted alone. The fact that they stood alone, against armies of bullies, made them all the more brave. But the bravest of all the brave cowboy knights did not stand alone. He had six companion "true" knights who stood beside him. Nevertheless, they were a small band of "true" knights vastly outnumbered by the bullies.

The cowboy knight in this case was Yul Brynner in *The Magnificent Seven* (1960), one of the greatest Western movies of all time. *The Magnificent Seven* is based on Akira Kurosawa's 1954 film, *The Seven Samurai,* although neither I nor anyone else in America seemed to know that at the time. In Kurosawa's film, a master older samurai is recruited by peaceful peasants to defend their small village against a marauding band of rogue samurai, the knights of medieval Japan. To do this, the old samurai, in turn, recruits six other samurai. Together, although vastly outnumbered, they successfully defend the peasant village. They did the right thing. They were "true" samurai. They were real men.

That is also the plot of *The Magnificent Seven.* Yul Brynner is an older gunfighter recruited by Mexican villeins...that is, peons...to defend their small village against a band of outlaw knights, I mean banditos, led by Eli Wallach. Brynner, in turn, recruits six other knights, that is, gunfighters, and together they defend the Mexican village. The movie was a huge hit and launched the Hollywood careers of actors who went on to become some of the biggest macho stars of the silver screen: Steve McQueen, Charles Bronson, and James Coburn. It even paved the way for Robert Vaughn, the dandiest of the Seven, to become "Napoleon Solo," the James Bond-type hero of the TV spy series, *The Man from U.N.C.L.E.*

But the most macho of the macho Seven was their leader, Yul Brynner, who was already an established star with an Oscar on his resume, so I tried to emulate Yul Brynner. I didn't shave my head -- but I tried to stand like him, move like him, walk like him. Yul Brynner walked with an easy hip-swinging gait which seemed to say he was totally confident that he could handle anything. Yul Brynner walked like a real man, I thought. And so I taught myself to walk like Yul Brynner, with a confident, easy, hip-swinging swagger which said, "I'm ready for anything and if you give me any shit I'll kick your ass." That's what it looked like to walk like a man.

In all these cases, the cowboy knights were idealized fictional creations who embodied the millennium-old knightly code of chivalry. Their universal and enduring popularity encouraged others than me to emulate them.

There is at least one other traditional code of conduct which we can say without doubt creates many real life paladins for the weak and oppressed. Instead of a mere handful of "true" knights, in this case we have an entire people of paladins. I am speaking of the Jews.

There was a class of men in ancient Israel who routinely played the role of paladins. These were the prophets, who sought to turn the power of various kings of Israel into the paths of righteousness. In a way, this was a precursor of the medieval code of chivalry, wherein the powerful were told that they should protect the powerless, instead of oppressing them. Perhaps the most famous incident in this tradition occurred when the Prophet Nathan confronted King David over his adultery with Bathsheba and the murder of her husband, Uriah.

Jesus, too, fulfilled this role of the prophets in the only passage in the New Testament wherein Jesus tells us how he felt about capital punishment. The story is told in John, 8:3-11. A woman found guilty of adultery is brought before Jesus by a crowd ready to stone her to death, for that was the Mosaic Law's punishment for adulterous women (Deuteronomy 17: 5-6). The woman's persecutors ask Jesus, should we kill her?

Jesus replies that, since Mosaic Law prescribes death for a woman who sleeps with a man not her husband, they should obey the law. But then Jesus goes on to add, "Let him who is without sin cast the first stone." The woman's would-be killers hesitate and look at each other. Every one of them knows that they have a guilty secret, that each of them has sinned. Every one of them knows they each deserve to be whipped or stoned for *something* they've done. And so, one by one, the would-be killers drop the stones from their hands and slink away in shame.

Eventually, the woman is left alone with Jesus. He looks around in mock surprise and says, "What? Hath no man condemned thee?"

The woman replies, "No man, Lord."

And Jesus says, "Neither do I condemn thee: Go, and sin no more."

Jewish tradition has not limited the role of paladins solely to the prophets nor to merely exhorting the powerful to be righteous and the murderous to be merciful. As noted in the story of the Golem and the Rhineland pogroms of the First Crusade, Jews have been a despised and oppressed people since antiquity, when the Diaspora sent Jews throughout the Roman Empire to live as strangers in a strange land.

Even before the Diaspora, they were an enslaved people in Egypt. Each year at Passover, they celebrate their liberation from Egyptian bondage and their exodus out of the land of the oppressor. At their Passover seders, Jewish parents not only remind their children of their ancient oppression, but encourage their children to think of others who, even still, suffer similar oppressions. Jewish children are taught that every Jew has a responsibility, a religious duty, in a sense, to save the world by defending the oppressed. Thus, in addition to inventing the Greatest Golem to defend themselves, Jews also taught that every one of them should be a real life, human-sized Golem. Because we live in a world of bullies, every Jew is instructed that it is his or her duty to be Paladin.

Another way of saying this is that every Jew, man and woman, should be "real man," a "mensch" -- and a "mensch" does the right thing. And, contrary to what the Athenians said at Melos, the right thing is to say that "justice" is not solely for the powerful who can enforce just treatment for themselves. "Justice" is for everyone, including the weak, who should be defended against the oppression of the powerful.

One consequence of this tradition, I think, has been the disproportionate number of Jewish participants in reform movements all kinds, regardless of time or country. Jews were disproportionately involved in the early European and American labor movements, the various socialist and communist movements, the Civil Rights Movement, and even the American New Left and anti-Vietnam War movements. As a people, Jews were relentlessly beaten and oppressed in all ages and nations so, as a people, because of their traditions and their teachings, they did not stand by silently as others were likewise beaten and oppressed. From their number has therefore come an entire pantheon of paladins to challenge the powerful bullies of the world.

And, unlike the cowboy knights of TV and Hollywood, these paladins actually existed. They were minor messiahs who would serve until the Messiah came -- but whose very existence as models for imitation made the actual Messiah unnecessary.

I wasn't a Jew.

But I'd been a boy soldier. I knew about "duty."

Duty

"Let your life be a counter friction to stop the machine....A minority is powerless while it conforms to the majority; it is not even a minority then; but it is irresistible when it clogs by its whole weight....If a thousand men were not to pay their tax bills this year, that would not be as violent and bloody a measure as it would be to pay them and enable the State to commit violence and shed innocent blood. This is, in fact, the definition of a peaceable revolution, if any such is possible....When the subject has refused allegiance, and the officer has resigned his office, then the revolution is accomplished."

-- Henry David Thoreau
On the Duty of Civil Disobedience

****

"Eric Davin, United States Army."

No one moved. No one said a word. Two hundred young men, black, white, and some brown, stood silently at rigid attention in ten rows in the large room, twenty men to a row. A profusion of American flags flanked the walls and blossomed into bouquets at the front. Before the flags stood two decorated Army sergeants. A third stood at the end of my row. All three sergeants were starring at me.

"Eric Davin, United States Army," one of the sergeants in front called out again.

It was my last chance to step forward. It was my last chance to avoid five years in prison.

The three Army sergeants kept starring at me. They knew what the 199 young men standing with me were going to do. Each of them was going to take a step forward, indicating his acceptance of induction. And from the moment each one did so, he would no longer be a civilian, protected by all the laws which protect civilians. Each would be a soldier, subject to the Uniform Code of Military Justice. Each would be under the command of the sergeants watching me.

But the sergeants who didn't know what I was going to do.

They were waiting. The 199 young men standing with me were waiting. Two years in the United States Army and possible deployment to Vietnam -- or five years in prison. Which was it going to be?

So easy to step forward, like everyone else. Step forward and be seen as a hero who did his duty. Step forward and be forever after an honored and respected Vietnam Era vet. Step forward and get all that financial aid for college, bonus points when you applied for a government job, the Veteran's Administration to take care of you when you're dying, and free burial in a national cemetery when you're finally dead. Step forward like everyone else.

Or stand there and stand alone. Stand there and give up all those perks for vets. Stand there and then go to prison for the next five years. Stand there and be forever reviled as a coward who dodged the draft.

It was my choice.

It wasn't too late to step forward.

****

On October 10th, 1969, I climbed the steps of the Cambridge City Hall at 6:30 a.m. Designed by noted architect H. H. Richardson in his distinctive nineteenth century Romanesque style, the Cambridge City Hall is an ancient building composed of big square rough hewn stones piled on top of each other. Contrary to my induction order, I had only the clothes I wore. And I had only enough money for a one-way subway ride. But I *had* brought my induction order. I had no desire to violate any more military orders than necessary.

When I left Miss Peet's house in the pre-dawn darkness to walk to the Cambridge City Hall, I had not disturbed her to tell her that I was to be drafted into the military that morning. I had not told anyone. Indeed, I hardly knew anyone in Cambridge that I might have told. I was still a stranger in town, and the town was a stranger to me.

It was gray and cold in Cambridge that October morning. I awoke at five o'clock and quietly showered, shaved, and dressed. I made my bed, straightened my books and papers on my Formica desk, and made sure I had my induction order. At six o'clock I stepped carefully down the creaking wooden stairs, trying not to awaken Miss Peet, and eased out the old front door.

I walked through a gate in the front yard's side fence and I was immediately in the back of the Cambridge Friends Meeting House. To my right were steps leading down to a basement room housing an office of the American Friends Service Committee. I was neither a Quaker nor a pacifist, but I'd visited the Quakers inside that office a few times since moving into Miss Peet's clapboard house. We had in common our opposition to the war and our opposition to the death machine I had now been called to serve. I saluted the dark door as I crunched past on the gravel driveway. Today, I said silently to the door, I go to fight Moloch.

Across a small grassy oval and directly opposite Longfellow's House was another house of religion, the Cambridge Mormon church. I ignored the Mormons as I walked past. I walked on down the broken and uneven red brick sidewalks of Brattle Street, past the Loeb Drama Center, until I reached Harvard Square. At six o'clock the Square was already beginning to stir. The Tasty, the small greasy spoon I'd visited on my first day in town, was already crowded. People were buying newspapers at Nini's Corner. Commuters were disappearing into the mouth of the subway station in the middle of the Square. The subway didn't stop at the City Hall, it traveled underneath it and beyond it into Central Square. I could've taken it and backtracked to City Hall, but I had enough money to ride the subway only once, so I walked through the Square and up Mass Ave toward the City Hall, arriving there just after 6:30.

Cambridge's City Hall is located on Mass Ave opposite the city's main post office. As a federal agency, the local draft board should have been in that federal post office building. But, it was not. Cambridge readily made room for the local draft board in its municipal facilities. In this way, the city of Cambridge was a willing cog in the death machine. But, most cities in America had this blood on its hands.

Despite the pre-dawn darkness, City Hall was open. I entered the front doors and climbed the stairs to Room 211-A. The hallway was already jammed with other inductees and their suitcases. I found a sergeant in charge and showed him my induction order. He checked my name off on a clip board. He eyed my empty hands. "Where's your bag?"

"I don't have one."

"You're gonna get tired of wearing those clothes after a couple of days. Line up in the hall with the others."

At seven o'clock the sergeant led us down the front stairs of the Cambridge City Hall and to several green Army busses lined up in front on Mass Ave. We climbed aboard the Army busses one-by-one and were driven through the morning rush traffic to the South Boston Army

Base. We were unloaded, lined up, stripped to our underwear, and processed. We were then given a pre-induction physical exam.

This was the most important part of the process, as far as I was concerned. When I went to trial, I intended to argue that I had to refuse induction as a last recourse, as all other avenues of redress had been exhausted. If I'd simply refused to show up at all, the U.S. Attorney in Boston could counter that I had not proven that induction refusal was my last recourse. I might have failed my pre-induction physical exam. If so, I would not have been inducted. Now, he could say, we'll never know if my refusal was really necessary to avert a claimed injustice.

So, now we *would* know. I had to give the military machine every possible chance to reject me before I could argue in court with any chance of success that I had no recourse but to refuse induction. It was a small technicality, but it was all I had.

An Army sergeant, followed by a team of doctors in white coats, strode into the waiting room where we draftees stood talking in our underwear. "Awright, shut the fuck up," he bellowed, "or *no one* goes into the Army today!"

There was instant silence. I knew then exactly where I stood in that crowd of inductees. I stood alone.

"Awright," the sergeant bellowed again. "Form lines in front of each of these doctors for your physicals!"

We lined up before the doctors. The lines moved quickly.

When I reached the head of my line, the doctor glanced up from his papers.

"Name?"

"Eric Davin."

"Has your physical condition changed since your previous physical?"

"Not to my knowledge."

He stamped the papers in front of him. "You're passed. Step aside."

I stepped aside.

And that was my pre-induction physical.

After dressing we were herded into a room filled with classroom desks. The decorated sergeants gave each of us a form covered in tiny print. It seemed to be a list of hundreds of political organizations. The form asked us to check off any organization to which we belonged. Most of the organizations were unknown to me, but some I knew. On the political far right there was the John Birch Society and the Minutemen. On the political far left there was the Communist Party and Students for a Democratic Society. In between were organizations like CORE, the NAACP and the ACLU.

I got up and returned my blank form to one of the decorated sergeant. "It is none of your business which political organizations I belong to," I told him. "I refuse to fill out this form"

I was instantly surrounded by the other decorated sergeants. "Do you intend to refuse induction today?" one asked. I was mildly surprised. It was the first time anyone had asked me that question. Evidently, they'd been through this routine before.

"Yes, I intend to refuse induction."

"Are you going to stage a demonstration of any kind?"

I knew the futility of that. I'd witnessed the sudden silence of the inductees awaiting their physical exams. It was clear to me that no minds would be changed this day.

I shook my head. "No, I'm not here to stage any kind of demonstration. I'm just here to refuse induction. If everybody else wants to go into the Army, that's their business. They've already made their decisions. Nothing I could say at this point would make any difference."

The hunched shoulders of the decorated sergeants relaxed. They became cordial. They even smiled. "Well," one said, "we still have to submit paperwork on you, including this form. Would you mind at least signing it at the bottom, so we can document that you were given this form?"

Paranoia flashed through me. What if they checked off political organizations after I signed the form? It could be a trick.

"OK, give it to me."

I took the form and drew a heavy dark "X" across its entire face. Then I signed it. I handed it back to the sergeant. "Thanks," he said. "We appreciate that. Most resisters are not as cooperative as you."

"I'm not here to cause trouble. I'm just here to refuse induction."

But, *would* I refuse induction? I'd been telling people that I'd refuse induction. But talk is cheap. You can *say* you'll do anything. No, you say, I will not join the death dealers. No, I will not plunge my hands into the blood of others. No, I will not serve evil by becoming a willing executioner for the Empire.

But, what will you do when everyone around you says you're wrong? What will you do when everyone around you is stepping forward to serve? And what will you do when you face five years in prison if you don't take that one easy step forward?

Does anyone *really* know, before the fact, if he will do the right thing?

Or will he do the easy thing?

So easy to step forward.

Just one step.

****

"Eric Davin, United States Army," the decorated sergeant in the flag draped hall called out once more. The three decorated sergeants waited for me to step forward. My fellow draftees waited for me to step forward.

A real man does the right thing.

Regardless of the consequences to himself.

That's how he earns his balls.

It's that simple.

And that hard.

I did not step forward.

The sergeant at the end of my line motioned to me. "Please step this way."

Was this a trick to get me to step forward?

I very deliberately stepped *backward* out of my line and followed the sergeant out of the flag draped hall to a small waiting room at the side. Behind me, the induction ceremony continued. One by one, names were called off, followed by, "United States Army."

One by one an inductee stepped forward.

They *all* stepped forward.

Eventually, a decorated sergeant came for me.

"The Commandant would like to see you."

I was led into an elevator and taken up to the plush office of the Commandant of the South Boston Army Base. The Commandant was sitting behind a shiny mahogany desk, his chest covered with military ribbons.

"Sir, this is the draftee who refused induction," the sergeant said.

"Thank you, sergeant. You may go."

I stood before the Commandant's desk, waiting.

He waved to a chair. "Have a seat, son."

I had a seat.

"Son, it's not too late to change your mind. Do you realize how serious this is?"

"Yes, sir, I do."

"But, do you, *really?* Think about what you're doing. If you go into the Army, it's only for two years. And when you come out, you'll qualify for college aid, you'll qualify for Veterans' Administration health benefits, all kinds of benefits. More than that, you'll be a respected military veteran who will be honored for having served his country in her time of need.

"But, if you refuse induction, you'll be ruining your life. You'll go to prison for five years. When you come out, people will call you a draft dodger and a coward. Could you live with that for the rest of your life?"

I cleared my throat before answering. "I don't care what other people call me. But, if I let the fear of prison frighten me into doing something I think is morally wrong, I know I'd be a coward in my own eyes for the rest of my life. And if I did something that was wrong just for those benefits you mention, I'd never be able to respect myself. My self-respect is more important to me than what others think of me. And, besides, I think I'm serving my country better by saying it's doing wrong, and going to prison for saying that, than by helping it murder people on the other side of the world who simply want to live in freedom."

"We have freedom of speech in America. You can say anything you want to say."

"Not in the military, I can't. You know the rules are different under the Uniform Code of Military Justice. Besides, when you want my body, when you want my assistance in committing a crime, then I have to put my body where my mouth is. I have to say no, I won't give you my body. I'm not going to kill for you and I'm not going to help you kill."

"But you don't seem like some kind of a radical. The sergeants tell me you've been very cooperative up to this point. Why are you doing this?"

"I'm doing it, sir, because I object to murder as a matter of conscience. That means I'm a Conscientious Objector, no matter what Selective Service says. I will not be an accomplice to murder. So I guess that does make me some kind of a radical."

"It seems to me it also makes you very foolish, because you are deliberately choosing to go to prison. It doesn't have to be that way. We still haven't done the paperwork. I'm giving you one last chance to save your life. It's not too late to change your mind."

"Thank you, sir, but no. I'd rather go to prison than serve in the military."

The Commandant sighed. "Well, then, so be it. I'm very sorry for you."

There was a knock on the door.

"Yes?"

The decorated sergeant who'd escorted me to the Commandant's office entered.

"Yes, sergeant?"

"Sir, we have a request to make of this young man."

"What is it?"

"Well," the decorated sergeant said, directing his comments to me as well as his Commandant, "if the volunteer Marine Corps doesn't meet its enrollment quota, it is authorized to dip into the draft pool to make up the difference. That happened today, sir. One of the inductees, a black man, was randomly chosen and inducted into the Marine Corps. He'll be shipped off today to the Marine basic training camp at Paris Island, South Carolina. Everyone else there will be gung-ho volunteers. It'll be hell on him down there."

"I'm sorry for him," I said to the decorated sergeant. "What's this have to do with me?"

"Well, you've been very cooperative in your induction refusal, and we appreciate that very much. Usually, resisters are very disruptive. So, we were wondering...we haven't done the paperwork yet. Would you mind being drafted into the Marine Corps in his place?"

I smiled. "It doesn't matter to me *which* branch of the military I refuse to serve in. They're all just as bad to me. Sure, I'll take his place."

The South Boston Army Base Commandant rose and leaned over his shiny mahogany desk to shake my hand. "I wish you luck."

"Thank you. I appreciate your offer."

Then I returned to the flag draped induction hall with the decorated sergeant. It was empty but for another decorated sergeant and one black man in civilian clothes. I walked up to the black civilian and asked, "Do you want to go into the Marine Corps?"

"No, I surely don't."

I smiled and shook his hand. "Then I'll be drafted into the Marine Corps in your place."

We faced front and stood side by side. The sergeant who had brought me down quickly called out my name and the branch of the military into which I was to be officially drafted:

"Eric Davin, United States Marine Corps."

I did not move.

The decorated sergeant did not call my name a second time. Instead, he quickly called out the name of the black man standing next to me, followed by, "United States Army."

The black man just as quickly stepped forward. Then he turned to me and smiled. "You saved my life." Then he left with one of the decorated sergeants.

"Well," the other one said to me. "You're still a civilian. We don't have any authority over you. Go home. Your file will be sent to your local draft board. They'll contact you concerning your trial."

Then he escorted me to the gate. When we reached it, he stopped and turned to me. "I've never made this return walk with anyone before. And I never thought I'd say this to anyone who refused induction, but -- good luck. And thanks for helping us save that guy from the Marines." He smiled and offered his hand.

I shook it.

That morning, a fleet of green Army busses from all over the Boston area had pulled up to this gate and disgorged hundreds of young men to be inducted into the Army and, for one, the Marine Corps.

In the afternoon, I walked out of the South Boston Army Base alone.

I caught the subway back to Harvard Square and climbed up to the Out of Town News traffic island. The Square was a hive of activity around me. I was lost in the crowd. The sky was still overcast. The sun was a pale winter disk leaking through flowing gray clouds. It was a late Friday afternoon. Soon, it would be dusk. Soon, I'd have to be at the Loeb, rehearsing the triptych as if nothing in particular had happened to me that day. We opened on the main stage in a month. Because the opening of *Morning, Noon, and Night* was to be a birthday blow-out for the Loeb, we were going to have a rock band on stage, warming up the crowd and providing ambiance as we performed. There were a lot of details to be coordinated. David Boorstin, our director, was feeling under pressure and becoming tense and anxious in rehearsal.

I walked down Brattle Street past the Brattle Street Theater, past the Blacksmith Shop, past the Loeb, past Longfellow's mansion to Willard Street. I opened the door at 8 Willard and walked into Miss Peet's low-ceilinged living room.

Miss Peet was sitting quietly on the couch, her hands folded in the lap of her shapeless cotton housedress, lost in her century-old thoughts. She looked up as I came in.

"Hello, dear," she said. "Did you have a nice day?"

Suddenly, as I stood there before her, black despair flooded over me as the day's events flashed through my mind. The Commandant of the South Boston Army Base was right, I thought. I'd just thrown away my life. And I'd just thrown away my relationship with Annie. I was headed for prison and I'd lost her. She'd be a different Annie by the time I came out in five years. My future looked like one big black pit into which I was falling. I felt alone and abandoned and lost. I felt defeated.

But I couldn't tell Miss Peet any of that. She wouldn't understand.

And then I remembered what the black draftee had said when he shook my hand after I'd taken his allotted place in the Marine Corps. "Yes, Miss Peet. I had a very nice day. I saved someone's life."

Miss Peet smiled at me. "That's nice," she said. Had she even heard?

Yes, I thought, it *is* very nice. And then I thought of Shana, and something she had once told me. According to the Talmud, Shana said, "Whoever saves one life, saves the world entire."

I hadn't been able to save Shana. Perhaps, I thought, I can't even save myself. But I saved *someone's* life today. And so Shana would've said I'd saved the world entire. And maybe she would've also said I'd been a mensch.

Farewell to the Sixties

"In the depth of winter, I finally learned that within me there lay an invincible summer."

-- Albert Camus

****

Five days after I refused induction I was swept up in the October 15th Moratorium on all business as usual in protest against the war. That bright sunny Wednesday morning I walked to Cambridge Common to participate in a start-up rally, one of many taking place all over the Boston region, indeed, all over the East Coast. As we gathered on Cambridge Common, Massachusetts Governor Francis W. Sargent was speaking to a crowd of 5,000 on the Lexington Green, where the Minutemen had met the British that April morning in 1775, thus launching the American Revolution. "This war is killing America's soul," Gov. Sargent told the new patriots assembled on the Lexington Green. The new patriots loudly agreed.

Newly-elected Congressman Michael J. Harrington addressed ten antiwar rallies in towns along the North Shore just above Boston. Brandeis University President Morris Abram spoke against the war before an audience of 400 attorneys at Boston's Faneuil Hall. Vermont Governor Philip Hoff who, just the year before had been the first Democratic governor to oppose the war, spoke at the University of Vermont saying the war was a "mistake" and called for an immediate troop withdrawal.

In New Haven, Connecticut, Mayor Richard Lee and Long Island Congressman Allard K. Lowenstein attacked the war before a crowd of 50,000. Yale University President Kingman Brewster, Jr. who, until recently, had been pro-war, was with them. Brewster told the crowd that, "It is not easy to stop short of victory in a cause for which so many have fallen in the line of duty. Let us say simply that we cannot tolerate the abuse of their memory as a justification for continuation of the killing."

And so it went, in rally after rally, event after event, too many to name.

As I walked through Harvard Square to get to the Common, about a ten-minute walk from where I lived with Miss Peet, I noticed every business in the Square was closed. Everything. Not one shop was open. Cambridge Common was covered with people. Not an inch of bare ground was visible. When we began marching out of the Common, through Harvard Square, then up Mass Ave toward MIT and Boston, it seemed like an endless river of people flowed down the street, pouring in from every Middlesex village and town. A skywriting plane traced a gigantic peace symbol in the cloudless sky above us, bright white against the blue. As the peace symbol floated over Boston, I took a picture of it.

Passing through Harvard Square I recognized the old man marching next to me, his wild white hair dancing in the breeze. It was psychologist Erik Erikson, along with his wife, Joan. His name hadn't always been "Erikson." He was raised in Germany as "Erik Homberger." When he moved to America, he left his past behind forever and changed his name to "Erik, Son of Erik" -- Erikson. He had no other father.

His book, *Gandhi's Truth*, had just been published and I had read it. In it, he tried to show the virtues of non-violent civil disobedience. It was his hope that "new models of fraternal behavior may come to replace those images of comradeship and courage that have been tied in the past to military service."

Now, as we marched through Harvard Square side-by-side, I asked, "Professor Erikson, why are you here today?"

He smiled at me, but didn't stop walking. "Because it's the right thing to do."

"Would you be willing to be arrested today, if it came to that?"

"Of course."

"Why?"

"Because it's the right thing to do."

And then I blurted it out. I don't know why. I'd told no one, and no one in that mass of tens of thousands of marchers flowing through Harvard Square knew my secret. "Professor Erikson, five days ago I was drafted into the military. I refused induction. I'm going to prison."

Erik Erikson looked at me as we walked and he reached over to touch the back of my arm just above the elbow. "What's your name?"

"Eric."

He smiled and squeezed gently. "Eric. You did the right thing." It felt like a benediction.

But then I was embarrassed that I'd even mentioned my secret. I wasn't seeking validation or a benediction from Erik Erikson, or anyone else, for what I'd done. I'd done it for the very reason that Erikson had said. It was the right thing to do. I didn't need to be praised for having done what was right, and so to have mentioned it seemed to devalue what I'd done. As Lao Tzu said, "Those who know don't talk. Those who talk don't know."

So I felt awkward walking next to Erik Erikson after having confessed. What was there to say after that exchange? I quickly snapped his picture, white head outlined against the shockingly blue sky, and increased my pace. He was soon lost in the mass of people.

After the we crossed the Charles River into Boston, our torrent of marchers merged into other huge rivers of humanity flowing from Brookline, Allston-Brighton, and other Boston neighborhoods. We clotted Commonwealth Avenue as we slowly shuffled our way up toward Boston Common. Someone in an apartment along Comm Ave had placed a gigantic speaker in his open window and was blasting out Phil Ochs' "I Ain't a-Marchin' Anymore."

By 3:30 p.m. an estimated 100,000 of us had gathered at the Common, ten percent of the one million Americans who rallied against the war on that day. And then I heard Harvard economist John Kenneth Galbraith, the man who, more than anyone else, had launched me on my dissident trajectory, say in person what I'd read in his pamphlet. This war was one we were not winning; this war was one we could not win; this war was one we should not *desire* to win. We were not just on the wrong side in Vietnam. We *were* the wrong side in Vietnam.

South Dakota Senator George McGovern followed him. "This is the highest form of patriotism," McGovern told us. "It is carried out by Americans who love their country enough to call her to a higher standard....To challenge the mistaken policies of our country is to pay it a high compliment -- because it is based on the faith that we can do better....So let us do our nation the high honor of serving not her power, but condemning her evil and giving her the truth. For it is still the truth that sets both men and nations free."

A month later, on November 12th, *Morning, Noon, and Night* opened on the main stage at Harvard. It was a smash hit and, for the next two weeks, we played to SRO audiences at the Loeb. Somehow, in the minds of many, the triptych seemed to be an elemental part of the times. The (student) critics, as the saying goes, raved. In the November 14th edition of *The Harvard Crimson*, Gregg J. Kilday said we actors "quickly establish an uncanny competence and flexibility that extends through most of the evening."

Harvard student Frank Rich, now a respected *New York Times* columnist, agreed in his November 17th *Harvard Crimson* review the Monday after our opening weekend. "A Mindblow at the Loeb," his headline read, "A Farewell to the Sixties." It was a long review, given prominent placement. "If you go to the Loeb this week," he began, "you have nothing to lose but your mind. And that might be the best thing that could ever happen to you.

"Whites, blacks, radicals, liberals, conservatives, heterosexuals, homosexuals, sado-masochists, women-liberators, male chauvinists, Wellesley girls: *Morning, Noon, and Night* will freak you all out. There will be fist-fights at the Loeb this week; nasty words and name calling; walkouts galore. Something is happening over there, and that something should not be missed.

"Exactly what is happening on Brattle Street are three one-act plays, all written by young Americans and all deeply rooted in the nightmarish decade that is now grinding to a halt. A decade of snipings and war, assassinations and drugs. *Morning, Noon, and Night* is not so much *about* these things as *of* them. And such is the stuff we are made of -- we and nightmares.

"The first of these one-actors, Israel Horovitz's *Morning,* is black in every sense. The set and costumes are black, the people are black (or white, as I'll explain in a second), the humor is black. It is a strange play, one that insecure whites and Uncle Toms will call racist...."

Frank Rich went on to synopsize the play, in which a black Harlem family wakes up one morning to discover that they are white. Complications ensue. I was playing head of the family.

"Playwright Horovitz lets everyone have it in *Morning,*" Frank Rich continued. "The play's language -- explicit and, as they say, coarse -- will probably send a good deal of people out of the theatre within a few minutes after the house lights dim. And the playwright's handling of dialects (the white actors switch back and forth between Harlemese and East Side-esque) is bound to scare a lot of whites into silence as the play goes on its hysterically funny way....As *Morning's* family changes its voice from an Amos 'n' Andy inflection to a John Lindsay or Wilson Pickett or Rap Brown inflection, the white audience is scared out of its wits. It doesn't know how to react....

"It is perhaps a cruel joke Mr. Horovitz is playing on the theatre-goer -- but a necessary one. It is exactly the kind of communications impasse he is dealing with that spawns the rhetoric that leads to real racism, law-and-order candidates, backlash and violence. It is no surprise that his play ends with a grotesquely scary and ecumenical ('Kill the white man! Kill the black man!') chant of murder.

"Terrence McNally's *Noon* does not have the apocalyptic ending of *Morning,* but it deals with very much the same problem in a different context, that of sex. Surely one of the funniest one-actors I have ever seen, *Noon* is about a wide variety of people (a nymphomaniac, a homosexual, an uptight heterosexual intellectual, and a middle-aged sado-masochist couple from Westchester) who find themselves thrown together in a New York loft....McNally's documentation of the sexual mores involved -- complete with whips and chains, undressing, and non-euphemistic language -- will...strike some people as obscene. That's their problem.

"*Night,* the final play of the trilogy, is in every way the third act of the evening. It is an answer to the chaotic world depicted in the first two plays, a goodbye-to-all-that farewell to the Sixties. It is both devastating and exhilarating, and an even bigger mind-blow than *Morning* or *Night.*

"The actors, each of whom has three meaty roles, show an amazing amount of versatility and are usually every bit as brilliant as the plays they are working with....In a cast of this quality, it is hard to single any one actor out as being above the rest."

According to the critics in their rave reviews, we blew the audience's minds at the Loeb in what was my main stage Harvard debut. Today, I wonder if anyone even remembers this triptych. Perhaps the plays were too much *of* their times. They were of the Sixties, and have faded with the passions and truths of the Sixties.

One such truth was My Lai. America discovered on November 12th, the same day we opened at the Loeb, what had taken place in that tiny Vietnamese village the morning of March 16th, 1968. On the morning of November 12th, 1969, *The Boston Globe* reported how American soldiers had poured into My Lai and killed every man, woman, and child they could find, perhaps 560, perhaps more. Americans read how American soldiers slit the throats of the Vietnamese, scalped them, cut out their tongues. They learned that, at the time, the U.S. military had recorded the events at My Lai as "well-planned, well-executed, and successful."

But, if this was what a "well-planned, well-executed, and successful" American military operation was like, then, as Galbraith had told us during the Moratorium, the war was one we should not *desire* to win. Because *we* were the wrong side. America really *was* as fucked up as the society we depicted on stage every night at the Loeb.

On November 13th, the day of our second performance and the day after the My Lai news was reported, another Moratorium began. Unlike the October Moratorium, which was designed to take place all over America, the November Moratorium took place only in Washington, D.C. The New Mobilization Committee to End the War in Vietnam massed up to 800,000 dissenters in the city. They marched down Pennsylvania Avenue to a rally at the Washington Monument. There, Coretta Scott King, Dr. Benjamin Spock, and Senator George McGovern urged demonstrators to continue speaking out against the madness.

The November Moratorium ran November 13-15, 1969. The most memorable event was the March Against Death, which began at 6:00 p.m. on the 13th. For the next 40 hours, 46,000 protestors filed past the White House, where Nixon cowered inside, each one carrying a placard with the name of an American soldier killed in Vietnam, or the name of a village destroyed by American troops, such as My Lai. As each protestor passed the White House, he or she stopped, called out the name on the placard, and moved on to the Capitol building, where he or she deposited the placard in one of 40 wooden coffins.

On November 20th *The Cleveland Plain Dealer* published the infamous photos of the My Lai massacre which Army photographer Ron Haeberle, using his personal camera, had taken that day in My Lai. The next day, *Life* magazine published them so that the entire nation could see what America was doing in Vietnam.

Earlier that year, Henry Kissinger, Nixon's Secretary of State, had warned Ho Chi Minh and other North Vietnamese leaders that Nixon planned to repudiate his "Vietnamization" program of decreasing American involvement in the war. Kissinger told Ho that Nixon would massively escalate the war, and use nuclear weapons against the North, unless the Vietnamese capitulated by November 1. At the time I was marching through Harvard Square with Erik Erikson in the October Moratorium, the American military had already planned a detailed campaign of nuclear war against the North. The Rostow Thesis was finally coming to fruition.

Of course, Ho Chi Minh and the Vietnamese leadership refused to capitulate. "Uncle Ho" died on September 3rd, at age 79, confident of ultimate victory in Vietnam, no matter what Nixon did, no matter what price needed to be paid, even that of enduring the Empire's nuclear onslaught. If you are truly willing to pay the cost of freedom, whatever that may be, no one can make you bend your knee.

The October and November Moratoria changed Nixon's plans. As we now know from his memoirs, they convinced Nixon that the antiwar movement had, in his words, so "polarized" America that he was politically unable to carry out his threat to unleash a nuclear holocaust against the people of Vietnam. At the time of the Moratoria, Nixon had claimed that he wasn't paying attention to us. He had more important things to do. He was busy, he said, watching the Redskins play football on TV.

We now know that he lied. We now know that, by marching in our hundreds of thousands on those days in the autumn of 1969, ordinary Americans stopped the nuclear Armageddon our leaders had planned.

But, we didn't know that at the time. We only knew that the war went on, that Americans and Vietnamese continued to die, and would do so for years to come. The antiwar movement had just won a great victory, it had saved the people of Vietnam from nuclear hellfire -- but it seemed that we had failed.

We seldom know the full ramifications of our actions. We just know that we must act. We act even if we think we will lose. We act because it's the right thing to do.

And sometimes, against all expectations, we win.

Morning, Noon, and Night ended its main stage run at Harvard's Loeb on November 22nd, the anniversary of the assassination which seemed to have launched the craziness of the Sixties. That night, before going out on stage, I listened to our rock band blasting away at stage right and I recalled the day my neighbor on 51st Street in Phoenix had jerked me awake to tell me that Kennedy had been shot that morning in Dallas. I'd been a Goldwater Republican at the time, and I viewed Kennedy's death as no great tragedy.

It all seemed so long ago and so far away. I seemed to have lived several lifetimes since then, become several different people over the course of the Sixties. And here I am, I thought, standing behind the curtains on the main stage at Harvard, waiting to go on, living yet one more life. And yet JFK's assassination was only six years ago to the very day. What a long strange trip it had been.

It's not over yet, I reminded myself. No one here knows anything about my other life as a draft resister, but I'm still going to prison when this applause dies away.

So be it, I thought.

And then I walked out on Harvard's main stage to say farewell to the Sixties.

That Christmas, Annie came home from Pitzer for the holidays. But this time, "home" meant Cambridge. Vern was there, housesitting a Harvard professor's home on Larch Road while the professor was on sabbatical in Europe.

I was also there. Annie deigned to stay with Vern in his borrowed West Cambridge manse, but she spent all of her time with me in my tiny room at Miss Peet's.

And, as had been true the Christmas before, which we'd shared with Richard Jones, we had almost no money. So we went to the Book Case, a well-stocked Harvard Square used book store on Church Street, and for a few pennies Annie bought me a battered old Webster's dictionary as my Christmas gift. Before giving it to me Annie wrote inside it, "To Eric, on this '69 Christmas in Cambridge -- You love words -- May this help you -- As a companion...."

I treasured the dictionary, and I treasured our time together, as I felt that Christmas of 1969 would be the last Christmas we would share for a long time. Perhaps it would be our last Christmas, ever. I still feared that Annie might not be there for me when I returned from prison.

Then, on December 18th, 1969, one day before my 23rd birthday, my draft board sent me the best birthday present I have ever received. "Upon advice of the Regional Attorney," Mrs. Dimmick wrote, "this local board has reopened your classification and classified you I-O. This action has the effect of cancelling your induction order and removing your delinquency."

And that was it.

Even though I was not a religious pacifist, even though I did not belong to a traditionally pacifist church, even though I was an atheist and I had refused to fight in the Empire's war simply because it was wrong and unjust, the S.S. System had decided against prosecuting me. The Regional Attorney had decided that there was a good chance the S.S. System would loose if it tried to prosecute me in the hostile jurisdiction of Boston, the scene of my "crime," where the federal courts had already established a track record of antiwar decisions.

And that would create a dangerous legal precedent which might help other draft resisters who were neither religious pacifists nor members of a traditionally pacifist church, but who were atheists who opposed the Empire's war simply because it was wrong and unjust.

And that would not be good for the Empire's war machine, the modern Moloch whose voracious hunger for young bodies had to be constantly fed.

Better to pretend nothing had ever happened.

So, because I refused to be inducted into the military machine, the S.S. System had cancelled my induction retroactively.

Because I was willing to go to prison for refusing to kill and help kill, the S.S. System reclassified me as a Conscientious Objector. I would *not* be going to prison, after all. I would not have to pay the cost of freedom -- because I had been *willing* to pay the cost of freedom.

America, it seems, can do the right thing when it wants to do so.

Or is forced to do so by a majority of Americans.

And, as Thoreau said when he opposed the Empire's war against Mexico, anyone who is right is already a "majority of one."

The Empire's war against the people of Vietnam went on.

But I had won this battle.

And the military draft was abolished in 1973.

And the war -- America's longest war -- ended in 1975.

And the people of Vietnam won the war.

Because they, too, had been willing to pay the cost of freedom.

And in 1977 President Jimmy Carter pardoned all draft resisters, including non-registrants and those in Canadian exile. They were free to come home.

Sometimes, Goliath falls.

And sometimes, love endures.

"....My deepest love to you," Annie had finished writing inside the used Webster's dictionary before giving it to me that Christmas in Cambridge.

I have it open now in front of me and I am reading her words.

Fight the Power

www.ingramcontent.com/pod-product-compliance
Lightning Source LLC
Chambersburg PA
CBHW080722300426
44114CB00019B/2460